Perspectives on American Book History

Studies in Print Culture and the History of the Book

Perspectives on American Book History

ARTIFACTS AND COMMENTARY

Edited by
SCOTT E. CASPER,
JOANNE D. CHAISON, AND
JEFFREY D. GROVES

University of Massachusetts Press, Amherst and Boston,
in association with
American Antiquarian Society, Worcester, Massachusetts,
and
The Center for the Book, Library of Congress, Washington, D.C.

Copyright © 2002 by University of Massachusetts Press
All rights reserved
Printed in the United States of America
LC 2001006911
ISBN 1-55849-316-6 (cloth); 1-55849-317-4 (paper)

Designed by Dennis Anderson
Set in Monotype Dante
Printed and bound by Sheridan Books

Library of Congress Cataloging-in-Publication Data

Perspectives on American book history : artifacts and commentary /
edited by Scott E. Casper, Joanne D. Chaison, and Jeffrey D. Groves.
    p. cm. — (Studies in print culture and the history of the book)

Includes bibliographical references
    ISBN 1-55849-316-6 (alk. paper) — ISBN 1-55849-317-4 (pbk. : alk. paper)
    1. Book industries and trade—United States—History—Sources.
2. Publishers and publishing—United States—History—Sources. 3. Books
and reading—United States—History—Sources. 4. Book industries and
trade—Social aspects—United States. 5. Publishers and
publishing—Social aspects—United States. 6. Books and reading—Social
aspects—United States. 7. United States—Intellectual life.
I. Casper, Scott E., 1964– II. Chaison, Joanne D., 1944– III. Groves, Jeffrey D.,
1959– IV. Series
    Z471 .P47 2002
002' .0973—dc21

                                                                    2001006911

British Library Cataloguing in Publication data are available.

Most of the documents and artifacts originating in the seventeenth, eighteenth, and nineteenth centuries that are reproduced in this book are courtesy of the American Antiquarian Society, unless otherwise indicated in the source notes. Items from the later nineteenth and twentieth centuries are reproduced courtesy of the individuals and institutions indicated in the source notes, are in the public domain, or fall under the doctrine of fair use. In a few cases an unsuccessful good-faith effort has been made to find the rights holder and obtain permission. The publisher welcomes information on these cases.

This book is published with the support and cooperation of the University of Massachusetts Boston, the American Antiquarian Society, Worcester, Massachusetts, and The Center for the Book, Library of Congress, Washington, D.C.

Founded in 1812, the American Antiquarian Society is a learned society and independent research library in Worcester, Massachusetts, with rich and deep holdings of books, pamphlets, broadsides, and newspapers printed in the United States through 1877, together with strong collections of manuscripts, graphic arts materials, and related reference and secondary materials. The Society's Program in the History of the Book in American Culture, established in 1983, has assumed a leadership role in the book history field in the United States. Among its activities are annual summer seminars and the sponsorship and production of the five-volume work *A History of the Book in America* (Cambridge University Press and AAS, in progress).

Encouraging the study of books and print culture is a principal aim of The Center for the Book in the Library of Congress, which was established in 1977 to stimulate public interest in books, reading, and libraries. Its program, sponsored primarily by private contributions, includes symposia, publications, and joint projects within the Library of Congress and with like-minded organizations outside the Library. For information about The Center for the Book's activities, its partnership networks throughout the United States and in many other countries, and its several dozen publications, consult its website: <http://www.loc.gov/cfbook>.

Contents

Preface   vii

1   Texts for the Times: An Introduction to Book History
ROBERT A. GROSS   1

2   Literacy and Reading in Puritan New England
JILL LEPORE   17

3   Print and Everyday Life in the Eighteenth Century
PATRICIA CRAIN   47

4   Publishing the American Revolution
RUSSELL L. MARTIN   79

5   The Book Trade Transformed
JEFFREY D. GROVES   109

6   Antebellum Reading Prescribed and Described
SCOTT E. CASPER   135

7   Publishing an Emergent "American" Literature
SUSAN S. WILLIAMS   165

8   Northern and Southern Worlds of Print
ALICE FAHS   195

9   Reshaping Publishing and Authorship in the Gilded Age
NANCY COOK   223

10   Print Cultures in the American West
JEN A. HUNTLEY-SMITH   255

11   Laboring Classes, New Readers, and Print Cultures
ANN FABIAN   285

12 The Industrialization and Nationalization of
    American Periodical Publishing
        CHARLES JOHANNINGSMEIER   311

13 Print and the Creation of Middlebrow Culture
        TRYSH TRAVIS   339

14 Out of the Mainstream and into the Streets: Small Press Magazines,
    the Underground Press, Zines, and Artists' Books
        ELLEN GRUBER GARVEY   367

15 Newspapers since 1945
        GLENN WALLACH   403

16 The Once and Future Book
        SCOTT E. CASPER, JOANNE D. CHAISON, AND JEFFREY D. GROVES   435

17 Resources for Studying American Book History:
    A Selective, Annotated Bibliography
        JOANNE D. CHAISON   441

    Contributors   459

Preface

LITERACY AND print have profoundly shaped the contours of modern human cultures. In what is now the United States the effects of print and literacy were widespread even at the beginning of the colonial period, and they continue in complex and powerful ways to this day. Over the last two decades, the history of the book (or the study of print culture, as it is also known) has emerged as an exciting and dynamic perspective for understanding developments in American history and literature. Some teachers have created undergraduate and graduate courses devoted solely to book history. Many more have incorporated a book history approach into their history and literature courses. Engaging book history in the classroom demands close attention to the products of print culture: books, magazines, newspapers, advertisements, and so on.

Perspectives on American Book History (*PABH*) is designed to fill the void that developed as American book history moved out of the archive and scholarly journal and into the classroom. Early in the development of this book we realized that we did not want to create a reader that merely reprinted scholarly essays. Rather, we wanted to provide students and teachers with "artifacts," primary texts and images that encourage discussion and interpretation, as well as with short commentary essays that model ways in which those artifacts can be used. Such a reader, we believed, could prepare students to do archival work in their own local libraries. Recognizing that not all libraries support book history research equally well, we also decided to develop a CD-ROM supplement for the book—an "Image Archive"—that would afford both teachers and students access to a rich collection of digital images as they consider the place of print culture in American history and literature.

While this book is organized chronologically, the word "perspectives" in the title should be taken to heart: this is not a definitive history of the book and print culture in North America. We have tried to create a sense of narrative from chapter to chapter, but many important developments, trends, and occasions do not make an appearance here. Nonetheless, for both undergraduate and graduate students, we believe that *PABH* will provide not only an effective and engaging introduction to print culture in the United States but also an intellectual framework for further inquiry.

Before using *PABH*, the reader should browse through it paying attention to several of its features. Except for chapters 1, 16, and 17, each chapter begins with a headnote, written chiefly by the editors, that situates the material historically. Artifact descrip-

vii

tions, also written by the editors, are grouped together at several points throughout the chapter, and the artifacts' original provenance or publication information appears in the source notes at the end. Artifacts appear in their original language, syntax, and spelling; we generally have not used "sic" to note conflicts with current usage or errors in the original. Chapter authors—each an expert in his or her field—selected the artifacts and wrote the commentary essays that interpret them. At the end of each chapter the reader will find bibliographical information about works cited in the commentary section and about other works germane to the chapter topic. Some works referred to incompletely in the bibliographies are preceded by asterisks: this designation indicates that readers can find full and annotated entries for those sources in chapter 17, "Resources for Studying American Book History." This annotated bibliography of standard reference works in the field will be helpful to students at any level as they begin library research projects. It can also assist teachers and librarians in acquiring reference works in book history. The Image Archive disk tucked into the back of the book can be used with either Microsoft or Netscape Web browsers. Before using the Image Archive extensively, the viewer should read the pages (linked from the home page) "Copyright and Fair Use," "Suggestions for Classroom Use," and "Technical Information about the Images."

DURING THE editing of this book, we have incurred many debts to individuals and institutions. With great pleasure, we acknowledge our primary debt to our contributors, an impressive group of scholars who are charting the future course of American book history. Paul Wright, our indefatigable editor at the University of Massachusetts Press, believed in and supported our project from the very beginning and continuously contributed to the improvement of the manuscript. We thank Paul and his outstanding colleagues—managing editor Carol Betsch, designer Dennis Anderson, and copyeditor Julia Gaviria—for their skill and patience in moving the project forward. The Center for the Book in the Library of Congress, and especially its director, John Cole, have contributed greatly to the publication of this book. We are most thankful for their support and confidence. Two summer research grants (Groves) from Harvey Mudd College supported the development of the Image Archive. The first of these grants allowed us to hire Levi Scoggins, a Harvey Mudd student, to design the CD and assist us in digitizing its images. Our work was also supported by a sabbatical leave from the University of Nevada, Reno (Casper), and a development leave from the American Antiquarian Society (Chaison). Funded by a Maguire Grant from Claremont Graduate University, David Parker, a doctoral candidate at that institution, assisted us with book illustrations and Image Archive editing in the closing phase of the project. Several institutions—The Libraries of the Claremont Colleges, the Special Collections Department at the University of Nevada, Reno, and the Huntington Library—have generously granted us permission to use materials from their collections. Michael Zinman, Stuart McConnell, and Randy Ringen graciously allowed us to borrow "artifacts" from their collections for reproduction in the Image Archive.

Otto Cortez, another Harvey Mudd College student, translated a selection from *El Clamor Publico* for chapter 10.

We are profoundly indebted to the American Antiquarian Society, the outstanding archive for research in American book history. Both this book and the CD-ROM that accompanies it depend on and are testimony to the strengths of the AAS collection. Archives, however, are no more useful than the guides who make them accessible, and we would like to note that the exceptional staff at AAS have been, in a sense, our co-researchers in putting this book together. We thank Georgia Barnhill, Nancy Burkett, Ellen Dunlap, Babette Gehnrich, Amanda Hegarty, John Hench, Thomas Knoles, Dennis Laurie, Laura Oxley, Caroline Sloat, Caroline Stoffel, and Laura Wasowicz. We especially thank Marie Lamoureux and Philip Lampi for their incomparable assistance throughout this project.

Finally, for their unwavering support and boundless encouragement, and for their advice, patience, and good humor, we thank Teresa Shaw, Gary Chaison, and other members of our families.

S. E. C.
J. D. C.
J. D. G.

Perspectives on American Book History

1

Texts for the Times
An Introduction to Book History

ROBERT A. GROSS

TEXTBOOKS have been a staple of American publishing ever since the late 1680s, when a Boston bookseller named Benjamin Harris issued *The New-England Primer* to inculcate literacy and piety in Puritan children. Upon the sales of such works—the *Primer* went into the millions over the course of the eighteenth century—were built the major publishing houses of nineteenth- and twentieth-century America (Beales and Monaghan, 383–84). Even so, *Perspectives on American Book History (PABH)* is special. Issued by a university press, it heralds the coming of age of the academic field known as the history of the book. At the start of a new millennium, five and a half centuries after Johannes Gutenberg's innovation and in the middle of an electronic revolution, books and the printed word more generally are at the center of an expansive interdisciplinary enterprise drawing scholars from the humanities and social sciences alike, in such areas as anthropology, bibliography, history, journalism, librarianship, literature, sociology, cultural studies, and communications, and ranging widely across time and space. Throughout the curriculum, courses and degree programs are springing up, conferences are being organized, research centers founded, journals and book series launched, all devoted to "studies in print culture and the history of the book." Now, with the publication of this collection, another milestone has been reached: the creation of an original reader through which to study key texts and episodes in the book history of the United States. By these steps, the field has become "hot," in the word of the *Chronicle of Higher Education* (Winkler). Predictions of the impending end of books in the age of the Internet notwithstanding, the study of communication through writing and print has established its place on the academic map.

A BRIEF HISTORY OF BOOK HISTORY

Why so much interest in a medium that has been a fixture of Western culture for well over five hundred years? The answer lies at the intersection of two communications revolutions. The first took place in the middle of the fifteenth century, when Gutenberg, a goldsmith from Mainz, Germany, developed the main techniques—casting metal type from molds, fixing type on paper with a wooden press, employing an oil-based ink to ensure a clear, indelible impression—for the mechanical reproduction of texts in hundreds and thousands of copies, dooming the handwritten book to oblivion. The second, dating from the last quarter of the twentieth century, replaces type, press, and ink with silicon chips, keyboards, monitors, and fiber optics to drive the networked computers through which millions of people, scattered all over the globe, can communicate with one another at any time of day or night. Rapidly transforming all areas of commerce and culture in a new information economy, this electronic revolution may well eliminate the common forms of the newspaper, the magazine, and the book, the last of which took on the distinctive character known as the codex—bound pages of handwritten and later printed text—some seventeen hundred years ago, with technological formats still in their infancy or not yet conceived (Kilgour, 81–97; Dewar).

The first revolution generated the history of the book as an intellectual endeavor, initially conducted by bibliographers, collectors, printers, and publishers, all interested in tracing the rise, expansion, and triumph of the press as an achievement of technology and a work of art (Hall, "On Native Ground"). Not until the middle of the twentieth century did academic historians discover the subject as a key to social and cultural history. The path was pioneered by the French scholars Lucien Febvre and Henri-Jean Martin, whose book *L'apparition du livre* (1958) remade the study of the book trades into *histoire du livre* and established France as the lively center of a dynamic field. At the heart of this inquiry were the causes and consequences of the introduction of the printed book into the world of early modern Europe, from the mid-fifteenth to the late eighteenth century. "We hope to establish how and why the printed book was something more than the triumph of technical ingenuity," Febvre and Martin announced at the outset, "but was also one of the most potent agents at the disposal of western civilisation in bringing together the scattered ideas of representative thinkers. . . . Fresh concepts crossed whole regions of the globe in the very shortest time. . . . [The] printed book was one of the most effective means of mastery over the whole world" (Febvre and Martin, 10–11). The advance of the book was bound up with the leading transformations of Western thought, from the waning of medievalism under the joint blows of Renaissance and Reformation to the rise of Enlightenment and Romanticism in the age of the French Revolution. Building on Febvre and Martin's example, such influential works as Elizabeth Eisenstein's *The Printing Press as an Agent of Change* (1979), Robert Darnton's *The Business of Enlightenment* (1979), and the first English edition of Carlo Ginzburg's *The Cheese and the Worms* (1980) offered concepts and methods to understand "the book as a force in history" (Darnton, *Business of Enlightenment*, 2). Book history helped to track the dissemination of ideas in learned and popular cultures, to recover lost *mentalités* of subordinate classes, and to assay the impact of print on the spread and uses of literacy, the production and communication of knowledge, the power of church and state, the growth of nationalism and the extension of empire, and the conduct of everyday life in the face-to-face rural communities in which the vast majority of humanity once lived. Such questions arose from the very circumstances under which printing was invented and spread. If the "shift from script to print" launched a "communications revolution," as Elizabeth Eisenstein asserted, what better realm to explore than "Gutenberg's galaxy" (Gross, "Communications Revolutions," 11)?

These interests were easily translated to other realms, particularly to early America. Historians such as David D. Hall and Richard D. Brown discerned cultures, notably in New England, where reading was a common practice, despite scarcities of type, presses, paper, and ink, where authority was linked to control over communications, and where the folklore of common people and the learning of elites flowed together in books, sermons, and common speech (Joyce et al.; Hall, *Worlds of Wonder*; Brown). Simultaneously, students of American literature were abandoning the New Critical notion that the meaning of a poem or novel inheres in its aesthetic design. They were branching out, under the impact of linguistic theories and a "new historicism," to investigate the material conditions under which writing is produced and the roles of the reader and of "interpretive communities" in making meaning from texts. These separate lines of inquiry soon came together in a series of influential books emphasizing the interplay of literary text and historical context. Cathy Davidson portrayed the striking transformation wrought by female readers of the novel in the wake of the American Revolution. Richard Brodhead incisively analyzed the cultural work done by such genres as the sentimental novel and the magazine travel essay in the construction of the nineteenth-century middle class. These studies have been pursued with increasing intensity, extended into the twentieth century, and abetted by such institutions as the American Antiquarian Society's Program for the History of the Book in American Culture and the Society for the History of Authorship, Reading, and Publishing. From them emerged in the 1980s and 1990s the new history of the book: a medium for teaching and scholarship well suited to the needs of a "media age."

The conjuncture of an intellectual trend in the academy with a new revolution in communications was soon evident. Febvre and Martin were among the first to foresee the changes on the horizon. "The book is a relative newcomer in western society," they declared. "It began its career in the mid-fifteenth century, and its future is no longer certain, threatened as it is by new inventions based on different principles" (Febvre and Martin, 10). To Eisenstein two decades later, the copying machine and the word processor betokened a democratic future where everyone could be a publisher. "We seem to be in the midst of yet another publishing revolution that very well may undermine current notions of intellectual property and bring us closer to the medieval experience of everyman serving as his own scribe" (Eisenstein, "From Scriptoria to Printing Shops," 40). Such developments in print were intertwined with more dramatic advances in communication, led by television, film, and ultimately the computer. In 1964 the Canadian oracle Marshall McLuhan, having limned "the making of typographic man" in *The Gutenberg Galaxy* (1962), announced that "the medium is the message." On that basis he determined that the mode of consciousness shaped by print—linear, sequential, detached, logical thinking—was giving way to a new, "cool," aural and visual mode stimulating all the senses and quickening involvement in a "globe" fast becoming, through the mass media, "a village" (McLuhan, *Understanding Media*, 5). McLuhan's slogan crystallized a growing awareness that the several divisions of the communications business—books, newspapers, magazines, radio, television, film—were all part of "the media." Since the 1960s, the dramatic growth of this conglomeration of national and multinational enterprises has been central to the expansion of American economic, political, and cultural power. "America's biggest export is no longer the fruit of its fields or the output of its factories," according to the *Washington Post*, "but the mass-produced products of its popular culture—movies, TV programs, music, books, and computer software" (Fahri and Rosenfeld). In this milieu, information and entertainment are ubiquitous. Under the aegis of huge corporate empires, diverse media are increasingly orchestrated to common ends. Only a handful of trade publishers remains independent and wholly devoted to print (Epstein; Schiffrin). The new age stirs excitement at the rich possibilities for popular enlightenment opened up by the World Wide Web. It also stirs alarm at the rapid colonization of cyberspace by commercial interests and the use of the new medium to propagate pornography, ignorance, and hate. Are we entering a golden age of literacy, where words, sounds, and images will combine to empower individuals and forge communities? Or are we merely raising modern mass culture onto a new plane, more powerful, alluring, and insidious than ever?

THE BUSINESS OF PRINT CULTURE

As the world's first mass medium, circulating across five centuries of history, books carry important messages about the past and significant clues to the future. Employing the methods and machines developed by Gutenberg, printers in early modern Europe produced multiple copies of books on a scale never before seen, as many as twenty million by the sixteenth century (Kilgour, 82). The surviving classics of antiquity and the newer works of Christendom were set in type and made available to more readers than they ever reached in their own times. Printing seized upon and popularized organizational devices, such as tables of contents and indexes, created in the latter years of the manuscript book, and thereby fostered the rationalization of knowledge. It was a solvent of Christian unity and traditional authority, putting the Bible in the hands of common men and women, and a constituent of new secular powers such as the nation-state, whose monarchs and subjects were knit together as readers of a common vernacular language. What the press built up, it also pulled down. Printers took gossip at court and grumbling among the people and put them into permanent form in cold type. Bound between covers, such reports systematized grievances against the old order and spurred desires for change. In the face of these challenges, custodians of power bewailed the expansion of the reading public and the influence of those who catered to its tastes. When the press was not distributing "lewd Ballads" and "corrupted tales in Inke and Paper," it was satisfying a "furious itch of novelty" and "general thirst after news" (Eisenstein, *Printing Press*, 130–31). To the black-robed dons in the pulpit and in the colleges, the danger was embodied in a new class, "the men of letters," who impertinently intruded themselves, by way of print, into relations between parents and children, clergy and laymen, rulers and subjects. Yet press and public were fickle. Printers and booksellers freely sold their services to the status quo, just as "the people" could applaud the suppression of critical voices. Printing was Janus-faced, its countenance turned toward liberty and authority, individuality and collectivity, tradition and change, depending on the shifting balance of forces in the economy, politics, and religion of the pre-modern European world (Eisenstein, *Printing Press*; Darnton, *Forbidden Best-Sellers* and *Literary Underground*; Anderson).

As in the Old World, so in the New. Printed books held out mixed possibilities for freedom and domination. *Perspectives on American Book History* reveals the multivocal discourse surrounding books and reading, from the Puritan founders of Massachusetts Bay, with their ideal of promoting piety through print, down to the latest entrepreneurs of online journalism, confident that the Internet will bring "continued growth and a bright future" (Sturm, ch. 15), despite alternative visions of the new medium as a free space for the expression of any and every opinion, unconstrained by copyright and the calculation of profit. In early America, magistrates and ministers were as determined to prescribe the proper uses of literacy and to confine the press within an orthodox frame as their counterparts across the ocean. But printing had its own imperatives. It could as readily prop up government by publishing the laws as undermine it with criticism and exposés of "those miscreants who, for the sake of private or public advantage to themselves, would sacrifice both their King and Country" (*Massachusetts Spy*, January 7, 1771). Even worse, books could give teenage boys illicit knowledge of the female sex and ruin the morals of young women with "licentious" tales of folly and vice (*Observations on Novel-Reading*, ch. 3 below). The fate of the social order evidently rested in the hands of mechanics at the press and tradesmen in the countinghouse. Hopeful that patriotic printers would advance civic virtue, Americans accepted that risk in the new republics they established in the states and in the national government created by the Constitution. They guaranteed liberty of the press, allowed free trade in books, encouraged authors and publishers with copyright laws, and promoted the circulation of newspapers with official advertising, printing contracts, and cheap postage. Time and again, throughout U.S. history, such optimism would be disappointed.

A recurring theme of *Perspectives on American Book History* is the constant tension between commerce and culture. In the relentless quest for profits, entrepreneurs have worked tirelessly, from the early nineteenth century on, to expand the literary marketplace and boasted of their ingenuity in transforming "obscure and seemingly useless manuscripts" into "thousands and tens of thousands of copies, beautifully printed, embellished, and bound, to instruct, entertain, and cheer many millions of readers" (Abbott, ch. 5 below). In their minds, the press was an essential instrument of democracy and enlightenment. By disseminating knowledge to the masses at low cost, they took authority from elites and empowered the people. But have writers and readers celebrated those efforts? Not very often. True, commercial publishing gave rise to a profession of authorship for women as well as men. But the economic terms of the trade, as recalcitrant writers like Herman Melville saw it, were too harsh. "Dollars damn me," complained the author of the unsalable *Moby-Dick*. "What I feel most moved to write, that is banned—it will not pay" (Melville, ch. 7 below). The marketplace rewarded only those who bowed to its demands. A similar lament rose up from the editors and writers for mass-circulation periodicals at the start of the twentieth century. Publishing for the millions may have spawned a host of new jobs, but for the novelist Jack London, authors' row was really a new Grub Street, where the imagination was ground down into "hack work" for the great newspaper syndicates (London, ch. 12 below). The choice was simple: conform or starve. London, admittedly, was hardly a reliable reporter, even of his own experience. And other figures, such as Mark Twain, embraced opportunities to get rich from writing and publishing.

Still, a chorus of discontent resounds from the diverse voices gathered in this book, from the mid-nineteenth to the late twentieth centuries. Far from democratizing knowledge, say the critics, the barons of the press have advanced their own power at the expense of the common good. In the boundless chase after dollars, publishers have fashioned a standardized national culture, as artificial as it is uniform. They have degraded art, punished creativity, and diminished local and regional diversity. They have turned news into entertainment and corrupted the channels of public information. As big businessmen, the dominant figures in the book trades have put the interests of capitalism over democracy. If they have made reading matter available cheaply to millions in ever-greater, more diverse supplies, they have done so on terms that drive out or dilute the best and appeal to the lowest common denominator. The publishing revolution betrayed its promise from the very start.

Capitalism is thus central to the story of American publishing. Like other businessmen in the American economy, the entrepreneurs of the book trade have been motivated chiefly by the pursuit of profit. The quest for markets and sales and the push for new technology have propelled every major wave of change in the publishing industry. *Perspectives on American Book History* documents these developments through the initiatives and opinions of the many participants in the literary marketplace. Though it may carry the name of a single author, a book is as much a collaborative product as a newspaper or magazine, born of the collective effort of diverse workers in a division of labor that has grown more and more elaborate over time. An extended circuit connects author to reader through multiple points: workingmen (and occasionally women) at the case and the press; paperfolders and leatherworkers in the bindery; the many middlemen of the trade—wholesalers, retailers, shippers, peddlers, and newspaper boys, among others; editorial personnel, including copyeditors, proofreaders, designers, illustrators, indexers, and publicists; the agents, lawyers, acquisition editors, and publishers who arrange the deals by which manuscripts become books in the first place; and the advertisers, marketers, book clubs, and reviewers who shape the reception of books in the marketplace and in readers' minds (Darnton, "What Is the History of Books?"). Whatever their location in the circuit, all of these persons have experienced, in varying ways, the competitive, commercial logic of the capitalist market.

Perspectives on American Book History traces the rise of the modern publisher, issuing books from a few urban centers for sale to readers scattered across an extensive republic, in the first part of the nineteenth century. The central challenge facing the first generation of booksellers (the original designation for a publisher) was to create and reach a national market. To that end, entrepreneurs such as Philadelphia's Mathew Carey promoted an annual trade fair, on a European model, where printers and booksellers could meet, exchange books, and forge regular ties. Through such gatherings, they hoped to overcome the formidable barriers to distributing their wares. It was equally urgent to cut the costs of production. Carey and others undercut the wages of journeymen printers by hiring semiskilled teenagers and women and by putting out jobs to cheaper workers in country shops. They pressed for technological innovations—the power press, the stereotype plate—to replace human labor with machines. By these means, they heightened productivity and gained flexibility. And they streamlined operations according to a systematic plan epitomized by the state-of-the-art Harper & Brothers in the 1850s.

These antebellum developments set the pattern for the next century and a half. During the Civil War, while Confederate printers were starved for type, ink, paper, labor, contributors, and ultimately readers, Union presses poured out a cornucopia of items designed to inform and inspire a population eager for news and stories from the front. In the Gilded Age the literary marketplace became still more complex, as subscription publishers emerged as major players, trade houses tried to fend off rivals, and ambitious authors such as Twain perfected methods of self-promotion and gambled on new technological devices. In the far west, as in the seaboard east, the publisher Hubert Bancroft followed the rationalizing model of the Harpers, and newspaper owners used cheap labor to break the power of unions. With the rise of big business, mass-circulation magazines and newspapers took advantage of new inventions (rotary and web presses, linotype machines, half-tone photographic reproduction) and improved communications (railroad, post office) to develop the modern formula for publishing: bundle up huge audiences and charge advertisers high rates for access to them. Literary syndicates fostered a national print culture by distributing standardized features and ads to diverse local and regional publications. In the 1920s the Book-of-the-Month Club and its "middlebrow" counterparts developed fresh ways to market books to hundreds of thousands of readers across the nation. Repelled by this commercial onslaught, some writers and editors sought refuge in "little magazines," which carved out a niche in publishing. But another alternative, the underground press of the Sixties, proved short-lived, eventually succumbing to the lure of profits (especially from sex ads). Today, publishing is undergoing the most far-reaching technological revolution since Gutenberg, driven, as ever, by the corporate quest for profit. Online news delivery, financed by onscreen advertising, is taking the press into uncharted realms, where print, image, and sound will be distributed to audiences in new forms at ever-greater speed. Doubtless, Mathew Carey would be pleased. The latest phase of America's communications industry has its roots in the capitalist quest for readers and profits that the onetime radical Irishman set loose.

It is easy to exaggerate the commercial character of American print culture. Though directed largely by private interests, publishing has served all sorts of non-pecuniary ends during our history. Puritans enlisted print in the evangelical campaign for souls. Government officials authorized publication of laws, lest ignorance excuse noncompliance. The Revolutionary generation aspired to create an informed citizenry, well-versed in the principles of republicanism and alert to violations of its rights. Political parties sponsored newspapers to broadcast their message, inspire supporters, and get out the vote. In the nineteenth century religious denominations and benevolent associations brought forth a huge publishing complex, employing cutting-edge technology to produce Bibles, tracts, and reform pamphlets in the millions, for the sake of converting readers to God, peace, temperance, antislavery, and other worthy causes. To combat the flood of "infidel books" (such as those by Voltaire and Thomas Paine), "foul and exciting romances," and sensational news from the mercenary "Satanic press," religious publishers dispatched evangelical peddlers to the dark corners of the land, with instructions to go from door to door handing out Bibles and tracts to starving souls at whatever price, if any, they could afford. Rather than worry about *"What will sell,"* the American Tract Society asked only what was needed. A pure channel was essential for divine truth (Nord, 243, 248).

Not everybody was so fastidious, even evangelicals. To many seekers after truth, the medium was definitely *not* the message. Ideally, the subjective experience of a text transcended its commercial existence as a commodity. Book-of-the-Month Club judge Henry Seidel Canby saw his mission as guiding "the general intelligent public" to unique and authentic encounters with literature, whatever the club's ads might say (Canby, ch. 13 below). What he craved in books was "deep reading," total immersion in a text. Such reading lifted the individual to a new state of thinking and feeling. "Reading for experience," Canby affirmed, "is the only reading that justifies excitement. . . . [It] is transforming. Neither man nor woman is ever quite the same again after the experience of a book that enters deeply into life" (Radway, *A Feeling for Books*, 294). Deep reading was, in fact, a secular conversion experience. In the pages of a book, the reader is born again. That ideal of communication, whereby two souls— author and reader—meet through the medium of print, links Canby back to the Puritan vision of the Bible as "the Voice of God" (Mather, ch. 2 below) and forward to Beat poets in Greenwich Village and to contemporary figures like Cindy O., who cruises the subways, the buses, and the streets of New York on the look-out for just the right person to receive her self-published zine *Doris*—"one to this girl who is laughing with her friend, one to that girl sad and alone on the last train of the night. . . . I want . . . to break—with this one small gesture—the crazy things we are taught; to keep distant and distrustful, alienated, lonely and safe" (Cindy O., ch. 14 below). In this ideology of reading, commerce can obtrude and distort the conduct of communications. But in the best of all worlds, it is immaterial to the reading experience.

Actually, the business of publishing *is* different from most commercial enterprises. Today, publishing companies are modern corporations, commonly subdivisions of giant media empires, conducting operations through a hierarchy of specialized departments, and buying and selling goods in national and global markets. They barely resemble the small, family-owned "houses" of the last century, where an ethos of gentility softened the hard edges of trade and editors treated their labor on manuscripts as a distinct craft, founded on civility and taste. It is unlikely that *Publishers' Weekly* would now complain, as it did in 1890, that "this is an age of ambition," whose aggressive spirit had tarnished the "dignity" of book publishing. "If literature and art are to be treated as common merchandise . . . it will make commonplace the manners of our people and their intelligence restricted to the counting room" (Coser et al., 17–18). Yet, in one fundamental respect, the book business has not changed significantly over the centuries. Its basic product is a singular good: an individual book, identified by a particular title, associated in most cases with a specific author, and promising to convey a unique experience to the reader. Bushels of wheat, tons of steel, the latest automobile models, and the newest computers: all are theoretically interchangeable within their category. If you've tried one, you've tried them all. Not so for books, each of which claims to offer distinctive satisfactions. That is precisely the dilemma of the book business, as it is for the movie industry. How can a new work, whose qualities and author are unknown to consumers, be marketed to an audience? "One of the films on this list of ten will be a big success," a Hollywood executive once told a reporter. "Which one?" "I have no idea" (Coser et al., 7). The same uncertainty besets publishing decisions. To limit their risks, publishers market successful authors like brand names ("If you liked Mark Twain's *Tom Sawyer*, you'll love his *Huck Finn!*"), tailor manuscripts to tried-and-true formulas, and gather up individual titles into popular categories, such as the *Hardy Boys* series and *Silhouette Romances*, counting on the whole to sell the parts (Radway, *Reading the Romance*). But the history of publishing is littered with failed predictions and unanticipated bestsellers. In the end, everything hinges on the specific book.

THE LIFE OF A BOOK

The same rule holds true in book history. The specific titles that issue from the press constitute the fundamental data of the field. They are the product of an industry whose cumulative output over the centuries is documented in a wide range of sources, including library catalogs, booksellers' advertisements, publishers' ledgers, copyright registers, inventories of estates, diaries and letters, and many more. Every item in that vast corpus has its own story, inscribed in the unassuming details of the title page. With the tools of bibliography, we can trace the career of a book across time and space. In such retrospective records as the *Eighteenth-Century Short Title Catalog,*

Charles Evans's *American Bibliography* and its continuation by Ralph R. Shaw and Richard H. Shoemaker, and the *National Union Catalogue of Pre-1956 Imprints* lie the essential clues for any title: its debut in print, revealed in the place and year of publication; its origins, indicated by the author, publisher, and/or printer; its format, length, and occasionally price; its popularity, as suggested by repeated printings and new editions; its adoption by new publishers and its translation into other languages; its last appearance before the public. The title page not only identifies a work but advertises it for sale. The marketing campaign is often carried out through a catchy title and a canny description of the author, noting his or her expertise, institutional affiliation, and previous works. It may also call attention to the genre. Then again, the book may never have been a commercial venture. The aspirations for a work are intimated in the mode of publication. It may have been sponsored by a church, eager to honor its pastor by paying to put his sermons into print. It may have been financed through advance subscriptions from private individuals, such as the wealthy, patriotic gentlemen whose names were printed along with Joel Barlow's epic poem, *The Vision of Columbus* (1787), with "His Most Christian Majesty" Louis XVI of France and "His Excellency George Washington, Esq." heading the list (Barlow; Charvat, 5–12). It may have come into print only through the initiative of the author, who hired the printer to issue the work. Such self-publishing was common in the seventeenth and eighteenth centuries, when gentlemen engaged in writing not for profit, but as a public service. Indeed, in the desire to avoid notice, the author may have opted to remain anonymous or to employ a pseudonym appropriate to the subject ("Solon" for a would-be lawmaker, "Publius" for a citizen, the *nom de plume* shared by the three authors of the *Federalist* papers, Alexander Hamilton, James Madison, and John Jay). Such clues point to the social standing and cultural significance of a book and its author. Taking many titles together, they can chart the conduct of the book trade, the popularity of books and genres, the geographical distribution of publishers, the social character of authorship in a particular period.

Consider the list of volumes shipped by the London bookseller Robert Boulter to the Boston merchant John Usher about 1682 (ch. 2 below). It is a sparse document, giving a shorthand description of each title and recording how many of each were sent. Altogether, 127 separate works, in 820 copies, made the Atlantic crossing. This was an unsolicited order, gotten up by the enterprising Boulter as a "mercantile adventure," in hopes of capitalizing on New Englanders' desire to feel connected to the world they had left behind (Ford, 12). What meanings can be extracted from this roster of obscure seventeenth-century books? The early twentieth-century historian Worthington C. Ford, who first put the list into print, decoded the entries and reconstructed their bibliographical identities. From this evidence he grouped the titles into genres and ranked them according to popularity. Religion claimed first place, amounting to half the consignment, followed by schoolbooks; such devout and useful works were sure to appeal to Puritans. Surprisingly, Boulter had also packed some 160 romances, tales, and other "small books and pleasant histories" into the crate (Spufford). Ford judged that a miscalculation of the market. When Usher sent his own orders to London in succeeding years, there was hardly a light tale among them. The contrast suggested the sober temperament of the Puritan fathers. "Boston was not inclined to frivolous reading, and the London book-lists of Usher did not encourage the cultivation of such a taste" (Ford, 50).

Perhaps so, but with a little more digging into the Boulter list, a richer, livelier story can be told. A veteran of the London book trade, Boulter had been in business for some seventeen years when he dispatched the literary cargo to the City upon a Hill. The shipment was assembled at an unusual moment in the book business. From 1679 to 1685, Restoration England was gripped by political crisis, fueled by fears of Popish plots and Protestant uprisings, as Whigs and Tories squared off in a run-up to the Glorious Revolution of 1689. Amid the rising tensions, in 1679 Parliament failed to renew the Press Act, under which books were carefully scrutinized before publication and those deemed dangerous to the state suppressed. Censorship was not effectively restored until 1685, when James II assumed the throne. In the interregnum, the presses clattered with dissent, in an outpouring of opinion not seen since the English Civil War (Jones, 197–233; Johns, 230–48). So many imprints flooded the market that the price of books went tumbling. In a bid to recoup his losses, Boulter selected a lively sample of books currently circulating in London and dispatched them to Puritan readers in Boston (Amory, 104–5). Most of the consignment had been published within the previous five years. It included an exposé of the "horrid popish plot" against Charles II (Smith) and a report of the trials of the conspirators (L'Estrange). Accompanying them was a narrative of similar Catholic schemes against Queen Elizabeth, originally published in the 1580s and now restored to print. Boulter also catered to the New Englanders' preferences in religion. Every work of divinity in the shipment—sermons, treatises, conversion narratives—had been carefully chosen for the audience. Nearly all of the clerical authors were nonconformists—Independents, Presbyterians, and an occasional Baptist—who had suffered for the sake of conscience. Some had given up office, rather than submit to the Church of England; others had been arrested for holding unauthorized religious meetings. To New England Puritans, who had been harried out of the land by Archbishop Laud, these were fellow martyrs in the cause of Christ. Massachusetts ministers regularly corresponded with their persecuted brethren, worried about their fate, and promoted their writings to parishioners (Bremer, 202–52). The works of a few—Joseph Alleine's *An Alarm to Unconverted Sinners*, Richard Baxter's *A Call to the Unconverted*—served as spiritual guides to anxious Christians for two centuries; Massachusetts readers helped make them "steady sellers" (Hall, *Worlds of Wonder*, 48–50). Clearly, Boulter knew his market.

Why, then, did he slip all those light romances and joke books into the mix? Protestants on both sides of the Atlantic were regularly cautioned against such reading. "When thou canst read," advised the Reverend Thomas White, "read no Ballads and foolish Books, but the Bible" (Hall, *Cultures of Print*, 51). Yet there they sat, alongside Latin textbooks for Harvard students, volumes of Ovid and Seneca for the learned, practical handbooks for merchants' clerks, and all those summons to salvation. One title surely stood out: *Guy of Warwick*, the tale of the "noble Exploits and Victories" of an English knight in the century before William the Conqueror. First recorded in an Anglo-Norman manuscript of the early thirteenth century, then translated into Middle English around 1300, the medieval legend began a long literary career as a 13,000-line poem celebrating the chivalry and piety of the steward's son who rose to become the Earl of Warwick. To earn the hand of the earl's daughter, Guy embarks on a quest for glory in tournaments and war on the Continent. Mission accomplished, he returns home to find England in danger from Irish dragons, come from the west, and Saracen giants in the employ of Danish invaders from the east. Wherever Guy goes, he leaves bodies in his wake. In the course of this bloody progress, the knight recognizes the vanity of worldly striving and pledges his life to God. No matter that he has won the fair Felice, the earl's daughter, as his bride. No sooner do they marry than Guy leaves home to roam the world as a hermit. The two are reunited only shortly before their deaths. This elaborate saga was originally composed for a select audience of barons, but it gained considerable popularity as a manuscript book, and when printing began in England, it was one of the earliest titles to be set in type. By the Tudor-Stuart era, Guy had become an English national hero, his adventures told and retold to popular audiences on the stage, in broadside ballads, quarto editions, and chapbooks—and much abbreviated in the process (Richmond; Simons). The romance was sung as a "ditty" at festival times, especially at Christmas, and in alehouses and "other places of base resort" (Richmond, 168). Guy was, it seems, a man for all classes, except for humanist critics and Puritan clerics. As early as 1572, one observer included *Guy* in a list of "harmful books whose vogue had passed with the darkness of papist belief" (Simons, 238). A century later, the pious author of a *History of Genesis* complained of *Guy*'s continuing popularity: "And yet how often do we see Parents prefer Tom Thumb, Guy of Warwick, Valentine and Orson, or some other foolish book, before the Book of Life" (Richmond, 163).

The brief entry for *Guy* on Boulter's list, along with *Valentine and Orson* and other romances, challenges easy judgments about the Puritans and print. Surely, Boulter knew such tales were targets of the culture war that reformers were waging in Old England and New. Was he simply aiming to clear his shelves of unsold books? Did he guess that a taste for light reading had survived the ocean crossing and taken root in the thin soil of the Puritan commonwealth? Unfortunately, we have no way to know. But this was not the last to be heard of *Guy* and his literary companions in New England book history. Around 1700 the Boston minister Cotton Mather was horrified to discover "Plays, and Songs, and Novels, and Romances, and foolish and filthy Jests, and Poetry prostituted unto Execrable Ribaldry" for sale at the booksellers, in plain view of female shoppers (Hall, "Readers and Writers," 127). The minister could take comfort that few colonial printers ever issued American editions of these objectionable works, but that did not stop their circulation in the countryside. Sometime during the decade before the American Revolution, a mischievous youth in the Connecticut Valley town of Hanover, New Hampshire, came across a copy of *Guy* and found it much to his liking. "The character of Guy, Earl of Warwick, was my favorite," he recalled. "I felt an enthusiastic ardor to tread the stage on which he had so fortunately exhibited. I often viewed myself at the head of armies, rushing with impetuosity into the thickest of embattled foes, and bearing down all who dared oppose me." The boy, the son of a strict Presbyterian minister, grew up to become the "notorious" rogue Stephen Burroughs, who won fame not for military exploits but for a wild career as a "confidence man" and criminal. In retrospect, Burroughs conceded that "reading and dwelling so much on those romantic scenes," at a time when his mind was so impressionable, "was attended with very pernicious consequences" (Burroughs, 9; Gross, "Confidence Man"). Such cautionary examples had little effect on printers. In the early republic, *Guy* obtained his own American editions, though his heyday was over. The brave knight fought his final battles in a cheap, illustrated children's book in 1847, one of "Grandfather Lovechild's Nursery Stories" issued by a Philadelphia publisher. In badly written verse, he bore the bourgeois message that "There's nothing in this work-day world / We may not win / If we be energetic, constant, brave / And free from sin." It is no wonder *Guy* lost his following. By the time he went out of print, he had been sanitized for the descendants of Puritans (Lovechild).

With *Guy of Warwick*, bibliography becomes a form of literary archaeology, as we probe the multiple layers of meaning buried in its record of publication and reader reception. Not all titles on Boulter's list nor in any of the other sources gathered in *Perspectives on American Book History* will be such rich sites for excavation. But every one has taken a journey along the various circuits connecting author to reader. One fascination of book history lies in retracing those steps and discovering fresh angles on general history in the details of a single publication or of a larger set of works, such as the shipment Boulter sent to Boston. That one "mercantile adventure" offers a glimpse into transatlantic trade. It reveals the breakdown of censorship in London. It highlights the culture wars of the seventeenth century, even as it suggests the fluidity of the book market, where romances and sermons mingled together. These findings are not restricted to any one time or place. Discovering such patterns can be a continuing source of instruction and entertainment. So, too, can delving into the business decisions of publishers, the ideologies of print, and the cultural practices of reading, to name just a few of the themes opened up by this collection. To dip into *Perspectives on American Book History* is to find surprises and pleasures on every page and to see the past through new eyes. So long as the written word furnishes such satisfactions, we need not worry about the future of books, whatever form they may ultimately take.

WORKS CITED

Alleine, Joseph. *An Alarm to Unconverted Sinners.* . . . London: N. Simmons, 1675.

*Amory, Hugh. "Printing and Bookselling in New England, 1638–1713." In *A History of the Book in America*. Vol. 1, *The Colonial Book in the Atlantic World*, edited by Hugh Amory and David D. Hall, 83–116.

Anderson, Benedict Richard O'Gorman. *Imagined Communities: Reflections on the Origin and Spread of Nationalism*. Rev. and exp. ed. London and New York: Verso Books, 1991.

Barlow, Joel. *The Vision of Columbus: A Poem in Nine Books*. Hartford: Hudson and Goodwin, for the author, 1787.

Baxter, Richard. *A Call to the Unconverted to Turn and Live. With the Addition of Some Prayers*. London: N. Simmons, 1674.

*Beales, Ross W., and E. Jennifer Monaghan. "Literacy and Schoolbooks." In *A History of the Book in America*. Vol. 1, *The Colonial Book in the Atlantic World*, edited by Hugh Amory and David D. Hall, 380–87.

Bremer, Francis J. *Congregational Communion: Clerical Friendship in the Anglo-American Puritan Community, 1610–1692*. Boston: Northeastern University Press, 1994.

Brodhead, Richard H. *Cultures of Letters: Scenes of Reading and Writing in Nineteenth-Century America*. Chicago: University of Chicago Press, 1993.

Brown, Richard D. *Knowledge Is Power: The Diffusion of Information in Early America, 1700–1865*. New York: Oxford University Press, 1989.

Burroughs, Stephen. *Memoirs of the Notorious Stephen Burroughs: Containing Many Incidents in the Life of This Wonderful Man, Never Before Published*. Boston: Charles Gaylord, 1840.

Charvat, William. *The Profession of Authorship in America, 1800–1870: The Papers of William Charvat*. Edited by Matthew J. Bruccoli. Columbus: Ohio State University Press, 1968.

Coser, Lewis, Charles Kadushin, and Walter W. Powell. *Books: The Culture and Commerce of Publishing*. New York: Basic Books, 1982; Chicago: University of Chicago Press, 1985.

Darnton, Robert. *The Business of Enlightenment: A Publishing History of the Encyclopédie, 1775–1800*. Cambridge, Mass.: Harvard University Press, 1979.

———. *The Forbidden Best-Sellers of Pre-Revolutionary France*. New York: W. W. Norton, 1995.

———. *The Literary Underground of the Old Regime*. Cambridge, Mass.: Harvard University Press, 1982.

———. "What Is the History of Books?" In Robert Darnton, *The Kiss of Lamourette: Reflections on Cultural History*, 107–35. New York: W. W. Norton, 1990.

Davidson, Cathy N. *Revolution and the Word: The Rise of the Novel in America*. New York: Oxford University Press, 1986.

Dewar, James A. "The Information Age and the Printing Press: Looking Backward to See Ahead." Essay by Rand Corporation analyst posted on the research center's website <http://www.rand.org/publications/P/P8014/>, December 5, 1999.

Eisenstein, Elizabeth L. "From Scriptoria to Printing Shops: Evolution and Revolution in the Early Printed Book Trade." In *Books and Society in History: Papers of the Association of College and Research Libraries Rare Books and Manuscripts Section Preconference, 24–28 June 1980, Boston, Massachusetts*, edited by Kenneth E. Carpenter. New York and London: R. R. Bowker, 1983.

———. *The Printing Press as an Agent of Change: Communications and Cultural Transformation in Early-Modern Europe*. 2 vols. Cambridge: Cambridge University Press, 1979; *The Printing Revolution in Early Modern Europe*. Abr. ed. Cambridge and New York: Cambridge University Press, 1983.

Epstein, Jason. *Book Business: Publishing Past, Present, and Future*. New York: W. W. Norton, 2000.

Fahri, Paul, and Megan Rosenfeld. "American Pop Penetrates Worldwide." *Washington Post*, October 25, 1998, A1, A26–27.

Febvre, Lucien, and Henri-Jean Martin. *The Coming of the Book: The Impact of Printing 1450–1800*, translated by David Gerard and edited by Geoffrey Nowell-Smith and David Wootton. London: New Left Books, 1976.

Ford, Worthington Chauncey. *The Boston Book Market, 1679–1700*. Boston: Club of Odd Volumes, 1917. Reprint, New York: Burt Franklin, 1972.

Ginzburg, Carlo. *The Cheese and the Worms: The Cosmos of a Sixteenth-Century Miller*, translated by John and Anne Tedeschi. Baltimore: Johns Hopkins University Press, 1980.

Gross, Robert A. "Communications Revolutions: Writing a History of the Book for an Electronic Age." *Rare Books and Manuscripts Librarianship* 13 (1998): 8–26.

———. "The Confidence Man and the Preacher: The Cultural Politics of Shays's Rebellion." In *In Debt to Shays: The Bicentennial of an Agrarian Rebellion*, edited by Robert A. Gross, 297–320. Charlottesville: University Press of Virginia, 1993.

*Hall, David D. "On Native Ground: From the History of Printing to the History of the Book." *Proceedings of the American Antiquarian Society* 93, pt. 2 (1983): 313–36. Reprinted in David D. Hall, *Cultures of Print: Essays in the History of the Book*.

*———. "Readers and Writers in Early New England." In *A History of the Book in America*. Vol. 1, *The Colonial Book in the Atlantic World*, edited by Hugh Amory and David D. Hall, 117–51.

———. *Worlds of Wonder, Days of Judgment: Popular Religious Belief in Early New England*. New York: Alfred A. Knopf, 1989.

Johns, Adrian. *The Nature of the Book: Print and Knowledge in the Making*. Chicago: University of Chicago Press, 1998.

Jones, J. R. *Country and Court: England, 1658–1714*. Cambridge, Mass.: Harvard University Press, 1978.

Joyce, William L., David D. Hall, Richard D. Brown, and John B. Hench, eds. *Printing and Society in Early America*. Worcester, Mass.: American Antiquarian Society, 1983.

Kilgour, Frederick G. *The Evolution of the Book*. New York: Oxford University Press, 1998.

L'Estrange, Roger, comp. *The History of the Plot, or a Brief and Historical Account of the Charge and Defence of Edward Coleman . . . Sir George Wakeman . . . ; Not Omitting Any One Material Passage in the Whole Proceeding*. London: R. Tomson, 1679.

Lovechild, Laurence. *Guy of Warwick*. Philadelphia: George B. Zieber, 1847.

Massachusetts Spy, January 7, 1771.

McLuhan, Marshall. *The Gutenberg Galaxy: The Making of Typographic Man*. Toronto: University of Toronto Press, 1962.

———. *Understanding Media: The Extensions of Man*. New York: McGraw-Hill, 1964.

*Nord, David Paul. "Systematic Benevolence: Religious Publishing and the Marketplace in Early Nineteenth-Century America." In *Communication and Change in American Religious History*, edited by Leonard I. Sweet, 239–69.

Radway, Janice A. *A Feeling for Books: The Book-of-the-Month Club, Literary Taste, and Middle-Class Desire*. Chapel Hill: University of North Carolina Press, 1998.

———. *Reading the Romance: Women, Patriarchy, and Popular Literature*. Chapel Hill: University of North Carolina Press, 1984.

Richmond, Velma Bourgeois. *The Legend of Guy of Warwick*. New York and London: Garland Publishers, 1996.

Schiffrin, André. *The Business of Books: How International Conglomerates Took Over Publishing and Changed the Way We Read*. London and New York: Verso Books, 2000.

Simons, John, ed. *Guy of Warwick and Other Chapbook Romances: Six Tales from the Popular Literature of Pre-industrial England*. Exeter, England: University of Exeter Press, 1998.

Smith, John. *The Narrative of Mr. John Smith, of Walworth in the County of Palatine of Durham, Gent., Containing a Further Discovery of the Late Horrid and Popish Plot. . . .* London: R. Boulter, 1679.

Spufford, Margaret. *Small Books and Pleasant Histories: Popular Fiction and Its Readership in Seventeenth-Century England.* Cambridge: Cambridge University Press, 1981.

Winkler, Karen J. "In Electronic Age, Scholars Are Drawn to Study of Print." *Chronicle of Higher Education,* July 14, 1993, A6–8.

2

Literacy and Reading in Puritan New England

JILL LEPORE

ENGLISH PURITANS—Protestants who wanted to "purify" the Anglican Church —held that all believers needed to read the Bible for themselves. As a result, Puritans were among the most highly literate segment of seventeenth-century English society. When thousands of them migrated to North America to found a "New England" in the 1620s and 1630s, they brought traditions of reading and writing. It took less than a decade for their leaders to found Harvard College (1636) and establish a printing press in Cambridge, Massachusetts (1639). For ordinary residents of Puritan New England, literacy primarily meant the ability to read the Bible and other religious materials (such as psalm books), but it also afforded the opportunity to read other works, notably practical guides such as almanacs. Those who could write as well as read (for the two skills were taught separately) could also keep diaries, write letters, or sign official documents—all of which helps explain why more written material survives from colonial New England than from any other part of English North America.

And *English* North America it was. It is too easy for us to imagine Puritans as the founders of what would—more than a century later—become the United States. They did not imagine themselves that way. In their own eyes, they were transplanted Englishmen and Englishwomen creating a New England. Their relation to books and reading confirmed this identity. Most of what they read—including their Bibles— was printed in England and shipped across the Atlantic. Their leaders, many of them educated in English colleges, corresponded with ministers and relations back home; their booksellers ordered hundreds of volumes from London. When such New England Puritans as Cotton Mather wrote books, they were likely to send them to London for publication. (Shorter works, such as pamphlets and schoolbooks, were more likely to be printed in Massachusetts.) Newspapers did not take hold until early in the 1700s, but the earliest ones were chronicles of European affairs, not compendia of local occurrences. Seventeenth-century New England was the western periphery of England.

At the same time, New Englanders found themselves in contact with the indigenous people of their adopted home: the Wampanoags, Narragansetts, Nipmucks, Pequots, and other Algonquian peoples. Much of their contact concerned land. The growing English colony sought to expand westward, and many Puritans saw acquiring Indian lands as bringing order to the wilderness. For John Eliot, Christianizing the native people mattered more. Eliot and other missionaries established Christian "praying towns" among the Indians in Massachusetts Bay and Plymouth colonies. Eliot also translated the Bible into Massachusett, an Algonquian language. After King Philip's War of 1675–77, the bloodiest conflict between the Massachusetts colonists and their native neighbors, several New Englanders wrote histories of the event. The story of the publication of those works provides another reminder of how New England stood between two other worlds: several of the histories were published in London, not Boston. And one of those published in Massachusetts, Mary Rowlandson's narrative of her captivity among the Indians, may well have been typeset by James Printer—a literate Indian who worked at the Cambridge Press.

ARTIFACTS

Studying literacy in seventeenth-century New England—or in any of early modern Europe and its colonies, for that matter—requires us to examine seemingly unfamiliar sources, often in unfamiliar language and spellings. The artifacts in this chapter exemplify many different kinds of sources, from which the careful reader can glean much about reading and writing among the inhabitants of colonial Massachusetts. The first three artifacts come from published materials. *The Whole Booke of Psalmes* (1640), often called the *Bay Psalm Book*, whose title page appears here, was the first English book printed in North America. Anne Bradstreet (1612?–1672), who wrote her poetry in Massachusetts but published it in London, was the daughter of one of the colony's first leaders. The two poems reproduced here, "Prologue" and "The Author to Her Book," both explore the tensions of being a woman writer in her society—at the same time that they testify to the levels of literacy that some women in that society attained. John Eliot's (1604–1690) Massachusett Bible (1661), in the Algonquian Indian language, was the first Bible printed in North America.

Anne Bradstreet, Two Poems (1650, 1678)[1]

"Prologue" (1650)

To sing of Wars, of Captains, and of Kings,
Of Cities founded, Common-wealths begun,
For my mean pen are too superiour things:
Or how they all, or each their dates have run
Let Poets and Historians set these forth,
My obscure Lines shall not so dim their worth.

But when my wondring eyes and envious heart
Great *Bartas* sugar'd lines, do but read o're
Fool I do grudg the Muses did not part
'Twixt him and me that overfluent store;

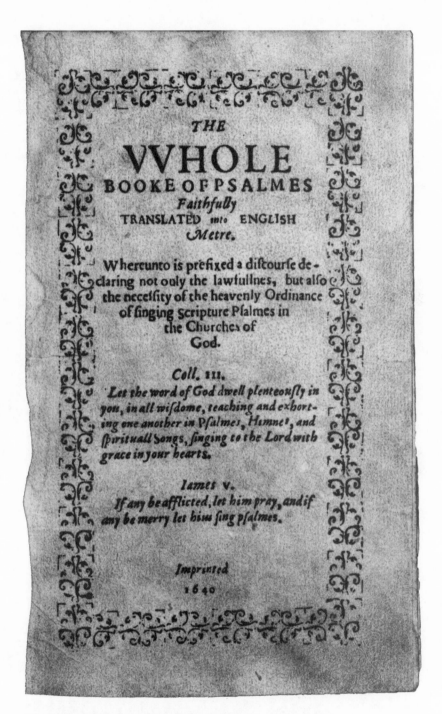

The Whole Booke of Psalmes (1640)[2]

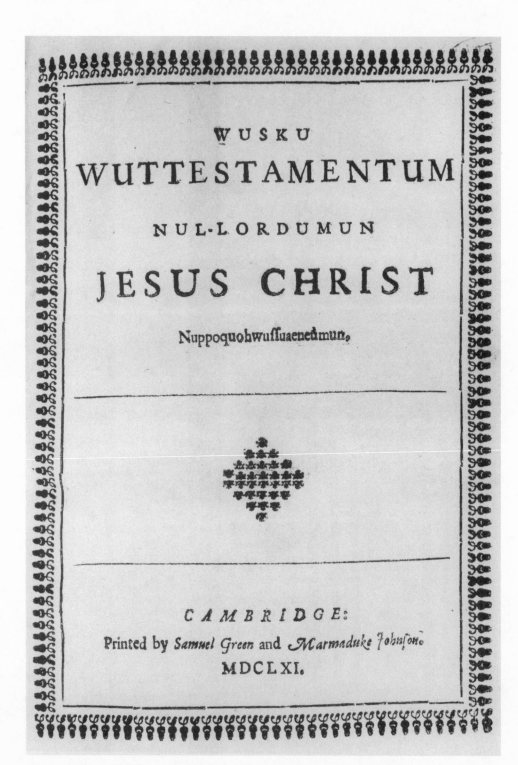

Wusku Wuttestamentum Nul-Lordumun Jesus Christ (1661)[3]

A *Bartas* can, do what a *Bartas* will
But simple I according to my skill.

From school-boyes tongue no rhet'rick we expect
Nor yet a sweet Consort from broken strings,
Nor perfect beauty, where's a main defect:
My foolish, broken, blemish'd Muse so sings
And this to mend, alas, no Art is able,
'Cause nature, made it so irreparable.

Nor can I, like that fluent sweet tongu'd Greek,
Who lisp'd at first, in future times speak plain
By Art he gladly found what he did seek
A full requital of his, striving pain
Art can do much, but this maxime's most sure
A weak or wounded brain admits no cure.

I am obnoxious to each carping tongue
Who says my hand a needle better fits,
A Poets pen all scorn I should thus wrong,
For such despite they cast on Female wits:
If what I do prove well, it won't advance,
They'l say it's stoln, or else it was by chance.

But sure the Antique Greeks were far more mild
Else of our Sexe, why feigned they those Nine
And poesy made, *Calliope*'s own Child;
So 'mongst the rest they placed the Arts Divine,
But this weak knot, they will full soon untie,
The Greeks did nought, but play the fools & lye.

Let Greeks be Greeks, and women what they are
Men have precedency and still excell,
It is but vain unjustly to wage warre;
Men can do best, and women know it well
Preheminence in all and each is yours;
Yet grant some small acknowledgement of ours.

And oh ye high flown quills that soar the Skies,
And ever with your prey still catch your praise,
If e're you daigne these lowly lines your eyes
Give Thyme or Parsley wreath, I ask no bayes,
This mean and unrefined ore of mine
Will make you glistring gold, but more to shine.

"The Author to Her Book" (1678)

Thou ill-form'd offspring of my feeble brain,
Who after birth did'st by my side remain,
Till snatcht from thence by friends, less wise than true
Who thee abroad, expos'd to publick view,
Made thee in raggs, halting to th' press to trudge,
Where errors were not lessened (all may judge)
At thy return my blushing was not small,
My rambling brat (in print) should mother call,
I cast thee by as one unfit for light,
Thy Visage was so irksome in my sight;
Yet being mine own, at length affection would
Thy blemishes amend, if so I could:
I wash'd thy face, but more defects I saw,
And rubbing off a spot, still made a flaw.
I stretcht thy joynts to make thee even feet,
Yet still thou run'st more hobling than is meet;
In better dress to trim thee was my mind,
But nought save home-spun Cloth, i'th' house I find
In this array, 'mongst Vulgars mayst thou roam
In Critick's hands, beware thou dost not come;
And take thy way where yet thou art now known,
If for thy Father askt, say, thou hadst none:
And for thy Mother, she alas is poor,
Which caus'd her thus to send thee out of door.

MULTIPLE WORLDS of reading and writing surrounded colonial New England. Richard Bourne (d. 1682), a missionary to the "praying" (that is, Christian) Indian towns of Plymouth, compiled a survey of those Indians' literacy in 1674: how many of each tribe could read and write. In reporting the results to Daniel Gookin of Boston (the document reproduced here), Bourne revealed the kinds of communication networks that connected ministers, missionaries, and other New Englanders to one another. The seven letters to and from Increase Mather (1639–1723) suggest how wide those networks could be, for Mather received correspondence not just from Plymouth but also from London and Dublin. These letters also referred to many aspects of print: the book shipments sent from a London printer to a Boston bookseller; the competing histories of King Philip's War (in which Alexander, mentioned in several letters, was an Indian sachem, Philip's brother). The page from the 1679 almanac of John Danforth (1660–1730) exhibits a genre that ordinary New Englanders knew well: Published annually, almanacs were a staple of the farmer's household or tradesman's shop, providing useful information about the weather, tides, and times of sunrise and sunset, as well as advice and short poetry. The 1683 book invoice listed titles sent to the Boston bookseller John Usher, along with the number of copies of each. Combined with bibliographical research, such invoices can often reveal what local booksellers thought their customers wanted to read. But Usher had not ordered this shipment—its contents suggest what a London bookseller imagined New Englanders wanted to read.

A Report on Literacy Rates among Massachusetts Indians (1674)[4]

Richard Bourne, of Sandwich, to Daniel Gookin,
Boston, September 1, 1674

To his much esteemed friend, Captain Gookin, in Cambridge.
Worthy Sir,

All due respects presented; according to your desire, signified in your letter unto myself, I have endeavoured to return you a particular answer, according to the short time I had to accomplish it in. . . . I hope it will occasion many to render thanks to God with myself, in respect of the grace in the gospel manifested among these poor, lost people. And for those that I have been conversant with, and employed amongst, these many years, you may please to see as followeth.

First there is Meeshawn, or near the head of the Cape, and at Punonakanit, or Billingsgate, that are praying Indians, that do frequently meet together upon the Lord's day to worship God; and likewise the rest as followeth; viz.

Men and women	51	} 72	
Young men and maids	21		
Of these seventy-two there is that can read Indian			25
And that can write there is			16

Potanumaquut, or Nawsett, or Eastham, there are praying Indians,

Men and women	24	} 44	
Young men and maids	20		
Of these forty-four there is that can read			7
That can write there is but			2

Manamoyik, there are praying Indians,

Men and women	42	} 71	
Young men and maids	29		
Of these seventy-one there is that can read			20
That can write			15
That can read English			1

Sawkattukett, Nobsquassit, Matakees, and Weequakut, praying Indians

Men and women	55	} 122	
Young men and maids	67		

Of these one hundred and twenty-two there is that can read — 33
That can write there is — 15
That can read English — 4

Satuit, Pawpoesit, Coatuit, Mashpee, Wakoquet, there is praying Indians

Men and women — 70 ⎱
Young men and maids — 25 ⎰ 95
Of these ninety-five there is that can read — 24
That can write — 10
That can read English — 2

Codtanmut, Ashimuit, Weesquobs, there is praying Indians

Men and women — 12 ⎱
Young men and maids — 10 ⎰ 22
Of these twenty-two there is that can read — 13
That can write — 7
That can read English — 2

Pispogutt, Wawayontat, Sokones, there is praying Indians

Men and women — 20 ⎱
young men and maids — 16 ⎰ 36
Of these thirty-six that can read — 20
That can write — 7

. . . We have and do want books exceedingly to carry on the work by those that are employed therein. I do not question but there is more than one hundred young ones, that are entered both in writing and reading, that are not put into this account. . . .

Thus I hope I have in general answered your queries according to the short time I had to accomplish these things in, considering the remoteness of several places, where I am conversant divers times. Thus I have given you a brief answer to your desires; intreating the blessing of the Lord to be with you and this great work for Jesus Christ which we have in hand: and rest

Yours in the service of Christ,
Rich. Bourne

Correspondence of Increase Mather (1676–1677)[5]

John Cotton, Plymouth, to Increase Mather, Boston, November 24, 1676

Rev^d & Deare Brother,

I have bin very sollicitous to answer your desires with reference to matter for your History, & did therefore goe on purpose to our Govr with your letter last Wednesday, who then promised me to devote the next day to waite upon you in looking for what he might have usefull in that respect, & speedily to write to you concerning Alexander, etc, & also he hath in his keeping something drawne up by our Secretary, which he intends to send you; or what is meet, out of it. Also I have desired & obtained of Major Bradford, a Booke in folio written by his father, which I shall send by the first opportunity by water; if I cannot send it by land. The Jour-nall of Plimouth beginnings I could send you, but I thinke it needs not, for you told me some passages in it; whence I conclude you have that booke. Major Bradford hath another printed Booke, which he thinks would well contribute to you. Its title is Good Newes from P. in N: E: But he cannot finde it. He will doe his endeavour speedily to helpe me to it. If he doe you shall soone have it. I told the Govr, the matter required hast. I hope you will very suddenly heare from him. . . .

Your Affectionate Brother,
John Cotton

The Major hath found the booke. Mr Clark posts away this Saturday sunset. I hope on Monday a man will bring you the books.

Richard Chiswell, London, to Increase Mather, Boston, February 16, 1677

S^r,

I rec'd yours of July 19th, & have in M^r. Usher's Cask p^r. Anderson, in the Ship Blessing, sent you all the books you wrote for, & have returned 8 of your Princi-ples, which I cannot sell, & having charged myself with them at 12^d. [per] book in my last accompt stated, I have discounted for them at the same rate in this.

I have added a few new things of good note which I hope you will be pleased with, the first of them is an answer to a Pamphlet I sent you in the last p[ar]cell, & which makes no small stir here at present. Hales of Eaton, & Stillingfleet are very famous. Walker of Baptism is said to be very learned & exceedingly well done. The two books of Contemplations were writ by the Lord Cheif Justice Hales, a person who for all kind of learning, Philosophy, Physick, Mathematicks, &c., as well as Law, (his proper profession,) and for most exemplary piety & untainted integrity & uprightness, has not le[ft] his fellow, nor was there, as tis believed, ever his fellow in our English Cou[rts] of Judicature before him, the whole nation mournes for the loss of him. That Great audit or Good Steward's account, in the first vollume, is a most lively & exact character of his life & practice to his dying day, & so great an honour & esteem doe all good men here beare to his memory, that I know not any two books have come forth these 20 yeares, that have sold so great a number in so short a time, as these two vollumes of his, though published without his consent, the one a little before he died, the other printing when he died, & I doubt not but when you have read them you will like them also.

S^r, I received the two coppies of your history of the Warrs in New Engl^d, for which I heartily thank you, & two also for your Brother, which I sent last week away for Dublin, but before these came to my hands (at least a month before) a friend of mine by accident met with the very first of them that came over to England & brought it to me, & caused it to be printed, but some people here made it too much their business to cry it downe, & sayd a better narrative was comeing, which did very much disappoint me, so that I never sold 5 hundred of them; yet as a token of my thankfullness to you for your respects, I have sent you two dozen of them: That they are without the Exhortation mentioned in the title is because the Coppy I received from my friend had it not, & there was not then another coppy come.

S^r, I rejoyce with you for that the Lord has been pleased so far to vanquish your enemies: Poore soules, Oh that their eyes were opened & they convinced how they resist their owne mercies, even the everlasting gospell, which the Lord has brought into their Land, & a people that wish & pray for their eternall happiness; sure the time will come that they shall be called, the Lord have compassion upon them, & hasten the accomplishment of those gracious promises that concern it. The God of Israel keep you, is the hearty prayer of

> Your ffriend & servant,
> Ric. Chiswell

I have sent a few books to Mr Usher without order, which I put in to fill up the Cask. You may see them at his shop, & I hope may help some of them off his hands, by recomending them to your publick Library, especially the new ones, which cannot be there already, p[ar]ticularly D^r. Caves Lives of the Fathers, & D^r. Cary's Chronologicall account of ancient time, which are both exceedingly well esteemed by the most learned & ingenious men here.

A Coppy

	£	s.	d.
Postage of 2 Pacquett wherein Letters for your Brothers	0.	1.	0
Dr Tuckneys Sermons, 4°.	0.	8.	0
Straight gate to heaven, 12°. bound,	0.	0.	8
Hotchkis reformation or ruine, 8°.	0.	2.	0
Discovery of Pigmies, 8°.	0.	1.	0
Horologicall Dialogues, 8°.	0.	1.	0
Hornes Cause of Infants maintained, 4°.	0.	1.	0
Whiston on Baptism, all 3 parts, 8°.	0.	5.	6.
State of Northampton, 4°.	0.	0.	3
Tozer's Directions to a godly life, 12°.	0.	1.	0

Barbets Chirurgery, 8°.	0.	6.	0
Leybournes Dialling, 4°.	0.	3.	0
Hook's Motion of the Earth, 4°.	0.	1.	0
Stephenson's mathemat. compendium, 12°.	0.	2.	6
8 First principles of New England, 4°. returnd	0.	8.	0
ADDED.—			
Pacquet of advices to the men of Shaftsbury, 4°.	0.	1.	6
King & L^d. Chancellor's Speeches.	0.	0.	6
Dr Stillingfleet's Letter to a Deist, 8°.	0.	2.	6
Mr Hales (of Eaton) his Tracts, 8°.	0.	2.	6
Hornecks Law of Consideration, 8°.	0.	3.	6
Walker of Baptism, 12°.	0.	3.	6
Rules of Health, 12°.	0.	1.	0
Family Physitian, 12°.	0.	1.	0
Judge Hale's Contemplations, 2 Vol. 8°.	0.	10.	0
24 Warrs of New England, 4°.	—	—	—
Catalogue No. 7. 8. 9. 10, fol.	—	—	—
	3.	7.	5

Nathaniel Mather, Dublin, Ireland, to Increase Mather, Boston, February 26, 1677

Dear Brother,

Yours of 8ber 13 was the latest that I recd from you and with it 3 of your historyes of the late war with the Indians, for which I heartily thank you & wish I had had more of them, for but 2 or 3 others that I hear of came to this kingdome & they were so acceptable that save that I kept one of them, to read it over a few hours, I have not yet been able to keep any of them in my hands. Indeed they were opened at the Custome house by his Matyes Commissioners, & one of them dd to the Lord Lieut, which his Excellency after hee had read it returned again. I bless the Lord for the sp^t that breaths all along in it. . . .

I much rejoyce in God's great mercy begun in your son Cotton. I heartily thank him for his map of New England. It helps mee much in understanding your & other narratives. One defect or two I observe in it, there is wanting a scale of miles & a compass, & if I have not forgotten (which it is like I may) the Blew hills are misplaced, for hee hath placeth them south from Dorchester, whereas according to my defaced idea of the Countrey, they were rather northward from it. . . .

I remayn Dear Br, Your most aff. Br.
N.M.

John Cotton, Plymouth, to Increase Mather, Boston, March 19, 1677

Rev^d & Deare Brother,

I could have desired to have kept your booke a few days longer, whereby it might have bin filled with marginal notes of Erratas. Our Govr & Magistrat had some cursory perusall of the booke, the mistakes are Judged to be many more then the truths in it. . . .

Pray for your Lov: Br:
J: C:

John Cotton, Plymouth, to Increase Mather, Boston, April 14, 1677

Rev^d & Deare Brother,

Soe much confidence I have in you, that I durst to put my life in your hands; how it comes to passe that you, my most intire friend, have endangered my losse of my best friends here, besides all that reproach those concerned in the Bay will lay upon me, you will enforme me in your next: I went last Wednesday to visit our Govr; who had lately recieved letters from Mr. Hubbert & Mr Dudley, informing thus: Mr. Hub: saith, Mr John Cotton one of your preachers hath written to his Brother Increase Mather, that some of your magistrates said there were as many mistakes or untruths in the booke as lines, this he had from Mr Allen, & Mr Thacher, who said he heard the letter read, & 1 of these ministers advised him to send to the Govr for satisfaction: Mr Dud: writes sharply & reproachfully of me for what I wrote to you: Our Govr is angry, & sent for the Treasurer, the day before, & possessed him as if he were the maine man whom I intended: but when I came to the Govr, I told his honour, that divers magistrates spake of mistakes in the booke: Mr D: & Mr H: desire our Govr to put an *Imprimatur*, & to assert the truth of the booke: I told the Govr; I hoped he would returne noe answer that should entrench upon the truth of my words, for I would assert that I had written nothing but the truth. . . . I am at a losse what to write at such a distance; my desire is that you would honestly tell me why you trusted J: A: havinge litle reason to expect but that he would make mischeife of it. I am certaine you intended noe harme to me, but if you doe not improove your piety & prudence to suppresse discourse of this subject, ——— . . . I am,

Your Affectionate Brother
John Cotton

I am in great trouble of spirit, & straitened for time, soe that I cannot write to you as I would about this matter, I lack to speake with you, I hope my letter you keep close; I finde noe magistrate disowne his words, & therefo truth is my friend, but I feare lest our Govr write some kinde of Attestation, etc. I dare not write what I thinke: Pray write to me, what the very sentence is, which I wrote about mistakes, *verba*[*tim.*]

Increase Mather, Boston, to John Cotton, Plymouth, April 21, 1677

Dear Brother,

I am sorry to hear what Mr H. hath written to your Governour concerning your letter to me which he never saw nor hath truly reported. If the generality of Reports in his Narrative should be like that in his [?], it is pitty. You say indeed in your letter, that some of your Magistrates said he was mistaken in asserting that Alexander dyed before he came halfeway home. And also that somebody (whether your selfe or who it is you doe noe express) judged there were many mistakes in what he had published. But you doe not write that there are as many mistakes as Lines in Mr H Narrative, much less that your Magistrates did any of them say so. Mr H hath therefore done wrong to you and others in so reporting of you. I did not divulge your letter onely Mr Th & Mr A. (being concerned in giving Imprimatur) were desired by Mr H. to enquire of me what mistakes I observed in his Narrative, therefore I read to them, what you wrote, but did not mention your Name, onely that I had received the letter from a minister in Plymouth Colony.

I was forward in encouraging Mr. H in his worke. And of my own accord gave a large Imprimatur to his Booke, but afterwards withdrew it partly because I understood there was more mistakes in it (and I am justly informed that in Connecticott they find much fault with it) than at first I thought there had been. And partly because He bid the printer set Mr Allen his name to my [?] & yet Mr A. never saw it to this day, which thing some take to be a degree of Forgery, had it bin done as was designed. Al so because I perceived so much of Adulation (as it seemed to me) as caused his discourse to be Nauseous & I believe modest & Humble Spirits can not but wish the style had bin otherwise. . . .

When you see your Govr, present my service to him. I doubt not, but when He is rightly informed, any hard thoughts which Mr H may by his misreport have occasioned concerning yourselfe will vanish.

John Cotton, Plymouth, to Increase Mather, Boston, June 25, 1677

Revd & Deare Brother,

Mr Shove was this day at my house; as he passed along to Barnstable, (for your booke he thankes you) & told me that in Mr H's history, things are strangely falsifyed, (I use his owne words) he much commends your History, & sayes had Mr H: followed your Narrative he had showed more truth; my request to you is, that you will prudently of your owne accord (unlesse you see weighty reason to the contrary) write a letter to Mr Shove, & desire him to acquaint you with the mistakes he knowes to be in that booke; I doubt not but he will readily grant your desires, for he freely asserts many things to be notorious, & if you had the particulars in writing, I believe it would be of good use: If you see meete to write to him, pray doe it now

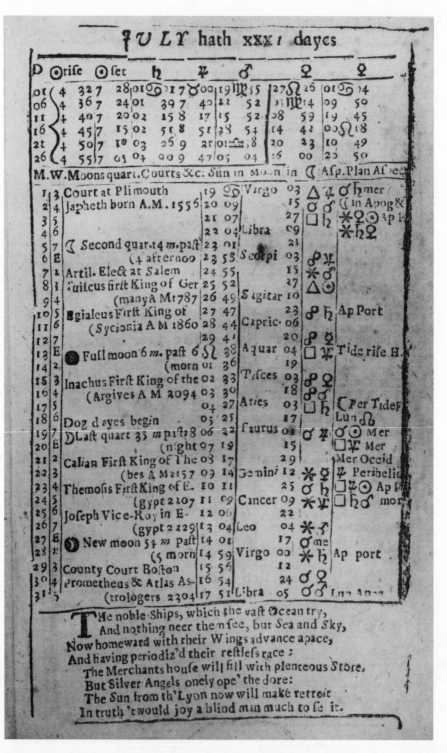

John Danforth, *An Almanack . . . for . . . 1679* (1679)[6]

by Mr. Clarke, & send it hither, because he will call next weeke, & soe you may soone have an answer:

Our due salutations to you & sisters & cousens, craving your prayers, etc., for me & mine, in great haste, I rest,

Your Affectionate Brother,
John Cotton

A Book Invoice (c. 1683)[7]

Books sent to John Usher of Boston without order by Robert Boulter of London.

12	Terrences	2	lyfe and death [of Joseph Alleine]
38	Bonds horrace	5	sincere Convert
13	erasmus Colloquies	9	sound beleevers
13	dyers worcks	1	owen on the sperit
22	apples of Gould	1	—— on the hebrews
3	Calamys ark	4	person of Christ
6	meads almost a Christian	16	boatswains art
10	foxes end of tyme	2	felthams resolves
3	faramond	1	Cooks marrow [of chirurgery]
4	brooks ark	8	Cotton on the Covenant
9	norwoods epitomy	3	queens Closet
15	bybles	4	winchester phrasis
12	Cocker Cockers tutours	16	Cap of gray hairs
4	Glasson of law	2	rarlerys remains
2	last part of the english rogue	2	Clelias
22	turky skins	13	sellers navigation
2	parismus	12	seamans Companion
1	destruction of troy	6	brooks remedies
1	Valentyn and orson	9	argalus and parthenia
4	Goulmans dictionarys	1	Assemblys annotations
15	dugarts Rhetorique	7	Clarks tutours
10	Complete modelist	2	Compleat Clark
4	Johnson arithmatick	6	burrougs Contentment
4	ovid metamorphosis	2	Collins on providence
4	esops in english	2	Everards workes
2	burroughs on matthew	6	Baxters Call
5	Carmichael on mortification	6	Doctrin of the byble
5	mitchells sermons	10	Wills Commonwealth
8	alleins allarm	2	reynolds on Murther
3	remaines [of Joseph Alleine]	1	pembrooks arcadia

3	Colliers divinity	1	Ceasars Commentary
2	Flavell on providence	2	leighs Caesars
3	touchstones [by John Flavell]	6	wise masters
12	smiths narrative	2	Erastus
12	Clarks formula	2	Unlucky Citicen
24	testaments	2	Rich Cabinet
6	senecas	1	Senecas moralls
3	Doolitles Catechis	9	Gentle Craft
2	Coles soveranity	1	Cambdens Elizabeth
3	Januas works	1	Miltons history
5	Culpepers dispensatory	6	Guy of Warwick
6	phisitian	6	Reynard fox
2	perfect politician	3	war with the Jews
6	ashwoods trade	1	Parys Narative
3	rythers plat [for mariners]	12	dr Faustus
1	baxter of Concord	6	tom reading
1	tanners art of physick	6	[Tom A] Lincolns
2	temples miscellanea	12	Joviall Garland
6	pearse of death	12	Crown Garland
3	douting Christian	6	Jack Newberry
2	Vertuous woman	4	absolute accoumpt
4	help to discours	6	Garlands of delight
18	flavell on the sacrement	6	fortunatus
24	vincents Catechis	6	royall arbours
6	alleins Catt	8	S[c]oggins jests
6	leis Catt	6	history of Joseph
6	Janewais life	6	Devill & Dives
4	Johnsons Deus Nobiscum	6	Booke of knowledg
3	watsons Contentment	4	Mandevills travells
6	pooles nullity [of the Romish Faith]	6	wise masters
12	—— Dialogues	3	wakemans tryalls
100	testaments	2	Langhams
1	Bacons works	3	dugdalls
1	Cloud witnesses	12	Procession
1	phillips dictionary	4	pack cards

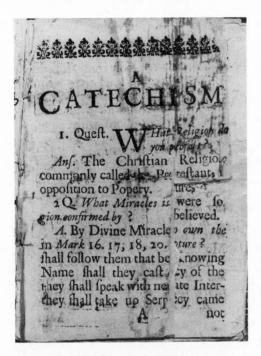

[Benjamin Harris], *The Protestant Tutor* (1685)[8]

Increase Mather in his library (1688)[9]

THE LAST five artifacts, all from the late seventeenth and early eighteenth centuries, offer still more varied glimpses at Puritan print culture. The tattered leaf of catechism, *The Protestant Tutor* (1685), from Benjamin Harris (d. 1716) illustrates the way many Puritan children learned their religion—by rote. Increase Mather's 1688 portrait displays the leading minister as he wanted to appear: with his books, in his cherished library. *The A, B, C of Religion* (1713) by his son Cotton Mather (1663–1728), like Harris's catechism, shows how schoolbooks promoted literacy and piety simultaneously. The *Boston News-Letter*, one of the first North American newspapers, was "Published by Authority." Without the authority of the colonial government, newspapers could not legally appear. (The first American newspaper, *Publick Occurrences* [1690], had not received "authority"—and was shut down after only one issue.) Finally, Jabes Wekit's land deed, written originally in Massachusett, illustrates another important use of literacy: the definition of property rights. Using such documents, along with the other evidence in this chapter, historians of the book seek to answer pivotal questions: Who could read and write? What did they read, and where did they get their books? And to what uses did they put their literacy: what did being literate *mean* in people's lives?

Cotton Mather, *The A, B, C of Religion* (1713)[10]

A Dead Child was once raised unto Life, by GOD, at the *Prayer* of an Holy Prophet unto Him. And in the Raising of this Child, we read, 2 King IV. 34. He *lay upon the Child, and* (first) *put his Mouth upon his Mouth; and* (then) *his Eyes upon his Eyes; and* (afterwards) *his Hands upon his Hands;—and the Child opened his Eyes.* We *Pray,* That the *Souls* of our Children may *Live.* If we are our Selves the true Children of *Abraham,* it will appear in this; we shall importunately *Pray* to God for our Children, *Oh! that they may Live in thy sight!* But *Praying* for them, is not all we have to do for them. The *Enlivening Word* of God must be applied unto them. We must apply the *Lively Oracles* of the Word, unto the *Mouthes,* and the *Eyes,* and the *Hands* of the Children. If our God please then to make an Application of it unto their *Hearts,* this will cause them to *Live.* Yea, tho' the Children are *Cast forth unto the Loathing of their Person,* and evenly *Dead,* and rotting and stinking in their Sin; yet, *O Lord, Thou wilt say unto them, Live; yea, thou wilt say unto them in their Blood, Live.* There is that Excellency in the Word of God, that it suits *all Ages.* It has *Milk* for the *Babes,* as well as *Meat* for the *Strong.* It instructs both the *Old* and the *Young,* to *Praise the Lord.* You have here a Psalm, of Lessons to be Learn'd by *Children;* even as soon as they learn their Letters. In the *Hebrew,* every Verse begins with a New Letter, according to the Order of the Alphabet; Perhaps, that so the *Hebrew Children* might have it as Early as they had their Alphabet. . . .

You have the *Word of God;* they that are yet but in the Capacity of *Children,* may perceive whose *Word* it is; that they have *God* speaking to them in it. He was a *Young Child,* who when the *Word* of God called upon him, said; 1 Sam. III. 10. Lord, *Speak, for thy Servant heareth.* One must be more Silly than a Child in the Schoolboyes Cloathes, who Paies no Regard unto the *Word of God.* There is in this Word, that which the *Angels themselves desire to look into;* and there is that which bespeaks Regards from the *Lowest Capacity. Children,* As soon as you can Read, you may take the Bible, and in Reading of it, think, *This is the Voice of God; God now Speaks unto me.*

New-England.　　　　　　　　Numb. 518.

The Boston News-Letter,

Published by Authority.

From Monday March 22. to Monday March 29. 1714.

By His EXCELLENCY,

Robert Hunter, Esq; Captain General and Governour in Chief of the Provinces of *New-York, New-Jersey,* and all the Territories thereon depending in *America,* and Vice Admiral of the same, &c.

A PROCLAMATION.

Whereas it hath been represented to Me by some of the Gentlemen of Her Majesty's Council of the Province of New-York, That in the Night, between the ninth and tenth Days of February last, Trinity-Church in that City was broke upon the Books of Divine Service, and the Vestments dedicated to that Use, carried out, Tore to pieces, and defiled with Ordure. And whereas such an Impious Outrage cannot be supposed to be perpetrated by any but such as are avow'd Enemies to Religion in General, or to the Civil and Religious Constitution of England in particular, or such as for filthy Lucre, or worse Purposes, may have, in appearance, conform'd to or complied with either, but by their Unchristian and Lewd Conversation, and their Dis-loyal and Seditious Conduct sufficiently manifest their Aversion to both. To the end therefore that the Actors, Abettors or Contrivers of such an Unexampl'd Affront to Religion and the Church of England may be detected, and the hellish Devices of those who may have endeavour'd to lead the Innocent with their own Guilt, may be disappointed, I have thought fit, by virtue of the Powers and Authorities granted to Me by Her Majesty's Letters Patents under the Broad Seal of Great Britain, to make, and order to be published this Proclamation, promising a Reward of Fifty five Pounds to any Person or Persons not guilty of the above recited Atrocious Crime, who shall make such Discovery of the same as may be sufficient for the Conviction of the Authors or Contrivers of that Impiety in a due Course of Law. And if any Person guilty of the same shall make such Discovery of his Accomplices, as is aforesaid, such Person is hereby entituled to, and promised the Reward above-mention'd, besides Indemnity and Pardon for himself and one more, such as he shall name, if more than two were guilty of or privy to the Fact.

Given under my Hand and Seal at *Burlington* in *New-Jersey* the third Day of *March,* in the Twelfth Year of Her Majesty's Reign, Annoq; Dom 1713.

By His Excellency's Command.　　　Ro. HUNTER.

GEO. CLARK.

GOD Save the QUEEN.

Cracow, August 27. There is Advice by an Express, that the Turkish Army has passed the Dniester, and that their Vanguard is arrived within 4 or 5 Leagues of Caminieck. King Stanislaus and the Palatine of Kiow have joined that Army, which is reported to be above 20000 Men. However, as these Advices have not been confirm'd by any Express from the General of the Crown, who is on the Frontiers with the Polish Army, 'tis hoped this Intelligence will prove false.

Madrid, August 28 N S. The Court being informed that some Genoese Ships had carried Provisions into Barcelona, have given notice to the Republick, that it should be look'd upon as an Act of Hostility, if they continued such Proceedings. We have received advice from Catalonia, that Four or five thousand of the Garrison of Barcelona had Sally'd out of the Town, but being warmly received by the Spanish Artillery, they retir'd with great precipitation: However, the Duke de Popoli had thought proper to remove his Camp to a greater distance from the Place, by reason of a Battery rais'd at a Convent of Capuchins, which play'd upon his Army with some Success. The Miquelets had taken Possession of the Passes of the Mountains, and made it very difficult to bring Provisions for the Army. Brigadier Ordegno had summoned the Isle of Majorca to submit to the King, but the Governour answer'd, He would not surrender till the Castilians had conquer'd the whole Province of Catalonia. Whereupon the Duke de Popoli has desired a Reinforcement of Troops, which will accordingly be sent him very speedily. The Cities of Mataro, Urgell, and Cardona have made their Submission to his Majesty, but the Citadel of the latter Place is preparing for a Defence, in case they should be besieg'd. General Almendaria has order'd the Walls of Manreza to be raiz'd, deliver'd up several Houses there to be Plunder'd by the Soldiers, and put to death those who were most Instrumental in perswading the Inhabitants to declare against the King.

Warsaw, August 29. The Sieur Buzeval, Minister of France,

arrived here two Days ago, as did also the Danish Adjutant Meyer, and both had this Day Audience of King Augustus. That Prince continues in this City, and will not set out for the Frontiers till he has certain Advice of the Motions of the Infidels, of which we have not yet any Account that can be depended upon. They write from Great Poland, that the Saxon Troops are marching with all speed for Sendomir, where his Majesty designs to review them. Notwithstanding Orders have been given to seize several Persons as being concerned in the late Conspiracy, we do not hear that any have been taken up, which makes us believe, that they had timely Notice given them of the discovery of their Plot, and so that they have made their escape. The Partisans of Stanislaus had design'd to rescue the Palatine of Russia on his way from hence to Saxony, and had got together to the number of 50 Horse; but they came four hours too late, and those that conducted him made so much hast, that they arrived at Koningstein without any opposition. Our Advices from the Frontiers do not confirm the arrival of the Turkish Forces at Choczin, as it was reported some days ago, but the General of the Crown has been inform'd that they are assembling near Bender, and that the Tartars are preparing to make an Irruption into our Territories, whereupon he has sent Orders to the Country People to remove their Effects into the Fortify'd Places, and hold themselves in a readiness to retire thither upon the first Advice they shall have of the march of the Enemy. The following Abstract of the Articles of the late Treaty between the Port and Muscovy has been made Publick here:

1. The Muscovite Troops shall march out of all the Territories of Poland within two Months, and shall not return thither upon any pretence whatsoever. 2. The Port shall be allow'd to procure a Passage to the King of Sweden thro Poland or Muscovy to his own Dominions under a Guard at the Charge of the Grand Signior, and the said Guard shall return without any hindrance or opposition 3. The Cossacks shall be restor'd to their ancient Privileges, and Kiow with all the Country on the other side of the Dnieper or Boristhenes, shall belong to the Czar, and the Country on the other side of that River to the Port. 4. Azoph shall return to the Turks, who are allowed to repair the Fortifications thereof, but Tagonrock shall be demolished. 5. The 60 Pieces of Cannon which the Muscovites have carried away from thence, shall be restor'd, or an Equivalent given for it, after which they shall be at liberty to take away the Iron Guns which they have left in Azoph. 6. According to the Peace concluded near the River Pruth, the Turks shall be at liberty to rebuild some Places in the Neighbourhood of Caminieck, that have been demolish'd. 7. The River Zamara shall be the Limits of Turkey, and that of Excess shall be the Frontier of Muscovy, and both Parties are allowed to build each a Fortress on their respective Frontiers; but Azoph and the Limits on that side shall remain in the same Condition. 8. All Acts of Hostility shall cease on both sides, and the Cossacks and other Countries belonging to the Czar are included in this Peace. 9. The Calmucks shall remain to the Czar, and the Crim Tartars to the Port, and these two Nations shall be hindred from committing any Hostilities. 10. The Pretensions of the Tartars of a Yearly Tribute shall be refer'd to another time. 11. This Peace shall continue for 25 Years, and may be prolong'd for a longer time.

Hamburg, August 29 N S. Two Days ago all the Avenues of this City were shut up by some Danish Troops. No Body was suffer'd to come in or go out of the Town, and the Posts were stopt till this Morning when these Disorders ceas'd, but the Cause of so extraordinary a Proceeding is not yet known. Yesterday the Ministers of Denmark, Prussia, and Hanover were in Conference with the Deputies of our Magistrates, in order to regulate our Commerce, and fix on some Place where Provisions and Merchandize should be examin'd before they are allow'd to pass in or out of the Town. Each of them propos'd a different Place, and they parted without coming to any conclusion. The King of Prussia has writ to several Princes to interpose with the King of Denmark to raise the Blockade of Tonningen, and to withdraw his Forces out of Holstein. His Majesty hath likewise caus'd a Declaration to be delivered to the Danish Ministers, in which he tells them he had hopes, for a long while, that the King their Master would have consented to one of the many Proposals that had been made to him upon this Subject; but finding now that it was in vain to expect it, and having receiv'd certain Information that Tonningen was reduc'd to the last Extremity, he thought himself obliged to take care of the Affairs of Holstein, in pursuance of his Engagements to that purpose. His Danish Majesty has intercepted a Letter from Baron Goertz to General Stabock, desiring

Transcription and Translation of Jabes Wekit's Land Deed[12]

Massachusett

1718 tha AbRni–20 · 1 tayss
nen Jabes wekkit yeu nummahtommattuo-
onk nuttinnummau ~~luttin~~ nuttohk ~~neohtag~~
~~hettammun mamunshabbat~~
thom bennas neahtag . mamunshabbat
baunussu . wessattummus somwe · en · sauw-
anniyeu paunussu stakkissohtug baunnus
nogque en nobattinniyeu : baunussu : wonk
stakkissohtug ~~bann~~ baunus · quen nogqee
en sinnattinniyeu baunus quen : nogque en
nogquttinniyeu . neit : watuhquashshau baunus . nen · Jabes wekkit: kuttinnummauwinn-
in ken thom pennas wame · nuttohk · kah : wame
mohtugquash mashkehtuash kah wame
nenoh attannegkik nomme ohke
nen bashshonnis wekkit : noowekontam
kauttohtauwun nuttohk kah kauttauwohkon
kah kauttohtauwun micheme kah michen

nen : Jabes . wekit . yeu : noomark X
nen : bashonnis wekkit yeu noomark X
nen sam tesken X
nen sam tanau X
waenninnuog

English

1718, April 21.
I, Jabes Wekkit, this is my bargain.
I conveyed my land ~~that lies at,~~
~~it is called Mamunshabbat,~~
to Thom Bennas, that lies at Manunshabbat.
The bounds are a red oak straight to the
southward; the bounds are a wooden stake; the bounds are
towards the southeast; the bounds are another
wooden stake; bounds a long way towards
the northward; bounds a long way towards
the southwestward; then the bounds come to the beginning.

1710

uy 18 tho Abrnl 20.1 doyst
nen Jabes wekkit yev nv mmahtommastvo
onk nv ttinnvmmav ettin nvttohk ~~nekeng~~
~~ketts~~ ~~nv~~ ~~nvmvnjsabbat~~
dhom bennas neahtag mamonjsabbot
bavnvjsv wessattvmmvj somwe enjavnv
anniyev pavnvjsv stakkijsohtvg bavnnv
negwe en nob attinniyev ibavnvjsv wonj
stakkijsohtvg ~~bavnj bavnvj~~ vvn no jgee
en jinnattinniyev bavnvj gvjrinogqejse en
noggvttinniyev neit watvhgvajkjhav bavnvj nen Jabej wekkit kvttinnvmmav vivn
in ken dhompennaj wame nvttohk kah wame
mohtvjgvvjk majkkehtvajk kah wame
nenoh attannegkik nomme ohke
nen bajhjhonnij wekkit noowekontan
kavttohtavvvn nvttohk kah kavttavvohkon
kah kavttohtavvvn michemekah michem

nen Jabej wekit yev noomark +
nen bajhjhonnij wekkit yev noomark O
nen jam tejken O
nen jamtanav +
waenninnvog

Jabes Wekit's Land Deed (1718)[13]

I Jabes Wekkit let you have it,
you Thom Pennas, all my land and all
trees, grass, and all
that grows there within the land.
I Bashshonnis Wekkit am content.
You own my land, and you use it
and you own it forever and ever.

I Jabes Wekit, this is my mark (X).
I Bashshonnis Wekkit, this is my mark (X).
I Sam Tesken (X).
I Sam Tanau (X).
Witnesses.

COMMENTARY: A BOOKISH FAITH

At about five o'clock in the morning of November 27, 1676, Boston was consumed by fire. Ignited by a carelessly placed candle and fueled by an autumn wind, the fire spread quickly from one house to another, the flames skipping almost across the harbor to Charlestown. Boston burned for hours. Driving rain ultimately halted the devastation, but before the fire stopped much of the town was in ashes. A church, several warehouses, and nearly fifty houses had been destroyed, leaving as many as eighty families homeless. Yet, despite it all, Increase Mather, Puritan minister of Boston, gave thanks to God. For though he saw his house burn to the ground, he had managed to rescue his most cherished possession: his library.

Hearing of the fire in Boston, Mather's friend John Bishop wrote to offer his condolences but most of all to inquire about Mather's many books: "I am sorry for your great affliction & losse, especially if your bookes should be burnt, as I hope they are not, for that losse would be greater & more irreparable then all the rest." And when William Goffe heard the story of the fire and of the providential rescue of the library, he, too, wrote to Mather: "I have desire to sympathise with you in your late fiery Tryall. But rejoyced much to hear that you had time to remove & secure your cheife treasure, I mean your Bookes" (Green, 47, 54; Bishop; Goffe).

Books were scarce in early New England, and they were precious. Since Protestantism required encountering God directly through reading the Scriptures, the most precious book of all was also the most popular: the Bible. A sixteenth-century English Puritan leader had admonished, "If (as hath been showed) all ought to read the scriptures then all ages, all sexes, all degrees and callings, all high and low, rich and poor, wise and foolish have a necessary duty therein" (Lake, 288). When the Puritan movement spilled over the Atlantic in the seventeenth century to found the colonies of New England, all members of the new society—including women, children, and even Indians—were expected to practice their piety by poring over the pages of their Bibles.

But did they? Were New Englanders "high and low, rich and poor, wise and foolish" all readers? Did ordinary men and women cherish their Bibles as much as Mather cherished his library, with the reverence so wonderfully illustrated in Jan Van der Spriett's portrait of the Boston minister? Puritan New England was, especially for its day, an unusually literate society, even a learned one, but was all reading put to spiritual purposes? What did Puritans really read? Or, more important, which Puritans read what? Historians have long debated the nature of the relationship between power and print in early New England. Did Puritan ministers such as Increase Mather, with his large, precious library, ultimately control the flow of information to less literate colonists? Or did growing literacy in seventeenth-century New England actually subvert clerical authority? A wealth of sources—from surviving imprints to letters to printers to library inventories—is available to help historians answer these questions. Ultimately, these sources suggest that literacy in Puritan New England at first reinforced but eventually toppled traditional notions of authority and power in society, setting the stage for the proliferation—and democratization—of print in the late eighteenth and nineteenth centuries.

Seventeenth-century New England was unlike any other colony in North America. Because of the unique nature of the "Great Puritan Migration" of the 1630s, New England society was top-heavy with intellectuals: by the 1640s, out of a population of twenty-five thousand, nearly a hundred New England men had attended Oxford or Cambridge, at least fifty of whom held advanced degrees (Wright, 16). The priorities of these men, the leaders of the New England colonies, led them to appropriate funds to establish Harvard College in 1636, to found a printing press in Cambridge three years later (the first printing press in the British North American colonies) and, soon after, to establish a second press in Boston. The books owned by these learned men constituted formidable libraries: when William Brewster died in 1643, he left a collection of nearly four hundred books. Men as wealthy as Brewster often also donated books to the growing Harvard College Library and, beginning in 1657, to a rival library in Boston.

These learned men (and a few women, too) read not only religious books but also political tracts and scientific treatises shipped to them from England. London booksellers, like Richard Chiswell and Robert Boulter, sent thousands of books across the Atlantic, some by special order, but most to be sold at bookshops in Boston (or what were usually coffeehouses doubling as bookstores). Alternatively, men of means such as John Winthrop Jr. could always import books from friends. Winthrop's friend Edward Howes sent him books from England year after year, writing, for instance, in 1632, "here I have sent you the Swedish Intelligencer which speakes wonder to the world; withall I have sent you your Archymedes and an Almenack, with a booke or two of other news besides" (Wright, 32). Winthrop read widely: he kept abreast of international developments and scientific advances and constantly increased his knowledge of ancient writers.

While vast libraries such as those of William Brewster, Increase Mather, and John Winthrop Jr. were, of course, unusual, most town ministers had at least a small library, and most families owned at least a Bible. In Boston, Puritan minister Thomas Shepard complained in 1673 that "in multitudes of Families there is . . . no Bible, or onely a torn Bible to be found," but his complaint seems to have been ill-founded (Shepard, 50). Historians studying seventeenth-century New England probate inventories (lists of the items in a household) have found that 59 percent of even the poorest New Englanders owned "religious books," as did 74 percent of the middling classes, and 100 percent of the well-to-do. Although probate inventories do not normally list the titles, or even the kinds of books in a household, families who owned just one or two books are most likely to have owned a Bible and a primer, or reading instruction book. When probate records, surviving library catalogs, and booksellers' inventories do list book titles, religious books always outnumber all other kinds and are followed only distantly by other kinds of reading (Main, 133–34; Hall, 170–71).

An invoice of books sent in 1683 to John Usher of Boston by Robert Boulter, a London bookseller, hints at the scope of reading material available to New Englanders. Painstaking comparison of the invoice with checklists and bibliographies of books known to have been in print in seventeenth-century England reveals that Boulter sent Usher titles ranging from *Aesop's Fables* ("4 esops in english") to Nicholas Culpeper's *Pharmacopoeia Londinensis: or the London dispensatory* ("5 Culpepers dispensatory"), a catalog of medical remedies. Some of what Boulter sent was fanciful, including *Mandeville's Travels* ("4 mandevills travells"), and some was downright scandalous, such as playing cards ("4 pack cards"), which were illegal in New England. A great deal of the material Boulter sent to Usher in Boston was religious, from scripture ("24 testaments") to books of religious instruction ("3 Doolitles Catechis") to sermons ("6 Baxters Call"—that is, Richard Baxter's *Call to the Unconverted*) to elegies of celebrated ministers ("2 lyfe and death [of Joseph Alleine]").

Boulter appears to have been guessing what to send Usher, and many of his guesses were wrong. Usher could not have sold the playing cards openly, and much of the fictional and fanciful reading material in Boulter's shipment would have been difficult to market in New England. If New Englanders had access to a wealth of printed material from England, they were nonetheless decidedly selective. Their preferences can be measured by comparing two invoices of Boston bookseller Hezekiah Usher (not to be confused with John Usher). In 1682 Usher received a shipment of books that he did not specifically order but that were selected by a London merchant for sale in New England. In 1685 Hezekiah Usher received another shipment, but this time *of books he requested*. Following his own instincts, and the tastes of London readers, the London merchant sent a fair amount of secular material in the 1682 shipment, including romances and histories. But, following Usher's orders in 1685, he sent many more religious books and schoolbooks (Ford, 44):

Hezekiah Usher's Invoices	1682	1685
Religious books	223	311
Schoolbooks	128	391
Bibles, testaments, catechisms, etc.	178	55
Law	4	36
Dictionaries	5	3
Arts: Navigation	60	50
Medicine	12	11
Cookery	5	—
Military	—	5
History, travel, biography	45	6
Romance, etc.	160	6
	820	874

New Englanders also put their reading preferences into practice in deciding what books to print themselves. After the Cambridge Press was founded in 1639, one of its very first productions was a new translation of the Psalms, *The Whole Book of Psalmes*, a work so popular it was reprinted seven times before 1700 (Hall, 23–24). With the notable exception of extremely practical annual almanacs, most of what came off the presses in Cambridge and Boston was religious: sermons, catechisms, prayer books. And the Cambridge Press's major, indeed monumental, production was John Eliot's complete translation of the Bible into Massachusett. (The amount of paper used to print two editions of this complete Bible in 1663 and 1685 was more than the total that had been used at the Cambridge Press since its founding in 1639.)

New Englanders brought or bought their own English-language Bibles from England (since the Cambridge, Massachusetts, press was not licensed to print the Bible in English) and they read them intently, memorizing lengthy passages and reading chapters over and over again. Because they lived in what one historian has called a "world of wonders," many Puritans also believed that the Bible had special magical powers. When young John Dane could not decide whether to migrate to New England or not, he used his Bible like a crystal ball: "I hastily toke up the bybell, and tould my fatther if whare I opend the bybell thare i met with anie thing eyther to incuredg or discouredg that should settle me. I oping of it, not knowing no more then the child in the womb, the first I cast my eys on was: Cum out from among them, touch no unclene thing." And off to New England he went. To some, the Bible also seemed to afford supernatural protection. During King Philip's War, in 1676, one colonist sat in the town common reading the Bible in the midst of an Indian attack, believing he could not be killed that way. Instead, he was the single casualty of the day (Dane, 154; Kingsley, 2:445).

Episodes like these remind us that Bibles were both books and objects of devotion. A Bible had sacred power even if one could not read it. But Puritan ministers preferred their parishioners to *read* the Good Book, not worship it. In Massachusetts

Bay Colony, fathers were required by law to give their children religious instruction, and most of that instruction consisted of reading aloud from the Bible or other religious texts, training children to read for themselves. After publication of *The Whole Book of Psalmes*, the Cambridge Press's earliest productions included spelling books and catechisms for children, both printed in the 1640s. So closely were literacy and piety connected that when Cotton Mather published a book to instruct children in "the Maxims of Religion" in 1713, he called it "The A, B, C of Religion."

Stressing, and in some cases legislating, literacy made a difference. New Englanders were considerably more literate than their English countrymen. By one estimate, about 60 percent of white men and 30 percent of white women in New England were literate in 1660, and the numbers only increased, leading to near-universal white male literacy by the end of the colonial era. But what "literacy" means in this context is confusing. Historians usually measure "signing literacy," the proportion of the population that signed documents with a written name rather than a mark. But, since reading was taught before writing, some who signed only with a mark may have been able to read, while others could sign their name but not actually write. And, to make matters more confusing, people who sign documents one year may be found using a mark the next (Lockridge, 13). Women's education, especially, was likely to stop after they learned to read. Women's literacy was meant to be passive; their quiet reading of the Scriptures was never to be a defiance of their minister's authority. Meanwhile, women who did write were always exquisitely conscious of just how far they were overstepping the bounds of their sex, as when Anne Bradstreet wrote in the prologue to her book of poetry, "I am obnoxious to each carping tongue / Who says my hand a needle better fits."

That so many women in New England even learned to read is testament to the power of the Puritan conviction of the importance of reading to religious expression. Even more startling evidence of this conviction can be found, however, in New Englanders' efforts to teach reading and writing to Indians. In New France, French Jesuit missionaries used books as tools of conversion, not by teaching Indians to read but by demonstrating the power of writing. To a people without writing, literacy is an awesome phenomenon, a kind of magical telepathic power, and Jesuits relied on demonstrations of "talking books" to convince Indians of the superiority of Europeans and the Christian faith. As Protestants, Puritan missionaries were unwilling to take this approach; instead, they believed that Indians could be brought to Christ only by being taught to read the Bible for themselves.

Beginning in the 1640s the Puritan minister John Eliot, of Roxbury, began learning the Massachusett language. Aided by Indian translators, interpreters, and teachers, Eliot painstakingly translated the Bible into Massachusett in the 1650s and 1660s. Even before the New Testament was printed in 1661, Eliot had printed a primer, a catechism, and a book of Psalms, all in Massachusett; the complete translation of the Bible was first printed in 1663. He used these books to teach Algonquians to read and write, first in Massachusett, then in English. Before his death in 1690, Eliot and his Indian assistants also translated and printed works of devotion popular in England, including Baxter's *Call to the Unconverted* and Lewis Bayly's *Practice of Piety*. With a veritable "Indian Library" in print, Eliot could recommend in 1669, in his *Indian Primer*, a sequential program of study:

Wa-an-tam-we us-seonk ogke-
tam-un-at. Cate-chi-sa-onk.
Ne-gon-ne og-kee-tash Primer.
Na-hoh-to-eu og-kee-tash
Ai-us-koi-an-tam-oe weh-kom-a-onk
Ne-it og-kee-tash Bible.

[Wise doing to read Catechism
first, next read Primer. Next
read Repentance Calling
next read Bible.]

(Eliot, *Indian*, 14)

Eliot's Indian converts lived in fourteen Christian Indian towns in Massachusetts Bay, and other missionaries established similar communities in Plymouth. Eliot often boasted of the success of his instructional and missionary efforts: in 1673, he declared that in the fourteen Christian Indian towns, "we have schools; many can read, some write, sundry able to exercise in publick" (Eliot, "Account," 127). But a contemporary survey of Christian Indian settlements in Plymouth Colony suggests that literacy rates in Indian communities were quite low. Of 462 converted Indians, 142 (31 percent) could read the Massachusett language, 72 (16 percent) could write, and 9 (2 percent) could read English. Christian Indian men and women, that is, were less literate than white English women. Still, that even this many Indians could read and write is undoubtedly significant. When compared, not with white women, but with black slaves in the south, the literacy of New England's Indians is particularly startling. Historians have only begun to consider its implications.

Native literacy survived well into the eighteenth century, as demonstrated by Jabes Wekit's land deed, written in Massachusett. Clearly, literacy had practical purposes for Indians, too. But, like English colonists, Christian Indians used their literacy mainly for devotional purposes. The Indian Bibles that survive today are filled with marginalia, notes written by their readers in the margins. Puritans, too, wrote in their books, often expressing the humility they felt before God and their unworthiness for salvation. Indians' marginalia is quite similar, but it is impossible to know whether the humility they expressed goes beyond that of a modest Christian and extends to a kind of racial self-hatred that might have been the consequence of being labeled as "savage heathen." One Wampanoag Indian from Martha's Vineyard wrote in the margins of his Indian Bible, "I am forever a pitiful person in the world. I am not able clearly to read this, this book" (Goddard and Bragdon, 423).

Puritan ministers in early New England wanted everyone to read, the rich and the poor, the young and the old, men, women, and Indians alike, so that all could read the Bible for themselves and seek their own salvation. But those same ministers did not want everyone to write. Writing—especially writing that appeared in *print*—was a different matter entirely. Licensors controlled the Cambridge and Boston presses, and determined what would, and would not, be printed. The Massachusetts General Court regularly banned books from England, as when in 1654 it ordered "that all & every the inhabitants of this jurisdiction that have any of the bookes in their custody that have lately been brought out of England under the names of John Reeves & Lodowick Muggleton [two Quakers] . . . & shall not bring or send in all such bookes now in their custody, to the next magistr, shall forfeit the sume of ten pounds for every such booke that shalbe found" (Shurtleff, 3:356).

How the Puritan elite controlled printing is dramatically illustrated in letters between Increase Mather and various friends, including his brother-in-law John Cotton. Mather, who had written a history of King Philip's War, published in both Boston and London, attempted to suppress a rival account of the same conflict written by William Hubbard, minister of Ipswich ("Mr H" in Mather's letters). In the end, Mather's efforts failed (and Hubbard's account was printed with an official imprimatur from the Governor and Council of Massachusetts Bay). But his machinations in that affair, like his daring rescue of his precious library in the Boston fire of 1676, reveal just how passionately Puritan leaders were willing to fight for the power of print.

SOURCE NOTES

[Unless otherwise indicated artifacts and documents are reproduced courtesy of the American Antiquarian Society (AAS), Worcester, Massachusetts.]

1. Anne Bradstreet, *Several Poems* (Boston, 1678), 3–4, 236.

2. *The Whole Booke of Psalmes* (Cambridge, Mass., 1640), title page.

3. *Wusku Wuttestamentum Nul-Lordumun Jesus Christ* (Cambridge, Mass., 1661), title page.

4. Richard Bourne to Daniel Gookin, in Daniel Gookin, "Historical Collections of the Indians in New England [1674]," *Massachusetts Historical Society Collections*, 1st ser., 1 (1792), 196–99.

5. "The Mather Papers," *Massachusetts Historical Society Collections*, 4th ser., 8 (1868), 7–9, 229–30, 232, 234–35, 239, 575–77; Increase Mather to John Cotton, Mather Family Papers, box 2, folder 9, American Antiquarian Society.

6. John Danforth, *An Almanack . . . for . . . 1679* (Cambridge, Mass., 1679).

7. Worthington Chauncey Ford, *The Boston Book Market, 1679–1700* (Boston: Club of Odd Volumes, 1917), 88–107.

8. *The Protestant Tutor* (Boston, 1685).

9. Jan Van der Spriett, *Increase Mather*, oil on canvas, 1688. Courtesy Massachusetts Historical Society, Boston, Mass., MHS neg. no. 1442.

10. Cotton Mather, *The A, B, C of Religion* (Boston, 1713), 1–3, 29–30.

11. *Boston News-Letter*, no. 519 (March 22–29, 1714).

12. Transcription and translation from Ives Goddard and Kathleen Bragdon, *Native Writings in Massachusett*, Memoirs of the American Philosophical Society, 185 (Philadelphia: American Philosophical Society, 1988), 47–49. Reproduced courtesy of the American Philosophical Society, Philadelphia, Pa.

13. Jabes Wekit, land deed, manuscript, 1718. Box 2, folder 2, Curwen Papers, American Antiquarian Society.

WORKS CITED

Bishop, John. Letter to Increase Mather, April 26, 1677. *Massachusetts Historical Society Collections*, 4th ser., 8 (1868): 298.

[Dane, John]. "John Dane's Narrative, 1682." *New England Historical and Genealogical Register* 8 (1854).

Eliot, John. "An Account of Indian Churches in New-England, in a letter written A.D. 1673." *Massachusetts Historical Society Collections*, 1st ser., 10 (1809): 127.

———. *The Indian Primer*. Cambridge, Mass., 1669.

Ford, Worthington Chauncey. *The Boston Book Market, 1679–1700*. Boston: Club of Odd Volumes, 1917.

Goddard, Ives, and Kathleen Bragdon. *Native Writings in Massachusett*. Memoirs of the American Philosophical Society, 185. Philadelphia: American Philosophical Society, 1988.

Goffe, William. Letter to Increase Mather, June 12, 1677. *Massachusetts Historical Society Collections*, 4th ser., 8 (1868): 159.

Green, Samuel A., ed. *The Diary of Increase Mather*. Cambridge, Mass.: John Wilson and Son, 1900.

Hall, David D. *Worlds of Wonder, Days of Judgment: Popular Religious Belief in Early New England*. New York: Alfred A. Knopf, 1989.

Kingsley, John. Letter to the Connecticut War Council, May 5, 1676. In *The Public Records of the Colony of Connecticut*, edited by J. Hammond Trumbull. 15 vols. Hartford, 1850–90.

Lake, Peter. *Moderate Puritans and the Elizabethan Church*. Cambridge: Cambridge University Press, 1982.

Lockridge, Kenneth. *Literacy in Colonial New England*. New York: W. W. Norton, 1974.

Main, Gloria. "The Standard of Living in Southern New England, 1640–1773." *William and Mary Quarterly*, 3d ser., 45 (January 1988): 124–34.

Shepard, Thomas. *Eye-Salve*. Cambridge, Mass., 1673.

Shurtleff, Nathaniel B., ed. *Records of the Governor and Company of the Massachusetts Bay in New England* (MCR). 5 vols. Boston, 1853–54.

Wright, Thomas. *Literary Culture in Early New England*. New Haven, Conn.: Yale University Press, 1920.

FOR FURTHER RESEARCH

Amory, Hugh. "Under the Exchange: The Unprofitable Business of Michael Perry, a Seventeenth-Century Boston Bookseller." *Proceedings of the American Antiquarian Society* 103, pt. 1 (1993): 31–60.

Axtell, James. *After Columbus: Essays in the Ethnohistory of Colonial North America*. New York: Oxford University Press, 1988.

Brown, Matthew P. "'BOSTON/SOB NOT': Elegiac Performance in Early New England and Materialist Studies of the Book." *American Quarterly* 50 (June 1998): 306–39.

Cressy, David. "Books as Totems in Seventeenth-Century England and New England." *Journal of Library History* 21 (Winter 1986): 92–106.

———. *Literacy and the Social Order: Reading and Writing in Tudor and Stuart England*. Cambridge: Cambridge University Press, 1980.

Derounian, Kathryn Zabelle. "The Publication, Promotion, and Distribution of Mary Rowlandson's Indian Captivity Narrative in the Seventeenth Century." *Early American Literature* 23 (1988): 239–61.

Dorsey, Peter A. "Going to School with Savages: Authorship and Authority among the Jesuits of New France." *William and Mary Quarterly*, 3d ser., 55 (July 1998): 399–420.

Finnegan, Ruth. *Literacy and Orality: Studies in the Technology of Communication.* Oxford: Oxford University Press, 1988.

Hall, Michael G. *The Last American Puritan: The Life of Increase Mather, 1639–1723.* Middletown, Conn.: Wesleyan University Press, 1988.

Kamensky, Jane. *Governing the Tongue: The Politics of Speech in Early New England.* New York: Oxford University Press, 1997.

Lepore, Jill. "Dead Men Tell No Tales: John Sassamon and the Fatal Consequences of Literacy." *American Quarterly* 46 (December 1994): 479–512.

———. *The Name of War: King Philip's War and the Origins of American Identity.* New York: Alfred A. Knopf, 1998.

Littlefield, George Emery. *Early Boston Booksellers, 1642–1711.* Boston: The Club of Odd Volumes, 1900.

Miller, Perry. *The New England Mind: The Seventeenth Century.* Cambridge, Mass.: Harvard University Press, 1953.

Morison, Samuel Eliot. *Intellectual Life of Colonial New England.* New York: New York University Press, 1956.

Nelsen, Anne Kusener. "King Philip's War and the Hubbard-Mather Rivalry." *William and Mary Quarterly,* 3d ser., 27 (October 1970): 615–29.

Ong, Walter. *Orality and Literacy: The Technologizing of the Word.* London: Methuen, 1982.

Watt, Tessa. *Cheap Print and Popular Piety, 1550–1640.* Cambridge: Cambridge University Press, 1991.

Winship, George Parker. *The Cambridge Press, 1638–1692.* 1945. Reprint, Freeport, N.Y.: Books for Libraries Press, 1968.

3

Print and Everyday Life in the Eighteenth Century

Patricia Crain

IN 1685 the young English printer William Bradford announced in Philadelphia that he had "brought that great Art and Mystery of Printing into this part of America." Over the next century, American printing continued to expand well beyond its New England beginnings. After Bradford offended Pennsylvania's Quaker council once too often, he left to found New York's first printing house in 1693. Further south, Virginia's royal governor William Berkeley thanked God in 1671 that "there are no free schools nor printing" in the colony, and hoped "we shall not have these [for a] hundred years, for learning has brought disobedience, and heresy, and sects into the world, and printing has divulged them." William Nuthead made the first attempt to start a printing press in Virginia in 1682, but the government of the colony quickly shut it down. And Virginia remained without its own printer for nearly half a century, until 1730. Nuthead moved to Maryland and opened the south's first long-lasting print shop in 1685.

By 1720 colonial America's most famous printer, Benjamin Franklin, had begun his career as an apprentice in his brother's Boston shop. But James Franklin ran afoul of the colonial government, was imprisoned for printing seditious material in 1722, and decamped to Rhode Island to start the first print shop there in 1727. Within a decade Benjamin was established in Philadelphia and was sending his own apprentices out to start printing houses elsewhere, including one of the earliest South Carolina shops in 1732. Bradford, Nuthead, the Franklins: North America's pioneering printers crossed colonial boundaries and were among the first colonists with intercolonial connections.

Genres of printed material multiplied just as printers themselves did. Schoolbooks and almanacs, among the staples of the earliest Massachusetts printers, proliferated. For local printers, these could become "steady sellers," assuring regular customers in a trade whose practitioners always operated on the margins of bankruptcy. Many of these printers, especially in cities, also published newspapers. More literary works—books of poetry and history, for example—still tended to be published in London and imported to the colonies, because few colonial printers could afford the risk if such works failed to find an audience. Not all colonial printing was in English: by mid-century Philadelphia boasted a thriving German-language press, which published a newspaper, pamphlets of various sorts, and the second Bible printed in North America (after John Eliot's 1661 Indian Bible).

47

New genres produced new concerns about the effects of print on readers. Newspapers routinely faced charges of seditious libel if they discussed local governments. When boys got their hands on manuals intended for midwives or married couples, such as *Aristotle's Master Piece*, the matter could end up in a disciplinary hearing. And as novels gained popularity in the colonies—first English ones such as Samuel Richardson's *Pamela*, and by the 1790s American ones as well—some Americans worried about whether the lures of fiction would corrupt the impressionable minds of readers, especially women. The proliferation of printing, of genres, and of reading itself could be cause for concern as well as celebration.

ARTIFACTS

Two colonial Americans' experiences of reading open this chapter. William Byrd (1674–1744) amassed Virginia's largest colonial library. Like the Mathers of Massachusetts, Byrd treasured books. His secret diaries attest to both his prodigious reading and his involvement in extensive networks of correspondence—the primary way elite colonists communicated with one another and received news in the early eighteenth century. Benjamin Franklin (1706–1790) was just twelve when he became an apprentice to his older brother James (1697–1735). In his autobiography, the younger Franklin recalled how his new trade encouraged his reading and writing—even if he was copying the "wretched" style of Grub Street, the London center of cheap publishing. (Franklin wrote the section of his autobiography reproduced below in 1771; the first American edition of the autobiography was not published until 1818.) At the age of twenty-two, Franklin composed his own epitaph. Like Byrd's diaries, this curious document suggests the way books could shape one's self-image.

William Byrd, *The Secret Diary of William Byrd of Westover* (1709)[1]

[June 16, 1709]

I rose at 5 o'clock and read a chapter in Hebrew and a little Greek. I neglected to say my prayers and ate milk for breakfast. Mr. Bland's boy brought me abundance of letters from Williamsburg, out of the men-of-war. I spent all the morning in reading them. My orders for being of the Council arrived among the rest. By these letters I learned that tobacco was good for nothing, that protested bills would ruin the country, that our trade with the Carolina Indians was adjusted in England, that my sister Braynes was [in prison by the cruelty of C-r-l-y], that my salary was in a fair way of being increased, that the College was like to be rebuilt by the Queen's bounty, that there was a probability of a peace next winter. I ate mutton for dinner. While we were at dinner, Colonel Harrison, Mr. Commissary, and Mr. Wormeley came to see us, but would not eat with us. They likewise brought me some letters. Captain Wilcox dined with us. His people brought me a box of [. . .] from P-r-c-r. I walked about the plantation. Mr. Wormeley and I played at billiards and I won half a crown. I said my prayers. All the company went away. I had good health, good thoughts, and good humor, thank God Almighty.

[June 17, 1709]

I rose at 5 o'clock and read some Greek in Josephus and perused some of my new books. . . .

[Aug. 12, 1709]

I rose at 5 o'clock and read two chapters in Hebrew and some Greek in Josephus. I said my prayers and ate milk for breakfast. I removed more of my books into the library. I read some geometry. I danced my dance. It was a very cold day but did not rain. Old Ben had his leg bathed in milk and mullein and found ease. I ate boiled shoat for dinner. In the afternoon I put up my books and then read some Greek in Homer and some Italian. In the evening I took a walk about the plantation. I neglected to say my prayers but had good health, good thoughts, and good humor, thanks be to God Almighty.

Benjamin Franklin, *Autobiography* (1818)[2]

This Bookish Inclination at length determin'd my Father to make me a Printer, tho' he had already one Son, (James) of that Profession. In 1717 my Brother James return'd from England with a Press & Letters to set up his Business in Boston. I lik'd it much better than that of my Father, but still had a Hankering for the Sea. To prevent the apprehended Effect of such an Inclination, my Father was impatient to have me bound to my Brother. I stood out some time, but at last was persuaded and signed the Indentures, when I was yet but 12 Years old. I was to serve as an Apprentice till I was 21 Years of Age, only I was to be allow'd Journeyman's Wages during the last Year. In a little time I made great Proficiency in the Business, and became a useful Hand to my Brother. I now had Access to better Books. An Acquaintance with the Apprentices of Booksellers, enabled me sometimes to borrow a small one, which I was careful to return soon & clean. Often I sat up in my Room reading the greatest Part of the Night, when the Book was borrow'd in the Evening & to be return'd early in the Morning lest it should be miss'd or wanted. And after some time an ingenious Tradesman Mr Matthew Adams who had a pretty Collection of Books, & who frequented our Printinghouse, took Notice of me, invited me to his Library, & very kindly lent me such Books as I chose to read. I now took a Fancy to Poetry, and made some little Pieces. My Brother, thinking it might turn to account encourag'd me, & put me on composing two occasional Ballads. One was called *Light House Tragedy*, & contain'd an Account of the drowning of Capt. Worthilake with his Two Daughters; the other was a Sailor Song on the Taking of *Teach* or Blackbeard the Pirate. They were wretched Stuff, in the Grub-street Ballad Style, and when they were printed he sent me about the town to sell them. The first sold wonderfully, the Event being recent, having made a great Noise. This flatter'd my Vanity. But my father discourag'd me, by ridiculing my Performances, and telling me Verse-makers were always Beggars; so I escaped being a Poet, most probably a very bad one.

Benjamin Franklin, "Epitaph" (1728)[3]

The Body of
B. Franklin,
Printer;
Like the Cover of an old Book,
Its Contents torn out,
And stript of its Lettering and Gilding,
Lies here, Food for Worms.
But the Work shall not be wholly lost:
For it will, as he believ'd, appear once more,
In a new & more perfect Edition,
Corrected and amended
By the Author.
He was born Jan. 6. 1706
Died   17

A COLONY'S government could be a printer's chief customer and obstacle. Governmental contracts to print the laws promised a most lucrative source of income. By 1729—after abandoning his apprenticeship (to his brother's chagrin) and laboring in a London printing house—Benjamin Franklin owned and ran a print shop in Philadelphia. He knew that many local citizens were clamoring for paper money, in an era when every issue of paper currency generated controversy. The following episode from his autobiography shows Franklin in his multiple worlds of words: debating the issue among his friends (the "Junto" was their literary society) and printing a pamphlet. Newspapers, another staple of eighteenth-century American printers, survived at the sufferance of local governments. Controversy could lead to a libel suit or a prison sentence, as Franklin's brother learned. Many papers played it safe, following a London model and simply chronicling European events. The pages reproduced here from James Franklin's *New-England Courant* and Andrew Bradford's (1686–1742) *American Weekly Mercury* illustrate the look of early American newspapers. John Markland's (d. 1735) *Typographia*, among the first books published when William Parks re-established Virginia printing in 1730, offers another striking example of the connections between printing and government. This long ceremonial poem celebrating King George and the royal governor of Virginia was an auspicious way for Parks to launch his business. The title page and frontispiece from *Der kleine Kempis*, published in Germantown, Pennsylvania, in 1750, serves as a reminder that English was not the only language used in colonial printing.

Benjamin Franklin, *Autobiography* (1818)[4]

About this Time [1729] there was a Cry among the People for more Paper Money, only 15,000£ being extant in the Province & that soon to be sunk. The wealthy Inhabitants oppos'd any Addition, being against all Paper Currency, from an Apprehension that it would depreciate as it had done in New England to the Prejudice of all Creditors. We had discuss'd this Point in our Junto, where I was on the Side of an Addition, being persuaded that the first small Sum struck in 1723 had done much good, by increasing the Trade, Employment, & Number of Inhabitants in the Province, since I now saw all the old Houses inhabited, & many new ones building, where as I remember'd well, that when I first walk'd about the Streets of Philadelphia, eating my Roll, I saw most of the Houses in Walnut Street between Second & Front streets with Bills on their Doors, to be let; and many likewise in Chestnut Street, & other Streets; which made me then think the Inhabitants of the City were one after another deserting it. Our Debates possess'd me so fully of the Subject, that I wrote and printed an anonymous Pamphlet on it, entitled, *The Nature & Necessity of a Paper Currency.* It was well receiv'd by the common People in general; but the Rich Men dislik'd it; for it increas'd and strengthen'd the Clamor for more Money; and they happening to have no Writers among them that were able to answer it, their Opposition slacken'd, & the Point was carried by a Majority in the House. My Friends there, who conceiv'd I had been of some Service, thought fit to reward me, by employing me in printing the Money, a very profitable Job, and a great Help to me. This was another advantage gain'd by my being able to write.

THE
New-England Courant.

From MONDAY January 29. to MONDAY February 5. 1722.

Aliud est maledicere, aliud accusare. Cic.

JUDICIOUS Author observes, That there is nothing in which Men more deceive themselves than in what the World call Zeal. There are so many Passions which hide themselves under it, and so many Mischiefs arising from it, that some have gone so far as to say, It would have been for the Benefit of Mankind, if it had never been reckoned in the Catalogue of Virtues. The fatal Effects of Zeal among our Selves, has almost perswaded me to be of this Opinion. A furious pretended Zeal, which only regards Matters of Opinion, has been improv'd against my self with a Design to destroy my Reputation and Interest amongst those who are Strangers to my Person: And that this Design might be the better carried on, some Persons have been so undutiful to the Reverend Dr. *Increase Mather*, as to perswade him to prefix his Name to an Advertisement in the last Weeks *News-Letter* and *Gazette*, wherein the mildest Appellation I meet with, is that of a wicked and cursed Libeller. This Charge I now lye under from the oldest Minister in the Country, and in order to clear my self I shall first give an Account of the first Cause of the Difference between us.

The Week before the *Courant* of *Jan.* 1. came out, a Grandson of Dr. *Increase Mather* brought me the following Account of the Success of Inoculation in *London*,

A Passage in the London Mercury*, Sept.* 16.
' Great Numbers of Persons in the City and the Suburbs ' are under the Inoculation of the Small Pox. Among the ' rest, the eldest Son of a noble Duke in Hanover Square, ' had the Small Pox inoculated upon him.

This he said his Grandfather desir'd me to insert in my next, and assur'd that he had transcrib'd it himself, and that it was Word for Word with the Account in the *London Mercury*. About Noon on the Day that the *Courant* came out, I saw the Four first Pages of the *London Mercury* of *Sept.* 16. and found nothing in them, but that *the eldest Son of a noble Duke in Hanover Square, had the Small Pox inoculated upon him INCOGNITO*. Here our young Spark was detected in a downright Falshood, and lost his Credit with *Couranto* ; and I had great Reason too to believe that the first Part of the above Paragraph was not in the other Half-Sheet of the *Mercury*, because both Passages related to Inoculation, and might (no doubt) have been as well inserted together. The next Week I inserted a Letter in the *Courant*, which asserted, that the former Part of the Passage, viz. *Great Numbers of Persons in the City and the Suburbs are under the Inoculation of the Small Pox*, was not to be found in the *London Mercury* of that Date, but at the same time inform'd us, that there were *some Accounts like it in a Weekly Mercury, which wanted Confirmation, and with the Addition of the Word Incognito*. So that tho' the Author of this Letter cou'd not find the former Part of the above Passage in the *London Mercury*, yet his main Design was to show, that those who sent the said Passage to me, design'd to impose on the Publick by leaving out the material Word *Incognito* ; and the Truth of this can be prov'd by many who have seen but the first Four Pages of the said *Mercury*. However, I am now inform'd by Gentlemen whom I dare believe, that the former Part of the said Passage is to be found in the last Half-Sheet of the *London Mercury* Sept 16. so that I have been impos'd on by both Sides, and shall take Care for the future, not to insert any thing in the *Courant* upon the Word of another.

I come now to consider the Doctor's Advertisement, and shall first observe, that those who first took the Advantage of my Credulity to deceive the World, (by leaving out the Word *Incognito*,) are those who now call me a cursed Libeller.

The Doctor first endeavours to clear himself of the Imputation of being one among the Supporters of the *Courant*, but at the same time acknowledges, that he had paid me for Two or Three of them. He might as well have said he had paid me for many more, as to have put me to the Trouble of proving it. Whether he remembers it or no, his Grandson *Biles*, by his Order, desir'd me to set him down as a Customer some Time ago ; but upon the Appearance of a Letter in the *Courant*, wherein a certain Clergyman was touch'd upon, he dropt it as a Subscriber, but sent his Grandson almost every Week for a considerable Time to buy them ; by which Method he paid more for the Paper and was more a Supporter of it, than if his Name had been continu'd in the List. At length, being weary with sending, he became a Subscriber again, and express'd no Dislike of the Paper till after Mr. *Musgrave* had publish'd his Grandson's Letter in the *Gazette* of *Jan.* 15. So that he both had and paid me for one Paper after that which he so much dislikes. The Truth of this I am ready to declare upon Oath, against the Testimony of all the Men in the Country. And that he has been a Subscriber, and consequently a Supporter of the Paper, the following Letter under his own Hand, will sufficiently prove.

Mr. Franklin,
' I Had Thoughts of taking your *Courant* (upon Tryal) for ' a Quarter of a Year, but I shall not now. In one of ' your *Courants* you have said that *if the Ministers of God ' are for a Thing, it is a Sign it is from the Devil,* and have ' dealt very falsly about the *London Mercury*. For these and ' other Reasons, I shall NO MORE be concerned with you.
Your well wishing, but grieved Friend,
I. Mather.

In the next Place he says, *In one of his vile Courants, he insinuates, that if the Ministers of God do approve of a Thing, it's a sign it is of the Devil, which is a horrid Thing to be related.*

The Words in the *Courant* are in a Dialogue (by an unknown Hand) between a Clergyman and Layman, and are exactly as follows.

Cl. But I find, all the Rakes in Town are against Inoculation, and that induces me to believe it is a right Way.

Laym. Most of the Ministers are for it, and that induces me to think it is from the D——l ; for he often makes use of good Men as Instruments to obtrude his Delusions on the World.

The Doctor must know, that Satan once stood up against Israel, and provoked *DAVID* to number the People. *Joab*, his wicked General, was not so easily provok'd to this Evil: The King's Word was abominable to him. This is Doctrine which I have often heard from the Pulpit, and if I am condemn'd for publishing it, I may venture to say (in the Words of the Doctor's Grandson, that I have Company of which I need not be *ashamed*.

Again, *And altho' in one of the* Courants *it is declared, that the* London Mercury Sept. 16. 1721. *affirms, That Great Numbers of Persons in the City and Suburbs are under the Inoculation of the Small Pox ; in his next* Courant *he asserts, That it was some busy Inoculator, that imposed on the Publick in saying so.*

I desire him to consider, that what I declared in one *Courant* was at his Desire, and what I asserted in the next was at the Instance of another ; so that I am but a Publisher of what one declares and another asserts.

Then, (after telling us that he has read those Words in the *London Mercury*,) he says, *And he doth frequently abuse the Ministers of Religion, and many other worthy Persons, in a Manner which is intollerable.*

One of these worthy Persons he hints at, has been since presented by the Grand Jury for cohabiting with a Woman as his Wife, who was never known to be so ; and another has not yet been able to clear himself of the Charge against him.

Again, *I can well remember, when the Civil Government could have taken an effectual Course to suppress such a cursed Libel.*

Here the Doctor calls the *Courant* a *cursed Libel*, and yet tells us the Government *cannot* suppress it ; by which he owns there is nothing in the Paper against Law, and plainly proves what he says to be a *Curse causeless*, which shall not come.

Again he says, *I cannot but pity poor Franklin, who tho' but a young Man, it may be speedily he must appear before the Judgment Seat of GOD, &c.*

I shall make no other Answer to this, than, That there is no Man living which doeth good and sinneth not, and that I expect and Hope to appear before God with safety in the Righteousness of Christ.

James Franklin, *The New-England Courant* (1722)[5]

Andrew Bradford, *The American Weekly Mercury* (1741/42)[6]

John Markland, *Typographia. An Ode, on Printing*, stanza IX (1730)[7]

Yet fair befal His Fame,
And may his Mem'ry long
In latest Annals live,
Who first contriv'd the *wondrous Frame*,
That to *dead Types* supply'd a *Tongue*,
And *Speech* to *lifeless Characters* could give.
O well was he employ'd the while,
And happy was the vent'rous Toil!
His Breast had compass'd some great Thought,
Tho' formless yet, and void,
His busy Faculties were all employ'd,
How future Ages might be surest taught,
By old Examples, long since done,
What Paths to follow, what to shun,
How vertue ev'n in Death befriends,
And how Ambition ends,
How *Socrates* instructed, *Caesar* fought;
Long Time, his swelling Breast
The great *Idea* had opprest,
'Till, fix'd at Length, he in a Rapture bid,
Come up a *glorious, great Design*,—And so it did.

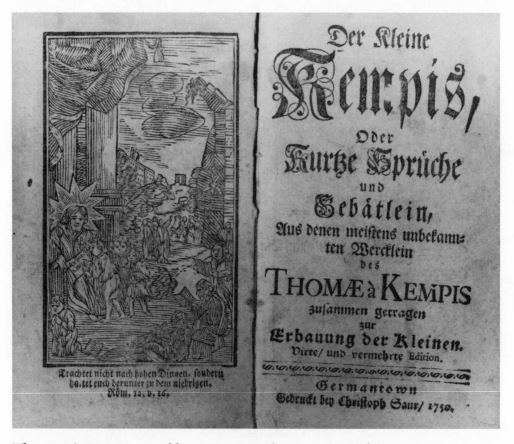

Thomas à Kempis, *Der kleine Kempis, oder Kurze Sprüche und Gebätlein* (1750)[8]

PRIMERS AND children's books were among the daily staples of ordinary colonists' reading. These were "good" books, upholding and inculcating cultural values—even if those values changed over time. *The New-England Primer*, originally published in the late 1600s and perhaps the most famous colonial schoolbook, was well known for its rhyming alphabet, complete with religious and moral messages: "Time cuts down all / Both great and small." A later children's book, *History of Giles Gingerbread* (1776?), demonstrates how the genre changed during the eighteenth century. Not all young people stuck to such prescribed reading, though. In the eyes of New England's clerical and legal authorities, improper books could shape immoral selves. In 1744, the famed Congregationalist clergyman Jonathan Edwards (1703–1758) documented the notorious "Bad Book Case," using townspeople's testimony about what local boys were illicitly reading.

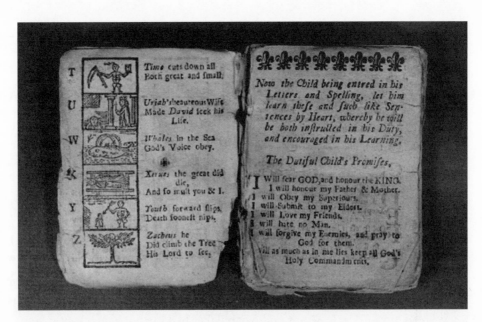

Image Alphabet, *The New-England Primer* (1727)[9]

Old Gaffer Gingerbread, *History of Giles Gingerbread.
A Little Boy who lived upon Learning* (1776?)[10]

Jonathan Edwards, "The Bad Book Case" (1744)[11]

Here Are Included the Testimonies against Oliver Warner, Given in the Spring, in the Year 1744

Rebeccah Strong testifieth that near five years ago the next May, Charles Wright and Timothy Root came into the shop, and [she] found 'em with a book that they were provoked about. Moses Sheldon asked whether we had seen such a book, mentioning the name. She had, at Dr. [Samuel] Mather's, concluding by the pictures that seemed to her to be these parts of a woman's body.

Timothy Root and Simeon [Root] and Moses Sheldon, often talking in a private way about a book, said something about a bible in a laughing way, that she concluded was that. When talking about the book, they talked about women and girls, and turn about and looked upon me, and said, "You had not need to be scared; we know as much about ye as you, and more too." When he (Moses Sheldon) inquired about the book, he asked me if it was not such an one, and I told him it was. "Well," says he, "that was the book that we had here, that you used to look after, and I have read it out." Uncle Moses said Noah Baker had the book, and kept it between his coat and the lining. Sarah Baker found it, and gave it to her mother. Moses Sheldon and those two Roots and Charles Wright. Timothy Root and Charles Wright chiefly used to talk much about such things as I suppose such books relate to.

Rachel Clap. Oliver Warner, Deacon Parsons' son, Medad Lyman wanted Aristotle, intended to find it. Simeon Root noised that he was sorry so that he had not read more. He told what was pictured out in the book. There the child is, lies all pictured out.

John Miller's wife. Delivered by younger sister. Isaac Parsons promises reformation. Never thought of the harm. He would totally and finally have done with it.

Mindwell [Miller]. Moses Sheldon: "I know a great deal more than you can think about the works of nature." Not above two months ago. Turned away and laughed.

Martha Clark. Ebenezer Bartlet: "What if I should say I sat 'till midnight reading one of them books." When he was talking about such books. "Don't you think I would sit up again if I had opportunity?"

Bathsheba [Negro]. At David Burt's, Noah Baker, Timothy Root and Elkanah Burt, reading in a book that they called "the bible" in a laughing way. All read in it. Timothy Root read most. (About the time that Noah Baker was married.) Read it before her [and] Naomi Warner. Laugh. Ready to kiss them, and catch hold of the girls and shook 'em. Timothy Root in particular. Called it "young folks' bible." The book was exceeding unclean to the top of baseness. The book what they read was about women. Samuel Burt's book, they said. It [was] about women's having children.

Had seen the book at Samuel Burt's once before. Timothy Root said at that time at Burt's, after the child is born they burn guts and garbages.

Hannah Clark with her in the street, and Oliver Warner met them. Said, "When will the moon change girls? I believe you can tell. I believe you have circles 'round your eyes. I believe it runs."

Medad Lyman and Oliver Warner knew what the girls was, what nasty creatures they was.

At another time, Oliver Warner and Medad Lyman reading in a base book, nasty book, about womenkind. At Moll Macklin's talk. John Macklin was there; he was worse than others that was there. Thankful Parsons was there. Dorothy Danks was there.

Joanna Clark. Oliver Warner, about a year ago: "When does the moon change girls? Come, I'll look at your [face] and see whether there be a blue circle 'round your eyes." Bathsheba Negro was with her. "I believe it runs."

Ebenezer Pomeroy, last lecture day night, when she groaned, said, "I believe you need the old granny. I have read in a book about that." John Lancton was with him.

Shadrach Bedartha. Oliver Warner asked me if I did not want a book that there had been talk about. I asked him who there be had such a book. He answered, "That is no matter to you." He offered to let me have it; offered it for ten shillings in money. He understood Oliver, and Oliver talked as though he supposed I understood him.

Elizabeth Pomeroy. Found a book in their house up the chimney, on the backside of the chimney on the press. No reason to think it was mother brought it in. The title, "The Midwife Rightly Instructed." Katherine Wright was with her. A new book.

Katherine Wright to the same. See Betty [Pomeroy] took it out. "Midwife Rightly Instructed," etc.

Experience Strong. A year or year and one half [ago], Ebenezer Bartlet at Jonathan Strong's house: "It might be necessary for young men to know such things." He owned that if he had had such a sense as he once had, he should have had no inclination to read such books.

Isaac Searl. Ephraim Wright talked to him and Oliver Warner too, that told him they would not have him tell more than he need, that they would not have him enlarge much upon it. Ephraim Wright told him he need not say a word, if he had not a mind to.

Mary Downing. Two years ago this summer at her mother's. Oliver Warner there. There was reading amongst them in a book. They made sport of what they read in the book. One or two more there; she could not certainly say who they was. They all did so. What they laughed and made sport of was about girls, things concerning girls that it is unclean to speak of. They seemed to boast as if they knew about girls, knew what belonged to girls as well as girls themselves. She took it that the book was about the same things that they talked of. They seemed by their talk to apprehend that they got what they knew about girls out of that book. They run upon the girls at that time, boasting how much they knew about them. Many other times here, talking after the same manner about what he knew about girls. He has talked to me himself about what he knew.

John Lancton, a fortnight ago last Friday, was at the farm where I was and was talking of such things, and he boasted that he had read Aristotle. He talked about his reading that book more than once; talked about the things that was in that book in a most unclean manner a long time. Betty Danks and Moll Waters there. He spoke of the book as a granny book. When I checked him, he laughed. He talked exceeding uncleanly and lasciviously, so that I never heard any fellow go so far. After he was gone, we—the young women that were there—agreed that we never heard any such talk come out of any man's mouth whatsoever. It seemed to me to be almost as bad as tongue could express.

IN THE second half of the eighteenth century, more Americans engaged in literary reading. Enjoying English novels and poetry, they made reading into more than just a vehicle for education, religious edification, or information. Phillis Wheatley (1753?–1784), an African American woman, wrote poetry that was published in London in 1773. Wheatley's work not only displayed her own creative gift but evidenced her wide reading as well. Like many American poets, she imitated contemporary English neoclassical models. But who would believe that the poems were her own work? In addition to her portrait and her poetry, the selection printed here includes the introductory material from her book: a letter from her master to the publisher and a list of the prominent New Englanders who testified to her authorship. Martha "Patty" Rogers (1761–1840) displayed the effects of her literary reading in an extensive diary that seems narratively and stylistically similar to the "sweet" novels she enjoyed. As it turned out, Rogers did not marry the Reverend William Woodbridge or Dr. Samuel Tenney, the two suitors mentioned here, or anyone else. Notably, Tenney later married Tabitha Gilman, who wrote a novel, *Female Quixotism* (1801), in which the central character seems to have been modeled on Rogers. Not everyone considered the widening audience for belles lettres a good thing. The first American-written novel, William Hill Brown's (1765–1793) *The Power of Sympathy* (1789), contained a long scene in which characters discussed proper and improper reading. Many early American novels (including the most popular one, Susannah Rowson's *Charlotte Temple*) included such scenes, possibly to answer the critics who lambasted fiction itself as a pernicious influence and a symbol of luxury in a nation supposedly governed by republican simplicity. The last artifact in this chapter, written by a Pennsylvania college student the same year *The Power of Sympathy* appeared, expressed just such a view.

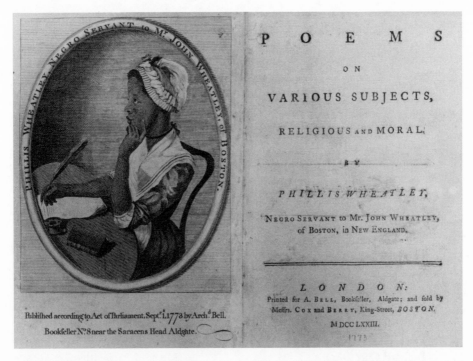

Phillis Wheatley, *Poems on Various Subjects, Religious and Moral* (1773)[12]

Phillis Wheatley, *Poems on Various Subjects. . . .* (1773)

The following is a Copy of a LETTER sent by the Author's Master to the Publisher.

PHILLIS was brought from *Africa* to *America,* in the Year 1761, between Seven and Eight Years of Age. Without any Assistance from School Education, and by only what she was taught in the Family, she, in sixteen Months Time from her Arrival, attained the English Language, to which she was an utter Stranger before, to such a Degree, as to read any, the most difficult Parts of the Sacred Writings, to the great Astonishment of all who heard her.

As to her WRITING, her own Curiosity led her to it; and this she learnt in so short a Time, that in the Year 1765, she wrote a Letter to the Rev. Mr. Occom, the *Indian* Minister, while in *England.*

She has a great Inclination to learn the Latin Tongue, and has made some Progress in it. This Relation is given by her Master who bought her, and with whom she now lives.

JOHN WHEATLEY.

Boston, Nov. 14, 1772.

To the PUBLICK.

AS it has been repeatedly suggested to the Publisher, by Persons, who have seen the Manuscript, that Numbers would be ready to suspect that they were not really the Writings of PHILLIS, he has procured the following Attestation, from the most respectable Characters in *Boston*, that none might have the least Ground for disputing their *Original*.

WE whose Names are under-written, do assure the World, that the POEMS specified in the following Page,* were (as we verily believe) written by PHILLIS, a young Negro Girl, who was but a few Years since, brought an uncultivated Barbarian from *Africa*, and has ever since been, and now is, under the Disadvantage of serving as a Slave in a Family in this Town. She has been examined by some of the best Judges, and is thought qualified to write them.

His Excellency Thomas Hutchinson, *Governor,*
The Hon. Andrew Oliver, *Lieutenant-Governor.*

The Hon. Thomas Hubbard,	*The Rev.* Charles Chauncy, *D.D.*
The Hon. John Erving,	*The Rev.* Mather Byles, *D.D.*
The Hon. James Pitts,	*The Rev.* Ed. Pemberton, *D.D.*
The Hon. Harrison Gray,	*The Rev.* Andrew Elliot, *D.D.*
The Hon. James Bowdoin,	*The Rev.* Samuel Cooper, *D.D.*
John Hancock, *Esq;*	*The Rev. Mr.* Samuel Mather,
Joseph Green, *Esq;*	*The Rev. Mr.* John Moorhead,
Richard Carey, *Esq;*	*Mr.* John Wheatley, *her Master.*

N.B. The original Attestation, signed by the above Gentlemen, may be seen by applying to *Archibald Bell,* Bookseller, No. 8, *Aldgate-Street.*

To MÆCENAS

MÆCENAS, you, beneath the myrtle shade,
Read o'er what poets sung, and shepherds play'd.
What felt those poets but you feel the same?
Does not your soul possess the sacred flame?
Their noble strains your equal genius shares
In softer language, and diviner airs.
      While *Homer* paints lo! circumfus'd in air,
Celestial Gods in mortal forms appear;
Swift as they move hear each recess rebound,
Heav'n quakes, earth trembles, and the shores resound.
Great Sire of verse, before my mortal eyes,

---

*The Words *"following Page,"* allude to the Contents of the Manuscript Copy, which are wrote at the Back of the above Attestation. [Note in original.]

The lightnings blaze across the vaulted skies,
And, as the thunder shakes the heav'nly plains,
A deep-felt horror thrills through all my veins.
When gentler strains demand thy graceful song,
The length'ning line moves languishing along.
When great *Patroclus* courts *Achilles'* aid,
The grateful tribute of my tears is paid;
Prone on the shore he feels the pangs of love,
And stern *Pelides* tend'rest passions move.

      Great *Maro's* strain in heav'nly numbers flows,
The *Nine* inspire, and all the bosom glows.
O could I rival thine and *Virgil's* page,
Or claim the *Muses* with the *Mantuan* Sage;
Soon the same beauties should my mind adorn,
And the same ardors in my soul should burn:
Then should my song in bolder notes arise,
And all my numbers pleasingly surprize;
But here I sit, and mourn a grov'ling mind,
That fain would mount, and ride upon the wind.

      Not you, my friend, these plaintive strains become,
Not you, whose bosom is the *Muses* home;
When they from tow'ring *Helicon* retire,
They fan in you the bright immortal fire,
But I less happy, cannot raise the song,
The fault'ring music dies upon my tongue.

      The happier *Terence** all the choir inspir'd,
His soul replenish'd, and his bosom fir'd;
But say, ye *Muses,* why this partial grace,
To one alone of *Afric's* sable race;
From age to age transmitting thus his name
With the first glory in the rolls of fame?

      Thy virtues, great *Mæcenas!* shall be sung
In praise of him, from whom those virtues sprung:
While blooming wreaths around thy temples spread,
I'll snatch a laurel from thine honour'd head,
While you indulgent smile upon the deed.

      As long as *Thames* in streams majestic flows,
Or *Naiads* in their oozy beds repose,
While *Phoebus* reigns above the starry train
While bright *Aurora* purples o'er the main,

---

*He was an *African* by birth. [Wheatley's note.]

So long, great Sir, the muse thy praise shall sing,
So long thy praise shall make *Parnassus* ring:
Then grant, *Mæcenas*, thy paternal rays,
Hear me propitious, and defend my lays.

Martha (Patty) Rogers, Diary (1785)[13]

Friday— jan— 7th— very pleasant. felt fatigued—Set to work—PM—finished Mr. Woodbridge's shirts and wrote to send with them—Mrs. Thurston called on me to go to Mrs. G She told me Mr T had greaved her, and treated her with Indignity— I spent the evening at Mrs. G— Mrs. T— told me she had talked with Mr. W—ge— he ask her how I did—whether I still thot of him? She Returned for answer, She belived I was <u>happy</u>! that I <u>still</u> had a particular Regard for him "well I hope it is nothing more" "I don't know how to act with regard to Patty I feel embarisst— I wish to treat her with <u>tenderness</u>! & yet I dare not" O! Sally how <u>happy</u> you make me by conversing on that dear <u>object</u> tis happiness to me, to reflect on those agreeable Scenes we have past together! I now at this moment feel every tender emotion arising in my Bosom!—We came home

Satterday—jan 8th very pleasant PM went to see my Sister—had an agreeable time—Came home at dark—read and went to Bed with a gratifull heart!

Sunday—jan 9th very pleasant Went to meeting all day. Coming home Doctor T[enney] offered me his arm. I went and dined with Sally—& we had some social chat—But one action in the day gave me <u>pain</u>—coming from meeting at Night D—r T—y overtook me, & I had the assurance to take his arm unast! how could I? how could I? But he is a person of so much goodness I doubt not he will forgive it. But take care my girl for the future! and not give ocation for those keen sensations! The D—r came and spent the evening with us, so I see he took no acception from my freedom—the evening past in good humour on all sides—

Monday—jan 10th very cold—felt very unwell—Sent the amiable Woodbridge his shirt and with it the a Letter— what the consequence will be, I know not—Read in a <u>Sweet novel</u> the D—r brought me it affected me so, I could hardly read it, and was often obliged to drop the Book to supress my greif! Went to Bed, Lay, and <u>thot</u> of the Lovely Woodbridge—Shed a <u>torrent</u> of tears at the <u>Recollection</u> of past Interviews with him.

"O! Why should Bliss depart so soon,
And friendship Stay to mourn,
Why the fond passions cling so fast,
When every joy is gone" Watts.

William Hill Brown, *The Power of Sympathy* (1789)[14]

"WHAT books would you recommend to put into the hands of my daughter?" said Mrs. *Bourn*, as she walked into the library—"it is a matter of some importance." "It is a matter of *more* importance," answered *Worthy*, "than is generally imagined, for unless a proper selection is made, one would do better never to read at all:—Now, Madam, as much depends on the choice of books, care should be taken not to put those in the way of young persons, which might leave on their minds any disagreeable prejudices, or which has a tendency to corrupt their morals."— "As obvious as your remark is," added Mr. *Holmes*, "it is evidently overlooked in the common course of education. We wisely exclude those persons from our conversation, whose characters are bad, whose manners are depraved, or whose morals are impure; but if they are excluded from an apprehension of contaminating our minds, how much more dangerous is the company of those books, where the strokes aimed at virtue are redoubled, and the poison of vice, by repeatedly reading the same thing, indelibly distains the young mind?"

"WE all agree," rejoined *Worthy*, "that it is as great a matter of virtue and prudence to be circumspect in the selection of our books, as in the choice of our company.—But, Sir, the best things may be subverted to an ill use. Hence we may possibly trace the cause of the ill tendency of many of the Novels extant."

"MOST of the Novels," interrupted my father, "with which our female libraries are overrun, are built on a foundation not always placed on strict morality, and in the pursuit of objects not always probable or praiseworthy.—Novels, not regulated on the chaste principles of true friendship, rational love, and connubial duty, appear to me totally unfit to form the minds of women, of friends, or of wives."

"BUT, as most young people read," says Mrs. *Bourn*—"what rule can be *hit upon* to make study always terminate to advantage?"

"IMPOSSIBLE," cried Miss, "for I read as much as any body, and though it may afford amusement, while I am employed, I do not remember a single word, when I lay down the book."

"THIS confirms what I say of Novels," cried Mr. *Holmes*, addressing *Worthy* in a jocular manner, "just calculated to kill time—to attract the attention of the reader for an hour, but leave not one idea on the mind."

"I AM far from condemning every production in the gross," replied *Worthy*; "general satire against any particular class, or order of men, may be viewed in the same light as a satire against the species—it is the same with books—If there are corrupt or mortified members, it is hardly fair to destroy the whole body. Now I grant some Novels have a bad tendency, yet there are many which contain excellent sentiments—let these receive their deserved reward—let those be discountenanced; and if it is impossible 'to smite them with an apoplexy, there is a moral certainty of their dying of a consumption.'— But, as Mrs. *Bourn* observes, most young persons read, I will therefore recommend to those who wish to mingle instruction with entertainment, method and regularity in reading. To *dip* into *any book* burthens the mind with unnecessary lumber, and may rather be called a disadvantage, than a benefit—The record of memory is so scrawled and blotted with imperfect ideas, that not one legible character can be traced."

"WERE I to throw my thoughts on this subject," said my good father-in-law, as he began to enter more warmly into the debate—drawing his chair opposite *Worthy*, and raising his hand with a poetical enthusiasm—"Were I to throw my thoughts on this subject into an Allegory, I would describe the human mind as an extensive plain, and knowledge as the river that should water it. If the course of the river be properly directed, the plain will be fertilized and cultivated to advantage; but if books, which are the sources that feed this river, rush into it from every quarter, it will overflow its banks, and the plain will become inundated: When, therefore, knowledge flows on in its proper channel, this extensive and valuable field, the mind, instead of being covered with stagnant waters, is cultivated to the utmost advantage, and blooms luxuriantly into a general efflorescence—for a river properly restricted by high banks, is necessarily progressive."

THE old gentleman brought down his hand with great solemnity, and we complimented him on his poetical exertion. "I cannot comprehend the meaning of this matter," said the penetrative Miss *Bourn*. "I will explain it to you, my little dear," said he, with great good nature—"If you read with any design to improve your mind in virtue and every amiable accomplishment, you should be careful to read methodically, which will enable you to form an estimate of the various topicks discussed in company, and to bear a part in all those conversations which belong to your sex—you see, therefore, how necessary general knowledge is—what would you think of a woman advanced in life, who has no other store of knowledge, than what she has obtained from experience?"

"I THINK she would have a sorry time of it," answered Miss.

"TO prevent it in yourself," said Mrs. *Bourn* to her daughter, "be assiduous to lay in a good stock of this knowledge, while your mind is yet free from prejudice and care."

"HOW shall I *go to work*, Madam," enquired the delicate daughter.

Mrs. *Bourn* turned toward Mr. *Holmes*, which was hint enough for the good old man to proceed.

"THERE is a medium to be observed," continued he, "in a lady's reading; she is not to receive every thing she finds, even in the best books, as invariable lessons of conduct; in books written in an easy, flowing style, which excel in description and the luxuriance of fancy, the imagination is apt to get heated—she ought, therefore, to discern with an eye of judgment, between the superficial and the penetrating— the elegant and the tawdry—what may be merely amusing, and what may be useful. General reading will not teach her a true knowledge of the world.

"IN books she finds recorded the faithfulness of friendship—the constancy of *true love*, and even that honesty is the best policy. If virtue is represented carrying its reward with it, she too easily persuades herself that mankind have adopted this plan: Thus she finds, when, perhaps, it is too late, that she has entertained wrong notions of human nature; that her friends are deceitful—her lovers false—and that men consult interest oftener than honesty.

"A YOUNG lady who has imbibed her ideas of the world from desultory reading, and placed confidence in the virtue of others, will bring back disappointment, when she expected gratitude. Unsuspicious of deceit, she is easily deceived—from the purity of her own thoughts, she trusts the faith of mankind, until experience convinces her of her errour—she falls, a sacrifice to her credulity, and her only consolation is the simplicity and goodness of her heart.

"THE story of Miss *Whitman* is an emphatical illustration of the truth of these observations. An inflated fancy, not restricted by judgment, leads too often to *disappointment* and repentance. Such will be the fate of those who become (to use her own words)

'Lost in the magick of that sweet employ,

'To build *gay scenes* and fashion *future joy.*'

"WITH a good heart she possessed a poetical imagination, and an unbounded thirst for novelty; but these airy talents, not counterpoised with judgment, or perhaps serious reflection, instead of adding to her happiness, were the cause of her ruin."

"I CONCLUDE from your reasoning," said I, "and it is, besides, my own opinion, that many fine girls have been ruined by reading Novels."

"AND I believe," added Mrs. *Bourn*, "we may trace from hence the causes of spleen in many persons advanced in life."

"YOU mean old maids, Madam," cries the sagacious Miss, "like my aunt *Deborah* —she calls all the men deceitful, and most women, with her, are no better than they should be."

"WELL said!" exclaimed *Worthy*, "the recollection of chagrin and former disappointment, sours one's temper and mortifies the heart—disappointment will be more or less severe in proportion as we elevate our expectations; for the most *sanguine tempers* are the soonest discouraged; as the highest building is in the most danger of falling."

"IT appears from what I have said," resumed Mr. *Holmes*, "that those books which teach us a knowledge of the world are useful to form the minds of females, and ought therefore to be studied."

I MENTIONED Rochefoucault's maxims.—

"DO they not degrade human nature?" enquired my father.

"THIS little book," answered *Worthy*, "contains much truth—and those short sketches traced by the hand of judgment, present to us the leading features of mankind." "But," replied my father, "that *interest should assume all shapes*, is a doctrine, which, in my mind, represents a caricature rather than a living picture." "It is the duty of a painter to produce a likeness," said *Worthy*.—"And a skillful one," cried my father, continuing the metaphor, "will bring the amiable qualities of the heart to light; and throw those which disgrace humanity into the shade." "I doubt," rejoined

Worthy, "whether this flattery will answer the purpose you aim to accomplish— You entertain a high opinion of *the dignity of human nature*, and are displeased at the author who advances any thing derogatory to that dignity. *Swift*, in speaking of these maxims, in one of his best poems, affirms,

'They argue no corrupted mind
'In him—the fault is in mankind.'"

"AS I began this subject," added I, "it shall be ended by one observation—As these maxims give us an idea of the manners and characters of men, among whom a young person is soon to appear; and as it is necessary to her security and happiness that she be made acquainted with them—they may be read to advantage."

"THERE is another medium," said Mr. *Holmes*, assenting to my observation, "to be noticed in the study of a lady—she takes up a book, either for instruction or entertainment; the medium lies in knowing when to put it down. Constant application becomes labour—it sours the temper—gives an air of thoughtfulness, and frequently of absence. By *immoderate reading* we hoard up opinions and become insensibly attached to them; this miserly conduct sinks us to affectation, and disgustful pedantry; *conversation* only can remedy this dangerous evil, strengthen the judgment, and make reading really useful. They mutually depend upon, and assist each other.

"A KNOWLEDGE of HISTORY which exhibits to us in one view the rise, progress and decay of nations—which points out the advancement of the mind in society, and the improvements in the arts which adorn human nature, comes with propriety under the notice of a lady. To observe the origin of civilization—the gradual progress of society, and the refinements of manners, policy, morality and religion—to observe the progression of mankind from simplicity to luxury, from luxury to effeminacy, and the gradual steps of the decline of empire, and the dissolution of states and kingdoms, must blend that happy union of instruction and entertainment, which never fails to win our attention to the pursuit of all subjects.

"POETRY claims her due from the ladies. POETRY enlarges and strengthens the mind, refines the taste and improves the judgment. It has been asserted that women have no business with *satire*—now satire is but a branch of poetry. I acknowledge, however, much false wit is sent into the world, under this general title; but no critick with whom I am acquainted ever called satire false wit—for as long as vice and folly continue to predominate in the human heart, the satirist will be considered as a useful member of society. I believe *Addison* calls him an auxiliary to the pulpit. Suffer me to enlarge on this *new idea*. Satire is the correction of the vices and follies of the human heart; a woman may, therefore, read it to advantage. What I mean by enforcing this point, is, to impress the minds of females with a principle of self correction; for among all kinds of knowledge which arise from reading, the duty of self knowledge is a very eminent one; and is at the same time, the most useful and important.

"OUR ordinary intercourse with the world, will present to us in a very clear point of view, the fallacious ideas we sometimes entertain of our own self knowledge.—

We are blinded by pride and self love, and will not observe our own imperfections, which we blame with the greatest acrimony in other people, and seem to detest with the greatest abhorrence; so that it often happens, while we are branding our neighbour for some foible, or vanity, we ourselves are equally guilty.

"RIDICULOUS as this conduct must appear in the eyes of all judicious people, it is too frequently practiced to escape observation.

"I WILL drop this piece of morality, with a charge to the fair reader, that when-ever she discovers a satire, ridiculing or recriminating the follies or crimes of man-kind, that she look into her own heart, and compare the strictures on the conduct of others with her own feelings."

Observations on Novel-Reading: In an Essay written by a member of the Belles-Lettres Society of Dickinson College, at Carlisle. In the Year 1789 (1792)[15]

Many booksellers and printers in this country are well aware of the rapid sale they can have for novels, and of the great gain they can thus make by a very quick con-version and return of their money; they are polite enough for their own pockets to encrease the number of these books daily as well by importation as reprinting; and are very ready to clear their consciences of indiscriminately distributing quantities of rank poison, instead of prescribing the reviving draught, or the mitigating pill.

I am a friend to the liberty of the press, but at the same time one of the greatest enemies to the abuse of that liberty: And I therefore cannot forbear thinking, that our STATE LEGISLATURES, or even the legislature of the UNITED STATES, would not act beneath their dignity, if they should, among other restraints on the *licentiousness* of the press, lay a very heavy duty on all novels whatsoever for the future—as well those imported, as those printed within their jurisdiction. This would not only tend in time to diminish the number of these books, if not stop the printing or importing of them altogether, but also to multiply more valuable books—to lower their prices, and by these means diffuse knowledge to a much greater extent than at present—This would be taxing a prevalent species of luxury—I may add *licentious* luxury, which is more prejudicial to the welfare of AMERICA than many others, on which the wisdom of THE HONORABLE OUR CONGRESS has already led them to lay a heavy impost.

COMMENTARY: GOOD NEWS AND BAD BOOKS

In 1728, the year that Cotton Mather died, Benjamin Franklin, then twenty-two and setting up as a printer in Philadelphia, wrote his own epitaph (reproduced above). Franklin's mock epitaph might be read as a real one for Cotton Mather, so strongly do the two men represent opposing print mores. The epitaph takes literally the familiar conceit of life as a book, focusing on the material object. The fleshly body becomes a "stript" book cover, and the "work" that will not be "wholly lost," as distinct from the book's torn-out pages, sounds like an orthodox "soul" transcending the corporeal and ready for God's corrections. But in Franklin's hands, "work" resonates with the everyday labors of the print shop and the painstaking toil of composing type, which Franklin learned beginning at age twelve when he was apprenticed to his brother James. The epitaph's wit lies in the fact that, as the printer, Franklin controls what comes off the press; the printer's practical authority over authors seems here to reach as far as the Author of all things. Years later, Franklin in a like mind would begin his last will and testament: "I, Benjamin Franklin, printer." Franklin's vocation as a printer and his workaday relationship to the materiality of print constituted the very fabric of his identity.

And what of the man who had actually died around the time Franklin was writing what was, in effect, his own professional birth announcement? While Cotton Mather had a mania for printed things (a 7,000–volume library) and an obsession for getting into print (he published some 400 works), his relation to print was grounded in the sermon tradition. The emphasis of his Harvard education was on acquiring the skills as well as the languages—Greek and Latin—of classical rhetoric, a system that privileged oral over written performance and was the typical training for the ministry in the seventeenth century. For Mather print was an alternative fluency to that of speech. (His stammer perhaps contributed to his desire to speak through print.) All of his publications—his detractors' accusations about his "innate Itch of writing" and his own fears of vanity aside—constitute a gloss on the only legitimate book, the Bible. As a rule, publication was part of his ministry, always sacredly motivated, always ancillary to oral performance or to spiritual experience.

Over the course of the eighteenth century, Mather's sacred and rhetorical orality, in which print is a supplement to speech, gave way to Franklin's more utilitarian mode. With increasingly secularized and steadily growing literacy, more and more people began to transact the business of everyday life through the medium of print. They signed off on legal forms, filled in bills of lading, had broadsides printed up, purchased tickets, exchanged currency. Authority gradually became invested not in a minister or a sacred text or an administrative office but, in somewhat disembodied ways, in printedness and in literacy themselves. These transformations, however, were gradual and varied with local conditions. Literacy rates rose for all groups in all regions during the eighteenth century, reaching about 90 percent for white men and women in the north. While only nine printers served the colonies in 1720, by 1760 there were forty-two, a third of them in the south and outside of the major northern cities (Warner, 32). Increased access to literacy and new uses of print transformed public life, as the proliferation of newspapers demonstrates. In addition, especially through the genres of children's literature and the novel, print also penetrated private life, influencing both intimate ties between individuals and the ways in which people reflected upon their own lives.

The most important new genre of this period was the newspaper, the form that Franklin cut his teeth on. Designed to transmit "Publick Occurrences Both Forreign and Domestick" (as the title of the first, one-issue American venture of 1690 put it), newspapers evolved from handwritten newsletters that postmasters circulated outward from cities to the provinces. Later, with access to a press, postmaster and printer often became one and the same. William Byrd's Westover, Virginia, diary describes what it meant to get the news some twenty years before Virginia saw its first local newspaper: face-to-face talk with people who might also deliver handwritten letters. The information Byrd received (mediated through his wry worldview) came in a flood of items of strictly private and more generally public interest commingled, with no distinctions made among them. This private communication network was both exclusive and cumbersome. Eventually a ready audience, shaped by the beginnings of the consumer revolution and the spread of commercial interests, made the newspaper into a staple, if not always stable, commodity of the press. Indeed, three-quarters of all printers between 1700 and 1765 printed newspapers (Copeland, 17).

At one time papers followed the *London Gazette* by announcing themselves "published by authority." John Campbell, the Boston postmaster responsible for the first sustained American newspaper, the *Boston News-Letter* (1704–76), used the phrase as did his rival at the *Boston Gazette* (1719–98) even though neither paper was an official government organ. Originally signifying government regulation, "published by authority" became a catchphrase for reliable information, coming from the metropolis. The phrase eventually fell into disuse as sources for information became more multiple and diffuse. These sources are represented by such traditional graphics of newspaper mastheads as ships, postboys, and Mercury (the god of commerce and muse of the news, whose name shares the same root with merchant and market). In the *American Weekly Mercury* (founded by Franklin's rival Andrew Bradford in 1719), the ships come and go in a bustling port, with the Union Jack at center. The factotum—the initial ornamented capital letter—of James Franklin's *New-England Courant* (1721–26) visually displays the relationship between circulation and content: the letter is embedded in and emerges from the network that circulates it. Between 1720 and 1770, 37 percent of news items (other than European events and state business) was shipping news; in 1760 the figure rose to 46 percent (Copeland, 40). Then as now, to a large extent the network that distributes the news is the news.

In conjunction with the domestic spread of literacy, newspapers filled needs created by the growth of a transatlantic network of commercial interests. Benjamin Franklin registers the resulting shift in authority in his satiric rules for the *New-England Courant* (January 29–February 5, 1722). Writing against the Boston clergy (Mather, of course, among them) and the administration that would soon jail his brother, Franklin presents a list of mock "Rules, which . . . will render your Paper not only inoffensive, but pleasant and agreeable." A send-up of ministerial sanctions, his rhetoric also smacks of courtesy books and children's catechisms. He signs his letter, not with the cosmopolitan, theatrical signatures of much *Courant* fare (such as Tom Penshallow and Philo Satyricus), but with "your hearty Friends and Wellwishers, A, B, C, &c." As he burlesques the letters of academic degrees by reducing them to the ABCs, Franklin playfully demonstrates that literacy has become invested with the power to organize and critique public behavior. This *Courant* article conveys the notion that those who know their letters and have access to a press can enter the debates of the day as well as anyone. Indeed, Franklin's own life and works would help create the conditions of the emerging public sphere, in which the printing press played the central role.

The career that Franklin self-consciously charts in his *Autobiography* spans to a striking degree the shifting range of opportunities provided by the period's literacy and print environments. While still a child, Franklin was apprenticed to his brother as a printer and became a devoted consumer of books. Like eighteenth-century college boys for whom the production and circulation of manuscript verses was a mark of gentility, Franklin was drawn to poetry. But for this working boy, poetry had to pay. He wrote, printed, and hawked his ballads on the street, in the long-standing folk tradition of the urban peddler, crying his wares on the lowest rung of the ladder of commerce. As his ambitions rose, Franklin got poetry to pay in a less direct fashion, "so far as to improve one's Language" (*Autobiography,* 41). By the time he had set up on his own, Franklin cannily grasped where the real money was to be had: literally in money itself. In a turn that extravagantly epitomizes the period's network of print, politics, and commerce, Franklin argued for paper money in a pamphlet from his own press and then gained the lucrative government contract to print the very currency he promoted.

Such government printing was a mainstay of the press across the colonies. But while all colonial printers were necessarily entrepreneurial, relying on emerging American commercial networks, southern printers tended to express more strictly imperial attitudes and allegiances. One of the first books from the new Williamsburg press in 1730 was John Markland's *Typographia: An Ode on Printing.* Its printer, William Parks, had established provincial papers in England and founded the first southern papers in America, the *Maryland Gazette* (1728) and, later, Williamsburg's *Virginia Gazette* (1736). *Typographia* celebrates King George and his Virginia stand-in, Governor Gooch, whose "Patronage and Encouragement" permit the art of printing to flourish: "Where GOOCH administers, AUGUSTUS reigns." Print is most interesting to the poet as a tool for extending the reach of George and Gooch, namely via "VIRGINIA's Laws." The job of the printer ("the careful Artist") is to supply "a *Tongue,/*And *Speech* to *lifeless Characters.*" In colonial Virginia, the oral world of legal rituals paralleled New England's ministerial orality (Isaac, 90–92). In *Typographia* legal orality finds an adjunct—and speech—in print. The poem is an ode to bureaucracy:

to management and administration invested in the person of Gooch, as George's representative. According to this ceremonial ode, print functions to circulate imperial power.

Legal printing—not only legislative business, but the job printing of certificates, deeds, contracts—was a significant part of many printers' livelihood, Franklin's as well as Parks's. Franklin's account books for 1730 to 1735 show that he printed 16,800 "blanks," a wide variety of legal forms to be filled in and signed by hand (Wroth, 225). As in the north, private southern colonial libraries were most likely to contain theological works. But the next most numerous category in the south was the law, both theoretical and practical. Not only did merchants and property owners have to know the rudiments of law for commercial transactions, but laymen sat on the courts in isolated areas (Davis, 31–32). William Parks printed the first American guide to local laws, George Webb's *Office and Authority of a Justice of the Peace* (1736).

Other books from Parks's press indicate a market for self-education: John Tennent's 1734 *Every Man His Own Doctor* and the first American cookbook, E. Smith's 1742 *Compleat Housewife* (Stiverson, 142). A 3,500–volume library could be supplied directly from London, to sustain William Byrd's classical reading, and his identity as an English aristocrat. But less aristocratic customers in Parks's Williamsburg bookstore were looking for something else. As these titles show, locally produced books were increasingly committed to an ethic of self-help and how-to. In the eighteenth century the Puritan habit of turning to the Bible for solace and aid, as well as revelation, began to extend to other kinds of print. In certain cases print could not only extend the reach of persons but could replace persons entirely, functioning not simply as supplements to social life but as surrogates. Books now offered instruction on physical tasks and deportment, previously the exclusive realm of person-to-person, body-to-body contact. These books, like the ready reckoners (guides to everyday arithmetic), letter-writing manuals, and literacy primers of the day, presented themselves as genial and knowledgeable acquaintances who would take on the role of "master" in master-apprentice and master-student relationships.

A book could supply all manner of information that had traditionally belonged within the domain of personal interaction. In Northampton, Massachusetts, during the so-called "bad books" case of 1744, teenage boys had gotten hold of midwife's manuals, including the notorious "Aristotle." Originally published in 1684, the steamily informative *Aristotle's Master Piece* was widely reprinted in England and America well into the nineteenth century. When the boys teased local girls with their newfound knowledge, Jonathan Edwards asked all concerned to account for themselves before a committee of the church. "[T]hey got what they knew about girls out of that book," Mary Downing testified, marking a striking intersection of the history of American sexuality with the history of American print culture. Midwifery books and marriage manuals, whether used by adults or as props for naughty boys, demonstrate the ways in which traditional knowledge, whether of birthing babies or of having sex, was now inflected by print. And when Northampton teenagers referred to "Aristotle" as "the bible," they were drawing on time-honored folk mockery while at the same time mirroring a new fact of life in the print market: in the place where *one* Bible once held sway, there were now *many* books.

Some of the same boys whose intimate lives were changed by "Aristotle" had previously experienced the shatteringly intimate effects of religious conversion, a phenomenon that was also being promoted in the print marketplace. By 1744 Jonathan Edwards's part in the Great Awakening, which peaked in Northampton in 1736, had virtually ended, though the itinerant evangelical preacher George Whitefield continued to stir religious enthusiasm on his tour of America, including the south, through 1745. Every stage of the Awakening had been fueled by publication and publicity. Edwards published all of his key sermons, often within months of delivering them. The debates surrounding Whitefield's Philadelphia visit in Bradford's *American Weekly Mercury* and Franklin's *Pennsylvania Gazette* in 1739 and 1740 allowed Franklin, always alert to the main chance, to solicit subscribers for Whitefield's *Sermons and Journals*, the most successful book Franklin ever published (Green, 102). Between 1739 and 1745 American printers published more works by Whitefield than by any other writer (Lambert, 128).

The children of Northampton, who knew so well how to read their "Aristotle," very likely got their letters from *The New-England Primer*, which introduced children not only to literacy but also to the many uses of print, not all of which were as orthodox as its Westminster Catechism might indicate. *The New-England Primer* was probably compiled in 1690 (the earliest extant editions date from 1727) by Benjamin Harris, whose eight-year residence in Boston resulted not only in the *Primer* but in America's first newspaper. The two were linked not only by proximity, as commodities available from Harris's London Coffee-House in Boston, but also in the ways in which they contributed to the spread of print in the coming years. The *Primer* depended on its official catechisms and other orthodox content to gain an audience. But its prestige was not strictly religious. Published as if it had the imprimatur of the highest civil power, its frontispiece changed over time, depicting first kings and queens of England, and after the Revolution such figures as George Washington and John Hancock. As potent as these respectable credentials were, they perhaps contributed less to the book's enormous staying power than did the *Primer*'s famous picture alphabet. These pictures and rhymes linked the daunting new world of print to a familiar old world of proverbial sayings and related visual images. Such phrases as "The Cat doth play/And after slay," and its cat-and-fiddle image, reached back at least two centuries. After about 1740 *The New-England Primer* was joined by other primers and children's chapbooks, which were first imported and then pirated and imitated by colonial printers. More playful and more secular than the *Primer*, these little books conveyed a more commercial ethic. In the *Giles Gingerbread* frontispiece reproduced here, an image of a peddler appears in the place of kings and statesmen. Learning is presented as something to be purchased and consumed; Old Gaffer Gingerbread sells "useful knowledge by the Pound." The story recounts how Giles learns the alphabet, motivated by a desire to become a great man, and the tale closes with a full-page alphabet, somewhat in the spirit with which Franklin had signed "A, B, C" to his *Courant* letter. Such entertaining fare sometimes incorporated catechisms as well, combining playfulness, pedagogy, and piety in the same text. These hybrid forms typify the chapbook genre. Similar meldings of sacred and secular, of the market-oriented and the civic-minded, appear in adult literature as well and shape the reading and writing customs of the period.

Like colonial American life, colonial American printing was conducted in a variety of languages. Sharing the expanding mid-Atlantic market with Benjamin Franklin and Andrew Bradford, among others, Christopher Sower served the German communities in Pennsylvania. In a career that paralleled Franklin's, Sower published a successful newspaper, Bibles, primers, catechisms, and tracts, including Whitefield's sermons—all in German. More complex is the relation of the indigenous people to literacy and print. Vernacular Indian languages were taught and printed throughout the eighteenth century. As their languages were transcribed for the first time, many Indians were both persuaded and coerced to become literate. Indians owned and annotated books, wrote deeds and wills, and in other ways made use of print and literacy (Goddard, 15). Nevertheless, in Anglophone New England as in the Spanish-dominated southwest, for the native population, literacy was "an instrument of colonization" (Gallegos, 92). In the Spanish territories of New Mexico and California, books circulated to missions, ranches, and military outposts from Madrid as well as Mexico City, which had established a vital book trade in the sixteenth century.

The European domination of both indigenous American and imported African cultures may have contributed to the growing prestige of print. Books—an exclusively European object—were regarded as signs of civilization. Portraits from the period routinely depicted ministers, book in hand, against book-laden backdrops. Edwards and Whitefield are both shown in such portraits. And ordinary people, including women and tradesmen, were increasingly posed with books as evidence of both literacy and piety. This symbol is of particular importance for Phillis Wheatley's 1773 *Poems*, whose frontispiece identifies her image with those of numerous other authors conventionally posed with book and pen. Slaves were in general excluded— sometimes by law, sometimes by custom—from what were for most whites becoming routines of literacy in the eighteenth century. But there were many exceptions to this rule. The Society for the Propagation of the Gospel in Foreign Parts, the Associates of Thomas Bray, and the Friends, among others, all operated schools for black students throughout New England, the middle colonies, and the upper south (Horton, 20–21). Informal teaching went on everywhere, though Georgia and South Carolina made it more difficult after the Stono slave rebellion in 1739. Wheatley struggled to get into print and had to go to London to do so. A Boston edition of her poems was not published until 1786, after her death. For her white publishers and audience, the image of the African American woman as author was regarded as inherently suspect. Consequently, eighteen "most respectable Characters in Boston" submitted Wheatley to an oral examination and signed a document guaranteeing her credit as an author. The security of the physical—the mouth and the hand— were required to underwrite Wheatley's appearance in print.

Many writers credited print with special powers: to reveal but also to disguise and deceive, to solace but also to seduce. The early American novel might almost be thought of as a laboratory in which writers and readers experimented with and analyzed these perceived powers. Benjamin Franklin was the first American to reprint a British novel, Samuel Richardson's *Pamela* (1744), but it failed commercially. Booksellers did better by importing novels from England, which accounted for the wide distribution, north and south, of Defoe's *Robinson Crusoe* (1719), Smollett's *Roderick Random* (1748), and Sterne's *Sentimental Journey* (1768), among others. Throughout the eighteenth century, the novel trailed other genres as a marketable commodity (Hall, 364). Nonetheless, the fierce antifiction rhetoric of conduct books and education tracts suggests that the novel was a vital feature of the cultural landscape, and a perilous one at that, especially for those perceived to be the most susceptible: women and children.

The first American novel, William Hill Brown's *The Power of Sympathy* (1789), is addressed "To the YOUNG LADIES of United Columbia . . . Intended to represent the specious causes, and to Expose the fatal consequences of SEDUCTION." An epistolary novel, its plot and multiple subplots revolve around seduction, susceptibility, and incest. In the excerpt printed above, Mr. Holmes speaks of print as a force that can overpower the unwitting, penetrating and shaping them without their permission or knowledge. Likened to a flood, print's power is naturalized and figured as irresistible in force, speed, and quantity: "[I]f books, which are the sources that feed this river [of knowledge], rush into it from every quarter, it will overflow its banks, and the plain will become inundated." The solutions to the uncontrollable flood of printed matter, this passage seems to say, are first, to establish a canon and methodical habits, which will strongly limit novel reading; and second, to *talk* about reading: *"[C]onversation* only can remedy this dangerous evil, strengthen the judgment, and make reading really useful." The dangers of print can be offset by insisting that print supplements face-to-face communication, as in the Wheatley example. One of the paradoxes of eighteenth-century attitudes is that while print was essential to the development of the public sphere, many people also viewed print as a medium of deception and seduction and as dangerously private.

Twenty-four-year-old Patty Rogers, of Exeter, New Hampshire, so finely attuned to the "sweet novel[s]" that come her way, is exactly the susceptible reader who invites the strictures expressed by Brown and by the Dickinson College student in the excerpt reprinted above. Tabitha Gilman Tenney, a romantic rival of Rogers, wrote one of the first American novels, *Female Quixotism* (1801). This novel's heroine, possibly modeled on Patty Rogers, draws her notions about love from novels, with comically disastrous effects (Davidson, 191–92). As tokens of courtship, novels expressed and inspired emotion. And as dictionaries of sensibility, they provided Patty Rogers with terms in which to think about her relationships. Her mental world is stocked not only with the catchphrases of the sentimental novel ("keen sensation," "a torrent of tears"), but also with the popular poetry of the day. No less than Benjamin Franklin, whose identity has been characterized as a "being-in-print" (Warner, 74), Patty Rogers shaped her consciousness in dialogue with her reading. Novels and poems gave form to the turbulent sensations of her young womanhood, and often her reading seems not merely to reflect but actually to create her thoughts and emotions.

Print became, to varying degrees and in a variety of ways, an adjunct to social life for virtually everyone in this period. For some, print *was* life. Such men as Mather, Byrd, Franklin, and Parks formed real and imagined communities through their reading, their writing, and through print's circulation networks. For the African American woman Phillis Wheatley, engagement with literacy and print led to the monumental practical consequence of manumission. The effects of print were not always so dramatic, nor was print necessary for all. Yet for almost everyone, print became a fact of life from the mid-century on; for nearly everyone it had become at least a factor in life. Pieces of paper—bills of lading, handbills, admission and lottery tickets, paper currency, funeral broadsides—joined the hardy staple books—almanacs, *The New-England Primer*, the Bible—as frequently encountered artifacts and as commodities that more and more people gained access to and learned to use. New print genres, specifically newspapers, children's literature, and the novel served to establish community, and, perhaps more fundamentally, contributed to new aspects of personality.

SOURCE NOTES

[Unless otherwise indicated artifacts and documents are reproduced courtesy of the American Antiquarian Society (AAS), Worcester, Massachusetts.]

1. William Byrd, *The Secret Diary of William Byrd of Westover 1709–1712*, edited by Louis B. Wright and Marion Tinling (Richmond, Va.: Dietz Press, 1941), 48–49. Reproduced courtesy The Dietz Press, Richmond, Va.

2. Benjamin Franklin, *The Autobiography and Other Writings* (New York: Penguin, 1986), 13–14, 71–72.

3. Benjamin Franklin, *Writings* (New York: Library of America, 1987), 91. Public domain material reproduced courtesy The Library of America, New York.

4. Benjamin Franklin, *The Autobiography and Other Writings* (New York: Penguin, 1986).

5. *New-England Courant* (Boston), no. 27 (January 29–February 5, 1722).

6. *American Weekly Mercury* (Philadelphia), no. 1155 (February 11–18, 1741/42).

7. John Markland, *Typographia: An Ode, on Printing* (Williamsburg, Va.: William Parks, 1730; facs. ed., Roanoke, Va.: Stone Printing, for presentation to the Members of the American Institute of Graphic Arts, 1926), 12.

8. Thomas à Kempis, *Der kleine Kempis, oder Kurze Sprüche und Gebätlein* (Germantown, Pa.: Christoph Saur, 1750), title page.

9. *The New-England Primer, Enlarged. For the more easy attaining the true reading of English. To which is added, Milk for Babes* (Boston: S. Kneeland and T. Green, 1727).

10. *History of Giles Gingerbread. A Little Boy who lived upon Learning* (Boston: Edes and Gill, [1776?]).

11. Jonathan Edwards, "The Bad Book Case," in *A Jonathan Edwards Reader*, ed. John E. Smith, Harry S. Stout, and Kenneth P. Minkema (New Haven, Conn.: Yale University Press, 1995), 172–75. Copyright © Yale University Press. Reproduced courtesy Yale University Press, New Haven, Conn.

12. Phillis Wheatley, *Poems on Various Subjects, Religious and Moral* (London: Printed for A. Bell, Bookseller, Aldgate; and sold by Messrs. Cox and Berry, King-Street, Boston, 1773), frontispiece and title page, 6–7, 9–12.

13. Martha (Patty) Rogers, Diary, Rogers Family Papers, Manuscripts Collection, American Antiquarian Society, Worcester, Mass.

14. William Hill Brown, *The Power of Sympathy: or, The Triumph of Nature. Founded in Truth*, 2 vols. (Boston: Isaiah Thomas, 1789), 1:39–61.

15. *Observations on Novel-Reading: In an Essay written by a member of the Belles-Lettres Society of Dickinson College, at Carlisle. In the Year 1789* (Philadelphia: Thomas Dobson, 1792), 57–58.

WORKS CITED

Copeland, David A. *Colonial American Newspapers: Character and Content*. Newark: University of Delaware Press, 1997.

Davidson, Cathy N. *Revolution and the Word: The Rise of the Novel in America*. New York: Oxford University Press, 1986.

Davis, Richard Beale. *A Colonial Southern Bookshelf: Reading in the Eighteenth Century*. Athens: University of Georgia Press, 1979.

Gallegos, Bernardo P. *Literacy, Education and Society in New Mexico, 1693–1821*. Albuquerque: University of New Mexico Press, 1992.

Goddard, Ives, and Kathleen Bragdon. *Native Writings in Massachusett*. Memoirs of the American Philosophical Society, 185. Philadelphia: American Philosophical Society, 1988.

Green, James. "Benjamin Franklin as Publisher and Bookseller." In *Reappraising Benjamin Franklin: A Bicentennial Perspective*, edited by J. A. Leo Lemay, 98–114. Newark: University of Delaware Press, 1993.

Hall, David D. "Books and Reading in Eighteenth-Century America." In *Of Consuming Interests: The Style of Life in the Eighteenth Century*, edited by Cary Carson, Ronald Hoffman, and Peter J. Albert, 354–72. Charlottesville: University Press of Virginia, 1994.

Horton, James Oliver, and Lois E. Horton. *In Hope of Liberty: Culture, Community and Protest Among Northern Free Blacks, 1700–1860*. New York: Oxford University Press, 1997.

Isaac, Rhys. *The Transformation of Virginia 1740–1790*. Chapel Hill: University of North Carolina Press, 1982.

Lambert, Frank. *"Peddler in Divinity": George Whitefield and the Transatlantic Revivals*. Princeton, N.J.: Princeton University Press, 1994.

Stiverson, Cynthia A. and Gregory A. "The Colonial Retail Book Trade: Availability and Affordability of Reading Material in Mid-Eighteenth-Century Virginia." In *Printing and Society in Early America*, edited by William L. Joyce, David D. Hall, Richard D. Brown, and John B. Hench, 132–73. Worcester, Mass.: American Antiquarian Society, 1983.

Warner, Michael. *The Letters of the Republic: Publication and the Public Sphere in Eighteenth-Century America*. Cambridge, Mass.: Harvard University Press, 1990.

Wroth, Lawrence. *The Colonial Printer*. 1931, 1938, 1965. Reprint, New York: Dover, 1994.

FOR FURTHER RESEARCH

Avery, Gillian. *Behold the Child: American Children and Their Books 1621–1922.* Baltimore, Md.: Johns Hopkins University Press, 1994.

Byrd, William. *The Commonplace Book of William Byrd II of Westover.* Edited by Kevin Berland, Jan Kirsten Gilliam, and Kenneth A. Lockridge. Chapel Hill: University of North Carolina Press for Omohundro Institute of Early American History and Culture, 2001.

Carson, Cary, Ronald Hoffman, and Peter J. Albert, eds. *Of Consuming Interests: The Style of Life in the Eighteenth Century.* Charlottesville: University Press of Virginia, 1994.

Clark, Charles E. *The Public Prints: The Newspaper in Anglo-American Culture, 1665–1740.* New York: Oxford University Press, 1994.

Crain, Patricia. *The Story of A: The Alphabetization of America from The New England Primer to The Scarlet Letter.* Stanford, Calif.: Stanford University Press, 2000.

Gilreath, James. "Books in the South and the Two-Culture Theory of Colonial Society: An Interpretive Essay." *Publishing History* 32 (1992): 51–62.

Gustafson, Sandra M. *Eloquence Is Power: Oratory and Performance in Early America.* Chapel Hill: University of North Carolina Press for Omohundro Institute of Early American History and Culture, 2000.

Hall, David D. *Cultures of Print: Essays in the History of the Book.* Amherst: University of Massachusetts of Press, 1996.

Haviland, Virginia, and Margaret N. Coughlan. *Yankee Doodle's Literary Sampler of Prose, Poetry and Pictures.* New York: Crowell, 1974.

Hayes, Kevin J. *A Colonial Woman's Bookshelf.* Knoxville: University of Tennessee Press, 1996.

Isaac, Rhys. "Books and the Social Authority of Learning: The Case of Mid-Eighteenth-Century Virginia." In *Printing and Society in Early America,* edited by William L. Joyce, David D. Hall, Richard D. Brown, and John B. Hench, 228–49. Worcester, Mass.: American Antiquarian Society, 1983.

Johnson, Julie Greer. *The Book in the Americas: The Role of Books and Printing in the Development of Culture and Society in Colonial Latin America.* Providence, R.I.: John Carter Brown Library, 1988.

Miller, Perry. *The New England Mind: From Colony to Province.* Cambridge, Mass.: Harvard University Press, 1953.

Monaghan, E. Jennifer. "Family Literacy in Early 18th-Century Boston: Cotton Mather and His Children." *Reading Research Quarterly* 26, no. 4 (1991): 342–70.

———. "Literacy Instruction and Gender in Colonial New England." *American Quarterly* 40 (March 1988): 18–41.

Mulford, Carla. Introduction to William Hill Brown, *The Power of Sympathy.* New York: Penguin, 1996.

Oswald, John Clyde. *Printing in the Americas.* 1937. Reprint, New York: Hacker Art Books, 1968.

Reilly, Elizabeth Carroll. "Common and Learned Readers: Shared and Separate Spheres in Mid-Eighteenth-Century New England." Ph.D. diss., Boston University, 1994.

Rice, Grantland S. *The Transformation of Authorship in America.* Chicago: University of Chicago Press, 1997.

Rosenbach, A. S. W. *Early American Children's Books.* New York: Kraus Reprint Corporation, 1966.

Scheick, William J. *Authority and Female Authorship in Colonial America.* Lexington: University Press of Kentucky, 1998.

Shields, David. *Civil Tongues and Polite Letters in British America.* Chapel Hill: University of North Carolina Press, 1997.

———. "The Manuscript in the British American World of Print." *Proceedings of the American Antiquarian Society* 102, pt. 2 (1993): 403–16.

Steele, Ian. *The English Atlantic 1675–1740: An Exploration of Communication and Community.* New York: Oxford University Press, 1986.

Weber, David J. *The Spanish Frontier in North America.* New Haven, Conn.: Yale University Press, 1992.

Welch, d'Alte. *A Bibliography of American Children's Books Printed Prior to 1821.* Worcester, Mass.: American Antiquarian Society, 1972.

Winterich, John T. *Early American Books and Printing.* Boston: Houghton Mifflin, 1935.

Wolf, Edwin, 2d. *The Book Culture of a Colonial American City: Philadelphia Books, Bookmen, and Booksellers.* Oxford: Oxford University Press, 1988.

4

Publishing the American Revolution

RUSSELL L. MARTIN

WHO "PUBLISHED" in North America around 1750? That is, who assumed the financial risks and made the business decisions that got words, pictures, and ideas into print? Not "publishers" in a later sense of the term—firms that primarily coordinated the creation of printed matter. Instead, a colonial work's publisher was the entity that financed its printing: a local or colonial government that paid to have its documents printed; a minister or religious organization that paid to publish sermons. The printer who took such jobs might also "publish" some works himself: almanacs, for which he could gauge an annual market; stationery and business forms; a newspaper. Beyond "steady sellers," book publishing lagged far behind because it was cheaper for a printer—who usually doubled as a bookseller—to import a few copies from England than to publish his own edition.

During the imperial crisis that began at the end of the Seven Years' War (or French and Indian War) in 1763 and culminated in the American Revolution (1775–83), printers came to play prominent roles. Many had long been connected to local governments: printing the laws or paper money, staffing the post office. Their newspapers had mainly chronicled European events. In 1695 Parliament had abandoned the Licensing Act, which required printers to be licensed by the government and thus legislated prior restraint on printing. But printers remained subject to legal charges of seditious libel *after* their publications appeared. In the most famous American case, New York's royal government tried printer John Peter Zenger in 1735 for material in his *New-York Journal*. Zenger's acquittal virtually ended such prosecutions in America, but elected colonial legislatures continued to suppress dissent, occasionally imprisoning authors or printer-publishers. The threat of prosecution—and, more important, the financial need to sell newspapers—kept most printers wary of controversy, at least until the Stamp Act. In the process of their ideological mobilization, American printers redefined "freedom of the press" along partisan lines. Studious avoidance of controversy gave way to political alignment, as Whigs (those who opposed British policies, and eventually supported the Revolution) argued that press freedom meant the liberty to challenge official "tyranny."

The creation of a republican form of government, in which the people (adult white males) elected representatives, encouraged a belief in an enlightened citizenry. If governmental power at home and monarchies abroad always threatened republican liberty, America needed educated citizens ready to meet the danger. Printer-publishers espoused this ideology wholeheartedly, for it confirmed their own importance. The number of printers in America more than doubled between 1764 and 1783; in those years, the number of newspapers grew from 23 to 58, and the volume of all printed material expanded even faster. Thomas Paine's best-selling *Common Sense* (1776) had encouraged the drive for American independence by employing plain English accessible to ordinary citizens. The 1787 Constitutional Convention may have occurred behind closed doors, but the ratification battle took place largely in print: supporters' and opponents' words appeared in newspapers and pamphlets. In the 1790s most American newspapers took sides in the new political battles between Federalists and Jeffersonian Republicans—all claiming to enlighten the public. Who belonged to that public, of course, remained a troublesome issue.

ARTIFACTS

Long before he became a leader of the colonial revolt against Britain, Benjamin Franklin (1706–1790) was a practicing printer. In that role, he explained his conception of "freedom of the press" in 1731. Franklin wrote his "Apology for Printers" shortly after the local clergy had taken offense at the wording of a handbill produced in his shop. Note Franklin's rationale for printing opinions on all sides: to what extent was it an ideological statement, and to what extent a strategy for economic survival in his precarious trade? The printer-publisher William Livingston (1723–1790) expressed the prevailing definition of "freedom of the press" in 1753: dangers could arise not only from censorship of the press but also from "licentiousness" in print. If the press had the freedom to "promote the common Good of Society," it did not possess an equal liberty to publish material "repugnant" to that common good. Livingston would later become a revolutionary leader in New Jersey, serving fifteen terms as the state's first elected governor and founding the *New Jersey Gazette* in 1777 to support the colonial revolt and condemn Loyalists.

Benjamin Franklin, "Apology for Printers," from
The Pennsylvania Gazette (1731)[1]

BEING frequently censur'd and condemn'd by different Persons for printing Things which they say ought not to be printed, I have sometimes thought it might be necessary to make a standing Apology for my self, and publish it once a Year, to be read upon all Occasions of that Nature. . . .

I request all who are angry with me on the Account of printing things they don't like, calmly to consider these following Particulars

1. That the Opinions of Men are almost as various as their Faces; an Observation general enough to become a common Proverb, *So many Men so many Minds*.

2. That the Business of Printing has chiefly to do with Mens Opinions; most things that are printed tending to promote some, or oppose others.

80

3. That hence arises the peculiar Unhappiness of that Business, which other Callings are in no way liable to; they who follow Printing being scarce able to do any thing in their way of getting a Living, which shall not probably give Offence to some, and perhaps to many; whereas the Smith, the Shoemaker, the Carpenter, or the Man of any other Trade, may work indifferently for People of all Persuasions, without offending any of them: and the Merchant may buy and sell with Jews, Turks, Hereticks and Infidels of all sorts, and get Money by every one of them, without giving Offence to the most orthodox, of any sort; or suffering the least Censure or Ill-will on the Account from any Man whatever.

4. That it is as unreasonable in any one Man or Set of Men to expect to be pleas'd with every thing that is printed, as to think that nobody ought to be pleas'd but themselves.

5. Printers are educated in the Belief, that when Men differ in Opinion, both sides ought equally to have the Advantage of being heard by the Publick; and that when Truth and Error have fair Play, the former is always an overmatch for the latter: Hence they chearfully serve all contending Writers that pay them well, without regarding on which side they are of the Question in Dispute.

6. Being thus continually employ'd in serving all Parties, Printers naturally acquire a vast Unconcernedness as to the right or wrong Opinions contain'd in what they print; regarding it only as the Matter of their daily labour: They print things full of Spleen and Animosity, with the utmost Calmness and Indifference, and without the least Ill-will to the Persons reflected on; who nevertheless unjustly think the Printer as much their Enemy as the Author, and join both together in their Resentment.

7. That it is unreasonable to imagine Printers approve of every thing they print, and to censure them on any particular thing accordingly; since in the way of their Business they print such great variety of things opposite and contradictory. It is likewise as unreasonable what some assert, *That Printers ought not to print any Thing but what they approve*; since if all of that Business should make such a Resolution, and abide by it, an End would thereby be put to Free Writing, and the World would afterwards have nothing to read but what happen'd to be the Opinions of Printers.

8. That if all Printers were determin'd not to print any thing till they were sure it would offend no body, there would be very little printed.

9. That if they sometimes print vicious or silly things not worth reading, it may not be because they approve such things themselves, but because the People are so vicious and corruptly educated that good things are not encouraged. I have known a very numerous impression of *Robin Hood's Songs* go off in this Province at 2 s. per Book, in less than a Twelvemonth; when a small Quantity of *David's Psalms* (an excellent Version) have lain upon my hands above twice the Time.

10. That notwithstanding what might be urg'd in behalf of a Man's being allow'd to do in the Way of his Business whatever he is paid for, yet Printers do continually discourage the Printing of great Numbers of bad things, and stifle them in the Birth. I my self have constantly refused to print any thing that might countenance

Vice, or promote Immorality; tho' by complying in such Cases with the corrupt Taste of the Majority, I might have got much Money. I have also always refus'd to print such things as might do real Injury to any Person, how much soever I have been solicited, and tempted with Offers of great Pay; and how much soever I have by refusing got the Ill-will of those who would have employ'd me. I have heretofore fallen under the Resentment of large Bodies of Men, for refusing absolutely to print any of their Party or Personal Reflections. In this Manner I have made my self many Enemies, and the constant Fatigue of denying is almost insupportable. But the Publick being unacquainted with all this, whenever the poor Printer happens either through Ignorance or much Persuasion, to do any thing that is generally thought worthy of Blame, he meets with no more Friendship or Favour on the above Account, than if there were no Merit in 't at all. . . .

I consider the Variety of Humours among Men, and despair of pleasing every Body; yet I shall not therefore leave off Printing. I shall continue my Business. I shall not burn my Press and melt my Letters.

William Livingston, "On the Use, Abuse and Liberty of the Press," from *The Independent Reflector* (1753)[2]

WHETHER the Art of PRINTING has been of greater Service or Detriment to the World, has frequently been made the Subject of fruitless Controversy. The best Things have been perverted to serve the vilest Purposes, their being therefore subject to Abuse, is an illogical Argument against their Utility. Before the Invention of the Press, the Progress of Knowledge was slow, because the Methods of diffusing it were laborious and expensive. The shortest Production was too costly to its Author; and unless the Writer had an opulent Fortune, or rich Patrons to pay off his *Amanuenses*, he was driven to the Necessity of retailing his Compositions. . . . It is otherwise since the Discovery of the Art of *Printing*. The most inferior Genius, however impoverished, can spread his Thoughts thro' a Kingdom. The Public has the Advantage of the Sentiments of all Individuals. Thro' the Press, Writers of every Character and Genius, may promulge their Opinions; and all conspire to rear and support the Republic of Letters. The Patriot can by this Means, diffuse his salutary Principles thro' the Breasts of his Countrymen, interpose his friendly Advice unasked, warn them against approaching Danger, unite them against the Arm of despotic Power, and perhaps, at the Expence of but a few Sheets of Paper, save the State from impending Destruction. . . . Such also are the Advantages of *Printing*, to the Philosopher, the Moralist, the Lawyer, and Men of every other Profession and Character, whose Sentiments may be diffused with the greatest Ease and Dispatch, and comparatively speaking at a trifling Expence. In short, as the glorious Luminary of the Heavens, darts its Rays with incredible Velocity, to the most distant Confines of our System, so the Press, as from one common Center, diffuses the bright Beams of Knowledge, with prodigious Dispatch, thro' the vast Extent of the civilized World.

Secrecy, is another Advantage, which an Author had not before the Art of *Printing* was discovered. As long as Power may be perverted, from the original Design of its being lodged with the Magistrate, for protecting the Innocent and punishing the Guilty, so long will it be necessary to conceal the Author who remarks it, from the Malice of the Officer guilty of so pernicious a Perversion; and by Means of this Art he may write undiscovered, as it is impossible to detect him by the Types of the Press.

It must indeed be confessed, that this useful Discovery has, like many others, been prostituted to serve the basest Ends. This great Means of Knowledge, this grand Security of civil Liberty, has been the Tool of arbitrary Power, Popery, Bigotry, Superstition, Profaneness, and even of Ignorance itself. The Press groans under the Weight of the most horrid Impieties, the most ruinous and destructive Principles in Religion and Politics, the idlest Romances, the most contemptible Fustian, Slander and Impotence. But to shut up the Press because it has been abused, would be like burning our Bibles and proscribing Religion, because its Doctrines have been disobeyed and misrepresented; or like throwing off all Law and Restraint, and sinking into a State of Nature, because the over-grown Power of the civil Ruler, abusing his Trust, has sacrificed the Lives and Properties of his Subjects, to lawless and tyrannical Sway. . . .

No Nation in *Europe*, is more jealous of the *Liberty of the Press* than the *English*, nor is there a People, among whom it is so grossly abused. With us, the most unbounded Licentiousness prevails. We are so besotted with the Love of Liberty, that running into Extreams, we even tolerate those Things which naturally tend to its Subversion. And what is still more surprizing, an Author justly chargeable with Principles destructive of our Constitution, with Doctrines the most abject and slavish, may proceed even with inveterate Malice, to vilify, burlesque and deny our greatest Immunities and Privileges, and shall yet be suffered to justify himself under the unrestrainable Rights of the Press. An Absurdity grossly stupid and mischievous. What! sap the Constitution, disturb the public Tranquility, and ruin the State, and yet plead a Right to such Liberty derived from the Law of that State! The *Liberty of the Press*, like Civil Liberty, is talked of by many, and understood but by few; the latter is taken by Multitudes, for an irrefreinable Licence of acting at Pleasure; an equal Unrestraint in Writing, is often argued from the former, but both are false and equally dangerous to our Constitution. Civil Liberty is built upon a Surrender of so much of our natural Liberty, as is necessary for the good Ends of Government; and the Liberty of the Press, is always to be restricted from becoming a Prejudice to the public Weal. . . .

Thus the Press will have all that Liberty which is due to it, and never be checked, but where its being unrestricted will prove an Evil, and therefore only where it ought to be checked. Liberty and Science may then spread their Wings, and take the most unbounded Flights. But should Tyranny erect its formidable Head, and extend its Iron Scepter, the Nation may publish, and any private Person represent the general Calamity with Impunity. Does Corruption or Venality prevail, the Patriot is at Liberty to inveigh and suppress it. The boldest Criminal lies open to Censure and Satire, and any Man may expose and detect him. The Divine may put Vice at a Stand; every Attack upon the publick Welfare may be reprehended, and every destructive Scheme baffled and exposed; for all Men are free in that Way, to defeat every Project that is detrimental to the Public. This Privilege is a great One, and we should all conspire to maintain it. This is the true LIBERTY OF THE PRESS, for which Englishmen ought to contend. Such a Liberty can never be dangerous, either to the Public, or their Ruler; but on the contrary may often be necessary. . . .

THE Press is for ever in the Mouths of Printers, and one would imagine, that as they live by its Liberty, they would understand its true Limits, and endeavour to preserve its rightful Extent. But the Truth is, there is scarce one in Twenty of them, that knows the one or aims at the other.

A PRINTER ought not to publish every Thing that is offered him; but what is conducive of general Utility, he should not refuse, be the Author a Christian, Jew, Turk or Infidel. Such refusal is an immediate Abridgement of the Freedom of the Press. When on the other Hand, he prostitutes his Art by the Publication of any Thing injurious to his Country, it is criminal,—It is high Treason against the State. The usual Alarm rung in such Cases, the common Cry of Attack upon the LIBERTY OF THE PRESS, is groundless and trifling. The Press neither has, nor can have such a Liberty, and whenever it is assumed, the Printer should be punished. Private Interest indeed has, with many of them, such irresistible Charms, and the general Good is so feeble a Motive, that the only Liberty they know and wish for, is of publishing every Thing with Impunity for which they are paid. . . .

BENJAMIN FRANKLIN was in London, serving as Pennsylvania's spokesman in the imperial capital, when Parliament proposed a Stamp Act for the colonies in 1765. Franklin knew by February that the act would pass, requiring that all legal documents, official papers, books, and newspapers be printed on stamped paper and taxed. Printers had to purchase the stamped paper, which would either increase the costs of their wares to customers or eat into their already scant profits. Either way, the Stamp Act spelled potential financial ruin. For some printers, the act also engendered ideological difficulty: should their newspapers oppose it or maintain the customary silence on controversial issues? Should they defy the law and print without the stamps? David Hall (1714–1772), who managed the day-to-day operations of the Philadelphia print shop Franklin still co-owned with him, explained both sets of difficulties to his absent partner. From the summer of 1765 on, some printers began to take stands against the Stamp Act, as the excerpt printed below from the *New-Hampshire Gazette* attests. The day before the act took effect, Hall's own *Pennsylvania*

Gazette joined the chorus. The Stamp Act was repealed in 1766. Two years later, the revolutionary leader Samuel Adams (1722–1803) recalled in the *Boston Gazette* how printers had mobilized against "tyranny," while the South Carolina printer Peter Timothy (c. 1725–1782) complained to Franklin about the consequences of not taking a stand.

Letters between Benjamin Franklin and David Hall (1765)[3]

London, Feb. 14. 1765
Dear Mr. Hall,

 . . . The Stamp Act, notwithstanding all the Opposition that could be given it by the American Interest, will pass. I think it will affect the Printers more than any-body, as a Sterling Halfpenny Stamp on every Half sheet of a Newspaper, and Two shillings Sterling on every Advertisement, will go near to knock up one Half of both. There is also Fourpence Sterling on every Almanack. . . .

My love to Cousin Molly and your Children. I am Yours affectionately

B FRANKLIN

Philadelphia Septemr. 6th 1765
Dear Sir.

 . . . We are all in a Ferment here, as well, as in the other Governments, about the Stamp Law taking, or not taking place. . . . there seems to be a general Discontent all over the Continent, with that Law, and many thinking their Liberties and Privi-leges, as English Men lost, or at least in great Danger, seem Desperate. What the Consequences may be, God only knows; but, from the Temper of the People, at Present, there is the greatest Reason to fear, that the Passing of that Law will be the Occasion of a great Deal of Mischief. . . .

In my last, you may remember, I told you, that all the Papers on the Continent, ours excepted, were full of Spirited Papers against the Stamp Law, and that be-cause, I did not publish those Papers likewise, I was much blamed, got a great Deal of Ill-will, and that some of our Customers had dropt on that Account. . . . I was in Hopes that, that Storm would have blown over, and that the People would have been Satisfied with the Arguments I used for not inserting these Pieces; but I find I am much mistaken; for as the Time of the Law taking place draws nearer, the more the Clamours of the People increase against me, for my Silence in the Paper; alledging, that as our Gazette, spreads more generally than all the other Papers put together on the Continent, our not Publishing, as the Printers of the other Papers do, will be an infinite Hurt to the Liberties of the People. And I have been told by many, that our Interests will certainly suffer by it; nay, Hints have been given, that in Case of the Peoples being exasperated I must stand to the Consequences. So that how to Behave, I am really at a loss, but believe it will be best to humour them in some Publications, as they seem to insist so much upon it. . . .

I am. Dear Sir Yours

D[avid] H[all]

Philadelphia October 14th. 1765
Dear Sir

. . . We Printers of News Papers here, Dutch and English, have been proposing to take the Advice of the ablest Council, how far we may, or may not, be safe in carrying on our Papers without the Stamps, which is the only Method, we think, we can take, tho' we imagine they will not Advise us to proceed, the Risk being so great; and if they should give it as their Advice that we should not go on, we must, of Consequence, stop, till the Act becomes general, or that we hear further from England; so that whether the Law takes place or not, the Confusion that Things will be in for some time, must be very great, and truly distressing.

To shew you that my Fears were not groundless, with respect to our Customers leaving off taking the Gazette, I am sorry Now to tell you, that we have already lost at least 500 of them, since the Resolves of the House of Commons were published relating to that Law; and if so many have dropt before, what may we not expect after the First of November [when the Stamp Act was to take effect]? . . . I am, Dear Sir, Yours most Affectionately,

D. H

The New-Hampshire Gazette, and Historical Chronicle (1765)[4]

To the PRINTERS.

I am just came to Town, and the first News I heard was, that the PRINTERS & Publishers are all frightened out of their Wits, (*not quite, but nearly such in North-America*) and that the Liberty of the PRESS was upon the verge of Destruction. As I know not what Ground there might be for these Assertations, I made some Enquiry, and found sure enough that you PRINTERS and Publishers have but too much Reason to be alarmed; for during the last Twelve Months, there have been no less than EIGHT Attacks upon the PRESS. Indeed this serious Business well deserves some sober Consideration, and in my Opinion, (would in any Times, but the present) make a Minister think so. However, I cannot think the People quite so lethargic as some Folks in Power tell me; they say the People are quite satisfied, are perfectly easy in their Minds, and sincerely believe that their Liberties and their Interests are *undoubtedly secure* in the Hands of the present Administration.—May be so.—Nobody desires to have Liberty of this Country securer than I do: But I cannot help saying, that this *Court Cant*, very ill agrees with certain very Public Transactions. Can our Liberties be secure, when that great and essential one of the PRESS is daily attacked, and PRINTERS and BOOKSELLERS are so terrified by uncommon Rigour, that they will neither Print nor Publish? . . .

The Pennsylvania Gazette (1765)[5]

We are sorry to be obliged to acquaint our Readers, that as the most UNCON-STITUTIONAL ACT that ever these Colonies could have imagined, to wit, The STAMP ACT, is feared to be obligatory upon us, after the First of November ensuing (the FATAL TO-MORROW) the Publishers of this Paper, unable to bear the Burthen, have thought it expedient to stop a While, in order to deliberate, whether any Methods can be found to elude the Chains forged for them, and escape the insupportable Slavery; which, it is hoped, from the just Representations now made against that Act, may be effected.—Mean while, we must earnestly request every Individual of our Subscribers, many of whom have been long behind hand, that they would immediately discharge their respective Arrears, that we may be able not only to support ourselves during the Interval, but be better prepared to proceed again with this Paper, whenever an Opening appears for that Purpose, which we hope will be soon.

[Samuel Adams], *Boston Gazette, and Country Journal* (1768)[6]

To the PRINTERS.

There is nothing so *fretting* and *vexatious*, nothing so justly TERRIBLE to tyrants, and their tools and abettors, as a FREE PRESS. The reason is obvious; namely, Because it is, as it has been very justly observ'd, in a *spirited* answer to a *spirited* speech, *"the bulwark of the People's Liberties."* For this reason, it is ever watched by those who are forming plans for the destruction of the peoples liberties, with an *envious* and *malignant* eye. If a villain is portraited and held up to the public, rather than fail in the attempt to cast an odium upon the press, they will even *own the character*, and pronounce it a libel. . . . It is not at all surprizing, that *your* press is hated, and *your* paper branded with the name of *"infamous,"* by *some* men: These are the men who formed and pushed to the utmost of their power, the late *detested Stamp-Act*: These are the men, who have been forging chains and manacles; and when they could not, after the most impudent attempt, *force* them upon the people, have with intollerable insolence endeavor'd to perswade them that they had better *put them on themselves*: But *your* Press has sounded the alarm; or to use the words of a *minion*, "rung the alarm bell": *Your* Press has spoken to us the words of truth: It has pointed to this people, their dangers and their remedy: It has set before them Liberty and Slavery; and with the most perswasive and pungent language, conjur'd them,

in the name of GOD, and the King, and for the sake of all posterity, to chuse Liberty and refuse Chains: Go on, for you have been already prosper'd. The People have listned with attention: They have pursued *such* measures as in spite of the slanderous tongues of their malicious enemies *must* and *will* be successful: While these measures have been taking, *your* Press has been incessantly calling upon all to be quiet; and patiently to wait for their political salvation—NO MOBBS— NO CONFUSIONS—NO TUMULTS—This has been the language of YOUR—*"infamous"* Paper—Let this be the language of ALL—*We* know WHO have abus'd us— We owe them *Contempt*, and we will treat them with it in full measure: But let not the hair of their scalps be touch'd: The time is coming, when they shall lick the dust and melt away.
POPULUS

Peter Timothy to Benjamin Franklin (1768)[7]

Chas. Town, So. Carolina, Sept. 3d. 1768.
Dear Sir,

. . . I should have done myself the Pleasure to write you frequently, but that I was constantly told you would be on your Return home before my Letters could reach England. . . . I could have given you from Time to Time a great deal of Intelligence—in such a confused Manner as my perplexed Head would have admitted, who find myself from the most *popular* reduced to the most *unpopular* Man in the Province; by taking upon me a Place in the Post-Office at the Time of the Stamp-Act; discontinuing Printing, while its Operation was in Suspence; and declining to direct, support and engage in the most violent Opposition—which so exasperated every Body that they have taken every Step to injure, and set up [Charles] Crouch (a worthless Fellow) against me, whom they support with their utmost Zeal and Interest. Ruduced to this Situation I have not been myself since Nov. 1765. Nor shall I recover, unless I quit the Post-Office when some other Occasion offers to distinguish myself in the Cause of America. . . .

AS THE imperial crisis escalated in the 1770s, printers found neutrality increasingly untenable. As Peter Timothy had learned, a partisan competitor could undermine a neutral printer's support among an increasingly Whig clientele. For Whig printers, freedom of the press now meant the liberty to censure the royal government, its local officials, and its actions—not the need to publish both sides. Printers such as New York's James Rivington (1724–1802), who argued for a free press open to the royal side of the story, found themselves stamped as Tory sympathizers even before some of them eventually sided with the Crown. In 1774 *Rivington's New-York Gazetteer* engaged in a war of words with John Holt's Whig *New-York Journal*; one salvo in that skirmish appears below. Colonial "committees of correspondence"—a name many Whig groups used to denote their inter-colonial print connections—boycotted Rivington's work, as seen in the 1775 Rhode Island resolution reproduced below. That November, an armed group from Connecticut invaded New York and destroyed Rivington's types, putting him out of business for over a year. Rivington returned to New York City, occupied by British troops, in 1777, with a new set of types and the title of King's Printer. Meanwhile, Whig printers became key players in the Revolution. The career of Peter Timothy, who re-established contact with Benjamin Franklin in 1777, exemplified how the older avoidance of controversy gave way to political involvement and self-aggrandizement. Thirty-three years later, Isaiah Thomas (1749–1831), printer and publisher of the *Massachusetts Spy* and an ardent Whig, wrote the first history of printing in America. From the vantage point of victory, Thomas explained how he and other printers had navigated the crisis.

Rivington's New-York Gazetteer (1774)[8]

Mr. RIVINGTON,

WHEN, in times of public difficulty, a Printer keeps his press free and open;—when his conduct shews, that he is unbiassed by the narrow views of a party, and unawed by the fear of personal resentment, he deserves to be esteemed as one of the most useful and valuable members of the community. But on the contrary, when it is obvious to the meanest capacity, that a News-paper is wholly employed in prosecuting party designs, tending to inflame the minds of the people against government, and by means thereof to introduce anarchy and confusion; the printer of such a paper, justly renders himself abhorrent to all good men, and may well be considered as a pest to society.

I was led into these reflections upon the perusal of some of the late NEW-YORK JOURNALS, printed by JOHN HOLT; and as great an advocate as I am for the freedom of the press, which I consider as one of the strongest bulwarks to the liberties of a free country; yet, I must confess, it gives me pain, when I behold such a flagrant perversion of so inestimable a privilege. To give a character of the NEW-YORK JOURNAL in a few words,—it is a receptacle for every inflammatory piece that is published throughout the continent.—With respect to foreign intelligence, those paragraphs that reflect highly on the Ministry and the Parliament, and tend to widen the breach between Great Britain and the Colonies, are industriously selected; but whatever is published with a view of conciliating their differences, any proposal towards an accommodation between them, is altogether inadmissible. This partiality is so glaring, that a Boy of ten Years old cannot fail observing it. The only excuse that can be made for such a conduct is, the extreme poverty of the printer,—that it was become necessary, in order to procure a temporary subsistence, to sell himself and his paper to the highest bidder. But even this I can by no means think sufficient to exculpate him. The common prostitute is held no less criminal, because want may have driven her to the necessity of making sale of her person, and of exposing her body for the horrid purpose of publick prostitution. . . .

I shall take my leave for the present of this *poor devil* of a Printer, whom no circumstance could have rendered an object of my notice, but his being the wretched Conductor of a more wretched news-paper. . . .

MERCATOR.

New-York, 9th August, 1774.

Resolution of Newport (Rhode-Island) Committee (1775)[9]

Resolved, That the freedom of the Press is of the utmost importance to civil society; and that its importance consists, "besides the advancement of truth, science, morality, and arts in general, in its diffusion of liberal sentiments on the administration of Government, its ready communication of thoughts between subjects, and its consequential promotion of union among them, where, by oppressive Officers, are shamed or intimidated into more honourable and just modes of conducting affairs". . . . But when, instead thereof, a Press is incessantly employed and prostituted to the vilest uses; in publishing the most infamous falsehoods; in partial or false representations of facts; in fomenting jealousies, and exciting discord and disunion among the people; in supporting and applauding the worst of men, and worst of measures; and in vilifying and calumniating the best of characters, and the best of causes; it then behooves every citizen, every friend to truth, science, arts, liberality of sentiment, to that union between subjects, upon which depends their security against oppression, to discountenance and discourage every such licentious, illiberal, prostituted Press.

And whereas, a certain *James Rivington*, a Printer and Stationer in the City of *New-York*, impelled by the love of sordid pelf, and a haughty domineering spirit, hath, for a long time, in the dirty *Gazetteer*, and in pamphlets, if possible still more dirty, uniformly persists in publishing every falsehood which his own wicked imagination, or the imaginations of others of the same stamp, as ingenious perhaps in mischief as himself, could suggest and fabricate, that had a tendency to spread jealousies, fear, discord, and disunion throughout this country; and by partial and false representations of facts, hath endeavoured to pervert truth, and to deceive and mislead the incautious into wrong conceptions of facts reported, and wrong sentiments respecting the measures now carrying on for the recovery and establishment of our rights, and the supporters of those measures; and particularly hath disgorged from his infamous Press, the most virulent, foul abuse, on the Members of the late Continental Congress—characters which, for wisdom, integrity, fortitude, and publick virtue, deserve, and have received, the applause of every inhabitant of this wide extended Continent, excepting a very few venal tools of a corrupt Administration. . . .

Resolved, therefore, That it is the opinion of this Committee, that no further dealings or correspondence ought to be had with the said *James Rivington*; and we recommend it to every person who takes his Paper, called *Rivington's Gazetteer,* immediately to drop the same; and also take the liberty to recommend a similar conduct towards him to the other Towns in the Colony.

Resolved, That this Resolution be printed in the next *Newport Mercury.*

Rivington's New-York Gazetteer (1775)[10]

Last Thursday was hung up by some of the lower class of inhabitants, at New-Brunswick, an effigy, representing the person of Mr. Rivington, the printer at New-York, merely for acting consistent with his profession as a free printer. . . .

TO THE PUBLIC.

The PRINTER has been informed, that a number of Bacchanalians, at Brunswick, flushed with the inebriating draughts, not of the juice of the Vine, but of New-England Rum, have lately sacrificed him to the *Idol of Licentiousness.* Lest this piece of heroism should not be sufficiently known, he has thought proper to exhibit a Representation of the scene in which he was thus offered up a Victim, that the fame of the exploit may spread from "Pole to Pole." From this publication too, these little, shabby, piddling politicians may know how much their vengeance is regarded: But while he consigns these snarling curs (who, he is well informed, were, and indeed could be no other, than the very *Dregs of the City*) to the same infamy with the *pediculous* Committee at *Freehold*; he begs leave to address himself to the respectable Public:

The Printer is bold to affirm, that his press has been open to publications from ALL PARTIES; and he defies his enemies to produce an instance to the contrary. He has considered his press in the light of a public office, to which every man has a right to have recourse. But the moment he ventured to publish sentiments which were opposed to the dangerous views and designs of certain demagogues, he found himself held up as an enemy to his country, and the most unwearied pains taken to ruin him. In the country wherein he was born he always heard the LIBERTY OF THE PRESS represented as the great security of freedom, and in that sentiment he has been educated; nor has he reason to think differently now on account of his experience in this *country. While his enemies make liberty the prostituted pretence of their illiberal persecution of him, their aim is to establish a most cruel tyranny, and the Printer thinks that some very recent transactions will convince the good people of this city of the difference between being governed by a few factious individuals, and the GOOD OLD LAWS AND CONSTITUTION, under which we have so long been a happy people.*

Peter Timothy to Benjamin Franklin (1777)[11]

Peter Timothy presents his most respectful and affectionate Salutes to his good Friend Doct. Franklin—whom he begs Leave (tho' late) to congratulate upon the high Honours Thirteen United Free and Independent States have conferred upon him, with a unanimous Voice. . . . Timothy has had a Thousand Things to communicate to his Friend; but so incessantly has he been engaged in public Affairs for full Four Years, that whenever he would make the Attempt (if he had been allowed Time to prosecute it) he was always at a Loss where to begin or where he should end, and has been thereby constantly discourage[d]. . . . I was both a Member of and Secretary to the Congresses, General Committee, Charles Town Committee; Chairman (and did all the Business) of the Committee of Observation and Inspection, in such a Manner as too many will remember; and also Secretary to the Councils of Safety, who, while they existed, sat Day and Night, without a single Day's Intermission—continually in Motion from Congress to Com^{ee}. from Com^{ee}. to Council. from Council to Inspection, & so on.—I say, if my Friend can have an Idea of the Labour I underwent in these Employments, without mentioning the incessant calls from one way or other besides, he would wonder how it was possible for one Man to go thro' it all and preserve his Senses—and admit that it was impossible to indulge an Inclination to private Correspondence.—However, as he has now broke the Ice, he proposes to go on, and will convey from Time to Time such Intelligence as in its Nature or Consequences may be important and be glad at all Times to receive and obey any Commands that his Friend may lay on him, or put it in his Power to continue a useful Member of the United States. . . .

> Your most affect. & obed. humb^e. Servt.
> Peter Timothy
> 12 June, 1777

Isaiah Thomas, *The History of Printing in America* (1810)[12]

It was at first the determination of Thomas that his paper should be free to both parties which then agitated the country, and, impartially, lay before the public their respective communications; but he soon found that this ground could not be maintained. . . . The tories soon discontinued their subscriptions for the [Massachusetts] Spy; and, the publisher was convinced that to produce an abiding and salutary effect, his paper must have a fixed character. He was in principle attached to the party which opposed the measures of the British ministry; and he, therefore, announced that the Spy would be devoted to the support of the whig interest. . . .

Writers of various classes, in the whig interest, furnished essays, which in a very considerable degree aided in preparing the public mind for events which followed.

Common sense in common language is necessary to influence one class of citizens, as much as learning and elegance of composition are to produce an effect upon another. The cause of America was just; and, it was only necessary to state this cause in a clear and impressive manner, to unite the American people in its support.

Several attempts were made by the government of the province to prosecute the printer, but without effect. . . . The printer had the further honor of being exhibited and burnt in effigy by the royalists of Northcarolina, and he was threatened with having a coat of tar and feathers by a regiment of British soldiers, which paraded before his house. . . .

Its publication ceased in that town [Boston] on the 6th of April, 1775, and on the 19th of that month, hostilities between Great-britain and America commenced. A few days before this event took place, its publisher sent, privately, a press and types to Worcester; and, on the 3d of the following May, the publication of the Spy was resumed, and was the first printing done in that town. The title of the paper, of course, was again altered; it was now "The Massachusetts Spy: Or, American Oracle of Liberty."—headed with, "Americans!—Liberty or Death!—Join or Die!" The day of publication at Worcester, was Wednesday.

THE AMERICAN Revolution added new meaning to the familiar refrain that printing diffused education beyond the elites, rehearsed in the *Essex Journal*'s 1773 statement and a poem about "The Art of Printing" that appeared in a 1774 Pennsylvania almanac (both reprinted below). Now that discussion was connected also to the Revolution's republican ideals, as printer Isaac Collins (1746–1817) explained when he revived William Livingston's *New Jersey Gazette* after the war. But those ideas about print and education did not apply to all Americans. Slavery still existed in every American state at war's end, even if scattered emancipation movements were gathering steam. Long-standing colonial slave laws in South Carolina (1740) and Georgia (1755) prohibited teaching slaves to write—a skill considered far more dangerous than reading (which religious institutions such as the Society for Propagating the Gospel actually encouraged among slaves). That danger was nowhere more apparent than in advertisements for runaway slaves. Many of those African Americans carried passes attesting to their freedom. When forged by the runaways themselves, these passes were analogous to the pseudonyms that literate, white authors attached to their pamphlets and newspaper articles in these same years: evidence of how print could obscure or transform individual identity.

The Essex Journal and Merrimack Packet: Or, the Massachusetts and New-Hampshire General Advertiser (1773)[13]

THE great Utility of a PRINTING Press, is so well known, at this Day, by the Generality of Mankind, that it would be judged incongruous in us to point out its Advantages.

NEWS-PAPERS, are so universally allowed to be of great Benefit to the Public, as they tend to INSTRUCT and ENTERTAIN their numerous Readers: By them we may learn the State of all Kingdoms and Nations, their Manners and Customs, and their various Agitations and Commotions; every striking Phaenomenon in Nature, every new Invention in the Arts and Sciences, and Husbandry, can be registered, and the Affairs of our own Country inserted; and occasionally interspersed with judicious Remarks, and Reflections, that Kings and Statesmen may know the Condition and Minds of the People; Gentlemen may be amused, and Merchants, Tradesmen and Husbandmen, at their leisure Hours, be agreeably entertained; and undoubtedly learn something beneficial.

We, therefore, intend to publish a Weekly News-Paper, and will spare no Pains or Cost, in our Power, to make it answer the Design of the Institution, and the Expectations of all those who may generously promote this Undertaking. And if the utmost CARE and ATTENTION and the GREATEST IMPARTIALITY, will entitle the Publishers of a News Paper to Encouragement, we flatter ourselves, the Inhabitants of the *Massachusetts-Bay* and *New-Hampshire,* and more particularly those in this Town and Country, will give THIS Paper a KIND Reception.

* * * * *

[advertisement]

Printing.

Those LADIES and GENTLEMEN who are desirous of seeing the curious ART of PRINTING, are hereby informed, that on MONDAY next the Printing Office, will be opened for their reception, and the Printers ready to wait on all who will do them the honour of their company. The business will be exhibited precisely at eleven o'clock in the forenoon, and at three in the afternoon. *December 4th, 1773.*

"The Art of Printing, a Poem" (1774)[14]

Hail mystick art! which men like angels taught,
To speak to eyes, and paint unbody'd thought!
Though deaf and dumb; blest skill, reliev'd by thee,
We make one sense perform the task of three.
We see, we hear, we touch the head and heart,
And take, or give what each but yields in part.
With the hard laws of distance we dispense,
And without sound, apart commune in sense:
View, tho' confin'd; nay rule this earthly ball,
And travel o'er the wide expanded All.
Dead letters thus with living notions fraught,
Prove to the soul the telescopes of thought;
To mortal life a deathless witness give,
And bid all deeds and titles last—and live.
In scanty life, eternity we taste,
View the first ages—and inform the last.
Arts—hist'ry—laws—we purchase with a look,
And keep, like fate, all nature in a book.

Isaac Collins, *The New-Jersey Gazette Will Be Revived on Tuesday the 9th Instant, on the Following Terms* (1783)[15]

The Printer thinks the Utility of a general Circulation of News-Papers is set in so plain and handsome a Light in the following short Essay, published in a late New-England paper, that he takes the Liberty of offering it to the *Consideration* of his Fellow-Citizens.

An ADDRESS to the CITIZENS of AMERICA, shewing the Necessity of encouraging a general circulation of NEWS-PAPERS, among all Classes and Denomination of People.

WITHOUT Knowledge among the People, Liberty and publick Happiness cannot exist long in any Country; and this necessary Knowledge cannot be obtained in any other Way than by a general Circulation of publick Papers.

    These are the Channels for all publick Information, by which we learn what Laws are made, what our Rulers are doing, what Events are taking Place in our Country, or among other Nations; also, what is to be bought or sold; Matters of Curiosity, Speculation, Amusement and Instruction; in short, publick Papers are the political Eyes and the civil Light of the People; without which they will grope in Darkness, and be a Prey to Tyrants. Ignorance is the dark Door at which Tyranny enters. Another vast Advantage which arises from the general Circulation of publick Papers, is, the Novelties they contain excite Youth to read them, whereby they are perfected in the Art of Reading, and at the same Time gain useful Knowledge. But this Source of Instruction is so fertile with publick Advantages and private Benefits, that they cannot be numbered. And all these vast and durable Benefits may be had very easily and cheap indeed; as one Paper may answer for two Families, the Expence may thereby be reduced so very small that Poverty itself will not be excluded the Privilege. Therefore, if any remain ignorant and neglect this cheap Information, they ought to consider that they are preparing themselves, and training up their Children, in that Path of Ignorance which leads to Slavery! Let no one conceive because the War is over, they shall have no interesting Concern in publick Affairs; and in order to save a trifling Expence, neglect to read the publick Papers: The People of all Classes are in this Matter, *"Penny wise, and Pound foolish."*

It ought forever to be remembered, that *Ignorance* pays more for *Folly*, than *Knowledge* gives for *Wisdom*; and that *Tyranny* taxes more for *Chains*, than *Liberty* demands for all the Blessings of *Freedom*. How astonishing then must the Conduct of a People be, who have spent their dearest Blood and Treasure to purchase the inestimable Jewel of Liberty, if they should neglect the Preservation of it, or their Heirs should sacrifice to *Ignorance* the sacred Inheritance.

Let us then arouse to Enquiry and Perseverance in the Pursuit of Knowledge; attend to the Conduct of all the Servants of the Publick, and be Inquisitive to know of them the State of our Nation, and the Reasons for all publick Measures; comparing their Information with the State of Matters exhibited in the publick Papers: Thus we may be wise, free and happy. But if to save a few Pence, or a little Time in reading publick Papers, we should neglect them, Ignorance may gradually overspread this new enlightened Country, and Tyranny advance as Knowledge decays, until Darkness and Slavery wrap this glorious Land in all the Horrors of despotick Sway.

CONSIDERATION.

Advertisement for a Runaway Slave, from *The Pennsylvania Gazette* (1788)[16]

RAN away on Tuesday, the 5th August, instant, from the subscriber, living in Talbot county, Maryland, a likely bright Mulatto Lad, named Damon, 21 years old, about 5 feet 6 inches high, slender and active, and well acquainted with the business of waiting in a house, to which he has always been used; he went off in an Oznabrigs shirt, trowsers and waistcoat, but as he is well supplied with a variety of clothing it is impossible to say how he may be dressed; is extreamly artful, much address must be used in taking, and great care in securing him when taken, otherwise he will certainly make his escape. He has been learning to read, and has succeeded in a small degree; has a scar on one of his legs, but it is not remembered which, occasioned by a scald or a burn. He will very probably change his name, and likely may assume the name of Mat or Matthias, as he was called by that name when a child. He may also have got a pass, as he is capable of any fraud of that sort. He has lately become very fond of strong liquor, and may now possibly indulge himself in it. Whoever will apprehend the said slave, and secure him in such a manner that the subscriber may get him again, shall receive a reward of *One Shilling a Mile* for every mile he may have got from home, and shall be generously rewarded if brought home and delivered to

ROBERT GOLDSBOROUGH, jun.

Maryland, Talbot county, August 12, 1788.

WHEN A convention of educated, influential men proposed a new Constitution for the United States in 1787, they submitted their document for ratification by the thirteen states. Some states approved it quickly, but in a few critical states the battle was closer and more difficult. To promote ratification in New York, Alexander Hamilton (1757–1804), as well as James Madison and John Jay, wrote a series of essays for publication in newspapers and in book form. To help answer the objection that the document contained no bill of rights, one of Hamilton's *Federalist* papers explained in the passage reproduced below why no such bill could guarantee "liberty of the press." The Constitution won ratification as proposed, but within three years a Bill of Rights—the first ten amendments—had been added, including the "freedom of the press" that had meant several different things over the previous six decades. In the 1790s, war between England and France threatened to tear the new nation apart. The Republicans, led by Thomas Jefferson, mobilized in opposition to the Federalist administrations of George Washington and John Adams and in support of the revolutionary alliance with now-revolutionary France. Newspapers were a crucial vehicle of the Jeffersonian opposition, notably Philadelphia's *American Aurora*, published by Benjamin Franklin Bache (1769–1798)—Benjamin Franklin's grandson. When Adams signed the Sedition Act in 1798, threatening opposition printers with prison and fines, Republicans cried tyranny. The *Aurora* led this charge, while the pro-administration *Columbian Centinel* offered a Federalist solution grounded in using, not shutting down, the press. The debates highlighted an essential truth about newspapers in the early republic: the vast majority espoused the tenets of one or another political party.

Alexander Hamilton, *The Federalist* No. 84 (1788)

On the subject of the liberty of the press, as much has been said, I cannot forbear adding a remark or two: In the first place, I observe that there is not a syllable concerning it in the constitution of this state [New York], and in the next, I contend that whatever has been said about it in that of any other state, amounts to nothing. What signifies a declaration that "the liberty of the press shall be inviolably preserved?" What is the liberty of the press? Who can give it any definition which would not leave the utmost latitude for evasion? I hold it to be impracticable; and from this, I infer, that its security, whatever fine declarations may be inserted in any constitution respecting it, must altogether depend on public opinion, and on the general spirit of the people and of the government.

United States Constitution, Amendment I (1791)

Congress shall make no law respecting an establishment of religion, or prohibiting the free exercise thereof; or abridging the freedom of speech, or of the press; or the right of the people peaceably to assemble, and to petition the government for a redress of grievances.

The Sedition Act (1798)[17]

An Act in addition to an act, intituled, "an act for the punishment of certain crimes against the United States". . . .

Sec. 2. *And be it further enacted,* That if any person shall write, print, utter or publish, or shall cause or procure to be written, printed, uttered or published, or shall knowingly and willingly assist or aid in writing, printing, uttering or publishing, any false, scandalous, and malicious writing or writings against the government of the United States, or either house of the Congress of the United States, or the President of the United States, with intent to defame the said government, or either house of the said Congress, or the said President, or to bring them or either of them into contempt or disrepute; or to excite against them, or either or any of them, the hatred of the good people of the United States; or to stir up sedition within the United States; or to excite any unlawful combination therein, for opposing or resisting any law of the United States, or any act of the President of the United States, done in pursuance of any such law, or of the powers in him vested by the Constitution of the United States, or to resist, oppose, or defeat any such law or act; or to aid, encourage or abet any hostile designs of any foreign nation against the United States, their people or government, then such person, being thereof convicted before any court of the United States, having jurisdiction thereof, shall be punished by a fine not exceeding two thousand dollars, and by imprisonment not exceeding two years. . . .

"The Spirit of the Press," from *American Aurora* (1798)[18]

There was a time, Citizens, when under the protecting influence of a Constitution ("which we once fondly hoped would be immortal,") we flattered ourselves, that *the liberty of the press* was a right too dear to Americans to be resigned with tameness, and too firmly secured to be violated with impunity. We will not say that time is past—but we will say that under the influences of an exaggerated and mischievous system of alarm, and the insidious pretexts of order and submission to the Laws, we have seen a system maturing, openly hostile to the spirit of freedom, and measures carried *in the face of our Constitution*;—for what?—to screen from scrutiny the conduct of your own Government, and to silence by an argument of force the remonstrances of reason; to wrest from your hands the weapon which conducted you to freedom, "a right inestimable to freemen, and formidable to tyrants only." To the laws of our country we owe that profound submission, which a Republican will never withhold. But *to the constitution* upon which alone those laws must be founded, and to the *people* for whose security it was established, we owe duties, still more sacred, and these we will never violate; fully confident that to no laws "abridging the freedom of speech or of the press," can submission ever be lawfully required,—and that the man who falls a victim to these will but seal the constitution with his blood.

Columbian Centinel (1798)[19]

FOR THE COLUMBIAN CENTINEL.

Mr. Russell,

Of all the great modern improvements, there are few which contribute more to social happiness, than the liberty of the press; while nothing perhaps is more destructive than its licentiousness. The liberty of the press diffuses knowledge, teaches us our just rights, is no inconsiderable restriction upon those who may have the power of invading them; & whenever the occasion may require it, rouzes the people to those energetic measures, which no tyranny can resist. The licentiousness of the press, excites murmurs and discontents, and a tardy and reluctant obedience to the laws, teaches irreligion and immorality; and weakens the arm of government, in the maintainance of public order, and in the public defense; yet so thin are the partitions which divide them; so difficult it is to say precisely where the one ends and the other begins . . . if we attempt to tear out all the ill, we destroy both the warp and the woof; the utmost then that we should expect, is to soften the evil which may not be averted; to mitigate what we cannot prevent, and to find some palliative for the licentiousness of the press, since we must not trust its liberty. . . . It is recommended for this purpose, that the President be empowered to give an adequate salary to one, or more printers, whose duty it shall be to read all the scandal circulated against government within their particular districts, to examine into the real state of the case, and to publish it with proper commentaries, forwarding an impression to each of those printers, whose papers may require such wholesome corrective; the delivery of the government papers may always be known by the officers of the post office, and a proper penalty may be annexed to the falsification, or the post-ponement of the pieces forwarded for publication, to which, indeed, one or more columns in every anti-government paper throughout the union, may be particular-ly reserved by law. . . .

The misfortune is, that the different papers have not an equal, and similar circu-lation, so as mutually to correct each other; whence it happens that the people very seldom have an opportunity of hearing both sides of many important questions; one side indeed, the worst side, they very generally hear, for persons inimical to the country have gone, and no doubt will go in future, to the expence of furnishing gratis, several thousand copies of the anti-government papers, and of having them delivered to their readers free of all charges*; and thus (notwithstanding the cheap-ness of newspapers in general) the difference between a small expence, and no ex-pence at all, is frequently sufficient to give a preference to the anti-government pa-pers, through which alone, a very great number of individuals obtain all that they know, of the state of public affairs. . . .

A NEW CUSTOMER.—No. 1

*To my own knowledge the Aurora has been delivered in this manner at *Legionville*, and at *Cincinnati*.

COMMENTARY: A REVOLUTION IN PRINT

"What a hard Case it is, that after this Day's Appearance upon the Stage of Action, I must Die, or submit to that which is worse than Death, be Stamp'd, and lose my Freedom." So began an extraordinary newspaper essay, "The Lamentation of the New-Hampshire Gazette," on October 31, 1765—the day before the Stamp Act took effect. The anonymous author of "The Lamentation" (perhaps Daniel Fowle, the paper's printer in Portsmouth, New Hampshire) assumed the voice of his newspa-per "and the Press in general" to protest British colonial policy. With its borders draped in black mourning bands, the newspaper's somber physical appearance was somewhat at odds with the prose's tone, at times whimsical and self-effacing, at times earnest and outspoken. The author recounted in impressive detail the "glori-ous Actions and heroick Atchievements" of printing history, from Gutenberg to the current troubles in the far-flung North American outposts of the British Empire. In this narrative, the printing press was a means of extending knowledge and power, both in the learned professions and in society at large. These benefits were possible, however, only if the press was free. Through personification, "The Lamentation" made the abstract principle of freedom of the press vivid: "Must I be thus *mark'd* or *Stamp'd*, which I look upon as a Mark of *Reproach*, and *Contempt*;—I cannot bear it —

Freedom, the Privilege of an Englishman, is the Element I love to swim in—*Slavery* I abhor, and the least Degree upon my natural Right, makes me jealous of what may be the Consequences, for Oppression makes a poor Country, and a desperate People." Readers were thus invited to take the cause of the newspaper as their own, to see any attempt to restrain the press as an infringement on their personal freedom and "natural Right."

These, indeed, were the basic questions of the American Revolution: What is freedom? What is slavery? What is natural right? For printer-publishers, the Revolution had twofold meaning. The printed word helped shape the Revolution itself, from the newspapers' protests against the Stamp Act to the phenomenal popularity of Thomas Paine's *Common Sense* to a proliferation of political pamphlets, broadsides, and newspaper articles about the leading questions of the day. At the same time, the Revolution, seen broadly as an imperial crisis that began in the mid-1760s and continued through the ratification of the Constitution a quarter-century later, helped reshape how printers envisioned themselves, their role in society, and the notion of "freedom of the press."

By the middle of the eighteenth century printers in London had lost much of their autonomy to the emerging profession of "booksellers"—the forerunners of modern-day publishers, who coordinated the financing and publication of books and hired printers to perform the mechanical labor of setting type and producing printed sheets. On the North American periphery of the British empire, however, printers retained a different self-image: as a valuable trade with "mysteries" known only to those who had entered it as apprentices, worked their way to journeyman status, and ultimately joined the ranks of master craftsmen who owned their own shops, as in other artisanal trades such as carpentry or shoemaking (Botein, 14–16). Unlike carpenters and shoemakers, however, printers had special gifts and faced unique problems. Printers considered themselves intellectuals among tradesmen, entitled to a place alongside professionals: witness Benjamin Franklin's pretensions to social status. At the same time, as Franklin put it in 1731, their "peculiar Unhappiness"—the danger of offending potential customers through what they produced for other customers—set them apart from "other Callings." The press itself, as well as the trade, possessed a power to awe the uninitiated. In the poem "The Art of Printing," the press has supernatural power: "Hail mystick art! which men like angels taught,/ To speak to eyes, and paint unbody'd thought!" In the first issue of the *Essex Journal and Merrimack Packet* (1773), Isaiah Thomas and Henry Walter Tinges suggested a similar mystery when they invited "LADIES and GENTLEMEN who are desirous of seeing the curious ART of PRINTING" to drop in at their office for an upcoming exhibition of the press itself in action.

As this advertisement should remind us, however, printing was also how printers and their families made a living. Most master printers lived on the edge of financial failure; Benjamin Franklin was the exception, not the rule. Economic necessity dictated many of the printer's decisions. Publishing his own editions of books was usually too risky; better to import some copies from England. Diversifying one's shop made sense: the colonial printer usually sold books and perhaps other goods, worked for the local government as a clerk or postmaster, and published a newspaper. Franklin's "Apology for Printers" admitted as much: opening his press and his newspaper columns to all points of view—or so he said—was a business decision far more than a libertarian or ideological one. In reality, most colonial printers practiced what Franklin described in his "Apology's" final item. They refused to print certain kinds of material, especially the politically controversial, except when taking a side might produce a financial windfall (as Franklin's brother James hoped in the 1720s and John Peter Zenger attempted in the 1730s). If colonial newspapers often seem like dull recapitulations of foreign events, that content probably owed much to their proprietors' financially motivated decisions not to offend (Botein, 20–22). Economics also help explain why those printer-publishers began to take political stands from the Stamp Act crisis in 1765 to the outbreak of war a decade later. As Franklin's partner David Hall and South Carolina printer Peter Timothy learned to their regret, neutrality could drive away subscribers in the heat of political crisis. Charleston men of means even helped Timothy's former journeyman Charles Crouch, "a worthless Fellow" in Timothy's estimation, set up a rival newspaper. The abandonment of neutrality, much like its earlier maintenance, cannot be fully understood outside the printers' own occupational context.

Still, printers did consider their trade a "calling," not just a livelihood. Their ideology of diffusing knowledge throughout the population proved especially consonant with the republican ideology of the Revolution. This notion had originated in the colonists' English heritage: after all, William Livingston in 1753 contrasted *English* freedom of the press against the censorship in the Ottoman Empire. The central republican idea that liberty waged a constant struggle against the encroachments of power—and that a free press provided a crucial check against tyranny—derived from English opposition thought of the 1720s and 1730s. Expressed in the much-republished "Cato's Letters" of John Trenchard and Thomas Gordon, that thought provided the germ of many an American revolutionary's resistance. This belief persisted after the Revolution, when Jeffersonian Republicans' response to the 1798 Sedition Act seemed to hark back to the seditious libel cases of the 1730s. Again and again, printers identified their calling with a republican system of government. As Isaac Collins's 1783 broadside put it, "publick Papers are the political Eyes and the civil Light of the People; without which they will grope in Darkness, and be a Prey to Tyrants. Ignorance is the dark Door at which Tyranny enters." This was freedom of the press as republican bulwark—not as libertarian invitation to all points of view, as the Whigs' treatment of Loyalist printer James Rivington revealed.

During the imperial crisis of the late 1760s and 1770s printers assumed new prominence. If, as John Adams recalled forty years later in a now-famous letter to Thomas Jefferson, "the Revolution was in the Minds of the People . . . before a drop of blood was drawn at Lexington," the printed word had effected the transformation. We tend to forget Adams's next sentence: "The Records of the thirteen Legislatures, the Pamphlets, Newspapers in all the Colonies, ought to be consulted during that Period, to ascertain the Steps by which the public Opinion was enlightened and informed concerning the Authority of Parliament over the Colonies" (Adams, 2:455). In disseminating information from one colony to another and creating inter-colonial consciousness, "committees of correspondence" were certainly important. Those letter-writing societies throughout the colonies had some roots in the networks of correspondence that Benjamin Franklin had established with fellow printers decades earlier—to coordinate supplies and business dealings. But the printed page probably played a more significant role in creating inter-colonial networks, facilitating the exchange of information, and unifying the far-flung colonies.

The Declaration of Independence provides a case study. On July 8, 1776, four days after it was adopted by the Continental Congress, the "self-evident truths" of this document were proclaimed to an assembled crowd in Philadelphia. In New York, the Declaration was read to George Washington's troops the next day. But most Americans learned of the political separation from Great Britain through printed sources. The Declaration was printed in at least seventeen American editions in 1776 and 1777, and in virtually all the newspapers. The first printing in Massachusetts, for example, occurred in the July 17 edition of Isaiah Thomas's *Massachusetts Spy* in Worcester. Moreover, the Declaration did not appear in a vacuum. When readers opened their *South Carolina & Georgia Almanack* for 1777, they found a text of the Declaration as well as the more mundane information—such as a calendar and advice about farming—that helped them to order their daily lives. But those same almanac readers had grown accustomed to political as well as practical advice over the years. William Pitt's "Speech for the Removal of the Stamp Act" was printed in the *Almanack* for 1767, "A Question of Taxation without Representation by a Gentleman of South Carolina" appeared in 1771, and "Liberty the Birthright of Man" was printed in 1775. The Declaration of Independence was part of an ongoing public debate in print not only in South Carolina and Georgia but in all the colonies.

Newspapers offered clear testimony to the unifying power of print. Colonial American printers had long filled their papers with stories and information copied from London newspapers. During the revolutionary crisis, those American papers increasingly copied from each other. Printers exchanged their papers and reprinted stories that first appeared a thousand miles away: citizens of South Carolina could thus read of the actions of legislatures or committees in New England. When the Rhode Island committee of correspondence endorsed the boycott of Loyalist publisher James Rivington's newspaper, it made sure to have its action published in the *Newport Mercury*—not just for the benefit of local citizens, but also for newspaper publishers and their readers throughout the colonies. Similarly, the very idea of an inter-colonial boycott of Rivington's New York newspaper implied that his paper, or the stories in it, were crossing colonial lines. By 1780 newspapers' titles reflected their politicization. Amid the ubiquitous and long-standing *Gazettes* and *Journals*, whose editorial content often expressed new ideological concerns, other newspapers' titles made explicit the aims of the Revolution, whether the emphasis was on geographical union (for instance, the Boston *Continental Journal*), political principles (the New York *Constitutional Gazette*), intended audience (the Philadelphia *Freeman's Journal*), or public function (the Elizabethtown *Political Intelligencer*). *Massachusetts Spy* became "The Massachusetts Spy: Or, American Oracle of Liberty," with "Americans!—Liberty or Death!—Join or Die!" in its masthead. What was true for the patriot side was also true for the loyalist, as the profusion of the titular word "royal" amply demonstrates.

The sheer number of American publications multiplied, too. The increase in production of books, pamphlets, and broadsides was impressive, growing from 340 surviving imprints for 1765 to close to 500 for 1770 and almost 1,000 for 1775. Production fell precipitously during the rest of the war years, and began rising again once peace was established in 1783, returning to 1,000 imprints by 1790. When compared to the more modest output of the first half of the eighteenth century, the publications of the Revolution must have seemed "innumerable" to John Adams or any other observer. A raw count of surviving American imprints is only a crude measure of the role of printed materials, of course; and we cannot forget the continuing role of imported books in shaping public opinion. Nevertheless, the increase (including exponential growth in the publications of local and state governments) tells part of the story of American politicization. So does the circulation of certain key works, such as *Common Sense* (1776), which sold 100,000 copies in its first four months.

Print also helped democratize the Revolution. Early in the imperial crisis, pamphlet authors tended to write for elite, educated men. Their work often contained untranslated phrases or whole sentences in foreign languages, generally Latin. They used pseudonyms that suggested classical learning. They developed technical, legal arguments about the unconstitutionality of Parliament's actions. Paine's *Common Sense* drew on a different style, adapted to a wider readership and replete with homespun allusions. As Isaiah Thomas remembered, "Common sense in common language is necessary to influence one class of citizens, as much as learning and elegance of composition are to produce an effect upon another. The cause of America was just; and, it was only necessary to state this cause in a clear and impressive manner, to unite the American people in its support." Certainly Thomas had the benefit of hindsight, but he described a more general shift in revolutionary rhetoric. Pseudonyms persisted, but many of them took forms suited to a classically learned *and* a less-educated audience: "Populus" (in the 1768 *Boston Gazette*), "Publius" (the pseudonym Hamilton, Madison, and Jay used in the *Federalist* essays). Pseudonymous authorship also befitted the public sphere of the new republic: Even if an author's identity was an open secret to many, pseudonymity and anonymity implied disinterested argument, in the name of the public good rather than that of the writer. William Livingston had anticipated the value of anonymity in 1753, when he noted how the printed word enabled an author to express dissent without fear of reprisal from corrupt magistrates: "[B]y Means of this Art he may write undiscovered, as it is impossible to detect him by the Types of the Press." Anonymous or pseudonymous print, therefore—not just print itself—could buttress the republican defense of liberty against power.

Democratization and an expanded public sphere had their limits. As one contemporary article put it, women were "Born for liberty, disdaining to bear the irons of a tyrannic government" (American Woman). The printed word helped focus attention on women's broadened roles in the newly established republican order—contributing to the revolutionary effort by saving their rags for paper mills, as well as by sacrificing English luxury items for homespun cloth. After the war, the ideology of "republican motherhood" required educated women who could raise the next generation of an enlightened citizenry. By 1800, female literacy rates were rising quickly. A few women even ran printing shops, usually after their husbands died: Clementina Rind in 1770s Virginia and Lydia Bailey in Philadelphia at the end of the century were examples. Nevertheless, women's place in republican America was clearly subordinate to men's, and one of the best ways to caricature an opponent was to label him "feminine."

Slavery, of course, represented the greatest blot on America's republican experiment. The *Boston Gazette* could proclaim in 1768 that the press had set before the people "Liberty and Slavery; and with the most perswasive and pungent language, conjur'd them . . . to chuse Liberty and refuse Chains." Isaac Collins could conclude his 1783 prospectus with the injunction that if the people neglected to read newspapers, "Darkness and Slavery [might] wrap this glorious Land in all the Horrors of despotick Sway." Revolutionary newspapers and pamphlets are striking for how often they mention slavery in the same breath with liberty—of persons and of the press. Such appeals to liberty appeared in the newspapers next to advertisements for the return of runaway slaves. For most African Americans, though, slavery was not a rhetorical flourish but an ever-present reality. Some were capable of enlisting the power of the press in their own cause, of turning the Englishman's language on its head. In a noteworthy circular letter sent to all town representatives in Massachusetts in 1773, four slaves simultaneously congratulated and challenged the provincial legislators:

> We expect great things from men who have made such a noble stand against the designs of their *fellow-men* to enslave them. We cannot but wish and hope Sir, that you will have the same grand object, we mean civil and religious liberty, in view in your next session. . . . as the people of this province seem to be actuated by the principles of equity and justice, we cannot but expect your house will again take our deplorable case into serious consideration, and give us that ample relief which, *as men*, we have a natural right to. (Bestes)

The questioning of human rights may have led to odd juxtapositions on the page, but it also led to Benjamin Rush's *An Address to the Inhabitants of the British Settlements in America, Upon Slave-Keeping* (1773) and other early abolitionist literature.

In the decades after the American Revolution, printers proudly remembered their role in winning America's independence. Isaiah Thomas's history of printing in America transferred that self-congratulation from the ephemeral pages of newspapers into a two-volume work designed for the eyes of posterity. Thomas could now boast that North Carolina "royalists" had burned him in effigy and that British soldiers parading in front of his house had threatened to tar and feather him. But by 1810, when Thomas wrote these words, printers in America's largest cities were experiencing another transformation in their trade. Some had turned decisively toward newspaper publishing, focusing on their political endeavors. Others—as well as entrepreneurs who had never worked as printers—moved toward a new kind of "publishing": book publishing along the model that British bookseller-publishers had pioneered in the mid-1700s. Those new publishers hired printers who remained in "the trade" to do their typesetting and printing. Bidding low to get these jobs, master printers took on more apprentices, who eventually became journeymen and glutted the market for print labor. Printing, in short, moved toward a capitalist wage system in which most journeymen stood little chance of owning their own shops. Printers looked increasingly like "mere mechanics," not the vanguard of an enlightened citizenry (Botein, 50–53). Seen in this light, perhaps Isaiah Thomas's *History of Printing in America* expressed nostalgia for printers' fading glory as much as optimism about the future of the trade he had helped create.

SOURCE NOTES

[Unless otherwise indicated artifacts and documents are reproduced courtesy of the American Antiquarian Society (AAS), Worcester, Massachusetts.]

1. *Pennsylvania Gazette* (Philadelphia), June 3–10, 1731, 1–2.

2. *Independent Reflector* (New York), no. 40 (August 30, 1753): 159–62.

3. Published in *The Papers of Benjamin Franklin*, vol. 12, ed. Leonard W. Labaree (New Haven, Conn.: Yale University Press, 1968), 65–66, 255–58, 319–21. Copyright © Yale University Press. Reproduced courtesy Yale University Press, New Haven, Conn.

4. *New-Hampshire Gazette, and Historical Chronicle* (Portsmouth), July 12, 1765, 3.

5. *Pennsylvania Gazette* (Philadelphia), October 31, 1765, 3.

6. *Boston Gazette, and Country Journal*, March 14, 1768, 2.

7. In *The Papers of Benjamin Franklin*, vol. 15, ed. William B. Willcox (New Haven, Conn.: Yale University Press, 1972), 200–201. Copyright © Yale University Press. Reproduced courtesy Yale University Press, New Haven, Conn.

8. *Rivington's New-York Gazetteer*, August 11, 1774.

9. "Newport (Rhode-Island) Committee," in *American Archives*, 4th ser., 2, ed. Peter Force (Washington, D.C., 1837–53), 11–12.

10. *Rivington's New-York Gazetteer*, April 20, 1775.

11. Douglas McMurtrie, ed., "The Correspondence of Peter Timothy, Printer of Charlestown, with Benjamin Franklin," *South Carolina Historical and Genealogical Magazine* 35 (October 1934): 128–29.

12. Isaiah Thomas, *The History of Printing in America* (Worcester, Mass., 1810), 1:378–79, 2:250–53.

13. *Essex Journal and Merrimack Packet: Or, the Massachusetts and New-Hampshire General Advertiser* (Newburyport, Mass.), December 4, 1773, 1, 3.

14. Anthony Sharp, *The Lancaster Almanack* (Lancaster, Pa., 1774).

15. Isaac Collins, *The New-Jersey Gazette Will Be Revived on Tuesday the 9th Instant, on the Following Terms* (broadside, 1783).

16. *Pennsylvania Gazette* (Philadelphia), August 20, 1788.

17. Signed by President John Adams, July 14, 1798; published in many newspapers, including *Columbian Centinel*, August 8, 1798.

18. *American Aurora* (Philadelphia), July 21, 1798.

19. *Columbian Centinel* (Boston), August 8, 1798.

WORKS CITED

Adams, John. *The Adams-Jefferson Letters: The Complete Correspondence between Thomas Jefferson and Abigail and John Adams*. Edited by Lester J. Cappon. Chapel Hill: University of North Carolina Press, 1959.

American Woman. *The Sentiments of an American Woman*. Philadelphia: John Dunlap, 1780.

Bestes, Peter, Sambo Freeman, Felix Holbrook, and Chester Joie. "Sir, The efforts made by the legislative. . . ." Circular. Boston, April 20, 1773.

Botein, Stephen. "Printers and the American Revolution." In *The Press and the American Revolution*, edited by Bernard Bailyn and John B. Hench, 11–57. Worcester, Mass.: American Antiquarian Society, 1980.

"The Lamentation of the New-Hampshire Gazette." *New-Hampshire Gazette, and Historical Chronicle* (Portsmouth), October 31, 1765.

FOR FURTHER RESEARCH

Adams, Thomas R. *American Independence: The Growth of an Idea. A Bibliographical Study of the American Political Pamphlets Printed between 1764 and 1776 dealing with the Dispute between Great Britain and her Colonies*. Providence, R.I.: Brown University Press, 1965.

Bailyn, Bernard. *The Ideological Origins of the American Revolution*. Cambridge, Mass.: Harvard University Press, 1967.

Bailyn, Bernard, and John B. Hench, eds. *The Press and the American Revolution*. Worcester, Mass.: American Antiquarian Society, 1980.

Brown, Richard D. *The Strength of a People: The Idea of an Informed Citizenry in America, 1650–1870*. Chapel Hill: University of North Carolina Press, 1996.

Davidson, Philip. *Propaganda and the American Revolution, 1763–1783*. Chapel Hill: University of North Carolina Press, 1941.

Ferguson, Robert. "Writing the Revolution." In *The Cambridge History of American Literature*, edited by Sacvan Bercovitch, 426–69. New York: Cambridge University Press, 1994.

Fliegelman, Jay. *Declaring Independence: Jefferson, Natural Language, and the Culture of Performance*. Palo Alto, Calif.: Stanford University Press, 1993.

Humphrey, Carol Sue. *"This Popular Engine": New England Newspapers during the American Revolution, 1775–1789*. Newark: University of Delaware Press, 1992.

Larkin, Edward. "Inventing an American Public: Thomas Paine, the *Pennsylvania Magazine*, and American Revolutionary Discourse." *Early American Literature* 33 (1998): 250–76.

Levy, Leonard W. *Legacy of Suppression: Freedom of Speech and Press in Early American History*. Cambridge, Mass.: Belknap Press of Harvard University Press, 1960. Revised as *Emergence of a Free Press*. New York: Oxford University Press, 1985.

Maier, Pauline. *American Scripture: Making the Declaration of Independence*. New York: Alfred A. Knopf, 1997.

Monaghan, E. Jennifer. "Reading for the Enslaved, Writing for the Free: Reflections on Liberty and Literacy." *Proceedings of the American Antiquarian Society* 108, pt. 2 (1998): 309–41.

Nord, David Paul. "Newspapers and American Nationalism, 1776–1826." *Proceedings of the American Antiquarian Society* 100, pt. 2 (1990): 391–405.

Rosenfeld, Richard N. *American Aurora: A Democratic-Republican Returns: The Suppressed History of Our Nation's Beginnings and the Heroic Newspaper That Tried to Report It.* New York: St. Martin's Press, 1997.

Sloan, William David, and Julie Hedgepeth Williams. *The Early American Press, 1690–1783.* Westport, Conn.: Greenwood Press, 1994.

Smith, Jeffery Alan. *Printers and Press Freedom: The Ideology of Early American Journalism.* New York: Oxford University Press, 1988.

Waldstreicher, David. *In the Midst of Perpetual Fetes: The Making of American Nationalism, 1776–1820.* Chapel Hill: University of North Carolina Press, 1997.

———. "Reading the Runaways: Self-Fashioning, Print Culture, and Confidence in Slavery in the Eighteenth-Century Mid-Atlantic." *William and Mary Quarterly,* 3d ser., 56 (April 1999): 243–72.

Wallett, Francis G. *Massachusetts Newspapers and the Revolutionary Crisis, 1763–1776.* Boston: Massachusetts Bicentennial Commission, 1974.

Warner, Michael. *The Letters of the Republic: Publication and the Public Sphere in Eighteenth-Century America.* Cambridge, Mass.: Harvard University Press, 1990.

Wood, Gordon S. *The Radicalism of the American Revolution.* New York: Alfred A. Knopf, 1994.

5

The Book Trade Transformed

JEFFREY D. GROVES

IN 1790 making a book entailed using materials, processes, and machines perfected three centuries earlier. By 1865, however, the technology of the book trade had changed dramatically. Machine-made paper, for instance, replaced hand-laid. Printing presses, once pulled by a strong arm, could now be powered by belt, shaft, and steam engine. Such new technologies helped to increase the amount of print produced, making books, magazines, and newspapers available more widely, and often more cheaply, than they had been before. The exploitation of new machines and methods, of course, was dependent on other developments in the book trade. For instance, the modern publisher, as distinct from the earlier master printer or bookseller, came into being in the early nineteenth century, functioning as an entrepreneur who coordinated the financing, production, and distribution of printed works. Change was not limited to the book trade. In 1790 the population of the United States was just under 4 million; by 1865, there were more than eight times that many Americans. National literacy rates climbed dramatically and public schools and libraries became major consumers of books. Transportation networks became more extensive and sophisticated through the use of new road systems, steamboats, canals, and railroads. An increasingly efficient postal system and the invention of the telegraph helped spread information of all sorts at greater speed across the country. New businesses such as advertising agencies and express companies helped to publicize and distribute the material of a growing print culture.

Publishers themselves proudly pointed to such developments as evidence of their own importance in the education of a young nation. These advances, they argued, were part and parcel of the American experience and helped to distinguish this energetic and innovative country from "the old world." Such progressive visions, however, were not completely shared by the laborers who worked for publishing entrepreneurs. Printers spoke often of the debilitating effects of the new "capital" on time-honored labor practices, of the fear that new machines would throw people out of work, of new wage policies that would create a more competitive and less remunerative labor market. Like workers in other fields, printers formed unions to represent their interests. Printers' unions, in fact, constituted one of the most energetic and well-organized sectors in the nineteenth-century American labor movement.

ARTIFACTS

As the transformation of the book trade began, booksellers, printers, and publishers were quick to comment on the benefits they provided and the problems they faced in distributing reading materials throughout an extensive and rapidly growing country. In his *Address to the Printers and Booksellers throughout the United States*, the pioneering Philadelphia publisher Mathew Carey (1760–1839) described his frustrations about the lack of a national book market and proffered a solution to this problem. "Parson" Mason Locke Weems (1759–1825), best known as the writer who created the story of George Washington and the cherry tree, earned his living as a peripatetic book peddler in the American countryside, selling the products of Carey and other publishers. Thanks to his firsthand encounters with consumers, he often wrote to Carey about what sold—and what did not. In the 1809 letter reproduced below, Weems elaborated on Carey's frustrations and forwarded a different idea about how to distribute books efficiently.

Mathew Carey, *Address to the Printers and Booksellers throughout the United States* (1801)[1]

The patriotic spirit of fostering domestic arts and manufactures, which, to the honor of our country, is rapidly spreading among our citizens, demands, from all persons interested in those arts and manufactures, suitable exertions to extend and improve their respective branches. To this measure, every honorable motive, public and private, powerfully impels them.

Considered merely as a manufacture, the printing business has strong claims to regard. It converts a raw material, originally of the greatest possible insignificance, into an article of high price. It moreover furnishes employment, immediately or remotely, to various other important manufactures. On the printer chiefly depend the paper-maker, the letter-founder, ink-manufacturer, book-binder, engraver, &c. Every step taken to advance or retard the progress of the first, must proportionately affect all the others. In this point of view, therefore, this business must be regarded as of primary importance, and entitled to the protection of every real friend to his country. But when it is viewed as the grand means of disseminating improvements in the arts and sciences, of the refinements of civil society, of all that can render life of real value, it rises to a degree of magnitude incalculably great.

That it has, since the peace of 1783, been extended to a degree very far beyond what its most sanguine patrons could have rationally anticipated, is obvious. But it is still susceptible of greater proportionable increase. By a proper system, in a few years hence, as many books may be annually printed in inland towns, where, ten years ago, there was no sign of a printing press, as were executed in Philadelphia at the organization of the general government.

The great extent of our country, the distance between the capitals of the manufacturing states, and the expense and trouble of journies for the purpose of exchanging the productions of the press of one state for those of the others, have hitherto interposed obstructions to the extension of this business, which have greatly cramped the enterprize of the individuals concerned in it. For every purpose of trade, there is an almost impassable barrier interposed between the booksellers of the western parts of Pennsylvania and those of the interior of Massachusetts, &c. The printers in Carlisle, Lancaster, and Pittsburg, are confined almost entirely to an intercourse with those of Philadelphia, to whose mercy they are but too much exposed. The same may be observed of the printers in the numerous small towns of Massachusetts, whose dealings are limited in a great degree to Boston; and the observation might be extended to almost every part of the Union.

Is there no mode of removing or diminishing these obstructions? of aiding the energies of a set of men whose public and private utility might be tripled or quadrupled? of counteracting the numerous disadvantages under which the less wealthy of the profession labour? of increasing to perhaps an incalculable extent, the value of the productions of American genius, so as to render the profession of an author as lucrative here as elsewhere . . . as lucrative in effect, as it is honorable, when directed to serve the best purposes of society? It is believed that there is, and a very efficacious one, of which the most sanguine expectations may be formed. It has the advantage of not being a novel project, hitherto unessayed. It is, in a word, to establish

A Literary Fair,

as nearly on the plan of those of Frankfort and Leipzic, as possible. The salutary operation of those fairs in the encouragement of literary talents, and in the rapid and wide-extended circulation of books, is too well known to require any detail. . . .

It is therefore hoped that all persons concerned in the bookselling business, from one extremity of the continent to the other, will concur in this plan, and give it a fair trial. . . .

Among its beneficial tendencies, a few shall be slightly glanced at.

At present, when a printer in a situation remote from any of our capitals, publishes a book, it generally lies dead on his hands, or he is almost wholly confined to one market in the exchange of it. And thus the article, however intrinsically valuable, becomes, by the superabundance, a mere drug. Instead of that regard to which honest industry, usefully employed, has so fair a claim, disappointment and loss are the discouraging issue. The consequence inevitably is, that the spirit of enterprize, from which great public and private benefit might accrue, is smothered under the incumbent weight, and sinks into torpor and inactivity.

But behold the cheering reverse. We will suppose the fair established, and all, or most of the printers and booksellers throughout the Union there assembled once a year. If the booksellers of Walpole, of Salem, of Newhaven, of Albany, of Hudson, of Baltimore, of Carlisle, of Lancaster, of Greensburg, of Alexandria, of Richmond, &c. &c. print books, and each brings a few hundreds of his own, they may in a day or two be converted into an extensive and valuable assortment suited for their respective markets; and thus their past industry will be requited, future exertions stimulated, and their means of supporting their families and of benefiting the community be vastly increased. . . .

But although this establishment will be far more serviceable to booksellers and printers in isolated situations, and in humble circumstances, than to those in large towns and in affluence, it by no means follows, that to the latter description it will be injurious, or even useless. Far from it. The advantages to them will be solid and considerable. Many a musty shopkeeper, which has long retained undisturbed possession of the shelves of a store in Boston, New-York and Philadelphia, would find a ready market, when transported to the banks of the Susquehannah, the Patomack, or the Santee. Besides, the great increase which must take place in the number of books printed, will inevitably multiply the business in every direction. . . .

Without further detail, it is proposed that the fair herein recommended, be held in the city of New-York; . . . that it begin on the first day of June, 1802; and continue for one or two weeks, as may be found necessary. . . .

Mason Locke Weems, Letter to Mathew Carey (1809)[2]

I sit down to write you a long letter. It pleases me much to find that you are getting to see things in the light in which they have long appear^d to me. I now & ever have enjoy'd the solace & support of principle in this most important of all human pursuits, I mean the dissemination of books. . . . You seem to think this grand enterprise is most to be advanc^d by subscription. Very greatly no doubt it is. . . . [Y]et I contend that in your circumstances it w^d be immensely wrong to have but one arrow in your quiver when you cou'd have two equally feather'd & sure. You have at least 80.000 Dollars worth of books on hand. Are you so fond of them as to be resolved that they shall never leave their shelves. Why let not some of your Charity begin at home? Those blessed books well written, and printed to go abroad and enlighten & exalt mankind. And cou'd those excellent dead Authors, who have so long been lying in state in your store, but lift up their voice they w^d break your midnight slumbers with lamentation & mourning at their doleful confinement. Well, now were you to open their prison doors & let the Captives loose, you cou'd no doubt, in way of Cartel obtain in exchange such a mass as w^d, in conjunction with those of *your own* now at press & printing, enable me with infinite ease to establish at least 150 to 200 stores of *about 200$ each*. You speak of *dead Capital*. But, in my opinion there is nothing to be dreaded on that score, provided your Capital be vested in the right books. And certainly there *are books* of that description; and of this, surely you and I must be Judges at this time of day. Indeed of this I have long been inform'd as you well know. For . . . I have been incessantly preaching to you about the *Right books*. And when I was with you in Philad^a, was I not constantly telling you that high pric^d books and books without name wou'd not do. Our

Country, said, I, is made up of the small fry. Give me a Seine of small meshes. It is but rare that I want to see an Author that stands higher than a dollar. Give me 50 Varieties, from 25 to 50 or 75 cents—*interesting subjects*—popular titles—fascinating frontispieces & showy bindings and I shall carry everything before me—especially if to these you add the Auxiliaries of numerous catalogues, & striking flourishes on the great pleasure & profits which the Farmers & their Boys & Girls may derive from education and Reading. Thank God I am now getting to be known by great numbers, who, I believe, will aid y[r] sales, especially if I cou'd have handsome circulars, address'[d] to my numerous acquaintance Legal, Theological, Medical, Military, Agricultural, &c &c and distributed at little or no expence. . . .

Content not yourself with one string to your bow when you can have two!! I repeat, that if Heaven shou'd restore the ancient order of things, Peace & Plenty, the good that you may do & the money that you may make, may greatly exceed anything that you first thought of. Weigh well my plan—SUBSCRIPTIONS & ORDERS hold perhaps the first place in my expectations—And next, metamorphose a great deal of your present stock—cut down your heavy ships into smaller craft—Turn (in the language of Vulcan) your old Sows into Pigs—I shall write again—I have a world to say.

WHILE IMPROVED transportation helped to open distant markets, publishing also had matured as a profession by mid-century. Evidence of that maturation appeared in the establishment of trade journals: magazines directed to publishers and booksellers, connecting the book trade into a network of shared information and values. The *American Publishers' Circular and Literary Gazette* printed an article in its first issue (1855) emphasizing the necessity of information exchange for a business based on the dissemination of texts. The same year, New York's publishers assembled at a book festival to display their wares and celebrate their success. In a speech at that festival, George Palmer Putnam (1814–1872), an influential publisher himself, summarized the historical growth of American publishing to a gathering of publishers and authors.

Anonymous, "The American Publishers' Circular," from *The American Publishers' Circular and Literary Gazette* (1855)[3]

That the Book Trade requires a better method of communication between its members than any other branch of business is self-evident. The Publisher, anxious to draw the attention of the Bookseller to his newly published, or forthcoming books, must necessarily, especially if his business is extensive, either advertise largely, or send circulars to his customers through the post-office. The latter expedient is both expensive and uncertain. The difficulty of ascertaining the precise location of all Booksellers seems insurmountable; and many of the circulars frequently never reach their destination. To advertise largely in either a daily or weekly newspaper (except in one exclusively devoted to the trade) is, when the object of the Publisher is to reach the eye of the Bookseller, almost as uncertain. . . .

It is absolutely necessary for the Bookseller to have as perfect a knowledge as possible of all books published, both in this and foreign countries, so that he need turn away no customer unsatisfied. The "Publishers' Circular" will give full and accurate lists of all new publications, American and foreign, in every number; together with literary intelligence, statistics, and various information connected with the publishing world.

It would undoubtedly relieve the Bookseller of a laborious task if he could obtain an insight into the contents of the books he sells without the necessity of thoroughly perusing them. It is almost absolutely necessary that he should do so, to enable him to represent the utility and merits of the work offered in an intelligent and reliable manner. To relieve the bookseller from this task, it is proposed to devote a portion of the paper to brief epitomes of all new publications sent for notice in its columns. The paper, however, will attempt no criticisms; it will simply record facts. The principal object of the paper, "to promote the acquisition and circulation of early and authentic intelligence on all subjects connected with Publishing and the Trade in Books," will be carried out with all possible faithfulness.

George Palmer Putnam, "Introductory Statistical Sketch" Presented at the New York Book Publishers' Association Festival (1855)[4]

The records of American Publications (*) for the twelve years ending in 1842 show an aggregate of 1115 different works. Of these 623 were original, and 492 were reprinted from foreign books. The full list of reprints would show very nearly the same number as the originals,—viz., an average of 52 of each, per annum.

In the year 1853 there were 733 new works published in the United States; of which 278 were reprints of English works, 35 were translations of foreign authors, and 420 (a large preponderance) were original American works—thus showing an increase of about 800 per cent. in less than twenty years. As the average increase of the population of the United States in the same time . . . scarcely reached 80 per cent., it appears that literature and the book trade advanced ten times as fast as the population. If we compare the *numbers* printed of each edition, the growth is still greater; for, 20 years ago who *imagined* editions of 300,000, or 75,000, or 30,000, or even the now common number of 10,000? Who would then believe in reaching 150,000 with a magazine or newspaper? . . .

One word about the Mechanical aspects of our progress in book-making. We have yet much to achieve. *Excelsior* is our motto. But . . . even now, we may point with pride to specimens of the "black art," not a whit behind the best across the

*Incomplete in the list of reprints. [Putnam's note.]

sea. If *every* specimen is not perfect, let it be remembered that the aggregate of the NEW books first manufactured in a single year is not less than two millions four hundred thousand. Putting aside school-books, Bibles, and society publications, the number of volumes printed and reprinted will reach eight millions! The school-books alone will swell the number twelve millions more. The number of volumes issued yearly from the gigantic establishment of Messrs. Harper alone has been estimated at more than a million of volumes; and the Philadelphia house of Lippincott sends forth books at an average of fifty cases per day the year round. Specimens, these, though large ones. And then consider, besides, the enormous bulk of reading matter issued by our two hundred periodicals and two thousand newspapers! Think of the eighteen thousand double, or thirty-six thousand single reams of paper, required yearly for a single magazine, which courses over the country, unprecedented in cheapness and attraction, at the rate of one hundred and fifty thousand per month. The wildest imaginings, at home or abroad, twenty years ago, would not have stretched so far as this. Why . . . the sheets from our book-presses alone, in a single year, would reach nearly twice round the globe; and if we add the periodicals and newspapers, the issues of our presses in about eighteen months would make a belt, two feet wide, printed on both sides, which would stretch from New York to the Moon!

PUBLISHED BOOKS and articles elaborated on Putnam's statistics about the "mechanical aspects" of publishing. In 1855 Harper & Brothers, one of New York's largest publishers, opened its new publishing factory and office, one of the most technologically advanced establishments of its day. The output of the Harpers' twenty-eight bed and platen presses, like the one pictured below, dwarfed the turn-out of most other American publishing houses. That same year, Jacob Abbott (1803–1879)—a popular Harper's author—wrote a "story book" (part of Harper's story-book series) celebrating the new operation. A decade later, Alfred Hudson Guernsey (1818?–1902) published an article in *Harper's New Monthly Magazine* about how the magazine itself was produced at the same New York printing plant. Along similar lines, James Gordon Bennett's New York *Weekly Herald*—a leading paper in America's largest city—described its own plant, complete with the newest Hoe presses, to its readers in 1845. Bennett (1795–1872), whose operation included a "job office" that printed small jobs such as theatrical programs, made a point of noting how publishing newspapers differed from making books. The novelty and success of these enormous printing factories gained nationwide attention, as an article from the St. Paul *Minnesota Pioneer* revealed: apparently its editor visited Bennett's establishment in 1852.

Jacob Abbott, "Type-Founding," from *The Harper Establishment* (1855)[5]

[W]e entered the casting-room, which was in the upper story of the building. There was a range of workmen all around the room, each busy casting type at this little machine. The machines had each its own separate furnace and reservoir of metal, so that they looked like so many little forges ranged in order all about the room. . . .

But I must describe the machine a little more particularly. It appeared to be complicated in its construction, but the principle of its operation, as is usually the case, indeed, with all great inventions, was very simple. The essential thing is a mould to cast the types in, made in parts, so as to open for the purpose of letting the type drop out, and then to shut up together again very closely and exactly. The several parts forming the mould are so connected with machinery worked by the crank that they are opened and shut again every time the crank is turned once round. . . .

It is by no means to be supposed, however, that because the operation of the machine thus described seems so simple, the artisan who works it has nothing to do but to turn a crank. This is, indeed, all the mechanical work that he has to perform, but in the exercise of judgment, skill, and discretion, he has a great deal to do. He must watch his furnace and his reservoir of melted metal, to see that the metal is always of the proper temperature. He must be careful, too, that he does not turn the machine too fast, for this would heat the mould too much, and thus prevent the perfect form of the type. He must continually keep his eye on the little orifice where the metal is ejected from the reservoir, to see that all is right there, and that no little globules of melted metal remain on the outside of it to prevent a perfect junction of the face of the mould with the outside surface. In a word, a person, to be a good type-founder, notwithstanding all the help he obtains from his machine, must be a man of great skill, careful judgment, and practical dexterity.

The metal, in being injected or forced into the mould, passes through an opening, which forms a sort of long, slender funnel, which enters at the lower end of the mould. This funnel itself, as well as the mould, becomes filled with metal, so that, when the type drops upon the paper below this metal remains attached to it in the form of a long and slender wedge-shaped projection called a jet. . . . This *jet* must, of course, be removed in the process of finishing the type. Indeed, the removing of it is the first step in the finishing process.

They *break* it off. . . . One would not suppose that there would be any thing particularly curious or interesting in so simple an operation as this, but I found it quite curious, on account of the great rapidity with which the boys, whose business it is, perform it, and the arrangements which were made to facilitate the work. . . .

The breaker is seated, when at work, at a sort of low table, with sides all around it, to prevent the types from falling upon the floor. . . . At one end of the table, within the box, is a great pile of types, with the jets attached to them, just as they come from the moulds. These the boy continually draws down upon the surface of the cushion, where he breaks off the jets from them with an inconceivably rapid motion of the fingers, and then separates the parts by pushing the jets one way and the types another. The boy whom I watched performed the operation so rapidly that, with the closest observation, I could not follow the motions of his fingers at all, or see by what means he contrived to accomplish the object. . . .

The next process to breaking was what was called rubbing. The rubbing was the work of women and girls. The room where this operation was performed had two or three long low tables extending through it from end to end, with what seemed to be a row of grindstones lying upon them. These stones were large and not very thick, and they were lying on their sides upon the tables. The upper surface of them seemed to be very level and flat, and were of about the roughness of sandpaper. Before each stone sat a female operative rubbing types. The object of this rubbing was to smooth the sides of the type, and to remove a little thin projection of metal which is apt to be left, after the casting, at the edges. . . .

The girl takes up a handful of types, and lays them down, side by side, on the stone. She takes ten or twenty at a time. She then lays two of her fingers across the types, and, by a sweep of her arm to and fro, she rubs them back and forth on the flat surface of the stone. This smooths and evens the under sides of the types. Then she brings the types to the edge of the stone, so as to allow the ends of the whole row to project a little, and by a very dexterous movement—so dexterous and quick, indeed, that you will have to look very closely to follow it—she turns them all over together, and then proceeds to rub the other side, and finally pushes them into a box ready near the stone to receive them. . . .

The next process is *setting*. This consists of the work of arranging the types in rows for inspection and for the final finishing. The setters are usually small girls. The types are taken up by them from a box, where they lie in bulk, and are placed in a row upon a long stick, like a yard-stick. It is astonishing to witness the rapidity of motion and the accuracy which these girls display in taking up and placing the types, arranging them all the same way, that is, with the same side toward them, and the letter faces all turned downward.

Alfred Hudson Guernsey, "Making the Magazine," from *Harper's New Monthly Magazine* (1865)[6]

The articles having been selected, and the order in which they are to appear fixed, they are sent to the "Composing Room," where they are "set up" in type. . . . Here the "copy" is given to a "compositor," or rather to a number of compositors, who proceed to put it into type.

The compositor's "case" consists of a shallow box two and a half feet long, and half as broad, divided into compartments for the different characters used. Two of these are required for the sorts in common use. These are placed in a sloping position on a stand, the upper case being more inclined than the lower. The lower case, as arranged for an ordinary work in English, has 54 boxes of different sizes; these contain the various small letters (hence styled "lower case letters"), the marks of punctuation, the figures, and spaces and "quadrats" of different sizes. The upper case has 98 boxes of uniform size. These contain the capitals, small capitals, and various characters which are in frequent use, such as parentheses, stars, and other signs of reference, dashes, dollar and pound marks, and so on, besides leaving a few boxes for characters which may be frequently wanted for special work. . . .

The tools of the compositor consist simply of the composing-stick with its rule, and a sharp-pointed bodkin for making corrections. . . . His copy lies before him, usually upon the small-cap side of the upper case. He reads a few words, as many as he can readily remember, and then proceeds to pick up the letters composing them, one by one, and putting it into the stick, keeping it in its place by a slight pressure of the thumb, until the line is nearly full. . . . If a very little more room is wanted, the compositor makes it by taking out the spaces between the words, and putting in thinner ones; or he reverses the process and puts additional space between the words. This process is called "justifying". . . . A good compositor will complete about three lines in five minutes, so that, deducting the time spent in justifying, he picks up nearly one letter a second, hour in and hour out. In addition, he has learned his copy by heart, though indeed he forgets the words as soon as he has set them up. He does not look at the face of the letter; he assumes that each will be in its proper box. Near the lower end of each type, and on the side below the bottom of the letter, are several deep "nicks." If the type is placed in the stick with the nicks on the outer side of the line it must be in the right position. . . .

Machines have been invented for setting and distributing type. By simply touching keys, as in playing upon an organ, the type, liberated one by one from receptacles, which may be considered the pipes of the organ, are made to glide in a continuous stream, forming themselves into words and sentences more rapidly than a man can write, much less "set them up;" but the lines must be "justified" by hand. . . . These machines are marvels of mechanical ingenuity; but it is still doubtful, taking into account conditions which only a printer can appreciate, whether they can do their work more economically than can be done by the compositor. . . .

If the work were to be printed directly from the type, the pages would be imposed into a sheet, locked up, and sent to press. Most newspapers and pamphlets are still printed from the type; but the Magazine and most books are printed from stereotype or electrotype casts. The process of stereotyping consists in taking a mould in plaster of Paris from a page of type, and then taking a cast in type-metal from that mould. The advantages of this method are numerous; the principal being that it obviates the necessity of laying out a large amount of dead capital for a long time. Thus, in "Liddell and Scott's Greek Lexicon" there was an interval of five years between the "composition" of the first sheet and the last, during all of which time the work was going on. If the work was to be printed from the type, the first sheet must have been printed as soon as it was ready, and so on to the end. But none of the work would be put into market until after the last sheet was printed, five years later. The paper and printing of each sheet would form so much dead capital during the interval. Moreover, the publishers would print as many copies as they would be likely to sell for ten years. Measuring from the time when the first sheet was printed until the last copy containing it was sold would be fifteen years, the average being just half that period. Interest, insurance, and storage during this time would fully equal the original cost of the sheets. But the pages being stereotyped, the printing of the first sheet need not be commenced until the last was ready. Then there would need to be printed at once only as many copies as would be likely to be wanted in a year; for whenever the edition was found to be running out it could be reprinted from the plates. Taking these and other considerations into account, the entire cost of a book of this kind, exclusive of binding, is reduced about one half by stereotyping it. An additional expense is indeed incurred in the outset; but it has become an axiom among publishers that "a book is not worth doing that is not worth stereotyping."

But the process of stereotyping has many defects, especially when applied to the reproduction of engravings. The plaster mould is not perfectly accurate; and the metal expands and contracts a little in heating and cooling. The difference in a page of type is hardly perceptible; but in an engraving, where each minute line should be faithfully reproduced, it becomes very evident. Stereotype casts of fine engravings are never satisfactory. Besides, the metal being soft, and the fine lines very faint, after a few thousand impressions have been taken the plate becomes "worn."

Stereotyping has within a few years quite generally, and in the Harper Establishment entirely, been laid aside for the somewhat more expensive but far more perfect process of electrotyping. . . .

[L]et us follow a page of the Magazine into the electrotyper's room. A sheet of wax is laid upon it, and it is placed under a powerful press, which forces the wax into the interstices of the page, producing a perfect mould. The face of this mould is covered with plumbago—commonly called black-lead—in order to give it a metallic surface. The mould is taken into the battery room. Here are a number of long narrow tanks, filled with a strong solution of sulphate of copper and a series of batteries. The positive pole of a battery is attached to a mould, the negative is attached to a copper plate, and both are placed in the tank. In an instant a thin film of copper appears on the surface of the mould. It is demonstrable that this is infinitely thinner than the thinnest gold-leaf. This coating increases momently, and in from two to twelve hours, according to the intensity of the operation, which is regulated by the electrotyper, it forms a "shell" of the required thickness: about that of a sheet of stout paper. The upper surface is a perfect facsimile of the original page, the minutest line and point of an engraving being reproduced with absolute precision. The under surface is exactly parallel with the upper. The shell looks as though one had with a series of punches stamped every line into a thin sheet of copper.

This thin shell would be crushed flat by the immense pressure of the printing-press. It must now be "backed up" with type-metal. Now this metal, even in a melted state, will not readily adhere to copper. But it will adhere to tin, and tin will adhere to copper. The shell, its back having received a thin coating of tin, is put face downward in a shallow iron dish, and held firmly in its place by a series of small elastic rods. The dish is then swung by means of a crane, so that it rests in a flat caldron filled with type-metal, kept in a melted state by a furnace. . . . When the plate has acquired the same temperature as the metal, so that both will contract equally in cooling, a quantity of the melted metal is dipped up with a ladle and poured over the plate, filling up every hollow and forming a solid backing. The plates, thus backed up, are considerably thicker than is required. They are passed through a planing-machine, which reduces them to a perfectly uniform thickness of about one-seventh of an inch. They are then carefully examined to see that they contain no imperfections; the edges are smoothed and beveled, and they are ready for the pressman, who is technically called the "printer."

Jacob Abbott, "The Press," from *The Harper Establishment* (1855)

A representation of [a power-press], as it stands in the great press-room of the Harper Establishment, is seen in the following page. . . . The girl who stands at it is called the feeder. She has a pile of damped paper on a stand over the press. The pile is inclined a little toward her, so as to make it easier for her to draw off the successive sheets. Under this pile of paper is the platen. We recognize it by the iron braces partially seen beneath the stand on which the paper is placed. . . . To the right, we see a part of the system of rollers by which the form is inked. The feeder has just placed a sheet to be printed on the inclined table before her. This table is called the *apron*. In a moment a set of iron fingers will come up from below, and, taking hold of the lower edge of the paper, will draw it in under the platen, between the platen and the form. The revolution of the machinery will then bring an immense power into operation, by means of cams and levers seen below, by which the bed of the press, with the form and sheet upon it, are pressed up for a moment with great force against the platen. This makes the impression. The form then descends again, and the sheet, by a very ingenious and peculiar mechanism, passes out *under* the apron on which the feeder originally placed it, toward the left, where the edge of it jumps up very mysteriously upon a series of endless tapes, which may be seen in the engraving through the fly-wheel. . . . From these it is taken up by a light frame, formed of long and slender rods of wood, and is carried over and laid down upon the pile at the extreme left of the engraving. Thus the work goes regularly on, with no attendance whatever except the placing of each successive sheet with the reach of the iron fingers which are to draw it into the machine.

Visitors who watch the motions of the press while it is performing its work are always particularly pleased with the life-like actions of the iron fingers that come up and take hold of the lower edge of the sheet of paper on the apron. . . .

There are nearly thirty of these presses in the great press-room, and there is something imposing and almost sublime in the calm and steady dignity with which the ponderous engines continue their ceaseless toil. There is, indeed, a real dignity and a real grace in the movements which they perform. The observer looks down the room from the elevated desk of the foreman, and surveys the scene with great interest and pleasure, wondering at the complicated massiveness of the constructions, and at the multitude of wheels, and pulleys, and bands that mingle and combine their motions with the revolutions of the machinery. . . .

Jacob Abbott, "Forwarding," from *The Harper Establishment* (1855)

When the sheets are folded, they are *gathered,* as it is termed; that is, a pile of each sort being laid out along a table, a girl takes from each pile one, and puts them together in the proper order, so as to form the book or pamphlet. . . .

Books that are to be bound are *sewed.* . . . To prepare the books for being sewed, the first step is to *saw* small grooves through the backs of them, deep enough to receive the bands of twine to which each sheet is secured. . . .

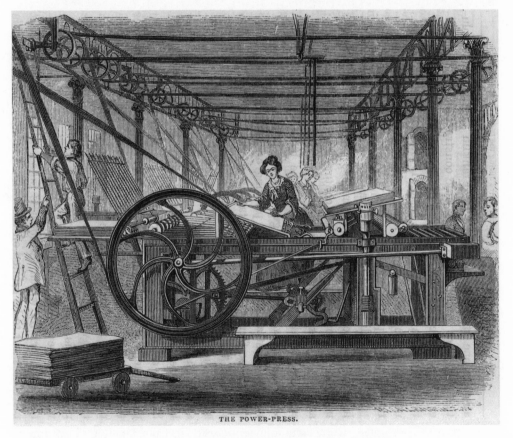

THE POWER-PRESS.

"The Power-Press," from *The Harper Establishment* (1855)

The sheets are then to be sewed. This operation is performed by great numbers of girls, seated at long tables, extending in rows along the room. . . . The sewing of the books is a great work. The ranges of tables devoted to it are so extensive as to furnish accommodations for one hundred girls, and each place is provided with a seat and a stool, that may both be raised or depressed, to suit the comfort and convenience of the occupant. . . . Every visitor who sees these girls at their work is struck with the extreme rapidity and dexterity of their movements, and with the healthy, and happy, and highly attractive appearance which they themselves and the scene of their labors exhibit. Indeed, so far as my observation goes, one of the chief subjects of remark with strangers, after coming away from a visit to the whole establishment, is the intelligent and manly bearing of the men who are employed in it, and the attractive appearance and lady-like manners of the girls.

Jacob Abbott, "The Distribution," from *The Harper Establishment* (1855)

The authors, whose writings the proprietors and conductors of this establishment bring before the public by the aid of the immense mechanical means and facilities they have at their command, and the still more immense business organization which they have built up, and which extends its ramifications to almost every city street and rural village or mountain hamlet throughout the land, are very numerous, and they occupy every variety of intellectual and social position. There are classical scholars who pursue their studies in learned libraries, and make profound researches into Greek and Roman lore. There are intrepid travelers, who follow whales in the Pacific Ocean, or lose themselves among the fields and mountains of ice in the Polar Seas. There are clergymen, who instruct the world with their expositions of Scripture, and of moral and religious truth; and statesmen, who discuss questions of politics; and novelists, who invent ingenious tales to furnish amusement and recreation for the weary and the solitary; and tourists, who give accounts of their tours; and embassadors, who relate the history of their embassies; and multitudes besides. The productions of all these, and of many others, come into this vast establishment each in the form of a single roll of obscure and seemingly useless manuscript, and then, a few weeks afterward, are issued in thousands and tens of thousands of copies, beautifully printed, embellished, and bound, to instruct, entertain, and cheer many millions of readers.

"The Herald Establishment," from *The Weekly Herald* (1845)[7]

THE COMPOSITOR'S ROOM.—This occupies the whole of the fifth or upper story of the building. There are twenty hands constantly employed here, and room for thirty more, when, on any extraordinary occasion its full strength is to be brought out. . . .

At one end of this great room stands the proof-reader and foreman's desks; on the opposite end nearly, a stone cistern, supplied with water; also, the necessary conveniences for the internal and external application thereof. In the centre of the inner side wall stands a time piece, to guide the operations of the men, and ensure that punctuality which is indispensable here. Against this wall, and running from one end to the other, is a long case for matter set up, or in process, and for matter to be distributed. Two or three feet from this, towards the longitudinal centre, and parallel to it, is a bench, on which are kept the *forms*, before and after they are sent to and received from the press-room; this bench or table has a number of drawers, in which are kept the implements and accessories used in preparing the *forms* for press, to and from which it is conveyed by the ingenious hoisting machine connecting the upper and lower extremities of the edifice.

The hours of work are from 10 o'clock, A. M., till 2 o'clock at night, out of which time are to be deducted one hour for dinner and two for tea. All this time is required to set up the great quantity of matter, for which the *Herald* cannot be approached by competition, for the system, order, and facilities that characterize this important department, as well as every other. It is not unfrequent to see twenty columns of new and original matter in the morning *Herald*, and that of the smallest type, whilst the evening edition will bring out of later news still, as much as the whole fresh matter of one of the penny papers; or as they are better called, hand-bills, which profess to tell the people, in the morning, something they do not know, but in nine cases out of ten such pretension is mere wind. There is a good deal said about the performance of the Harpers in book printing, but after all, what is it to the feats done in the *Herald* newspaper printing establishment, where there has been often as much matter set up within the compass of one working day, and published in the next *Herald* as would make a book of three hundred and fifty octavo pages. Let the bookmakers match that, if they can.

"The New York Herald Establishment," from *The Minnesota Pioneer* (1852)[8]

On a recent visit to the city of New York, we made a short visit to Mr. Bennett's establishment, the greatest printing concern in the Union whence newspapers issue. Although we had heard much of it, we soon saw that the half had not been told us. We were struck—as a practical printer naturally would be—with the magnitude of the composing room, which easily and conveniently accommodates one hundred compositors, and where one of the most important of the various branches of the industrial world is carried on with a regularity and precision that are perhaps thoroughly comprehensible of the craft. The press department is on the same magnificent scale. It has four of Hoe's fast presses, each costing $12,000, and each capable of throwing off twelve thousand impressions per hour, a speed without which even the proprietor of the Herald might find it impossible to accomplish his great undertakings. The job office attached to the establishment is one of the most extensive and well supplied in the country. There is printed the theatrical work of the city, and similar matters, in a style that is not to be surpassed. All over the establishment—in the intellectual and business departments as well as in the mechanical—are evidences of the care of a controlling mind of the first class. The history of the newspaper press may be challenged to furnish anything more remarkable than that of the Herald, which now stands at the head of American journals, after having struggled for some years against greater adverse influences than any other paper ever encountered. As a faithful chronicle of the age, it is not to be competed with.

AS PUBLISHERS waxed eloquent about their growing businesses and impressive technologies, workers actively organized to advocate for their own positions. These print workers were not alone: during America's early industrial revolution, laborers in other trades also began to organize for better wages and conditions. The "Introductory Remarks" to the Constitution of The Typographical Association of New York recounted the history of this printers' union. In a published address to New York printers, Franklin J. Ottarson, an officer of another printers' association, addressed the tension between the new unions and established master printers such as John F. Trow. A short article from the *Protective Union*, a newspaper associated with an active typographical union in Boston, described the union reaction that began in the 1830s when women and children were hired to do the work traditionally reserved for men. As we contemplate the nineteenth-century transformation of the book trade, the voices of workers present a necessary counterweight to the enthusiastic rhetoric of the publishers.

Anonymous, "Introductory Remarks" to the Constitution of The Typographical Association of New York (1833)[9]

The Typographical Association of New York was instituted on the 17th day of June, 1831. It may not be deemed improper to state some of the causes which led to its formation; and, in doing this, it will be necessary to revert to the condition of the printing business for some years past.

In the year 1809 the New York Typographical Society was formed, for the purpose of sustaining a uniform scale of prices, and of affording pecuniary relief to the sick and distressed of its own members, their widows and orphans. This institution has continued to the present time; but the principal object of its first formation has long since ceased to claim any part of its attention. In 1812, war occurring between this country and Great Britain, the business suffered extremely, and continued in a depressed state until 1815 or 1816, when it was found necessary to call a general meeting of the journeymen in the city, to take into consideration the propriety of revising the scale of prices; and after considerable debate between employers and employees, a scale was agreed upon, which was adopted by the New York Typographical Society. The demands of the workmen were very generally acceded to, and for some three or four years business was very brisk.

In the year 1818 the society was incorporated by an act of the legislature, and, being prohibited by the terms of its charter from interfering with the scale of prices, it became merely a mutual benefit institution.

In the meantime, the seeds of declension in the trade were gradually sown, and the fruit began to appear in various ways. Some printers from a distance, having heard that business was good, and, being determined to obtain it at all hazards, located themselves among us; and to secure a sufficient quantity of work commenced operations on terms that could not be afforded, if they wished to obtain a fair remuneration for their labor, or act honestly by the workman. The consequence was, that while a few grew rich at the expense of the journeymen, old-established printers, who had before paid honorable prices, were obliged to reduce their charges for work, or lose much of their business; and as their receipts were diminished, the wages of the journeymen were by degrees reduced, until, instead of a uniform scale of prices, every man was compelled to work for what he could obtain.

Another cause of depression was the practice, which then prevailed, and has continued more or less to the present time, of employing runaway or dismissed apprentices for a small compensation. These were called two-thirds men, and have always proved a great pest to the profession. . . .

The trade, also, as far as pressmen are concerned, had suffered extremely by the applications of machinery to that branch of the business; and while a few individuals were growing rich, as they asserted, for the benefit of the public at large, many who had spent from five to seven years of the flower of their lives in acquiring a knowledge of their profession, were left without employment, or were obliged to resort to some business with which they were unacquainted, and thus constrained to serve a sort of second apprenticeship.

Matters continued in this condition for a number of years. Meantime the business of stereotyping had increased to a great extent; and the numerous improvements in the art, or rather the motto of multum in parvo literally reduced to practice, rendered it every year more and more difficult for compositors to support themselves and their families. The disgrace of some employers, every advantage was taken of the necessities of the workmen, and impositions were continually practiced upon them.

Men, however, when borne down by oppression, rise in their strength, and assert their rights. The journeymen printers of the city of New York, from a sense of justice to themselves, and those employers who had uniformly paid honorable prices, resolved to unite as an association for the purpose of elevating the business to a proper level. Numbers of them were engaged on the several daily newspapers of this city at prices deemed sufficient when there was little labor and scarcely any competition, but which were found totally inadequate when all vied with each other to present the latest news to the readers. To accomplish this, the workmen were almost entirely deprived of their rest for nights together.

Scarcely any employment can be more laborious than that of publishing a daily morning newspaper. Many of the offices are in the most crowded parts of the city; and, not having been built for the purpose, are illy calculated to afford a good circulation of air, or what is next in importance, good light. To the injurious effects of these and similar causes, many of the most worthy of the profession have fallen victims; and others, after a short endurance, have found their faculties so impaired, and their constitutions so debilitated, as to be rendered incapable of undertaking any other permanent employment for their future support. It requires the united exercise of the mental and bodily labor of the persons employed, for nearly the whole night, and a considerable portion of the day; being seldom able to allot more than seven hours to rest and refreshment. To be thus confined for such a length of time, inhaling the stagnant air of a printing office, is sufficient to enervate a man of the most vigorous constitution.

Under all these circumstances, a general meeting of the trade was called about the 1st of June, 1831, at which a committee was appointed to draw up a just and equitable scale of prices. The committee made their report to an adjourned meeting, which adopted it; and on the 17th day of the same month the Typographical Association of New York was established, and a constitution and by-laws framed for its government.

A circular to the employing printers was forthwith issued, covering the new scale of prices, and respectfully asking them to accede to it. Most of them, to their honor, saw the justice of the demand, and promptly awarded the wages asked for. There were some, however, both among the book offices and daily newspapers, who altogether refused, and have managed, from that time to the present, by a constant change of workmen . . . to evade the demands for a fair compensation. It is a source of consolation, after all, that the expenses of those establishments where the prices are not paid are greater than those where they are, owing to the incompetency and dishonesty of those employed.

Franklin J. Ottarson, "Address" Prepared on Behalf of the Franklin Typographical Association (1844)[10]

The corresponding secretary of the Franklin Typographical Association having been duly appointed by the board of managers to confer with certain printers concerning prices, respectfully submits the following report:

Saturday morning, July 20, I called on John F. Trow, the corporation printer, and stated to him that I had been appointed by the association to inquire of him if there was any truth in the rumor that he was about to reduce prices in his book office. He answered me very haughtily, "Suppose there is?" I said that I did not come to explain why he should not reduce prices, but merely to ask what truth there was in the rumor. Again he replied, "Suppose there is?" I asked him if that was his only answer. He replied that he acknowledged no right in the association to ask him questions; that the association had been the cause of difficulty in his office, and that he was determined to "set his face against" this or any other association that should assume the right of dictation as to what men should receive for their labor. . . . He held that he had the right to pay what he pleased for work, and that no one had a right to say a word in the matter. . . .

Printers of New York! have you no interest in this matter? A portion of your number, by great exertion formed an association—upon a liberal and benevolent plan—have adopted a scale of prices to which these very men acceded, and which every honorable employer considers fair and just. . . .

If you who are not members of our association would come up and join—if you would help yourselves fight your own battles—we might give such an answer as would effectually convince Mr. John F. Trow, and others of his belief, that free and independent men, men who earn an honest livelihood by the sweat of their brow, have a right to dictate to fellow-men—aye though their names be not blazoned six several times in gorgeousness of gold leaf and black paint upon the walls of a four-story building.

But if the mass of journeymen printers will remain idle in this business—if they will shun all opportunity for benefiting themselves—then they must submit to be insolently told that they have no right to ask a fair return for their labor, that they must take what their masters choose to offer, and be silent; they must be content to cringe before the soulless tyrant who by any means may happen to possess control over a case of type and a rickety press; they must be content to live or die, to feast or starve, as the greed and avarice of the employer may dictate.

Anonymous, from *The Protective Union* (1850)[11]

Every *religious* paper in Boston, except the Trumpet and the Pilot, refuses to pay the prices as established by the Printers' Union. The Trumpet is a Universalist, and the Pilot a Catholic paper. All honor to them!—Cincinnati Nonpareil

We suppose that the Nonpareil obtained its information from the union, but we are very sorry that it should have been misled. We are informed that the Pilot is the only religious paper in this city which pays its workmen the established prices. All honor to the Pilot! The other religious papers generally employ girls and boys at half price, and a sprinkling of journeymen, to whom they give but about two-thirds price. The journeymen would not object to the employment of girls, if they were paid full wages, but they are used as instruments to oppress the former.

COMMENTARY: INTERPRETING PUBLISHER ARTIFACTS

IN 1801 Mathew Carey, an energetic and ambitious Philadelphia printer and book-seller, distributed a broadside address that described the geographical challenges faced by the eighteenth- and early-nineteenth-century American book trade. The "great extent" of the United States, Carey noted, hampered the shipment of printed goods from one city to another, and the business consequences of this limitation were "discouraging." Lacking a national publishing center like London, a city in which the vast majority of English publishing was concentrated, American printers and booksellers found it difficult to think beyond their own regions. Carey himself, with the aid of Parson Weems, had been trying for some years to build a distribution network that would carry his books far beyond the Philadelphia area, but up to the date of his broadside the results of his efforts had been disappointing.

Carey's proposal for overcoming the geographical obstacle he faced was both creative and sensible: because there was no main origin of supply from which to distribute printed goods to the country, then "the country" should be brought on a temporary basis to an arbitrary center—a "literary fair" at which printers and booksellers from all around the United States could congregate to establish trade relationships, exchange goods, and circulate information that would help to open new markets for printed material. Carey's idea was clearly persuasive, for between 1802 and 1805 five fairs were held, one in Philadelphia, one in Newark, and three in New York. Thereafter, however, the fairs vanished, in part because country printers used these occasions to flood urban markets with cheap reprints (thus motivating city booksellers to withdraw from the fairs), in part because of an economic depression associated with the Napoleonic wars, and in part because book fairs were not a customary feature of the English publishing system on which the American trade largely modeled itself (Winship, "Getting the Books Out," 14–15).

Carey's plan for a regular meeting of the book trade did not last five years into the nineteenth century, but within fifty years of the fairs' demise his precocious desire for a national book market was to a large extent realized. Several of the artifacts repro-duced in this chapter date from 1855, each depicting a massively changed American publishing scene from the one Carey knew at the turn of the century. The column from the *American Publishers' Circular and Literary Gazette* describes the inception of a trade journal and organization that attempted to be national in scope, offering publishers and booksellers from all parts of the country the opportunity to gather "early and authentic intelligence" about the book trade. George Palmer Putnam's 1855 address to 600 publishers, booksellers, and authors shows them how much they had increased book, magazine, and newspaper production in the last twenty-five years, and urges them to be patriotically proud of their exertions. Jacob Abbott's book *The Harper Establishment* and the New York *Weekly Herald*'s self-congratulatory description of its newspaper plant are meant to awe the reader with the technological and productive wonders of what were then two of the world's most advanced pub-lishing facilities.

In the first half of the nineteenth century, the modern publisher came into being. This increasingly well-capitalized entrepreneur coordinated and took the risks for the financing, production, and distribution of books and magazines but did not necessarily own the means for making and transporting print products (Winship, *American Literary Publishing*, 13–15). Additionally, during the same period developments in printing technology, transportation, shipping, and communication, as well as rising literacy and education rates, worked with a fitful but growing economy to enable publishers to exploit an expansive, increasingly national market for printed matter. Regional interests did not vanish, of course: American publishing remained to a significant extent decentralized, with important new publishing interests cropping up in cities like Cincinnati, Chicago, and San Francisco as the country expanded to the west. Still, publishers in long-established print culture centers such as Philadelphia, Boston, and especially New York largely surmounted the geographical distances and regional mentalities that seemed so limiting to Carey. Indeed, across the nation, publishers began to seek out particular but distant audiences by specializing their wares. For instance, religious publishing boomed in the antebellum United States. The American Tract Society, founded in 1825 and dedicated to distributing Protestant publications through a sophisticated network of traveling booksellers, published almost a million volumes in 1855 and thus rivaled even Harper & Brothers in size and productivity (Tebbel, 508, 513–14). Specialization was not limited to religion. Several publishers, such as McLaughlin Brothers, served the rapidly growing market for children's books and games. Others, such as Oliver Ditson, published the sheet music that was greatly in demand throughout the nineteenth century.

As we look back at it with knowledge of these many developments, Carey's broadside seems particularly interesting because it allows us to measure changes in nineteenth-century publishing. Using a source merely to index change, however, can be misleading. Artifacts such as Carey's broadside or Putnam's speech are typically much richer than such limited use would suggest. Book historians must constantly remind themselves that the texts they interpret have rhetorical features that must be addressed alongside the "facts" extracted from those texts. Carey's broadside is an exercise in rhetoric from its opening sentence. Rather than merely making commonplace observations about the difficulties of the book trade, Carey also seems determined to weave a particular perspective into his address, a perspective that during the nineteenth century became a standard view for publishers to take of their social utility and status. There is, Carey writes at the beginning of his address, a "patriotic spirit" in the early republic for the "fostering of domestic arts and manufactures." For a country such as the United States, which had sprung into national being only recently, domestic manufacture was an important economic issue. As a contributor to the national good, Carey argues, printing should be held in especially high regard. Not only does the printer convert materials "of the greatest possible insignificance" into marketable items, providing many jobs in related industries along the way, but he is also of "primary importance" because print products can educate, refine, and acculturate the citizens of a new country. With these claims, Carey positions printing on a high rung of the social ladder, arguing for its dominance among American manufactures. The printer, he suggests, is one of the greatest of patriots, to be lauded as a servant of the public good.

Carey's rhetoric foreshadows the development of a dominant publishing ideology in the United States. If we again jump to 1855 and look at some of Jacob Abbott's chapters from *The Harper Establishment*, we see that Carey's claims have been internalized at the Harper firm, allowing that extremely competitive and successful publishing house to sublimate its economic purpose by focusing the reader's attention on its service to the republic. In 1855 Harper & Brothers had just recently rebuilt its printing house following a disastrous fire in 1853. The Harper book factory was now an advanced industrial plant (both architecturally and organizationally) that allowed books to be created on something like an assembly line. In describing this plant, Abbott is both enthusiastic and thorough in his descriptions of book-making processes. As he details the various technologies that would have seemed quite advanced to his contemporary readers, he impresses us with the seemingly objective tone of his descriptions. We must remind ourselves, however, that there is much more going on in his text than the mere recounting of technical information.

Like Carey, Abbott makes an implicit argument throughout *The Harper Establishment* concerning the status of publishers, an argument that is perhaps most clearly seen in the last chapter of the book, "The Distribution." In that chapter, Abbott decisively shifts the authority for textual production from the author to the publisher. Publishers, we learn, enable authors to reach a national audience. Without the "aid of the immense mechanical means and facilities" that publishers can offer writers, and without the distribution network to which the publisher allows access (a network that "extends its ramifications to almost every city street and rural village or mountain hamlet throughout the land"), the author would have no readers. In fact, the author's production, we are told, is an "obscure and seemingly useless manuscript" that has no value until it arrives in the publisher's hands, after which it can "instruct, entertain, and cheer many millions of readers." To the extent that authors have the potential to instruct, entertain, and cheer, publishers are the necessary agents for the realization of that potential. Publishers, Abbott implies, are themselves active in this role for the American public, and thus they have an important function (one anticipated in Carey's rhetoric) in the education of a young country. This conception of the publisher's activities spread quickly in the nineteenth century. Some publishers, such as James T. Fields, George Palmer Putnam, James Gordon Bennett, and James Harper, became as famous and as celebrated as many of the authors they published.

Interestingly, while Abbott describes the publisher as a servant of the public good, he also unintentionally provides information that helps us to critique that rhetorical stance. Throughout *The Harper Establishment*, Abbott frequently refers to the men, women, boys, and girls who work in the printing industry. He expresses amazement at their speed in completing repetitive tasks and suggests that the moral good of publishing is demonstrated in their individual characters. In his chapter on "Forwarding," for instance, Abbott writes that the girls (young, unmarried women, not necessarily children) who sew book bindings for the Harpers display a "healthy, and happy, and highly attractive appearance" to "every visitor." Indeed, Abbott claims, "one of the chief subjects of remark with strangers, after coming away from a visit to the whole establishment, is the intelligent and manly bearing of the men who are employed in it, and the attractive appearance and lady-like manners of the girls." Not only is print culture good for the nation and democracy, but laboring in a publishing establishment also seems to confer desirable qualities on workers.

If we read between the lines of Abbott's book, we might be tempted to discount his cheery description of labor conditions at Harper & Brothers. Looking at the chapter on "The Press," for example, we see that Abbott clearly intends his description of the bed and platen press to be celebratory, to suggest how publishers have put great mechanical forces at the service of American readers. Mechanical presses, after all, produce great quantities of reading material, and the more there is to read, the text seems to imply, the better for democracy. If, however, we look carefully at Abbott's description, we see a disquieting set of metaphors that force us to wonder if the Harpers' workers were really as happy as Abbott depicts them. First, Abbott represents the press room from the "elevated desk of the foreman," a manager who oversees production rates and who would have been much more interested in product than in the manners that workers displayed in the factory. Second, the "girl" who is pictured operating the press is reduced to a function. She is "the feeder" of the press, a worker whose monotonous job, hour after hour, day after day, is to place one sheet of paper after another onto the apron of the press—the rest of the printing process is completed mechanically. Third, the press itself is described in animate terms. It possesses "iron fingers" that have "a life-like action," it exhibits a "great power," and yet it also displays "a real dignity and a real grace in the movements" that it performs. The machine, in fact, is "sublime," mysterious but fascinating in its operation. By the time we reach the end of Abbott's laudatory passage, the machine has assumed a more human character than the seemingly mechanical operative who feeds it.

Compare Abbott's description with a contemporary sketch about labor conditions. In April 1855 Herman Melville, who published most of his novels with the Harpers, brought out "The Paradise of Bachelors and the Tartarus of Maids" in *Harper's New Monthly Magazine*. (Indeed, Abbott may allude to Melville in "The Distribution" chapter of *The Harper Establishment*, for Melville was an "intrepid traveler" who "follow[ed] whales in the Pacific Ocean.") In the second half of Melville's sketch, the narrator visits a New England paper factory of the sort that might have supplied paper to the Harpers. The workers in this factory are primarily young women, and the narrator is appalled at the conditions under which they labor. Their work is repetitive, monotonous: "At rows of blank-looking counters sat rows of blank-looking girls, with blank, white folders in their blank hands, all blankly folding blank paper" (675). Machines dominate the scene:

Not a syllable was breathed. Nothing was heard but the low, steady, overruling hum of the iron animals. The human voice was banished from the spot. Machinery—that vaunted slave of humanity—here stood menially served by human beings, who served mutely and cringingly as the slave serves the Sultan. The girls did not so much seem accessory wheels to the general machinery as mere cogs to the wheels. (675)

The young women, full of "unrelated misery" (675) and working in extremely unhealthful conditions, show none of the qualities that Abbott insists the workers at the Harper establishment display. Melville, of course, may be grinding his own rhetorical axe; it would be as unwise to take his description at face value as it is to trust Abbott unquestioningly. Other evidence, however, suggests that Abbott may not be painting an accurate picture of the labor relations at the Harper establishment.

Prior to the nineteenth century, printing had typically been the domain of male workers. Starting in the 1830s, however, and corresponding to some extent with the rise in union activity among printers, women began to find their way into press rooms, sometimes as replacements for striking male workers. During the 1850s, the question of whether women should be allowed in the printing workplace was heated. Organizations such as the New York Typographical Union No. 6 were beginning to organize effectively and to use collective bargaining and strikes as negotiating tools for higher wages, shorter hours, and better working conditions. Printers' unions, in fact, were forming national networks in much the same way that publishers were, with local unions reporting to a national coordinating body. One of the most vexing questions debated by union members was whether women should work as printers (especially as compositors) and, if so, whether they should be allowed to join the union. Many male printers felt that when a woman joined the work force, wages went down generally (women were typically paid less for their work), and a job was lost for a man who might have a family to support. While Harper & Brothers obviously employed many women, Abbott acts as if the contemporary discussion about female workers did not exist and thus erases the labor tensions in the printing industry.

From sources like those in this chapter, then, we can cull at least two kinds of information. The first is largely descriptive, the second rhetorical and ideological. By carefully considering the first, we can come to understand the actual processes through which print was produced and distributed in the nineteenth-century United States. By reading between the lines of the second, we can penetrate to the concepts and practices that motivated people who worked in the book trade, both as publishers and as print laborers. Examining the history of print culture demands that we utilize both kinds of information thoroughly.

SOURCE NOTES

[Unless otherwise indicated artifacts and documents are reproduced courtesy of the American Antiquarian Society (AAS), Worcester, Massachusetts.]

1. Mathew Carey, *Address to the Printers and Booksellers throughout the United States* (Philadelphia: Mathew Carey, 1801).

2. Mason Locke Weems, *Mason Locke Weems, His Works and Ways: Letters, 1784–1825*, vol. 2, ed. Emily Ellsworth Ford Skeel (New York: n.p., 1929), 396–400.

3. "The American Publishers' Circular," *American Publishers' Circular and Literary Gazette* (New York) 1 (September 1, 1855), 1.

4. George Palmer Putnam, "Introductory Statistical Sketch," *American Publishers' Circular and Literary Gazette* (New York) 1 (September 29, 1855), 67–68.

5. Jacob Abbott, *The Harper Establishment; Or, How the Story Books Are Made* (New York: Harper & Brothers, 1855), 76–82, 119–22, 130–33, 160. The subsequent artifacts by Abbott are from the same source.

6. Alfred Hudson Guernsey, "Making the Magazine," *Harper's New Monthly Magazine* 32 (December 1865), 7–13.

7. "The Herald Establishment," *Weekly Herald* (New York), August 30, 1845, 273–74.

8. "The New York Herald Establishment," *Minnesota Pioneer* (St. Paul), September 23, 1852, 2.

9. "Introductory Remarks," in *A Documentary History of the Early Organizations of Printers*, ed. Ethelbert Stewart (Indianapolis: International Typographical Union, 1907), 42–45.

10. Franklin J. Ottarson, "Address," in *A Documentary History of the Early Organizations of Printers*, ed. Ethelbert Stewart (Indianapolis: International Typographical Union, 1907), 75–76.

11. *Protective Union* (Boston), January 12, 1850, 51.

WORKS CITED

Melville, Herman. "The Paradise of Bachelors and the Tartarus of Maids." *Harper's New Monthly Magazine* 10 (April 1855): 670–78.

Tebbel, John. *A History of Book Publishing in the United States*. Vol. 1. New York: R. R. Bowker, 1972.

Winship, Michael. *American Literary Publishing in the Mid-Nineteenth Century: The Business of Ticknor and Fields*. Cambridge: Cambridge University Press, 1995.

*———. "Getting the Books Out: Trade Sales, Parcel Sales, and Book Fairs in the Nineteenth-Century United States." In *Getting the Books Out*, edited by Michael Hackenberg, 4–25.

FOR FURTHER RESEARCH

Ballou, Ellen. *The Building of the House: Houghton Mifflin's Formative Years*. Boston: Houghton Mifflin, 1970.

Charvat, William. *Literary Publishing in America, 1790–1850*. Philadelphia: University of Pennsylvania Press, 1959. Reprint, with afterword by Michael Winship, Amherst: University of Massachusetts Press, 1993.

Comparato, Frank E. *Books for the Millions: A History of the Men Whose Methods and Machines Packaged the Printed Word*. Harrisburg, Pa.: Stackpole, 1971.

Crouthamel, James L. *Bennett's New York Herald and the Rise of the Popular Press*. Syracuse, N.Y.: Syracuse University Press, 1989.

Exman, Eugene. *The Brothers Harper: A Unique Publishing Partnership and Its Impact upon the Cultural Life of America from 1817 to 1853*. New York: Harper & Row, 1965.

Gilreath, James. "American Book Distribution." *Proceedings of the American Antiquarian Society* 95, pt. 2 (1985): 501–83. Reprinted in *Needs and Opportunities in the History of the Book: America, 1639–1876*, edited by David D. Hall and John B. Hench, 103–85. Worcester, Mass.: American Antiquarian Society, 1987.

*Green, James N. "From Printer to Publisher: Mathew Carey and the Origins of Nineteenth-Century Book Publishing." In *Getting the Books Out*, edited by Michael Hackenberg, 26–44.

*Groves, Jeffrey D. "Judging Literary Books by Their Covers: House Styles, Ticknor and Fields, and Literary Promotion." In *Reading Books: Essays on the Material Text and Literature in America*, edited by Michele Moylan and Lane Stiles, 75–100.

Gura, Philip F. "Early Nineteenth-Century Printing in Rural Massachusetts: John Howe of Greenwich and Enfield, ca. 1803–45, with a Transcription of His 'Printer's Book,' ca. 1832." *Proceedings of the American Antiquarian Society* 101, pt. 1 (1991): 25–62.

John, Richard R. *Spreading the News: The American Postal System from Franklin to Morse*. Cambridge, Mass.: Harvard University Press, 1995.

Kinane, Vincent. "'Literary Food' for the American Market: Patrick Byrne's Exports to Mathew Carey." *Proceedings of the American Antiquarian Society* 104, pt. 2 (1994): 315–32.

MacKellar, Thomas. *The American Printer: A Manual of Typography*. Philadelphia: L. Johnson & Co., 1866.

Nord, David Paul. "Free Books, Free Grace, Free Riders: The Economics of Religious Publishing in Early Nineteenth-Century America." *Proceedings of the American Antiquarian Society* 106, pt. 2 (1997): 241–300.

Pretzer, William S. "The Quest for Autonomy and Discipline: Labor and Technology in the Book Trades." In *Needs and Opportunities in the History of the Book: America, 1639–1876*, edited by David D. Hall and John B. Hench, 13–59. Worcester, Mass.: American Antiquarian Society, 1987.

Remer, Rosalind. *Printers and Men of Capital: Philadelphia Book Publishers in the New Republic*. Philadelphia: University of Pennsylvania Press, 1996.

Schiller, Dan. *Objectivity and the News: The Public and the Rise of Commercial Journalism*. Philadelphia: University of Pennsylvania Press, 1981.

Sutton, Walter. *The Western Book Trade: Cincinnati as a Nineteenth-Century Publishing and Book-Trade Center*. Columbus: Ohio State University Press, 1961.

Tucher, Andie. *Froth and Scum: Truth, Beauty, Goodness, and the Ax Murder in America's First Mass Medium*. Chapel Hill: University of North Carolina Press, 1994.

Winship, Michael. "Printing with Plates in the Nineteenth-Century United States." *Printing History* 5, no. 2 (1983): 15–26.

Zboray, Ronald J. *A Fictive People: Antebellum Economic Development and the American Reading Public*. New York: Oxford University Press, 1993.

6

Antebellum Reading Prescribed and Described

Scott E. Casper

AS NEW technologies and publishing arrangements expanded and transformed the book trade, a wider range of Americans read than ever before. Literacy among northerners, which had been nearly universal among white men in the colonial period, became virtually universal among native-born men *and* women by 1850. Literacy rates among southern whites, although never as high, increased as well. The expansion of literacy had several sources. The republican ideology of the Revolution called for an educated citizenry, including literate women as "republican mothers." Evangelical Christianity, which emphasized the individual's personal relationship with God, promoted reading (particularly of the Bible and religious tracts) across class, gender, and color lines. In a burgeoning commercial economy, too, correspondence, newspapers, and agricultural periodicals assumed greater importance for farmers and merchants connected to local or regional markets. A rising number of northern states and communities developed public schools and school systems between 1790 and 1860, spurred by reformers who proclaimed the republican, Christian, and economic benefits of universal education. Southern states and localities did not follow suit, largely because the south's population was far more dispersed than the north's, because reform movements took less hold in the south, and because wealthy planters preferred to have their children educated at home and at private boarding schools. Across the nation, libraries (usually private associations or enterprises run from a newspaper office or bookstore) provided access to a far wider variety of books than most Americans could have afforded to purchase for themselves.

To some Americans, the diffusion of literacy harbored potential dangers. Many critiques centered on what people were reading. Rising literacy fostered new forms and genres of print: women's magazines and domestic novels; exposés of crime or the underside of urban life. Newspapers had been predominantly political since the revolutionary years, and most editors had aligned themselves with a political party or faction. Beginning in the 1830s, however, new kinds of urban newspapers emerged alongside the partisan press that continued to dominate rural and small-town journalism. Sometimes called the "penny press" (even though many cost two cents an issue), papers such as the New York *Sun* emphasized sensationalism and refused to take sides in politics, while others such as the New York *Tribune* offered less sensational, but similarly less partisan, reportage. Older warnings about the invidious effects of novels, especially on women, declined by the mid-nineteenth century but never disappeared entirely. Now a new kind of caution emerged: What effect would sensationalism, in fiction or in the news, have on readers? A different question—slave literacy—vexed southerners: not what reading material was available, but who was allowed to read. Would literacy promote slaves' desire for freedom? Although many states passed laws against teaching slaves to read or write, some southern ministers argued that literacy was essential to evangelizing slaves. In any event, thousands of enslaved people did learn to read and write, far more than scholars have traditionally assumed.

For historians of reading, the central—and the most difficult—question is this: How did people read? In other words, what did Americans make of what they read? It is easy to assume, for instance, that people read for escape, to transcend their everyday circumstances. The opposite is equally possible: that reading was embedded in everyday religious, economic, and secular life. The diaries, letters, and narratives of ordinary and extraordinary readers begin to provide answers.

ARTIFACTS

As ever more Americans read the rapidly multiplying, increasingly diverse products of printers and publishers, writers greeted them with prescriptions: what they should read, how they should read, even how they should treat their books. In many cases these suggestions appeared in advice or "conduct of life" manuals that also included prescriptions about behavior, character, and dress. William A. Alcott's (1798–1859) *The Young Man's Guide*, written by a prolific author of advice literature (including also *The Young Woman's Guide to Excellence*), contained wide-ranging hints for men in their teens and twenties who sought to "make themselves." *The Mother's Book*, the product of the well-known abolitionist author and editor Lydia Maria Child (1802–1880), offered advice on child raising, especially to mothers of a new middle class in cities and towns. W. P. Atkinson (1820–1890) originally delivered his lecture "Books and Reading" to workers in a Cambridge, Massachusetts, factory where he had established a library. Libraries could be found in many New England factories of the early industrial revolution, when workers were generally native born and lived in boardinghouses run or sanctioned by the factory owners.

William A. Alcott, *The Young Man's Guide* (1833)[1]

I do not propose, in a work of this kind, to recommend to young men what particular books on any subject they ought to study. First, because it is a matter of less importance than many others, and I cannot find room to treat of every thing.

He who has the determination to make progress, will do so, either with or without books, though these are certainly useful. But an old piece of newspaper, or a straggling leaf from some book, or the monument itself—and works of nature as well as of art, will be books to him. Secondly, because there is such an extensive range for selection. But, thirdly, because it may often be left to the reader's own taste and discretion. He will probably soon discover whether he is deriving solid or permanent benefit from his studies, and govern himself accordingly. Or if he have a friend at hand, who will be likely to make a judicious selection, with a proper reference to his actual progress and wants, he would do wrong not to avail himself of that friend's opinion.

I will now mention a few of the particular studies to which he who would educate himself for usefulness should direct his attention.

1. GEOGRAPHY.

As it is presumed that every one whom I address reads newspapers more or less, I must be permitted to recommend that you read them with good maps of every quarter of the world before you, and a geography and correct gazetteer at hand. When a place is mentioned, observe its situation on the map, read an account of it in the gazetteer, and a more particular description of it in the geography. . . .

2. HISTORY.

It is deemed disgraceful—and ought to be—for any young man at this day to be ignorant of the geography and history of the country in which he lives. And yet it is no uncommon occurrence. However it argues much against the excellence of our systems of education, that almost every child should be carried apparently through a wide range of science, and over the whole material universe, and yet know nothing, or next to nothing, practically, of his own country. . . .

8. NOVELS.

As to NOVELS it is difficult to say what advice ought to be given. At first view they seem unnecessary, wholly so; and from this single consideration. They interest and improve just in proportion as the fiction they contain is made to resemble reality; and hence it might be inferred, and naturally enough, too, that reality would in all cases be preferable to that which imitates it. But to this it may be replied, that we have few books of narrative and biography, which are written with so much spirit as some works of fiction; and that until those departments are better filled, fiction, properly selected, should be admissible. But if fiction be allowable at all, it is only under the guidance of age and experience;—and here there is even a more pressing need of a friend than in the cases already mentioned.

On the whole, it is believed to be better for young men who have little leisure for reading, and who wish to make the most they can of that little, to abandon novels wholly. If they begin to read them, it is difficult to tell to what an excess they may go; but if they never read one in their whole lives, they will sustain no great loss. Would not the careful study of a chapter of Watts's Improvement of the Mind, be of more real practical value than the perusal of all that the best novel writers,— Walter Scott not excepted,—have ever written?

9. Of newspapers.

Among other means both of mental and moral improvement at the present day, are periodical publications. The multiplicity and cheapness of these sources of knowledge renders them accessible to all classes of the community. And though their influence were to be as evil as the frogs of Egypt we could not escape it.

Doubtless they produce much evil, though their tendency on the whole is believed to be salutary. But wisdom is necessary, in order to derive the greatest amount of benefit from them; and here, perhaps, more than any where else, do the young need the counsels of experience. I am not about to direct what particular newspapers and magazines they ought to read; this is a point which their friends and relatives must assist them in determining. My purpose is simply to point to a few principles which should guide both the young and those who advise them, in making the selection.

1. In the first place, do not seek for your guide a paper which is just commencing its existence, unless you have reason to think the character of its conductors is such as you approve.

2. Avoid, unless your particular occupation requires it, a business paper. Otherwise your head will become so full of 'arrivals' and 'departures,' and 'prices current,' and 'news,' that you will hardly find room for any thing else.

3. Do not take a paper which dwells on nothing but the details of human depravity. It will indeed, for a time, call forth a sensibility to the woes of mankind; but the final result will probably be a stupidity and insensibility to human suffering which you would give much to remove.

4. Avoid those papers which, awed by the cry for *short* and *light* articles, have rendered their pages mere columns of insulated facts or useless scraps, or what is still worse, of unnatural and sickening love stories.

Lastly, do not take a paper which sneers at religion. It is quite enough that many periodicals do, in effect, take a course which tends to irreligion, by leaving this great subject wholly out of sight. But when they openly sneer at and ridicule the most sacred things, leave them at once. 'Evil communications corrupt' the best 'manners;' and though the sentiment may not at once be received, I can assure my youthful readers that there are no publications which have more direct effect on their lives, than these unpretending companions; and perhaps the very reason is because we least suspect them. Against receiving deep or permanent impressions from the Bible, the sermon, or the *book* of any kind, we are on our watch, but who thinks of having his principles contaminated, or affected much in any way, by the newspaper? Yet I am greatly mistaken, if these very monitors do not have more influence, after all, in forming the minds, the manners, and the morals (shall I add, the *religious character*, even?) of the rising generation, than all the other means which I have mentioned, put together.

Lydia Maria Child, *The Mother's Book* (1831)[2]

The books chosen for young people should as far as possible combine amusement with instruction; but it is very important that amusement should not become a necessary inducement. I think a real love of reading is the greatest blessing education can bestow, particularly upon a woman. It cheers so many hours of illness and seclusion; it gives the mind something to interest itself about, instead of the concerns of one's neighbors, and the changes of fashion; it enlarges the heart, by giving extensive views of the world; it every day increases the points of sympathy with an intelligent husband; and it gives a mother materials for furnishing the minds of her children. Yet I believe a real love of reading is not common among women. I know that the new novels are very generally read; but this springs from the same love of pleasing excitement, which leads people to the theatre; it does not proceed from a thirst for information. For this reason, it has a bad effect to encourage an early love for works of fiction; particularly such as contain romantic incidents. To be sure, works of this kind have of late years assumed so elevated a character, that there is very much less danger from them than formerly. We now have true pictures of life in all its forms, instead of the sentimental, lovesick effusions, which turned the heads of girls, fifty years ago. But even the best of novels should form the *recreation* rather than the *employment* of the mind; they should only be read now and then. They are a sort of literary confectionary; and though they may be very perfect and beautiful, if eaten too plentifully, they do tend to destroy our appetite for more solid and nourishing food. The same remarks apply in a less degree, to children's forming the habit of reading nothing but stories, which are, in fact, *little novels*. To prevent an exclusive and injurious taste for fiction, it is well to encourage in them a love of History, Voyages, Travels, Biography, &c. . . . I am aware that all cannot afford to buy books freely; but I believe there are very few in this land of abundance, who do not spend in the superfluities of dress and the table, more than enough to purchase a valuable library. Besides, ample means of information are now furnished the public by social libraries, juvenile libraries, Lyceums, &c. I can hardly suppose it possible that any person can really want a book, in this country, without being able to obtain it. . . .

Of late years, the circulating libraries have been overrun with profligate and strongly exciting works, many of them horribly exciting. I have a deep prejudice against the whole class. The greater the genius displayed, the more dangerous the effects. The necessity of fierce excitement in reading is a sort of intellectual intemperance; and like bodily intoxication, it produces weakness and delirium. The Pelham novels, the works of Byron, Maturin, Lewis, and Mrs. Radcliffe are of this description. They have a most unhealthy influence upon the soul. . . .

Historical works of fiction may be read in connexion with history to great advantage, at any time from fourteen years of age to twenty. There is an edition of Shakspeare, called The Family Shakspeare, in which impure sentences are entirely omitted; the historical plays in this edition would give a strong additional interest to the history of the periods they illustrate. Sir Walter Scott has furnished a novel for almost all the interesting reigns in English History. These works are not professedly religious or moral.—They are pictures of life just as it is—giving a distinct idea of the manners, costume, and superstitions, of various ages. Their influence is never in opposition to good; and to a thinking mind they afford abundant food for reflection, as well as an inexhaustible fund of amusement.

Amid the multiplicity of modern books, the old standard works are too much neglected. Young people had better read Plutarch's Lives, and Anarcharsis' Travels in Greece, than to read fifty of the best miscellaneous productions of the day. To read every new thing fosters a love of novelty and a craving for excitement; and it fritters away time and intellect to little purpose. Such books as I have recommended strengthen the mind, and fill it with something solid. They are particularly valuable on account of the classical information they contain. Every woman should have some classical knowledge. I do not mean that they should study Latin and Greek. I merely mean that they should have general information of the government, customs, religion, &c., of the ancients; and the reason I think it desirable is, that they cannot understand the allusions in good English books without some such knowledge. . . .

To conclude, I would suggest that it is better to have a few good books than many middling ones. It is not well for young people to have a great variety. If there are but few books in the house, and those are interesting, they will be read over and over again, and well remembered. A perpetual succession of new works induces a habit of reading hastily and carelessly; and, of course, their contents are either forgotten, or jumbled up in the memory in an indistinct and useless form.

Franklin said wisely, 'Any book that is worth reading once, is worth reading twice;' and there is much good sense in the Roman maxim, 'Read *much*, but do not read *many* books.'

W. P. Atkinson, *Books and Reading: A Lecture* (1860)[3]

At the request of the Treasurer of a Massachusetts manufacturing company, I some time ago selected and purchased a collection of books for the use of the hands employed in his mills, and last winter was invited by them to give one of a course of lectures before a society for mutual improvement which they had formed in connection with their library. . . . Lest any reader should feel surprised at the character of many of the books I have occasion to mention, as being above the level of the readers for whom the library was intended, I ought perhaps to say that nearly all the persons employed in these mills are Americans, chiefly from the country towns of New England, and have, therefore, almost without exception, received the elements of a good English education in New England common schools. . . .

It is all very well for people who have plenty of spare time, and who never knew what it was to work in their lives, to talk about working people spending all their leisure hours in instructive study; but let them do a hard day's work once, and see if at the end of it they feel exactly like sitting down to master some difficult subject requiring close attention, and hard and continuous thought; and no study is of much avail without these. It is a physiological absurdity. The limbs cannot be tired without tiring the whole system. The mind does not exist apart, independent of the body, as you would suppose from hearing some people talk about it; whatever fatigues the body, fatigues, to a greater or less extent, the brain also. . . .

I do not think it reasonable, then, to expect of the majority of hard-working people a great amount of intellectual exertion in their leisure hours, because their strength has already been expended in other ways. A moderate amount of real mental labor, they can and ought to perform; for without it they will be in danger of degenerating into dull drudges,—their minds running to waste, while their bodies grow stronger. But I do think—and here I differ from many good, but over-strict people—that light reading for amusement merely, is not only harmless, but eminently useful. It is a refreshment to the mind which will render it healthier and happier, to get, I do not care how interested—the more interested the better—in a really good novel. It is better than medicine to have a good hearty laugh over something really entertaining. Those long-visaged persons who preach that this world is nothing but a scene of woe, and who think that nothing can be good unless it is very solemn, *may* be sincere, but for one I must be permitted to consider them sadly mistaken. . . .

I therefore put into your library a pretty large collection of good novels, and I am not sorry to see that you have been very diligent in the perusal of them. I gave you Scott and Cooper, Dickens and Thackeray, Kingsley and Reade, Miss Edgeworth, and Jane Austen, and Charlotte Bronte, Mrs. Gaskell and Miss Muloch, not to mention others of lesser note. And what a store of innocent pleasure do these names call up! Here is another world into which we can step aside to enjoy ourselves after our daily work in the real world is done. How are our imaginations stimulated, often our best feelings called out, by these marvellous creations of genius! And when we have had our recreation in this shadowy realm, we return refreshed again to our real world of sober duty. No doubt you may abuse this, as you may abuse any other good gift. If novel-reading takes you off from duty, leads to discontent with daily life, turns your head with romantic notions that can never be realized,—and novel-reading may do all this,—or, if instead of an occasional amusement, you make novel-reading the only occupation of your minds,—why, then you are abusing novel-reading, and showing yourself to be a deplorably weak and silly person. . . .

When I speak, then, of reading for amusement, I mean wholesome, not unwholesome reading. And I would set my standard high; I would throw aside merely silly books, though they may be ever so easy reading. There is no telling how much good you may do yourself by discrimination, how much harm by carelessness, even in light reading. Silly sentimentality and second-hand romance, what trash they are! Laura Matilda and her magnificent lover, the Count, and that darling sentimental correspondence, and the wedding at St. Bride's—how sweet it was! and that gentlemanly and romantic pirate, and that high-souled and high-spirited high-wayman,—how delightful! and what double-distilled nonsense! Depend upon it, you will spoil your appetite if you read trash. What sort of a digestion would you have if you were to feed on slops and sugar candy?

TWO VISUAL artifacts—a religious primer published by the American Tract Society and a page from an early sensational novel—exemplify several new forms of print that captured wide readerships. Religious publishers, such as the American Tract Society and the American Sunday-School Union, were among the most prolific publishers in the mid-nineteenth century. On one of its own title pages, reproduced here, the ATS offers a vision of how and where its books might be read. The cheap urban newspapers of the 1830s and 1840s appealed to a growing population of readers, although scholars disagree about whether they drew a predominantly working-class audience. Many of them won their audience by covering scandals, grisly murders, and other sensational stories. Unlike earlier newspapers—and the political papers that continued to dominate outside America's largest cities—these new papers employed their own reporters to cover events. In the process, they helped redefine what was "news." In *The Quaker City* (1845), his sensational novel about Philadelphia, the working-class newspaperman George Lippard (1822–1854) employed rhetoric and told stories much like the ones in the paper he published. Lippard's novel sold hundreds of thousands of copies in the mid-nineteenth century and stayed in print for decades.

The other three selections come from readers themselves. Michael Floy (1808–1837), an evangelical Methodist, lived in New York, worked at his family's nursery business, and belonged to various religious and reform societies. Julia A. Parker (1818–1852), originally a Vermonter, moved south to Germantown, Pennsylvania (near Philadelphia), in 1841 to teach at a girls' academy. Edward Jenner Carpenter (1825–1900), a doctor's son from a farming community, kept his journal during the year he worked as an apprentice cabinetmaker in Greenfield, a town in western Massachusetts. None of these readers' reflections was published during his or her own lifetime.

Excerpts from the Diary of Michael Floy (1833–37)[4]

October 20, 1833. Cold rainy weather throughout the day and evening. I went to Church twice & was chorister both in the morning & afternoon. The Sunday school was well attended considering the state of the weather, but I think it requires a person of pretty firm muscle to manage a Sunday school of youngsters, and I find I have continual need of a prayer or else I would soon be discouraged. I forgot to mention that last Friday I finished the Rambler. I intend now to confine myself to reading biographies and I accordingly began yesterday with (my favorite) Doddridge's Life of

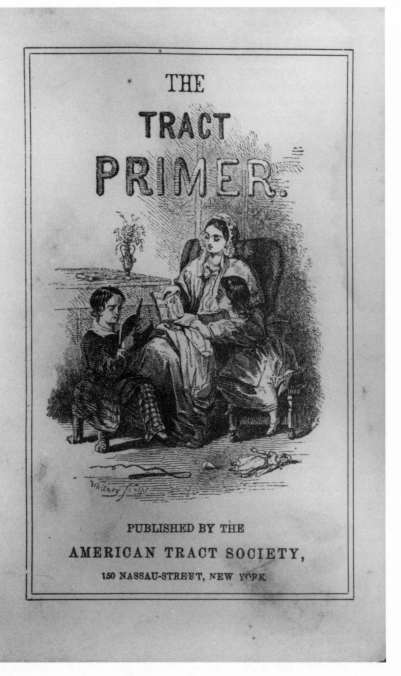

The Tract Primer (c. 1848)[5]

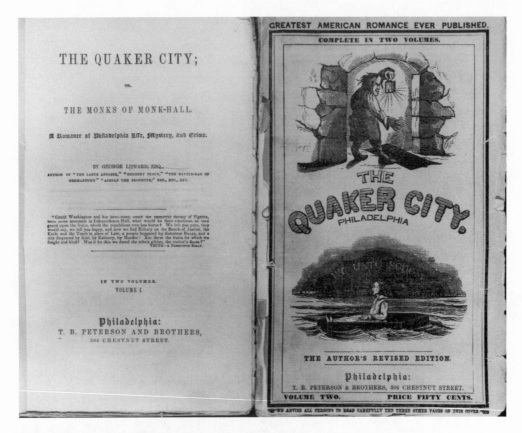

George Lippard, *The Quaker City* (c. 1858)[6]

Col. Gardiner. The dedication I think is beautifully done. I read the Bible & Testament (carrying the latter always about me) every day in the Week, and on Sundays I have not time to read any thing else. I was particularly struck with reading the 17th chap. of I Chronicles; what gratitude to his God, & ardent piety is there displayed by David.

October 22, 1833. Not much rain today, altho the weather is not clear, and no sun to be seen. I have not much to do on such days as this and yesterday, but I endeavor to employ my time in reading, and such is my thirst for knowledge, that I can truly say I esteem it above all earthly goods; and I keep no money in my pocket very long, for when I see a book that takes my fancy, have it I must. And altho I have purchased a great lot of Books, I do not regret that I have done so, because I generally purchase what I conceive is useful. I never read a novel in my life and I do not think I ever will, for I find so many books daily published that are of real use, that all my leisure time is not sufficient for reading even them.

Our woman Margaret has gone away, having taken to herself a husband. There was no class meeting in the Evening, and I did not choose to go to the Love feast in Allen-st. I this day finished reading Doddridge's Life of Gardiner and can truly say I have derived much benefit from the perusal; and I feel very thankful for enjoying such privileges of reading as I now have.

November 1, 1834. Same as yesterday. Recovering very slowly from my fever, continuing my fever-powders. Cold is very bad yet. Made an end of Lord Chesterfield today. The first volume I like the best, containing as it does pleasing and instructive letters on History to his son, and written in an elegant style. I admire them much, and yet these his lady had the greatest doubts about publishing. . . . The following [in Chesterfield] is most wicked advice: "In the course of the world a man must be able to accost and receive with smiles these whom he would rather meet with sword. In courts he must turn himself inside out. All this may, nay must be done." Again: "Never show the least symptom of resentment which you cannot gratify, but always smile when you cannot strike."

Reading over and over such advice as the above (for many of the letters are mere repetitions), I was glad to come to the end of them. His son, the dear young man, did not seem to relish such advice, notwithstanding it came from a parent, but appeared only anxious to improve his mind, and no doubt did so. What more could the lord want? Oh, he must be a man of pleasure, a gallant. Nonsense! could he not be polite, gentlemanly, easy, frank, without being an adulterer, a hypocrite, a duellist? I am surprised at his lordship's sense, for common sense he undoubtedly had. Some passages of the letters are very fine and contain good advice, expressed as I said before in an excellent style, very similar to that of Cobbett of the present day. I do not approve of some words made use of by Chesterfield. Perhaps he used some of them to show his lordly style. . . .

I am, however, determined after reading his lordship's injunctions to apply myself more to the art of pleasing than before. Nature has given me the faculty. I find that constant intercession at a throne of grace in behalf of all mankind makes me more and more interested in every person's welfare, even with the most humble beggar. If I can act out this principle so as to suit myself to all ages, ranks, conditions, this in my opinion constitutes politeness.

March 27, 1835. Somewhat rainy and quite warm. Went to Court for the last [for possible jury duty], but they were still at the same case as yesterday, so the remainder of the Jurors were discharged. The Court was thronged, the case being that of seduction: the "lady" as deep in the mud as her suitor in the mire, in my opinion. The action was brought by the father of the lady. He had hardly paid that attention to the girl's virtue which was incumbent upon him, for it was proved that on one occasion when there was a great racket among the gentleman and lady, the old fellow came out of his bed and told them not to make such a noise, adding "Do you think I keep a whore house?" . . . I fully believe the novels and romances have made a greater part of the prostitutes in the world, to say nothing of the many miserable matches. Many rush right into the married life after reading novels; they will do the same, they will be gallant, heroic, chivalric; but they find it to be a different matter from what they expected; they fret and foam but they are tied fast, and the poor lady is made miserable for life. This is supposing the best, but suppose the gentleman has no design to marry; he wins the heart of the foolish creature, seduces her, and then leaves her to her fate. Such things happen almost daily, and all, I believe, in consequence of novels.

April 25, 1836. Cold easterly wind. Went to Harlaem; finished heading down the Peach trees. Took up more than $100 worth of trees. Many orders were perplexing, but thanks to my mathematical head I was perfectly composed while about them. Bought a lot of young Plums & Cherries from Mr. Brown. In the Rail car coming down, saw a poor looking man and forlorn wife; a baby was in her arms; he would gape at it with the most endearing looks, then read a book which upon examination I found to be one of Harpers' Family Library, the Life of Sir Isaac Newton!

May 30, 1836. Finished Paulding's Life of Washington in 2 vols. It contains some valuable and original information concerning this great man. His [Paulding's] great care, however, to write high sounding sentences, pretty similes (altho some are hackneyed enough), gaudy tropes, has almost if not altogether ruined the work. Strange he had not more sense than to write so; but this is pretty much the case with all the American authors I have read. . . . I may be thought too severe in thus criticising a work which constitutes Nos. 75, 76 of the Family Library. Here then is a specimen or two. "Mount Vernon was thronged with visitors: it was the shrine where his countrymen came to pay their devotions." Is this a heathenish, Mohammedan, or blasphemous sentence? Oh no, it is only a highly figurative sentence. Then away with such figures in a Christian country! . . . Another matter: the work is spread out into two volumes of large type, so that there is more reading in *one* of the other numbers of the Family Library, but all the numbers are 50 cts. each, so the price is $1. Why charge so high? The reason is, Mr. Paulding has a copy right.

Excerpts from the Letters and Journal of Julia A. Parker (1837–41)[7]

Letters to "My Dear E."

Acworth, March 9, 1837

I received your letter from the hand of our friend, Mr. F— a few days since. With joy and gratitude I perused it, as a new pledge of my friend's affection. Yet let me ask, why did you not present yourself, instead of this consolatory bit of paper?— Why, my dearest, you cannot know the disappointment my heart experienced, when I was obliged to give up the hope of seeing you now, for months to come. . . .

You mentioned The Memoirs of Josephine, published by the Harpers. It is on my list for perusal. In our judgment of that incomparable woman, we agree. . . . My own reading for the past winter, has been occasionally, of the kind termed fictitious, which you dislike. Yet I must beg leave to differ from you, on the ground of its utility, as well as that of its moral tendency. I must deny the assertion of the poet, that

> 'Eyes dazzled by fiction's gaudy rays,
> In modest truth no light or beauty sees.'

I have just finished Fay's 'Norman Leslie.' It is a beautiful and instructive work of the kind. The hero is not a character entirely enveloped in the mantle of perfection, —thus robbed of *all* faults; but excellent and not unworthy of admiration. It abounds in fine description of natural scenery, and presents withal, some striking traits of American character. Some day when time hangs heavily, or passes too slowly, turn to the chaste and enchanting pages of 'Norman Leslie.'

I have spent the winter very, very pleasantly,—with my books has the time been mostly passed; what very kind friends they are; my reading has been both entertaining and instructive. Never in three months have I accomplished so much. We received The Republic of Letters last autumn, a selection of the best standard literature and English classics; it has received an attentive perusal. . . .

January, 1840

. . . I spend much of the time in reading and study. I have been laughing, weeping, and making merry over the pages of Waverley. I am now reading Chalmers' Treatise; also the life of Schiller, the great champion of German literature, a character full of interest, marked by such love of moral excellence, such devotion and success in intellectual pursuits. Since reading his life, and a criticism of his work, together with some other of the German authors, I feel a very strong desire of acquiring a perfect knowledge of that language which has become the vehicle of such transcendent elevation and originality of thought. . . .

I think of spending the remaining part of the winter in Keene [New Hampshire], with two prominent objects in view,—to exchange the isolation of our little village for something more animated, and to pursue my literary schemes more successfully.

May, 1840

I am reading Bancroft's History at present. We may congratulate ourselves in at length producing a historian worthy to write our unequalled history. So successfully commenced, it must proceed with increasing interest. Fortunate is the country that produces such a historian, but doubly fortunate the historian who has such a country to write. The bare facts of American history far transcend in pathos and interest the reality, the fable, the poetry, that lend such charm to the historic pages of Greece and Rome.

Have you read that inimitable work of Dickens, Nicholas Nickleby? Never did the pen of any writer present humanity with so much of meanness, selfishness, and vice, on the one hand, and such ethereal purity and excellence, on the other. Does truth preside over these delineations? Can human character sink to such frightful degradation? *Pardonnez-moi*, but I can scarcely believe that such a character as Squeers can be based upon the real: if so, it would be delightful to see him, or any of his stamp, tied to a whirlwind that had started in pursuit of a comet.

If you have not read the book, please do so, by my especial request.

Journal (written as a schoolteacher near Philadelphia)

June 28, 1841. Another day has gone. Nothing unusual has diversified it. The school duties completed, read portions of the life of Madam De Staël. She was a most interesting woman. I love to read of the splendid qualities that made up her character. What compliment, that Bonaparte dared not have her in his dominions by reason of her powerful influence.

July 5, 1841. Read from the Memoir of Margaret Davidson. Was intensely interested. Such astonishing powers of mind, developed at so early an age, I never conceived of before. The inimitable pen of Irving has embalmed her sweet memory for ever. She was, indeed, all that was lovely, as well as intellectually great. A sparkling gem in the constellation of American Literature.

July 10, 1841. Spent an hour this morning in the school-room relating to the young ladies some of the prominent characteristics of Margaret Davidson. They seemed much interested.

> 'Lives of goodness much remind us
> We can make our lives sublime.'

July 24, 1841. Read some extracts from the Biography of Madame De Staël in school this morning. I cannot contemplate a mind like hers without the most ardent longing to turn aside from the beaten track of life, and explore those rich fields of observation, those secret recesses of thought, that the gifted *few* alone may enter. I feel immortal longings rise within me. I would consecrate my life, yea, my whole life, to improvement,—to the perfection of my whole nature. Would that I were the favored child of knowledge, placed in the midst of her treasures, initiated into her deep mysteries. Surely I would be what I am not.

July 29, 1841. Was particularly struck with a few lines in the 'Editor's Table,' in the 'Lady's Book.' The writer speaking of the advancement of society, remarks, that in nothing is it so strikingly manifest, as in the fact, that during the last fifteen or twenty years, more has been written on the subject of female education, than all that has been written previously by any nation, or in any age of the world;—and that, too, in a style, and from motives so entirely different. One being to make her the theme of ridicule and satire; the other from a desire to elevate her as a social and moral being, preparing her for the high destiny assigned her by heaven, to be the gentle minister of virtue, the guide and director of mind from its first opening, and through its successive developments.

September 15, 1841.—Read 'Stephens's Travels in Central America.' How happy I am while reading a book like this. I have lived to-day only with the past. I envy the author the terrible dangers he passed; for what comparison do they bear with the satisfaction and interest one must feel in exploring the time-worn monuments of a people who have ceased to exist, and who have no place on the page of history.

December 10, 1841.—Commenced reading Boswell's Life of Johnson. Have been much interested. I love to read the life of a distinguished man. It is pleasant to dwell on those specimens of humanity, who have traced out for themselves a glorious path to fame, and done honor to the race.

What so noble, so commanding, as a mind that can originate beautiful thoughts, —thoughts that penetrate other minds with an omnipotent power, and unseal the passion fountains of the soul, kindling in the before torpid spirit an inextinguishable love of excellence, a thirst for higher things than the dull realities of life! Such a mind is indeed a ray from heaven, a spark of the Infinite and Eternal Spirit.

Excerpts from the Journal of Edward Jenner Carpenter (1844–45)[8]

Friday March 1st [1844]. According to my Fathers advice when I came here, which I have long neglected, I have concluded to commence a Journal and write down every night what has occurred during the day worthy of note. . . . I began today to take the Hampden Washingtonian of Mr. Eastman for which I am to pay him 75 cts. at the end of the year.

Sunday March 3rd. It has been a very pleasant day the snow disappears rapidly. I have been reading this evening a story called The Insubordination or the Shoemakers Daughters, an American story of real life by T. S. Arthur which I think is good.

Sunday March 10th. I staid in the shop in the forenoon & read some old Saturday Couriers alone Dexter having gone home.

I read today in the Saturday Courier a recipe for curing a burn viz. "Take a table spoonful of lard, half a table spoonful of spirits of turpentine, and a piece of rosin as big as a walnut, and simmer them together till melted, and then let them cool." Also a recipe for the Sick head ache. . . .

10 o'clock in the evening. After dinner I thought I would get ready and go to meeting but it being rather late before I got ready, I concluded that I would stay in the shop and read some old papers that I borrowed of Uncle Jo.

Thursday March 14th. Very pleasant & warm. I read tonight a story called Easy Nat or Boston bars and Bostons boys. It is the life of three boys during their apprenticeship one of them was Easy Nat who was led into drunkenness & all sorts of dissipation by his brother apprentice & afterwards became a Washingtonian & the other apprentice set his masters house on fire & then cut his throat. This shows the evil of drunken Companions. I finished the Bureau today that I begun a week ago last Monday. . . .

Tuesday March 26th. It has been the most pleasant day we have had this year.
   I went down to the Literary Club this evening and them debate on the question "Is novel reading beneficial["] did not stay till it was decided. I then came up to the shop & read 2 or 3 stories in the Saturday Courier besides some anecdotes puzzles & the like.

Thursday March 28th. It has rained considerable this afternoon & evening. I began this evening to read a novel called The Mysteries of Paris & as I have been considerably taken up with it I cannot write any more tonight

Thursday June 6th. Pretty fair day, not very warm, good day to work. Joseph K. Moore, George N. Allen, Henry A. Willis & myself wrote a letter tonight to Messrs Wilson & Co N.Y. to have them send us 4 copies of their Despatch one year only. It is a large monthly paper, only 25 cts a year   The first one I suppose will come the 1st of July.

Tuesday July 9th. Very pleasant, but it looks a little like rain this evening. . . . Mr. Eastman got out an Extra Gazette this morning with the news that Joe Smith the Mormon was dead. He was in jail with two others awaiting their trial for treason, & there was a guard place inside & outside of the jail, they fired upon the guard on the inside with some pistols they had in their possession and then went to get out of a window when he was shot through with more than a hundred balls, one of the other prisoners (Hirym Smith Joe's brother) was killed & the other prisoner was badly wounded. This happened June 26th at Carthage Ill. The Extra says also that they are having another riot in Philadelphia, & it is feared that there will be considerable bloodshed. . . .

Monday August 19th. A rainy day, & it is needed for it was getting rather dry & dusty. . . . I began a Panell end Bureau with double Ogee drawer this morning. I went into the Democrat office tonight & bought a book called the Omnibus of Modern Romance, it contains six novels, for which I paid 25 cents. I began one tonight called the "Game of life," the scene is laid in London & vicinity, & I think it is good so far as I have read.

Saturday March 1st [1845]. We had a snow squall this morning but it cleared off quite pleasant, but not as warm as it has been, the snow has gone so much that the boys have been playing ball today.

I began this Journal a year ago today, & the more I write in it the more I like to. I also began to take the Washingtonian a year ago today, for which I paid 75 cts. Dexter is going to take it in the year coming. Last night when I got into the shop I found a letter from my cousins David E. & Jonathan Alexander. It was 3 o'clock before I went to bed last night & I am rather sleepy tonight. I recived a paper from Jane Slate this week & I must send her one in return. My postage bill counts up considerable.

SHOULD SLAVES be taught to read and write? To what purposes might they put these skills? The debate over slaves' literacy escalated after several well-publicized slave revolts led by literate African Americans: Denmark Vesey's (led by a free black man) in 1822, Nat Turner's nine years later. Abolitionists, black and white, seized upon literacy as part of their crusade: the denial of literacy represented another inhumanity within the south's "peculiar institution." Meanwhile, attempting to quell further incitements to slave revolt, President Andrew Jackson's postmaster general forbade abolitionists from sending their literature in the United States mail. Frederick Douglass (1818–1895), a former slave who had escaped from Maryland, was already a nationally prominent abolitionist lecturer by the time he wrote his *Narrative*. In it he explained how he learned to read and write—and taught others to read as well—despite laws that forbade the teaching of slaves. Finally, two passages from Harriet Beecher Stowe's (1811–1896) *Uncle Tom's Cabin*, the best-selling American novel before the Civil War, illustrate how fiction could capture contemporary debates about literacy and reading. Douglass and Stowe both considered slavery evil, but they implied different notions of how enslaved people might use the printed word.

Frederick Douglass, *Narrative of the Life of Frederick Douglass, An American Slave* (1845)[9]

Very soon after I went to live with Mr. and Mrs. Auld, she very kindly commenced to teach me the A, B, C. After I had learned this, she assisted me in learning to spell words of three or four letters. Just at this point of my progress, Mr. Auld found out what was going on, and at once forbade Mrs. Auld to instruct me further, telling her, among other things, that it was unlawful, as well as unsafe, to teach a slave to read. To use his own words, further, he said, "If you give a nigger an inch, he will take an ell. A nigger should know nothing but to obey his master—to do as he is told to do. Learning would *spoil* the best nigger in the world. Now," said he, "if you teach that nigger (speaking of myself) how to read, there would be no keeping him. It would forever unfit him to be a slave. He would at once become unmanageable, and of no value to his master. As to himself, it could do him no good, but a great deal of harm. It would make him discontented and unhappy." These words sank deep in to my heart, stirred up sentiments within that lay slumbering, and called into existence an entirely new train of thought. It was a new and special revelation, explaining dark and mysterious things, with which my youthful understanding had struggled, but struggled in vain. I now understood what had been to me a most perplexing difficulty—to wit, the white man's power to enslave the black man. It was a grand achievement, and I prized it highly. From that moment, I understood the pathway from slavery to freedom. It was just what I wanted, and I got it at a time when I the least expected it. Whilst I was saddened by the thought of losing the aid of my kind mistress, I was gladdened by the invaluable instruction which, by the merest accident, I had gained from my master. Though conscious of the difficulty of learning without a teacher, I set out with high hope, and a fixed purpose, at whatever cost of trouble, to learn how to read. The very decided manner with which he spoke, and strove to impress his wife with the evil consequences of giving me instruction, served to convince me that he was deeply sensible of the truths he was uttering. It gave me the best assurance that I might rely with utmost confidence on the results which, he said, would flow from teaching me to read. What he most dreaded, that I most desired. What he most loved, that I most hated. That which was to him a great evil, to be carefully shunned, was to me a great good, to be diligently sought, and the argument which he so warmly urged, against my learning to read, only served to inspire me with a desire and determination to learn. In learning to read, I owe almost as much to the bitter opposition of my master, as to the kindly aid of my mistress. I acknowledge the benefit of both.

. . . I was now about twelve years old, and the thought of being *a slave for life* began to bear heavily upon my heart. Just about this time, I got hold of a book entitled "The Columbian Orator." Every opportunity I got, I used to read this book. Among much of other interesting matter, I found in it a dialogue between a master and his slave. The slave was represented as having run away from his master three times. The dialogue represented the conversation which took place between them, when the slave was retaken the third time. In this dialogue, the whole argument in behalf of slavery was brought forward by the master, all of which was disposed of by the slave. The slave was made to say some very smart as well as impressive things in reply to his master—things which had the desired though unexpected effect; for the conversation resulted in the voluntary emancipation of the slave on the part of the master.

In the same book, I met with one of Sheridan's mighty speeches on and in behalf of Catholic emancipation. These were choice documents to me. I read them over and over again with unabated interest. They gave tongue to interesting thoughts of my own soul, which had frequently flashed through my mind, and died away for want of utterance. The moral which I gained from the dialogue was the power of truth over the conscience of even a slave-holder. What I got from Sheridan was a bold denunciation of slavery, and a powerful vindication of human rights. The reading of these documents enabled me to utter my thoughts, and to meet the arguments brought forward to sustain slavery, but while they relieved me of one difficulty, they brought on another even more painful than the one of which I was relieved. The more I read, the more I was led to abhor and detest my enslavers. I could regard them in no other light than a band of successful robbers, who had left their homes, and gone to Africa, and stolen us from our homes, and in a strange land reduced us to slavery. I loathed them as being the meanest as well as the most wicked of men. As I read and contemplated the subject, behold! that very discontentment which Master Hugh had predicted would follow my learning to read had already come, to torment and sting my soul to unutterable anguish. As I writhed under it, I would at times feel that learning to read had been a curse rather than a blessing. . . .

Mr. Freeland was himself the owner of but two slaves. Their names were Henry Harris and John Harris. The rest of his hands he hired. These consisted of myself, Sandy Jenkins, and Handy Caldwell. Henry and John were quite intelligent, and in a very little while after I went there, I succeeded in creating in them a strong desire to learn how to read. This desire soon sprang up in the others also. They very soon mustered up some old spelling-books, and nothing would do but that I must keep a Sabbath school. I agreed to do so, and accordingly devoted my Sundays to teaching these my loved fellow-slaves how to read. Neither of them knew his letters when I went there. Some of the slaves of the neighboring farms found what was going on, and also availed themselves of this little opportunity to learn to read. It was understood, among all who came, that there must be as little display about it as possible. It was necessary to keep our religious masters at St. Michael's unacquainted with the fact, that, instead of spending the Sabbath in wrestling, boxing, and drinking whisky, we were trying to learn how to read the will of God; for they had much rather see us engaged in those degrading sports, than to see us behaving like intellectual, moral, and accountable beings. . . .

I held my Sabbath school at the house of a free colored man, whose name I deem it imprudent to mention; for should it be known, it might embarrass him greatly, though the crime of holding the school was committed ten years ago. I had at one time over forty scholars, and those of the right sort, ardently desiring to learn. They were of all ages, though mostly men and women. I look back to those Sundays with an amount of pleasure not to be expressed. They were great days to my soul. . . . They came because they wished to learn. Their minds had been starved by their cruel masters. They had been shut up in mental darkness. I taught them, because it was the delight of my soul to be doing something that looked like bettering the condition of my race. I kept up my school nearly the whole year I lived with Mr. Freeland; and, beside my Sabbath school, I devoted three evenings in the week, during the winter, to teaching the slaves at home. And I have the happiness to know, that several of those who came to Sabbath school learned how to read; and that one, at least, is now free through my agency.

Harriet Beecher Stowe, *Uncle Tom's Cabin* (1851)[10]

[Sold down the Mississippi River, the enslaved Tom is on a boat headed toward New Orleans.]

When there seemed to be nothing for him to do, he would climb to a nook among the cotton-bales of the upper deck, and busy himself in studying over his Bible,—and it is there we see him now. . . .

He saw the distant slaves at their toil; he saw afar their villages of huts gleaming out in long rows on many a plantation, distant from the stately mansions and pleasure-grounds of the master;—and as the moving picture passed on, his poor, foolish heart would be turning backward to the Kentucky farm, with its old shadowy beeches. . . .

In such a case, you write to your wife, and send messages to your children; but Tom could not write,—the mail for him had no existence, and the gulf of separation was unbridged by even a friendly word or signal. . . .

As for Tom's Bible, though it had no annotations and helps in margin from learned commentators, still it had been embellished with certain way-marks and guide-boards of Tom's own invention, and which helped him more than the most learned expositions could have done. It had been his custom to get the Bible read to him by his master's children, in particular by young Master George; and, as they read, he would designate, by bold, strong marks and dashes, with pen and ink, the passages which more particularly gratified his ear or affected his heart. His Bible was thus marked through, from one end to the other, with a variety of styles and designations; so he could in a moment seize upon his favorite passages, without the labor of spelling out what lay between them;—and while it lay there before him, every passage breathing of some old home scene, and recalling some past enjoyment, his Bible seemed to him all of this life that remained, as well as the promise of a future one.

[Months later, the angelic white child Eva St. Clare and her self-centered mother Marie converse.]

"Mamma," she said, suddenly, to her mother, one day, "why don't we teach our servants to read?"

"What a question child! People never do."

"Why don't they?" said Eva.

"Because it is no use for them to read. It don't help them to work any better, and they are not made for anything else."

"But they ought to read the Bible, mamma, to learn God's will."

"O! They can get that read to them all *they* need."

"It seems to me, mamma, the Bible is for every one to read themselves. They need it a great many times when there is nobody to read it."

"Eva, you are an odd child," said her mother. . . .

"Here's poor Mammy!" said Eva. "She does love the Bible so much, and wishes so she could read! And what will she do when I can't read to her?"

Marie was busy, turning over the contents of a drawer, as she answered.

"Well, of course, by and by, Eva, you will have other things to think of besides reading the Bible round to servants. Not but that is very proper; I've done it myself, when I had health. But when you come to be dressing and going into company, you won't have time. See here!" she added, "these jewels I'm going to give you when you come out. I wore them to my first ball. I can tell you, Eva, I made a sensation." . . .

"Are these worth a lot of money, mamma?"

"To be sure, they are. Father sent to France for them. They are worth a small fortune."

"I wish I had them," said Eva, "to do what I pleased with!"

"What would you do with them?"

"I'd sell them, and buy a place in the free states, and take all our people there, and hire teachers, to teach them to read and write. . . . I'd teach them to read their own Bible, and write their own letters, and read letters that are written to them. . . ."

COMMENTARY: CREATING "INTELLECTUAL, MORAL, AND ACCOUNTABLE BEINGS"

For those who prescribed what their fellow Americans should read, literacy could degrade as well as enlighten. Falling in with the wrong sorts of books, magazines, and newspapers could ruin individuals' character as surely as associating with the wrong sorts of companions could. Conversely, proper reading—both the works one selected and the ways one read them—could strengthen men's and women's, boys' and girls' morality, intellect, patriotism, and right habits. Prescriptions for reading between the Revolution and the Civil War took myriad forms: sermons, conduct manuals, letters from parents to their children, even an 1855 book called *Confessions and Experience of a Novel Reader*. This proliferation of advice undoubtedly reflected the contemporary increase in printed materials. More of everything was being published every year: books in dozens of genres, magazines, newspapers, religious tracts, political pamphlets, advertisements. More people were reading, too. Women figured prominently among the new readers; by the 1840s, so did working-class Americans across the northeast. But much of the advice to readers presumed something else:

SCOTT E. CASPER

that individuals possessed the freedom and the responsibility to make their own moral choices, no less than their own literary ones. Derived from evangelical religion, encouraged by a democratic political system, and strengthened as many Americans migrated from traditional agricultural families to growing towns and cities, the concept of free agency—intellectual, moral, economic—pervaded American life in the early republic. This new sense of agency carried with it a sense of awesome responsibility: of accountability for one's own morality or immorality, success or failure, character or degradation. Hence the fears that the wrong reading would make the wrong sorts of Americans. Hence too, however, the sense that the right reading could expand opportunities for people of all classes, both sexes, and diverse occupations.

The most prolific disseminators of the printed word, the religious tract societies that distributed hundreds of thousands of tracts annually from the 1820s on, championed the centuries-old belief that reading had a moral purpose. Some of these societies became the most vocal critics of novel reading. At the same time, much of their literature employed the conventions of fiction by the 1840s: vivid storytelling about believable characters (who resisted or overcame temptation, or suffered direly for not doing so). Even as colporteurs (traveling agents who sold or gave away tracts) encouraged readers to peruse books in traditional ways—carefully, repeatedly, as one might read the Bible—they also helped democratize religious reading during the Second Great Awakening, carrying their wares to many people who had never owned books before. The moral purpose of reading figured also in the concept of "domesticity," the emerging idea of women's roles that works such as Lydia Maria Child's *The Mother's Book* prescribed. In the domestic ideal, women bore the principal responsibility for their children's education. The middle-class home, newly separated from the world of economic production and presumably insulated from the competitive world of the marketplace that threatened men's moral fiber every day, became the setting for children's moral instruction. Books would be a central vehicle of that instruction: not just those that mothers read to or with their children, but also the books (such as Child's) mothers read in order to develop their own moral and didactic instincts.

As Julia Parker's reading illustrates, however, it is inaccurate to assume that women read predominantly for moral lessons or that women's reading served primarily to confine them in new, domestic roles. Parker did study religious books as she experienced a spiritual awakening in the early 1840s, but these were only a fraction of her reading. More often she read secular works that advanced her literary and intellectual ambitions: leading novels of the day, magazines such as *Godey's Lady's Book* that espoused the cause of an educated American womanhood, biographies of authors who had inspired her. Those authors were mostly women of intellect, whose accomplishments provided models for Parker and her students in Philadelphia. Other American women shared Parker's thirst for learning and her sense that intellectual development allowed women to transcend their daily obligations. Women formed literary societies, social libraries, and reading classes; they described and recommended books in their letters to female friends. As one historian puts it, "reading women made books a site for experiments in personal transformation" (Kelley, 403). So did many men, of course—but men had a wider variety of other outlets for self-formation, and women perhaps more than men embraced reading explicitly for its intellectual opportunities.

Men's transformations through reading more frequently occurred as parts of a multifaceted process that mid-nineteenth-century Americans called "self-making." At its simplest, this process was economic: the struggle to find and learn a vocation or trade. Reading could play a role here. In addition to literary and religious fare, the young New Yorker Michael Floy perused books on flower breeding, presumably in order to advance his family's nursery business. Young urban clerks and aspiring merchants could read periodicals directed to them, such as Freeman Hunt's *Merchant's Magazine and Commercial Review*; farmers could find dozens of agricultural periodicals. Much advice in these occupational magazines and newspapers was practical. At the same time, they aimed higher: to the reader's intellect and character. Agricultural magazines sometimes ran stories of farmers who established reading rooms, implying the importance of reading. *Merchant's Magazine* devoted considerable attention to the character traits that young men needed to cultivate: honesty, sobriety, steady habits, an aversion to speculation. Beyond the occupational periodicals, fiction for young men also carried moral lessons. Edward Jenner Carpenter, a young apprentice cabinetmaker in western Massachusetts, described the temperance lessons he took from stories like "Easy Nat, or Boston Bars and Boston Boys." Michael Floy's reading for character formation was more complex. Much of it consisted of religious books: Philip Doddridge's *Life of Col. James Gardiner* told the biography of a "Christian soldier" prominent in the eighteenth century, and at least five of Floy's books came from New York's Methodist publishing house. But Floy also read Lord Chesterfield's *Letters to His Son*, a guide to the formation of "polite" character that had been popular among America's colonial gentry and remained widely read in the plantation south. Chesterfield's advice pertained largely to manners: how one could be admired in public. This emphasis on surface appearance annoyed Floy (as did some of the book's eighteenth-century language), but he kept reading anyway. In the end, he interpreted Chesterfield through his own evangelical reformer's frame of reference: he would define "politeness" as being "more and more interested in every person's welfare, even with the most humble beggar." The sorts of self-formation that books recommended were not always the lessons that readers imbibed.

Of course, women and men did not inhabit wholly separate worlds of books. Some genres (recipe books, farming manuals) certainly appealed to one gender. Others—novels (notably Walter Scott's), biographies, histories, literary magazines—found both male and female readers. At the level of experience, we can see men and women reading together and influencing each other's choices. Kentucky-born Sarah Hill married transplanted Vermonter Calvin Fletcher in 1821; together they made their home in the new town of Indianapolis, Indiana. Calvin became his wife's tutor, prescribing for her the sort of "masculine" reading he did: rhetoric, poetry, science, arithmetic, even Chesterfield—but virtually no novels. Only after Sarah began raising children did their spheres diverge: hers into daily routine (and away from books), his into legal practice (Brown, 190–93, 235–40; Thornbrough and Riker, 1:43–102, 3:25–81). Even households whose members each had their own reading fare may have enjoyed reading together in annual gift books of poetry and fiction, novels, or magazines that included a variety of material suited to the whole family. Mary and Daniel Child of Boston engaged in just such companionate reading. Although he read far more than she did, much of his reading was aloud—probably to her, their children, and other family members. Their interests ranged widely and often reflected their shared everyday lives and concerns: Unitarian sermons and tracts (many written by ministers they had heard), reform literature, even a scientific essay about comets on a winter night when they saw one (Zboray and Zboray, "Reading and Everyday Life"). Frederick Douglass's 1845 *Narrative* reveals another setting where women and men came together over books: the Sabbath school Douglass surreptitiously conducted for slaves near his master's plantation.

Douglass's *Narrative*, contemporaneous slave narratives, and many later interviews of former slaves illustrate how enslaved Americans prized literacy. Writing particularly for a northern, white audience, Douglass emphasized the connection between literacy and freedom. After all, by 1845 many northern cities and towns had widespread public schooling, and northern whites had nearly universal literacy. This audience would be outraged that southern states made it a crime to teach slaves to read or write, just as it would be shocked by Douglass's images of African Americans sold away from their families or whipped mercilessly. Denial of literacy, disrespect for family, and cruel punishment would all resonate with the very middle class that in these years read together, enshrined the home as a haven of morality, and eschewed corporal punishment. In fact, most southern laws against teaching slaves were relatively recent, enacted in the wake of Nat Turner's rebellion, which seemed to exemplify the dangers of literate blacks. Only Virginia, Georgia, and the Carolinas banned the teaching of slaves for the entire period from 1830 to 1865, and Virginia's law prohibited only the assembly of slaves for teaching, not education of slaves individually by their masters. Literacy laws were rarely enforced in court. But Douglass's book was more than brilliant abolitionist rhetoric: it also showed the multiple ways slaves valued literacy as a hallmark of freedom. First, reading the Bible connoted a kind of spiritual freedom. Second, the process of learning to read often involved tricking one's master: asking to hear the same biblical passage again and again, then examining the book later and figuring out the letters and syllables; finding odd times and places to peruse books or take lessons from literate fellow slaves or free blacks. Finally, the ability to write could advance one's physical progress toward freedom: masters especially feared slaves who could write and thus could forge the passes that allowed them off their plantations, as did Douglass himself.

Douglass's *Narrative* also offered glimpses of how slaves could learn to read and write, and what they could make of their reading. Like free people, many slaves had religious motives for education: literacy meant learning to read the Bible, not just hear it from the mouths of white ministers or their own literate preachers. Some southern ministers recognized the incongruity of Christianizing slaves without educating them: Did not evangelical Protestantism depend upon every individual's familiarity with the Bible? Charles Colcock Jones, a minister who embraced reform movements (women's rights, Cherokee rights) and established a Presbyterian and Baptist mission for Georgia blacks, wrote a book calling for *The Religious Instruction of Negroes in the United States* in 1847. A slave owner himself, Jones apparently taught his own slaves to read and write, even if his book advocated only oral instruction because of southern literacy laws (Cornelius, 35–36). The specific book from which Douglass learned how to argue against slavery, *The Columbian Orator*, was a popular textbook in the early republic: schoolchildren read its speeches and stories to learn the arts of reading, rhetoric, and oratory. More than most children, Douglass found meaning in those speeches—and in the story of the articulate runaway slave, he found an example that suited his condition as clearly as "Easy Nat" suited Edward Jenner Carpenter's. Easy Nat and the runaway slave shared a significant characteristic: both exemplified how the individual must assume responsibility for his own freedom, whether from drink or from bondage.

Different forms and genres of print, then, fostered particular kinds of self-formation: intellectual development, moral improvement, liberty from chattel slavery. And books that meant something to one audience, whether Chesterfield's *Letters to His Son* or *The Columbian Orator*, could possess very different meaning for readers in other circumstances. Two sorts of reading contexts are critical. We might call the first "nonliterary": the ways in which personal or social circumstances affect what and how people read. Frederick Douglass's condition as a slave, Julia Parker's as a woman seeking intellectual fulfillment and as a schoolteacher hoping to inspire her students, Michael Floy's as an urban evangelical in a period of reform movements, Edward Jenner Carpenter's as an apprentice living among other apprentices and participating in political rallies and debating clubs: such circumstances affected the ways these young men and women read. Nonliterary contexts also shaped where and with whom people actually did their reading: in family parlors, workplaces, newspaper offices, railway cars. The other sorts of contexts are "literary": the ways in which people's particular access to print culture influenced the choices and meanings they made. It is important, for instance, that Floy could buy books directly from the Methodist publishing house in New York while Carpenter depended upon friends and relatives to send him newspapers from other cities and towns. Americans who borrowed books from libraries or discussed books in literary clubs experienced reading collectively. Literary context also included the forms and genres in which one received print. Floy, for example, read numerous volumes in the Harper's Family Library series, published by one of America's emergent capitalist firms of the 1830s. Carpenter often described stories from the newspapers—a very different sort of reading, which contained diverse articles closely juxtaposed. Understanding readers' contexts is essential if we are to consider books within people's everyday lives, not just as intellectual experiences or escapes from those lives.

The problem for historians of the book lies in the fragmentary evidence of nine-teenth-century Americans' reading. Letters, diaries, and published memoirs—much of the evidence in this chapter—survive from only a tiny fraction of readers. The readers who wrote such documents came from a limited swath of American society: not merely the literate, but those with the time and the inclination to record their thoughts. Most slaves, even those who could read and write, had little such time or inclination. Hence our surviving records come largely from published narratives like Douglass's and interviews conducted with former slaves long after emancipation (many of them as part of the Federal Writers Project in the 1930s). Similarly, historians have suggested that members of the working classes constituted a primary audience for several cheap forms of print, such as sensationalistic penny newspapers and dime novels. Few such readers left evidence to prove or disprove this claim, even if much of those works' contents seems intended for laboring audiences. Edward Carpenter may have been an apprentice when he kept his diary, but this physician's son did not follow the cabinetmaking trade for long: a few years after he kept his diary in 1844–45, he moved north to Brattleboro, Vermont, where he opened a bookstore and became town librarian for nearly thirty years. Carpenter's diary, with its emphasis on self-culture and self-making, suggests another gap in our knowledge: to this point, most scholarship on actual antebellum readers focuses on the northeast. Did southerners and westerners, especially in rural places, share the reading experiences and responses of their contemporaries in rural New England, Boston, New York, or Philadelphia?

Even the extant documents require sensitive reading if we are to comprehend the light they shed on print culture. For instance, slave narratives tended to minimize the extent of reading among slaves in order to reinforce the point that slavery denied human beings this fundamental right. Young men and women in their teens and twenties often kept diaries expressly to record their progress toward character or education, and some intended these diaries to be read by a parent. They may well have written about their reading in phrases suited to the project of self-improve-ment: witness Michael Floy's statement that he had "derived much benefit" from Doddridge's *Life of Gardiner*. Other descriptions of books copied the language of the books themselves. Young readers sometimes incorporated the flowery prose of novels into their own diary entries. Moreover, these Americans read—and wrote about their reading—amid myriad prescriptions about what and how to read, from parents, ministers, advice manuals, lectures, and magazines. In short, many readers' diaries were themselves literary endeavors.

Novels such as *Uncle Tom's Cabin* also offered scenes of reading and writing. Indeed, such scenes were as commonplace in antebellum fiction as discussions about novel reading had been in novels of the 1790s and early 1800s. In lamenting Tom's inability to write letters to his family, Harriet Beecher Stowe evoked an experience increasingly familiar to antebellum white Americans. Migration—as far west as California—was separating members of white families, even as commerce was dividing enslaved fam-ilies. But thanks to a national postal system (the largest department of the federal government), literate people could maintain contact with newly distant friends and relations. Like Edward Jenner Carpenter, they could send and receive newspapers in the mail, too. Tom's exclusion from this experience was certainly characteristic of most slaves, but Stowe was not merely aiming to describe his deprivation. This scene pressed her political point: Slavery violated the bonds of family. If fiction can help us understand debates over reading, it—even more than readers' diaries—must be read with the author's perspective in mind. In Stowe's case, that perspective was less subversive than Frederick Douglass's: whereas the former slave stressed how literacy could pave the path to freedom, the northern white author imagined slave literacy largely in terms of Bible reading and familial communication.

Historians of the book have recently begun to explore other sorts of evidence. Using the circulation records of nineteenth-century libraries, several scholars have analyzed what people checked out, thus providing a window onto communal reading practices. For instance, the patrons of the Washington County Farmers' and Mechanics' Library in rural Cambridge, New York, checked out predominantly histories, biographies, and the historical novels of Walter Scott and Jane Porter when the library opened in 1817. Some of these works were so popular that members borrowed the first volume and found the second already checked out when they returned for it. By the 1840s far fewer books were being checked out—perhaps the library's collection had not kept pace with new literary tastes—and the remaining members were borrowing sensational true-life stories of pirates, criminals, and steamboat disasters (Washington County Records). Such records do not tell us who within a library member's household actually read the borrowed book, but they do reveal the circulation of books among people who had paid to join a community of readers. Postal records provide another fruitful source. Many local nineteenth-century post offices kept records of newspapers and magazines that arrived by mail; where these records survive, they too offer a sense of how members of a local community maintained connections to larger worlds of communication through periodical reading (Thomas, 99–141). Where people left no accounts of their reading, sometimes other observers did: itinerant booksellers, notably the agents of the religious tract societies, sent letters back to their employers about how people responded to them and their books. Because these agents often traveled to areas where books were scarce, their reports offer glimpses into worlds far from the cosmopolitan readers most likely to leave diaries (Nord).

The meanings and the contexts of reading cannot be understood apart from each other. Nineteenth-century writers prescribed particular courses of study for specific audiences, from aspiring professionals to young women to working-class men. Many men and women read for the same reasons those writers prescribed. More often, however, individuals' reading choices and habits emerged in the circumstances of their daily lives. Whether they read for pure escape, for moral or intellectual edification, for solutions to practical concerns, or for advancement in their occupations, their reading helped shape those lives.

SOURCE NOTES

[Unless otherwise indicated artifacts and documents are reproduced courtesy of the American Antiquarian Society (AAS), Worcester, Massachusetts.]

1. William A. Alcott, *The Young Man's Guide* (1833; reprint, Boston: T. R. Marvin, 1846), 209–22.

2. Lydia Maria Child, *The Mother's Book* (Boston: Carter, Hendee & Babcock, 1831), 86–97.

3. W. P. Atkinson, *Books and Reading: A Lecture* (Boston: Crosby, Nichols, Lee, & Co., 1860), note; 18–21.

4. Michael Floy, *The Diary of Michael Floy Jr., Bowery Village 1833–1837*, ed. Richard Albert Edward Brooks (New Haven, Conn.: Yale University Press, 1941), 6–7, 115–16, 147–48, 232, 239. Copyright © Yale University Press. Reproduced courtesy Yale University Press, New Haven, Conn.

5. *The Tract Primer* (New York: American Tract Society, ca. 1848).

6. George Lippard, *The Quaker City* (Philadelphia: T. B. Peterson and Brothers, ca. 1858).

7. E. Latimer, ed., *Life and Thought: Cherished Memorials of the Late Julia A. Parker Dyson*, 2d ed. (Philadelphia: Claxton, Remsen, Hafflefinger & Co., 1871), 11–12, 42–44, 58–79.

8. Edward Jenner Carpenter, "Journal," March 1, 1844–June 30, 1845, Manuscripts Collection, American Antiquarian Society, Worcester, Mass.

9. Frederick Douglass, *Narrative of the Life of Frederick Douglass, An American Slave* (Boston: Anti-Slavery Office, 1845), 33–34, 39–40, 80–82.

10. Harriet Beecher Stowe, *Uncle Tom's Cabin; or, Life Among the Lowly* (Boston: John P. Jewett & Co., 1852), 1:209–11, 2:67–69.

WORKS CITED

Brown, Richard D. *Knowledge Is Power: The Diffusion of Information in Early America, 1700–1865.* New York: Oxford University Press, 1989.

Confessions and Experience of a Novel Reader . . . By a Physician. Chicago: Wm. Stacy, 1855.

Cornelius, Janet Duitsman. *When I Can Read My Title Clear: Literacy, Slavery, and Religion in the Antebellum South.* Columbia: University of South Carolina Press, 1991.

Kelley, Mary. "Reading Women/Women Reading: The Making of Learned Women in Antebellum America." *Journal of American History* 83 (September 1996): 401–24.

Nord, David Paul. "Religious Reading and Readers in Antebellum America." *Journal of the Early Republic* 15 (Summer 1995): 241–72.

Thomas, Amy M. "Who Makes the Text? The Production and Use of Literature in Antebellum America." Ph.D. diss., Duke University, 1993.

Thornbrough, Gayle, and Dorothy L. Riker, eds. *The Diary of Calvin Fletcher.* 9 vols. Indianapolis: Indiana Historical Society, 1972–83.

Washington County (N.Y.) Farmers' and Mechanics' Library Records. Manuscripts Collection, American Antiquarian Society, Worcester, Mass.

Zboray, Ronald J., and Mary Saracino Zboray. "Reading and Everyday Life in Antebellum Boston: The Diary of Daniel F. and Mary D. Child." *Libraries & Culture* 32 (Summer 1997): 285–323.

FOR FURTHER RESEARCH

Augst, Thomas. "The Business of Reading in Nineteenth-Century America: The New York Mercantile Library." *American Quarterly* 50 (June 1998): 267–305.

Brown, Richard D. *The Strength of a People: The Idea of an Informed Citizenry in America, 1650–1870.* Chapel Hill: University of North Carolina Press, 1996.

Casper, Scott E. *Constructing American Lives: Biography and Culture in Nineteenth-Century America.* Chapel Hill: University of North Carolina Press, 1999.

Clark, Christopher, ed. "The Diary of an Apprentice Cabinetmaker: Edward Jenner Carpenter's 'Journal' 1844–45." *Proceedings of the American Antiquarian Society* 98, pt. 2 (1988): 303–94.

Dickinson, Cindy. "Creating a World of Books, Friends, and Flowers: Gift Books and Inscriptions, 1825–1860." *Winterthur Portfolio* 31 (Spring 1996): 53–66.

Doherty, Linda J. "Women as Readers: Visual Representations." *Proceedings of the American Antiquarian Society* 107, pt. 2 (1997): 335–88.

Gilmore, William J. "Peddlers and the Dissemination of Printed Material in Northern New England, 1780–1840." In *Itinerancy in New England and New York: The Dublin Seminar for New England Folklife, Annual Proceedings, 1984.* Boston: Boston University Press, 1986.

———. *Reading Becomes a Necessity of Life: Material and Cultural Life in Rural New England, 1780–1835.* Knoxville: University of Tennessee Press, 1989.

Glynn, Tom. "Books for a Reformed Republic: The Apprentices' Library of New York City, 1820–1865." *Libraries & Culture* 34 (Fall 1999): 347–72.

Gross, Robert A.. "Much Instruction from Little Reading: Books and Libraries in Thoreau's Concord." *Proceedings of the American Antiquarian Society* 97, pt. 1 (1987): 129–88.

———. "Reconstructing Early American Libraries: Concord, Massachusetts, 1795–1850." *Proceedings of the American Antiquarian Society* 97, pt. 2 (1987): 331–451.

Gutjahr, Paul. *An American Bible: A History of the Good Book in the United States, 1777–1880.* Stanford, Calif.: Stanford University Press, 1999.

Halttunen, Karen. *Murder Most Foul: The Killer and the American Gothic Imagination.* Cambridge, Mass.: Harvard University Press, 1998.

*Harris, Michael H. "'Spiritual Cakes Upon the Waters': The Church as a Disseminator of the Printed Word on the Ohio Valley Frontier to 1850." In *Getting the Books Out: Papers of the Chicago Conference on the Book in 19th-Century America*, edited by Michael Hackenberg, 98–120.

Hayes, Kevin J. "Railway Reading." *Proceedings of the American Antiquarian Society* 106, pt. 2 (1997): 301–26.

Henkin, David. *City Reading: Written Words and Public Spaces in Antebellum New York.* New York: Columbia University Press, 1998.

Jaffee, David. "The Village Enlightenment in New England, 1760–1820." *William and Mary Quarterly*, 3d ser., 47 (July 1990): 327–46.

Kaser, David. *A Book for a Sixpence: The Circulating Library in America.* Pittsburgh: Beta Phi Mu, 1979.

Lehuu, Isabelle. *Carnival on the Page: Popular Print Media in Antebellum America.* Chapel Hill: University of North Carolina Press, 2000.

Leonard, Thomas C. "News at the Hearth: A Drama of Reading in Nineteenth-Century America." *Proceedings of the American Antiquarian Society* 102, pt. 2 (1993): 379–401.

Machor, James L., ed. *Readers in History: Nineteenth-Century American Literature and the Contexts of Response.* Baltimore, Md.: Johns Hopkins University Press, 1993.

Perlmann, Joel, and Dennis Shirley. "When Did New England Women Acquire Literacy?" *William and Mary Quarterly*, 3d ser., 48 (January 1991): 50–67.

Stewart, David M. "Cultural Work, City Crime, Reading, Pleasure." *American Literary History* 9 (Winter 1997): 676–701.

Zboray, Ronald J., and Mary Saracino Zboray. "'Have You Read. . . ?' Real Readers and Their Responses in Antebellum Boston and Its Region." *Nineteenth-Century Literature* 52 (September 1997): 139–70.

7

Publishing an Emergent "American" Literature

SUSAN S. WILLIAMS

IN 1820 Sydney Smith, an English clergyman and critic for the *Edinburgh Review*, asked a question that would almost immediately become notorious on the western side of the Atlantic. "In the four quarters of the globe," Smith queried, "who reads an American book?" Despite its smug tone of superiority, some implications of Smith's question were valid: the American book market was dependent in many ways on the English one, and the younger country had not yet established a coherent literary tradition to call its own. Indeed, many Americans seem to have believed that without such a tradition the nation could never be culturally independent from England.

For the next several decades, authors, critics, and publishers in the United States responded vigorously to the challenge in Smith's question by trying to produce "great" literature that was also particularly "American." Some writers, like Nathaniel Hawthorne, tried to elevate American materials, to create out of the country's Puritan past a literary myth that would inform the present. Others, like Walt Whitman, attempted bold stylistic experiments intended to create an American idiom. Harriet Beecher Stowe's *Uncle Tom's Cabin*, a panorama of American society and a critique of American slavery, sold hundreds of thousands of copies. By 1870 the validity of Smith's claim seemed to have evaporated—not only did Americans produce and market hundreds of thousands of American books each year, but authors, critics, readers, and publishers had established a national "canon," a body of important literary works and a constellation of "great" authors. This canon allowed Americans to claim that their literature—indeed, their culture—had come of age.

In the process of creating an American literature, authors and publishers developed new relationships and new ways of practicing their business. Early in the period, there was a genteel quality about these relationships, a sense that those involved in the book trade were all gentlemen and should behave as such. But as the century wore on and the economics of publishing became more and more clear to those who wanted to have their texts published, and as more and more women entered the literary marketplace and challenged male authority in it, the genteel sheen of publishing began to wear off, leaving behind it an emergent, professional market for the written—and printed—word.

ARTIFACTS

During the first half of the nineteenth century American authors struggled to understand themselves, both as authors and as citizens of the United States, in comparison to England and its rich, centuries-old literary tradition. The opening artifacts in this chapter display three examples of such comparison. An anonymous contribution to the *United States Literary Gazette*, published in 1825, defined literary greatness as a quality that transcends national boundaries, but then concluded by associating a particular mode of writing, "the prophetic," with the United States. (The *United States Literary Gazette*, a semi-monthly periodical of literary news and criticism, appeared between 1824 and 1826. Its contributors included such prominent American writers as William Cullen Bryant and Henry Wadsworth Longfellow.) By mid-century Ralph Waldo Emerson (1803–1882) ranked among America's foremost literary men, thanks in large part to his famous lectures on both sides of the Atlantic. In his 1844 essay "The Poet," Emerson found great potential but little originality in American literature. Criticizing American authors for too slavishly following English models, he exhorted them to "chaunt our own times and social circumstances." Herman Melville (1819–1891) was also well-known by then, but not primarily for the now-classic *Moby-Dick*. Rather, Melville had won popularity for his South Seas adventure novels, including *Typee* and *Omoo*. In his 1851 review of Hawthorne's *Mosses from an Old Manse*, Melville argued that American authors must and do succeed on the basis of their own originality and national vision.

"Authors and Writers," from *The United States Literary Gazette* (1825)[1]

Authors never die. The good and the evil they do, alike live after them. The body may be dead, but the mind lives; on earth too; and will live. Men's minds, as others know them, are known by what they say, do, and write. We have had men amongst us who never wrote any thing, but who, nevertheless, acted widely upon others by conversation alone. They thought as deeply, and as accurately, and talked with the same precision and order, as if they were thinking for writing, or were actually writing. Their opinions were sought for, where they might be useful, and were as accessible as if they were on the bookseller's counter, or in the library. These were strictly authors. They are, however, necessarily short-lived. Their records are not permanent. They are not the property of the whole, and which the whole will find a common pride and interest to preserve, and to preserve unadulterated. They are the property of a few, which the few will appropriate, and may alter and deform without mercy, and without fear. It is melancholy to see the mind thus dying to its own age, and to the future. If we have felt safer while such a mind was with us and near us, when danger was abroad, or anticipated, we have lost much when we have lost it. We have acquired a habit of dependence, and have felt it to be the direct and useful product of the greater and better power of another. It has been a useful dependence, for its quality has been to make our own minds stronger and better. There has been an advantage to us, perhaps, that these men have not written. Their honest and sound views have not been submitted either to vulgar impertinence, or party malevolence. The sharp, and sometimes effective, criticism of lesser minds, or the encounter of as strong, differently, and, it may be, less prudently directed, has not hurt our faith, or diminished our confidence. We have reposed delightedly and usefully beneath the protection of a fine mind, and, it may be, for the time, have not been disquieted, that we have had so few with us. The influence that has been so limited and personal, however, might have been felt every where. In its degree perhaps less vividly, but in its amount far greater. Above all, if these men had written, they would have survived the grave.

Men are known, it was said, by what they do. The men about whom we have written, were known in this way, and a wide and useful influence was exerted by their actions. It is a property of such minds to be consistent with themselves. They have been cautious in their decisions, and what is truth with them, is not unfrequently one of its nearest approximations. Theirs has been a study of human experience in its varieties and causes. The distinctions they have made, have proceeded out of the actual differences of things. What such men were or thought years ago, or yesterday, in regard to the great questions of human concern, they would be, or think to-day. They have taught us what, and how they are; and if they have seemed different beings to us at any time, the change has most probably belonged to our own minds, not to theirs. . . .

But these men have not written. They gave their minds to perishing records, the memories of men. A few years, and it will be difficult to remember their faces. If we remember their thoughts, it may not be to better our own, or to act by them.

Men, in the third place, are known by what they write. This remark wants large qualification. Writers are authors by emphasis, in common speaking. But all who write are not so. Few men give us what others have not given us before. Other men's thoughts have passed through their minds, it is true, but they have come out as they went in. It is rare that they get even a new costume, and if they do, how frequently are they only deformed by it. These are writers. An author is one whose mind has not been the highway of other men's thoughts, but a soil into which they have been cast, like seed into the good ground, and where they have died in the upspringings and full harvest of higher and brighter thoughts. The observation of men and of nature has done the same thing. An affinity, if the term be allowed, has, in these men, subsisted between their own minds and the minds of other men. And they have detected motive, where other men have only been taken with the conduct. They thus take us in their works to the deep springs of human action, and show to us all its sources, whether pure or impure, however wickedly selfish, or honourably disinterested. These men are authors, for they are eminently *producers*; for when they have written, the world has got something which it had not before. These are rare men. Ages have passed away without them. When they have appeared, it has been sometimes accidentally, and the world has not known its own; and they have had no other reward but the incommunicable one, which a fine mind always has, and always must have, in the noble company of its thoughts. The works of such men have been a legacy to all posterity. And how sacred has been the entail; how careful have we been of the patrimony, and how jealous lest its fame should become the property of another.

The authors of whom we write never repeat themselves. Let characters or incidents be as numerous as they may, a real individuality is preserved every where. You constantly perceive that the various beings created are conscious of their own identity, and act in consequence of it; and that the distinctions between them belong as naturally to this consciousness as they do to the same thing in actual life. Shakespeare was pre-eminent in this character of original authorship. His dead, and equally his living, never appear again when he has done with them, either to push us from our stools, or jostle us in our way. The ghost of Banquo appears indeed to the disturbed imagination of his own Macbeth; but it had no form or being to Shakespeare's mind any more than it had to the vision of the royal guests. When Hostess Quickly tell us that Sir John is dead, and how he died, the association of the winding-sheet, the coffin, the pall, and the grave, is inevitable, and we no more look for his return on earth again, than we should for an acquaintance, or accustomed neighbour, after he is buried.

Some writers who have been once original, seem to have fallen in love with their first fine conception, and ever after hanker for it as for a first love. Let now the variety be intended to be never so great, and names, ages, and temperaments differ as they may, we always detect some limb, some feature, or some peculiarity of the first, given or transfused into all its successors. Their minds are like the philosopher's stone, whatever is touched becomes gold.

Great authors have, finally, a property in their own minds, which other men have not. Other men, and their thoughts and doings, and all external nature, it is true, have their effects upon them. But they have minds too, and in virtue of the very superiority of these over others, bring more to pass of a strictly original character, than the combined suggestions, and other operations, of all the matters of mere observation.

Writers have been divided into various classes. We have spoken of two; —those who are authors and those who are not. There is another class we mean to glance at. This embraces writers who are honest, and writers who are not. We have no concern with the purposes or motives of men when they write or print, for a bad book may not have proceeded from a bad motive, or a useful one from the best. Honest authors are not so to themselves only, but to their age, and to their country. There is a real weakness in written hypocrisy. A man may walk before us, and talk before us too, and be nothing he seems. But the mind and heart of the whole community stir at the false histories of the writing author. And this they do, whether the falsehood be found in the glozing of sin, in excessive panegyric, or in caricature vice. . . .

We have spoken of authors who have been true to their own character, to their age, and to the world. There are other classes; we have room to speak of but one more. This class is peculiar to our own country. It has in a measure been made by the country, its institutions, and prospects, and deserves to be named. It belongs to us; and however little we have been allowed to appropriate of letters, we may safely claim this. If we should name it, *we* should call it the *prophetic* class of authors. This will serve to distinguish them at once from all writers within a reasonable antiquity, and will surely distinguish them from all the moderns. Our writers, whether imaginative or historical, are prophetic. They go habitually before the time. They live in the future of their own minds. They are with a population which cannot be numbered. The blessings of our institutions are upon all. A mass of intellectual power and physical strength occupies the distance, to a degree at times almost oppressive to us, who are comparatively few and powerless. Now there is no harm in this, and while the future continues in futurity, we would class ourselves among the faithful.

Sometimes, however, this vast and remote future seems to approach nearer than it should upon the borders of the present, and sometimes our writers and talkers seem to think, and to feel, that it has actually reached us, and that we are now what a few centuries may make us. In this there may be great evil. If our legislators get it, they may legislate for what is not; changing and overturning what belongs to us, to make way for what belongs to nobody. Our financiers may get it, and we may be taxed in advance, and be called wealthy, because every body may be hereafter. It would sometimes seem that the inspiration of our writers was getting transfused into the mass, and that we are living in the future, whether we will or no. We are getting at last at abuses, which have been the protection and happiness of our fathers and ourselves, but which will never be tolerated in the times to come. A strange sort of benefaction is thus to be substituted for present good, the incalculable good of a vast future.

If this be in any measure true, if *we* are to realize prophecies, or are realizing them already, we should look to it, and very seriously. Human life is getting longer, it is said, than it used to be, but it will hardly carry us as far as our writers are disposed to do. We may be losers in the bargain, and what is thus lost to us, will be lost to our successors, however remote, or however numerous. They were safe prophets in the British parliament, who foretold the liberty of these already, and could not long want the other. Prophets are not safe now however, our prophetic writers; for we have both liberty and prosperity, and it is for these, and for these alone, we should give our minds in the fulness of their best powers; and if we are true to our best interests, those which have been long proved, and found so, our posterity will be blessed without prophesy.

Ralph Waldo Emerson, "The Poet" (1844)[2]

I look in vain for the poet whom I describe. We do not, with sufficient plainness, or sufficient profoundness, address ourselves to life, nor dare we chaunt our own times and social circumstance. If we filled the day with bravery, we should not shrink from celebrating it. Time and nature yield us many gifts, but not yet the timely man, the new religion, the reconciler, whom all things await. Dante's praise is, that he dared to write his autobiography in colossal cipher, or into universality. We have yet had no genius in America, with tyrannous eye, which knew the value of our incomparable materials, and saw, in the barbarism and materialism of the times, another carnival of the same gods whose picture he so much admires in Homer; then in the middle age; then in Calvinism. Banks and tariffs, the newspaper and caucus, methodism and unitarianism, are flat and dull to dull people, but rest on the same foundations of wonder as the town of Troy, and the temple of Delphos, and are as swiftly passing away. Our logrolling, our stumps and their politics, our fisheries, our Negroes, and Indians, our boasts, and our repudiations, the wrath of rogues, and the pusillanimity of honest men, the northern trade, the southern planting, the western clearing, Oregon, and Texas, are yet unsung. Yet America is a poem in our eyes; its ample geography dazzles the imagination, and it will not wait long for metres. If I have not found that excellent combination of gifts in my countrymen which I seek, neither could I aid myself to fix the idea of the poet by reading now and then in Chalmers's collection of five centuries of English poets. These are wits, more than poets, though there have been poets among them. But when we adhere to the ideal of the poet, we have our difficulties even with Milton and Homer. Milton is too literary, and Homer too literal and historical.

Herman Melville, "Hawthorne and His Mosses," from *The Literary World* (1850)[3]

Let America, then, prize and cherish her writers; yea, let her glorify them. They are not so many in number as to exhaust her good-will. And while she has good kith and kin of her own, to take to her bosom, let her not lavish her embraces upon the household of an alien. For believe it or not, England, after all, is in many things an alien to us. China has more bonds of real love for us than she. But even were there no strong literary individualities among us, as there are some dozens at least, nevertheless, let America first praise mediocrity even, in her own children, before she praises (for everywhere, merit demands acknowledgment from every one) the best excellence in the children of any other land. Let her own authors, I say, have the priority of appreciation. I was much pleased with a hot-headed Carolina cousin of mine, who once said,—"If there were no other American to stand by, in literature, why, then, I would stand by Pop Emmons and his 'Fredoniad,' and till a better epic came along, swear it was not very far behind the Iliad." Take away the words, and in spirit he was sound.

Not that American genius needs patronage in order to expand. For that explosive sort of stuff will expand though screwed up in a vice, and burst it, though it were triple steel. It is for the nation's sake, and not for her authors' sake, that I would have America be heedful of the increasing greatness among her writers. For how great the shame, if other nations should be before her, in crowning her heroes of the pen! But this is almost the case now. American authors have received more just and discriminating praise (however loftily and ridiculously given, in certain cases) even from some Englishmen, than from their own countrymen. There are hardly five critics in America; and several of them are asleep. As for patronage, it is the American author who now patronizes his country, and not his country him. And if at times some among them appeal to the people for more recognition, it is not always with selfish motives, but patriotic ones.

It is true, that but few of them as yet have evinced that decided originality which merits great praise. But that graceful writer [Washington Irving], who perhaps of all Americans has received the most plaudits from his own country for his productions,—that very popular and amiable writer, however good and self-reliant in many things, perhaps owes his chief reputation to the self-acknowledged imitation of a foreign model, and to the studied avoidance of all topics but smooth ones. But it is better to fail in originality, than to succeed in imitation. He who has never failed somewhere, that man cannot be great. Failure is the true test of greatness. And if it be said, that continual success is a proof that a man wisely knows his powers,—it is only to be added, that, in that case, he knows them to be small. Let us believe it, then, once for all, that there is no hope for us in these smooth, pleasing writers that know their powers. Without malice, but to speak the plain fact, they but furnish an appendix to Goldsmith, and other English authors. And we want no American Goldsmiths; nay, we want no American Miltons. It were the vilest thing you could say of a true American author, that he were an American Tompkins. Call him an American and have done; for you cannot say a nobler thing of him. But it is not meant that all American writers should studiously cleave to nationality in their writings; only this, no American writer should write like an Englishman or a Frenchman; let him write like a man, for then he will be sure to write like an American. Let us away with this leaven of literary flunkeyism towards England. If either must play the flunkey in this thing, let England do it, not us. While we are rapidly preparing for that political supremacy among the nations which prophetically awaits us at the close of the present century, in a literary point of view, we are deplorably unprepared for it; and we seem studious to remain so. Hitherto, reasons might have existed why this should be; but no good reason exists now. And all that is requisite to amendment in this matter, is simply this: that while freely acknowledging all excellence everywhere, we should refrain from unduly lauding foreign writers, and, at the same time, duly recognise the meritorious writers that are our own; —those writers who breathe that unshackled, democratic spirit of Christianity in all things, which now takes the practical lead in this world, though at the same time led by ourselves—us Americans. Let us boldly contemn all imitation, though it comes to us graceful and fragrant as the morning; and foster all originality, though at first it be crabbed and ugly as our own pine knots. And if any of our authors fail, or seem to fail, then, in the words of my Carolina cousin, let us clap him on the shoulder, and back him against all Europe for his second round. The truth is, that in one point of view, this matter of a national literature has come to such a pass with us, that in some sense we must turn bullies, else the day is lost, or superiority so far beyond us, that we can hardly say it will ever be ours.

BY MID-CENTURY American publishers printed hundreds of American titles each year. Even if most of those books did not live up to Emerson's and Melville's ideal of an "authentic" American voice, the book-buying public nonetheless began to develop a hunger for a national literature. Publishers envisioned themselves as crucial to their authors' success, as well as to the development of American nationalism. Reminiscing about his long publishing career in 1871, James T. Fields (1817–1881) narrated his version of how Nathaniel Hawthorne's *The Scarlet Letter* came to be published— a story in which Fields implied that the author's genius depended for its expression on the publisher's facilities. Fields's relationship with Hawthorne (1804–1864) is also suggested by a photograph, taken in the early 1860s, of the author with Fields and his publishing partner, William D. Ticknor (1810–1864). Or maybe authors needed acquaintance with more than their publishers; perhaps hands-on experience at the printing press would benefit them. So argued Nathaniel Parker Willis (1806–1867), a New York editor and writer whose newspaper the *Home Journal* gained wide readership in the 1850s—and who had begun his career as a printer. The selection reproduced here appeared in a North Carolina newspaper—testimony to how New York literary culture was coming to pervade the entire nation.

James T. Fields, *Yesterdays with Authors* (1872)[4]

I came to know Hawthorne very intimately after the Whigs displaced the Democratic romancer from office. In my ardent desire to have him retained in the public service, his salary at that time being his sole dependence, —not foreseeing that his withdrawal from that sort of employment would be the best thing for American letters that could possibly happen, —I called, in his behalf, on several influential politicians of the day, and well remember the rebuffs I received in my enthusiasm for the author of the "Twice-Told Tales." One pompous little gentleman in authority, after hearing my appeal, quite astounded me by his ignorance of the claims of a literary man on his country. "Yes, yes," he sarcastically croaked down his public turtle-fed throat, "I see through it all, I see through it; this Hawthorne is one of them 'ere visionists, and we don't want no such a man as him round." So the "visionist" was not allowed to remain in office, and the country was better served by him in another way. In the winter of 1849, after he had been ejected from the custom-house, I went down to Salem to see him and inquire after his health, for we heard he had been suffering from illness. He was then living in a modest wooden house in Mall Street, if I remember rightly the location. I found him alone in a chamber over the sitting-room of the dwelling; and as the day was cold, he was hovering near a stove. We fell into talk about his future prospects, and he was, as I feared I should find him, in a very desponding mood. "Now," said I, "is the time for you to publish, for I know during these years in Salem you must have got something ready for the press." "Nonsense," said he; "what heart had I to write anything, when my publishers (M. and Company) have been so many years trying to sell a small edition of the 'Twice-Told Tales'?" I still pressed upon him the good chances he would have now with something new. "Who would risk publishing a book for *me*, the most unpopular writer in America?" "I would," said I, "and would start with an edition of two thousand copies of anything you write." "What madness!" he exclaimed; "your friendship for me gets the better of your judgment. No, no," he continued; "I have no money to indemnify a publisher's losses on my account." I looked at my watch and found that the train would soon be starting for Boston, and I knew there was not much time to lose in trying to discover what had been his literary work during these last few years in Salem. I remember that I pressed him to reveal to me what he had been writing. He shook his head and gave me to understand he had produced nothing. At that moment I caught sight of a bureau or set of drawers near where we were sitting; and immediately it occurred to me that hidden away somewhere in that article of furniture was a story or stories by the author of the "Twice-Told Tales," and I became so positive of it that I charged him vehemently with the fact. He seemed surprised, I thought, but shook his head again; and I rose to take my leave, begging him not to come into the cold entry, saying I would come back and see him again in a few days. I was hurrying down the stairs when he called after me from the chamber, asking me to stop a moment. Then quickly stepping into the entry with a roll of manuscript in his hands, he said: "How in heaven's name did you know this thing was there? As you have found me out, take what I have written, and tell me, after you get home and have time to read it, if it is good for anything. It is either very good or very bad, —I don't know which." On my way up to Boston I read the germ of "The Scarlet Letter"; before I slept that night I wrote him a note all aglow with admiration of the marvellous story he had put into my hands, and told him that I would come again to Salem the next day and arrange for its publication. I went on in such an amazing state of excitement when we met again in the little house, that he would not believe I was really in earnest. He seemed to think I was beside myself, and laughed sadly at my enthusiasm. However, we soon arranged for his appearance again before the public with a book.

This quarto volume before me contains numerous letters, written by him from 1850 down to the month of his death. The first one refers to "The Scarlet Letter," and is dated in January, 1850. At my suggestion he had altered the plan of that story. It was his intention to make "The Scarlet Letter" one of several short stories, all to

Photograph of Nathaniel Hawthorne, James T. Fields (left),
and William D. Ticknor (right)[5]

be included in one volume. . . . [B]ut I persuaded him, after reading the first chapters of the story, to elaborate it, and publish it as a separate work. After it was settled that "The Scarlet Letter" should be enlarged and printed by itself in a volume he wrote to me:— . . . .

"As regards the size of the book, I have been thinking a good deal about it. Considered merely as a matter of taste and beauty, the form of publication which you recommend seems to me much preferable to that of the 'Mosses.'

"In the present case, however, I have some doubts of the expediency, because if the book is made up entirely of 'The Scarlet Letter,' it will be too sombre. I found it impossible to relieve the shadows of the story with so much light as I would gladly have thrown in. Keeping so close to its point as the tale does, and diversified no otherwise than by turning different sides of the same dark idea to the reader's eye, it will weary very many people and disgust some. Is it safe, then, to stake the fate of the book entirely on this one chance? A hunter loads his gun with a bullet and several buckshot; and, following his sagacious example, it was my purpose to conjoin the one long story with half a dozen shorter ones, so that, failing to kill the public outright with my biggest and heaviest lump of lead, I might have other chances with the smaller bits, individually and in the aggregate. However, I am willing to leave these considerations to your judgment, and should not be sorry to have you decide for the separate publication.

" . . . If 'The Scarlet Letter' is to be the title, would it not be well to print it on the title-page in red ink? I am not quite sure about the good taste of so doing, but it would certainly be piquant and appropriate, and, I think, attractive to the great gull whom we are endeavoring to circumvent."

"Printers and Authors," from *North Carolina Standard* (1849)[6]

N. P. Willis, in the Home Journal, thus lays claim to his right as one of the brotherhood of Faustus:

If there was an apprenticeship to the trade of authorship, it would be as essential that a young author should pass a year as a compositor in a printing office, as that a future sea-captain should make a voyage before the mast. It is not alone that he would thus learn the importance of properly preparing his "copy" for the printers, by a legible penmanship and knowledge of the signs, marks, and abbreviations by which proof is corrected. These are matters, an acquaintance with which, on the part of the author, would save much time and vexation, and prevent serious blunders. The chief advantages would be to the author himself. There is no such effectual analysis of style as the process of type-setting. As he takes up letter by letter, of a long or complex sentence, the compositor becomes most critically aware of where the sentence might have been shortened to save his labor. He detects repetitions, becomes impatient of redundancies, recognizes careless or inappropriate use of expletives, and soon acquires a habit of putting an admiring value on clearness and brevity. We venture to say that it would alter the whole character of American literature, if the authors, (of our fluent nation!) were compelled, before legally receiving a copy-right, to have given one year to labor at the compositor's case. We have said nothing of that art of nice punctuation, which is also acquired in a printing office, and by which a style is made as much more tasteful as champagne by effervescing.

Journeymen Printers are, necessarily, well-instructed and intelligent men. It is a part of a proof reader's duty to mark a "query" against every passage in a new book which he does not clearly comprehend. Authors who know what is valuable, profit by these quiet estimates of their meaning; and many a weak point, that would have ruined a literary reputation, if left uncorrected for the reviews to handle, has been noiselessly put right by a proof-reader's unobtrusive "qu?" Of most books, indeed, we would rather have the criticism of the workmen in the office where it was printed, than of the reviewers who skim and pronounce upon it.

We speak with some little authority on this subject, not only because father and grandfather of our own were printers and newspaper editors before us, but because we have ourselves profited by the disciplines of which we speak. A rebellion against Greek and Latin in boyhood, was very sensibly met by the putting of us to work at the compositor's case, and we did not leave it to resume an education, till, (after two years' practice) we could "set and distribute" like a journeyman. Our labor was upon the religious newspaper, the Boston Recorder, and we well remember the gratification with which we obtained the exclusive privilege of setting from the manuscript of Rev. Richard Storrs, one of the contributors—the style was so seizable by the memory and so invariably brief and to the point. Whatever may have been the merit of our own style of writing since, we are convinced that we owe, at least its freedom from certain defects, to the training we received while so small as to stand perched upon two type-boxes at a "brevier case."

REPLYING IN 1868 directly to Sydney Smith's challenge from several decades earlier, Henry C. Carey (1793–1879) returned to the importance of the publisher in literary production. A former publisher himself who became one of America's foremost political economists, Carey argued that literature had become established in the United States to a large extent because of publishers' exertions. Carey's lineage might have foretold his remarks: his father was Mathew Carey, the pioneering publisher of the early nineteenth century. Numerous authors disputed the publishers' claim to credit for American literary greatness, however. In a letter to Hawthorne from 1851, Herman Melville reported that he constantly compromised the quality of his fiction in order to make a living from it: that, in his memorable phrase, "Dollars damn me." Two subsequent artifacts—an 1841 letter from Edgar Allan Poe (1809–1849) to Fitz-Greene

Halleck, and an 1850 letter from Hawthorne to Emerson—show the way in which the proliferation of magazines, a potentially lucrative source of income for authors, began to affect the profession of authorship during this period. Sophia Hawthorne's (1809–1871) 1851 letter about her husband illustrates the connections between American authors and European publishers by mid-century. By then, Europeans *were* reading American books—not just the other way around.

H. C. Carey, *Letters on International Copyright* (1868)[7]

Forty years since, the question was asked by the "Edinburgh Review," Who reads an American book? Judging from the facts here given, may we not reasonably suppose that the time is fast approaching, when the question will be asked, Who does *not* read American books?

Forty years since, had we asked where were the *homes of American authors*, we should generally have been referred to very humble houses in our cities. Those who now inquire for them will find their answer in the beautiful volume lately published by Messrs. Putnam and Co., the precursor of others destined to show the literary men of this country enjoying residences as agreeable as any that had been occupied by such men in any part of the world; and in almost every case, those homes have been due to the profits of the pen. Less than half a century since, the race of literary men was scarcely known in the country, and yet the amount now paid for literary labor is greater than in Great Britain and France combined, and will probably be, in twenty years more, greater than in all the world beside. With the increase of number, there has been a corresponding increase in the consideration in which they are held; and the respect with which even unknown authors are treated, when compared with the disrespect manifested in England towards such men, will be obvious to all familiar with the management of the journals of that country who read the following in one of our principal periodicals:—

"The editor of Putnam's Monthly will give to every article forwarded for insertion in the Magazine a careful examination, and, when requested to do so, will return the MS. if not accepted."

Here, the competition is among the publishers to *buy* the products of literary labor, whereas, abroad, the competition is to *sell* them, and therefore is the treatment of authors, even when unknown, so different. Long may it continue to be so!

Such having been the result of half a century, during which we have had to lay the foundation of the system that has furnished so vast a body of readers, what may not be expected in the next half century, during which the population will increase to a hundred millions, with a power to consume the products of literary labor growing many times faster than the growth of numbers? If this country is properly termed "the paradise of women," may it not be as correctly denominated the paradise of authors, and should they not be content to dwell in it as their predecessors have done?

Herman Melville, letter to Nathaniel Hawthorne, June 1[?], 1851[8]

In a week or so, I go to New York, to bury myself in a third-story room, and work and slave on my "Whale" while it is driving through the press. *That* is the only way I can finish it now,—I am so pulled hither and thither by circumstances. The calm, the coolness, the silent grass-growing mood in which a man *ought* always to compose,—that, I fear, can seldom be mine. Dollars damn me; and the malicious Devil is forever grinning in upon me, holding the door ajar. My dear Sir, a presentiment is on me,—I shall at last be worn out and perish, like an old nutmeg-grater, grated to pieces by the constant attrition of the wood, that is, the nutmeg. What I feel most moved to write, that is banned,—it will not pay. Yet, altogether, write the *other* way I cannot. So the product is a final hash, and all my books are botches.

Edgar Allan Poe, letter to Fitz-Greene Halleck, June 24, 1841[9]

I need not call your attention to the signs of the times in respect to Magazine literature. You will admit the tendency of the age in this direction. The brief, the terse, and the easily circulated will take place of the diffuse, the ponderous, and the inaccessible. Even our Reviews are found too massive for the taste of the day—I do not mean for the taste of the merely uneducated, but also for that of the few. In the meantime the finest minds of Europe are beginning to lend their spirit to Magazines. In this country, unhappily, we have no journal of the class, which can either afford to compensate the highest talent, or which is, in all respects, a fitting vehicle for its thoughts. In the supply of this deficiency there would be a point gained; and the project of which I speak has originated in the hope of supplying it.

Nathaniel Hawthorne, letter to Ralph Waldo Emerson, 1850[10]

In the matter of this projected magazine, I am afraid I cannot do much; and am therefore glad that it is of very little consequence whether I do anything.

The remuneration, which the publishers could afford to offer, must necessarily be small. Now, Graham has made me an offer (which I declined) of $100 for a brief article. I have tempting offers, likewise, from the Tribune, for a long story to be published in chapters. This being the case, and being dependent on my pen, I certainly could not be a frequent contributor to the new magazine. I have no faith whatever in its success; so that I should not feel as if I were doing anybody good, while doing myself harm. No instance is known to me of a magazine, here or in England, succeeding purely on its literary merits—though these claims are not undesirable to have, in aid of, and incidental to others, which the public regards more.

Sophia Hawthorne, letter to Louisa Hawthorne, December 1, 1851[11]

Mr. Fields who is abroad writes of splendid fame in England which [Nathaniel Hawthorne] has won by the Scarlet Letter &c, & Barry Cornwall has written him a beautiful note & sent him his Poems, all of which you shall see & will enjoy when you come. I have for you also a very handsome English edition of the Scarlet letter sent to Nathaniel by the Publishers—or rather for you I have one of the same sent by Ticknor—for the other we must keep as a trophy. There have been several different editions of both Scarlet letter & House of 7. G. published in London, & Twice-told tales—& one of each we have. Also Nathaniel received the other day from Prussia a translation of the Scarlet Letter—as a gift from the translator, with a letter. The great Leipsic house of Tauchniss has also sent him proposals. So you see that all the world is on its knees at his feet & he is fast becoming Crowned King in the realm of Letters & Genius.

DURING THE nineteenth century women made advances as authors but simultaneously maintained a second-class status in comparison to their male counterparts. American literary anthologies began to appear in the 1840s, but books such as *The Prose Writers of America* included mostly works by men. The frontispiece and title page to John S. Hart's (1810–1877) 1852 anthology, *The Female Prose Writers of America*, depicted a contemplative, educated woman of the upper classes as a model American reader and writer. A dozen years later an American reprint of an English magazine article from 1864 both played on and deflated this ideal. Women, it held, were more suited to the delicate, the refined, the pure, than to the degrading realities of the authorial profession. In her 1847 book, *Woman in America*, Mrs. A. J. Graves argued that women can contribute to the development of literature, but that they should write out of their own domestic experience. By 1870, however, many American women had become best-selling authors, often by writing distinctly outside of any immediate domesticity. The closing excerpt from Virginia Penny's (b. 1826) *How Women Can Make Money* focused on what women authors had accomplished by that day and what they had to look forward to in the future as professional authors.

Frontispiece and Title Page, from John S. Hart, *The Female Prose Writers of America* (1852)[12]

"Literary Women," from *Littell's Living Age* (1864); reprinted from *The London Review*[13]

Nothing is harder than to make a clever woman understand why men in general entertain a strong objection to feminine authorship. She sees that her brothers and her other friends dislike the idea of her devoting her energies to literature; and she repeats to herself that the feeling is a selfish one, and unworthy of sensible men. In the present day, it happens that women are carrying off splendid laurels in the literary world; and feminine enthusiasts may point without reproach to the author of "Romola" and "Adam Bede" as conferring as high distinction by her genius upon the entire sex as Miss Austen did a generation or two ago by her delicate and admirable works. They argue, accordingly, —though perhaps unconsciously, —that literature is a field where women do succeed, and therefore must be a field that should be open to all women. In their hearts they half accuse the other sex of a secret desire to keep so rich a soil for their own use. The common talk about blues and literary women they regard as vulgar and ungenerous, and are ready to break a lance with anybody who does not bid them to indulge their tastes for writing; to go up to the magazines and to the publishers and prosper. Women whose lot in life is to marry and be at the end of a house, require no employment of the kind. Literature would interfere with their domestic duties and ties, without bringing them any corresponding advantages. But there are many others who have no household life to look forward to, which is not cheerless and inadequate. They see no object before them at all corresponding in worthiness to the secret energy and sentiment of which they are conscious within themselves. Why should they not take an occupation that seems ready to their hands, and for which they possess a certain capacity and a distinct liking?

At first sight it seems obvious that women of sensibility and education have many qualities most suitable for and marketable in the world of print. In the first place, they have a keen perception of what is noble and ignoble in character, and an unlimited power of appreciating nicely fine traits and symptoms of what is evil as well as of what is good. Like children, they appear to be able to tell by instinct when a coarser atmosphere enters the room in company with this person or with that; and will read at a glance whether the latest comer belongs to the category of the wheat or of the tares. If their powers of compression and repression were equal to their powers of expression, women would possibly be the greatest orators in the world. Montaigne says that every woman is, in a greater or less degree, a rhetorician. The observation seems a just one, the more we examine it by the light of social experience. Some of the best talkers, both in England and in other countries, belong to the softer sex; and a man may envy and in vain desire the wonderful versatility with which a feminine mind passes through every shade and phase of sentiment, and rings the changes on every chord. This mental susceptibility makes women take the lead in society, when their genius and training are of a high order. They are pre-eminently fitted to be the centre of conversation and social intercourse, a post that requires infinite flexibility and variety in those who fill it. The refinement which is natural to women always, and which is especially developed by the whole course of their education in modern times, serves as a corrective to what otherwise might be a dangerous charm, and prevents them from allowing their enthusiasm and their spirits to run into excess. All these characteristics would be very valuable in a literary career; and it is no wonder that those who are endowed with them should feel very often an uncontrollable impulse to gratify what appears to be an instinctive taste.

Yet literature is not a profession to which English gentlemen are pleased to see their sisters and their daughters turn. There is an indistinct feeling at the bottom of their dislike of feminine authorship, which tells them that literary work has a tendency to wear off some of the delicate bloom which is perhaps the finest part of a woman's natural character. To understand by long experience the meannesses of the world, to comprehend the various ways in which men undergo moral declension and decay, and yet to be able to take a broad and comprehensive view of life

after all the destruction of one's ideals and utopias, is part of the necessary qualification for a great writer. The women who attain to it must attain to it by undergoing a defeminizing process; after which they gain much strength and breadth of
view at the sacrifice of that nameless beauty of innocence which is by nature the
glory of the woman, and which it is the object of English feminine training to preserve intact. . . .

If women were wise they would understand that they have a mission quite as
grand as that of literary authorship. It is the mission of keeping alive for men certain ideas, and ideals too, which would soon pass out of the world in the rush and
hurry of material existence if they were not fed and replenished by those who are
able to stand aloof from the worry and vexations of active life. When society ceases
to have the means of creating its own ideas, it must decay. Civilization is nourished
by the imaginative wealth that the world possesses and renews for itself from time
to time; and those treasures of imagination which we call ideas are mainly dependent on the social position occupied by women. Ideas of purity, unselfishness, and
devotion, in the words of the poet, are the hinges of the gate of life; and if women
were to become as men, the sacred fire would soon become extinct. The heathens
of old fitly expressed this truth by the images of the eternal flame of Vesta, which
it was the duty of her priestesses to maintain unimpaired and on which the welfare
of Rome herself depended.

Mrs. A. J. Graves, *Woman in America* (1841)[14]

An English writer has said "that there are many readers among American women,
but that *thinkers* are rare." The time is near at hand, we hope, when there will be no
ground for this reproach; when our women will show that they can think as well
as read. The same remark has been applied by another European writer to the men
of our country; and the want of original character—of nationality in our native
literature, has been frequently alleged against us. We certainly have some original
writers, but nothing that can claim to be considered a national literature. In the
literature of England we found "a model which accorded with the ideas and habits"
still prevalent among us; and, as Madame De Staël remarks, "wherever this is the
case, the mind is more inclined to adopt than to create. Necessity alone can produce
invention." Our political writers, indeed, found no model in the political writings
of England, the principles advanced in them being opposed to the genius of our
government; and necessity has given to us something like a national political literature. But not so with the polite literature of England: that we found in many
respects so much in accordance with our manners and sentiments, that we adopted
it as our own. Still, there is even in this a great deal which is unsuited to us as republicans, and which operates unfavourably upon our national character. We need a
literature truly and properly our own—one in conformity with our government
and social institutions: a literature exposing the folly and the inconsistency of the

anti-republican fashions, tastes, and opinions which we have derived from the literature and manners of the Old World. Our authors should unite in building up a social fabric, the proportions of which shall all be in perfect keeping with the simple majesty of the Doric Temple we have reared to liberty and equal rights.

To the literary females of our country a mission of the deepest interest is intrusted. It is for them to elevate the intellectual character of their sex; to make them truly republican women; to endeavour to provide for them a sound, healthful, and invigorating literature, adapted to their condition as the daughters of this great and free nation. Let them come forward, then, to the noble task of instructing their countrywomen in the high duties which pertain to them; and, above all things, let them be teachers of truth and reality.

But, if fictitious writings cannot be wholly dispensed with, let our works of this kind be at least American. Let no woman of genius among us so far abuse the gifts bestowed upon her as to furnish additional incentives to the already inordinate desire for wealth and luxury, by high-wrought descriptions of fashionable life, with its splendid mansions gorgeously furnished, and their richly-attired inmates; but draw her models from our humble or our truly refined homes; in short, from our genuine American women. Fashionable society in all countries possesses the same general characteristics, and we must look elsewhere for original national character. And in our national female character there is a rich mine for our writers as yet unexplored, which will amply reward all who seek for its virgin ore. . . . In eliciting the hidden stores of thought and feeling shut up in the heart of many a woman in humble life, we shall be surprised by beautiful revelations of character, more full of originality and deep interest than are to be found in the creations of the most gifted genius. If our writers would exhibit models of genuine refinement, and of simple, graceful elegance, let them study that domestic circle where, by the intellectual elevation of the mother and her daughters, home is made so lovely and attractive as to take from the gayeties of fashion all their fascination; where cultivated intellect and taste, and pure, unaffected feeling, communicate an indescribable charm to manners and conversation; and where piety sheds its crowning grace over all, giving to the natural character a spiritual life, holier and brighter than aught that belongs to earth.

Virginia Penny, *How Women Can Make Money* (1870)[15]

Many superior works of fiction have been written by ladies of America, some of which have been translated into the languages of Europe and introduced into those countries. Many of our fair countrywomen have distinguished themselves by their poetical effusions, and quite a number have published their poems in book form. Mrs. Everett Green, author of the "Lives of the Princesses of England," is now employed by the English Government upon state papers. Research into historical data, and the nice, careful arrangement of details, are well fitted to the patience of woman. . . . The success of women in works of fiction is unquestioned. This class of books requires less time, less study, and less money, and rewards the authors pecuniarily better than any other kind of work, considering, of course, the comparatively small amount of application required. As the females of our land become more generally educated, and have more leisure for the cultivation of their minds, no doubt more attention will be devoted to literary effort. The easy, natural manner of female authors is a marked feature. Different motives prompt to authorship—love of fame, wealth, influence, and a desire to do good. Persons are generally prompted to write by feeling that they know more of some particular subject than most people, or something entirely unknown or unthought of by any one save themselves. Some collect and arrange information obtained from books, observation, or experience, or all combined. E. Hazen says: "The indispensable qualifications to make a writer are—a talent for literary composition, an accurate knowledge of language, and an acquaintance with the subject to be treated . . .". Of all studies, the quiet and contemplative kind are most favorable to long life. Those of an exciting nature produce a reaction, sometimes, of the physical as well as intellectual powers.

COMMENTARY: CREATING A "PARADISE OF AUTHORS"

The first thing to notice about the artifacts in this chapter is how little they take for granted. What exactly does it mean to be an author? What does it mean to be an American author? What distinctions, if any, can we make between male and female authorship? Who is the appropriate audience for literature? These artifacts repeatedly ask these questions, and as they do so, they show quite vividly the extent to which the status of literature, and of American literature in particular, was in flux during the middle of the nineteenth century. Given this flux, it is not surprising that when one writer, Margaret Fuller, sat down in 1846 to write an essay titled "American Literature," she had in her very first sentence to concede that "some thinkers may object to this essay" on the grounds "that we are about to write of that which has, as yet, no existence" (122).

As the previous chapters have shown, American literature was in fact well established by 1846, already providing a rich legacy for writers, readers, and publishers on both sides of the Atlantic. But it had not fared as well among foreign critics. Although American works such as *Charlotte Temple* and *The Sketch Book* were popular with British audiences, many British magazines complained about the inferior quality of American literature. In 1819 one critic in *Blackwood's Magazine* had gone so far as to claim that "the human mind has suffered a deterioration by being transported across the Atlantic." The reasons for this deterioration could easily be catalogued:

> There is nothing to awaken fancy in that land of dull realities; it contains no objects
> that carry back the mind to the contemplation of early antiquity; no mouldering ruins

to excite curiosity in the history of past ages; no memorials, commemorative of glorious deeds, to call forth patriotic enthusiasm and reverence; it has no traditions and legends and fables to afford materials for romance and poetry. ("On the State of Learning," 647)

In citing such a list, this critic was giving voice to a kind of cultural imperialism that assumed that the United States did not yet have a cultural life sufficiently rich to produce a national literature. It was not true, of course, that America lacked a history; its colonial period, its growing regional diversity, and the history of Native Americans—among other topics—offered uniquely "American" subjects. But the prevailing critical consensus was that American writers had not yet produced any "great" literature, literature that would put it on the map, culturally speaking.

In spite of—or perhaps because of—this consensus, American writers began in the 1830s and 1840s to make a strong push for American literary nationalism: for the creation of a literature that would be distinctively American and that would be a source of pride for its citizens. Two groups of writers in particular—the Transcendentalists (based in Massachusetts) and "Young America" (based in New York)—worked to become cultural cheerleaders, encouraging readers to support American writers and exhorting writers to rise to the challenge of creating "great" literature. Much of the campaigning for literary nationalism was conducted in magazines. The Transcendentalists produced the *Dial*, while Young America received support in John Louis O'Sullivan's *United States Magazine and Democratic Review*. At the same time, other magazines criticized the goals of the literary nationalists, creating the "literary wars" of the 1840s. In particular, the *Knickerbocker*, and its editor Lewis Gaylord Clark, ridiculed the idea of an original "American Genius," instead endorsing universal literary values that extended beyond national boundaries (Bell, 57–58).

Nevertheless, the literary nationalists inspired a number of writers of the period, including Margaret Fuller, who also edited the *Dial*. Given this affiliation, it is worth noting that she ends her essay on "American Literature" on an optimistic note. "The future is glorious with certainties for those who do their duty in the present," she proclaims, "and, lark-like, seeking the sun, challenge its eagles to an earthward flight, where their nests may be built in our mountains, and their young raise their cry of triumph, unchecked by dullness in the echoes" (Fuller, 142).

Fuller's Romantic call is emblematic of the prophetic strain of the literary nationalists. The writers and thinkers invested in creating a distinctively American literature saw themselves not only as builders of a literary tradition but also as prophets who could usher America into a new era of democratic freedom and individualism. As early as 1825, the *United States Literary Gazette* had been explicit in defining American writers as prophets who "go habitually before the time" and "live in the future of their own minds." They use their imaginations, in other words, to create a particular vision of the future. This vision, in turn, creates for them a form of cultural immortality. Unlike mere "writers," who cannot see beyond their own time, authors can provide national leadership; on the one hand they are heroically solitary artists, but on the other they are "producers" of a vibrant national, and communal, culture. The artistic and the social are, in this sense, inextricably joined for the literary national-ists. Fine art and democratic values go hand in hand, just as do prophetic writers and patriotic readers.

One of Fuller's fellow Transcendentalists, Ralph Waldo Emerson, is today per-haps the best-known of the writers who called for the cultural independence that was at the heart of American literary nationalism. His essay "The Poet," published in 1844, was exuberant in naming all of the subjects that could be incorporated into an indigenous literature. His list of the American subjects waiting to be "sung" in poetry makes a pointed contrast to the list of "lacks" in the *Blackwood's* essay; instead of focusing on America's lack of history and tradition, Emerson reveled in all of the subjects that were just waiting to be mined by authors. (Emerson would, I believe, have shared the *Gazette's* distinction between writers and authors.) Walt Whitman was so inspired by this essay that he began to work on what would become perhaps the seminal collection of antebellum American poetry, *Leaves of Grass*. "I was simmering, simmering, simmering; Emerson brought me to a boil," Whitman is claimed to have said (in Loving, 195 n.5). Indeed, Whitman was so taken with Emerson as a prophetic mentor that in the second edition of *Leaves of Grass* he reprinted (without permission) a congratulatory letter from Emerson.

Other writers rose to the challenge of literary nationalism as well. Herman Melville, although a somewhat reluctant adherent to the Young America movement, nevertheless began to champion "originality" rather than slavish imitation of for-eign sources. In "Hawthorne and His Mosses," he not only promoted Nathaniel Hawthorne as an important American writer but also, like Emerson, identified writing as a form of prophecy. He made it clear that individual writers were "representative" men, in the sense that whatever they wrote individually would also inevitably reflect on the country as a whole. "It is for the nation's sake, and not for her authors' sake, that I would have America be heedful of the increasing greatness among her writers," he wrote. To write as an American was to have more at stake than personal success or aesthetic satisfaction; it was a form of national advancement.

And signs of this advancement did in fact begin to appear. Between 1850 and 1855 Americans produced such a distinguished body of literature that the period has come to be called the "American Renaissance": a literary awakening parallel to that in England after the Middle Ages. The critic who coined this term, F. O. Matthiessen, did so in 1941, at the beginning of World War II, when Americans were again partic-ularly preoccupied with showing their national strength on all levels. But even in the nineteenth century, critics noted the marked increase in the production of American literature. In *Letters on International Copyright*, H. C. Carey went so far as to call the United States a "paradise of authors," a place where "literary men" are well paid, held in high critical esteem, and are eagerly courted by their publishers. In this view, American cultural life had not deteriorated by virtue of going across the Atlantic. Indeed, the influence was beginning to be reversed. British writers were treated with "disrespect" in their own country, while in the United States even "unknown" writers were receiving due respect and consideration.

In his *Letters*, Carey makes clear that the growing success of American writers could not be separated from economic and material concerns. If the American Renaissance was in some sense a product of an ideological movement toward literary nationalism, it is also the case that this movement was facilitated by a number of changes in the publishing industry during this time. An increasingly extensive railway system helped to distribute books across the country from the three main publishing centers of Philadelphia, New York, and Boston. Changes in printing technology made it less expensive to publish books and also created a greater range of formats for books, from "keepsake" volumes bound in sumptuous leather to inexpensive editions available, for instance, in train stations. These changes were accompanied by other technological innovations as well, including improved lighting and better reading glasses, which helped readers as well as writers (Zboray, 14–16). These material conditions, while not in any simple way "producing" the American Renaissance, are nonetheless a vital consideration in accounting for the phenomenal growth in publishing in the middle of the nineteenth century.

Even as this growth created new opportunities for the publishing industry, it also created new challenges for the authors themselves. The range of publishing opportunities helped foster an increasingly diverse literary market: a market that distinguished between elite, highly educated audiences and more popular or mass ones; between children's literature and adult literature; and among different genres (didactic novel, "moral" literature, inspiring biographies, history, and so on). Although bookstores did not yet have as many sections as Borders and other "superstores" do now, they nevertheless were beginning to categorize literature in new ways. And that meant that authors, in turn, began to ally themselves with particular "niche" audiences. They also had to decide how much they wanted economic considerations to influence their choice of audience. While Herman Melville was working on *Moby-Dick* (1851)—an American classic that sold miserably during his own time—he had to will himself to write according to his own artistic standards rather than financial ones. "Dollars damn me," he wrote to Hawthorne; "What I feel most moved to write, that is banned, —it will not pay. Yet altogether, write the *other* way I cannot." Melville's first novels, *Typee* (1846) and *Omoo* (1847), were South Seas adventure stories that sold relatively well, but we see in this letter his frustration with the fact that economic and aesthetic considerations created two conflicting goals. Some writers, such as Henry David Thoreau, managed to be "prophets in the marketplace," but others, such as Melville, saw the demands of prophecy and of the marketplace as being diametrically opposed (Fink).

Publishers, sensing the growing diversity of the literary market, began to see it as an opportunity rather than a limitation. Some publishers, such as Boston's William D. Ticknor and James T. Fields, made a pointed effort to recruit distinguished authors and to market them as such. They were "genteel" publishers who saw themselves in league with the goals of literary nationalism, as they worked with authors to promote great American works. Ticknor and Fields were particular champions of Nathaniel Hawthorne. The photograph of the three of them together shows them as gentlemanly colleagues, but in fact Ticknor and Fields were crucial in converting Hawthorne from a moderately successful writer of short stories and children's books into a celebrated American writer. By Fields's own account, *The Scarlet Letter* was published because he traveled from Boston to Salem to beg Hawthorne to write a longer work for Ticknor and Fields to publish. Hawthorne first demurred, but then gave Fields the manuscript of *The Scarlet Letter*; Fields read it on the train home and immediately decided to publish it.

This story is no doubt largely rhetorical, but it goes a long way in showing the importance of publishers to the production of American writing in the middle nineteenth century. It was the publishers who determined the pay scales of writers; publishers who often recruited writers for particular ends; publishers who decided increasingly to advertise books as distinctively "American." Indeed, one firm, Wiley and Putnam, issued a "Library of American Books," which included, among other things, Fuller's *Papers on Literature and Art*. Ironically, the series included selections not only from American writers but also editions of the standard British writers Spenser (edited by Caroline Kirkland) and Chaucer (edited by Charles Deshler). So too did the list of authors published by Ticknor and Fields include not only Hawthorne, Emerson, and Thoreau but also British writers such as Dickens, Thackeray, and Robert Browning (Winship, 20). As Sophia Hawthorne attests, Ticknor and Fields also helped promote American writers abroad, creating an international celebrity that made Hawthorne a "Crowned King in the realm of Letters & Genius." Such celebrity, in turn, helped the cause of American literary nationalism. If an American writer could be a literary "King," then it was more difficult to claim that American literature did not exist.

As American literature began to have a better national and international reputation, publishers became increasingly committed to "buying American." As they did so, they also became more attuned to the demands of their reading audience. For instance, when Edgar Allan Poe—both a writer and an editor—wanted to establish a new magazine in 1841, he did so in part because he knew that magazines, and the short stories that filled them, would appeal to readers with limited amounts of leisure time. Poe felt that readers had neither the time nor the attention span to read and digest long works, and so he was prepared to offer this proto-MTV generation shorter, more easily accessible works. Publishers, readers, and authors worked together, then, to form what Robert Darnton terms a "communications circuit" (30–31). None of them dictated market tastes completely, but neither did they work in isolation from one another. If Ticknor and Fields encouraged Hawthorne to write longer novels rather than short stories, they were in turn responding in part to what they perceived as an opportunity to market high-quality American literature; and Hawthorne in turn used that opportunity to do his best writing. Throughout the rest of his career, he remained ambivalent about his ideal audience, sometimes wishing it to be popular and extensive and at others wishing it to be only a trusted friend. But whatever his ambivalence, he was also aware, as he wrote to Emerson, that he was financially "dependent on [his] pen," and for that reason had always to keep in mind that magazines, and by extension all writing, very rarely succeeded "purely on its literary merits."

Hawthorne was particularly aware of the competition he faced from women writers, whom he infamously described in a letter to Fields as the "damned mob of scribbling women." The context for his remark was his frustration at the fact that Maria Cummins's domestic novel *The Lamplighter* (1854) was selling so much better than his own works, and it may reveal his unhappiness with his publishers' marketing techniques as much as it does his disdain for women writers (Baym). Indeed, at other points in his letters, Hawthorne sings the praises of certain women writers, such as Fanny Fern and Grace Greenwood. Nevertheless, his comment shows that the increasing diversity of the literary market was helping to create a distinction between women's domestic writing and men's more "serious" pursuits. More often than not, women's writing was lumped together with popular writing, although in fact some women—such as Margaret Fuller—were just as serious about their art as Hawthorne and Melville were.

It is telling that when H. C. Carey describes America as a "paradise of authors," he notes in the same sentence that America is also "properly termed 'the paradise of women.'" The implication seems to be that these two paradises—of authors and of women—are more likely to be parallel than intersecting; women may provide a ready audience for authors, but women authors present a particular anomaly. Carey acknowledges that such women are being well paid, and are succeeding in the marketplace, but he also seems to will authorship to be something other than "women's work." It is here that the notion of author as prophet again becomes particularly meaningful. If authors are cultural prophets, then their work is valuable and productive. If they are writing merely for entertainment, then they are engaging in a form of nonproductive work: a form of work that, for male writers at least, threatens to make them seem weak members of society. The call for literary nationalism, that is to say, was also a call to make writing a viable occupation—and profession—for men and for women. Prior to the mid-nineteenth century, the predominant model for authorship was that of the genteel amateur, the person who wrote in his spare time but had another profession as well (Buell, 58–64). As authorship became more profitable, thanks to advances in the publishing industry, writers began to identify themselves as professionals. Yet they were also a particular kind of professional: one who, because of their ability to prophesy and to engage in original thought, deserved, like ministers, to be given a privileged place in their society. As Carey put it, they deserved due "consideration."

Women writers demanded a different kind of consideration. For one thing, they had to combat the opinions of some critics who argued that writing was not an appropriate occupation for women. As the anonymous author of "Literary Women" put it, writing required nothing short of a "defeminizing process." This process was particularly unfortunate given the fact that women already had "a mission quite as grand as that of literary authorship," that of "keeping alive for men certain ideas, and ideals too," which can only be preserved if one is "aloof from the worry and vexations of active life." This separate-spheres ideology posited that women were valuable when they provided a moral center within the private home, while men were valuable when they actively pursued their work in the public realm. This ideology was so influential in part because it was so pervasive. In fact, the essay on "Literary Women" was first published in England in the *London Review*, and then reprinted in Philadelphia in a weekly magazine, *Littell's Living Age*. This transatlantic printing history reminds us again that American literary nationalism needs to be understood in an international context; the push for a distinctively American writing occurred alongside a publishing culture that extended well beyond national boundaries.

Yet the vision of women writers put forward in "Literary Women" probably did have a special resonance in America, since it made an implicit connection between women and prophecy. Ironically, the stance of detachment that the essay promotes— a stance of standing aloof from the worries of everyday life in order to promote certain ideas—is exactly the stance of the prophetic author. As the *Literary Gazette* had put it, such authors have the ability to reveal "the deep springs of human action," and "to live in the futures of their own minds." They, too, stood apart from the vexations of daily life, thinking about future ideals rather than petty details. In this sense, women provided a possible model for the American author-as-prophet. Rather than women becoming "defeminized" by trying to write like men, the logic of prophecy necessitated that it would be better if men would learn to act more like women, separating themselves from the public world in order to record their future visions.

If women in this sense provided a model for the prophetic strain of literary nationalism, they contributed to literary nationalism in other ways as well. Although F. O. Matthiessen focused his study of the American Renaissance on the literary outpouring of five male writers (Hawthorne, Melville, Emerson, Thoreau, and Whitman), an astonishingly large volume of writing during the 1850s was produced by women, contributing to what Joyce Warren has termed "the (other) American traditions." Much, though certainly not all, of this writing centered on domestic life and the vicissitudes of courtship, marriage, and child rearing. Local in its details and realistic in its concern with everyday life, such writing was, by definition, "American" in its subject matter. Domestic writing about the home, in other words, was also often domestic in the sense of defining itself as concerned with American issues rather than foreign ones. Some classic domestic novels, such as Susan Warner's *The Wide, Wide World* or Louisa May Alcott's *Little Women*, portray characters who travel to Britain or Europe, but they do so only to return to America at the end. In this sense, as Mrs. A. J. Graves put it, "in our national female character there is a rich mine for our writers as yet unexplored, which will amply reward all who seek for its virgin ore" and will produce "beautiful revelations of character, more full of originality and deep interest than are to be found in the creations of the most gifted genius." Graves takes some key terms of literary nationalism—genius, originality, national character—and shows how applicable they are to women's sphere: the domestic, in short, becomes equivalent to the national.

This conjunction is perhaps nowhere more apparent than in the illuminated frontispiece to Hart's *Female Prose Writers of America*. This page presents a kind of iconography of the woman writer, subsuming individual differences into a picture of a single woman who, with the American flag, symbolizes patriotism and service to country. She leans on the flag, holding a bouquet of flowers rather than a pen; there are books and musical scores at her feet but they are less obvious than the lyre beside her and the pomegranates above her. The lyre associates her with the Greek muses, while the pomegranates associate her with Persephone, the goddess of fertility and eternity. The other thing that one notices about this frontispiece and its accompanying title page are the emphasis they put on nature. Our eyes quickly go from the foreground to the background, with its tranquil and almost sublime landscape of mountains and lakes. These women are not unnatural, this iconography wants to insist; instead they are working in a way that is both natural and unabashedly American.

Yet even as women writers allied themselves—and were allied by their publishers and by critics like Hart—with the goals of literary nationalism, they, no less than their male counterparts, worried about the market value of their writing. Writing, particularly of fiction, offered them a way to make a living that required little up-front capital and could be quite remunerative. As Virginia Penny puts it, the writing of fiction "requires less time, less study, and less money, and rewards the authors pecuniarily better than any other kind of work." Many fiction writers, of both sexes, would probably have taken exception to Penny's further claim that such writing also requires a "comparatively small amount of application." But Penny's explicit discussion of money—compared, say, to Melville's contorted "dollars damn me" letter—suggests that for some women, at least, writing to a particular market became a source of satisfaction rather than conflict. As writers, they could assume crucial roles as prophet and producer of ideas while also making no apologies for making money from it. In part this was because they had fewer options for alternative careers than did their male counterparts; in part it was because many of the most successful women writers (Susan Warner, Maria Cummins, and Louisa May Alcott among them) were single and were realistic about their needs to support themselves; and in part it was because their traditional gender roles made authorship—with its threat of nonproductive labor—need less justification for women than it did for men.

In certain ways, then, women writers contributed a great deal to making authorship a viable profession in this country. As it came to be defined in the mid-nineteenth century, this profession aspired both to be prophetic and to succeed in an increasingly diverse market; to be aloof and yet intimately connected to the patriotic goals of the nation; to be peculiarly "American"—or domestic—and yet also to increase the recognition of American writers abroad. Such aspirations, in turn, created a literary culture increasingly distinguished by certain hierarchies of taste: for authors over writers, prophets over "mere" recorders of the here and now, originality over imitation. Although at times there also seemed to be a hierarchy valuing male writers over female ones, the artifacts included in this chapter ultimately tell a different story.

American literary nationalism, in this view, was not simply the province of *the* American Renaissance and its most famous writers. Instead, it was a cultural enterprise shared, to varying degrees, by readers, authors, and publishers, and by men and women, as they worked together to create a profession of authorship that would increase the national and international visibility of American writers in the later nineteenth century. After the Civil War, writers very rarely had to question, as Margaret Fuller did, the existence of American literature. The terms under which that literature would come to be viewed were still in flux, and it was not until well into the twentieth century that American literature became institutionalized as a viable academic field. But by the later nineteenth century, American literature had not only "emerged" but flourished; it was, indeed, a "paradise of authors."

SOURCE NOTES

[Unless otherwise indicated artifacts and documents are reproduced courtesy of the American Antiquarian Society (AAS), Worcester, Massachusetts.]

1. "Authors and Writers," *United States Literary Gazette* 1 (March 1825): 346–47.

2. Ralph Waldo Emerson, "The Poet," in *Essays: Second Series*, 2d ed. (Boston: Phillips, Sampson, 1852), 9–45.

3. Herman Melville, "Hawthorne and His Mosses," *Literary World* 7 (1850): 125–27, 145–47.

4. James T. Fields, *Yesterdays with Authors* (Boston: James R. Osgood, 1872), 48–52.

5. Caroline Ticknor, *Hawthorne and His Publisher* (Boston and New York: Houghton Mifflin, 1913).

6. "Printers and Authors," *North Carolina Standard* (Raleigh), April 18, 1849, 1.

7. Henry C. Carey, *Letters on International Copyright*, 2d ed. (New York: Hurd and Houghton, 1868), 68–69.

8. Herman Melville, *The Writings of Herman Melville*, ed. Lynn Horth, vol. 14, *Correspondence* (Chicago: Northwestern University Press and the Newberry Library, 1993), 191. Copyright © Northwestern University Press. Reproduced courtesy Northwestern University Press, Evanston, Ill.

9. Edgar Allan Poe, *The Complete Works of Edgar Allan Poe*, ed. James A. Harrison, vol. 17, *Letters* (New York: Thomas Y. Crowell, 1902), 89–91.

10. Nathaniel Hawthorne, *The Centenary Edition of the Works of Nathaniel Hawthorne*, ed. Thomas Woodson et al., vol. 16, *The Letters, 1843–1853* (Columbus: Ohio State University Press, 1985), 379. Reproduced courtesy of Ohio State University Press, Columbus, Ohio.

11. Ibid., 511.

12. John S. Hart, *The Female Prose Writers of America* (Philadelphia: E. H. Butler, 1852).

13. "Literary Women," *Littell's Living Age* 25 (1864): 609–10.

14. Mrs. A. J. Graves, *Woman in America* (1841; New York: Harper & Brothers, 1847), 188–92.

15. Virginia Penny, *How Women Can Make Money* (Philadelphia: McKinney & Martin, 1870), 2–5.

WORKS CITED

Baym, Nina. "Again and Again, The Scribbling Women." In *Hawthorne and Women: Engendering and Expanding the Hawthorne Tradition*, edited by John L. Idol Jr. and Melinda M. Ponder, 20–35. Amherst: University of Massachusetts Press, 1999.

Bell, Michael Davitt. "Beginnings of Professionalism." In *The Cambridge History of American Literature*. Vol. 2, 1820–1865, edited by Sacvan Bercovitch and Cyrus R. K. Patell, 11–73. Cambridge: Cambridge University Press, 1995.

Buell, Lawrence. *New England Literary Culture*. New York: Cambridge University Press, 1986.

Darnton, Robert. "What Is the History of Books?" In *Reading in America: Literature and Social History*, edited by Cathy N. Davidson, 27–52. Baltimore, Md.: Johns Hopkins University Press, 1989.

Fink, Steven. *Prophet in the Marketplace: Thoreau's Development as a Professional Writer*. Princeton, N.J.: Princeton University Press, 1992.

Fuller, S. Margaret. *Papers on Literature and Art*. Part 2. New York: Wiley and Putnam, 1846.

Loving, Jerome. *Emerson, Whitman, and the American Muse*. Chapel Hill: University of North Carolina Press, 1982.

Matthiessen, F. O. *American Renaissance: Art and Expression in the Age of Emerson and Whitman*. New York and London: Oxford University Press, 1941.

"On the State of Learning in the United States of America." *Blackwood's Edinburgh Magazine* 4 (March 1819): 641–49.

Warren, Joyce, ed. *The (Other) American Traditions: Nineteenth-Century Women Writers*. New Brunswick, N.J.: Rutgers University Press, 1993.

Winship, Michael. *American Literary Publishing in the Mid-Nineteenth Century: The Business of Ticknor and Fields*. Cambridge: Cambridge University Press, 1995.

Zboray, Ronald J. *A Fictive People: Antebellum Economic Development and the American Reading Public*. New York: Oxford University Press, 1993.

FOR FURTHER RESEARCH

Barnes, James J. *Authors, Publishers and Politicians: The Quest for an Anglo-American Copyright Agreement, 1815–1854*. Columbus: Ohio State University Press, 1974.

Baym, Nina. *Feminism and American Literary History*. New Brunswick, N.J.: Rutgers University Press, 1992.

———. *Novels, Readers, and Reviewers: Responses to Fiction in Antebellum America*. Ithaca, N.Y.: Cornell University Press, 1984.

Boyd, Anne E. "'What! Has She Got into the "Atlantic"?': Women Writers, the *Atlantic Monthly*, and the Formation of the American Canon." *American Studies* 39 (Fall 1998): 5–36.

Brodhead, Richard H. *Cultures of Letters: Scenes of Reading and Writing in Nineteenth-Century America*. Chicago: University of Chicago Press, 1993.

———. *The School of Hawthorne*. New York: Oxford University Press, 1986.

Charvat, William. *The Profession of Authorship in America, 1800–1870*. Edited by Matthew J. Bruccoli. 1968. Reprint, New York: Columbia University Press, 1992.

Conrad, Susan Phinney. *Perish the Thought: Intellectual Women in Romantic America, 1830–1860*. New York: Oxford University Press, 1976.

Coultrap-McQuin, Susan. *Doing Literary Business: American Women Writers in the Nineteenth Century*. Chapel Hill: University of North Carolina Press, 1990.

Dauber, Kenneth. *The Idea of Authorship in America: Democratic Poetics from Franklin to Melville.* Madison: University of Wisconsin Press, 1990.

Geary, Susan. "The Domestic Novel as a Commercial Commodity: Making a Best Seller in the 1850s." *Papers of the Bibliographical Society of America* 70 (July–September, 1976): 365–93.

———. "Harriet Beecher Stowe, John P. Jewett, and Author-Publisher Relations in 1853." In *Studies in the American Renaissance, 1977,* edited by Joel Myerson, 345–67. Boston: Twayne, 1978.

Gilmore, Michael T. *American Romanticism and the Marketplace.* Chicago: University of Chicago Press, 1985.

Greenspan, Ezra. *George Palmer Putnam: Representative American Publisher.* University Park, Pa.: Pennsylvania State University Press, 2000.

Homestead, Melissa J. "Every Body Sees the Theft: Fanny Fern and Literary Proprietorship in Antebellum America." *New England Quarterly* 74 (June 2001): 210–37.

Kaplan, Amy. "Manifest Domesticity." *American Literature* 70 (September 1998): 581–606.

*Kearns, Michael. "The Material Melville: Shaping Readers' Horizons." In *Reading Books: Essays on the Material Text and Literature in America,* edited by Michele Moylan and Lane Stiles, 52–74.

Kelley, Mary. *Private Woman, Public Stage: Literary Domesticity in Nineteenth-Century America.* New York: Oxford University Press, 1984.

Miller, Perry. *The Raven and the Whale.* New York: Harcourt, Brace, 1956.

Newbury, Michael. *Figuring Authorship in Antebellum America.* Stanford, Calif.: Stanford University Press, 1997.

Reynolds, David S. *Beneath the American Renaissance: The Subversive Imagination in the Age of Emerson and Melville.* Cambridge, Mass.: Harvard University Press, 1989.

Samuels, Shirley, ed. *The Culture of Sentiment: Race, Gender, and Sentimentality in Nineteenth-Century America.* New York: Oxford University Press, 1992.

Spencer, Benjamin T. *The Quest for Nationality: An American Literary Campaign.* Syracuse, N.Y.: Syracuse University Press, 1957.

Tonkovich, Nicole. *Domesticity with a Difference: The Nonfiction of Catharine Beecher, Sarah J. Hale, Fanny Fern, and Margaret Fuller.* Jackson: University Press of Mississippi, 1997.

Widmer, Edward L. *Young America: The Flowering of Democracy in New York City.* New York: Oxford University Press, 1999.

Williams, Susan S. "'Promoting an Extensive Sale': The Production and Reception of *The Lamplighter.*" *New England Quarterly* 69 (June 1996): 179–200.

Ziff, Larzer. *Literary Democracy: The Declaration of Cultural Independence in America.* New York: Viking Press, 1981.

8

Northern and Southern Worlds of Print

ALICE FAHS

THE CIVIL WAR wrought staggering destruction on the disunited states. Between 1861 and 1865 more than a million men (in a nation of thirty million people, half of whom were women) died or were left grievously wounded. By war's end, much of the south lay in ruins. Northern towns and farms suffered less, because most of the conflict occurred in the Confederate States of America. Still, northerners no less than southerners knew this war firsthand. Their own experiences, letters from their relatives at the front, and newspapers that reported the war in words and pictures all brought the war home to Americans. Faced with the destructiveness of the Civil War, we can easily ignore the creative energy that war unleashed. Examples abound: the newspapers (the most famous being the heavily illustrated *Harper's Weekly*), Mary Chesnut's voluminous diaries reflecting on the conflict, Winslow Homer's drawings and paintings of war scenes, and later fiction such as Stephen Crane's *The Red Badge of Courage*. Significantly, much of this energy emerged in print: from children's books to patriotic envelopes, in words and in pictures, published and unpublished.

The proliferation of print in the Civil War reflected sectional differences that had existed long before the conflict began in 1861. For instance, the overwhelming bulk of the nation's publishing industry was in the north (as artifacts in the previous chapters suggest). Southern authors generally sought northern publishers for their work. The best-selling American authors, and the ones whose work would later become part of the American literary "canon," hailed predominantly from the northeastern states. And northerners, on average, were far more literate than southerners. During the war, these antebellum differences would translate into a northern print culture far more vibrant than its southern counterpart: northern publishers flourished, introducing new literary genres and giving old genres new twists—while southern magazines faced paper shortages, and southern readers had to make do without the northern books and periodicals they had come to enjoy.

Nonetheless, the wartime experience also revealed common threads, north and south. Union and Confederate diaries alike recorded the all-consuming interest in war. Northerners and southerners wanted the latest war news. Citizens of both regions, in other words, demanded and produced unprecedented amounts of print. And when the war ended, several million African Americans, newly liberated from slavery, would express similar desires, as education and literacy were now the coin of American citizenship.

ARTIFACTS

The selections in this chapter reveal how deeply involved northerners and southerners were in a world of print during the war, whether as readers, authors, editors, or critics. Southerners experienced literary anxieties and hopes, especially as they faced a new world of print scarcity. What would southerners read when blockades made northern books and magazines harder to get—and when Confederate patriotism rendered them suspect? Three women's diaries suggest the concerns and answers. Kate Stone (1841–1907) was twenty when war broke out and lived on a large cotton plantation in northeast Louisiana. Ella Gertrude Clanton Thomas (1848–1889), the wife of a planter, lived near Augusta, Georgia, during the war. The famous diarist Mary Chesnut (1823–1886), whose diary is considered one of the finest literary achievements of the war, lived in Columbia, South Carolina, at the time she made the entry reprinted here. Southern periodicals, although hard pressed to survive the war, expressed most bluntly the desire for a southern literature. The *Southern Literary Messenger*, founded in 1834, was the most illustrious and venerable literary magazine in the south. George William Bagby (1828–1883) edited the *Messenger* during the war, leading the call for southern literary nationalism—but also revealing the impediments to that objective. The *Southern Monthly*, a war magazine begun in September 1861, lasted only nine months.

Diary of Kate Stone (1861–1863)[1]

May 23, 1861. Tonight a little fire was pleasant and we all gathered around it to hear Mr. Newton read the papers. Nothing but "War, War" from the first to the last column. Throughout the length and breadth of the land the trumpet of war is sounding, and from every hamlet and village, from city and country, men are hurrying by thousands, eager to be led to battle against Lincoln's hordes. Bravely, cheerily they go, willing to meet death in defense of the South, the land we love so well, the fairest land and the most gallant men the sun shines on. May God prosper us. Never again can we join hands with the North, the people who hate us so. We take quite a number of papers: *Harper's Weekly* and *Monthly*, the *New York Tribune*, *Journal of Commerce*, *Littell's Living Age*, the *Whig* and *Picayune* of New Orleans, and the Vicksburg and local sheets. What shall we do when Mr. Lincoln stops our mails?

The Northern papers do make us so mad! Even Little Sister, the child of the house, gets angry. Why will they tell such horrible stories about us? Greeley is the worst of the lot; his wishes for the South are infamous and he has the imagination of Poe. What shall we do when our mails are stopped and we are no longer in touch with the world?

December 25, 1863. Mrs. Lawrence has been kind about lending us her books, but we have about finished her library. Have read history until I feel as dry as those old times. Have nearly memorized Tennyson and read and reread our favorite plays in

Shakespeare. Fortunately he never grows old. We hope Mr. McGee will be able to get *Harper's* to us. We wrote to him for it. That would keep us stirred up for awhile at least. The literature of the North is to us what the "flesh pots of Egypt" were to the wandering Israelites—we long for it.

Diary of Ella Gertrude Clanton Thomas (1861)[2]

July 21, 1861. I have read nothing new for some time. The Blockade has prevented the importation of new Books and loyal as I am and wish to be I think that for a time this will prove a serious inconvenience. I do not mean just at present for if we read "the signs of the times" and keep posted in political events we will have little time for anything else—but after the war is over, or if it continues for some time what shall we do for Books? It is true we all have standard books in our library, many of which will repay a second perusal with a more matured mind but our people are generally new to the making of Books and for some time we will miss the delightful pleasure of culling over half a dozen new Books to see which we shall read first—Yet why are we dependent upon the north? The two books which have created most sensation in the novel reading portion of the country for some time have been *Adam Bede, The Mill on the Floss* and *Beulah*. The two former by Miss Evans of England and the latter by Miss Evans of Mobile—and we have plenty of talent lying latent in the South to make for us a glorious name. We have one great drawback—indolence—to contend against. Say what we may it is more this than indifference or anything else which prevents so many from improving their God given talent. Unless urged by the spur of adversity and dependence they are too apt to bury their talent, willing to be entertained but not willing to do anything themselves towards entertaining. . . .

Diary of Mary Chesnut (1862–1865)[3]

June, 1862. Now, for the first time in my life, no book can interest me. But life is so real, so utterly earnest—fiction is so flat, comparatively. Nothing but what is going on in this distracted world of ours can arrest my attention for ten minutes at a time.

January 15, 1864. Every Sunday Mr. Minnegerode cries aloud in anguish his litany. "From pestilence and famine, battle, murder, and sudden death," and we wailed on our knees, "Good Lord, deliver us." And on Monday and all the week long, we went on as before, hearing of nothing but battle, murder, sudden death. Those are the daily events. Now a new book—that is the unlooked-for thing, the pleasing incident in this life of monotonous misery.

March 11, 1864. Today read *Blithedale*. *Blithedale* leaves such an unpleasant impression. I like pleasant, kindly stories now. We are so harrowed by real life.

Tragedy is for hours of ease.

March 12, 1864. John Thompson sent me a New York *Herald* only three days old.

March 12, 1865. We are surprised to see by the papers that we had behaved heroically in leaving everything we had to be destroyed—without one thought of surrender. We had not thought of ourselves from the heroic point of view.

The Southern Literary Messenger (1861–1864)[4]

June 1861. The paper on which the present number of the Messenger is printed, is far inferior to that we are in the habit of using. Cut off, as we are, from our regular manufacturer, we must ask our friends to make due allowance. Ere long we will be an *independent* people,—relying upon and helping ourselves, instead of building up our enemies. Again, we say, dear friends, help us, that we may be enabled to continue on our way.

We take pleasure in informing our Southern friends that Messrs. HENRY L. PELOUZE & CO., have established a Type Foundry in Richmond, and are prepared to supply those in want, with printing material generally. Should the Southern printers give them proper encouragement, we have no doubt that they will, in time, establish a foundry here equal to any in the Northern cities.

August 1861. Literary journals of a high order must be sustained at the South, if we would have an actual and not merely a nominal independence of the North—and in the Messenger we have a periodical just suited to the wants of Southern men. Let Southern writers rally to its support—let Southern subscriptions flow in to the publishers—and the Messenger will not only sustain its former enviable reputation, but will become the spokesman of Southern sentiment, and will discharge in the South the offices discharged in Great Britain by the English Reviews.

Letter from "a lady of Jackson, Mississippi," August 1861. The 'Messenger' comes addressed to my husband, I am your constant reader indeed, for there is hardly a line, in any number, that I do not peruse; the early and determined stand you took in favour of the Secession of Virginia, even enhanced the respect I have long had for the 'Messenger,' and I trust that though the present crisis has lost you Northern patronage, it will not be long before Southerners, who have wasted their money to pay for the demoralizing trash, sent forth by the Northern press, will awake to a full sense of the duty they owe to themselves and to Southern Literature. I have not paid for a Northern Periodical or Newspaper for twelve years—(and *we* are always *paying* subscribers)—the antipathy I have felt for the tone of Northern publications, is of long standing, and has continued to grow with age; when the 'Messenger' was reduced in price, I verily thought that the subscribers to Northern periodicals will now be left without excuse, but it was not so, our beautiful sunny South was still tied to the wheels of Northern publishers; I trust that the Literary bonds will fall with the political ones, and that henceforth we may have the patriotism to sustain our own literature.

September 1861. During these war times, the Messenger comes tardily to its subscribers. They will pardon inevitable delays. When the Editor, the type setters and the pressmen are gone to "fight the battles of their country;" when paper is scarce and printing ink is mean, we feel not so much regret in appearing late in the day, as pride in being able to appear at all. We think we shall not only survive the war, but, at its close, (provided it be not too long off,) be able to make the Messenger all that the most fastidious subscriber could ask. If we do our part, we shall not be compelled to solicit subscriptions by the worn out appeal to Southern patriotism. Southern patriotism never was proof against Northern newspapers and picture magazines. If the angel Gabriel had gone into the very heart of the South, if he had even taken his seat on the top of the office of the Charleston Mercury and there proclaimed the immediate approach of the Day of Judgment, that would not have hindered the hottest secessionist from buying the New York Herald and subscribing for Harper's Magazine. Southern patriotism is, and has always been, a funny thing—indeed the funniest of things. It enables a man to abuse the Yankees, to curse the Yankees, to fight the Yankees, to do everything but quit taking the Yankee papers. Nothing less than a battery of 10-inch Columbiads can keep Southern patriotism away from Yankee papers. Even that is doubtful. We suspect that the animating impulse which will ere long carry the Army of the Potomac into Washington City, will, when it is analyzed, be found to be, merely the inappeasable desire of Southern patriotism to obtain a copy of Bonner's Ledger.

Having this just conception of Southern patriotism, we shall act accordingly. Arrangements have been made to combine in the *Messenger* all of the most trashy, contemptible and popular features of *Harper, Godey, Frank Leslie*, the *Herald, Home Journal, Ledger, Yankee Notions, Nick-Nax, Budget of Fun*, and the *Phunny Phellow*. We shall have nothing but pictures. We shall have nothing but the latest news and the fashions. Diagrams of baby clothes, worked slippers, edgings, frills, cuffs, capes, furbelows, furaboves, and indeed all the most interior and intricate feminine fixings, shall be supplied in much profusion. We shall pay particular attention to woodcuts, representing bonnets, cloaks, *basquines, robes de* all sorts, etc. We shall furnish every month not less than 1800 different photographic views of the proper way to do up the back hair. We shall devote eleven-ninths of each number to crochet work and fancy pin-cushions. Meantime we shall devote our entire space to riddles, charades, acrostics, and questions in arithmetic. But the greater part of the magazine shall be given to little dabs of light literature *a la* Fanny Fern. Our exclusive exertions, however, shall be strained for the procurement of tales, stories, narratives, novels, novellettes, serials and serialettes, including Edward Everialettes and the like. We shall buy Sylvanus Cobb. We shall purchase Emerson Bennett. We shall offer any sum for Mrs. Emma E.D.N.O.P.Q.R.S.T.U.V.W.X.Y.Z. Southworth. Any lady having more initials than Mrs. Southworth, shall be ours at all hazards and to the last extremity. No expense shall be spared. We shall rent N. P. Willis by the year. We shall lease the remainder of the natural lives of all novelists in all parts of the world. We shall, in a word, satisfy, and if possible satiate the depraved taste of Southern patriotism.

November 1861. In common with other Southern interests, and especially with publications, THE MESSENGER has felt, and still feels, severely, the pressure of the war. While newspaper after newspaper has been suspended, and even the staunchest journals have been compelled to retrench and economise; while DeBow's *Review* is published but once in two months, THE MESSENGER has steadily held its own, despite of bad ink, a scarcity of paper and of printers, a great falling off in contributions, and almost a suspension in payments. This cannot last. Willing to make any reasonable sacrifice for the sake of sustaining the oldest and most neglected literary journal in the South, the proprietors of THE MESSENGER do not feel themselves called upon to do so solely and entirely out of their own purses. They feel that the most ardent and patriotic supporters of Southern literature would hardly expect them to perform an act at once so noble and impossible. They know they have done their duty and more than their duty. While hundreds and thousands of wealthy and cultivated gentlemen have indulged in grandiloquent professions of devotion to the cause of Southern letters, they—practical printers, earning their bread by daily work at the case—have contented themselves with the simple but potent eloquence of hard money, paid out of not over full pockets. This is said in no boastful spirit. It is a plain truth, told in mere justice to themselves. If no adequate return has been made to them for all they have done, they have derived comfort from the assurance that the neglect of the Magazine, which they had published for twelve or thirteen years, was due not so much to Southern indifference to them, and to native literature, as to that habit of dependence on the North, from which nothing less than the horrors of war could ever have delivered us. The war has come, Northern newspapers and magazines have been totally cut off, yet THE MESSENGER is in no better plight than before. . . . The publishers of THE MESSENGER will oppose this "stubborn" state of "things" with one more effort. They will send out, with the present number, bills against all who are indebted to them, with the simple, earnest request, "Pay me that thou owest." They have no begging to do. They have no more appeals to Southern patriotism to make. All they want is the money that is due them.

April 1862. Never were we so "put to it" for suitable contents for our [Editor's] Table. The Yankees have penetrated so far into the Confederacy—have menaced so many interior points, that our correspondents have had neither leisure nor inclination to furnish contributions. So great indeed are the distractions of the times, that the

Editor himself, whose sole duty, according to general belief, is to cater to the Table, has found it impossible to perform his task in a manner at all satisfactory. Driven to the wall for "matter," he has made some selections from old English writers, which he hopes will be deemed not altogether inappropriate to the "situation." The Messenger is not all it should be, but such as it is, it shall continue to greet our readers until the Confederate Metropolis shares the fate of Nashville and New Orleans.

January 1864. THE MESSENGER has passed into other hands. Of this the public has been apprized by the daily prints. It may not be generally known, however, that the new Proprietors, whose debut is made in the present number, are young gentlemen brim-full of energy and ambition, with abundant means, and, above all, imbued with correct opinions in regard to the proper mode of developing a literary journal. They intend to make THE MESSENGER, both externally and internally, far more inviting than it has heretofore been; to pay for contributions; to advertise liberally; to secure agencies in all the principal cities and towns of the Confederacy; to enlist the best and brightest talent in the land; and, while upholding a lofty standard of literature, so to enliven and invigorate the old magazine, as to enlist the favour and attract the admiration of all classes of society, except such as delight in productions intrinsically low and puerile. Their ideal is high, but at the same time popular, and it is their purpose to leave nothing undone which can ensure the public approval and establish at once their own reputation and that of the magazine.

They are prepared to do what their predecessors have not done and were not able to do; that is, to impart to the business management that energy and system without which no enterprise can or ought to prosper, and to give to the editorial department that undivided attention which a first class magazine imperatively demands. And here the former Editor and Proprietors think fit to say a word in self defence, as well from natural impulse as to forestall criticism detrimental to themselves, which the certain and rapid improvement of the magazine will be sure to provoke. Owning a printing establishment, the incessant engagements of which occupied nearly their whole time and means, the Proprietors could devote only intervals of leisure to THE MESSENGER. Long experience had taught them not to place too much confidence in the Southern demand for literature; they were unwilling to give up a certainty for an uncertainty. . . . The circulation of THE MESSENGER was small, so small, and the cost of publication, latterly, so heavy, that the pay of the Editor was trifling, and that of contributors merely nominal. It may excite surprise, and will no doubt sound laughable when we state that, in times of peace, the Editor's salary was but $300,—a pitiful sum, truly, which was increased during the past year to $400, or, allowing for present depreciation, just Twenty Dollars in coin, for editing the leading and, in fact, the only Southern magazine for a whole year. . . .

Under all these disadvantages, it is something to the retiring "management" that they have been able to keep alive THE MESSENGER during three years of terrible war, and in spite of a depreciated currency and a great scarcity of paper. This they think they may justly claim, and they care to claim no more.

A better and brighter era has dawned on the magazine, which for thirty years has stood in the front of Southern periodicals. New life is to be infused into it and a true system to be adopted. . . . A bright career, beset with some difficulties, it is true, is before them [the new editors]; but the time is not distant, when they will look back upon the revelations made in this, our parting editorial, as a curious and instructive legend of Southern literature in its early and struggling stages.

It remains only for the former Editor and Proprietors to make their bow. With best wishes alike for their old subscribers and contributors, and for the new Proprietors; with kindliest remembrance of the associations, past and present, which now terminate; and, above all, with profoundest aspirations for the success of that great and sacred cause on which all Southern literature depends, they bid their friends and readers a cordial, hearty, hopeful farewell. . . .

The Southern Monthly (1862)[5]

Soldier or Civilian who would see our Confederacy truly free, extend your aid to build up an INDEPENDENT SOUTHERN LITERATURE! By fostering and encouraging it, you erect an enduring bulwark for Liberty that will defend you where armies are powerless. Give it your support now—it will repay you a thousand fold. Gallant armies on the battle-field defend you against open foes—the Press, properly sustained, will do no less; it will protect you against more dangerous, because insidious ones. Call forth by active encouragement talented writers "to the manor born," and, "gallant as an army with banners," will they, in the dissemination of pure influences, and high aspirations, and true principles, fight the good fight of loyalty to OUR country against the wily Northmen, who have spread broadcast over our fair land their noxious exhalations, through the medium of those Northern Periodicals, heretofore so much patronised by us. We offer you the "SOUTHERN MONTHLY" as an exponent of SOUTHERN SENTIMENTS, SOUTHERN POLICY and SOUTHERN INSTITUTIONS. . . . Such is our programme—may we not hope for a large audience? We ask a full house. We look for 20,000 subscribers.

IN CONTRAST, the selections on northern popular literary culture suggest a world of print abundance—and some critics' disgust with that culture. As the war broke out, George William Curtis (1824–1892), novelist, writer, and reformer, became the political editor of the highly influential *Harper's Weekly*, in addition to his editorial duties for *Harper's Magazine*. His article from August 1861, and the 1861 diary of Sarah Butler Wister (1835–1908)—a prominent Philadelphian whose father was a slaveholder —suggest how the publishing and print trades contributed to Union pageantry early in the war. Before long, however, it became possible to poke fun at what seemed like publishers' wartime opportunism. Orpheus C. Kerr (Robert Henry Newell [1836–1901]) was a Civil War humorist who parodied Civil War culture, especially through his invention of the hapless Mackerel Brigade. His sketches appeared in the weekly New York Sunday *Mercury* before being published in book form in 1862. Kerr employed light satire, but the *Round Table*, a New York critical journal begun in January 1864, expressed harsher sentiments about war literature. Unlike its southern counterparts, the *Round Table* outlived the war.

George William Curtis, from *Harper's New Monthly Magazine* (1861)[6]

The flags flying every where are still the symbol of the only topic of talk and interest. The soldiers come and go. The sons of many States, East and West, resident in New York, receive their brothers and friends who arrive, with military pomp, salute them, feast them, bless them, and send them on their way. The green islands near the city whiten with the increasing camps. The children play in the streets dressed like Zouaves, with little muskets for toys. The beat of the drum, the bugle-call, the shrill, passionate shock of martial music fill the air by night and day. The bookshops have only placards of books of tactics and the drill. The windows glow with portraits of the heroes. The photograph galleries are crowded with living soldiers looking at pictured soldiers upon the walls. The piles of brick and rubbish in the streets are covered with posters bearing a charging Zouave for illustration, and with General Orders, and calls for recruits, and notices of warlike meetings. The theatres revive old battle melodramas and invent new. The passengers in the streets wear badges, rosettes, and cockades of the trinity of patriotic colors. In shawls, in cravats, in ribbons, the same tricolor appears. Shops are suddenly opened on every hand for the sale of camp stores and military equipage. The newspapers are crowded with various details of the same general subject. Reports, speculations, guesses, indignation, criticism; and in the midst of the cloud the sharp dart of the truth flashing home into a hundred hearts. The crowds assemble daily before the bulletins of the newspaper offices, and the excitement of important news flutters along Broadway or Nassau Street like the widening ripples in water. You feel something in men's motions; you see something in the general manner of the throng in the street before you read it recorded upon the board or in the paper. There is but one thought and one question. The people are soldiers. The country is a camp. It is war.

Diary of Sarah Butler Wister (1861)[7]

Chestnut Street is a sight; flags large & small flaunt from every building, the drygoods shops have red white & blue materials draped together in their windows, in the ribbon stores the national colors hang in long streamers, and even the book sellers place the red, white, and blue bindings together.

Orpheus C. Kerr, *The Orpheus C. Kerr Papers* (1862)[8]

Letter LII.

Washington, D.C., June 25th, 1862.

Early in the week, I took my usual trip to Paris, and found Company 3, Regiment 5, Mackerel Brigade, making an advance from the further shore of Duck Lake, for sanitary reasons. It was believed to be detrimental to the health of the gay Mackerels to be so near a body of pure water, my boy, for they were not accustomed to the element.

"Thunder!" says the general, brushing off a small bit of ice that had adhered to his nose, "they'll be drinking it next."

Captain Samyule Sa-mith was ordered to command the advance; but when he heard that the Southern Confederacy had two swivels over there, he was suddenly taken very sick, and cultivated his bed-clothes.

When the news of the serious illness of this valiant officer got abroad, my boy, there was an immediate rush of free and enterprising civilian chaps to his bedside.

One chap, who was an uncombed reporter for a discriminating and affectionate daily press, took me aside, and says he:

"Our paper has the largest circulation, and is the best advertising mejum in the United States. As soon as our brother-in-arms expires," says the useful chap, feelingly, "just fill up this printed form and send it to me, and I will mention you in our paper as a promising young man."

I took the printed form, my boy, which I was to fill up, and found it to read thus: "BIOGRAPHICAL SKETCH OF THE LATE _____.

"This noble and famous officer, recently slain at the head of his_____ (I put the word 'bed' in this blank, my boy), was born at _____ on the _____ day of _____, 1776, and entered West Point in his _____year. He won immortal fame by his conduct in the Mexican campaign, and was created brigadier-general on the ___ of _____, 1862."

These printed forms suit the case of any soldier, my boy; but I didn't entirely fill this one up.

Samyule was conversing with the chaplain about his Federal soul, when a tall, shabby chap made a dash for the bedside, and says he to Samyule:

"I'm agent for the great American publishing house of Rushem & Jinks, and desire to know if you have anything that could be issued in book-form after your lamented departure. We could make a handsome 12mo book," says the shabby chap, persuadingly, "of your literary remains. Works of a Union Martyr—Eloquent Writings of a Hero—Should be in every American Library—Take it home to your wife—Twenty editions ordered in advance of publication—Half-calf, $1.—Send in your orders."

Samyule looked thoughtfully at the publishing chap, and says he:

"I never wrote anything in my life."

"Oh!" says the shabby chap, pleasantly, "anything will do—your early poems in the weekly journals—anything."

"But," says Samyule, regretfully, "I never wrote a line to a newspaper in all my life."

"What!" says the publishing chap, almost in a shriek—"never wrote a line to a newspaper? Gentleman," says the chap, looking toward us, suspiciously, "this man can't be an American." And he departed hastily.

Believing, my boy, that there would be no more interruptions, Samyule went on dying; but I was called from his bedside by a long-haired chap from New York. Says the chap to me:

"My name is Brown—Brown's Patent Hair-Dye, 25 cents a bottle. Of course," says the hirsute chap, affably, "a monument will be erected to the memory of our departed hero. An Italian marble shaft, standing on a pedestal of four panels. Now," says the hairy chap, insinuatingly, "I will give ten thousand dollars to have my adver-tisement put on the panel next to the name of the lamented deceased. We can get up something neat and appropriate, thus:

WE MUST ALL DIE;
BUT
BROWN'S DYE IS THE BEST.

"There!" says the enterprising chap, smilingly, "that would be very neat and moral, besides doing much good to an American fellow-being."

I made no reply, my boy; but I told Samyule about it, and it excited him so that he regained his health.

"If I can't die," says the lamented Samyule, "without some advertising cuss's making money by it, I'll defer my visit to glory until next season."

And he got well, my boy—he got well.

The Round Table (1864)[9]

January 9, 1864. "Romances of the War." In the minds of most men a certain digni-fied solemnity connects itself inseparably with the idea of war. The gorgeous trap-pings of man and beast, the flapping of sanctified banners, the masses of moving humanity, the impressive effect of the

"—thunder of guns and the roll of drums
And an army marching by,"

are all fraught with a high degree of something akin to sublimity. And especially is the battle-field a subject of awe. Beside its horrid heroism and terrible splendor all commonplace emotions seem hollow and heartless, though they may be earnest enough for everyday wear. In such company, then, flippancy becomes appalling.

Yet there is a sort of literature, based upon that prurient hunger for "sensation" which demands a nightly supper of bleeding hearts and water, that carries its flippancy and its commonplaces to the battle-field, and flaunts them in affected bombast above the fallen heroes who lie there, happy, it may be, in an eternal immunity from such trash. We mean the so-called "Romances of the War" so much in vogue among magazines and "story papers" during the two sorry years just past. . . .

If there be no other reason, this wholesale demoralization of "light writing" should weigh heavily as an inducement for the termination of hostilities. The horrors of war are numerous and great, but its romances, so-called, are hardly better; and we sincerely implore all young ladies and gentlemen of budding talent and limited experience to refrain, henceforth, from doing feeble violence to our noble language in their frantic endeavors to gild the fine gold of heroism, and paint, with unctuous carmine and rose-pink,

"—the blood-red blossom of war, with a heart of fire!"

January 23, 1864. "Shoddy Literature." It is generally fancied that great events bring out great expressions. Is this tremendous epic we are now living to bring forth naught but trash unutterable and bombast? Are we to have nothing better than the well-behaved nonsense of Mr. Parton, and the dreary dribble of Mr. Morford, to mark, in literature, these days and nights of blood and fire, these broken hearts, these sundered kinsfolk, these robes of mourning that go trailing from the rocks of Eastport to the sands of the Rio Grande? Are there no sweet singers nor manly scribes left in our land?

Well, let us wait. Perhaps some of the hands that are smiting the enemy now, may smite the harp-strings when peace has robbed the saber of its occupation. Perhaps some of the brains that are now planning campaigns may write brave histories when campaigning is over. Meanwhile, we must be patient, and read as little as possible of this balderdash.

PRESIDENT LINCOLN'S Emancipation Proclamation, announced in September 1862, made abolition a Union war aim. But some northerners, especially African Americans, had envisioned emancipation as the war's outcome from the start. After Congress abolished slavery in Washington, D.C., in 1862, James Madison Bell (1826–1902) celebrated in verse. Bell, an African American poet, lived in San Francisco during the war. Lincoln's proclamation inspired African American poet and novelist Frances Ellen Watkins Harper (1825–1911) to write the verses reprinted here. Harper's poem appeared in *The Freedmen's Book*, a tribute to the emancipated slaves edited by the abolitionist writer Lydia Maria Child (1802–1880) at war's end. Emancipation did not end racism; indeed, some northerners conjured up nightmares of freed ex-slaves migrating to the north and taking white workers' jobs. For William Wells Brown (1815–1884), biography offered a vehicle to celebrate African Americans' achievements—and to prove their equality to white Americans. Born a slave in Kentucky, Brown published sixteen books after escaping north and was a popular antislavery lecturer. Reprinted here are his letter to abolitionist Gerrit Smith proposing his book of African American biographical sketches, and part of the book's preface. Even as African Americans placed their own aspirations in print, commercial publishers produced novels about slaves and slavery. In her letters to Will Harbert, Elizabeth Boynton (1845–1925)—who lived in Crawfordsville, Indiana, when war broke out—suggested the appeal of that popular literature. Like many abolitionist women, Boynton became a prominent activist for woman's suffrage after the war.

James Madison Bell, "Abolition of Slavery in D.C.," from *The Pacific Appeal* (1862)[10]

Thank God! from our old ensign
    Is erased one mark of shame,
Which leaves one less to rapine,
    One less to blight our fame.
For two and sixty summers
    Has our broad escutcheon waved,
Amid the ceaseless murmurs
    And wails of the enslaved;
But in the blest hereafter
    Shall our oft afflicted ears,
Be solaced with bright laughter,
    With gladsome praise and cheers.
For freedom's altar's basis
    More permanent shall be,
When rid the gaunt embraces
    Of fell barbarity.

Frances E. W. Harper, "President Lincoln's Proclamation of Emancipation, January 1, 1863" (1865)[11]

It shall flash through coming ages,
　　It shall light the distant years;
And eyes now dim with sorrow
　　Shall be brighter through their tears.

It shall flush the mountain ranges,
　　And the valleys shall grow bright;
It shall bathe the hills in radiance,
　　And crown their brows with light.

It shall flood with golden splendor
　　All the huts of Caroline;
And the sun-kissed brow of labor
　　With lustre new shall shine.

It shall gild the gloomy prison,
　　Darkened by the nation's crime,
Where the dumb and patient millions
　　Wait the better-coming time.

By the light that gilds their prison
　　They shall see its mouldering key;
And the bolts and bars shall vibrate
　　With the triumphs of the free.

Though the morning seemed to linger
　　O'er the hill-tops far away,
Now the shadows bear the promise
　　Of the quickly coming day.

Soon the mists and murky shadows
　　Shall be fringed with crimson light,
And the glorious dawn of freedom
　　Break refulgent on the sight.

William Wells Brown, letter to Gerrit Smith proposing a book (1862)[12]

Boston, September 4, 1862
Hon Gerrit Smith.

My dear Sir.— I am getting out a book of 250 pages, a synopsis of the contents of which, I enclose. We think here that it is just the work needed for the hour, to place the Negro in a right position before the country, especially the working classes. We are trying to get it out in as cheap a form as possible, so as to receive for it a wide circulation. I have spent in it what little I had and need more funds to bring it out. I have never asked for a donation for myself from anyone, and do not ask it for myself now. If you feel that you can give me any assistance in getting out the book, I will send you enough copies to make the *advance* good, at least in *paper*.
With fresh remembrance of my visit to your house, I would beg to be kindly mentioned to your family.

Respectfully and truly yours,
Wm. Wells Brown

William Wells Brown, *The Black Man, His Antecedents, His Genius, and His Achievements* (1863)[13]

The calumniators and traducers of the Negro are to be found, mainly, among two classes. The first and most relentless are those who have done them the greatest injury, by being instrumental in their enslavement and consequent degradation. They delight to descant upon the "natural inferiority" of the blacks, and claim that we were destined only for a servile condition, entitled neither to liberty nor the legitimate pursuit of happiness. The second class are those who are ignorant of the characteristics of the race, and are the mere echoes of the first. To meet and refute these misinterpretations, and to supply a deficiency, long felt in the community, of a work containing sketches of individuals who, by their own genius, capacity, and intellectual development, have surmounted the many obstacles which slavery and prejudice have thrown in their way, and raised themselves to positions of honor and influence, this volume was written. . . .

If this work shall aid in vindicating the Negro's character, and show that he is endowed with those intellectual and amiable qualities which adorn and dignify human nature, it will meet the most sanguine hopes of the writer.

Elizabeth Boynton, Letters to Will Harbert (1864)[14]

February 20th, 1864. I may be too sanguine and yet it seems *reasonable* to hope that the war will terminate in a few months—and yet much as I long for you and your manly love yet I do not wish for any peace that will leave a *slave* in our land. God

209

grant that when that dawn of peace shall come that wherever our starry flag floats it shall wave o'er free men and *free men alone*—I sometimes shudder when I think what an *horrible* institution "American Slavery" *is*—how long before we can say *was*—I have just finished that new story "Cudjo's Cave" and I wonder how men with any minds can think for an instant that slavery is aught but a *curse.*

March 5th, 1864. You have doubtless noticed criticisms upon a new book called "Peculiar" the hero of the book being a slave named by his master "Peculiar Institution." I read it last week and it has given me more intense views of that most enormous evil of the nineteenth century, American Slavery, than I have ever had before—and when I closed the book and . . . thought of all the evils attendant upon slavery I thanked God that I had been called on to give him who is dearer to me than all else, to a war that will eventually produce its overthrow. Sometimes I feel very brave, feel as though I could if called to do it give you up forever to my country. I feel equal to the spirit of the age we live in—feel, as an American woman should—at others alas, love obtains the mastery of patriotism, selfishness predominates over love for country and I weep bitter tears at our separation and feel that if you were once more with me a whole world of wars could not, should not take you hence— It is not that I love my country less, but you the more.

THE FINAL artifact (on the facing page) is a piece of sheet music, *Barbara Frietchie*, a song based on a poem by John Greenleaf Whittier (1807–1892) written in 1863. The sheet music, however, was not published until 1879: sixteen years after the end of the war, the literature it generated continued to inhabit the American imagination.

John Greenleaf Whittier and Elizabeth Sloman, *Barbara Frietchie* (1879)[15]

COMMENTARY: THE CIVIL WAR AS
A POPULAR LITERARY EVENT

"Men cannot think, or write, or attend to their ordinary business," Oliver Wendell Holmes reported from Boston in the fall of 1861. "They stroll up and down the streets, they saunter out upon the public places" (347). War fever had produced a "nervous restlessness of a very peculiar character." In South Carolina, Mary Chesnut confided to her diary that she had "tried to rise above the agonies of everyday life" by reading Emerson. "Too restless," she concluded of her failed attempt in June of 1861. "Manassas on the brain" (72).

Both north and south, war permeated the wide-ranging set of practices and beliefs that constituted popular literary culture. War changed what people read, what was available to read, and how, where, and with what expectations they read it. It altered the plans and prospects of publishers, pushing some to the brink of failure while giving new energy to a few well-positioned firms. It reshaped literary careers, forcing established authors to reconsider their writing plans, inspiring new authors to enter the literary marketplace, and deeply affecting what both found possible to imagine. Most profoundly, war catalyzed a rethinking of prevailing beliefs about the connecting links between literature and society, and between individual and nation. In the south, war produced an urgent discussion of the place of literature within the larger project of nation building, and of the role of the patriotic reader within a larger literary culture. In the north, an explosion of war-related popular literature and patriotic print goods, part of an expansive commercial culture of war, tightly bound the individual to the nation and yet, ironically, complicated attempts to fix the meanings of the war. North and south, war became not just an obsessive, all-consuming subject, but also a mode of perception and way of life that disrupted and reorganized authors' and readers' conceptions of their place within a larger literary marketplace.

Reading habits, for instance, changed dramatically with the onset of war, a fact that numerous observers noted both north and south. Newspapers suddenly became an urgent necessity of life. In Boston Oliver Wendell Holmes reported that one person he knew always went through the "side streets on his way for the noon extra,—he is so afraid somebody will meet him and tell the news he wishes to read, first on the bulletin-board, and then in the great capitals and leaded type of the newspaper." The newspaper was "imperious," according to Holmes. "It will be had, and it will be read. To this all else must give place. If we must go out at unusual hours to get it, we shall go, in spite of after-dinner nap or evening somnolence" (347, 348). From South Carolina Mary Chesnut concurred, commenting simply, "We haunt the bulletin board" (354).

At the same time, reading the newspaper displaced other forms of literary culture. "In times like the present," the *Southern Literary Messenger* commented in November, "very little interest is felt in literature. Nothing that does not relate to the war itself is read" (395). In the north Holmes reported that an "illustrious author" had confessed that he "had laid down his pen," unable to "write about the sixteenth century" while the nineteenth "was in the very agony and bloody sweat of its great sacrifice" (347).

Many authors, in fact, found that the onset of war disrupted their plans. In Charleston the poet Henry Timrod lamented that he had "planned several poems of length," but that "all of them, I am afraid, will remain the skeletons which they are as yet, until more peaceable times." By the end of 1861, with the dual impact of the end of northern mail service and a blockade of southern ports, Timrod bemoaned the disappearance of literary culture as he had known it: "No new books, no reviews, no appetizing critiques, no literary correspondence, no intellectual intelligence of any kind! Ah! It is a weary time!" (Hubbell, 9–10).

Authors and publishers in the north, too, found that they needed to shift their plans as a result of war. Inevitably, the public absorption in war interrupted and created havoc with established literary institutions and practices. Book publishers, for instance, saw their world change dramatically with the onset of war. As the trade journal of the publishing industry commented, "the entire absorption of public interest by current events has caused a nearly complete cessation in the demand for new books, and publishers have in consequence discontinued their usual issues" (*American Publishers' Circular*, 229). There was abundant evidence of the truth of this remark: while in July of 1860 the Boston publisher Ticknor and Fields, for instance, had had some thirty volumes in press, in July of 1861 its cost books showed that the firm had only four in production. Longfellow remarked on visiting Ticknor and Fields's "Old Corner" bookstore, "Nothing alive but the military. Bookselling dead." After a second visit he noted that "the 'Corner' looks gloomy enough. Ticknor looks grim and Fields is fierce. Business is at a standstill. So much for war and books" (Tryon, 252, 253). In Concord a worried Louisa May Alcott, who wished to submit a story to the *Atlantic Monthly*, recorded in her diary in November that editor James T. Fields had told her "he has Mss. enough on hand for a dozen numbers & has to choose war stories if he can, to suit the times." She declared that "I will write 'great guns' Hail Columbia & Concord fight, if he'll only take it for money is the staff of life & without one falls flat no matter how much genius he may carry" (Alcott, 72).

Alcott's comment suggested a developing reality of wartime popular literary culture: just as the early disruption of war initially affected both north and south in remarkably similar ways, so too did both sections rapidly begin to produce war literature to respond to readers' all-absorbing interest in the conflict. But this effort exposed deep economic and cultural divisions between the two sections, divisions that would only deepen over the course of the war. First and foremost was the fact that most major publishing firms and presses were in the north, not in the south. The 1860 census made the disparity dramatically clear: it counted 986 printing offices in New England and the middle states, only 151 in the south. Of these, the 21 presses in Tennessee produced the most work—yet Tennessee fell under Union control early in the war. There were 190 bookbinders in New England and the middle states, only 17 in the south. No printing presses were manufactured in the south, meaning that it would be difficult if not impossible to replace broken presses (*Manufactures*, cxxxii–cxlv). At the same time, on the eve of the war there were only a few established southern book publishers, including West & Johnston and J. W. Randolph of Richmond; S. H. Goetzel of Mobile; Evans & Cogswell of Charleston; and Burke, Boykin & Co. in Macon. Few other firms, except for religious publishers, were of any considerable size. Among the few established periodicals were the *Southern Literary Messenger*, the *Southern Monthly*, and the *Southern Field and Fireside*. Yet relatively few southerners read these periodicals, instead depending on northern books and periodicals for their reading matter.

This dependence on northern literature was a fact that many commentators now deplored even more strongly than they had during the antebellum period. "Not one Southern book" had lain on the southern parlor table before the war, the *Southern Monthly* claimed in a scathing editorial in its inaugural September 1861 issue. Instead the *Atlantic Monthly*, with "Harriet Beecher Stowe's last novel *continued*" and "Holmes' ingenious diatribes against our country," lay next to "the arrant Harper," while "on chair and sofa" lay "*Ledger* and *Mercury*" (2). Writing in the *Southern Field and Fireside*, Ella Swan scolded southern women, accusing them of having "united with the entire North in supporting a literature at war with your dearest interests." Were not "Southern papers, periodicals and books as worthy of your patronage?" The *Charleston Courier* said simply that "our patronage of magazines published at the North has heretofore been both a folly and a shame" (2).

As such comments made clear, the act of reading itself now took on a strongly ideological cast in the south. Suffused with nationalistic aims, reading was less a private than a public, patriotic act, a vital part of the "creation of Confederate nationalism" (Faust). Furthermore, being a patriotic Confederate involved not only what one did read but also what one did not. It demanded not just the embrace of southern literature but also the repudiation of northern literature—the two were intimately intertwined. Throughout the war, for instance, it was commonplace to begin discussions of southern literature with denunciations of northern literature; northern works pandered to popular taste, they were "trashy," "poisonous," "contemptible." Never one to shrink from hyperbole, the *Southern Illustrated News* in the fall of 1862 called "Yankee literature," with "a very few exceptions, the opprobrium of the Universe." Yankee books were "of the worst possible description," merely a "very bad imitation of the most indifferent class of English literature." Southern literature would come "in due time," and when it did, it would "in no way resemble the Yankee abortion" (September 13, 5).

Yet even as southerners denounced northern literature, it remained a powerful standard against which the south would define itself. Throughout the war, attacks on northern literature did not so much dislodge its power within southern cultural life as shift the terms on which that power was organized through an increasingly ritualized negation. At the same time, attempts to define what constituted a specifically southern literature were often vague: the *Southern Monthly* simply argued for a literature that would reflect "Southern institutions, Southern principles, and Southern interests" (September 1861, back cover). On only one point were commentators clear concerning what these "principles" and "interests" were: Southern literature would provide a positive view of slavery. Indeed, from the outbreak of war the very definition of southern literature was racialized and politicized, as numerous writers made explicit linkages between southern literary nationalism and a defense of slavery.

Although war drastically reshaped the landscape of established literary culture in the south, many commentators argued that it offered unparalleled opportunities for new expressions of literary nationalism. "We must have a periodical literature," the *Charleston Courier* said. "The need is great and it is felt. Forced from our dependence on the North, we must see to it, that we meet this pressing demand with cheerfulness, earnestness, and liberality" (2). The *Southern Monthly* stressed the importance of increasing the number of southern book publishers, "by the sustainment of which alone are we to have a flourishing and healthy literature. It will be found that they go hand in hand, and when the one languishes, the other etiolates and withers" (November 1861, 231–32).

Such comments envisioned war as an exhilarating opportunity finally to create an independent southern literature. Indeed, in the first years of war southerners established several new periodicals that sought to create a distinctive southern literature. As southern war fortunes ran high in 1862, so too did southern literary ambition. Ironically, literature was often explicitly modeled on despised northern counterparts, despite denials that this was so. The *Southern Illustrated News*, for instance, begun in September 1862, was meant to be a southern answer to such popular northern weeklies as *Frank Leslie's Illlustrated Newspaper* and *Harper's Weekly*. Like those periodicals, the *Southern Illustrated News* provided an eclectic group of war-related features including stories, profiles of generals, editorials on the war, humorous sketches of life in camp, reflections on women's home-front role, and war poems. By far the most important aspect of the *News* in its own reckoning, however, was its claim to be "Illustrated." But here its ambitions far outreached its capabilities, emphasizing the extreme difficulties under which Confederate publications were to labor throughout the war. The *News* promised to provide illustrations "honestly and faithfully drawn and engraved by competent and experienced artists." The first issue of the weekly, however, contained only one illustration, a small, crude engraving of Stonewall Jackson in the center of the first page. With a certain amount of defensive bluster, the *News* said that "we expect each week to increase the number of engravings, yet our aim shall be, not number, but quality" (September 13, 4).

A central problem for the *News* was finding experienced artists and engravers in the south. The *News* may have promised illustrations, but it simply did not have the personnel to produce them: within only a few weeks of its first issue it advertised "Wanted Immediately—Two competent Wood Engravers" (September 13, 5). Some months earlier, the *Southern Monthly* had admitted defeat in its own quest to be illustrated. "With no small feeling of chagrin, and some of shame, we are forced to confess that a well-illustrated magazine *cannot* yet be produced in the South," it said in March of 1862. "Good artists we can procure, but good engravers on wood are scarce among us, and even if they were more numerous, the wood itself is not to be had" (580).

Unlike the *Southern Monthly*, the *Southern Illustrated News* eventually did manage to "do better" by hiring several competent artists, including one who had been "actively and prominently engaged on Frank Leslie's Pictorial" (October 4, 8). Yet the illustrations in the *News* remained sparse and remarkably crude by northern standards. They underscored a distinct and important difference between the popular literary culture of war north and south. In the north the war was imagined visually in *Harper's Weekly, Frank Leslie's Illustrated Newspaper*, dozens of other publications and forms of print ephemera, and photographs exhibited in galleries such as Mathew Brady's New York gallery. In the south the literary war remained primarily a war of words, not pictures; of poetic images and oratorical flourishes, rather than painted or engraved representations.

This was not for southern lack of interest in a visual war: in mid-1862 a Richmond "Confederate Reading Room" advertised "YANKEE PICTORIALS OF THE WAR." These had been received from "a party just arrived from the North." Monthly subscribers paid fifty cents, while a single admission—"good for all day"—cost ten cents (*Daily Richmond Examiner*). As this advertisement revealed, war hardly annihilated interest in northern periodicals, despite the expressed hopes of numerous southern publications. Indeed, war may have intensified interest in northern "pictorials." Not only were they the only visual representations of the war available in the south, but they were so scarce as to be especially valuable commodities. Certainly numerous southern diaries record the receipt of a northern "pictorial" as a rare and noteworthy event.

In myriad ways northern literature continued to hold power for southern readers, writers and publishers, who sometimes even measured their own worth in a northern mirror. The *Southern Illustrated News*, for instance, which excoriated the "Yankees" at every opportunity, was jubilant when *Frank Leslie's Illustrated Newspaper* gave it a negative notice. *Leslie's* had reprinted one of the *News'* diatribes against the north, sarcastically commenting that "the South is going to have an art as well as a literature of its own," and noting that the *Southern Illustrated News* was "called illustrated, because it has one picture—an archaic portrait of Stonewall Jackson" (*Frank Leslie's Illustrated Newspaper*).

Yet the *Southern Illustrated News* professed to be triumphant at this notice. "We ask no greater triumph," the *News* said, "than that of knowing we have excited the ire of these immaculate Yankees, the Harpers and Leslie, for with the advent of the 'Southern Illustrated Newspaper' they clearly perceive that the prospect for the circulation of their miserable sheets ever again in the South, is poor indeed. Hence, we welcome their criticism and abuse of us as a bright harbinger" (October 11). The *News* even claimed, falsely, that "in New England and New York, the exigencies of the war, and the closing up of the Southern market, have well nigh extinguished authorship and its lights, from the little farthing candle of Mr. James Russell Lowell to the bright gas burner of Dr. Oliver Wendell Holmes." In contrast, the *News* boasted—again falsely—that one southern firm, West & Johnston, had produced more new books "during the past year, than any firm in Yankee land, not excepting our friends Sharper & Brothers of New York." The *News* concluded with satisfaction that "there has been a healthy stimulus given to literary production among us" (November 8).

It was true that war stimulated southern literary production. Indeed, war inspired an outpouring of poetry from amateur poets, many of them women, who contributed poems to local newspapers. At the same time, several publishers produced cheap war novels, while printers produced numerous Confederate broadsides. But it was equally true that war simultaneously threatened the very existence of southern literature. "But for the capture of Nashville by the Yankees, whereby the large stereotype foundry of that city was lost to us for the war," the *Southern Illustrated News* informed its readers, "many valuable fresh books and new editions of old ones would have been brought out in a style highly creditable to the taste and enterprise of the South." The *Southern Monthly*, located in Memphis, Tennessee, alerted its readers in April of 1862 that it had moved to Grenada, Mississippi, as the "occupation of Memphis by the Abolitionists" was "within the bounds of possibility." It promised, nevertheless, that the *Monthly* "will cease but with the Confederacy that gave it birth" (April 1862). Instead it ceased publication, forever, the next month. As problems with paper supply became increasingly desperate during the war, several popular periodicals, including the *Southern Illustrated News*, were forced to suspend publication for weeks at a time, while some printers published broadsides on the back of wallpaper. Under the exigencies of war the venerable *Southern Literary Messenger*, founded in 1834, was sold in January 1864 and published its last issue in June that same year. Most popular publications quietly folded with the defeat of the Confederacy, as readers and authors returned to their dependence on northern literature.

The situation was far different in the north, which on the eve of the war boasted a mature literary marketplace capable of distributing a wide variety of literature to a far-flung national market. While war initially caused a temporary paralysis of publishing, it quickly became a catalyst for an extensive print culture of war, including patriotic ephemera. From the start of the war in the north, it was possible to connect buying a wide range of goods with being loyal to the nation. For example, patriotic envelopes became a craze early in the war. Printed with flags and a variety of patriotic cartoons and illustrations, such envelopes were initially popular because they provided individuals with a means of displaying—and sending—their patriotism, but within months patriotic envelopes had accrued additional meaning as "collectibles." By late June of 1861 one printer advertised "400 different styles of patriotic envelopes," and several vendors began to stress their collectibility, offering collectors' albums in which to store and display them, such as the "Union and Patriotic Album" and "Illustrated Envelope Holder" (Grant). Although the rage for envelopes subsided by mid-1862, while it lasted this fad powerfully demonstrated a significant difference between north and south in the ability to produce a war-related print culture. Patriotic envelopes were an early wartime fad in the south as well as the north—one among many indications that southern nationality and northern nationality remained culturally linked during the war. Yet southern printers created only a few hundred different designs for patriotic envelopes over the course of the war, while northern printers created at least ten times that number with literally thousands of such designs offered for sale, many of them extraordinarily intricate.

As in the south, the public's all-absorbing interest in the war stimulated a new, war-related print culture in the north. But the more developed consumer economy of the north allowed printers and publishers to create a far more elaborate, visually decorative and theatrical war. The two major northern illustrated weeklies, *Frank Leslie's Illustrated Newspaper* and *Harper's Weekly*, presented extensive illustrations of the war, hiring a corps of "special artists," including the young Winslow Homer, to go into the field and produce sketches from which engravings would be made. Homer himself also produced a series of collectible souvenir cards depicting "Life in Camp" for the printer Louis Prang during the war. Similarly, Currier & Ives produced numerous sentimental war-related lithographs, such as "The Soldier's Dream of Home," and distributed them to a wide audience, while numerous music publishers produced elaborate illustrated sheet music for war songs, as well. While sheet music was also popular in the south, there was simply no Confederate parallel to the richly decorative northern war.

Once the initial shock of the outbreak of war had passed, popular magazines such as *Harper's Monthly*, *Harper's Weekly*, *Arthur's*, *Peterson's*, and the *Atlantic Monthly* began to produce an extensive war literature of stories and poems—at virtually the same moment, in the summer and fall of 1861, that southern publishers began to cast about for such basics as paper and ink. As war, patriotism, and commerce fused within the northern literary marketplace, publishers and authors began to issue a variety of genres of war literature—everything from war romances to war histories to children's war novels to volumes of war poetry to memorial volumes commemorating soldiers who had died in battle. By the start of 1862 several subscription firms began to engage in the project of publishing richly illustrated popular subscription histories of the war, even as it was still being fought. In the spring of that year some publishers already had agents in the field soliciting orders from northern customers; several of their resulting war histories sold hundreds of thousands of copies to a far-flung northern audience in small towns and rural areas. By 1863 and 1864 the market for war literature in the north even extended to children: in the last two years of the war an extensive juvenile war literature, consisting of war stories stressing an adventurous boys' war, began to appear. In the north, in short, the war proved to be a highly marketable commodity within a thriving literary marketplace. Indeed, the speed with which the war was transformed into a saleable commodity was captured in humorous form by the writer Robert Henry Newell, who under the nom de plume Orpheus C. Kerr began to publish parodies of the excesses of northern war-related print culture. At the same time, several critics bemoaned what they saw as the "shoddy" (a word invented during the war) quality of popular war literature.

Although war had at first been a disruption to northern popular literary culture, it increasingly instead fueled an entire sub-genre of "war literature." As the trade journal of the publishing industry marveled in 1864, the war had added "a new and imposing department to our literature." Not only were publishers issuing "military treatises of all kinds, original and republished," but they were also publishing "biographical publications, histories of the war, journals of officers, narratives, war-novels, and war poems," and "political treatises and pamphlets without number" *(American Literary Gazette*, 406). Though this list was imposing, it in fact failed to mention several war-related publications, including juvenile war literature, war humor, war romances, and illustrated ephemera. Still, the point was clear: war was surprisingly prosperous for printers and publishers in the north.

This flood of northern popular war literature revealed that the war's print meanings were constructed in a variety of different ways for different imagined readerships. An extensive feminized war literature, for instance, insisted that a central meaning of the war was women's suffering on the home front as they waited for news of husbands, brothers, or lovers. Juvenile war literature, in contrast, portrayed a war of individualized adventure, high spirits, and daring boyish deeds. In the wake of emancipation in 1863, a few African American authors, including James Madison Bell and Frances Ellen Watkins Harper, published war poetry that celebrated black freedom. Others, including prominent abolitionist William Wells Brown, published works celebrating the achievements of African Americans. Several white northern authors also published popular novels, including John Townsend Trowbridge's *Cudjo's Cave* and Epes Sargent's *Peculiar*, that explored the new place of African Americans in American life. At the same time, racialized sheet music often portrayed blacks with a crude visual vocabulary drawn from minstrelsy, revealing the persistence of racial stereotypes within northern culture. Each of these print wars created a different "imagined community" of nationhood in wartime, yet they were knit together through adherence to patriotic Unionism (Anderson).

Northern publishers and authors did not face the difficulties of southerners in producing war literature; nor did they engage in the same soul-searching over definitions of a new national literature. They assumed, in fact, that northern literature was already a national literature, and rarely paid much attention to the literary struggles of their southern counterparts. Indeed, if popular memories of wars could be determined solely by the volume of print culture produced during a conflict, then the cause of the north clearly won the popular literary as well as the battlefield war.

Yet the ongoing creation of popular memories of war is a far more slippery process than such an accounting would suggest. Later in the century, new political and cultural imperatives produced a deep nostalgia for the Confederacy within national popular magazines. The political project of reconciliation, accompanied by a white nostalgia for the slaveholding south, helped to produce a new set of literary memories of the war that celebrated the "Lost Cause" of the Confederacy. Far from this nostalgia being confined to the south, it was expressed in the most popular national magazines of the 1880s and 1890s, including *Century Magazine* and *McClure's*, both published in New York. Ironically, then, it was northern magazines and books that eventually became the mouthpieces for the southern literary nationality that southerners during the war so desperately wanted to create.

SOURCE NOTES

[Unless otherwise indicated artifacts and documents are reproduced courtesy of the American Antiquarian Society (AAS), Worcester, Massachusetts.]

1. Kate Stone, *Brokenburn: The Journal of Kate Stone, 1861–1868*, ed. John Q. Anderson (1955; reprint, Baton Rouge: Louisiana State University Press, 1995), 14, 270. Copyright © Louisiana State University Press. Reproduced courtesy Louisiana State University Press, Baton Rouge, La.

2. Ella Gertrude Clanton Thomas, *The Secret Eye: The Journal of Ella Gertrude Clanton Thomas, 1848–1889*, ed. Virginia Ingraham Burr (Chapel Hill: University of North Carolina Press, 1990), 188–89. Copyright © Virginia Ingraham Burr and Gertrude T. Despeaux. Reproduced courtesy of University of North Carolina Press, Chapel Hill, N.C.

3. Mary Chesnut, *Mary Chesnut's Civil War*, ed. C. Vann Woodward (New Haven, Conn.: Yale University Press, 1981), 359, 540, 581, 585, 755–56. Copyright © Yale University Press. Reproduced courtesy of Yale University Press, New Haven, Conn.

4. *Southern Literary Messenger* 32 (June 1861): 481; 33 (August 1861): 160; 33 (September 1861): 237; 33 (November 1861): 395; 34 (April 1862): 266; 38 (January 1864): 61–62.

5. *Southern Monthly* 2 (May 1862): back cover.

6. George William Curtis, "Editor's Easy Chair," *Harper's New Monthly Magazine* 23 (August 1861): 411.

7. Sarah Butler Wister, "Sarah Butler Wister's Civil War Diary," ed. Fanny Kemble Wister, *Pennsylvania Magazine of History and Biography* 102, no. 3 (1978): 277. Reproduced courtesy of *Pennsylvania Magazine of History and Biography*, Philadelphia, Pa.

8. Orpheus C. Kerr [Robert Henry Newell], *The Orpheus C. Kerr Papers* (New York: Blakeman & Mason, 1862), 378–82.

9. *Round Table*, January 9, 1864, 59; January 23, 1864, 91.

10. *Pacific Appeal* (San Francisco) April 26, 1862, in *Black Abolitionist Papers, 1830–1865*, reel 14 (Sanford, N.C.: Microfilming Corp. of America, 1981), microfilm.

11. Lydia Maria Child, *The Freedmen's Book* (1865; reprint, New York: Arno Press, 1968), 250–51.

12. William Wells Brown to Gerrit Smith, September 4, 1862, in *Black Abolitionist Papers, 1830–1865*, reel 14 (Sanford, N.C.: Microfilming Corp. of America, 1981), microfilm.

13. William Wells Brown, *The Black Man, His Antecedents, His Genius, and His Achievements* (1863; reprint, New York: Arno Press, 1969), 5–6.

14. Elizabeth Boynton Harbert Papers, Henry E. Huntington Library, San Marino, Calif. Reproduced courtesy of The Huntington Library, San Marino, Calif., Harbert Addenda, Box 5(3).

15. John Greenleaf Whittier and Elizabeth Sloman, *Barbara Frietchie* (New York: William A. Pond, 1879).

WORKS CITED

Alcott, Louisa May. *The Selected Letters of Louisa May Alcott*. Edited by Joel Myerson and Daniel Shealy. Boston: Little, Brown, 1987.

American Literary Gazette and Publishers' Circular 2 (April 15, 1864).

American Publishers' Circular and Literary Gazette 7 (July 20, 1861).

Anderson, Benedict. *Imagined Communities: Reflections on the Origin and Spread of Nationalism*. London: Verso, 1983.

Charleston Courier as quoted in the *Southern Field and Fireside,* May 18, 1861, 2.

Civil War Envelope Collection. Collection of Graphic Arts, American Antiquarian Society, Worcester, Mass.

Daily Richmond Examiner, July 26, 1862.

Faust, Drew Gilpin. *The Creation of Confederate Nationalism: Ideology and Identity in the Civil War South.* Baton Rouge: Louisiana State University Press, 1988.

Frank Leslie's Illustrated Newspaper 15 (September 27, 1862).

Grant, Robert W. *The Handbook of Civil War Patriotic Envelopes and Postal History.* Hanover, Mass.: Robert W. Grant, 1977.

Holmes, Oliver Wendell. "Bread and the Newspaper." *Atlantic Monthly* 8 (September 1861): 346–52.

Hubbell, Jay B., ed. *The Last Years of Henry Timrod, 1864–1867.* Durham, N.C.: Duke University Press, 1941.

Manufactures of the United States in 1860; Compiled from the Original Returns of the Eighth Census. Washington, D.C.: Government Printing Office, 1865.

Southern Field and Fireside 2 (May 18, 1861).

Southern Illustrated News 1 (September–November 1862).

Southern Literary Messenger 33 (November 1861).

Southern Monthly 1 (September 1861–April 1862).

Ticknor and Fields, Rough Cost Book, 1860 and 1861. Ticknor and Fields Archives, Houghton Library, Harvard University.

Tryon, Warren S. *Parnassus Corner: A Life of James T. Fields, Publisher to the Victorians.* Boston: Houghton Mifflin, 1963.

FOR FURTHER RESEARCH

Aaron, Daniel. *The Unwritten War: American Writers and the Civil War.* New York: Alfred A. Knopf, 1973.

Blight, David. *Race and Reunion: The Civil War in American Memory.* Cambridge, Mass.: Belknap Press of Harvard University Press, 2001.

Butchart, Ronald E. *Northern Schools, Southern Blacks, and Reconstruction: Freedmen's Education, 1862–1875.* Westport, Conn.: Greenwood Press, 1980.

Fahs, Alice. "The Feminized Civil War: Gender, Northern Popular Literature, and the Memory of the War." *Journal of American History* 85 (March 1999): 1461–94.

———. *The Imagined Civil War: Popular Literature of the North and South, 1861–1865.* Chapel Hill: University of North Carolina Press, 2001.

———. "The Market Value of Memory: Popular War Histories and the Literary Marketplace, 1861–1868." *Book History* 1 (1998): 107–39.

Faust, Drew Gilpin. *Mothers of Invention: Women of the Slaveholding South in the American Civil War.* Chapel Hill: University of North Carolina Press, 1996.

Foster, Frances Smith, ed. *A Brighter Coming Day: A Frances Ellen Watkins Harper Reader.* New York: The Feminist Press, 1990.

Fredrickson, George M. *The Inner Civil War: Northern Intellectuals and the Crisis of the Union.* New York: Harper & Row, 1965.

Goodrich, Lloyd. *The Graphic Art of Winslow Homer.* New York: New York Museum of Graphic Art, 1968.

Harper, Frances Ellen Watkins. *Complete Poems of Frances Ellen Watkins Harper*. Edited by Maryemma Graham. New York: Oxford University Press, 1988.

Hubbell, Jay B. *The South in American Literature, 1607–1900*. Durham, N.C.: Duke University Press, 1954.

Jones, Jacqueline. *Soldiers of Lights and Love: Northern Teachers and Georgia Blacks, 1865–1873*. Chapel Hill: University of North Carolina Press, 1980.

Kaser, David. *Books and Libraries in Camp and Battle: The Civil War Experience*. Westport, Conn.: Greenwood Press, 1984.

Masur, Louis P. *The Real War Will Never Get in the Books: Selections from Writers during the Civil War*. New York: Oxford University Press, 1993.

McPherson, James M. *The Negro's Civil War: How American Blacks Felt and Acted during the War for the Union*. 1965. Reprint, New York: Ballantine Books, 1991.

Morris, Robert Charles. *Reading, 'Riting, and Reconstruction: The Education of Freedmen in the South, 1861–1870*. Chicago: University of Chicago Press, 1981.

Moss, William. *Confederate Broadside Poems: An Annotated Descriptive Bibliography*. Westport, Conn.: Meckler, 1988.

Parrish, T. Michael, and Robert M. Willingham Jr. *Confederate Imprints: A Bibliography of Southern Publications from Secession to Surrender*. Austin, Texas: Jenkins Publishing Co., 1987.

Silber, Nina. *The Romance of Reunion: Northerners and the South, 1865–1900*. Chapel Hill: University of North Carolina Press, 1993.

Stevenson, Louise. *The Victorian Homefront: American Thought and Culture, 1860–1880*. New York: Twayne, 1991.

Wilson, Edmund. *Patriotic Gore: Studies in the Literature of the American Civil War*. New York: Oxford University Press, 1966.

Yoder, Jacob E. *The Fire of Liberty in Their Hearts: The Diary of Jacob E. Yoder of the Freedmen's Bureau School, Lynchburg, Virginia, 1866–1870*. Edited by Samuel L. Horst. Richmond: Library of Virginia, 1996.

9

Reshaping Publishing and Authorship in the Gilded Age

Nancy Cook

MOST MID-NINETEENTH-CENTURY publishers envisioned themselves as part of "the trade." In business terms, this meant that they sold their publications wholesale to booksellers, who in turn retailed those books to their customers. But "the trade" was as much an idea as a set of business practices. Reinforced by such periodicals as the *American Publishers' Circular and Literary Gazette* (1855) and *Publishers' Weekly* (1872), publishers and booksellers came to think of themselves as a confederacy of gentlemen: businessmen to be sure, but also colleagues with established protocols. Among these was an extralegal system called "the courtesy of the trade," designed to address the lack of international copyright. Before 1891 only Ameican citizens could hold a United States copyright. Foreign books, then, could be reprinted by American publishers without having to pay royalties to their authors. "Trade courtesy" attempted to keep publishers from undercutting one another by printing the same work: a foreign book, trade courtesy dictated, usually belonged to the American publisher that first produced it or purchased the right to do so from its author or its original European publisher. Between 1845 and 1870 this system functioned fairly smoothly.

After the Civil War, the trade encountered rising tensions. New publishing firms challenged older firms that had become associated through trade courtesy with particular authors and works (such as Ticknor and Fields with Tennyson). These new firms, often called "pirates" by the older firms, disregarded trade courtesy and printed any noncopyright work that they thought would sell. At the same time, an old business practice—subscription publishing—revived after the Civil War. Rather than divide wholesaling from retailing, firms that specialized in subscription publishing sent agents door-to-door to sell their books directly to consumers. Agents used a prospectus—an incomplete sample of the book for sale—to gather subscriptions. Books were later delivered to the purchasers. Subscription publishers could predict sales and adjust production accordingly. The more elite and well-established trade publishing houses, fearing that these newer firms would cut into their markets, labeled them upstarts. Religious publishing, too, had long differed from the "regular" book trade. From the founding of the Methodist Book Concern (1789), the African Methodist Episcopal Book Concern (1817), and the American Tract Society (1825), religious publishers had relied heavily upon networks of traveling agents to distribute their books. These "colporteurs" distributed many of those works free of charge or for whatever a consumer could afford. By the mid-nineteenth century the American Tract Society produced more volumes annually than any trade publisher. In the 1880s the Methodist Book Concern built a new office and bookstore in the same New York neighborhood as numerous commercial firms. Religious publications—schoolbooks, tracts, magazines, and more—existed alongside, not within, the regular trade, even if their distribution methods resembled those of the subscription houses.

Meanwhile, new technologies helped change book and magazine production. Chromolithography and various methods of reproducing photographs made illustrations more profuse and affordable to print. In the 1880s the invention of the Linotype mechanized typesetting. In the 1890s case-making machines increased the speed with which a book could be bound. And paper manufactured from wood pulp, introduced in the 1860s, dominated the market by century's end.

Because of the changes and tensions in the publishing world, the second half of the century was a challenging time for American authors. Authors as well as publishers participated fully in the endless debates about intellectual property rights before the 1891 Chace Act committed the United States to international copyright. In these years, too, popular authors became celebrities: their publishers marketed them virtually as brand names, using the new techniques of visual reproduction to show readers what their favorite writers looked like. As William Dean Howells astutely observed, an author now had to be a "man of business" as well as a "man of letters." The commentary essay and many of the artifacts in this chapter focus on the career of Mark Twain (1835–1910). As a writer, Twain's experiences are illuminating not because his career was representative. In fact, most authors had careers vastly different from his. Rather, Twain engaged the publishing world as a man both of letters and of business. Twain was a literary artist who cherished the complex textures of language and the imaginative consequences of narrative, but he was also a professional writer who expected to profit from his labor. And unlike many of the professional writers who preceded him, Twain tried energetically to take advantage of new technologies and business practices to enrich himself. Unfortunately, Twain's literary genius did not translate into business acumen. Still, his failures, when viewed alongside his successes, help illuminate the evolution of publishing and authorship in the Gilded Age.

ARTIFACTS

Subscription publishing vexed trade publishers throughout the last third of the century. *The Gilded Age*, written by Mark Twain and Charles Dudley Warner (1829–1900), gave its name to the era; it was published by the American Publishing Company, one of the leading subscription firms. Twain and Warner's 1873 contract for the book displays the kind of complex business arrangements by which authors brought their works before the public. Magazines published by and for regular trade publishers and booksellers, such as *Trade Circular Annual*, *Publishers' Weekly*, and the *Literary World*, routinely castigated subscription firms—usually cloaking their own commercial motives in arguments about literary value. But the subscription publishers could fight back: in an 1874 newspaper interview, Elisha Bliss (1822–1880), president of the American Publishing Company, argued that his methods served democracy and education by bringing the world of print to towns and villages that lacked their own bookstores. While this battle emphasized ideological points, Mark Twain got down to business in an 1887 letter to Charles L. Webster, the head of the subscription firm Twain had created himself. Here Twain assumed that authorship was a business, and clarified the potential advantages of subscription publishing for authors. Twain himself published by both trade and subscription—illustrating how the ideological distinctions between the two forms did not always hold.

Elisha Bliss, Contract for *The Gilded Age* (1873)[1]

This agreement made between Samuel L. Clemens & Charles Dudley Warner both of City of Hartford & State of Connecticut as parties of the first part & The American Publishing Co. of said city of Hartford as party of the second part Wittnesseth—

The said parties of the first part, being the authors of a manuscript for a proposed book, to be called *"The Gilded Age"*; in consideration of the agreements hereinafter made by the party of the second part, stipulate to furnish to the said party of the second part the said manuscript as soon as they desire it, in sufficient quantity to make a volume of about 600 pages printed octavo pages (small pica) & that they will not use or suffer any portion of the matter of said mss. to be used by others, but give the said party of the second part full control of it with full & exclusive right to publish the same so long as they the said party of the second part shall fulfill their part of this contract, & the copyright of said matter, having been or to be taken out in the names of said authors, it shall be held by them subject to their stipulations in this contract. The said party of the first part also agree to do all necessary proof reading & render other ordinary & usual assistance in bringing out the book, & to give all possible aid in its sale—

The party of the second part agrees to publish said book as soon as practicable for them to do so, commencing upon the work without unnecessary delay. The book is to be after the style of "The Innocents Abroad" & to equal it in the quality of its paper, binding, engravings & printing—The engravings inserted to be mutually acceptable to the said Warner & to E. Bliss Jr. Prest. of said American Publishing Co.

The said party of the second part also agrees to use their best efforts to sell said book, to print & distribute among their agents notices of the book, reviews &c & in large cities they shall instruct their agents to use introductory cards or circulars stating the object of their visit—

A sheet of extracts to be sent with copy of the book to editors, said extracts to be selected by the said Warner who shall also furnish a list of newspapers, from which he in connexion with the said E. Bliss. Jr. shall select such as they may deem proper, (say 500 more or less as they may agree,) to whom the said party of the second part shall within 12 months from issue of the book send free copies at their own expense, with sheets of extracts. Copies of the book with extracts to be sent to the leading papers and periodicals of the great cities from first edition printed—

And the party of the second part farther agrees to pay to the parties of the first part a royalty upon all books sold, of *Ten* per cent on the subscription price, one half of said sum or *Five* (5) per cent of the same to be paid to the said Clemens, and one half or *Five* (5) per cent of the same to be paid to the said Warner, a statement of sales & settlement of royalty to be made every three months after the issue of the book, said settlement to be made at office of said Company or sent upon order of the respective parties.

No royalty is to be paid upon any book given by said party of the second part or their agents to editors or others to advance the sale of the book—a list of such gifts to be rendered to parties of the first part if it is required by them—

It is farther agreed that no books shall be issued to any party (except to editors as above provided, to parties for reviews & recommendation—and to agents as sample copies to canvass with)—until enough are printed and bound to fill all orders on hand at once unless it be with the consent of said Warner.

This contract executed
at Hartford May 8. 1873.

Saml. L. Clemens.
Chas. D. Warner
E. Bliss Jr. prest.
American Publishing Co.

"Subscription Publishers and Underselling," from *Trade Circular Annual* (1871)[2]

The *Nation* recently contained some well-timed remarks upon the subscription publishers, and the worthless character of most of the books which they foist by thousands upon the public. It remarked, with justice, that, in certain cases, to publish a book by subscription was not only allowable, but beneficial alike to the public and to the publishers. Encyclopedias and works of that character, published in parts or volumes, in which the cost of production is immense, would often meet with but a limited sale if it were not for the personal canvassing of the agents, and, by a quick return of the outlay, enable the publisher to complete what might otherwise be beyond his means, or, at any rate, be an unprofitable speculation.

This is a perfectly legitimate branch of the publishing trade, and indirectly assists the regular bookseller; for, by promoting the love of literature, and by increasing the number of readers, it necessarily increases the number of bookbuyers. But with the greater number of the books published by the regular subscription houses the case is different. These books are often absolutely worthless, and this is not only true with regard to the nature of their contents, but also extends to their manufacture, in which paper, print, and binding are usually of the commonest and worst description. How buyers can be found for such books is a puzzle, for, beyond their title, there is nothing attractive about them, and yet they sell by thousands. We should imagine the people who buy them resemble the man who bought a Webster's dictionary to amuse himself with during the long winter evenings, and who, when he had read it half through, observed that it was a very good book, only he could not quite make out the plot.

"The Subscription Book Trade," from *Publishers' Weekly* (1872)[3]

A great proportion of the books issued to-day from Hartford, the headquarters of this business for the whole country, are either actually bad or very like humbug. A gorgeous binding, usually in very bad taste, thick but cheap paper, outrageously poor wood-cuts, the largest type with the thickest leads, add up into a very big, gaudy book which a glib tongue or persistent boring cheats folks into buying at five dollars, when the reading matter which it contains, if worth anything, would make about a dollar-and-a-half book in the regular trade. So that the business, as now conducted, is mainly bad. Yet it is very true that it is attaining enormous proportions. It is by no means destined to kill the regular trade, but there is no doubt that it is already hurting the latter very much. Many of the regular houses indeed are engaging in it, through branches of their firms, and thus "going over to the enemy. . . ."

S. R. Crocker, "Subscription Books," from *The Literary World* (1874)[4]

We are sorry to see an increasing tendency on the part of some of our best writers to appeal to the public through the agency of publishers of subscription books, so called. . . .

Authors as a class are not satisfied with the pecuniary reward given them by publishers, which is generally ten per cent on the retail price of the book. They think, and not unreasonably, that four hundred and fifty dollars—which would represent the author's share of the profits on a one-dollar-and-fifty book which reached a sale of 3,000 copies—is not a sufficient payment for the labor of six months, or it may be, a year. . . . The subscription plan offers certain important advantages, the chief of which is in the fact that a book is pushed into currency by the combined personal efforts of many experienced and dauntless men, while a book published in the regular way must depend mainly upon its own merits for its success. A subscription publisher having agreed to publish a certain book, that would be sold by the regular trade at one dollar and a half, makes it up in such a way—with thick paper, large type, and cheap illustrations—that it will bear the price of three dollars. Through the efforts of his agents, he sells from four to twenty times as many copies as the regular dealer would sell; and of course he can afford to allow the author a larger royalty. It would seem, in view of these facts, that the subscription plan was the only true way of publishing books. But several considerations are to be taken into account. Subscription books are in bad odor, and cannot possibly circulate among the best classes of readers, owing to the general and not unfounded prejudice against them as a class.

Consequently an author of established reputation, who resorts to the subscription plan for the sake of making more money, descends to a constituency of a lower grade and inevitably loses caste. . . . For this loss no money could compensate.

But the injury resulting from the adoption of the subscription plan by our best writers would not be limited to themselves, but would affect seriously our whole literature. This plan operates directly against the principle that the sale of a book should be proportioned to its merits, and makes these quite subordinate to the arts of importunity and trickery . . . of which almost every reader has had personal experience, as characteristic of the book-canvasser.

Elisha Bliss, "Subscription Books," from *New York Tribune* (1874)[5]

Mr. Bliss, speaking for the American Publishing Company: I do not think there ought to be any antagonism between the trade and ourselves. I do not think we can interfere with each other if each keeps his own ground. Speaking for my own firm our books, as a general thing, are books that are written expressly for us. We select good authors and pay high copyrights, and our books are often such as the trade would never have published. I know there are publishers in our branch of the book business who compile books that are worthless, costing but little and sold at a high price. The subscription book trade confines itself to its own books and does not sell any trade books. Instead of injuring the regular book business I think we create a thirst for knowledge and thus increase the sale of all kinds of books. In the little towns where there are no bookstores the book agent induces the people to buy. One book thus sold is read with avidity by the whole household, and when another agent comes it is ready to buy another book. In that way a nucleus is formed for hundreds of thousands of little libraries throughout the country, which never would have existed except for the book agent. . . .

Correspondent—Do you think the subscription book business is dying out?

Mr. Bliss—I do not. I think there are more books now being sold by subscription than ever before. Our trade last year was the largest of any year since we have been in business.

Mark Twain, Letter to Charles L. Webster & Co. (1887)[6]

Hartford
18 September 1887

Dear C. L. W. & Co:

Here is a systematic and orderly scheme which I have worked at a good deal, the last two days, and have finally got it to suit me. It cannot be easily improved, if at all. It has some advantages:

1. This system of royalties can be proposed without a blush, to the biggest author, and also to the littlest one. (Try it on the cook book.)

2. By it we *cannot* lose on any book which is important enough for us to be willing to publish it.

3. It gouges no author, and it permits no author to gouge us.

The system will vary but in one case. When we *know* an author will sell more than say 60,000, we may possibly have to promise an addition of 1 per cent to the 12 after a sale of that number.

I have put in those trade and subscription statistics, purposely that they may be *used* in talking with authors, in order that they may see the fairness of sinking the plates and paying only 5 and 6 per cent royalties on the first 20,000 copies sold. The statistics are not guesses, they are *facts* within my personal knowledge (provided the Sherman one is right—I got it from General Grant). If you will familiarize yourselves with these facts and arguments, and use them, you will be able to capture *any* author's book, it makes no difference who he is.

Please keep the scheme private, and study it. But let no clerk see it. Don't typewriter it. We don't want to give away a good idea to other publishers.

SLC

Just and Equable Scheme of Royalties.

An itemized and accurate account shall be kept, showing just what the "plant" or plates of a book cost us.

When receipts have *repaid* us that, the payment of royalties *shall then begin*, but not sooner. We will "sink the plates" always.

ROYALTIES
(estimated on a $3.50 book,
And paid on cloth basis, only.)

	Author gets	
On the first 10,000 copies,	5%————	$1750
" second " "	6%————	$2100
" third " "	10%————	$3500
	Total	$7,350

On all above 30,000 copies, the author to receive a royalty of 12 *per cent*.

On first 10,000, we deduct $5,000 office expenses and $1750 for author, leaving $3,250 profit. On second 10,000 we clear about $5,000; on third, about $6,500; on the rest, $5,800, or nearly 60% of the profit.

"TRADE" METHODS.

The average book-seller hardly ever orders more than 3 copies of a new book. (Do not take our word, but go and ask.) These go over the counter the first day, and he orders no more. He tells the customer he is "out," and proposes to take the customer's order. The customer doesn't care enough about it, and no sale is made.

RESULT, AND ARGUMENT.

Bret Harte's greatest sale was on his first book, "The Luck of Roaring Camp," when he was at the zenith of his popularity. This sale was 26,000 copies in 2 years. The price was $1.25 a copy, the royalty was 10%, or 12 ½ cents on each book. Result to Harte in 2 years, about $3,000!

We can sell 3 copies of *any* book where the trade can sell 1. Moreover, we always charge about a third more for a book than the trade can venture to ask for it. In this case we would have sold 75,000 and charged $2 a copy. And we should have handed Harte $15,000 instead of $3,000. . . .

General Sherman's book—$7 a set—sold 25,000 sets, and he got $25,000, or 50 cents a volume. Assisted by such a name as the General's, we should have quadrupled that sale easily, and paid him $80,000 in royalties, instead of $25,000.

The "Innocents Abroad," sold by subscription 160,000 copies at $3.50. Royalty all through, 5 per cent. Result to the author, about $30,000. By our graduated system of royalties, he would have received $62,000.

Very few authors can sell an edition of 3,000 in the trade aside from those above enumerated. Those who can do it can be counted on the fingers of the two hands.

The author of The Innocents Abroad tried 2 books in the trade. One of them sold 6,000 copies, the other sold 10,000. Total, 16,000. He has tried 10 books by subscription. Total sales, 618,000 copies.

RELIGIOUS PUBLISHING came of age in the nineteenth century. As early as the late 1850s a correspondent in the *American Publishers' Circular and Literary Gazette* criticized religious publishers for violating the courtesy of the trade (while recognizing that the religious "Societies" mostly published works that commercial firms did not). On February 11, 1890, at 7:30 p.m., the Methodist Book Concern held a service to dedicate its new Publishing and Mission Building in New York. Numerous leading ministers and other dignitaries addressed the audience. They described the new building in providential terms and summarized the century-long history of their publishing efforts. Equally important, they revealed the vertical integration of their endeavors: under one roof, the Book Concern would produce books and magazines, encourage authors, coordinate the distribution efforts of its traveling agents, and offer reading rooms for the faithful.

"Religious Publishing Societies," from *The American Publishers' Circular and Literary Gazette* (1857)[7]

To the Editor of the Publishers' Circular:

I am not one of those who regard our Religious Publishing Societies with distrust, or as unduly interfering with the legitimate prosecution of our trade. On the contrary I have always held that they have, in a large measure, advanced our interest by creating demands which we have helped to supply. Especially is this true in the department of children's books. It has been argued by the friends of these institutions, that they were created for the purpose of supplying what otherwise could not, or would not be furnished: and this is certainly true, and so long as they have done this they have had, as they deserved to have, the good will and wishes of the trade.

Of late, however, there has been a disposition on the part of certain of these Societies, to travel out of the original sphere, and become in many respects, nothing more or less, than great book establishments, with a plentiful supply of means, enabling them to manufacture, and to sell, "at greatly reduced prices." This, perhaps, would not be so much a matter for complaint, if they always continued to give the public what no one else would furnish. But a recent announcement or two, in the "Circular," proves the contrary. Here is a case in point:

Three years ago a publisher of this city purchased for a fair sum the advance sheets of an English book. The author was unknown here, and he took it on its intrinsic merits, himself being the judge. By that law of courtesy, which is an honor to the American trade, he was secured by his mere announcement, from any rival edition by a bookselling house. He assumed all the risk, and made a market for the work. It proved to be a good one—he had quite a sale—indeed an increasing one, and is, perhaps, selling better now, than during the first year of its re-publication. And *now* it is seized by one of the Societies—they want it—they did not before— and so do not hesitate to avail themselves of his capital, and his enterprize, to his disadvantage—for they will not only reprint upon him, but will undersell him. One would think that the fairer course would have been to purchase an edition, if it was an essential want, at a fair price. This is occasionally done, to the benefit of all parties. . . .

I say nothing of the disposition on the part of some of these Societies to reprint upon each other. That is a matter of their own: but they are bound to give us booksellers a better example. There is room enough, and work enough for us all. So it seems at least to one who has been in the book-trade in this city [New York] for more than a quarter of a CENTURY.

Speeches at the Dedication of the Publishing and Mission Building of the Methodist Episcopal Church, New York (1890)[8]

Prayer by Rev. Dr. W. F. Whitlock:

We bless thee that thou hast heard the prayers of thy people and brought prosperity and great power to these [religious] organizations. We thank thee, Father, for the work that they are now accomplishing; that in this center of thought and Christian activity there are going out influences and agencies that are blessing millions of homes. We thank thee that they are blessing not only the Church at home, but the Church abroad. We thank thee that here thy Church finds defense and instruction and encouragement. We thank thee that here is interpreted thy word, and that these interpretations are carried to very many of those who are teaching and studying thy truth. For all these things we praise thy name.

We bless thee, our heavenly Father, that thou didst put it into the hearts of those in more immediate authority to select this site and to build this structure. . . .

Address by Bishop E. G. Andrews:

Naturally to-night we take happy notice of the fact that great progress has been made during the century which now closes in the history of the Book Concern and during the seventy years of our Missionary Society organization.

The enterprise of establishing a publishing house required in the then weak and struggling Methodist Church no ordinary faith and courage. No wonder that they called it a *Book Concern*. Possibly some have not seen the appropriateness of this title. But, sir, you are a business man, and I beg to submit this proposition to you: Given a new and wholly untried business, given a total borrowed capital of $600, given the expenditure of the entire capital upon the printing and binding of books by sundry job-offices in Philadelphia; given the distribution, on credit, of all these books in the saddle-bags of itinerants from Massachusetts to Georgia; given a new enterprise thus conditioned, and could any one devise a better name for it than Book *Concern*? . . . We do not have that sort of Concern to-day. Trusting to the combined wisdom of Book Agents, of local committees, of the Book Committee and of the Missionary Board, all entering on the use and sustentation of this structure, with large accumulated capital and unquestioned credit, we are under no apprehension of financial embarrassment. . . .

No, sir, we have no concern about the stability of this Book Concern. But there are some things about which we are concerned. . . . We are concerned that the profits of this great establishment shall provide Methodism with a literature the very best that Methodism with money can furnish. We are concerned that our Sunday-school literature shall be, not feebly-good, but strong, surpassing any thing of the kind which the world now knows—instructive, attractive, inspiring, and ennobling to our youth. We are concerned that our periodical literature shall be delivered from the localisms and personalisms and general narrowness which, out of the conditions and relations of our church papers have heretofore seemed almost inevitable.

These are some of our concerns. May we not hope that these, also, like the former financial concern, may soon be allayed? And then if we can drop, even now as we enter this new edifice, the old and unattractive title, and substitute for it the simple title *Book House*, or, if any prefer, *Publishing House*, this also will not a little increase with some of us the pleasure with which we hail this hour.

Address by M. D'C. Crawford, D. D.:

But what is the true business of our publishing house? Is it not to make our literature the best possible, and give it to our whole Methodist population at the lowest market rates? Nay, if possible, undersell the market! I would then take the profits of the Book Concern and buy more brains to put in our periodicals and in our books. I would make them better and at the same time cheapen them. I am not criticising the men who make our periodicals. They are doing noble work. But there are not enough of them. It takes several men to make a modern metropolitan religious weekly, or a first-class review, or a popular Sunday-school journal. We need more editorial force. So, too, I think there should be a larger outlay for authorship, in order to increase the list of books which will commend themselves to the literary public and make the imprint of the house a guarantee of excellence.

Never before in the history of the Church has there been a *chance* for a satisfactory retail Methodist book-store in this city. Now we have an elegant room, and I trust it will be fitted up and so conducted as to compare favorably with any book-store in the land. Our people desire it and are entitled to it. It is their duty to come here and buy books.

SUBSCRIPTION AUTHORS depended on steady promotion, and sometimes that promotion occurred within the very books they wrote. Witness the portrait of Mark Twain from *The Innocents Abroad* (1869), a widely-circulated image that helped to make Twain one of the most recognizable Americans of his time. This "Poet Lariat" ostensibly depicted the object of Twain's scorn, the "farmer poet" Bloodgood Cutter—but the image itself was a caricature of Twain. In every good promotion, everything led back to the author—even images supposedly of someone else. Louisa Conrad, who had met Twain in 1867, asked him for a contribution for her scrapbook; in his response, he characteristically worked multiple angles. He had been planning his own self-pasting scrapbook, which he was to patent only a few years later. Here he satisfied his fan's request and perhaps primed her for his own forthcoming superior product, which would remain a moneymaker into the 1890s. The Self-Pasting Scrapbook represented Twain at his self-promoting best: it brought him many favorable notices in the press and a steady income for years. The frontispiece from an 1886 *Life of Mark Twain* came, in fact, from a pamphlet biography (just three inches square) distributed in packs of Duke's Cigarettes. This biography, part of a series called "Histories of Poor Boys who have become rich, and Other Famous People," emphasized Twain's successes as both man of letters and man of business: it listed the titles

"POET LARIAT."

Mark Twain as "Poet Lariat," *The Innocents Abroad* (1869)[9]

of many of his books, but also detailed his own publishing firm of C. L. Webster & Co., including the $350,000 it had earned Mrs. Ulysses S. Grant from publishing her husband's memoirs. (The portrait in this pamphlet was of a younger Twain.)

Mark Twain, Letter to Louisa Conrad (1873)[10]

RECIPE FOR MAKING A SCRAPBOOK
UPON THE CUSTOMARY PLAN
  Some rainy afternoon, get out the pasteboard box you keep your scraps in, & look over your collection. This will occupy some hours. Next day, buy a handsome folio scrap-book, with leaves of all shades & varieties of color—also get a bottle of

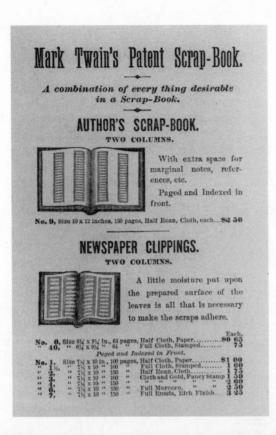

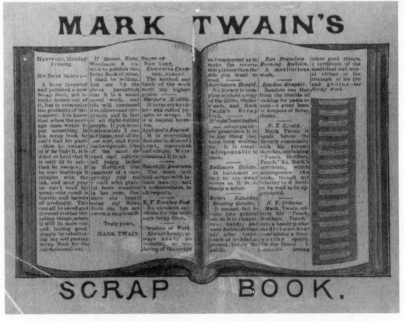

Mark Twain, Advertisement for a Self-Pasting Scrapbook (1878)[11]

Frontispiece, *Life of Mark Twain* (1886)[12]

mucilage. Now work an hour & cover two or three pages with choice selections; & then be called suddenly away. After a day or two, prepare to resume. You will now find that the pages are hopelessly warped; that the mucilage has soaked through & made the print almost illegible, & that colored leaves are a hateful thing in a scrapbook.

Now buy a new book, with pure white, stiff leaves—& get one ounce of good gum tragicanth. Leave a dozen flakes of the gum soaking in a gill of water over night; in the morning, if the gum is too thick & stiff, add water, but precious little of it, for the paste should not be thin. Paste in a page or two of scraps, & then iron them dry & smooth, or else leave the book under pressure.

You will be satisfied with your work this time. Now labor with enthusiasm for three days, heaving in poetry, theology, jokes, obituaries, politics, tales, recipes for pies, poultices, puddings,—shovel them in helter-skelter, & every-which-way, first-come-first-served—but *get them in*. During the next few days, cool down a little; during the next few, cool down altogether & quit.

While the next six months drift by, cut out scraps occasionally & throw them loosely in between the leaves of the scrap-book, & say to yourself that some day you will paste them. Meantime, mislay your gum tragicanth & lose your brush.

By & by that scrapbook will begin to reproach you every time your eye falls upon it; it will accuse you, it will deride your indolence; it will get to intruding itself with studied & offensive frequency & persistence; it will rob you of your peace by day & your rest by night. It will haunt your very dreams & say: "Look at me & the condition I am in."

And at last that day will come which is inevitable in the history of all scrap-books —you will carry it up to the grave-yard of musty, dusty, discarded & forgotten literature in the garret; & when you next see it you will be old, & sad, & scarred with the battle of life, & will say, "Ah, well a-day. It is but the type of all the hopeful efforts & high ambitions of the morning & the noontide of my pilgrimage—each so gallantly begun, & each in turn so quickly humbled & broken & vanquished!"

Yr. Friend,
Saml. L. Clemens.
Hartford, March 1873.

236

BOOKS, OF COURSE, were part of an international market—one made more contentious by the absence of an American international copyright law. In the early 1890s the New York firm of Funk & Wagnalls sued the city's *Evening Post* for libel. The newspaper had accused the publisher of "piracy" and "theft" for publishing the *Encyclopedia Britannica* (an English work) without paying for the copyright. The trial gave Henry Holt (1840–1926) and other publishers the opportunity to explain "the courtesy of the trade," the extralegal practice that had governed the reprinting of foreign authors before 1891. (The *Post* won.) Throughout the 1870s and 1880s American publishers and authors pushed for international copyright. In its 1879 article, "The New Outlook on Copyright," *Publishers' Weekly* expressed optimism about a new proposal by Harper & Brothers for an international commission of authors and publishers. Three years later America's premier political cartoonist Thomas Nast (1840–1902) drew "Innocence Abroad in Search of a Copyright," representing Mark Twain's recent trip to Canada to protect the copyright for his book *The Prince and the Pauper*. (According to an 1879 *Publishers' Weekly* article, Canada had imposed tariffs to deter the importation of foreign books—while unscrupulous Canadian publishers were flooding the United States with cheaper editions of American books.) In this cartoon, lines such as "Copy-Rights Granted Here Because Authors Are So Green and Never Grow Stale," "(We) Cabbage All We Can From the Yankees," and "Authors Are Small Potatoes," all linked United States–Canadian economic relations, especially agricultural ties, to issues of intellectual and cultural property. Once the Chace Act passed in 1891, Henry Loomis Nelson (1846–1908) described what international copyright meant and suggested its importance to the growing worldwide market for printed matter.

Testimony by Henry Holt, from *Publishers' Weekly* (1893)[13]

Question. What is the courtesy of the trade?

Answer. Not to jump another publisher's claim.

Q. How?

A. By reprinting a book already his.

Q. How is such a claim established?

A. First by arrangement with the author or his representative. In the absence of such arrangement, by first announcement of the intention to publish.

Q. How long have these claims been acknowledged?

A. Forty or fifty years I presume. I found the system in operation when I entered the trade thirty years ago.

Q. Is not the observance of trade courtesy confined to a few houses who form a sort of trust?

A. Not at all. There is no close corporation about it; anybody is welcome who will behave himself.

Q. But as a matter of fact is it not restricted to a few influential and well-established houses?

A. By no means. I was not very "influential" or "well established" thirty years ago (and may not be now for that matter), but I never had any trouble in getting my rights respected while I respected the rights of other people. The Harpers and Appletons and others of the heaviest houses in the trade have readily given up books to which I had the prior claim.

Q. Under the courtesy of the trade has not the person who first reprints an author's book here a right to all his subsequent books?

A. Yes, if he paid for the first one.

Q. That's an exception then to the "first announcement" rule?

A. Yes; nearly all the rules have exceptions. I could give you exceptions to that exception, and farther exceptions to those exceptions. Trade courtesy is as full of exceptions as the law itself. It has grown up as a mass of decisions in particular cases, just as the common law has. But nevertheless the general principles hold in most cases.

Q. How long has it been held that payment for the first book was essential to establishing a right to later ones?

A. I first heard of it about five years ago, I think. Probably about that time it was agreed in some dispute that a publisher ready to pay an author had a right as against a publisher who had never paid him. I remember that when I first heard of it I thought we were getting ahead.

Q. Why should there be any questions regarding rights from "first announcement?" Why should there not always be an arrangement with the author?

A. There generally has been with established authors. But there are many books by new and uncertain authors that are not worth negotiating for—especially under the disadvantages of the distance to Europe. Such books are a field for experiment, and if a publisher concluded that one was worth experimenting with, though not worth paying for in advance of experiment, the rights from his first announcement were intended to secure him the fruits of his experiment, if successful. But of late years there has grown up a set of publishers who let others do the experimenting and pay for the failures, and then steal the successes.

"The New Outlook on Copyright," from *Publishers' Weekly* (1879)[14]

The recent discussions of international copyright, and especially the draft of a treaty, with the accompanying letter of Messrs. Harper, . . . it is reasonable to hope, made entirely plain . . . that the so-called opposition in this country to international copyright was rather and chiefly opposition to such a form of international publishing-right as should give to English publishers an advantage, decided and absolute, over American publishers in the American market. That American publishers have not been willing to pay English authors is not true. In fact, under "the courtesy

Thomas Nast, "Innocence Abroad in Search of a Copyright," from *Harper's Weekly* (1882)[15]

of the trade" a system of remuneration had grown up, so closely equivalent to copyright returns, in the case of books from which the publisher himself got a return, that in the enjoyment of the substance of international copyright the form had become to those most interested but a secondary matter. The chief sufferers were American authors, who have vainly looked to English publishers, as a class, for any courtesy at all. . . .

The Harper draft, which is put forward as a suggestion for the consideration of the proposed commission, is especially useful as furnishing a definite basis for practical discussion. Those who have been for years persistently active in promoting international copyright without conditions, among whom several publishers have held a leading place, may find it matter for congratulation that the essential agreement of such houses as Messrs. Harper and Appleton promises a speedy consummation of international copyright. . . .

Henry Loomis Nelson, "United States Copyright to Foreign Authors," from *Harper's Weekly* (1891)[16]

The Constitution of the United States (I., 8) declares that "The Congress shall have Power to promote the Progress of Science and useful Arts, by securing for limited Times to Authors and Inventors the exclusive Right to their respective Writings and Discoveries." Copyright is the absolute control which the law gives to the author of his work of art or literature. Under the copyright law he is defended by the government against the unauthorized reproduction of his book, his picture, his chart, dramatic or musical composition, engraving, painting, drawing, or statue. The ideas and fancies, the facts and reasoning, of a writer or an artist are not protected. Nothing comes within the intent of a copyright law except the form in which the author clothes the product of his research, his fancy, or his imagination. Mr. Howells's copyright, for example, covers his stories as he tells them. Any one else may tell the same stories in a different way, without being guilty of an infringement on Mr. Howells's copyright. . . .

It will be seen that copyright limits as well as protects the author's property. It is not an extensive right. . . . Yet even this small right has been always denied by the United States to foreign authors and artists. The law passed March 4th (An Act to amend the Revised Statutes relating to Copyright) does not grant it without limitations. It simply bestows upon authors, whether native or foreign, the exclusive privilege of selling their own works for the statutory term of years, provided they print their books in the United States from type set in this country. . . .

The amended law, however, is a very important gain over the old and discreditable state of affairs, of which authors on both sides of the ocean have bitterly complained ever since America became a market for works of art and literature.

THE LAST ARTIFACTS in this chapter describe the intense competition to produce the first functional typesetting machine. The Linotype machine, illustrated here, won the race. Its inventor, Ottmar Mergenthaler (1854–1899), gave a speech in 1885 connecting his achievement to the history of American print technologies. The Linotype proved so successful that it was still being used well into the second half of the twentieth century. Its unsuccessful competitor, the Paige Compositor, was an extremely complex apparatus, as the illustration and a 1903 description suggest. Unfortunately for its investors—among them Mark Twain—the Paige Compositor proved impractical, and they lost millions of dollars trying to develop and market the machine.

"The Linotype Machine" (1902)[17]

Ottmar Mergenthaler, Speech to Linotype Investors (1885)[18]

You have come here to witness the operation of a new composing machine, and in as far as we are working in a field which is strewn with the wrecks and failures of former efforts in the same direction you will probably ask, "Are you going to have more success than those who have gone over that field before you; and if so, why?" My answer is, "Yes, we are going to have full success for the reason that we have attacked the problem in an entirely different way than did those who have failed."

...I knew the direction in which others had attempted to solve the problem, and was careful not to fall into the same rut which had led every previous effort into failure and ruin. We make and justify the type as we go along, and are thereby relieved from handling the millions of little tiny types, which have proved so troublesome to my predecessors who have failed. We have no distribution, yet we have a new type for every issue of a paper, an advantage which can hardly be overrated.

The Paige Compositor, from *Scientific American* (1901)[19]

I am convinced, gentlemen, that unless some method of printing can be designed which requires no type at all, the method embodied in our invention will be the one used in the future; not alone because it is cheaper, but mainly because it is destined to secure superior quality. . . .

It is a great result, but, gentlemen of the Board, to you it is due as much as to me. You have furnished the money, I only the ideas; and in thus enabling me to carry this invention to a successful end you have honored yourselves and your country.

I say you have honored your country, for every one will know that this invention has been originated in the land which gave birth to the telegraph, the telephone, the Hoe press and the reaper; everybody will know that it came from the United States, though comparatively few will know the name of the inventor.

John S. Thompson, "Composing Machines—Past and Present (No. V)," from *The Inland Printer* (1903)[20]

Perhaps the most wonderful typesetting machine ever invented was the Paige Compositor, the product of the brain of James W. Paige, of Hartford, Connecticut. Certainly no machine has a more interesting history. Mr. Paige first conceived the idea for his typesetting machine in 1873, and in the following year he completed a composing machine, without provision for justification or distribution. He then constructed an independent distributor. In 1881 a combined setter and distributor was completed. . . . In 1887 another machine was constructed in which was incorporated an automatic justifying device. In 1892 the apparatus was removed to Chicago, and two years later work was started on a commercial machine, which was installed in the office of the Chicago *Herald* in 1894. After several months' trial, during which time the machine was again partially reconstructed, work was abandoned, and the apparatus . . . was presented to Columbia University, the earlier Paige machine going to Cornell University. . . .

Before the first Paige machine was constructed the promoters had spent $1,300,000. Probably another million was expended before the end came. Mark Twain was bankrupted by investing in Paige machine stock. The history of the Paige patents is unique. The first application filed contained 204 sheets of drawings, with over a thousand separate views. . . . There were no less than 18,000 separate parts, with about eight hundred shaft bearings, with cams and springs innumerable.

In every way the Paige was a most remarkable piece of mechanism. Its complications were such as to demand the attendance of experts, and the impossibility of training mechanics to the degree of skill required made it a commercial impossibility. . . . The model machines constructed were built for handling but one size of type, though the machine could easily have been made interchangeable. The Paige Compositor, nine feet long and weighing over three tons, was run by a quarter-inch round belt and required but one-twelfth horse-power.

COMMENTARY: MARK TWAIN—THE COMPLEX WORLD OF A SUCCESSFUL AUTHOR

More than any other major American author in the nineteenth century, Mark Twain attended to the making of his own success. Twain was perhaps the most financially successful author of his era. Moreover, his reputation as a literary artist has blossomed since his death: today his books are taught in nearly every high school and college in the United States, and he has generated an enormous body of scholarship. It might seem that nothing about Twain remains to be analyzed, said, or written. Book history methods, however, allow for a new understanding of precisely those aspects of Twain's career that "everybody knows to be true." Rather than confirming that Twain was a kind of schizophrenic, torn between art and commerce, who squandered his own genius, a history-of-the-book approach reveals that his genius was dependent upon commerce—that his artistic and commercial successes were more integrated than previously believed. This is not, however, completely a success story. Twain was a man of his time; his successes typify the period, but so do his failures. All the changes in late-nineteenth-century publishing practice reflected aspects of American culture at large—highly competitive, intensely speculative, and suffering or enjoying explosive growth. True to the volatility of his era, Twain's involvement in the business of publishing as author, publisher, and financial backer of various machines was not always profitable.

Each decade between the Civil War and World War I saw at least some period of economic decline. People in all aspects of the book trade worried not only about fluctuations in business cycles, but also about the viability of publishing itself. Publishers regularly lamented that theirs was the "worst business in the world" (Sheehan, 3). They responded in many cases by trying to control more elements in the publication process, seeking several ways to make their businesses profitable. Sometimes they tried vertical integration, becoming their own printers and general agents or distributors, in addition to the more narrowly defined role of the publisher. As often as not, the added demands of keeping presses running got them into even more trouble: inventory exceeded demand, and capital was tied up in inventory.

Nevertheless, the number of publishers rose from 400 in 1859 to more than 1,500 in 1913 (Sheehan, 22–23). Not only were more publishing firms in business, but they also were publishing more titles per year than they had earlier in the century. From roughly 1,000 titles published in 1829, by the early 1890s the number had swelled to approximately 5,000 new titles a year, outstripping the nation's capacity to purchase, much less read, so many books. During the Gilded Age, the competitive spirit often dominated, even over common sense. For most publishers, the back list—the catalogue of previously published works, with their costs already recouped—made the profits, since current books were difficult to make pay. Yet the competitive frenzy, especially by the late 1880s, coaxed publishers into adding cost-draining new titles to an already swollen list. Different editions of the same title, often pirated, competed in an already glutted marketplace. While the range of titles sometimes spoke to a new, more diverse reading public, in times of economic strife the market was saturated with unsold books. Publishers felt competition to be everywhere, and castigated those publishers they imagined were hurting the book business. Trade publishers were particularly critical of the big subscription publishing houses.

Though subscription publishing had a long history before the 1860s, after the Civil War it became big business. Subscription firms produced books best known for their bulk (often weighing in at five pounds or more), copious if not always artful illustrations, and gaudy bindings. Armed with prospectuses containing sample pages and bindings, an army of canvassers peddled these books door-to-door, took orders, and returned later with the book for delivery and payment. Subscription books were expensive. At a time when many books were sold for fifty cents, subscription books often started at $2.75 and went as high as $10.00. Yet many sold exceedingly well, into the hundreds of thousands of copies, and royalties to authors were generally higher than those paid by trade publishers.

The more successful subscription publishing became, the more fire it drew from the trade publishing industry and its journalistic outlets. The trade press sneered at the cheaply produced, forgettable books peddled to backwater rubes who fell victim to the hard-sell agent and the gilt bindings. It was not literature, they said. It was not manufactured by "real" publishers, gentlemen such as Appleton or the Harpers, they said. It gave books a bad name and made people avoid legitimate booksellers, they said. When the trade press imagined two very distinct markets for books, subscription publishers followed suit. They claimed that they did not take business from the trade; rather, they performed a kind of missionary work, spreading literacy to the hinterlands, offering access to American culture for those outside the reach of the bookstore. Both sides exaggerated, and both mischaracterized their readers.

Many reasons for such animosity have been suggested. Subscription firms rarely gave out large numbers of complimentary review copies, which annoyed reviewers who were used to receiving them. While subscription firms often used newspapers to advertise for canvassers, they rarely spent money on advertisements for their books, and so were not as friendly with newspapers as many trade publishers were. Subscription publishers reprinted old material, sometimes under the guise of a new title, and so received some of the ire directed at the cheap reprint and pirate publishers. Subscription books featured the sensational or the timely, and hence were considered lowbrow and vulgar. More to the point, subscription publishers paid better royalties: with an army of canvassers promoting one book, that book often enjoyed extremely strong sales. The promise of big returns tempted trade publishing stalwarts such as Harriet Beecher Stowe to try their luck with the subscription publishers. Despite the rhetoric of animosity, however, throughout the period subscription and trade publishers mimicked each other's practices when it suited their needs. The rhetoric also obscures the fact that most large publishers had a subscription division of some sort by century's end.

In a Gilded Age characterized by cutthroat practices across a range of industries, where bigger was touted as better, many businesses turned to trusts—alliances under one management of companies or divisions that sought to control whole industries —in order to eliminate the competition. A horizontally integrated trust might seek to control a range of media, much as contemporary entertainment conglomerates own newspapers, television and radio stations, magazines, networks, and motion picture companies. A vertically integrated trust might seek to control all stages of a product's development and distribution, as did the Standard Oil Company (whose operations included oil wells, refining plants, and consumer sales) in the 1890s. John W. Lovell, who had early success in the late 1870s and early 1880s with cheap paperback and clothbound reprints, invited a number of publishers in the cheap book trade to join in a book trust. The United States Book Company bought plates and stock for cash and company shares, and more than twenty publishers joined the trust. At first, trade publishers were hopeful that the United States Book Company might stem the proliferation of cheap reprints, and so help the book industry become more profitable for everybody. Even *Publishers' Weekly* was modestly supportive:

> The Lovells have gradually worked their way up from indifferently made to better-made novels, from pirated works to books published by arrangement with foreign authors and publishers, and to American copyright literature. For a year or more the regular publishing houses, with a few exceptions, have done little more than keep up appearances in the line of foreign fiction, and during that time the Lovells more and more have pushed to the front. (February 1890, in Madison, 56)

By 1893 the trust was bankrupt, and the disposal of stock to satisfy creditors produced a glutted market where books wholesaled for as little as one cent.

Often with greater success than the Lovells, book publishers engaged in horizontal integration, becoming magazine publishers. Though this was not uncommon before the Civil War, many more publishers joined the fray after the war, hoping that each business would strengthen the other. Some publishers, notably the Harpers and James R. Osgood, had multiple magazine ventures. One big advantage to magazine-owning publishers was the practice of serializing novels, which often gave subsequent book publication just the boost it needed for brisk sales.

Mark Twain aspired to success as an author within this complex matrix of art and commerce. In 1867 his first book was published. After the manuscript had been rejected by a few publishers, Twain's friend from California, Charles Henry Webb, then in New York, agreed to see the book published. *The Celebrated Jumping Frog of Calaveras County, and Other Sketches* sold for $1.00 in paper covers and $1.50 in cloth. Though more than 1,500 copies were bound in the first month of sales, and more than 4,000 copies had been sold by 1870, Twain apparently earned no royalties from it. While *The Jumping Frog* failed to make a substantial dent in the already vast national book market, it had some success in England, selling more than 40,000 pirated copies by 1873 (*Letters* 2:48–49, 58). With this first book Twain learned both to be more careful about contracts (he had only an oral agreement for a ten percent royalty from Webb) and to be wary of the costs of book piracy. By the time Twain returned from a European trip aboard *The Quaker City* in the late 1860s, readers knew him from a series of humorous dispatches that had been widely circulated in American newspapers. These letters had attracted the attention of Elisha Bliss, head of the Hartford, Connecticut, subscription house, the American Publishing Company. Bliss suggested that Twain rework the newspaper letters into a *"humorous* work," and referred him to the company's success with the work of Albert Deane Richardson, a newspaperman and acquaintance of Twain (*Letters* 2:162). Twain saw an opportunity for success where *The Jumping Frog* had failed, and began an intermittent, though ultimately lifelong commitment to subscription book sales.

During his career Twain worked with highbrow and lowbrow publishers, established houses and fly-by-night concerns, trade publishers, pamphlet producers, magazines, and newspapers. In seeking financial success, he made use of nearly every mode of publication available. Beginning with *The Innocents Abroad* (the book about his *Quaker City* trip), published in 1869 by the American Publishing Company, Twain brought out the majority of his titles by subscription. Disillusioned with that company by the early 1880s, Twain entered into a subscription arrangement with trade publisher James R. Osgood. When Osgood's business failed, Twain started his own Charles L. Webster & Company in 1884. While the subscription method was well-suited to certain kinds of books—histories, miscellanies, Bibles, and topical books— Twain pioneered using the subscription method to sell novels. Although demanding extraordinary output of him (for subscription books generally ran to at least 600 printed pages), the method paid far better than trade royalties, making him rich by the 1880s (see Hill).

Taking a few quotations from Twain about subscription books and their readers, and reading them against the often vitriolic castigations of subscription books found in the press, some scholars have suggested two very different kinds of readers for trade books and subscription books. All this feeds quite neatly into readings of Twain as a rough, self-educated westerner uncomfortably settled with an eastern, moneyed wife. In these narratives of Twain's career, he struggles between his desire for acceptance by the literary and social elite, and his almost homespun dedication to be the "people's author," the favorite of the farmer and the rural rubes. While such readings have attended to the public rhetoric, particularly represented by trade press vehicles such as *Publishers' Weekly*, they have exaggerated the divisions between methods of publication. In fact, Twain used both methods to serve his ends. Throughout his career, he alternated between subscription and trade publication, hoping to reach as wide an audience as possible. He also published in a number of different magazines and supplemented his magazine production with pieces for newspaper syndication. He knew the audience each periodical addressed and how each periodical publication would affect his image and reputation. Sometimes he published in magazines targeted for young people, sometimes in such highbrow literary journals as the *Atlantic*. But he always paid attention to both the bottom line and his desired audience. Most often he saw periodical publication as a way to prime a prospective book audience for an upcoming work. Along the way he encouraged a great many other writers to use various methods of publication to suit different kinds of texts and audiences. As a subscription publisher, Twain alternately dumped slow books into the trade or railed against retailers such as John Wanamaker, who managed to get copies of briskly selling books away from canvassers and into his stores, undercutting the retail price in the bargain.

Mark Twain's engagement with the publishing industry, both as author and as publisher, reveals many of the issues that publishers faced, including the critical issue of vertical integration. In many ways Twain's career paralleled those of his financier or "robber baron" friends and acquaintances. In late-nineteenth-century America Twain most closely approached the concept of "author as trust": in his texts and his business practices, he found ways to absorb and otherwise appropriate his competition. In his travel books he borrowed freely from the work of others, turning bland travelogue to parody while filling out the large number of manuscript pages subscription books demanded. He used his newspaper and magazine columns to promote his own books, blurring the distinctions between "news" and advertising. And he became the publisher of other writers in order to fuel the publishing firm he started. Like the larger publishing houses, Twain's firm had to keep the front office busy, so Charles L. Webster & Company began to publish other authors. From his days with the American Publishing Company, Twain had learned the hazards of promoting or canvassing too many titles at once, but he failed to manage the Webster & Company list and releases profitably. Occasionally Twain the author delayed his own books to appease Twain the publisher, who had made too many commitments to other authors. Eventually the company failed, as did many other firms in this economically volatile period. Nevertheless, Twain was ready with a scheme to meet this setback. Pledging to honor his debts at par when many other failed publishers had returned only a few cents on the dollar of indebtedness, he announced a world tour of speaking engagements to earn his way out of debt (see esp. *Mark Twain's Correspondence with Henry Huttleston Rogers*).

At times, Mark Twain seemed the master of both vertical and horizontal integration, the tools of big business throughout the period. For most of his career, he used serialization to help promote his books, although he resented the practice when the American Publishing Company wanted him to contribute regularly, and for little or no pay, to its own short-lived periodical, the *American Publisher*. This unpleasant experience did not dampen Twain's enthusiasm. Rather, it seems to have spurred him to become a sharper negotiator for his own serial rights in several leading magazines. Twain saw the advantages gained by the publishing firms that had their own magazines, and as co-owner of Charles L. Webster & Company, he entertained notions of starting his own periodical. He proposed to his company's director, Fred Hall, that they launch an *"inexpensive"* magazine, with 20,000 copies to start. They would give away what they could not sell, sending copies to all the newspapers for free publicity in the form of favorable notices. Twain thought the magazine, tentatively titled "The Back Number," could contain articles culled from back issues of earlier periodicals (*Letters to His Publishers*, 355–56). Thus he could obtain the material without paying copyright, and like other publishers he would have a venue for advertising his own company's list of titles. Outside advertising would pay for the magazine's production. Twain promoted this idea, like countless others, to his cohorts, but soon dropped it.

Twain pioneered in myriad ways. Always interested in reaching out to new readers, always seeking a larger audience, he dabbled in almost every type of publication and sold his work at a remarkable range of prices. When reading matter for railroad travel became the rage, Twain issued pamphlets such as *Punch, Brothers, Punch* (1878). He called for one proposed pamphlet of his travel correspondence (already published by a newspaper syndicate) to declare on its cover, "Printed in Big Type for Railroad Use" (*Letters to His Publishers*, 286). When he realized that the $2.75 price for *A Connecticut Yankee in King Arthur's Court* was keeping the book from a potentially larger readership, he modified his marketing plans accordingly. He proposed a twenty-five-cent edition to sell heavily to "Labor Clubs," which had ordered other authors' titles by the hundred thousands (*Letters to His Publishers*, 295).

Not content with success in just the book and serial business, Twain sought to reach Americans by means other than prose texts. He agreed (then later declined) to write copy for a chromolithographed calendar. He enjoyed considerable success with his "Mark Twain's Patent Scrap Book," a largely empty book with pre-glued paper, to which one could paste items by simply moistening the scrap book pages (Budd, *Our Mark Twain*, 63–66). Kept largely by girls and young women, scrapbooks blurred the distinctions between advertising and more personal content, for they were often composed of artfully arranged advertising trade cards. By the 1880s they enjoyed significant popularity (Garvey, 16–50). Twain's scrapbook served his own interests in several ways. It gave him better access to the market of girls and young women, a segment not overly fond of his "boys'" books. It promoted his image as a man with his finger on the pulse of American culture, for newspapers gave considerable coverage to the clever way he responded to the American scrapbook fad. And it encouraged the collection of Mark Twain's authorized memorabilia and printed ephemera—postcards, trade cards, and tobacco cards bearing his likeness, as well as autographs and newspaper clippings. He also developed and attempted to manufacture board games.

The proliferation of print media, along with the rapid growth of a consumer class, helped raise the artist to celebrity status. Magazine and newspaper features offered details about authors' and painters' daily lives, studios or studies, and families, all for an increasingly inquisitive public. Many writers and artists either encouraged or at least tolerated such publicity, for it worked to their financial advantage. Having worked at a newspaper as compositor, reporter, and editor, Mark Twain was perhaps the most adept figure of his time at negotiating the press to his advantage. Whether giving frequent interviews to small-town and big-city reporters or donning his trademark white suit on his 1906 trip to the Capitol, Twain kept his name and image before the public and kept harried reporters everywhere well supplied with copy. In time, he grew to rely on newspapers as a means of connecting with his audience between books, as he relied on his camaraderie with newsmen to control what was said about him in the press. Photography aided Twain immeasurably as he parlayed his image into an American icon, becoming at times the most recognized person in America. Beginning with *The Innocents Abroad*, Twain's books reproduced his image in the form of caricature. By the mid-1870s, when Twain's work was before the public in book form, in magazines, in newspapers, and on the lecture circuit, his image was before the public in other ways too: in cartoons, in sheet music, in the "Celebrated Mark Twain Cigars." Although not all of these images were authorized (prompting Twain to seek to trademark his own name and image), he carefully managed who took his picture and when—encouraging flamboyant settings (Mark Twain in bed!) and clothing (the white suits) that kept him in the public eye. In an era before press agents and public-relations firms, Twain showed other writers and would-be celebrities how to manage one's publicity.

Even as they worked to attain and maintain celebrity status, authors such as Twain were particularly vexed by the frequent piracy of their work. With the breakdown of older business practices, developed and perpetuated by the established trade publishers, authors were increasingly at risk from "free market" business practices. As long as the highbrow publishers—headed by "gentlemen" such as Putnam, Appleton, Scribner, Holt, Ticknor and Fields—held power, they operated more often than not on the basis of "trade courtesy." In this system, even without international copyright an American publisher paid fees to a European author for the rights to publish the author's works in the United States. Generally other American publishers would not then publish competing or pirated editions of these works. This aspect of trade courtesy worked best for established writers with whom publishers anticipated a continuing relationship. The more established houses continued to cling to the idea of the literary profession as genteel, with relations between author and publisher based on friendship and mutual trust. But the foreign author, the unknown author, or the author who worked outside the coterie of literary society might find that trade courtesy was not universal. With new technology and an explosion in the number of publishers, there were fewer incentives to play the gentlemen's way. High-speed presses were expensive and needed to be working to pay back the investment, so demand increased for material to print. Upstart publishers resented the antidemocratic trade courtesy, seeing it as a kind of trust or syndicate that shut newcomers out. While many publishers, large and small, continued to practice one or more principles of trade courtesy, others increasingly ignored it and freely pirated European printed material. They offered American readers cheap reprints of popular European works, shoving the more expensive native material into the remainder bin (figuratively if not literally). By the 1880s writers and publishers alike felt that piracy was holding national literature back. Publishers were reluctant to pay American authors for original material, when piracy had driven prices down and boosted demand for more cheap European titles. Without international copyright, the literati contended, there would never be American literature as such.

Twain's sales in the United States suffered considerably from the importation of pirated Canadian imprints of his works. Although he went to great lengths to secure English copyright for his books, English copyright failed to protect against Canadian piracy. While canvassers for the American Publishing Company pushed *The Adventures of Tom Sawyer* beginning at $2.75, Canadian publishers were dumping pirated copies into the United States for $1.00 in cloth and as little as fifty cents in paper. There was no authorized cheap edition available in the States. Twain calculated and stewed over such losses for years, claiming they amounted to about $5,000 per year. In 1882 he filed suit "against the Belford publishers of Toronto and Chicago . . . based on his trademark claim; he believed that, although his *novels* could be piratically printed and sold, the trade name, 'Mark Twain,' could not be stolen and used without his consent" (Doyno, 188–89). His suit was unsuccessful.

As the case of Canadian piracy shows, the copyright problem affected more than European authors' pocketbooks and American sensibilities. While Mark Twain was among the most aggressive pursuers of his copyrights, other authors and publishers shared his concern. In 1886 one of the leading highbrow magazines, *Century*, published the views of forty-four American authors on international copyright. These authors compared their lack of rights to slavery, prejudice, and physical oppression. They saw in international copyright a chance to slip the yoke of European cultural imperialism, a way to encourage national identity and pride in American youth (Doyno, 194–96). In his statement Twain set the stakes high. He urged *Century* readers to "look at non-existent International Copyright from a combined business and statesmanship point of view, and consider whether the nation gains or loses by the present condition of the thing." To him, the influx of foreign texts offered "an ounce of wholesome literature to a hundred tons of noxious." Furthermore, lack of international copyright mocked the very rhetoric of nationalism: "Thus we have this curious spectacle: American statesmen glorifying American nationality, teaching it, preaching it, urging it, building it up—with their mouths; and undermining it and pulling it down with their acts" (in Doyno, 197–98). Twain continued to be active in the battle for international copyright, and his correspondence reveals many of the consequences of weak intellectual property rights for U.S. authors.

With the passage of international copyright legislation in 1891, European authors had to be compensated for the use of their texts. By 1900 many in the publishing business believed that the legislation had aided American authors significantly. With pirating under control, publishers competed for titles on a more-or-less even playing field, scrambling for works by American authors. In this newly altered marketplace, many authors found more bargaining power. More of them hired literary agents to handle increasingly complex negotiations over copyright, magazine serialization, newspaper syndication, and theatrical rights—and to command better terms for the publication of their work. Twain, whose work was already in demand, continued to try to secure and control the rights to publication of his own works. While his attempt at trademark was unsuccessful, ultimately he managed to protect much of his work by establishing the Mark Twain Company in 1908 (Budd, *Mythologizing of Mark Twain*, 79).

As his experimentation with several modes of publication, his own stint as a publisher, his avid interest in the art of promotion, and his attempts to create a "Mark Twain Trust" demonstrate, Twain was engaged in nearly every aspect of the publishing business. He also worked to develop printing and publishing technologies. Twain's early working life included frequent stints in newspaper and printing offices, where he learned the mechanics of publishing firsthand. Throughout his career his fascination with the technology of publishing cost him a fortune. Among the inventions Twain backed were the infamous Paige typesetter and the Kaolatype illustrating process. Both these projects, while ultimately not successful, were part of a number of competing products designed to cut costs while improving quality during printing. Although Twain routinely backed the wrong horse in the technology wars that raged within the publishing industry, his instincts about the role of technological development in the growth of publishing were right. When these technologies were developed more successfully by others, they helped bring about significant and lasting changes in publishing. As the man whose book title *The Gilded Age* has come to name both a period of American history and a cultural style, Twain participated visibly, even notoriously in the age of excess: the age of robber barons, conspicuous consumption, and genteel sensibilities. While his attempt to profit as financier from developing technologies failed miserably, he was enormously successful as an author in turning technology to his advantage, especially new techniques of illustration and photographic reproduction.

The records Mark Twain left, especially his letters to his publishers, employees, and financial and literary advisors, reveal a dizzyingly complex world for the successful author. Late in life he seems to have grasped some of the difficulties of having tried to be both author and publisher, recognizing the conflicts between the two roles. "All publishers are Columbuses[,]" he said, and "[t]he successful author is their America. The reflection that they—like Columbus—didn't discover what they started out to discover, doesn't trouble them. All they remember is that they discovered America; they forget that they started out to discover some patch or corner of India" (Twain, *Autobiography*, 253–54). As author rather than publisher, Twain, too, was a kind of Columbus, for in seeking to become a successful author, he also became a canonical one.

SOURCE NOTES

[Unless otherwise indicated artifacts and documents are reproduced courtesy of the American Antiquarian Society (AAS), Worcester, Massachusetts, or the author.]

1. Elisha Bliss, "Contract for *The Gilded Age*," in *Mark Twain's Letters*, ed. Lin Salamo and Harriet Elinor Smith, vol. 5 (Berkeley: University of California Press, 1997), 635–36. Copyright © Regents of the University of California. Reproduced courtesy of the University of California Press, Berkeley, Calif.

2. "Subscription Publishers and Underselling," *Trade Circular Annual for 1871* (New York: Office of the Trade Circular and Literary Bulletin, 1871), III.

3. "The Subscription Book Trade," *Publishers' Weekly* 2 (July 25, 1872): 93–94.

4. S. R. Crocker, "Subscription Books," *Literary World* 5 (August 1874): 40.

5. Elisha Bliss, "Subscription Books," *New York Tribune*, October 28, 1874, 8.

6. Mark Twain to Charles L. Webster & Co., *Mark Twain's Letters to His Publishers*, ed. Hamlin Hill (Berkeley: University of California Press, 1967), 232–34. Copyright © Regents of the University of California. Reproduced courtesy of the University of California Press, Berkeley, Calif.

7. "Religious Publishing Societies," *American Publishers' Circular and Literary Gazette* 3 (March 28, 1857): 193.

8. *Centennial of the Methodist Book Concern and Dedication of the New Publishing and Mission Building of the Methodist Episcopal Church* (New York: Hunt & Eaton, 1890), 9–10, 13–15, 25.

9. "Poet Lariat," from Mark Twain, *The Innocents Abroad* (Hartford, Conn.: American Publishing Co., 1869).

10. Mark Twain to Louisa Conrad, in *Mark Twain's Letters*, ed. Lin Salamo and Harriet Elinor Smith, vol. 5 (Berkeley: University of California Press, 1997), 303–4.

11. Mark Twain, *Punch, Brothers, Punch and Other Sketches* (New York: Slote, Woodman & Co., 1878).

12. *Life of Mark Twain* (Park Plains, N.Y.: Knapp & Co., 1886), frontispiece. Reproduced courtesy Lilly Library, Indiana University, Bloomington, Ind.

13. "The Evening Post's Libel Suit," *Publishers' Weekly* 43 (February 25, 1893): 359–61.

14. "The New Outlook on Copyright," *Publishers' Weekly* 15 (March 22, 1879): 339–40.

15. Thomas Nast, "Innocence Abroad (in Search of a Copyright)," *Harper's Weekly* 26 (January 21, 1882): 37. Reproduced courtesy of The Huntington Library, San Marino, Calif.

16. Henry Loomis Nelson, "United States Copyright to Foreign Authors," *Harper's Weekly* 35 (March 14, 1891): 197.

17. John S. Thompson, *The Mechanism of the Linotype* (Chicago: Inland Printer Co., 1902; rev. 6th ed., 1916).

18. *Biography of Ottmar Mergenthaler and History of the Linotype, Its Invention and Development* (Baltimore, 1898), 17–18.

19. "The Paige Compositor," *Scientific American* 54 (March 9, 1901): 145.

20. John S. Thompson, "Composing Machines—Past and Present. No. V," *Inland Printer* 30 (February 1903): 697–99.

WORKS CITED

Budd, Louis J. "A 'Talent for Posturing': The Achievement of Mark Twain's Public Personality." In *The Mythologizing of Mark Twain*, edited by Sara deSaussure Davis and Philip D. Beidler, 77–98. University: University of Alabama Press, 1984.

———. *Our Mark Twain: The Making of His Public Personality*. Philadelphia: University of Pennsylvania Press, 1983.

Doyno, Victor A. *Writing Huck Finn: Mark Twain's Creative Process*. Philadelphia: University of Pennsylvania Press, 1991.

Garvey, Ellen Gruber. *The Adman in the Parlor: Magazines and the Gendering of Consumer Culture, 1880s to 1910s*. New York: Oxford University Press, 1996.

Hill, Hamlin. *Mark Twain and Elisha Bliss*. Columbia: University of Missouri Press, 1964.

Madison, Charles A. *Book Publishing in America*. New York: McGraw-Hill, 1966.

Sheehan, Donald. *This Was Publishing: A Chronicle of the Book Trade in the Gilded Age*. Bloomington: Indiana University Press, 1952.

Twain, Mark. *The Autobiography of Mark Twain*. Edited by Charles Neider. New York: Harper & Row, 1959.

———. *Mark Twain's Correspondence with Henry Huttleston Rogers 1893–1909*. Edited by Lewis Leary. Berkeley: University of California Press, 1969.

———. *Mark Twain's Letters*. Vol. 2, edited by Harriet Elinor Smith and Richard Bucci. Berkeley: University of California Press, 1990.

———. *Mark Twain's Letters to His Publishers 1867–1894*. Edited by Hamlin Hill. Berkeley: University of California Press, 1967.

FOR FURTHER RESEARCH

Arbour, Keith. *Canvassing Books, Sample Books, and Subscription Publishers' Ephemera 1833–1951 in the Collection of Michael Zinman*. Ardsley, N.Y.: Haydn Foundation for the Cultural Arts, 1996.

Ballou, Ellen. *The Building of the House: Houghton Mifflin's Formative Years*. Boston: Houghton Mifflin, 1970.

Barnes, James J. *Authors, Publishers and Politicians: The Quest for an Anglo-American Copyright Agreement, 1815–1854*. London: Routledge & Kegan Paul, 1974.

Compton, F. E. *Subscription Books*. Pamphlet, fourth of the R. R. Bowker Memorial Lectures. New York: New York Public Library, 1939.

*Cook, Nancy. "Finding His Mark: Twain's *The Innocents Abroad* as a Subscription Book." In *Reading Books: Essays on the Material Text and Literature in America*, edited by Michele Moylan and Lane Stiles, 151–78.

———. "Marketing Mark Twain, or, Samuel Clemens and the Selling of *The Innocents Abroad*." Ph.D. diss., State University of New York–Buffalo, 1991.

Dickinson, Leon T. "Marketing a Best Seller: Mark Twain's *Innocents Abroad*." *Papers of the Bibliographical Society of America* 41 (Second Quarter 1947): 107–22.

Goble, Corban. "Mark Twain's Nemesis: The Paige Compositor." *Printing History* 18, no. 2 (1998): 2–16.

Gribben, Alan. "Autobiography as Property: Mark Twain and His Legend." In *The Mythologizing of Mark Twain*, edited by Sara deSaussure Davis and Philip D. Beidler, 39–55. University: University of Alabama Press, 1984.

*Hackenberg, Michael. "The Subscription Publishing Network in Nineteenth-Century America." In *Getting the Books Out: Papers of the Chicago Conference on the Book in 19th-Century America*, edited by Michael Hackenberg, 45–75.

Hart, James D. *The Popular Book: A History of America's Literary Taste*. Westport, Conn.: Greenwood Press, 1976.

McGill, Meredith L. "The Matter of the Text: Commerce, Print Culture, and the Authority of the State in American Copyright Law." *American Literary History* 9 (Spring 1997): 21–59.

Murray, Jeffrey S. "A Gift for the Gab: Hawking Books in the Hinterland." *Biblio* 3 (July 1998): 14–16.

Papovich, J. Frank. "Popular Appeal and Sales Strategy: The Prospectus of *The Innocents Abroad*." *English Language Notes* 19 (September 1981): 47–50.

Thomas, Amy M. "'There Is Nothing So Effective as a Personal Canvass': Revaluing Nineteenth-Century American Subscription Books." *Book History* 1 (1998): 140–55.

Twain, Mark. *Mark Twain, Business Man*. Edited by Samuel Charles Webster. Boston: Little, Brown, 1946.

———. *Mark Twain on Writing and Publishing*. New York: Book-of-the-Month Club, 1994.

"The Type-Composing Machine Upon Which Mark Twain Lost His Fortune." *Inland Printer* 17 (April 1896): 55.

Wells, Daniel A. "Mark Twain Allusions in the Boston 'Literary World': An Annotated List of Citations, 1870–1904." *Resources for American Literary Study* 24 (1998): 22–48.

West, James L. W., III. "Book-Publishing 1835–1900: The Anglo-American Connection." *Papers of the Bibliographical Society of America* 84 (December 1990): 357–75.

10

Print Cultures in the American West

JEN A. HUNTLEY-SMITH

AS THE UNITED STATES added new territories throughout the nineteenth century, the location of the "West" changed. In the colonial and revolutionary periods
the American west had been the Appalachian region; in the early 1800s it was the "Old
Northwest" (the Great Lakes region) and the "Old Southwest" of Arkansas, Alabama,
and Mississippi. The Louisiana Purchase of 1803 and the Mexican-American War of
1846–48, plus several smaller acquisitions, extended United States dominion across
the continent and over the people already living there, Native Americans and Mexican
Americans. Technological innovations, notably the transcontinental telegraph (1862)
and railroad (1869), improved connections between east and west: now information,
books, and magazines (along with people) could reach the Pacific states quickly.

For more than a century historians have asked this question: What is distinctive,
or "western," about the American west? Print culture provides paradoxical answers.
In one sense, eastern patterns migrated west. Easterners brought reading tastes with
them, and bought a variety of reading materials published in New York or Boston.
They also read local (that is, western) newspapers, but this too replicated eastern
habits. Like the south before and during the Civil War, settlers in the west were eager
for and dependent on the national print culture emanating from the eastern publishing
centers, even if they also hoped to build a western regional identity. Meanwhile, hardly
retreating from "civilization," publishers—especially in San Francisco—operated by
the latest business methods: separating editor from printer, employing cheap female
labor to undercut journeymen's wages and power, marketing aggressively. In another
sense, the west exhibited new tendencies. Instant communities, places such as mining
towns established in boom periods, sought to build infrastructures fast, complete
with print shops and newspapers. Here we do not see the incremental development
of the east and middle west.

In the west, too, polyglot people encountered each other, and print often became
the medium of that encounter. Ever since Columbus, Europeans had used the printed
word to assert dominion over places and people unfamiliar with European languages.
In the west, Anglo-Americans did the same, but so did others: newspapers in Spanish
and Chinese appeared within a decade of California's statehood (1850). For Native
Americans especially, the proper extent of assimilation remained a vexing question:
How fully should Native people adopt Euro-American ways, including the use of
English? By the end of the century another group of Americans—tourists—also

encountered the west. Railroad companies employed the printed word and image to lure travelers to a place they depicted as "new," even if people had been living there for centuries.

ARTIFACTS

Given the central role of linguistic encounters in the history of the American west, it should not be surprising that many groups used newspapers (which were relatively easy to establish, although difficult to make profitable) to represent their cultural backgrounds, evolving social positions, and political interests. The first three artifacts suggest the variety of newspaper publishing in California during the 1850s. Ferdinand Cartwright Ewer (1826–1883) came west for the 1849 gold rush but soon became a newspaper editor. A dozen years later he reminisced about the economic and political aspects of newspaper publishing in the new state of California. In doing so, he demonstrated how print publicized new towns and regions—and may actually have helped to shape settlement patterns in California. Several advertisements from a Chinese-language newspaper, the *Oriental* (San Francisco), suggest not only how the newspaper could help form communities of readers, but also how other linguistic communities sought to use such papers for financial gain. Francisco P. Ramirez's (b. 1837) prospectus from the first issue of *El Clamor Publico* (Los Angeles) illustrates how the newspaper mediated between the long-established, Spanish-speaking Californio population (whom Ramirez addressed) and a recently arrived culture that quickly dominated the economy and politics of the state.

Ferdinand Cartwright Ewer, Diary/Reminiscence (1850/1861)[1]

23 Years old

Jan 1st

With much diffidence in my ability I take charge of the Pacific News today. Salary $480 a month. I discharged J. Judson Ames from the post of City Reporter & placed James B. Devoe in his position. He soon desiring to go to N. Y. recommended Gen. Winchester formerly partner with Park Benjamin in the N. Y. literary paper, the New World, and I gave him the position. The News was owned then in equal shares by Col Allen (who was in N. Y.) having left his brother Major Allen with power of Attorney to act for him, and Mr. Falkner who when he left for N. Y. a month or two before had left Mr. Chas Eames with the editorship & responsibility of the concern. Mr. Eames put me in his place so that I stood as responsible for the entire management of the sheet & as the representative of Mr. Falkner. . . .

It was not long before Major Allen & Gen. Winchester began to sell the influence of the paper to various interests who were glad enough to purchase its columns. I was kept in the dark and when I had left the office for the night Winchester

& Allen would insert little paragraphs to further their designs. This gave me a good deal of trouble. And kept me at the office watching. A coolness grew up between me & them. Winchester went up the river (Sacramento) to the scene of where two rival towns were in process of starting viz Marysville at the mouth of the Yuba & Feather Rivers & Yuba City near by. He decided that Yuba City would be *the* place— took from them (as I learned) for himself & Allen a bribe in town lots for the "news." Came back & in his items of intelligence came out glaringly for the advantages of Yuba City. Allen tried to get me into the bargain offering me 20 or 30 lots. I told him I would have nothing whatever to do with such business. That such arrangements in addition to be dishonest would ruin the paper (which was the leading one on the Coast). The "assistance" was rendered by newspapers in such instances by means of bringing the favorite of the rival towns into prominent mention and so directing public attention to them & sending the travel there. I told Allen & Winchester that Falkners paper should enter into no such chicanery so long as I had the management of it. That I should not mislead the public, but should make the paper a reflex of the times. I had no objection to news & letters from Yuba City if that was *the* place. I left for up river to see for myself which spot would be likely to take the precedence. (At this time there was a rivalry between Benicia & San Francisco for the post of the great Bay City—also between Sacramento & Sutterville for the post of the leading Entrepot & depot of the Sacramento valley—also between Marysville & Yuba City higher up—and between San Joaquin City & some other place on the San Joaquin) I went up the river to Yuba City leaving word that no "puff" of any kind for any city speculation should appear in the columns while I was gone. My determination was to give news, not to use the paper for private speculations. On examination I judged & determined that Marysville was going to be *the* place north of Sacramento and returned. During my absence two violent puffs for Yuba & San Joaquin Cities appeared in the columns. I was powerless. Allen had a power of attorney from one of the partners & I had nothing to show that I was indeed acting for the other. . . . I resigned my post as Editor. This alarmed Allen & he begged me to stay & yielded the whole charge of the paper into my hands. I brot it out daily & enlarged it. My position was unpleasant—there being a coldness between Allen & myself—he had very materially injured the reputation of the paper already—and I determined to leave at the first opportunity.

Advertisements from *The Oriental* (1855)[2]

Francisco P. Ramirez, "Martes, Junio 19, De 1855," from *El Clamor Publico* (1855)[3]

Hoy saludámos respetuosamente al público. Suplicámos á nuestros patronos que reciban muchísimas gracias por la liberal suscricion con que nos han favorecido. Aunque sea duro decirlo, los extrangeros han mostrado mucho mas ardor para suscribirse á nuestro periódoco que los mismos Californios; sentímos profundamente esto y descamos que se presenten cuanto antes para que no quede sobre ellos semejante oprobio. Está enteramente dedicado á sus intereses, y á ellos, mas que à nadi-eles corresponde soportar nuestra empresa. ¡Qué lástima que muchos individuos a quienes interesa soportar estas empresas, se desentienden absolutamente de hacerlo y se contentan con no desear para su país ninguna clase de mejoras. Californienses! debeis persuadiros que la libertad de la imprenta es la mejor garantía para un pueblo, ye que el nuestro mas que ninguno necesita de sus auxilios. Esta es una verdad comprobada y que no necesita de ejemplos para justificarla. Trabajémos de acuerdo, prestad vuestra cooperacion y yá vereis los felices resultados que producirá. Nada es mas justo que mirar por la conservacion de nuestros propios intereses; aquel que vigila sobre ellos es digno de prosperar; pero el que se desentiende aun de las cosas mas útiles—el que por un error incurre en la falta de no tomar parte en los asuntos de interés público, ese ni es buen ciudadano, ni merece justamente que los demás se desvivan por protejerle.

Hace mucho tiempo desde que intentamos publicar en esta ciudad un periódico en Castellano, pero las muchas dificultades que se nos presentaban nos hicieron renunciar nuestra intencion: hasta que lo pusimos por obra, y EL CLAMOR PUBLICO es el primer fruto de nuestros trabajes. Se publicará en pequeña forma durante algunos meses, y si nuestros amigos nos soportan y animan, entonces lo haremos mas grande, ó lo publicarémos dos veces á la semana.

La bandera que seguimos es la bandera INDEPENDIENTE y no el pendon de ningun partido ó secta religiosa, y todas nuestras convicciones políticas se reducen à este único y estrañable deseo—*El progreso moral y material dentro de la esféra y del órden*. EL CLAMOR PUBLICO está edificado sobre el sólido cimiento de las ideas liberales, y sus columnas estaràn siempre abiertas para la discucion imparcial de todos los asuntos de interés público.

Persuadidos de que el público recibirá, con agrado nuestros esfuerzos, en adelante harémos todo lo posible para captarnos su estimacion. Sostendrémos a la Constitucion de los Estados Unidos, estando convencidos que solo bajo ella tendrémos libertades, y en donde solo se puede hallar felicidad : y combatirémos todo lo que esté opuesto á su espíritu magnánimo y grandiosas ideas.

* * * * *

No hay cosa tan buena recibir un periódico. Con el los niños aprenden a leer, arrastrados por la natural curiosidad de saber lo que pasa; con él los mas grandes aprienden á portarse como hombres de bien; con, el en fin se pasa un buen rato, y con su lectura se olvidan los pesares y los negocios de esta vida. Muchas personas se han estrañado al saber el infimo precio de la suscricion a este periódico—es verdad que es muy barato, pero consideremos la presente escacés del numerario tanto en esta ciudad como en todo el Estado.

[Today, we respectfully greet our public. We ask our patrons to accept our many thanks for the generous diligence with which they have supported us. Although it is hard to say, the foreigners have shown much more ardor for subscribing to our newspaper than the native Californios; we are profoundly hurt by this neglect and would like the natives to step forward so that such a disgrace will not hang over them. This newspaper is dedicated entirely to their interests, and it is their responsibility, more than anyone else's, to support our undertaking. It is a shame that many individuals who should be interested in supporting this enterprise would take absolutely no part in doing so and would remain content without a desire for the betterment of their country! Californians, you should be convinced that the liberty of the press is the best guarantee for a community, and that our community, more than any other, needs the aid of such liberty. This is a proven fact that needs no examples for justification. Let us work together, let us cooperate, and we will see the fortunate results it will produce. Nothing is more just than to look out for the conservation of our own interests; he who guards them is worthy of prosperity; but he who ignores even the most useful things—he who for some mistake fails to take part in public matters—is neither a good citizen, nor justly deserves that others do their best to protect him.

We have long tried to publish a newspaper in Castillian in this city, but the many difficulties that presented themselves made us renounce these intentions until such time as we could undertake their execution. *El Clamor Publico* is the first fruit of our work. A small version will be published for some months, and if our friends support and encourage us, then we shall make it bigger or publish it twice a week.

The flag we follow is the *Independent* flag and not the banner of any party or religious sect, and all our political beliefs can be reduced to this desirable wish—*The moral and material progress within our sphere and of social order. El Clamor Publico* is edified by the foundations of liberal ideas, and its columns will always be open for impartial discussion of all matters of concern to the public.

Convinced that the public will receive our efforts with approval, from now on we shall do everything possible to capture its esteem. We shall uphold the Constitution of the United States, being convinced that only under it shall we have liberties, and only in it can we find happiness. We shall combat all that opposes its magnanimous spirit and grand ideas.

* * * * *

There is nothing better than receiving a newspaper. With it, children learn to read, dragged by their natural curiosity to know what is happening; with it, the older ones learn to behave like good men; with it, in conclusion, you enjoy yourself, and by reading it you forget the affairs and business of this life. Many people have been surprised upon learning the ridiculously low price for a subscription to this newspaper—it is true that it is very cheap, but that is because we are taking into consideration the current scarcity of cash in this city as well as in the whole state.]

WHAT DID literary relations between east and west look like? Westerners certainly read books and magazines written and published in New York and Boston. Rachel Haskell's diary (1867), written in a Nevada mining camp, reveals how thoroughly she and her family were steeped in print culture. Some of her reading was produced locally. But much of it came to her from the east in the pages of magazines such as *Harper's New Monthly Magazine*. Two selections from Mark Twain's *Roughing It* (1872) show how established literary traditions were appropriated in the west, but also how printing became important to the Nevada mining economy. In the first selection, Twain (1835–1910) describes the interrelations of mining, job printing, and newspapers. In the second, he narrates the composition of a serial novel—one part sentimental, two parts gothic—for a Virginia City literary newspaper. Not just the products, but also the processes of eastern print culture spread quickly to the west. In 1874 Mrs. J. W. Likins (b. ca. 1825) published an account of her experiences as a subscription book agent in San Francisco—a new market for eastern publishers. Notably, Likins described her experience collecting subscriptions for Twain's *Roughing It*. The west did not depend entirely on eastern publishers for its literary goods. In fact, the west very quickly developed a sophisticated publishing economy that countered expectations by exporting western publications to eastern markets. An advertisement for a San Francisco publisher, A. L. Bancroft & Company, depicts a publishing enterprise reminiscent of the Harper establishment Jacob Abbott had described in 1855. The San Francisco firm's founder, Hubert Howe Bancroft (1832–1918), reminisced in his 1891 memoir—published, ironically, by Harper & Brothers in New York—about what occurred inside the building pictured in the advertisement.

Rachel Haskell, Diary (1867)[4]

Sunday Mar. 3rd. Got up late as usual these stormy times. Breakfast noon. I washed boys, a good scouring all over, dressed them, then went thru my own toilet. Ella read Gulliver's Travels aloud to boys. While Mr wrote in sitting room Mr. H. read in kitchen. I lay on sofa and enjoyed myself in said quiet position reading a book called "Light" by Alfred Mondet, till supper was nearly ready. Mr. H. keeps it going on stove. Washed dishes alone. Mr. H. talking in kitchen, Ella playing on piano some pleasant airs. Both ministers sick, so no church today. Came to sitting room, sat on a stool near piano while Ella accompanied songs by the family in chorus. Drew table in front of stove, resumed reading of "Light" while children with bright happy faces filled up the gaps. Mr. H. after playing on floor with two younger ones lay on the lounge and read likewise. Finished my book, pleasant writing but not extra deep. Ella read colored pictures.

Monday 4th. Looked a bit calmer and cooler, brighter in the morning. Sun shining cheerfully. Work thru, gave Ella lesson on new page of Linda March. We have been rather musical today, piano open all the time. Bud played a waltz wonderful, we had no idea he had caught even the air of. Is very fond of picking out tunes. Changed my calico dress and lay on sofa, while Ella read aloud some back pages of this. Have taken it easy today. Not sewing, only read "Enterprises." Seemed inclined to snow a little again this evening. Table mountain invisible and even Chalcedony somewhat hazy. Supper waiting on the gents who stay rather late up town. Mr did not come to supper. In evening Mr. H. read at table, while I lay on sofa and heard Dudley and Harry recite the multiplication table and count figures. Did not feel very brisk so took Maney and went to bed. In the night Mr. H. waked up eloquent in repeating a speech he dreamed he was delivering to a Nev. assembly. Sac[ramen]to was the especial theme. . . .

Monday 11th. Sprinkled last weeks clothes for ironing, made yeast. Ella ironed while I cut out new fashioned sacque. Paid $1.00 for schooling on bublining. Was interrupted by the arrival of one of the newly arrived Carsonites; Mr. Medley (really) looking fat and rubicund as Kris Kingle. Mr. Chapin came in shortly after bearing a loaf of very nice cake made by himself. He stayed to Supper. How comfortable and cozy the sitting room did look this evening by twilight. The shelves laden with books, spec- imens, minerals, shells. The Piano, the Sewing Machine, comfortable sofa and easy chair, with healthy, happy, prattling, chippy, little children all from Manie to Ella (again). I with Guitar in hand and Mr. Chapin looking at pictures in "Home Scenes." I played on the Piano for Mr. C. Later Mr. Mac Naten and Tannahill came in. Sat up late for return of Mr. H. I reading "Newcomes" and Ella "Cripple of Antioch." We heard a most piteous wail of wind that seemed like a groan of the Spheres or the wail of a lost soul. Twice or thrice repeated, then died away into a perfect calm. We went to bed without Mr. H. who did not return till after 12 o'clock, ostensibly wait- ing for the mail

Sat. 16th. Scrubbed kitchen again which looked terrific by this morning. Made bread and set doughnuts—all tardy in rising. Sat in entry and read the Dodge Club in Harper, Ella sewed some on machine while I sat at back window in sitting room enjoying the view and sewing Birdies velvet pants which proved too short in the legs. Jim Poor went to skating pond on horseback. Waited supper on Mr. H. who did not come. While seated at table, Mr. Ricker, his man Josh, and Chapin called. Made to give up frying doughnuts and sit in front room. Passed a pleasant evening. Mr. R. brot us a nice mince pie, had quite a talk with him. Mr. Chapin recd two pieces of music, both of which he presented to us, "What are the wild waves saying," and "Bonnie Eloise." Also a pack of author cards to the children which we played with much zest. After our callers left, we sat up quite late children and all, warmed our mince pie and enjoyed eating it much. I read "Newcomes" in bed till three o'clock in morning. Birdie and Maney awake playing around me. Mr. H. did not come home all night. But I thought of other things. Ella's dress I must make for Odd fellows ball and so forth so I experienced no particular harassment. . . .

Tuesday Apr. 2nd. Storming again. Snowing but melting soon as it touches Terra Firma. Mr. H. getting wood. I swept and made bed after getting breakfast then thought I should write this up from last Tuesday before I forgot events which are so slight it is hard to keep the sum. Mr. H. in and eating a lunch which his exercise on the hills has no doubt given him appetite for. I am still troubled with soreness and weakness of eyes. Do nothing for it. I must write some letters. Was writing balance of afternoon to my father. Mr. McNaughton came in which interrupted me somewhat. Mr. H. writing, too, so we talked by turns to visitor. Got up and hurried supper on table, mashed potatoes, bacon, eggs and slaw. Mr. Mc N. sat down with us. Maney very cross after supper. Made poor head way in writing tho tried to stay at it. Mr. H. put his face in window on return from town to view his family frightened me and amused children very much. Read the Enterprises and continuation of Clark-Rees breach of promise case, verdict with five thousand dollars for her. Read also of Mr. Peabodys continued munificence and was struck with an insane idea which I revolved all night, scarcely sleeping. Heard a step in the night which filled me with intense fear for few moments.

Wednesday Apr 3rd. Not an agreeable morning, or breakfast. Felt wearied and excited and no appetite. Maney crying as usual for the breast refusing other food. Mr. H. washed dishes. I mixed bread, have made biscuit for couple of weeks. Tacked and patched torn place on Ella's room carpet. Gave some clothes to washman, mended a little while nursing Maney whom Ella kept on porch seesawing long while Mr. H read Enoch Arden aloud to me. I cried, he laughed at me but I saw his eyes were filled with tears also. We both blubbered over the story and laughed at each other for so doing. Have my bread baked; looks nice. Before getting supper wrote the letter I revolved in my mind last night. Have not yet dispatched it but most assuredly will. Have some hope!—Fried doughnuts after supper, children poking in dough of their own cutting. We sit around the table, they looking at maps and I writing this, with Maney squealing so.

Mark Twain, *Roughing It* (1871)[5]

The city and all the great mountain side were riddled with mining shafts. . . . True, not ten of these mines were yielding rock worth hauling to a mill, but . . . nobody was discouraged. . . . Every one of these wild cat mines—not mines, but holes in the ground over imaginary mines—was incorporated and had handsomely engraved "stock" and the stock was salable, too. It was bought and sold with a fever-ish avidity in the boards every day. You could go up on the mountain side, scratch around and find a ledge (there was no lack of them), put up a "notice" with a gran-diloquent name in it, start a shaft, get your stock printed, and with nothing whatever to prove that your mine was worth a straw, you could put your stock on the market and sell out for hundreds and even thousands of dollars. To make money, and make it fast, was as easy as it was to eat your dinner. Every man owned "feet" in fifty differ-ent wild cat mines and considered his fortune made. Think of a city with not one solitary poor man in it! One would suppose that when month after month went by and still not a wild cat mine (by wild cat I mean, in general terms, any claim not located on the mother vein, i.e., the "Comstock") yielded a ton of rock worth crushing, the people would begin to wonder if they were not putting too much faith in their prospective riches; but there was not a thought of such a thing. They burrowed away, bought and sold, and were happy.

New claims were taken up daily, and it was the friendly custom to run straight to the newspaper offices, give the reporter forty or fifty "feet," and get them to go and examine the mine and publish a notice of it. They did not care a fig what you said about the property so you said something. Consequently we generally said a word or two to the effect that the "indications" were good, or that the ledge was "six feet wide," or that the rock "resembled the Comstock" (and so it did—but as a general thing the resemblance was not startling enough to knock you down). If the rock was moderately promising, we followed the custom of the country, used strong adjectives and frothed at the mouth as if a very marvel in silver discoveries had transpired. If the mine was a "developed" one, and had no pay ore to show (and of course it hadn't), we praised the tunnel; said it was one of the most infatuating tun-nels in the land; driveled and driveled about the tunnel till we ran entirely out of ecstacies—but never said a word about the rock. We would squander half a column of adulation on a shaft, or a new wire rope, or a dressed pine windlass, or a fascinating force pump, and close with a burst of admiration of the "gentlemanly and efficient Superintendent" of the mine—but never utter a whisper about the rock. And those people were always pleased, always satisfied. Occasionally we patched up and varnished our reputation for discrimination and stern, undeviating accuracy, by giving some old abandoned claim a blast that ought to have made its dry bones rattle—and then somebody would seize it and sell it on the fleeting notoriety thus conferred upon it. . . .

* * * * *

We expected great things of the Occidental. Of course it could not get along without an original novel, and so we made arrangements to hurl into the work the full strength of the company. Mrs. F. was an able romancist of the ineffable school— I know no other name to apply to a school whose heroes are all dainty and all per-fect. She wrote the opening chapter, and introduced a lovely blonde simpleton who talked nothing but pearls and poetry and who was virtuous to the verge of eccen-tricity. She also introduced a young French Duke of aggravated refinement, in love with the blonde. Mr. F. followed next week, with a brilliant lawyer who set about getting the Duke's estates into trouble, and a sparkling young lady of high society who fell to fascinating the Duke and impairing the appetite of the blonde. Mr. D., a dark and bloody editor of one of the dailies, followed Mr. F., the third week, introducing a mysterious Roscicrucian who transmuted metals, held consultations with the devil in a cave at dead of night, and cast the horoscope of the several heroes and heroines in such a way as to provide plenty of trouble for their future careers and breed a solemn and awful public interest in the novel. He also introduced a cloaked and masked melodramatic miscreant, put him on a salary and set him on the midnight track of the Duke with a poisoned dagger. He also created an Irish coachman with a rich brogue and placed him in the service of the society-young-lady with an ulterior mission to carry billet-doux to the Duke.

About this time there arrived in Virginia a dissolute stranger with a literary turn of mind—rather seedy he was, but very quiet and unassuming; almost diffident, indeed. He was so gentle, and his manners were so pleasing and kindly, whether he was sober or intoxicated, that he made friends of all who came in contact with him. He applied for literary work, offered conclusive evidence that he wielded an easy and practiced pen, and so Mr. F. engaged him at once to help write the novel. His chapter was to follow Mr. D.'s, and mine was to come next. Now what does this fellow do but go off and get drunk and then proceed to his quarters and set to work with his imagination in a state of chaos, and that chaos in a condition of extravagant activity. The result may be guessed. He scanned the chapters of his predecessors, found plenty of heroes and heroines already created, and was satisfied with them; he decided to introduce no more; with all the confidence that whisky inspires and all the easy complacency it gives to its servant, he then launched himself lovingly into his work: he married the coachman to the society-young-lady for the sake of the scandal; married the Duke to the blonde's stepmother, for the sake of the sensation; stopped the desperado's salary; created a misunderstanding between the devil and the Roscicrucian; threw the Duke's property into the wicked lawyer's hands; made the lawyer's upbraiding conscience drive him to drink, thence to *delirium tremens,* thence to suicide; broke the coachman's neck; let his widow succumb to contumely, neglect, poverty and consumption; caused the blonde to drown herself, leaving her clothes on the bank with the customary note pinned to them forgiving the Duke and hoping he would be happy; revealed to the Duke, by means of the usual strawberry mark on left arm, that he had married his own long-lost mother and destroyed his long-lost sister; instituted the proper and necessary suicide of the Duke and the Duchess in order to compass poetical justice; opened the earth and let the Roscicrucian through, accompanied with the accustomed smoke and thunder and smell of brimstone, and finished with the promise that in the next chapter, after holding a general inquest he would take up the surviving character of the novel and tell what became of the devil!

It read with singular smoothness, and with a "dead" earnestness that was funny enough to suffocate a body. But there was war when it came in. The other novelists were furious. The mild stranger, not yet more than half sober, stood there, under a scathing fire of vituperation, meek and bewildered, looking from one to another of his assailants, and wondering what he could have done to invoke such a storm. When a lull came at last, he said his say gently and appealingly—said he did not rightly remember what he had written, but was sure he had tried to do the best he could, and knew his object had been to make the novel not only pleasant and plausible but instructive and—

The bombardment began again. The novelists assailed his ill-chosen adjectives and demolished them with a storm of denunciation and ridicule. And so the siege went on. Every time the stranger tried to appease the enemy he only made matters worse. . . .

[He] . . . was peremptorily discharged, and his manuscript flung at his head. But he had already delayed things so much that there was not time for some one else to rewrite the chapter, and so the paper came out without any novel in it. It was but a feeble, struggling, stupid journal, and the absence of the novel probably shook public confidence; at any rate, before the first side of the next issue went to press, the Weekly Occidental died as peacefully as an infant.

An effort was made to resurrect it, with the proposed advantage of a telling new title, and Mr. F. said that The Phenix would be just the name for it, because it would give the idea of a resurrection from its dead ashes in a new and undreamed of condition of splendor; but some low-priced smarty on one of the dailies suggested that we call it the Lazarus; and inasmuch as the people were not profound in Scriptural matters but thought the resurrected Lazarus and the dilapidated mendicant that begged in the rich man's gateway were one and the same person, the name became the laughing stock of the town, and killed the paper for good and all.

Mrs. J. W. Likins, *Six Years Experience as a Book Agent: Including My Trip from New York to San Francisco via Nicaragua* (1874)[6]

During that period, I worked in all parts of the city, on several books; among them, "Knots Untied," a work written by a New York detective; "Garnered Sheaves," by Richardson; "Poetry and Songs," by William Cullen Bryant; "Cuba, with Pen and Pencil"; "Life of Barnum," and "Woman's Pilgrimage in the Holy Land.". . .

While I was canvassing for the "Life of Barnum," on California Street, I went down three or four steps into a large room, where there were quite a number of little offices divided by railings, each containing a desk and one or two chairs. In the farther end of the room was one quite large office, with four or five men in it. I will not call them gentlemen; they do not deserve that title.

When I first entered, I noticed them whispering, looking toward me, blinking and winking, as though they thought I was very green, and they could play almost any kind of a prank upon me. When I went up to them, one took my order book from my hand very impolitely, looked it all through, saying, "Barnum is an old humbug; still my friends and I will each take a copy, to help you along. We are all friends, and strangers in the city, and will not remain but a few days. Will you bring the books to our rooms, and can you bring them immediately?" I told him the books were ready to be delivered right away, I would comply with his request, providing he would give me the directions. Two of them pretended to sign their names in my order book. One's address was the Cosmopolitan, the other the Occidental Hotel.

I felt confident at once they were fictitious names; but I thanked them all the same, thinking inwardly, you will find I am not so green after all. I stopped at several of the smaller offices. As I left the room and passed up the steps, one of the pretended gentlemen who had not signed for the book, was standing outside, and said, "Madam, if you will tell me where you live, I will call at the house and buy a book." I told him I lived in San Francisco. He replied, "Well, I declare, that is satisfactory." "It is all the satisfaction you will get from me, sir," and I passed on.

I went directly to the hotels, and found no such persons stopping there. I was very much annoyed and studied for some time what course to pursue, made up my mind to find out their real names, and compel them take the books if there was any law to do so. In three hours from that time I knew who they were; as to who gave me the information, it is no fellow's business. I secured four copies of the books, in two styles of binding, and watched the office for several days before I could catch them all in. When I did, I marched through the room, with my four books, into their office. I addressed them politely, calling them by their right names, saying, "You mentioned no style of binding, so I have brought both; you can take your choice."

They seemed very much confused, made several efforts to say something, but did not succeed. They took the best binding, and paid me for them, all the time trying to laugh; said one of them, "You are a Yankee woman, sure enough." I told him he was very much mistaken, for I was a Southerner, and was now even with them. Feeling as though I was victorious, I left the room. . . .

On the first of March I called in Mr. Roman's bookstore, to secure territory for Mark Twain's book, "Roughing It." They gave me Santa Clara county, and a portion of the City. The book was not expected from the East for several days; so I worked on miscellaneous books until its arrival.

One day, when I was in the Subscription Department at Roman's, I was introduced to two ladies, one of them medium size, the other very small. When I learned they were canvassers, just starting in the business, I pitied them, although they looked smart enough to fight their own battles; for I knew the trials they would have to contend with.

When I commenced on Mark Twain's "Roughing It," I found the *small* lady had the district in the City adjoining mine. There was an M. B. we both had to contend with; *his* district was one side of Market, and one of Mission, from the Bay to Sixteenth street. Instead of working on his *own* district, he was like a wandering Jew, over all creation, and caused me to receive a great deal of abuse; when I contended for my rights, I found a great many in *my* district who had patronized *him*; they told me he came into their offices, which were many of them four or five blocks from his territory, to obtain their orders, and they could not very well refuse him, as he was a friend of theirs. It grieved me very much to think he would act so, when he knew my circumstances, and I had taken him for an honest gentleman. . . .

I had much to annoy me, notwithstanding this was the most salable book I had ever worked on. In many of the stores on Front Street, I took from three to five orders a day. In canvassing Battery street, I went up stairs in a building occupied by Government employees. In the front room were half a dozen gentlemen, who treated me kindly, but said when I insisted upon their buying a book, "I cannot; my wages are too small, and I do not feel able." I passed into the office. There was a gentleman I will call Mr. W., who had patronized me heretofore. Off from this room was a small private office; the door was open; seated inside was a gentleman, whom I politely asked to subscribe for Mark Twain's "Roughing It." He said, "I would be pleased to do so, to assist you, but I have already subscribed for a copy." "You will please to excuse me, sir," I replied, "but where did you buy, and who of?" He had not time to reply, when I heard a peculiar noise, something like a big bull-frog croaking. I looked around, wondering how it came in the room. There I be-held, seated in a chair at a desk, a being, something in the form of a man, but in reality looking more like a frog. . . . "What in the h— d— m— is it your business, where he got the book? Any one has as much right in this city, as you have. . . . I can tell you d—m plainly where he bought the book; it was in this office, and I bought one too from a Mr. B——, and it is none of your d——d business." I tried to explain to him how the territory was divided; it only seemed to enrage him the more, to think I would dare to speak in the presence of the majestic frog. . . .

I next visited the Custom House, but found it impossible, under my present ex-cited state of mind, from the abuse I had just received, to solicit any more that day; so I returned to my home, where I remained for several days. When I commenced work again, I determined to ask no questions, when any one said they had already purchased the book. I was five weeks working my district in the city, and was more successful than I had ever anticipated; I would often think that I myself was most assuredly ROUGHING IT.

Hubert Howe Bancroft, *Literary Industries: A Memoir* (1891)[7]

The business [H. H. Bancroft and Company] was now one of the most extensive of the kind in the world. It was divided into nine departments, each in charge of an experienced and responsible head, with the requisite number of assistants, and each in itself as large as an ordinary business in our line of trade. But this was not enough. Thus far it was purely a mercantile and publishing house. To make it per-fect, complete, and symmetrical, manufacturing must be added. This I had long been ambitious of doing, but was prevented by lack of room. Now this obstacle was removed, and I determined to try the experiment. The mercantile stock was brought up and properly arranged in the different departments on the first and second floors

268

Advertisement for A. L. Bancroft & Co. (1885)[8]

and basement, on one side of the new building. These rooms were each thirty-five by one hundred and seventy feet. On the third and fourth floors respectively were placed a printing-office and bookbindery, each covering the entire ground of the building, seventy-five by one hundred and seventy feet. To accomplish this more easily and economically several small establishments were purchased and moved with their business into the new premises, such as a printing, an engraving, a lithographing, and a stationery establishment. A steam-engine was placed in the basement to drive the machinery above, and an artesian well was dug to supply the premises with water. A department of music and pianos was also added. My library of Pacific coast books was alphabetically arranged on the fifth floor, which was of the same dimensions as the rooms below. Then I changed the name of the business [to A. L. Bancroft & Company], the initial letters only, my responsibility, however, remaining the same. The idea was not eminently practicable, I will admit, that I should expect to remain at the head of a large and intricate business, involving many interests and accompanied by endless detail, see it continue its successful course, and at the same time withdraw my thoughts and attention from it so as to do justice to any literary or historical undertaking. "How dared you undertake crossing the Sierra?" the pioneer railroad men were asked. "Because we were not railroad men," was the reply. . . .

In 1859, one William H. Knight, then in my service as editor and compiler of statistical works relative to the Pacific coast, was engaged in preparing the *Hand-Book Almanac* for the year 1860. From time to time he asked me for certain books required for the work. It occurred to me that we should probably have frequent occasion to refer to books on California, Oregon, Washington, and Utah, and that it might be more convenient to have them altogether. I always had a taste, more pleasant than profitable, for publishing books, for conceiving a work and having it wrought out under my direction. To this taste may be attributed the origin of half the books published in California during the first twenty years of its existence as a State, if we except law reports, legislative proceedings, directories, and compilations of that character. Yet I have seldom published anything but law-books that did not result in a loss of money. Books for general reading, miscellaneous books in trade vernacular, even if intrinsically good, found few purchasers in California. The field was not large enough; there were not enough book buyers to absorb an edition of any work, except a law-book, or a book intended as a working tool for a class. Lawyers like solid leverage, and in the absence of books they are powerless; they cannot afford to be without them; they buy them as mill-men buy stones to grind out toll withal. Physicians do not require so many books, but some have fine libraries. Two or three medical books treating of climate and diseases peculiar to California have been published in this country with tolerable success; but the medical man is by no means so dependent on books as the man of law—that is to say, after he has once finished his studies and is established in practice. . . . Poetry has often been essayed in California, for the most part doggerel; yet should Byron come here and publish for the first time his *Childe Harold,* it would not find buyers enough to pay the printer.

Even Tuthill's *History of California,* vigorously offered by subscription, did not return the cost of plates, paper, presswork, and binding. He who dances must pay the fiddler. Either the author or the publisher must make up his mind to remunerate the printer; the people will not till there are more of them, and with different tastes.

HUBERT HOWE BANCROFT was not just a publisher. He also wrote dozens of well-researched volumes of western American history and became one of America's great book collectors. Unlike most collectors, he bought Mexican rare books, as he explained in the section of his memoir reproduced here. To what extent was his collecting an act of preservation, and to what extent (to use his words) was it "ransacking" exotic "treasures"? Similarly, what was at stake when white, Protestant missionaries took Native American children away from their families to missionary schools? One of those children was Zitkala-Sä (1876–1938), a Yankton Sioux woman from Dakota Territory who later taught for a time in one of those schools in Pennsylvania. Writing for the well-known Boston literary magazine the *Atlantic Monthly* in 1900, Zitkala-Sä reminded her readers that literacy could be a two-edged sword. While it spread the ideas and values of a dominant culture and sped the assimilation of minority cultures, it also provided them the means to speak against that very process. A very different kind of encounter occurred when the west became a tourist playground. Many Americans—predominantly white people of the middle and upper classes—traversed the vast distances between Chicago and California for pleasure. On their journeys, through their railroad (and, later, automobile) windows, they saw what had once been "frontier." Railroad companies published guidebooks, postcards, and maps to encourage and romanticize these adventures. In 1887 the Denver & Rio Grande Railroad published *Rhymes of the Rockies*, a presentation booklet given to passengers on the railroad's popular Colorado and Utah routes. The general passenger agent for the line, S. K. Hooper (1841–1923), wrote the preface included here, and hundreds of thousands of copies in at least twenty editions were distributed under his auspices.

Hubert Howe Bancroft, *Literary Industries: A Memoir* (1891)[9]

[In the process of putting together his library of western Americana, Bancroft has just returned from a very successful European buying trip.]

Now, I thought, my task is done. I have rifled America of its treasures; Europe I have ransacked; and after my success in Spain, Asia and Africa may as well be passed by. I have ten thousand volumes and over, fifty times more than ever I dreamed were in existence when the collecting began. My library is a *fait accompli.* Here I will rest.

But softly! What is this inch-thick pamphlet that comes to me by mail from my agent in London? By the shade of Tom Didbin, it is a catalogue! Stripping off the cover I read the title-page: *Catalogue de la Riche Bibliotheque de D. Jose Maria Andrade.* . . .

Seven thousand books direct from Mexico, and probably half of them works which should be added to my collection! What was to be done? Here were treasures beside which the gold, silver, and rich merchandise found by Ali Baba in the robbers' cave were dross. A new light broke in upon me. I had never considered that Mexico had been printing books for three and a quarter centuries—one hundred years longer than Massachusetts—and that the earlier works were seldom seen floating about book-stalls and auction-rooms. . . . In making his collection Señor Andrade had occupied forty years; and being upon the spot, with every facility, ample means at his command, a thorough knowledge of the literature of the country, and familiarity with the places in which books and manuscripts were most likely to be found, he surely should have been able to accomplish what no other man could.

And then again, rare books are every year becoming rarer. In England particularly is this the case. Important sales are not so frequent now as fifty years ago. . . . During the past half century many new public libraries have been formed both in Europe and America, until the number has become very large. These, as a rule, are deficient in rare books; but . . . the managers of public libraries are more and more desirous of enriching their collections with the treasures of the past; and as institutions seldom or never die, when once a book finds lodgement on their shelves the auctioneer rarely sees it again. Scores of libraries in America have their agents, with lists of needed books in their hands, ready to pay any price for any one of them. Since there is but a limited number of these books in existence, with a dozen bidders for every one, they are becoming scarcer and dearer every year. . . .

Again I asked myself, What was to be done? Little penetration was necessary to see that this sale at Leipsic was most important; that such an opportunity to secure Mexican books never had occurred before and could never occur again. . . .

Shutting my eyes to the consequences, therefore, I did the only thing possible under the circumstances to secure a portion of that collection: I telegraphed my agent in London five thousand dollars earnest money, with instructions to attend the sale and purchase at his discretion. . . . Though my agent, Mr. Whitaker, was not very familiar with the contents of my Library, he was a practical man, and thoroughly versed in the nature and value of books, and the result of his purchase was to enrich my collection with some three thousand of the rarest and most valuable volumes extant.

Zitkala-Sä, "An Indian Teacher Among Indians," from *The Atlantic Monthly* (1900)[10]

"My Mother's Curse Upon White Settlers"

One black night mother and I sat alone in the dim starlight, in front of our wigwam. We were facing the river, as we talked about the shrinking limits of the village. She told me about the poverty-stricken white settlers, who lived in caves dug in the long ravines of the high hills across the river.

A whole tribe of broad-footed white beggars had rushed hither to make claims on those wild lands. Even as she was telling this I spied a small glimmering light in the bluffs.

"That is a white man's lodge where you see the burning fire," she said. Then, a short distance from it, only a little lower than the first, was another light. As I became accustomed to the night, I saw more and more twinkling lights, here and there, scattered all along the wide black margin of the river.

Still looking toward the distant firelight, my mother continued: "My daughter, beware of the paleface. It was the cruel paleface who caused the death of your sister and your uncle, my brave brother. It is this same paleface who offers in one palm the holy papers, and with the other gives a holy baptism of firewater. He is the hypocrite who reads with one eye, 'Thou shalt not kill,' and with the other gloats upon the sufferings of the Indian race." Then suddenly discovering a new fire in the bluffs, she exclaimed, "Well, well, my daughter, there is the light of another white rascal!"

She sprang to her feet, and, standing firm beside her wigwam, she sent a curse upon those who sat around the hated white man's light. Raising her right arm forcibly into line with her eye, she threw her whole might into her doubled fist as she shot it vehemently at the strangers. Long she held her outstretched fingers toward the settler's lodge, as if an invisible power passed from them to the evil at which she aimed.

"Retrospection"

Leaving my mother, I returned to the school in the East. As months passed over me, I slowly comprehended that the large army of white teachers in Indian schools had a larger missionary creed than I had suspected.

It was one which included self-preservation quite as much as Indian education. When I saw an opium-eater holding a position as teacher of Indians, I did not understand what good was expected, until a Christian in power replied that this pumpkin-colored creature had a feeble mother to support. An inebriate paleface sat stupid in a doctor's chair, while Indian patients carried their ailments to untimely graves, because his fair wife was dependent upon him for her daily food.

I find it hard to count that white man a teacher who tortured an ambitious Indian youth by frequently reminding the brave changeling that he was nothing but a "government pauper."

Though I burned with indignation upon discovering on every side instances no less shameful than those I have mentioned, there was no present help. Even the few rare ones who have worked nobly for my race were powerless to choose workmen like themselves. To be sure, a man was sent from the Great Father to inspect Indian schools, but what he saw was usually the students' sample work *made* for exhibition. I was nettled by this sly cunning of the workmen who hoodwinked the Indian's pale Father at Washington.

My illness, which prevented the conclusion of my college course, together with my mother's stories of the encroaching frontier settlers, left me in no mood to strain my eyes in searching for latent good in my white co-workers.

At this stage of my own evolution, I was ready to curse men of small capacity for being the dwarfs their God had made them. In the process of my education I had lost all consciousness of the nature world about me. Thus, when a hidden rage took me to the small white-walled prison which I then called my room, I unknowingly turned away from my one salvation. . . .

For the white man's papers I had given up my faith in the Great Spirit. For these same papers I had forgotten the healing in trees and brooks. On account of my mother's simple view of life, and my lack of any, I gave her up, also. I made no friends among the race of people I loathed. Like a slender tree, I had been uprooted from my mother, nature, and God. I was shorn of my branches, which had waved in sympathy and love for home and friends. The natural coat of bark which had protected my oversensitive nature was scraped off to the very quick.

Now a cold bare pole I seemed to be, planted in a strange earth. Still, I seemed to hope a day would come when my mute aching head, reared upward to the sky, would flash a zigzag lightning across the heavens. With this dream of vent for a long-pent consciousness, I walked again amid the crowds.

At last, one weary day in the schoolroom, a new idea presented itself to me. It was a new way of solving the problem of my inner self. I liked it. Thus I resigned my position as teacher; and now I am in an Eastern city, following the long course of study I have set for myself. Now, as I look back upon the recent past, I see it from a distance, as a whole. I remember how, from morning till evening, many specimens of civilized peoples visited the Indian school. The city folks with canes and eyeglasses, the countrymen with sunburnt cheeks and clumsy feet, forgot their relative social ranks in an ignorant curiosity. Both sorts of these Christian palefaces were alike astounded at seeing the children of savage warriors so docile and industrious.

As answers to their shallow inquiries they received the students' sample work to look upon. Examining the neatly figured pages, and gazing upon the Indian girls and boys bending over their books, the white visitors walked out of the schoolhouse well satisfied: they were educating the children of the red man! They were paying a liberal fee to the government employees in whose able hands lay the small forest of Indian timber.

In this fashion many have passed idly through the Indian schools during the last decade, afterward to boast of their charity to the North American Indian. But few there are who have paused to question whether real life or long-lasting death lies beneath this semblance of civilization.

S. K. Hooper, *Rhymes of the Rockies* (1902)[11]

Wherever Nature appears in her grander moods, her inspiration stirs the heart and the imagination, and whether it be the "Banks and Braes o' Bonnie Doon," the Crags of the "Rio de Las Animas," "The Royal Gorge," the rocky declivities of "Ben Venue" or the cleft summit of "The Mount of the Holy Cross," the poetic spirit is invoked and a rhythmic offering laid upon the altar of the muses. The picturesque countries of the old world have been immortalized in song, and to show that Colorado, one of the newest portions of the new world, has not failed to inspire the same sentiments in the hearts of none the less sincere poets, this book has been prepared. Upon these pages are presented a few of the contributions to poetic literature incited by beholding scenes grander and more varied than those of Scotland, Italy or Switzerland, all the more valuable because spontaneous and therefore expressive of genuine emotions. In order that nothing may be lacking in the conveying of a vivid impression, pictures which are works of art supplement the poems, and to further assist the imagination of those who have not beheld these scenes and to refresh the memory of those who have beheld them, brief but accurate descriptions have been added. In a work of this character, brevity must be observed and only typical poems and scenes have been selected. The mid-continent region traversed by the Denver & Rio Grande and the Rio Grande Western possesses without doubt the most magnificent scenery in the world, and the difficulty has been, not what to select, but what to omit. As it is, this book must be considered as only a hint as to what exists in the wonderland of the Rocky Mountains, and its object will be attained if it excite an intelligent interest in the most picturesque portion of our country.

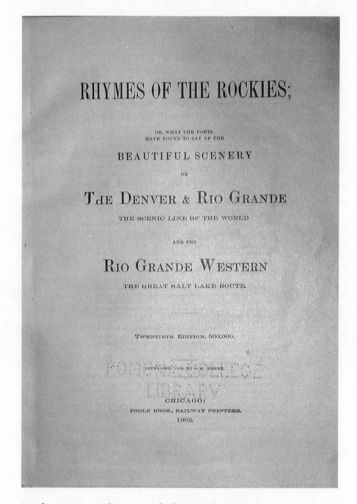

Title Page, *Rhymes of the Rockies* (1902)

COMMENTARY: TERRITORIAL ENTERPRISES: PRINT CULTURE AND THE WEST

Long before James Marshall discovered gold at Sutter's Mill in 1848, California hosted a diverse population of Spanish, Russian, Aleut and more than a hundred Native American language groups. After the gold strike immigrants flocked to the west coast, coming not only from the eastern seaboard of the United States, but also from such distant places as France, Chile, the Canton and Fukien provinces of China, Germany, Britain, and Mexico. Even though a polyglot culture developed from this immigration, it was nonetheless dominated by English-language institutions.

In the process of asserting military authority during the Mexican-American war in 1846, the United States Navy deployed the only printing press in California, an elderly Ramage locked away in a Monterey storage cabinet, to establish California's first newspaper. Newspaper historian Edward C. Kemble likened the American adoption of the Ramage press to a liberation, imagining the "wonder and delight with which the hidden and dusty old type . . . broke the thraldom of their fettered speech" to perform "honest service in the King's English" (Kemble, 53). Within a decade this solitary newspaper had multiplied to more than five hundred; during the previous century of Spanish and Mexican rule, the northern frontiers had produced fewer than six. Kemble's chauvinistic rhetoric notwithstanding, this contrast does not prove that the United States was more literate than Mexico. Mexico, in fact, had established a thriving book trade centered in Mexico City. Instead, the contrast reveals the centrality of print to a broad range of values, institutions, and power structures fundamental to Anglo-American culture.

Print culture in the American west was not only a feature of the institutions spread by settlers, but also an essential vehicle for their efforts to assert power over a cultural and physical landscape marked by diversity. Kemble supports this suggestion when he celebrates the substitution of English print culture for the "fustian verbiage" of Spanish (Kemble, 55). Francisco Ramirez supports it as well. Around 1855 Ramirez founded the Spanish-language *El Clamor Publico* in Los Angeles on the assumption that Anglos manipulated print to deprive Californios and Spanish-speaking immigrants of their civil and property rights. From German Catholics to Cherokee immigrants, non-English speakers quickly adapted print culture to their own ends. The existence of *El Clamor Publico* and numerous other non-English newspapers after 1848 illustrates one dimension of the interplay between culture and print in the American west. In addition, missionaries and others attempted to assimilate "foreigners" into Anglo culture by publishing bilingual papers, as did William Speer with the *Oriental*. Despite the *Oriental*'s assimilationist mission, Speer advocated strenuously for Chinese civil and cultural rights, both in the pages of the paper and later during political agitation for Chinese exclusion. At the same time, Speer's bilingual advertising both illustrates the economic needs of even the most idealistic publications, and implies the ultimate assimilation of even the most "foreign" into cultures of consumption.

As outsiders came into the west from other parts of the country and the world, residents abandoned farming and other enterprises to seek instant wealth in the gold fields. In 1848 Oregon's first paper, the *Spectator*, closed down temporarily because "[t]hat 'gold fever' which has swept about 3,000 of the officers, lawyers, physicians, farmers, and mechanics of Oregon into the mines of California, took away our printer also" (Turnbull, 45). Indeed, many indigenous publishers downplayed reports of gold strikes in other areas out of the well-founded fear of losing subscribers or workers to "gold fever." At the same time, many individuals who came to the gold fields to make their fortunes quickly realized that their original trades might serve them better, and so abandoned mining to provide services to miners. Among these were printers, publishers, and booksellers, including Hubert Howe Bancroft, who met his father at the Yuba River in 1852 while awaiting his first shipment of books. Bancroft, like his competitor Anton Roman, became a prominent regional publisher and bookseller centered in San Francisco. Likewise, Ferdinand Cartwright Ewer sailed to California in 1849 as part of a gold-mining company, but the company dissolved within weeks of his arrival and Ewer turned to newspaper editing out of destitution.

As editor for the *Pacific News*, Ewer discovered one of the powerful connections between newspaper publishing and western development: "It was not long before [owners] Major Allen & Gen. Winchester began to sell the influence of the paper to various interests who were glad enough to purchase its columns." Although Ewer claimed to be shocked at this manipulation of the press, the "booster" activities of the *Pacific News*'s proprietors differed only in degree from those of most western newspapers in the 1850s. Indeed, the publishing industry was integrated into the increasingly complex and specialized western economy on a number of levels. To begin with, westerners were disproportionally literate, with only a 7.1 percent illiteracy rate, compared to the nationwide rate of 20 percent (Pomeroy, 153). In most of the west, the industrial quality of the mining-based economy fueled indigenous job printing: receipts, blank forms, bills, stationery, and the stock certificates that made Mark Twain a "paper" millionaire. Mining's industrial structure also supported a largely urban settlement pattern, which in turn fostered the growth of local newspapers.

Most newspapers were the products of job printing offices, which supplied local communities with any number of essential tools and services. In addition to job and newspaper printing, these offices frequently carried books, blank books, maps, map-making and surveyor tools, and the legal forms necessary for land-rights, water-rights, and mineral-claims procedures. Because printers/publishers/editors often came to their profession from legal or administrative backgrounds, they frequently served their communities as scribes, notary publics, and ad hoc lawyers while pursuing their publishing careers. R. H. Taylor, editor of the Marysville *Herald*, served as a notary public and scribe for the town during his years as editor and proprietor, but within a few years had moved on to become a lawyer in the mining town of Downieville (Kemble, 178). Indeed, for many ambitious souls, the role of a newspaper editor or proprietor was simply one step toward a more lucrative political, legal, or real-estate career. In 1858 Edward Kemble claimed that one in every five (male) westerners had been associated with a newspaper at some point in his career. Although this claim is probably exaggerated, it nevertheless illustrates the ephemeral quality of the newspaper job in the overall careers of many westerners and suggests the ephemeral quality of newspapers themselves. Of the more than five hundred newspapers established in the first decade of California newspaper publishing, only about one hundred still existed in 1858 (Kemble, Appendix A).

Newspapers in the west served a variety of interests and promoted particular rhetorical styles for conveying information. Editors frequently engaged in pitched verbal battles with one another, giving rise to the "Oregon Style" of newspaper invective: "The last Oregonian is a proud sheet! The editor's courage . . . has oozed out at his fingers' ends, and his swaggering is converted into the vilest obscenity and filth, unrelieved by one particle of decency, sense, or wit," wrote *Statesman* editor Asahel Bush of his rival Thomas Dryer in 1851. "We cannot get down to the depths he has sunk to answer him, for we will not sully our columns with vulgarity and slang. When he rises, we will endeavor to pay him our respects. And, he must inevitably come up again, for it is an unvarying law that filth rises as it rots" (Turnbull, 83). Contentiousness was nothing new for American newspapers, but in the west the rhetoric achieved new heights of viciousness, and sometimes resulted in celebrated outbreaks of violence, even murder. Perhaps the most famous case was the murder of James King of William, editor of the San Francisco *Daily Evening Bulletin*, who

> saw fit to make a newspaper attack on J. P. Casey, an ex-convict from the State Prison of New York, and a professional ballot-box stuffer; and on the 14th ensuing, Casey shot King down in the open street, in broad daylight. King died; the Vigilance Committee took possession of the city; the whole State sympathized with the movement; and the Bulletin being the chief organ of the Committee, was in demand everywhere. (Kemble, 83)

Behind the often romanticized figurative and literal duels between editors, newspapers frequently sought to ruin each other economically, even by setting up temporary "dummy" papers to draw off their rivals' advertising and subscription revenue. Cutthroat economic and cultural competition intertwined with, reflected, and perhaps even fueled deep and bitter conflicts over all aspects of western development.

While transience characterized life throughout the American west, by the 1860s some western communities began to experience more settled, domestic characteristics than the early mining camps possessed. In the late 1860s Rachel Haskell kept a diary of her life in Aurora, Nevada. In it, she reveals how her family, transplanting domestic comforts into the Great Basin outback, was steeped in American print culture. Rachel, her husband, her children, and visitors to their home read on a daily basis. Her diary reveals that local or regional newspapers were important in these communities even though they had access to newspapers, magazines, and story papers published nationally. She and her family "read the Enterprises," the Virginia City *Territorial Enterprise*, regularly, even though Aurora was nearly a hundred miles away from Virginia City. In addition to locally published newspapers, Haskell also probably purchased sheet music from a San Francisco firm such as A. L. Bancroft's or Anton Roman's. She, her children, and their many visitors frequently "took up the guitar" or "picked out a tune" on the piano. Sheet music and instruments were important publishing components of the larger concerns such as Bancroft's, who devoted an entire floor of his establishment to music. The Haskells also read a great deal of fiction, ranging from William Makepeace Thackeray's *The Newcomes: Memoirs of a Most Respectable Family* to Jonathan Swift's *Gulliver's Travels*, as well as numerous sentimental and evangelical works, published both serially and in book form.

Book publishing and distribution in the nineteenth-century west was a tricky business proposition, as Bancroft discovered: "Even Tuthill's *History of California*, vigorously offered by subscription, did not return the cost of plates, paper, presswork, and binding. . . . Either the author or the publisher must make up his mind to remunerate the printer; the people will not . . ." (Bancroft, 87). Like newspaper publishers, however, book publishers in the west succeeded by diversifying. Bancroft kept afloat by publishing law books, and in addition to sheet music, firms such as his succeeded by publishing city directories, textbooks, almanacs, and other ephemera. In addition, larger firms such as Bancroft and Roman aggressively solicited customers through the efforts of foot canvassers such as Mrs. J. W. Likins, whose autobiography, *Six Years Experience as a Book Agent*, offers a colorful description of the trade. Likins and her fellow agents were each assigned territories for the books they sold and pursued subscriptions by engaging with individuals at home, at work, on the street, and in trains. Both Bancroft and Roman sold the products of eastern publishers, such as Mark Twain's *Roughing It,* as well as their own publications.

A visitor to the Haskell home, J. Ross Browne, observed that among the tasteful furnishings, "The tables were covered with books and periodicals, among which I observed a Magazine that takes the lead in civilizing new countries, but of which special mention would be superfluous" (in Lillard, 82). Browne probably refers here to *Harper's New Monthly Magazine,* not only because he wrote this comment in *Harper's,* but also because Rachel mentions reading James De Mille's serialized story "The Dodge Club" in *Harper's.* It is unsurprising that the Haskells would be reading eastern magazines: they were an extremely literary family, and magazine publishing arrived relatively late in the western publishing scene. Early western magazines were not remunerative enough to employ their own literary staff but required the dedication of leisure time to succeed: F. C. Ewer edited *The Pioneer,* the first literary magazine located in San Francisco, while holding down a day job as a customs-house official in 1854. James Mason Hutchings, publisher of *Hutchings' California Magazine,* relied on unpaid contributions of articles and artwork to fill the pages of his illustrated periodical. In the first decades such periodicals rarely lasted more than four or five years. In 1868 Anton Roman began publishing one of the first successful regional periodicals, the *Overland Monthly.* In 1869, however, the railroads brought new life to magazine publishing in the west. The Southern Pacific, for instance, sponsored *Sunset* magazine, designed as promotional reading material for tourists and settlers riding the Sunset Express. Magazines sponsored by railroads differed sharply from their literary predecessors in that splashy illustrations, rather than indigenous prose, dominated their content.

The arrival of railroads after 1869, like the gold rush two decades prior, had a dramatic impact on western publishing as it did on other business sectors of the west. The corporations building and financing the roads engendered bitter conflict over land claims and workingmen's rights to wages, bitterness that frequently expressed itself in ethnic violence. Many vented their anger at the Chinese, who built the railroads for much lower rates than whites commanded. Anti-Chinese hostility gathered strength in the 1860s and 1870s, and was reflected in the pages of the newspapers as well. The Sacramento *Union*, originally pro-railroad and sympathetic to the Chinese, modified its position to maintain its readership and advertising revenue. Additionally, the initial

completion of the transcontinental railroad brought intense competition from eastern markets, which dumped goods stockpiled during the Civil War in San Francisco
at cutthroat prices, threatening the local economy. Bancroft observed that "prices in
San Francisco fell far below remunerative rates, and the question with our jobbers
was, not whether they could make as much money as formerly, but whether they
could do business at all" (Bancroft, 84). The economic downturn of 1869 was a disaster for many San Francisco printers, who had previously enjoyed some of the highest
wages in the United States. More than 150 were out of work late that year, and in
August the Typographical Union went on strike to recoup some of their earlier rates.
Publishers refused to meet the Union's demands, and hired women printers and
compositors as well as patronizing the Women's Co-Operative Printing Union to
take up the slack during the eleven-day strike. As a result, women printers gained a
foothold in northern California's print industry previously denied them. The price,
however, was decades of hostility and exclusion from the powerful male Typographical Union (Levenson, 120–21).

Still, women made important contributions to western print culture. Although
women were underrepresented in most western states throughout the nineteenth
century, they played active roles in all levels of western printing and publishing—
from the literary mothers and consumers such as Rachel Haskell to the printers of San
Francisco; from the tireless booksellers such as Mrs. Likins and the literary writers
such as Ina Coolbrith and Mary Austin to the numerous unnamed schoolteachers
who cultivated literacy and the taste for literature. Although some of these women
were simply struggling to earn a living, others saw themselves, like Browne's charac-
terization of *Harper's*, as taking "the lead in civilizing" the new country of the west.

Browne's association between the act of "civilizing" western territories and the
print culture embodied in *Harper's* magazine might help us to understand why so
many individuals, against terrific odds, worked to establish their newspapers, bookshops, and magazines. At the same time, Zitkala-Sä's encounters with both print
culture and white western settlement raise more provocative questions. Zitkala-Sä,
a Yankton Sioux girl born in 1876, went east as an eight-year-old child to attend missionary schools for Indians, and became a teacher in one of those schools in her early
twenties. Zitkala-Sä wrote a series of autobiographical essays in the *Atlantic Monthly*
from 1900 to 1902. They mark a turning point in her career, an interlude in the literary
circles of New York and Boston, between her earlier life as a schoolteacher and her
subsequent work as an advocate for Indian cultural, political, legal, and economic
rights. The "tribe of broad-footed white beggars" cursed by Zitkala-Sä's mother were
miners flooding into the Dakota territories in the 1870s and 1880s, continuing the
cycle of mineral rushes that began in California in 1848 and served so powerfully
to shape western print culture. Zitkala-Sä further reminds us that the "civilizing"
influences of print culture could create tensions and opportunities for those who
were the educators' and reformers' intended beneficiaries. Throughout her life
Zitkala-Sä felt that her education in white culture, the "white man's papers," divided
her in painful ways from her own Sioux culture and traditions, especially from her

own mother. Nevertheless, Zitkala-Sä used that education as a powerful tool to preserve those traditions and to advocate for Indian rights. Her essays in the *Atlantic Monthly*, the prestigious eastern literary journal, illustrate not only her own troubled encounters with white "civilization," but her ability to utilize her experience in creating a "new way of solving the problem of my inner self"—a solution grounded in the turn-of-the-century literary world of eastern publishers and writers.

Zitkala-Sä traversed among and between the worlds of Indian and white, between west and east, between literary artistry and government advocacy. Her course reminds us that the story of American print culture intersects and overlaps with lines of power, and that race, ethnicity, and region complicate this relationship. In what ways did print culture serve those who attempted to assert power over the western cultural and physical landscape, and in what ways could it undermine those attempts? How did print culture reflect or shape shifting relationships among communities within the west? Between the west and other regions of the country? In western publishing, "the daily fitful utterance of communities" simultaneously reflected and helped shape the difficult course of Anglo western settlement (Kemble, 44).

SOURCE NOTES

[Unless otherwise indicated artifacts and documents are reproduced courtesy of the American Antiquarian Society (AAS), Worcester, Massachusetts, or the author.]

1. Ferdinand Cartwright Ewer, Diary, 1861. Kemble Manuscript Collections, California Historical Society, San Francisco. Reproduced courtesy of California Historical Society, North Baker Research Library Manuscript Collection, VMS 21.

2. *Oriental* (San Francisco) 1, no. 17 (April 28, 1855), 2.

3. Francisco P. Ramirez, "Martes, Junio 19, De 1855," *El Clamor Publico* (Los Angeles) 1, no. 1 (June 19, 1855), 2.

4. Richard G. Lillard, ed., "A Literate Woman in the Mines: The Diary of Rachel Haskell," *Mississippi Valley Historical Review* 21 (June 1944): 81–98. Reproduced courtesy of Organization of American Historians.

5. Mark Twain, *Roughing It* (Hartford, Conn.: American Publishing Company, 1872), 306–8, 361–68.

6. Mrs. J. W. Likins, *Six Years Experience as a Book Agent: Including My Trip from New York to San Francisco via Nicaragua* (San Francisco: Women's Printing Union, 1874), 104–11.

7. Hubert Howe Bancroft, *Literary Industries: A Memoir* (New York: Harper & Brothers, 1891), 81–82, 87–88.

8. John S. Hittell, *Hittell's Hand-Book of Pacific Coast Travel* (San Francisco: A. L. Bancroft & Co., 1885), [276].

9. Bancroft, *Literary Industries*, 96–101.

10. Zitkala-Sä, "An Indian Teacher Among Indians," *Atlantic Monthly* 85 (March 1900): 381–86.

11. S. K. Hooper, *Rhymes of the Rockies; Or, What the Poets Have Found to Say of the Beautiful Scenery on the Denver & Rio Grande* (1887; reprint, Chicago: Poole Bros., Railway Printers, 1902), [1], [3].

WORKS CITED

Kemble, Edward C. *A History of California Newspapers, 1846–1858*. Reprinted from the Supplement to the Sacramento *Union*, December 25, 1858, edited by Helen Harding Bretnor. Los Gatos, Calif.: The Talisman Press, 1962.

Levenson, Roger. *Women in Printing: Northern California, 1857–1890*. Santa Barbara, Calif.: Capra Press, 1994.

Pomeroy, Earl. *The Pacific Slope: A History of California, Oregon, Washington, Idaho, Utah, and Nevada*. New York: Alfred A. Knopf, 1965.

Stratton, Porter A. *The Territorial Press of New Mexico, 1834–1912*. Albuquerque: University of New Mexico Press, 1969.

Turnbull, George S. *History of Oregon Newspapers*. Portland, Ore.: Binfords & Mort, 1939.

FOR FURTHER RESEARCH

Armstrong, Robert D. "'The Matter of Printing': Public Printing in the Western Territories of the United States." *Journal of Government Information* 21, no. 1 (1994): 37–47.

Ashton, Wendell J. *Voice in the West: Biography of a Pioneer Newspaper*. New York: Duell, Sloan & Pearce, 1950.

Barth, Gunther Paul. *Instant Cities: Urbanization and the Rise of San Francisco and Denver*. New York: Oxford University Press, 1975.

Cloud, Barbara. *The Business of Newspapers on the Western Frontier*. Reno: University of Nevada Press, 1992.

Dary, David. *Red Blood and Black Ink: Journalism in the Old West*. New York: Alfred A. Knopf, 1998.

Etulain, Richard. *Re-imagining the Modern American West: A Century of Fiction, History, and Art*. Tucson: University of Arizona Press, 1996.

*Goff, Victoria. "Spanish-Language Newspapers in California." In *Outsiders in 19th-Century Press History: Multicultural Perspectives*, edited by Frankie Hutton and Barbara Straus Reed, 55–70.

*Harlan, Robert D. "Printing for the Instant City: San Francisco at Mid-Century." In *Getting the Books Out: Papers of the Chicago Conference on the Book in 19th-Century America*, edited by Michael Hackenberg, 121–36.

Holliday, J. S. *The World Rushed In: The California Gold Rush Experience*. New York: Simon & Schuster, 1981.

Huntley-Smith, Jen A. "'The Genius of Civilization': Print Technology in the Nineteenth-Century American West." In *Western Technological Landscapes*, edited by Stephen Tchudi, 37–50. Reno: Nevada Humanities Committee, 1998.

*Huntzicker, William E. "Chinese-American Newspapers." In *Outsiders in 19th-Century Press History: Multicultural Perspectives*, edited by Frankie Hutton and Barbara Straus Reed, 71–92.

Knight, Oliver. "The *Owyhee Avalanche*: The Frontier Newspaper as a Catalyst in Social Change." *Pacific Northwest Quarterly* 58 (April 1967): 74–81.

Knobloch, Frieda. *The Culture of Wilderness: Agriculture as Colonization in the American West*. Chapel Hill: University of North Carolina Press, 1996.

Murdock, Charles A. "History of Printing in San Francisco." *Pacific Printer & Publisher* 35 (May 1925): 365–66.

Robbins, William G. *Landscapes of Promise: The Oregon Story, 1800–1940*. Seattle: University of Washington Press, 1997.

Schwantes, Carlos A. "Landscape of Opportunity: Phases of Railroad Promotion of the Pacific Northwest." *Montana: The Magazine of Western History* 43 (Spring 1993): 38–51.

Steiner, Michael, and David Wrobel, eds. *Many Wests: Place, Culture, and Regional Identity*. Lawrence: University Press of Kansas, 1997.

*Stern, Madeleine B. "Dissemination of Popular Books in the Midwest and Far West during the Nineteenth Century." In *Getting the Books Out: Papers of the Chicago Conference on the Book in 19th-Century America*, edited by Michael Hackenberg, 76–97.

———. Introduction to Mrs. J. W. Likins, *Six Years as a Book Agent: Including My Trip from New York to San Francisco via Nicaragua*. San Francisco: Women's Printing Union, 1874. Reprint, San Francisco: Book Club of California, 1992.

*Sun, Yumei. "San Francisco's *Chung Sai Yat Po* and the Transformation of Chinese Consciousness, 1900–1920." In *Print Culture in a Diverse America*, edited by James P. Danky and Wayne A. Wiegand, 85–97.

11

Laboring Classes, New Readers, and Print Cultures

ANN FABIAN

ON THE EVE of the Civil War, the United States census counted 31 million white and black residents. Sixty years later, the nation's population had more than tripled, to nearly 106 million. The nation's center of gravity had shifted to the cities: in 1860 only a fifth of all Americans lived in urban places (2,500 or more inhabitants), but the 1920 census registered a majority (51.2 percent) urban population. America's enormous population growth resulted largely from immigration: between 1865 and 1915, 25 million immigrants came to the United States. By the 1890s these new Americans were predominantly arriving from new places: southern and eastern Europe, not just England, Ireland, or northern Europe. The new immigrants swelled the nation's industrial work force, laboring in hopes of establishing their families in America or returning home with money they could never have earned in their native countries. For those who wanted to stay in the United States, learning English—and especially having their children do so—ranked as a high priority.

Institutions proliferated to meet immigrants' desires for education, as well as to direct the nature of their "Americanization." Public schools multiplied, especially in cities. By 1900 thirty-one states and territories required some level of school attendance for all children. By 1914 there were more than 12,000 high schools in the United States, a dramatic increase from only 100 in 1860. The public-library movement also flourished in the last third of the nineteenth century. Whereas most libraries before the Civil War had been private institutions, now public libraries opened their doors free of charge. Controversy ensued over precisely what kinds of books people should read, exacerbated now by the millions of new readers and the glut of cheap publications, such as dime novels, that catered to them. But those very dime novels, and the "fiction factories" that published them, were yet another institution of "Americanization." Meanwhile, newspapers published in Yiddish, Polish, Italian, and myriad other languages at once provided ties to immigrants' native lands *and* introduced readers to American customs and issues.

Former slaves, and their children and grandchildren, envisioned education as a symbol of their freedom and a key to new opportunities. Within the south, black school systems emerged during Reconstruction. Southern schools were segregated, to be sure; black schools generally received less funding than white ones; and southern public schools generally lagged behind northern ones in number and quality. Still, African Americans now possessed opportunities for formal education that they had not had before the war. Their leaders, many of them graduates of new black colleges and universities, debated what form that education should take: Should freed people and their children study to gain an economic foothold in practical skills, or should their education focus on the liberal arts? For these new readers, like their immigrant contemporaries in America's cities, questions of what to read mattered as much as access to the education they prized.

ARTIFACTS

In 1921 the librarian of the Seward Park Branch of the New York Public Library sent a letter in Yiddish welcoming newcomers to the Lower East Side neighborhood of America's most polyglot city. For Shenah Pessah, the young immigrant woman in "Wings" (1920)—a short story by the second-generation Polish-American writer Anzia Yezierska (1885–1970)—the library in New York was also a world governed by forbidding middle-class propriety. Dorothy Richardson (1882–1955), a doctor's daughter from Pennsylvania, worked as a journalist in New York in the 1890s. Her book *The Long Day: The Story of a New York Working Girl* read like an autobiographical novel but was more likely the product of good investigative journalism; in the selection reprinted here, she described books and ideas in the workplace. Richardson's working girls may have enjoyed dime novels, but many middle-class reformers (including librarians) wondered whether this cheap literature had any value. The most famous of these reformers, Anthony Comstock (1844–1915), who spent decades seeking to regulate "improper" reading, explained his objections to dime novels in the 1883 selection included here.

Letter from the Acting Branch Librarian, Seward Park Branch, New York Public Library (1921)[1]

August 12, 1921
Miss Florence Overton,
Supervisor of Branches.
New York Public Library
476 Fifth Avenue
New York City
My dear Miss Overton:

I am herewith sending a copy, with the English translation, of the letter which we send to the newly arrived, whose names we obtain from the Hebrew Immigrant Aid Society. One of our assistants [is] going to their files and selecting those who have settled in our community. The enclosed may not be sufficiently useful to send to our English friends. It however represents a part of the work we are doing to make strangers to our shores feel at home and contribute somewhat to their happiness.

Very truly yours,
Acting Branch Librarian

The New York Public Library
Circulation Department
Seward Park Branch, 192 East Broadway
My dear

The Seward Park Branch of the New York Public Library is located near your home at 192 Broadway. You are welcome at this institution of your new fatherland, which is free for all citizens of New York. If you can not yet speak English, you will find a librarian who speaks your language and will show you how to join the library. There are books in Yiddish, Russian, Hebrew, German, French, as well as English, with simple books for those who wish to learn the language. You may read and study in the rooms at any time from nine o'clock in the morning until nine o'clock at night. A special room for children is open from three until six o'clock on school-days and from nine to six o'clock on Saturdays.

You and your family are cordially invited to visit the library and to become members.

> Very sincerely yours,
> Branch Librarian

Please bring this letter with you.

Anzia Yezierska, "Wings" (1920)[2]

When they entered the library, Shenah Pessah halted in awe. "What a stillness full of thinking! So beautiful, it comes on me like music!"

"Yes. This is quite a place," he acquiesced, seeing again the public library in a new light through her eyes. "Some of the best minds have worked to give us this."

"How the book-ladies look so quiet like the things."

"Yes," he replied, with a tell-tale glance at her. "I too like to see a woman's face above her clothes."

The approach of the librarian cut off further comment. As Mr. Barnes filled out the application card, Shenah Pessah noted the librarian's simple attire. "What means he a woman's face above her clothes?" she wondered. And the first shadow of a doubt crossed her mind as to whether her dearly bought apparel was pleasing to his eyes. In the few brief words that passed between Mr. Barnes and the librarian, Shenah Pessah sensed that these two were of the same world and that she was different. Her first contact with him in a well-lighted room made her aware that "there were other things to the person besides the dress-up." She noticed their well-kept hands on the desk and she became aware that her own were calloused and rough. That is why she felt her dirty finger-nails curl in awkwardly to hide themselves as she held the pen to sign her name.

Dorothy Richardson, *The Long Day:*
The Story of a New York Working Girl (1905)[3]

"Don't you never read no story-books?" Mrs. Smith asked, stirring the paste-pot preparatory to the afternoon's work. She looked at me curiously out of her shrewd, snapping dark eyes as she awaited my answer. I was conscious that Mrs. Smith did n't like me for some reason or other, and I was anxious to propitiate her. I was pretty certain she thought me a boresome prig, and I determined I'd prove I was n't. My confession of an omnivorous appetite for all sorts of story-books had the desired effect; and when I confessed further, that I liked best of all a real, tender, sentimental love-story, she asked amiably:

"How do you like 'Little Rosebud's Lovers'?"

"I've never read that," I replied. "Is it good?"

"It's fine," interposed Phœbe; "but I like 'Woven on Fate's Loom' better—don't you?" The last addressed to Mrs. Smith.

"No, I can't say that's my opinion," returned our vis-à-vis, with a judicious tipping of the head to one side as she soused her dripping paste-brush over the strips. "Not but what 'Woven on Fate's Loom' is a good story in its way, either, for them that likes that sort of story. But I think 'Little Rosebud's Lovers' is more interesting, besides being better wrote."

"And that's just what I don't like about it," retorted Phœbe, her fingers traveling like lightning up and down the corners of the boxes. "You like this hot-air talk, and I don't; and the way them fellows and girls shoot hot-air at each other in that there 'Little Rosebud's Lovers' is enough to beat the street-cars!"

"What is it about?" I asked with respectful interest, addressing the question to Mrs. Smith, who gave promise of being a more serious reviewer than the flippant Phœbe. Mrs. Smith took a bite of gingerbread and began:

"It's about a fair, beautiful young girl by the name of Rosebud Arden. . . ."
[Mrs. Smith recounts the story of Rosebud and then the conversation among the women resumes.]

"Hot air!" from the irrepressible Phœbe.

I felt that courtesy required I should agree upon that point, and I did so, conservatively, venturing to ask the name of the author.

Mrs. Smith mentioned the name of a well-known writer of trashy fiction and added, "Did n't you never read none of her books?"

My negative surprised her. Then Phœbe asked:

"Did you ever read 'Daphne Vernon; or, A Coronet of Shame'?"

"No, I have n't read them, either," I replied.

"Oh, mama! Carry me out and let me die!" groaned Mrs. Smith, throwing down her paste brush and falling forward in mock agony upon the smeared table.

"Water! Water!" gasped Phœbe, clutching wildly at her throat; "I'm going to faint!"

"What's the matter? What did I say that was n't right?" I cried, the nature of their antics showing only too plainly that I "put my foot in it" in some unaccountable manner. But they paid no attention. Mortified and utterly at sea, I watched their convulsed shoulders and heard their smothered giggles. Then in a few minutes they straightened up and resumed work with the utmost gravity of countenance and without a word of explanation.

"What was it you was asting?" Phœbe inquired presently, with the most innocent air possible.

"I said I had n't read the books you mentioned," I replied, trying to hide the chagrin and mortification I felt at being so ignominiously laughed at.

"Eyether of them?" chirped Mrs. Smith, with a vicious wink.

"Eyether of them?" warbled Phœbe in her mocking-bird soprano.

It was my turn to drop the paste-brush now. Eye-ther! It must have slipped from my tongue unconsciously. I could not remember having ever pronounced the word like that before.

I did n't feel equal, then and there, to offering them any explanation or apologies for the offense. So I simply answered:

"No; are they very good? Are they as good as 'Little Rosebud's Lovers'?"

"No, it ain't," said Mrs. Smith decisively and a little contemptuously; "and it ain't two books, eye-ther; it's all in one—'Daphne Vernon; or, A Coronet of Shame.'"

"Well, now I think it is," put in Phœbe. "Them stories with two-handled names is nearly always good. I'll buy a book with a two-handled name every time before I'll buy one that ain't. . . ."

"What kind of story-books do you read, then?" they demanded. To which I replied with the names of a dozen or more of the simple, every-day classics that the school-boy and -girl are supposed to have read. They had never heard of "David Copperfield" or of Dickens. Nor had they ever heard of "Gulliver's Travels," nor of "The Vicar of Wakefield." They had heard the name "Robinson Crusoe," but they did not know it was the name of an entrancing romance. "Little Women," "John Halifax, Gentleman," "The Cloister and the Hearth," "Les Misérables," were also unknown, unheard-of literary treasures. They were equally ignorant of the existence of the conventional Sunday-school romance. . . . I spoke enthusiastically of "Little Women," telling them I had read it four times and meant to read it again some day. Their curiosity was aroused over the unheard-of thing of anybody ever wanting to read any book more than once, and they pressed me to reciprocate by repeating the story for them, which I did with great accuracy of statement, and with genuine pleasure to myself at being given an opportunity to introduce anybody to Meg and Jo and all the rest of that delightful March family. When I had finished, Phœbe stopped her cornering and Mrs. Smith looked up from her label-pasting.

"Why, that's no story at all," the latter declared.

"Why, no," echoed Phœbe; "that's no story—that's just everyday happenings. I don't see what's the use putting things like that in books. I'll bet any money that lady what wrote it knew all them boys and girls. They just sound like real, live people; and when you was telling us about them I could just see them as plain as plain could be—could n't you, Gwendolyn?"

"Yep," yawned our vis-à-vis, undisguisedly bored.

"But I suppose farmer folks likes them kind of stories," Phœbe generously suggested. "They ain't used to the same styles of anything that us city folks are."

Anthony Comstock, *Traps for the Young* (1883)[4]

Parents mourn that the child's mind does not go out after noble things. They cannot understand why it is thus. The companion of the child's mind is exerting its sway, and the evil one is spreading his kingdom. What I have said applies more directly to the deluge of cheap sensational stories than to the higher grades of novel reading.

In novel reading, however, in general, the tendency is from the higher to the lower rather than from the lower to the higher. There are grave questions in the minds of some of our best writers, and of our most thoughtful men and women, whether novel reading at its best does not tend downward rather than upward. Some have questioned whether persons reading such authors as Mrs. Southworth and Alexander Dumas advance in time to George Eliot and Sir Walter Scott. This grade is not discussed here. We consider only the purely sensational works of fiction. These create an appetite that is seldom surfeited. The mind grows by what it feeds upon. Something more highly colored and exaggerated is sought after. The imagination is walled in like a canal, and thoughts run down the grade until the mind is emptied of lofty aims and ambitions, and the soul is shrivelled. . . .

How many parents ever stop and reflect, in sober earnest, that the minds of their children are active and open to anything exciting; that the bright budding intellect grasps with eagerness every topic of thought that fancy paints? How often we hear from children, "Oh, tell us a story!" How frequently the group of romping boys and girls are subdued by a story, and how charmed a child becomes with but a simple tale or anecdote! Anything marvelous or exciting is quickly appropriated. Parents forget that they are expected and designed by all-wise Providence to think and decide in these matters for their children.

Light literature, then, is a devil-trap to captivate the child by perverting taste and fancy. It turns aside from the pursuit of useful knowledge and prevents the full development in man or woman of the wonderful possibilities locked up in the child! Why rob the future ages of the high order of men and women, which would of necessity appear if the children of to-day were properly cared for and developed in keenest intellect and highest morals?

Aside from the enslavements to imagination and taste from this class of publications, alarmingly prevalent, many of the stories, though free from crime, lack a moral, contain insinuations against truth, justice, and religion, and favor deceit and lying. The tone is not elevating. They pave the way for that which is worse. If children must have stories, let parents provide those that have a high moral tone—stories where the hero is not a thief, murderer, or desperado, but a moral hero, whose chief trait of character is standing for the right. Teach the children to emulate deeds of heroism; to stand for the right even though the heavens fall; never to be sneered or laughed into doing a mean thing, nor neglecting duty. . . .

A word about bound books.

Recently I purchased a book offered for sale on the railroads, and recommended by the newsboy on the train on the Lake Shore and Michigan Southern Railroad as the "boss book," the "fastest selling book of the day." The web of the story consisted of four murders, three highway robberies, two burglaries, one blackmailing scheme, three attempts to murder women, one attempt to poison a young woman, two conspiracies to ruin a pure girl, one den of counterfeiters in full blast, two gambling hells, one confidence game, one brothel, procurers abducting a young girl for a rich man, three cases of assault and battery, one street fight, two dens of thieves, one forced marriage, two suicides, and oaths, lies, wine-drinking, smoking cigars, et cetera. The character that figured throughout all this was a beautiful young wife, who was the murderess and principal actor in all these horrible and disgusting scenes.

Again, these stories give utterly false and debasing ideas of life. All high moral purposes are made to give way to self-gratification. The great safeguard of human society—reverence to law—is broken down. Disobedience to parents is encouraged. The healthful restraint of parental authority is treated as a species of tyranny which the hero first chafes under, then resists, and lastly ignores. . . .

Again, these stories breed vulgarity, profanity, loose ideas of life, impurity of thought and deed. They render the imagination unclean, destroy domestic peace, desolate homes, cheapen woman's virtue, and make foul-mouthed bullies, cheats vagabonds, thieves, desperadoes, and libertines. They disparage honest toil, and make real life a drudge and burden. What young man will serve an apprenticeship, working early and late, if his mind is filled with the idea that sudden wealth may be acquired by following the hero of the story? In real life, to begin at the foot of the ladder and work up, step by step, is the rule; but in these stories, inexperienced youth, with no moral character, take the foremost positions, and by trick and device, knife and revolver, bribery and corruption, carry everything before them, lifting themselves in a few short weeks to positions of ease and affluence. Moral courage with such is a thing to be sneered at and despised in many of these stories. If one is asked to drink and refuses, he is set up and twitted till he yields or is compelled to by force. The idea of doing anything from principle is ridiculous in the extreme. As well fill a kerosene-oil lamp with water and expect a brilliant light. And so, in addition to all else, there is early inculcated a distaste for the good, and the piercing blast of ridicule is turned upon the reader to destroy effectually all moral character.

OUTSIDE NEW YORK, too, people hard at work made time for reading. In James Weldon Johnson's (1871–1938) novel *The Autobiography of an Ex-Colored Man* (1912), the narrator described his work as a "reader" for Spanish-speaking cigar makers in Florida, who like Dorothy Richardson's workingwomen managed to squeeze their reading into days of labor. In 1905 an Illinois farm woman took the time to write about her relations to books and reading for the editors of the New York *Independent*. In this piece, published as "One Farmer's Wife," note how easily the editors dismiss her literary aspirations. This dismissal of working people's cultural aspirations also forms the heart of the next selection, Anzia Yezierska's "An Immigrant Among the Editors." Culture reflected disparities of class, and by the end of the nineteenth century many critics and educators were wondering about how best to educate children for a life of labor. The excerpt reproduced here from Booker T. Washington's (1856–1915) autobiography, *Up from Slavery* (1901), defended his concrete approach, disparaging mere "book learning" in favor of industrial education for young African Americans. Washington, the founder of the Tuskegee Institute where students learned practical skills such as carpentry and brick making, was America's foremost African American educator at the turn of the twentieth century. He engaged in a long debate with the great sociologist W. E. B. Du Bois (1868–1963), who insisted that the life of the mind should be open to all. Du Bois wrote *The Souls of Black Folk* two years after Washington's autobiography, arguing for a very different kind of education for African Americans.

James Weldon Johnson, *The Autobiography of an Ex-Colored Man* (1912)[5]

After I had been in the factory a little over a year, I was repaid for all the effort I had put forth to learn Spanish by being selected as "reader." The "reader" is quite an institution in all cigar factories which employ Spanish-speaking workmen. He sits in the centre of a large room in which the cigar-makers work and reads to them for a certain number of hours each day all the important news from the papers and whatever else he may consider would be interesting. He often selects an exciting novel and reads it in daily installments. He must, of course, have a good voice, but he must also have a reputation among the men for intelligence, for being well posted and having in his head a stock of varied information. He is generally the final authority on all arguments which arise, and in a cigar factory these arguments are many and frequent, ranging from the respective and relative merits of rival baseball clubs to the duration of the sun's light and energy—cigar-making is a trade in which talk does not interfere with work. My position as "reader" not only released me from the rather monotonous work of rolling cigars, and gave me something more in accord with my tastes, but also added considerably to my income.

"One Farmer's Wife," from *The Independent* (1905)[6]

(The champions of most of our industrial classes, coal miners, factory girls, garment workers and household servants, are numerous and voluble, but the hardships of farmers' wives rarely appear in print. For that reason we are glad to be able to add to our series of representative "personal confessions" the following narrative of an Illinois farmer's wife. It was not originally submitted to us in its present form, but was a brief account of farm life from a woman's point of view, and was sent in to us at the suggestion of the correspondence school mentioned in the text. The article was unavailable as it stood, but it seemed to have "possibilities," so we returned the manuscript to her with the suggestion that she write a truthful narrative of her life and "tell everything." In response to the request we received the following article, which we publish without change. We hope that the money received for it and the joy of seeing it in print will not induce the author to neglect entirely her domestic duties to attempt a literary career. We discuss the article in our editorial columns. —EDITOR.)

I have been a farmer's wife in one of the States of the Middle West for thirteen years, and everybody knows that the farmer's wife must of a necessity be a very practical woman, if she would be a successful one.

I am not a practical woman and consequently have been accounted a failure by practical friends and especially by my husband, who is wholly practical. . . .

I always had a passion for reading; during girlhood it was along educational lines; in young womanhood it was for love stories which remained ungratified because my father thought it sinful to read stories of any kind, and especially love stories.

Later, when I was married, I borrowed everything I could find in the line of novels and stories, and read them by stealth still, for my husband thought it a willful waste of time to read anything and that it showed a lack of love for him if I would rather read than talk to him when I had a few moments of leisure, and, in order to avoid giving offense and still gratify my desire I would only read when he was not at the house, thereby greatly curtailing my already too limited reading hours.

In reading miscellaneously I got glimpses now and then of the great poets and authors, which aroused a great desire for a thorough perusal of them all; but up to the present time I have not been permitted to satisfy this desire. As the years have rolled on there has been more work and less leisure until it is only by the greatest effort that I may read the current news.

It is only during the last three years that I have had the news to read, for my husband is so very penurious that he would never consent to subscribing for papers of any kind and that old habit of avoiding that which would give offense was so fixed that I did not dare to break it.

The addition of two children to our family never altered or interfered with the established order of things to any appreciable extent. My strenuous outdoor life agreed with me, and even when my children were born, I was splendidly prepared for the ordeal and made rapid recovery. I still hoed and tended the truck patches and garden, still watered the stock and put out feed for them, still went to the hay field and helped harvest and house the bounteous crops; still helped harvest the golden grain later on when the cereals ripened; often took one team and dragged ground to prepare the seed-bed for wheat for weeks at the time, while my husband was using the other team on another farm which he owns several miles away. . . .

This is a vague, general idea of how I spend my time; my work is so varied that it would be difficult, indeed, to describe a typical day's work.

Any bright morning in the latter part of May I am out of bed at four o'clock; next, after I have dressed and combed my hair, I start a fire in the kitchen stove, and while the stove is getting hot I go to my flower garden and gather a choice, half-blown rose and a spray of bride's wreath, and arrange them in my hair, and sweep the floors and then cook breakfast.

While the other members of the family are eating breakfast I strain away the morning's milk (for my husband milks the cows while I get breakfast), and fill my husband's dinner-pail, for he will go to work on our other farm for the day.

By this time it is half-past five o'clock, my husband is gone to his work, and the stock is loudly pleading to be turned out into the pastures. The younger cattle, a half-dozen steers, are left in the pasture at night, and I now drive the two cows a half-quarter mile and turn them in with the others, come back, and then there's a horse in the barn that belongs in a field where there is no water, which I take to a spring quite a distance from the barn; bring it back and turn it into a field with the sheep, a dozen in number, which are housed at night. . . .

I have not eaten breakfast yet, but that can wait; I make the beds next and straighten things up in the living room, for I dislike to have the early morning caller find my house topsy-turvy. When this is done I go to the kitchen, which also serves as a dining-room, and uncover the table, and take a mouthful of food occasionally as I pass to and fro at my work until my appetite is appeased.

By the time the work is done in the kitchen it is about 7:15 a.m., and the cool morning hours have flown, and no hoeing done in the garden yet, and the children's toilet has to be attended to and churning has to be done.

Finally the children are washed and churning done, and it is eight o'clock, and the sun getting hot, but no matter, weeds die quickly when cut down in the heat of the day, and I use the hoe to good advantage until dinner hour, which is 11:30 a.m. We come in, and I comb my hair, and put fresh flowers in it, and eat a cold dinner, put out feed and water for the chickens; set a hen, perhaps, sweep the floors again; sit down and rest, and read a few moments, and it is nearly one o'clock, and I sweep the door yard while I am waiting for the clock to strike the hour. . . .

[And so her work continues throughout the day.]

It is now about 9 o'clock p.m., and after a short prayer I retire for the night.

As a matter of course, there's hardly two days together which require the same routine, yet every day is as fully occupied in some way or other as this one, with varying tasks as the seasons change. . . .

I have always had an itching to write, and, with all my multitudinous cares, I have written in a fitful way, for several papers, which do not pay for such matter, just because I was pleased to see my articles in print.

I have a long list of correspondents, who write regularly and often to me, and, by hook and crook, I keep up with my letter-writing, for, next to reading, I love to write and receive letters, tho my husband says I will break him up buying so much writing material; when, as a matter of course, I pay for it out of my own scanty income. . . .

I must admit that there is very little time for the higher life for myself, but my soul cries out for it, and my heart is not in my homely duties; they are done in a mechanical, abstracted way, not worthy of a woman of high ambitions; but my ambitions are along other lines.

I do not mean to say that I have no ambition to do my work well, and to be a model housekeeper, for I would scorn to slight my work intentionally; it is just this way: There are so many outdoor duties that the time left for household duties is so limited that I must rush through them, with a view to getting each one done in the shortest possible time, in order to get as many things accomplished as possible, for there is never time to do half as much as needs to be done.

All the time that I have been going about this work I have been thinking of things I have read; of things I have on hand to read when I can get the time, and of other things which I have a desire to read, but cannot hope to while the present condition exists.

As a natural consequence, there are, daily, numerous instances of absent-mindedness on my part; many things left undone that I really could have done, by leaving off something else of less importance, if I had not forgotten the thing of the more importance. My husband never fails to remind me that it is caused by my reading so much; that I would get along much better if I should never see a book or paper, while really I would be distracted if all reading matter was taken from me.

I use an old fashioned churn, and the process of churning occupies from thirty minutes to three hours, according to the condition of the cream, and I always read something while churning, and tho that may look like a poor way to attain self-culture, yet if your reading is of the nature to bring about that desirable result, one will surely be greatly benefited by these daily exercises.

But if one is just reading for amusement, they might read a great deal more than that and not derive any great benefit; but my reading has always been for the purpose of becoming well informed; and when knitting stockings for the family I always have a book or paper in reading distance; or if I have a moment to rest or to wait on something, I pick up something and read during the time. I even take a paper with me to the fields.

I often hear ladies remark that they do not have time to read. I happen to know that they have a great deal more time than I do, but not having any burning desire to read, the time is spent at a neighbor's house gossiping about other neighbors. . . .

The minister who performed the marriage ceremony for us has always taken a kindly interest in our fortunes and, knowing my literary bent, has urged me to turn it to account; but there seemed to be so little time and opportunity that I could not think seriously of it, altho I longed for a literary career; but my education had been dropped for a dozen years or more, and I knew that I was not properly equipped for that kind of a venture.

This friend was so insistent that I was induced to compete for a prize in a short story contest in a popular magazine not long since, tho I entered it fully prepared for a failure.

About that time there came in my way the literature of a correspondence school which would teach, among other things, short story writing by mail; it set forth all the advantages of a literary career, and proposed properly to equip its students in that course for a consideration.

This literature I greedily devoured, and felt that I could not let the opportunity slip, tho I despaired of getting my husband's consent.

I presented the remunerative side of it to him, but he could only see the expense of taking the course, and wondered how I could find time to spend in the preparation, even if it should be profitable in the end; but he believed it was all humbug; that they would get my money and I would hear from them no more.

When I had exhausted my arguments to no avail, I sent my literary friend to him, to try his persuasive powers. The two of us, finally, gained his consent, but it was on condition that the venture was to be kept profoundly secret for he felt sure that there would be nothing but failure, and he desired that no one should know of it and have cause for ridicule.

Contrary to his expectations, the school has proven very trustworthy, and I am in the midst of a course of instruction which is very pleasing to me; and I find time for study and exercise between the hours of eight and eleven at night, when the family are asleep and quiet. I am instructed to read a great deal, with a certain purpose in view, but that is impossible, since I had to promise my husband that I would drop all my papers, periodicals, etc., on which I was paying out money for subscription before he would consent to my taking the course. This I felt willing to do, that I might prepare myself for more congenial tasks; I hope to accomplish something worthy of note in a literary way since I have been a failure in all other pursuits. One cannot be anything in particular as long as they try to be everything and my motto has always been: "Strive to Excel," and it has caused worry wrinkles to mar my countenance, because I could not, under the circumstances, excel in any particular thing.

I have a few friends who are so anxious for my success that they are having certain publications of reading matter sent to me at their own expense; however, there's only a very limited number who know of my ambitions.

My friends have always been so kind as not to hint that I had not come up to their expectations in various lines, but I inwardly knew that they regarded me as a financial failure; they knew that my husband would not allow the money that was made off the farm to be spent on the family, but still they knew of other men who did the same, yet the wives managed some way to have money of their own and to keep up the family expenses and clothe themselves and children nicely anyhow, but they did not seem to take into account that these thrifty wives had the time all for their own in which to earn a livelihood while my time was demanded by my husband, to be spent in doing things for him which would contribute to the general proceeds of the farm, yet would add nothing to my income, since I was supposed to look to my own resources for my spending money. . . .

I might add that the neighbors among whom I live are illiterate and unmusical, and that my redeeming qualities, in their eyes, are my superior education and musical abilities; they are kind enough to give me more than justice on these qualities because they are poor judges of such matters.

But money is king, and if I might turn my literary bent to account, and surround myself with the evidences of prosperity, I may yet hope fully to redeem myself in their eyes, and I know that I will have attained my ambition in that line.

Anzia Yezierska, "An Immigrant Among the Editors" (1923)[7]

Ever since I began to read the American magazines one burning question has consumed me: Why is it that only the thoughts of educated people are written up? Why shouldn't sometimes a servant girl or janitress or a coal-heaver give his thoughts to the world? We who are forced to do the drudgery of the world, and who are considered ignorant because we have no time for school, could say a lot of new and different things, if only we had a chance to get a hearing.

Very rarely I'd come across a story about a shop-girl or a washerwoman. But they weren't real stories. They were twisted pictures of the way the higher-ups see us people. They weren't as we are. They were as unreal as the knowledge of the rich about the poor. Often I'd read those smooth-flowing stories about nothing at all, and I'd ask myself, Why is it that so many educated people with nothing to say, know how to say nothing with such an easy flow of words, while I, with something so aching to be said, can say nothing?

I was like a prison full of choked-in voices, all beating in my brain to be heard. The minute I'd listen to one voice a million other voices would rush in crying for a hearing, till I'd get too excited and mixed up to know what or where.

Sometimes I'd see my brain as a sort of Hester Street junk-shop, where a million different things—rich uptown silks and velvets and the cheapest kind of rags— were thrown around in bunches. It seemed to me if I struggled from morning till night all my years I could never put order in my junk-shop brain.

Ach! If only I had an education, I used to think. It seemed to me that educated people were those who had their hearts and their heads so settled down in order that they go on with quiet stillness to do anything without getting the rest of themselves mixed up and excited over it. They had each thought, each feeling, laid out in separate shelves in their heads. So they could draw out one shelf of ideas while the rest of their ideas remained quiet and still in the orderly place inside of them.

With me my thoughts were not up in my head. They were in my hands and feet, in the thinnest nerves of my hair, in the flesh and blood of my whole body. Everything hurt in me when I tried to think; it was like struggling up toward something over me that I could never reach—like tearing myself inch by inch from the roots of the earth—like suffering all pain of dying and being born.

Booker T. Washington, *Up from Slavery* (1901)[8]

The individual who can do something that the world wants done will, in the end, make his way regardless of his race. One man may go into a community prepared to supply the people there with an analysis of Greek sentences. The community may not at that time be prepared for, or feel the need of, Greek analysis, but it may feel its need of bricks and houses and wagons. If the man can supply the need for those, then, it will lead eventually to a demand for the first product, and with the demand will come the ability to appreciate it and to profit by it.

About the time that we succeeded in burning our first kiln of bricks we began facing in an emphasized form the objection of the students being taught to work. By this time it had gotten to be pretty well advertised throughout the state that every student who came to Tuskegee, no matter what his financial ability might be, must learn some industry. Quite a number of letters came from parents protesting against their children engaging in labour while they were in school. Other parents came to the school to protest in person. Most of the new students brought a written or a verbal request from their parents to the effect that they wanted their children taught nothing but books. The more books, the larger they were, and the longer the titles printed upon them, the better pleased the students and their parents seemed to be.

I gave little heed to these protests, except that I lost no opportunity to go into as many parts of the state as I could, for the purpose of speaking to the parents, and showing them the value of industrial education. Besides, I talked to the students constantly on the subject. Notwithstanding the unpopularity of industrial work, the school continued to increase in numbers to such an extent that by the middle of the second year there was an attendance of about one hundred and fifty, representing almost all parts of the state of Alabama, and including a few other states.

W. E. B. Du Bois, *The Souls of Black Folk* (1903)[9]

The function of the Negro college, then, is clear: it must maintain the standards of popular education, it must seek the social regeneration of the Negro, and it must help in the solution of problems of race contact and coöperation. And finally, beyond all this, it must develop men. Above our modern socialism, and out of worship of the mass, must persist and evolve that higher individualism which the centres of culture protect; there must come a loftier respect for the sovereign human soul that seeks to know itself and the world about it; that seeks a freedom for expansion and self-development; that will love and hate and labor in its own way, untrammeled alike by old and new. Such souls aforetime have inspired and guided worlds, and if we be not wholly bewitched by our Rhinegold, they shall again. Herein the longing of black men must have respect: the rich and bitter depth of their experience, the unknown treasures of their inner life, the strange rendings of nature they have seen, may give the world new points of view and make their loving, living, and doing precious to all human hearts. And to themselves in these the days that try their souls, the chance to soar in the dim blue air above the smoke is to their finer spirits boon and guerdon for what they lose on earth by being black.

I sit with Shakespeare and he winces not. Across the color line I move arm in arm with Balzac and Dumas, where smiling men and welcoming women glide in gilded halls. From out the caves of evening that swing between the strong-limbed earth and the tracery of the stars, I summon Aristotle and Aurelius and what soul I will, and they come all graciously with no scorn nor condescension. So, wed with Truth, I dwell above the Veil. Is this the life you grudge us, O knightly America? Is this the life you long to change into the dull red hideousness of Georgia? Are you so afraid lest peering from this high Pisgah, between Philistine and Amalekite, we sight the Promised Land?

THE EXTRAORDINARY next set of selections appeared in testimony taken in the early 1880s by the United States Senate Committee on Education and Labor and published in 1885 by the Government Printing Office. On September 18, 1883, the journalist Jennie Cunningham Croly ("Jennie June") explained to committee members that working girls needed a basic elementary education and practical training—and that they took pleasure in being outdoors or in reading sensational fiction during their rare moments of leisure. Frank K. Foster, a printer and labor organizer from Cambridge, Massachusetts, testified about changes in the trade and the social costs of an unstable workforce, as well as the physical strains of the labor behind the printed page. On November 22, 1883, the senators ventured to the Alabama countryside and questioned a teacher, C. S. Giddens, and several young scholars in a "Colored School" in Opelika. African American witnesses, in sessions conducted in Birmingham and Columbus, seemed reticent to voice complaints about political and social strife, but one after another they described their community's hunger for education.

Senate Committee on Education and Labor,
Report of the Committee of the Senate upon the Relations between Labor and Capital, and Testimony Taken by the Committee (1885)[10]

[Testimony of Jennie Cunningham Croly ("Jennie June").]

FEW RECREATIONS FOR WORKING GIRLS

By the CHAIRMAN:

Q. As to the large numbers of these poor girls that you speak of, what opportunities are there for them in the way of recreation, in the way of reading or any of the ordinary pleasures or relaxations in life? —A. Well, in the first place, such girls do not care much about sitting down to read. If they have half a day of spare time they want to get out of doors, they want air. These poor girls do not see daylight only a little while perhaps on Saturday afternoon or on a public holiday, such as the Fourth of July, or occasionally on a Sunday; in all probability, not even then. . . .

THE READING OF WORKING GIRLS

And as for reading they want something very different from what have in their daily lives, and so they run to the story papers that contain flashy stories; they tell about the fine ladies and how many dresses they have, and that tell about the worst murders and the most exciting incidents that they can get. And I do not blame them for it. They are crazy for something that is outside of themselves, and which will make them forget the hard facts of their daily lives.

[Testimony of Frank K. Foster.]

The members of the printing trade in Massachusetts occupy in the trade quite a large variety of positions, relatively. The wages paid to printers there vary all the way from $8 or $9 a week to $20 or $25 a week for male labor; the last-named sum being, of course, the wages paid for those who hold especially remunerative situations. And those working on the morning newspapers. The special reason for the difference in wages in these instances may, perhaps, be owing chiefly to the unhealthiness of the occupation, and its tendency to shorten life—the strain on the vitality and physical well-being of those engaged in night work. Then, again, the much more severe competition that those engaged in day work, especially in book work, have to meet from the large influx from the British provinces of Canada, Nova Scotia, Prince Edward Island, Newfoundland, New Brunswick, and Quebec, where prices are lower, and also the introduction of late, though not to a large extent, of female labor in the part of the trade pertaining directly to setting type. These elements come in direct competition with many men who have served an apprenticeship at the trade, and as a large portion of the work consists of type setting, the competition is very severe. Those who receive the largest wages are enabled to support their families in comparative comfort, provided they are industrious and economical; but at the present rates of living, the large majority of printers in Massachusetts find it difficult to live up to the traditions of their craft, to support their families and educate their children in a manner that they hold becoming to printers and to American citizens. . . .

The occupation is undoubtedly one of the most injurious, as regards the physical welfare of those employed in it, of any of the skilled trades, so called. The tables of mortality, so far as I have seen them, place the death rate among printers about the highest of any of the trades. This is owing in large measure to the necessity to which they are subjected of inhaling the antimony or black lead that collects in the type especially where the electrotyping process is used, as in book-making, and breathing air from which the oxygen has been exhausted by the consumption of gas in night-work, and the unnatural condition of the laborer who has to work during the night. . . .

The printers patronize the theater, I think, to a considerable extent, many of them at least once a week; and if a man belongs to a fraternal society of any description he of course attends the festivities, the "sociables," or dances that are organized by the society. . . . He is generally a reader—almost universally, I think—and where possible he patronizes the library and reading-room to a considerable degree. The reading-rooms and the various places provided for intellectual gratification are taken advantage of, I think, by a larger percentage of printers than of those belonging to any other trade. The nature of his pursuit gives the printer a taste for knowledge, and unless prevented by intemperate habits or unusual social conditions he pursues information through all available channels as far as he can conveniently and consistently with his physical comfort and his command of time. I may say, however, in this connection that the occupation as a general thing leaves the body and mind in a condition of lassitude, so that after a day's or a night's work it is difficult, unless the individual possesses extraordinary stamina, to do a great deal in the way of acquiring knowledge.

[A "Colored School."]

POOR COUNTRY SCHOOLS.

Q. How is it out in the country? —*A.* Oh, it is mighty poor in that way out there.

Q. Poorer than it is here? —*A.* Yes, sir; poorer than it is here. They run the schools out there about three months, and the rest of the time the children are out on the farms. The wages of the people is so poor they cannot pay teachers.

MONEY WANTED FOR THE SCHOOLS—POLITICS LET ALONE.

Q. If the Government would allow you to have some money for your schools that would be a good thing wouldn't it? —*A.* Oh, yes.

Q. I suppose you colored people do not pay much attention to politics now? —*A.* No, sir; we do not pay much attention to those things now. . . .

Q. I suppose the colored people have talked that over among themselves and have come to the conclusion that they had better turn their attention to making money and let politics go for one or two generations? —*A.* Yes, sir.

Q. Is that so generally? —*A.* No, sir. In Montgomery County the colored people take an active part, and also down in Coffee and Dale, they take an active part, because they are more able.

Q. I think it is the best way for you colored people to stick right to work and to try to get some education and to get some property, and that you say is the general idea of the colored people? —*A.* Yes, sir; I think so. . . .

Q. How old are those three women that I see over there studying their lessons? —*A.* All of those three are married ladies.

Q. About what age do you take the oldest to be? —*A.* About forty-seven or forty-eight.

Q. Have they children? —*A.* Only one of them.

Q. Are they learning to read? —*A.* Yes, sir; very well.

Q. Which is the oldest one? —*A.* The one sitting on the left.

Q. What is their object in learning to read at their age? —*A.* Well, their object is just to learn to read and write, so they can act for themselves.

Q. How long have they attended school here? —*A.* About seven months.

Q. How much longer will they attend? —*A.* They will attend probably three or four months longer.

At the request of the chairman, the teacher called up two or three of his pupils to show their proficiency. One of them, a little girl, read a passage from a text-book on civil government, after which she was questioned, as follows:

By the CHAIRMAN:

Q. How old are you? —*A.* I do not know my age.

Q. What is your name? —*A.* Mamie White.

Q. What is the name of the book you have been reading from? —*A.* Civil Government.

Q. How many pages are in it? —*A.* Two hundred and forty.

Q. Where was that book made? —*A.* I don't know, sir.

Q. Do you know how they make a book? —*A.* No, sir.

Q. Do they make books anywhere in this town? —*A.* Not as I know of.

Q. What is a book made of? There is paper in it, is there not? —*A.* Yes, sir.

Q. What else is there in the book? There is reading in it, is there not? —*A.* Yes, sir.

Q. How do they put the reading on to the paper? —*A.* They print it on.

Q. Do you know anything about how printing is done? —*A.* No, sir.

Q. Do you know who was the first man that printed? —*A.* No, sir.

Q. Is there not a good deal of printing done in this country? —*A.* Yes, sir.

Q. You go to school here? —*A.* Yes, sir.

Q. What makes you go to school? —*A.* To learn to read.

Q. Will it be of any use to you to know how to read? —*A.* Yes, sir.

Q. What use will it be to you? —*A.* It will be of use to me when I get larger and older.

Q. You have found out, I suppose, that folks who can read and write get along better than those who can't? —*A.* Yes, sir.

COMMENTARY: LIVES OF LABOR, LIVES OF THE MIND

On a November afternoon in 1883 the members of the Senate Committee to investigate relations between labor and capital walked into a classroom of a "colored school" in Opelika, Alabama. Imagine the well-dressed white men, the young scholars and the shabby classroom. A little girl, Mamie White, was called to the front of the class to read from her textbook *Civil Government*. How she felt about reading aloud, we do not know. Nor do we know how well she read or what she read, for the senator who questioned her did not ask her what she thought of the contents of *Civil Government*. He wondered, rather, if she knew how or where the book had been made; if she knew who had invented the art of printing.

Brief as it was, this exchange between a grown man and a little girl suggests one way to begin to think about the ways class shaped encounters with "print culture." Encouraged by her textbook, the little girl may have imagined herself grown into a citizen of her state. The senator, however, saw her grown into a worker in Alabama's paper mills—a book maker, perhaps, but not a reader or writer of books. While a book may have "reading in it," he reminded her, someone (a typesetter, a printer) put the "reading on to the paper." And before that, someone, perhaps an Alabaman like her, had run a machine in a mill that produced the paper. The senator's line of inquiry leads us straight back to the labor behind the printed word.

Before he left the room, the man asked the little girl a last question: "You have found out, I suppose, that folks who can read and write get along better than those who can't?" Mamie agreed. But just what did the senator mean by getting along better? And what did Mamie mean when she assented to his assertion?

Although the American educational system fostered widespread literacy, as she grew up the little girl would likely learn that her fine skills as a reader and thinker, while they certainly made it easier to read a sign or sign a name, would be blunted by hard realities of economic and social inequality. Like the politicians tramping around the Alabama countryside, educators and guardians of genteel culture worried about what the men and women of the new laboring classes would read and how they would interpret what they did read. Some wondered whether it was right to encourage a taste for extensive reading and high literature among those who were meant to labor with their hands. Were readers better workers or were readers, like the "farmer's wife" who sometimes neglected her chores to read and to write, prone to distraction, driven to discontent, or drawn to socialism?

Some hoped that working-class readers would "get along better" by reading the books that would make them better workers, learning to extract information from technical manuals and to draw inspiration from model biographies, the Bible, and tracts on good behavior. Certainly, reading skills could be deployed in the pursuit of "useful knowledge," the kind of information that had long been staple fare in philanthropic institutions, like the Apprentice's Library in Philadelphia (Lewis).

In some quarters, the idea of useful knowledge took on new significance. At his Tuskegee Institute, Booker T. Washington devised a plan for educating students that emphasized technical skills rather than "book learning." The books that symbolized learning to the parents of so many of his students represented foolish aspiration to him. Time and again, he cautioned young African Americans against a reading he considered so highbrow it ill suited them for the lives of manual labor most white employers allotted to them. Although those who read the classics might be those best able to envision a better future for their communities, as W. E. B. Du Bois so often argued, Washington encouraged his students to get along better by working in the present rather than reading and dreaming of a better future. In effect, Washington collapsed race into class, and offered well-trained, native-born, African American workers to employers.

Washington defended his plan as a good deal for workers and their bosses, but Du Bois saw it as a bad bargain, a plan that left all Americans, black and white, with a world sadly diminished. Although the brief selection reprinted here hardly does justice to Du Bois's eloquent assertions of the importance of culture, he knew the country would pay dearly if a people lost intellectual aspiration. Du Bois knew that the senator who could only imagine a little girl grown into a worker in a paper mill lived, as surely as she did, in a world made poorer by his diminished vision.

Nevertheless, Washington's strident defense of a life of labor over the life of the mind suggests just how threatening some found the idea of a literate and thinking working class. Some of those who read, whether Greek classics or technical manuals, no doubt eventually worked their way into the managerial and professional positions that had come to characterize the middle class. Others probably stayed loyal to class and community and perhaps, like Du Bois, came to question a social or racial order built to serve the interests of so few.

Sometimes books themselves (and not their content) seemed to transform those who encountered them. In Anzia Yezierska's story "Wings," the narrator learns lessons about dress, makeup, and cleanliness just by going into a library. According to some New York City librarians an encounter with books could extend the reach of genteel culture. To their great satisfaction, one mother testified: "You don't know how much better my Sammy is since he gets books. Before he was rough and noisy and hit all the little ones so much. Now he has manners and keeps himself clean" (*Results Not Shown by Statistics*, 15).

But newly mannerly Sammy may have had his mind on girls and dancing and not on pleasing librarians. It is easiest to find the testimony of teachers and librarians, but workingmen and women, immigrant and native born, found their own uses for books and reading. Reading itself might also be something other than a silent, solitary, and private act. Those who read aloud in the workplace developed alternatives to silent reading, turning print into speech and drawing the literate and illiterate into a single group of listeners. Although middle-class librarians urged working-class patrons toward the silent practices of "true" reading, there were other ways to approach printed matter. Working-class reading rooms, such as those patronized by the Cambridge printer Frank K. Foster and his friends, offered an alternative to the strict propriety enforced in most public and private libraries.

Even self-improvement did not have to meet the agenda proposed by middle-class reformers; nor did immigrant reading necessarily dissolve barriers around traditional ethnic communities. Some immigrants found in print culture the means to preserve in a new country practices they had known at home. The foreign-language press both advertised the modern commodities of a new life and announced the traditional gatherings of the old. And some surely found in their reading not the means to climb the ladder into the middle class or to preserve traditional cultures but rather the ideas that inspired them to challenge an economic system based on harsh inequalities of class, race, or gender. Tracts by socialists, anarchists, and labor leaders urged workers to question promises of equality and assurances of mobility, to turn their alternative reading practices to oppositional ends.

Workers also read newspapers, sometimes, as James Weldon Johnson noted, selecting one from among them to read the news aloud while others worked. While constrained budgets no doubt induced some to share papers at workplaces and in boardinghouses, one study of the expenditures of Massachusetts mill families, completed in 1890, found that 77 percent of households reported spending money on newspapers. Immigrant editors circulated the news in native languages, using papers to create for readers a shared sense of community and class (Nord, 162). Another study of workingmen's families, published in 1909, determined that most of the money spent on reading matter went for newspapers. The New York *Journal* and *World* were most popular with English-speaking readers; Russians, Austrians, and Italians bought papers in their own languages (Chapin, 211–14).

Before papers arrived in working-class households, they had passed through the hands of pressmen and typesetters—workers whose labor, as Frank K. Foster described it, had grown more physically arduous with mechanization and with the rising demand for morning papers. The decisions that assured a steady supply of printed goods meant harder work for printers. Machines undercut demands for skilled labor, and, as Foster remarked, publishers tried to meet competition from

Canada by offering women low wages to set type. Although journeymen printers might easily afford to buy the cheap books and newspapers they produced, their labor was worth far less than it had been. Publishers also found a cheap means of distribution in cities. Papers passed from the presses into the hands of newsboys, the ubiquitous street urchins of print culture.

It is easy to see the role of class in the debate over "useful" reading, in the labor behind print, and in the newspapers designed for specific groups of readers, but class appears as well in debates about the proliferation of "cheap fiction," of dime and half-dime novels, of story papers. The debate over novel reading that occupied teachers and preachers in the early years of the nineteenth century took on new life after the Civil War. Once again, the imaginary power of fiction seemed to threaten religious and moral authority by encouraging sympathy for the sinner. Nevertheless, most library directors succumbed to pressure from readers and shelved some novels alongside more serious works of history and biography. Public librarians sometimes tried to limit the circulation of fiction, permitting patrons to check out two books at a time, provided only one was a novel (Garrison, 67–74).

Women of the middle class seemed particularly vulnerable to the lures of sentimental fiction, but the novels respectable librarians chose surely seemed to librarians and their proper clients preferable to the great mass of cheap books and story papers that had been rolling off the presses since the early 1860s. The brief selection from Dorothy Richardson's novel, *The Long Day*, captures the differences between the sentimental reading of a middle-class woman and that of her working-class sisters. The narrator confesses to an "omnivorous appetite" for tender, sentimental love stories. And an exchange begins among the working girls that, rather than revealing their shared readings, makes visible their cultural differences, differences conveniently measured by an "either" and an "or." Not only does the narrator astound them with her "eyether," she hears the "or" so common in dime-novel titles as joining the titles of two books rather than title and subtitle of one. Finally, her retelling of *Little Women* inspires in her workplace friends only a dismissive "Why, that's no story—that's just everyday happenings."

Cheap fiction seemed to be everywhere (except for schoolrooms and respectable libraries). Dime novels and story papers were available at railway bookstalls, at street-corner newsdealers, and in hundreds of thousands of working-class households. In the mid-1860s a writer for the staid and stodgy *North American Review* marveled at the nearly 5 million Beadle's Dime Books that had been put in circulation in a mere five years. Each month publishers Beadle and Adams issued a new novel—an adventure set in the American west, a detective story set in an eastern city, or the saga of a tramping worker—and a single novel might sell as many as 40,000 copies. Plots were often so similar that readers may have used publishers' numbering systems to tell stories apart. The bulk confused the ministers, teachers, writers, and librarians who saw themselves as cultural authorities. They knew they could hardly hope to master such a mass of material, and they worried that a whole realm of culture had expanded beyond their reach (Everett, 303–9).

For the proponents of genteel culture, the sheer volume of cheap fiction was as disquieting as its content. Even if they could dismiss the stories as worthless tripe, the very thought of a printed world they did not know and would not or could not master threatened to undermine the cultural authority they had marked out as their own. Women of all classes or, as Anthony Comstock claimed, young men, appeared particularly defenseless against the lures of cheap reading. While Comstock believed in the power of high literature, a belief he shared with the "farmer's wife," he was also afraid that books, now so ubiquitous and so easy to afford, could lead boys into worlds rich in sexual fantasy but poor in lofty ideas and good discipline.

In turning to cheap fiction, women, children and workers all escaped the discipline and decorum thought to be built into the best books. A fledgling world of mass culture held for workers at least the promise they could make of their readings their own meanings without the intervention and influence of those who considered themselves the arbiters of culture.

To compound the beleaguered expert's dilemma in the 1870s and 1880s, workers devoured melodrama, romance, and adventure in the weekly story papers put out by big commercial publishers in New York and Chicago. Take, for example, the *Saturday Journal*, "a popular paper for pleasure and profit," published in the 1870s and 1880s by Beadle and Adams. The paper ran stories in installments, extending an adventure over several weeks. Each issue also offered dozens of short melodramatic vignettes (many of them submitted by readers), a column on women's fashion, portraits of "Talked About People" (including the publisher Sinclair Tousey and the merchant Horace B. Claflin), and a column addressed to "Readers and Contributors" in which editors answered readers' questions about beauty, romance, agriculture, housekeeping, story writing, and American history. Story papers helped introduce immigrants to America and rural people to the conventions of city life. One column from June 11, 1881, for example, advised one reader to spurn a suitor who had jilted her, another to use caution with toxic depilatories; other columns answered queries on the history of the Wisconsin territory, on laws regulating American citizenship, and on the "undesirable" ornaments in handwriting.

Studying these diverging imaginary worlds, some scholars contend that even the wildest tales of intrigue, adventure, and disguise can be read as allegories of class struggle. Cheap fiction, they acknowledge, may have offered readers escape from the daily grind, but a close examination of the forms of escape that workers chose suggests that there has been more to reading than simple diversion. The literary scholar Michael Denning insisted that workers, particularly native-born white workers, found in plots of dime novels imaginary solutions to the real problems they faced. Denning argues that workers whose lives were defined by factory labor discerned in dime novels an allegory of a lost republic, a country where independent artisans were figures of respect. In even the most fantastic tales of knights and cowboys, working-class readers perhaps found a language that helped them imagine an egalitarian world of justice and cooperation.

What native-born white women, immigrants, and African Americans made of their reading may be more difficult to say. What we do know for sure is that workers in great numbers consumed cheap books and papers. And that the presence of workers as consumers posed a challenge to a culture designed to suit the tastes of elites. While some men and women of wealth withdrew into the museum boardrooms and symphony halls designed as sanctums of high culture, a burgeoning mass culture, composed in part of cheap print, spun out beyond their control. When Anthony Comstock launched his crusade against dangerous books, he repeated some of the old arguments about the dangers of reading novels. While some dismissed sensational fiction as simple escape, Comstock saw in it a symbolic universe so potent it lured readers, particularly young men, to certain destruction. Comstock may represent an extreme form of concerns about working-class reading, but it must have struck some that a struggle over culture could be class struggle waged by other means.

So when Mamie White assented to the senator's assertion that those who could read got along better than those who could not, it was by no means clear what the two had agreed upon. For students interested in exploring what the artifacts of print culture may reveal about the experience of class, the ambiguities in the exchange between the senator and the little girl are rich indeed.

SOURCE NOTES

[Unless otherwise indicated material is considered to fall under fair use or to be in the public domain, or a good-faith effort has been made to locate the copyright holder.]

1. Unsigned letter from the Acting Branch Librarian to Miss Florence Overton, Supervisor of Branches, August 12, 1921. History File, Archives of the Seward Park Branch of the New York Public Library. Reproduced courtesy Archives of the Seward Park Branch of the New York Public Library, Astor, Lenox, and Tilden Foundations.

2. Anzia Yezierska, "Wings," in Yezierska, *Hungry Hearts* (Boston: Houghton Mifflin, 1920), 13.

3. Dorothy Richardson, *The Long Day: The Story of a New York Working Girl* (New York: Century Co., 1905), 75–86.

4. Anthony Comstock, *Traps for the Young* (New York: Funk & Wagnalls, 1883), 11–12, 24–25.

5. James Weldon Johnson, *The Autobiography of an Ex-Colored Man* (Boston: Sherman, French & Company, 1912), 73–74.

6. "One Farmer's Wife," *Independent* (New York) 58 (February 9, 1905), 7–12.

7. Anzia Yezierska, "An Immigrant Among the Editors," in Yezierska, *Children of Loneliness* (New York: Funk & Wagnalls, 1923), 154–55. Reproduced courtesy of Persea Books, New York. Copyright © 1991 Louise Levitas Henriksen.

8. Booker T. Washington, *Up from Slavery* (New York: Doubleday, Page & Co., 1901), 155–56.

9. W. E. B. Du Bois, *The Souls of Black Folk; Essays and Sketches* (Chicago: A. C. McClurg & Co., 1903), 75–76.

10. United States Senate, Committee on Education and Labor, *Report of the Committee of the Senate upon the Relations between Labor and Capital, and Testimony Taken by the Committee*, 4 vols. (Washington, D.C.: Government Printing Office, 1885), 1:41–42, 47, 613–14; 4:651–52.

WORKS CITED

Chapin, Robert Coit. *The Standard of Living among Workingmen's Families in New York City*. New York: Charities Publications Committee, 1909.

Denning, Michael. *Mechanic Accents: Dime Novels and Working-Class Culture in America*. New York: Verso, 1987.

Everett, William. "Beadle's Dime Books." *North American Review* 99 (July 1864): 303–9.

Garrison, Dee. *Apostles of Culture: The Public Librarian and American Society, 1876–1920*. New York: The Free Press, 1979.

Lewis, John Frederick. *History of the Apprentices' Library of Philadelphia, 1820–1920: The Oldest Free Circulating Library in America*. Philadelphia: Privately printed, 1924.

Nord, David Paul. "Working-Class Readers: Family, Community, and Reading in Late Nineteenth-Century America." *Communications Research* 13 (April 1986): 156–81.

Results Not Shown by Statistics in the Work of The Public Libraries of Greater New York—Compiled by the New York Public Library, the Brooklyn Public Library and the Queens Borough Public Library—Printed for the Budget Exhibit of the City of New York. New York, 1910.

Saturday Journal (New York) 12 (June 11, 1881): 4.

FOR FURTHER RESEARCH

Brodhead, Richard H. *Cultures of Letters: Scenes of Reading and Writing in Nineteenth-Century America*. Chicago: University of Chicago Press, 1993.

Dimock, Wai Chee, and Michael T. Gilmore, eds. *Rethinking Class: Literary Studies and Social Formations*. New York: Columbia University Press, 1994.

Erickson, Paul J. "Judging Books by Their Covers: Format, the Implied Reader, and the 'Degeneration' of the Dime Novel." *ATQ*, n.s., 12 (September 1998): 247–63.

Harrison, Jonathan Baxter. "Workingmen's Wives." In *Certain Dangerous Tendencies in American Life, and Other Papers*. Boston: Houghton, Osgood and Company, 1880.

Hoerder, Dirk. *The Immigrant Labor Press in North America, 1840s–1970s: An Annotated Bibliography*. 3 vols. New York: Greenwood Press, 1987.

Hoggart, Richard. *The Uses of Literacy*. 1957. Reprint, New Brunswick, N.J., and London: Transaction Publishers, 1992.

Jacobson, Matthew Frye. *Special Sorrows: The Diasporic Imagination of Irish, Polish, and Jewish Immigrants in the United States*. Cambridge, Mass.: Harvard University Press, 1995.

Joselit, Jenna Weissman. "Reading, Writing, and a Library Card: New York Jews and The New York Public Library." *Biblion: The Bulletin of the New York Public Library* 5 (Fall 1996): 97–117.

Kaestle, Carl, and Helen Damon-Moore et al. *Literacy in the United States: Readers and Reading since 1880*. New Haven, Conn.: Yale University Press, 1991.

*McHenry, Elizabeth. "Forgotten Readers: African-American Literary Societies and the American Scene." In *Print Culture in a Diverse America*, edited by James P. Danky and Wayne A. Wiegand, 149–72.

Ohmann, Richard. *Selling Culture: Magazines, Markets, and Class at the Turn of the Century*. New York: Verso, 1996.

Pawley, Christine. *Reading on the Middle Border: The Culture of Print in Late Nineteenth-Century Osage, Iowa*. Amherst: University of Massachusetts Press, 2001.

Rasche, William Frank. *The Reading Interests of Young Workers*. Chicago: University of Chicago Libraries, 1937.

Rose, Jonathan. *The Intellectual Life of the British Working Classes*. New Haven, Conn.: Yale University Press, 2001.

Van Slyck, Abigail A. *Free to All: Carnegie Libraries and American Culture, 1890–1920*. Chicago: University of Chicago Press, 1995.

*Vecoli, Rudolph J. "The Italian Immigrant Press and the Construction of Social Reality, 1850–1920." In *Print Culture in a Diverse America*, edited by James P. Danky and Wayne A. Wiegand, 17–33.

Waples, Douglas, and Ralph Tyler. *What People Want to Read About: A Study of Group Interests and a Survey of Problems in Adult Reading*. Chicago: University of Chicago Press, 1931.

12

The Industrialization and Nationalization of American Periodical Publishing

Charles Johanningsmeier

AFTER THE Civil War, periodicals became increasingly important to the development of American print culture. Magazines proliferated in number and kind, with their millions of subscribers spread across the nation and their variety constantly growing. By 1900 there were numerous magazines targeted at particular audiences, such as families, women, and children, and many others devoted to specialized topics, such as science, religion, and agriculture. A new kind of general-audience magazine, the inexpensive monthly such as *Cosmopolitan*, *McClure's Magazine*, and *Munsey's*, focused on contemporary issues and personalities, contained many high-quality illustrations, and featured advertisements prominently. By the turn of the century such magazines were cheap enough that they had become a typical part of almost every middle-class household.

Newspapers worked on an even larger scale than magazines, circulated with impressive efficiency across the nation: helped along by revenues from the ever bolder advertisements they carried, newspapers became the print form most responsible for leading the United States into a new mass-media era. To achieve new rates of circulation, newspapers took advantage of new technologies and modes of communication. Ever faster presses printed news communicated telegraphically from around the country and the world, and newspapers were distributed by an increasingly extensive and efficient rail system, allowing them to reach far beyond the cities in which they originated. Newspaper syndicates reached national audiences with identical news stories, features, and advertisements, a development that encouraged Americans to think beyond their own regions, to imagine themselves as citizens of a country with a shared body of information. Starting in 1861 "readyprint" or "patent inside" services began to offer both urban and rural newspapers the possibility of carrying national news and advertising. These services worked by supplying small newspapers with sheets on which two pages had already been printed with news and advertisements; the other half of the sheet remained blank. The printer, who typically lived and worked a great distance from the readyprint provider, could then fill in the other two pages with local news and ads. During the second half of the nineteenth century small newspapers proliferated in rural areas across the country, and thus a variety of companies competed to sell them readyprint sheets. Starting in the 1870s some syndicates began to offer "plate service": rather than selling half-printed sheets, these companies distributed stereotyped printing plates. Using such plates, local newspaper editors could exercise more freedom in designing their papers, since the printing plates could be cut and used wherever they seemed to fit best. Finally, in the 1880s "galley-proof" syndicates came into being. Rather than distributing heavy bundles of half-printed sheets or heavy boxes of printing plates, these firms distributed text that could be edited and typeset at the local paper.

Before the early 1900s, when "chain" newspaper owners such as Edward W. Scripps or William Randolph Hearst owned multiple newspapers in different cities and could reproduce common material in each one, newspaper syndicates made it increasingly possible for the same short story, serial novel, Woman's Page, Children's Page, or news feature to appear across the country in between twenty and a hundred newspapers on the same day. Syndicates thus revolutionized the circulation of print—and in the process of doing so disrupted many traditional relationships between authors, publishers, and readers.

ARTIFACTS

The growing importance of the periodical press, especially the newspapers, seemed very threatening to many traditional supporters of "book culture." In 1887 an anonymous writer (many newspaper and magazine writers during this period remained anonymous) compared books, magazines, and newspapers and concluded that the periodical had become the superior format for the general reader. In the same year, Allan Forman (1860–1914) admitted that newspaper syndicates in some ways depressed the printing trade, but that overall they were of great service to the country. Both of these pieces appeared in the *Journalist*—a periodical with particular interest in the topic of journalism itself. A 1913 cover and table of contents from the *American Magazine* provides a sense of both the style and the content of the magazines that were increasingly to be found in middle-class households. Early in the new century, several popular periodicals staked out a new mission: exposing corruption in government and business. This journalism, nicknamed "muckraking" by President Theodore Roosevelt, helped clean out several cities' municipal governments and most famously, in Upton Sinclair's 1906 novel *The Jungle* (first serialized in the Socialist newspaper *Appeal to Reason*), revealed the working conditions in meat-packing plants. Lincoln Steffens (1866–1936), among the foremost muckrakers, wrote for *McClure's Magazine*; his collected articles on municipal corruption appeared as *The Shame of the Cities* (1904).

"Books, Magazines and Newspapers," from *The Journalist* (1887)[1]

It is not by pandering to a crude and unwholesome taste that the magazines and newspapers succeed in winning so many readers while books of all kinds are left to gather dust on the dealers' shelves. They induce the public to give them preference by furnishing at a trifling cost matter which is quite equal in every way to that found in current books. It is hardly too much to say, in fact, that the average literary merit of such publications is superior to that of the majority of books. The progress that has been made in this respect is one of the wonders of the century, and things are easily done nowadays which were out of the question twenty years ago. There was a time when magazines were made for the "saving remnant" of culture and leisure, and newspapers were careless of all interests save those of a political nature; but that time has clearly gone by. These aggressive and potent forces now appeal to every taste and give attention to every interest, and the result is that when their contents are read and digested, the public has little desire or necessity to peruse new books.

The Sunday edition of a great daily paper contains as much reading matter as an ordinary book, and covers all topics of general importance. A book must be exceptionally good to gain the attention of the patrons of such a paper; and it cannot be doubted that where so much entertainment and instruction may be had for five cents, the number of those who are willing to pay a dollar for a bound volume must steadily decrease. We have outlived the superstition that there can be no literature in the true sense of the word except in the form of books. The development of the magazines and newspapers has reached a point where it is manifestly absurd to entertain a notion of that sort. It will no longer do to sneer at publications which have invaded the literary domain to an extent that enables them to anticipate the triumphs of the book-makers and provide the people with the choicest wares at merely nominal prices. . . .

There will always be books, of course, but they will never again have the influence that they once had in the shaping of popular thought and the adjustment of literary values. We really do not have time anymore to read books. The magazines and newspapers supply us with all that we can conveniently consume in the way of useful and valuable information; and the books, as a rule, may be disregarded without any danger of serious loss. . . . We can not read everything; and so, being compelled to make [a] choice, we take those publications which are at once both the cheapest and the best adapted to our practical wants.

[Allan Forman], "Journalistic Centralization," from *The Journalist* (1887)[2]

There is complaint loud and deep among newspaper men against the centralizing process, which finds expression in patent insides and outsides, news bureaus, plate matter, illustrated-article bureaus and syndicates. At first sight, it would seem as if their opposition were well founded. It is dispiriting to see the avenues of income closed up, one by one, to those who have long enjoyed their benefits. And this, and even more, has been done by the centralization referred to. It is obvious to all whose journalistic experience covers more than twenty years:

1. That the patent inside and outside displace, and therefore do the work of at least twenty thousand compositors, pressmen, stereotypers, reporters and space-writers.

Front Cover and Table of Contents (opposite),
from *The American Magazine* (1913)[3]

2. That plate matter and syndicate articles, though still in their infancy, have already driven at least a thousand writers out of business and have reduced the income of two thousand more by not less than fifty per cent.

3. That the new system is deteriorating the value of petty local news, and substituting for it matters of only general interest.

4. That the new system is killing individuality of local papers, bringing all publications using plate or syndicate matter to about the same level and pattern.

The specifications are more than borne out by the facts. . . .

Yet, on the other hand, the careful observer sees in the new system but another expression of the spirit of the age—labor-saving, expense-reducing, time-sparing

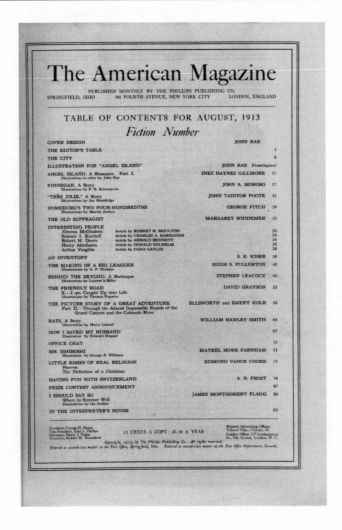

The American Magazine

PUBLISHED MONTHLY BY THE PHILLIPS PUBLISHING CO.
SPRINGFIELD, OHIO   381 FOURTH AVENUE, NEW YORK CITY   LONDON, ENGLAND

TABLE OF CONTENTS FOR AUGUST, 1913
Fiction Number

COVER DESIGN	JOHN RAE	
THE EDITOR'S TABLE		5
THE CITY		9
ILLUSTRATION FOR "ANGEL ISLAND"	JOHN RAE	Frontispiece
ANGEL ISLAND, A Romance. Part I.	INEZ HAYNES GILLMORE	11
Illustrations in color by John Rae		
FINNEGAN, A Story	JOHN A. MOROSO	17
Illustrations by F. E. Schoonover		
"TRÈS JOLIE," A Story	JOHN TAINTOR FOOTE	24
Illustrations by Jay Hambidge		
HOMEBURG'S TWO FOUR-HUNDREDTHS	GEORGE FITCH	29
Illustrations by Martin Justice		
THE OLD SUFFRAGIST	MARGARET WIDDEMER	32
INTERESTING PEOPLE		
Ximena McGlashen	Article by ROBERT H. MOULTON	33
Sumner I. Kimball	Article by CHARLES A. HARBAUGH	34
Robert H. Davis	Article by ARNOLD BENNETT	34
Henry Abrahams	Article by DONALD WILHELM	36
Arthur Voegtlin	Article by DANA GATLIN	38
AN INVENTORY	S. E. KISER	39
THE MAKING OF A BIG LEAGUER	HUGH S. FULLERTON	40
Illustrations by G. P. Hoskins		
BEHIND THE BEYOND, A Burlesque	STEPHEN LEACOCK	46
Illustrations by Lejaren à Hiller		
THE FRIENDLY ROAD	DAVID GRAYSON	53
X.—I am Caught Up into Life		
Illustrations by Thomas Fogarty		
THE PICTURE STORY OF A GREAT ADVENTURE	ELLSWORTH and EMERY KOLB	58
Part II.—Through the Almost Impassable Rapids of the Grand Canyon and the Colorado River		
RATS, A Story	WILLIAM HAWLEY SMITH	64
Illustrations by Harry Linnell		
HOW I SAVED MY HUSBAND		67
Illustration by Edward Hopper		
OFFICE CHAT		70
MR. ISHIBOSHI	MATEEL HOWE FARNHAM	71
Illustration by George A. Williams		
LITTLE RIMES OF REAL RELIGION	EDMUND VANCE COOKE	77
Heaven		
The Definition of a Christian		
HAVING FUN WITH SWITZERLAND	A. B. FROST	78
PRIZE CONTEST ANNOUNCEMENT		87
I SHOULD SAY SO	JAMES MONTGOMERY FLAGG	88
Where to Summer Well		
Illustrations by the Author		
IN THE INTERPRETER'S HOUSE		92

President, George H. Hazen
Vice-President, John S. Phillips
Secretary, Henry J. Fisher
Treasurer, Robert M. Donaldson

15 CENTS A COPY: $1.50 A YEAR

Western Advertising Offices:
Tribune Bldg., Chicago, Ill.
London Office: 3-7 Southampton
St., The Strand, London, W. C.

and co-operating. Like all new great movements, while it works some evil, it also works some good. It is but fair, therefore, to enumerate its good as well as its bad results:

1. It reduces cost to a great extent, and so brings a better press within the reach of the poorest.

2. It increases the number of papers published and enables the smallest town to have a self-supporting newspaper.

3. It increases the number of readers by millions.

4. It supplies the best thought of the most expert writers at a rate so cheap that it is bound to supplant the careless writing of local hacks, so prevalent in the past.

5. It brings the latest discoveries, inventions, researches and ideas before the entire nation simultaneously, and so undermines superstition, ignorance and bigotry.

6. It compels all publishers to take a high level—intellectual, literary, social and moral; all editors to be more cautious in their supervision, and all writers to be more careful as to their facts and their composition.

7. It enables the editor of a country paper to devote more time to his local pages and make a better paper, both of general and local news, for his readers, at less cost.

These are the main benefits. Others there are, but of less importance. Upon the whole, the impartial student of history as it is made should rejoice in the success of such concerns as the American Press Association, the Kellogg Newspaper Company, the American Press Syndicate, Bacheller & Co., S. S. McClure, the Franklin File Bureau, the bureaus of William F. G. Shanks, Joseph Howard, Jr., Julian Ralph, Col. J. Armoy Knox, and others of lesser note.

Lincoln Steffens, "The Shame of Minneapolis," from *McClure's Magazine* (1903)[4]

Whenever anything extraordinary is done in American municipal politics, whether for good or for evil, you can trace it almost invariably to one man. The people do not do it. Neither do the "gangs," "combines," or political parties. These are but the instruments by which bosses (not leaders; we Americans are not led, but driven) rule the people, and commonly sell them out. . . .

Well, Minneapolis got its old mayor back, and he was indeed "reformed." Up to this time [Albert Alonzo] Ames had not been very venal personally. He was a "spender," not a "grafter," and he was guilty of corruption chiefly by proxy; he took the honors and left the spoils to his followers. His administrations were no worse than the worst. Now, however, he set out upon a career of corruption which for deliberateness, invention, and avarice has never been equaled. It was as if he had made up his mind that he had been careless long enough, and meant to enrich his last years. He began promptly.

Immediately upon his election, before he took office (on January 7, 1901), he organized a cabinet and laid plans to turn the city over to outlaws who were to work under police direction for the profit of his administration. He chose for chief his brother, Colonel Fred W. Ames, who had recently returned under a cloud from service in the Philippines. But he was a weak vessel for chief of police, and the mayor picked for chief of detectives an abler man, who was to direct the more difficult operations. This was Norman W. King, a former gambler, who knew the criminals needed in the business ahead. King was to invite to Minneapolis thieves, confidence men, pickpockets and gamblers, and release some that were in the local jail. They were to be organized into groups, according to their profession, and detectives were assigned to assist and direct them. The head of the gambling syndicate was to have charge of the gambling, making the terms and collecting the "graft," just as

King and a Captain Hill were to collect from the thieves. The collector for women of the town [prostitutes] was to be Irwin A. Gardner, a medical student in the Doctor's office, who was made a special policeman for the purpose. . . . John Fitchette, better known as "Coffee John," a Virginian . . ., the keeper of a notorious coffee-house, was to be captain of police, with no duties except to sell places on the police force.

And they did these things that they planned — all and more. The administration opened with the revolution on the police force. The thieves in the local jail were liberated, and it was made known to the Under World generally that "things were doing" in Minneapolis. The incoming swindlers reported to King or his staff for instructions, and went to work, turning the "swag" over to the detectives in charge. Gambling went on openly, and disorderly houses [of prostitution] multiplied under the fostering care of Gardner, the medical student. But all this was not enough. Ames dared to break openly into the municipal system of vice protection. . . .

EDWARD W. BOK (1863–1930), editor of the *Ladies' Home Journal*, was not won over by the newspaper syndicates. In his 1895 essay "The Modern Literary King," he attacked what he believed was the tendency of syndicates to encourage literary competition, to drive authors to write for money rather than for art. In his 1893 essay "The Man of Letters as a Man of Business," William Dean Howells (1837–1920), one of the leading American authors as well as a past editor of the *Atlantic Monthly*, took a more measured view of magazine and newspaper publication; he also provided fascinating details about how authors at this time made—or failed to make—a living from their writing. Also in 1893, the prominent New England local-color author Mary E. Wilkins Freeman (1852–1930) embodied the relationship of letters to business when she negotiated serial and royalty terms with her publisher, Harper & Brothers. Jack London (1876–1916), another famous novelist of the period, published *Martin Eden* in 1909. In its pages London satirized the limitations of writing for the syndicates, even though he experienced few such limitations himself.

Edward W. Bok, "The Modern Literary King," from *The Forum* (1895)[5]

The one thought of the author of to-day is to make matter out of mind. The successful writer of the present, once he has secured the eye of the public, feels that he must keep himself and his work before the eye of that public. He must produce and go on producing whether impulse or inspiration comes to him or not. He must, he feels, produce just so much work. He is sincere and conscientious in the hope that what he does will be good work. But if it happens to be otherwise, which is more than likely, he feels that he is not altogether to blame. The work must be produced. It is not a case of *can*; it is simply and purely one of *must*. He is in a feverish race: he needs keep in the procession and as near the head of it as he can. He is driven by a force he neither understands nor stops to analyze. He must eke out his living by his pen, and there lies the root of the evil. Not only does his present belong to another, but his future is mortgaged. He contracts to write books for delivery within the next two, three, or five years, quite unmindful of the question whether there will be a book in him to write, or a story in him to tell, or not. He is simply "under contract": his time, his brain, his mind is mortgaged. . . .With one or two rare exceptions—so rare that they can be counted upon the fingers of a single hand, with fingers to spare—the successful authors of the day are under the thraldom of the modern literary king,—the almighty dollar. . . .

Competition, rightly directed, is always healthful and developing, but a mad, reckless, and senseless competition is injurious. And this is the kind of competition now raging in regard to literary wares. It has nothing healthy about it, nothing stable. The whole thing is on a false basis. It is misleading to the author, it is unfair to the public, and it is rapidly becoming ruinous to the publisher. It is a mad race, honeycombed at every step with pitfalls into which authors, editors, and publishers are tumbling each year. It began with misconception, and it must sooner or later end in misconception if nothing worse. . . .

The monetary basis of literary wares is unquestionably wrong, and the public suffers because of it. The literature given to the people is born of the mart and not of the study. Everything about it has the flavor of money, money, money. . . . The dollar is the curse of our literature to-day. It has become the juggernaut of the author. It is the modern literary king.

William Dean Howells, "The Man of Letters as a Man of Business," from *Scribner's Magazine* (1893)[6]

As I have hinted, it is but a little while that he [the American man of letters] has had any standing at all. I may say that it is only since the war that literature has become a business with us. Before that time we had authors, and very good ones; it is astonishing how good they were; but I do not remember any of them who lived by literature except Edgar A. Poe, perhaps; and we all know how he lived; it was largely upon loans. They were either men of fortune, or they were editors, or professors, with salaries or incomes apart from the small gains of their pens; or they were helped out with public offices; one need not go over their names, or classify them. Some of them must have made money by their books, but I question whether any one could have lived, even very simply, upon the money his books brought him. No one could do that now, unless he wrote a book that we could not recognize as a work of literature. But many authors live now, and live prettily enough, by the sale of the serial publication of their writings to the magazines. They do not live so nicely as successful tradespeople, of course, or as men in the other professions when they begin to make themselves names; the high state of brokers, bankers, railroad operators, and the like is, in the nature of the case, beyond their fondest dreams of pecuniary affluence and social splendor. . . . Still, they do very fairly well, as things go; and several have incomes that would seem riches to the great mass of worthy Americans who work with their hands for a living—when they can get the work. Their incomes are mainly from serial publication in the different magazines; and the prosperity of the magazines has given a whole class existence which, as a class, was wholly unknown among us before the war. It is not only the famous or fully recognized authors who live in this way, but the much larger number of clever people who are as yet known chiefly to the editors, and who may never make themselves a public, but who do well a kind of acceptable work. These are the sort who do not get reprinted from the periodicals; but the better recognized authors do get reprinted, and then their serial work in its completed form appeals to the readers who say they do not read serials. The multitude of these is not great, and if an author rested his hopes upon their favor he would be a much more embittered man than he now generally is. But he understands perfectly well that his reward is in the serial and not in the book; the return from that he may count as so much money found in the road—a few hundreds, a very few thousands, at the most. . . .

The young author who wins recognition in a first-class magazine has achieved a double success, first, with the editor, and then with the best reading public. Many factitious and fallacious literary reputations have been made through books, but very few have been made through the magazines, which are not only the best means of living, but of outliving, with the author; they are both bread and fame to him. If I insist a little upon the high office which this modern form of publication fulfils in the literary world, it is because I am impatient of the antiquated and ignorant prejudice which classes the magazines as ephemeral. They are ephemeral in form, but in substance they are not ephemeral, and what is best in them awaits its resurrection in the book, which, as the first form, is so often a lasting death. . . .

Whether the newspapers will become the rivals of the magazines as the vehicle of literature is a matter that still remains in doubt with the careful observer, after a decade of the newspaper syndicate. . . . It was not till the Sunday editions of the great dailies arose that there was any real hope for the serial in the papers. I suspect that it was the vast demand for material in their pages—twelve, eighteen, twenty-four, thirty-six—that created the syndicate, for it was the necessity of the Sunday edition not only to have material in abundance; but, with all possible regard for quality, to have it cheap; and the syndicate, when it came into being, imagined a means of meeting this want. . . .

[The newspaper syndicate] has placed a good many serial stories, and at pretty good prices, but not generally so good as those the magazines pay the better sort of writers; for the worse sort it has offered perhaps the best market they have had out of book form. . . . It has enlarged the field of belles-lettres, certainly, but not permanently, I think, in the case of the artistic novel. As yet the women, who form the largest, if not the only cultivated class among us, have not taken very cordially to the Sunday edition, except for its social gossip; they certainly do not go to it for their fiction, and its fiction is mainly of the inferior sort with which boys and men beguile their leisure. . . .

The syndicate has no doubt advanced the prosperity of the short story by increasing the demand for it. We Americans had already done pretty well in that kind, for there was already a great demand for the short story in the magazines; but the syndicate of Sunday editions particularly cultivated it and made it very paying. I have heard that some short-story writers made the syndicate pay more for their wares than they got from the magazines for them, considering that the magazine publication could enhance their reputation, but the Sunday edition could do nothing for it.

Mary E. Wilkins (Freeman), Letters to Harper & Brothers (1893)[7]

Randolph, Mass.
May 31. 1893.

Dear Sirs,

I am very glad that you are pleased with my story of Pembroke.

While, of course, I would not say positively that no error has been made on my own part, yet my estimate of the number of words in the story, is still in the neighborhood of eighty thousand. The estimate of the copyist was 79,420, and I paid for the work at that rate.

With regard to terms: the price I had proposed to Mrs. Sangster [editor of *Harper's Bazar*] in the event of the story being used in the "Bazar", was $2500. At my estimate of the number of words, that is thirty dollars per thousand, and at yours, it is not much over. Since the lowest price I am now offered for shorter work is fifty dollars per thousand, this seems to me a fair comparative price, and I hope that you may consider it so.

I am very glad to have arrangements made for the simultaneous publication in England.

Trusting that the terms I mention, may be satisfactory to you, I am very truly yours.

Mary E. Wilkins.

* * *

Randolph, Mass.
June 9. [18]93.

Dear Sirs,

I am pleased that you find my terms, $2500 for serial rights of Pembroke in "The Weekly" satisfactory.

With regard to the publication of Pembroke in book form, could you kindly consider the payment of fifteen instead of ten percent royalty for the first thousand copies?. That is the arrangement which Mr. Osgood made with me for the English editions.

320

I should be greatly obliged if you could see your way toward giving me this larger royalty upon this book.

> I am very truly yours
> Mary E. Wilkins

* * *

> Randolph, Mass.
> June 14th 1893.

Dear Sirs,

The terms which you mention for the publication in book-form of Pembroke, are quite satisfactory, and I am much obliged to you for acceding to my request for larger royalty. . . .

I return herewith the Agreement.

> I am very truly yours
> Mary E. Wilkins.

Jack London, *Martin Eden* (1909)[8]

"But the upshot of it all—of my thinking and reading and loving—is that I am going to move to Grub Street. I shall leave masterpieces alone and do hack-work—jokes, paragraphs, feature articles, humorous verse, and society verse—all the rot for which there seems so much demand. Then there are the newspaper syndicates, and the newspaper short-story syndicates, and the syndicates for the Sunday supplements. I can go ahead and hammer out the stuff they want, and earn the equivalent of a good salary by it. There are free-lances, you know, who earn as much as four or five hundred a month. I don't care to become as they; but I'll earn a good living, and have plenty of time to myself, which I wouldn't have in any [regular, salaried] position.

"Then, I'll have my spare time for study and for real work. In between the grind I'll try my hand at masterpieces, and I'll study and prepare myself for the writing of masterpieces. . . ."

The inhuman editorial machine ran smoothly as ever. He folded the stamps in with his manuscript, dropped it into the letter-box, and from three weeks to a month afterward the postman came up the steps and handed him the manuscript. Surely there were no live, warm [magazine] editors at the other end. It was all wheels and cogs and oil-cups—a clever mechanism operated by automatons. He reached stages of despair wherein he doubted if editors existed at all. He had never received a sign of the existence of one, and from absence of judgment in rejecting all he wrote it seemed plausible that editors were myths, manufactured and maintained by office boys, typesetters, and pressmen. . . .

Encouraged by his several small sales, Martin went back to hack-work. Perhaps there was a living in it, after all. Stored away under his table were the twenty storiettes which had been rejected by the newspaper short-story syndicate. He read them over in order to find out how not to write newspaper storiettes, and in so doing, reasoned out the perfect formula. He found that the newspaper storiette should never be tragic, should never end unhappily, and should never contain beauty of language, subtlety of thought, nor real delicacy of sentiment. Sentiment it must contain, plenty of it, pure and noble, the "For-God-my-country-and-the-Czar" and "I-may-be-poor-but-I-am-honest" brand of sentiment.

Having learned such precautions, Martin consulted "The Duchess" for tone, and proceeded to mix according to formula. The formula consists of three parts: (1) a pair of lovers are jarred apart; (2) by some deed or event they are reunited; (3) marriage bells. The third part was an unvarying quantity, but the first and second parts could be varied an infinite number of times.

IN THE 1880s and 1890s several controversies swirled around newspapers and newspaper reading. In "Use and Abuse of Newspapers," A. H. Plumb (1829–1907) argued that Sunday newspapers destroyed the "spirit and habit of public worship which is indispensable to the general welfare." The anonymous writer of "Sunday Papers Eulogized," on the other hand, claimed that Sunday newspapers served the common good in myriad ways. On a different issue, the anonymous author of "The Newspaper Side of Literature" suggested that newspapers, in pandering to a low common denominator, often failed to live up to their reportorial and stylistic potential. Margaret Lawless, an inveterate newspaper reader from Ohio, protested by letter in 1891 about the increasing homogeneity of syndicate-dependent newspapers. Several years earlier, however, Adelaide Cilley Waldron had come to a different conclusion: for families that received only one newspaper, the syndicate improved the quality of their reading experience. The anonymous author of "The Point of View" held that, while newspapers and mass-produced literature may have seemed to swamp readers with too much reading, these products also taught readers how to be selective as they educated themselves about the world around them. Finally, two illustrations from Lincoln Steffens's "The Business of a Newspaper" show how new technologies were quickly utilized by newspaper publishers to distribute their products as quickly and widely as possible.

A. H. Plumb, "Use and Abuse of Newspapers," from *Our Day* (1891)[9]

The Sunday newspaper is always and necessarily venal. Such an affirmation is a matter of judgment, and of course incapable of absolute proof. The reasons which prompt its utterance, however, will be given, and can be taken for what they are worth. They relate chiefly to the manifest influence of the Sunday newspaper in destroying that spirit and habit of public worship which is indispensable to the general welfare. This influence is so clearly calamitous that it seems impossible that intelligent men can be induced to perpetuate it except by the very large pecuniary profit the publication brings. . . .

No one of the Sunday newspapers has more than the merest modicum of religious reading; all of them have everything that week-day newspapers have, only more of it, to more fully engross the mind and chain it down to the lower regions of thought, the more ignoble and harmful views of human life.

Now the publisher of the Sunday newspaper who does all this for the sake of money, does what he cannot justify, and what brands him and his paper as venal, as unpatriotic. His paper is one of the most powerful of all modern forces in working for the neglect and abolition of all public worship, and the consequent degradation of the moral sense, the corruption of morals, and the loosening of the moral fabric. If every one were to take to reading the Sunday newspaper and were unchecked by other agencies, public worship would go; the Sunday civil rest-day would go; religious and moral restraints in the absence of public worship would be found ineffective to hold the baser elements of society in check, and the very safety of the republic would be endangered.

"Sunday Papers Eulogized," from *The Newspaper Maker* (1896)[10]

In a talk on Sunday newspapers, delivered at Music Hall, Boston, on Sunday, March 22, James Logan Gordon said:

The Sunday newspaper is the most remarkable literary production that the world ever saw. It comes to you every Sunday morning full of the active life of the world, with its energy, its cares and its humor. The Sunday newspaper is a reflex of the commercial world, it is distinctly a family paper, which the daily paper is not.

The Sunday newspaper comes into the home on Sunday morning, the father reads it, the wife peruses it over her husband's shoulder, and the children use it as a carpet, cut out the illustrations to adorn the walls.

The Sunday newspaper is the friend of the American home and the friend of Christian homes. The Sunday newspaper comes around just at a time when the American has time to read and cogitate. . . .

It stimulates thought, and where thought is stimulated bigotry cannot exist, intolerance goes out of the door, and more than that the Sunday newspaper is a great agent against the evils of ignorance, the mother of bigotry and intolerance. . . .

If a pastor declines to compete with the Sunday newspaper, I would say to that pastor, tender your resignation, and in so doing advise the church to retain the city editor of the paper having the largest circulation in the community.

I am ashamed of the church that is afraid to have the church of Christ compete with anything and everything.

"The Newspaper Side of Literature," from *The Century* (1888)[11]

How much of an improvement have we in Hoe's wonderful presses, in the steam which drives them, and in the electricity which makes the modern newspaper "the history of the world for a day"? Its reader has his ten pages a day and perhaps thirty-two pages on Sundays; he has hundreds of thousands of advertisements a year, and is himself numbered among hundreds of thousands of readers; he has daily news of the passing illnesses of crowned heads, the daily happenings of every corner of his own and other countries, everything that may be called "new," no matter how inane or evil. He lays his newspaper down and rises bewildered by a phantasmagoria of unconnected facts relating to every part of the universe, with his taste vitiated by slang, bad English, loose information, everything which can dissipate his mental energies, and with his heart, it may be, corrupted by grosser evils. Is he a clearer-headed, a wiser, or a better man than the New Yorker of just a hundred years ago, who, folding up his "Independent Gazetteer" and not caring a jot that he had not heard from Boston in two days or from North Carolina in two weeks, went quietly home to meditate on or discuss an essay of Hamilton, Madison, or Jay? . . .

It would be unfair to ignore the fact that some of our newspapers do exert the best literary influence on their readers, and conscientiously subordinate other features of their work to their duties as educators. But the typical modern newspaper, to meet the taste which it has created, must surrender whole columns to writers who aim only at being amusing, and often succeed only in being pert, slangy, or scandalous; and it must find or invent "news" items which have about as lofty an influence on the minds of readers as the wonders of the fair had on the mind of Moses Primrose. A continual flood of such matter is not to be offset or corrected by an occasional brilliant editorial, or a half-column speech by a public man, or a "syndicate" story by a good writer. And the effects are cumulative: such newspapers are steadily training a large number of readers to false standards in the only literature of which they have close and daily experience; and the newspapers themselves are as steadily being forced to an adoption of these false standards. In brief, the newspaper of the past, by reason of its lack of opportunity, was compelled to restrict its readers to matter of permanent educational value; the newspaper of the present, through its superabundance of opportunity, is too often training its readers out of all knowledge of or care for educational standards. . . .

With all its faults the newspaper of to-day is a tremendous power for good; for the perpetuation of freedom; for the criticism and reform of government; for the betterment of social conditions. The daily press has reformed many things, and ought to be, and is, fully able to reform itself.

Margaret Lawless of Toledo, Ohio, "A Reader's Protest Against Syndicates," from *The Writer* (1891)[12]

I am a newspaper reader,—I have always been,—would always wish to continue one: like all other habits formed in youth, the newspaper habit is absolute master in its own sphere. I like to read my daily paper, morning and evening. I like also certain weeklies of good standing. I like my own local papers and my state papers; and last, but not least, a fair share of denominational news,—or rather, I did like all these things,—but now —

Is it fair, is it just, that after blinking away a tear over a pathetic little tale in the *Morning Sunrise* this morning, this afternoon I should come across the same tale precisely in the *Evening Shades*, and to-morrow, being Sunday, I'm morally certain that I shall come upon it in the *Sunday Press*; and while I am indignantly turning this over in my mind, I slip the wrapper from a favorite messenger from the Western wilds, and lo! here I find the same letter from New York, the same letter from Washington, the same "Household," down to the tomato catsup and the ham omelet, that I perused yesterday in the *Weekly Giant* of the nearest metropolis! Though a newspaper reader, I am a busy woman, and I know that Monday, when my religious paper comes, I shall have to begin sifting over again, and my resentment grows. . . .

Have we not had pretty near enough of it? There has been some talk of the newspapers displacing magazines in popular favor. Never, while they go on in the ways of the syndicate. We will fly to the magazines with more profound love than ever. We *know* that the leading article in the *Thunderer* will *not* be duplicated in the *Cloud Burst*. We may follow with peace and an untroubled breast the fortunes of the good people in the serials which are taking their winding way through the pages of those great magazines, for we are morally certain that we shall meet them in no other place until they have attained to the dignity of book covers, and then we may seek or shun as we have learned to love or weary of them, but not in a half dozen different newspapers. Blessed, then, be the magazine which gives us such a sense of stability and security, and perish the syndicates which are spoiling our writers and teaching us to fritter, to idle, to gossip, to be vulgar, pushing, greedy, and crazy for notoriety.

Adelaide Cilley Waldron, "Business Relations Between Publishers and Writers," from *The Writer* (1887)[13]

I may find it provoking when seven out of ten of my weekly papers have the same serial, or short story, or extracts from special correspondence, but perhaps the family next door has only one weekly and no daily paper; surely the well-written articles bought by a good syndicate are better for my neighbor's instruction and amusement than would be the trash possibly served to him otherwise.

"The Point of View," from *Scribner's Magazine* (1893)[14]

The contemporary reader is thought to be in pretty deep waters, and doubts are now and then expressed as to his ability to keep his head above them. A century ago there was a little library of classics that he read at more or less, and if he could lay hands on a weekly newspaper he read that, too. Two generations ago he was taking a daily paper, and perhaps an eclectic magazine made up from the British monthlies. The civil war upset his habits and set him to reading all the newspapers he could afford to buy, and weekly picture-papers and a monthly magazine besides. The cheapening of the cost of white paper and the lowering of the price of "news" has confirmed him in the habits he learned then. Such an amount of reading is offered him now for two cents that he feels that he cannot afford to take in less than two or three newspapers, and the magazines are so cheap and so admirable that he must read one or two of them every month. And all the time books keep tumbling out from the presses faster than ever, and, of course, a man who thinks that he has a mind is bound to feed it part of the time on books. No wonder that the contemporary reader is embarrassed, and complains that he cannot keep up, and wants to know what to do about it. . . .

[Today's reader] must teach himself to take his literature in the same enlightened manner, reading according to his appetite and his necessities, as he would eat; not gorging himself because the market is generous; not eating a pie for breakfast nor beginning his dinner with coffee, but taking things as they ought to come.

And especially, if he is an intelligent man and wants to make the most of his day, he must read his newspapers with intelligence, doing it quickly while his mind is fresh, wresting the news out of them like the meat from a nutshell, and discarding the rest. It is easy for him, if he allows himself to do so, to read the newspapers and nothing else, just as it is a simple matter to support life on hog and hominy. But if he is going to read to the best purpose he must have a system about his reading analogous to that which regulates his diet. If he reads the newspapers as he ought to read them, and does not spend his eyes on "miscellany" and spun-out gossip, he will have time to get through them and keep the run of the magazines besides. If he reads the best of what is in the magazines he will read most of the best new fiction before it gets between covers, and will supplement usefully the current information that he gets from the newspapers. If he reads in the magazines only what appeals to him, he will still have time every day to read something in a book; and if he makes a point of reading something, however little, every day in a book that is worth reading, his library will be bound to pay him high interest on its value.

Above all things the modern must adapt his reading, in bulk and quality, to his personal circumstances and individual wants. The very multitude of new books destroys the obligation to read many of them. There is nothing any longer except the Bible and Shakespeare that the contemporary American need blush not to know. If he has intelligence and reasonable culture the presumption will be that if he has not read this it was because he was busy reading that, or was more profitably occupied than in reading either.

W. R. Leigh, "Interior of a Newspaper Train," from *Scribner's Magazine* (1897)[15]

W. R. Leigh, "A Modern Composing Room," from
Scribner's Magazine (1897)[16]

COMMENTARY: THE INDUSTRIALIZATION AND
NATIONALIZATION OF AMERICAN PERIODICAL PUBLISHING

For the most part, the trends in American periodical publishing begun before the
Civil War continued for approximately fifteen years afterward. Until 1880 periodical
publishing remained a relatively small-scale enterprise: the available printing technology was incapable of producing large numbers of newspapers, magazines, and
story papers, and the distribution systems in place limited the circulation of most
print products to local or at best regional audiences. In addition, no large cadre of
professional writers existed to supply periodicals with material to print. Newspaper
reporting was neither a profitable nor respectable occupation, and few American
essayists and fiction authors could support themselves solely with their writing.
Book royalties usually amounted to little more than a pittance (typically 10 to 15 percent of retail price), and in the absence of an international copyright agreement
(which would not come until the Chace Act of 1891), most magazines chose to print
British authors' works, which they could pirate from British books and periodicals
for free or for small honoraria.

After 1880, however, periodical publishing began the process of becoming a large-scale, highly capitalized industry that greatly resembled other industries of the period. The wide-scale use of a number of technological innovations allowed periodical publishers to mechanize their plants and print unprecedented numbers of their issues that, because of the economies of scale, were much cheaper than before and thus could reach new classes of readers. In addition, the railroads by this time had extended their reach to most areas of the country, allowing periodical publishers to regularize delivery of their time-sensitive products to millions more readers than had been possible previously. Supplying the growing number of print outlets with material were thousands of American writers who believed (often mistakenly) that authorship was a relatively easy way to make a living. At the same time, like the managers of many other businesses and corporations of the period, more periodical editors and publishers attempted to control the supply of material from authors and the sale of periodicals to consumers.

Some welcomed these developments, but others did not. Long before the debates over the effects of radio, movies, and television on listeners and viewers, Americans engaged in a vigorous and extensive debate as to whether the flood of periodicals and the organization of periodical publishing along corporate models were harming or benefiting authors and readers. The issues involved were acknowledged by contemporaries to be quite complex, and students of American culture today continue to investigate them in hopes of better understanding the ways in which mass media shape our society.

During the first decade after the Civil War the monthly magazine field changed very little from what it had been previous to the war; still dominant were *Harper's Monthly Magazine* (founded in 1850), the *Atlantic Monthly* (1857), and *Godey's Lady's Book* (1840), although there were a few significant newcomers such as *Lippincott's* (1868) and *Scribner's Monthly* (1870). For the most part, all of these magazines contained few illustrations and printed long essays, articles, and serial fiction by either "old guard" New England authors or British authors. All were published in Boston, New York, and Philadelphia, required a high literacy level for comprehension, and cost the relatively high price of about thirty-five cents per issue or four dollars per year. These factors, along with the limitations of the distribution system, restricted their audience to primarily genteel, northeastern readers.

The literary weeklies or "story papers" fared better in the first postwar decade. These physically large, newspaper-like periodicals sold for about five or six cents and enjoyed the preferential postal rates usually reserved for newspapers. Each issue contained about four to eight pages of miscellaneous materials, including a few news items, correspondence, and sometimes five to eight different serial fiction installments or short stories. The leaders in this field were *Frank Leslie's Illustrated Newspaper* (1855) and Robert Bonner's New York *Ledger* (1855). Extremely popular with soldiers during the war, they enjoyed circulations in the hundreds of thousands per issue until the late 1870s, when their increasing number, competition from dime novels, and the introduction of the Sunday newspaper dramatically cut into their sales and influence.

What was most clear in the postwar decades, however, was that America had been permanently transformed into a country of newspaper readers. During the war, people clamored for news from the battlefields, and a great many newspapers were founded to meet this desire. In 1860 there were 387 daily newspapers in the United States and 3,173 weekly papers, and in 1870 there were 574 dailies and 4,295 weeklies; by 1880, however, there were 971 daily newspapers and 8,633 weeklies (Dill, 28). In 1880 at least one newspaper was published in 2,073 of the 2,605 counties in the United States (North, 73). By the turn of the century, a number of major cities had more than ten daily newspapers. The country was, in short, flooded with newsprint.

In the 1880s newspaper publishers began a major campaign to expand their readership by reaching more women—who, as the controllers of household spending in most American families, were the readers that advertisers valued most. The Sunday edition was created almost solely for the purpose of exposing women to more advertisements. Newspaper editors consequently cast about for material that would make the Sunday edition acceptable reading for women and for Christian families who were not supposed to engage in worldly behavior or work on the Sabbath. The galley-proof syndicates in particular helped editors by providing a smorgasbord of features suitable for reading by the entire family.

It is still unclear whether these newspapers in fact attracted a great number of women readers, but they appealed strongly to working-class readers. The latter became avid readers of the Sunday newspaper not only because this was the working person's sole day of leisure, but also because, despite the Sunday edition's increase in size from about eight pages in the early 1880s to forty-eight pages or more after the turn of the century, its price remained usually only five cents—a veritable bargain of print. As a result, the circulation of the Sunday edition of each paper was usually higher than that of the daily edition. To cite just one example, in 1899 the *Boston Globe* circulated an average of 190,743 copies Mondays through Saturdays in October, but the *Boston Sunday Globe* had a circulation of 253,182 (Advertisement, 1). It is commonly estimated that an average of four people read each Sunday newspaper, so this means that roughly one million people were reading each issue of the *Sunday Globe* in this month. By the turn of the century and in the following decade most major metropolitan dailies east of the Mississippi, selling for the low price of one to three cents daily, regularly measured their circulations in the hundreds of thousands.

Joining the newspapers in the late 1880s and early 1890s were a group of new mass-market monthly magazines that, compared to their relatively staid predecessors, were not only cheaper (five to fifteen cents per copy) but also contained more fiction, illustrations, advertising, and news features dealing with contemporary issues. In short, these new magazines had taken the Sunday newspapers as their models (Mencken, 175). Such magazines included the *Ladies' Home Journal* (1883), *McClure's Magazine* (1893), and the *Saturday Evening Post* (whose focus changed dramatically after Cyrus Curtis purchased it in 1897). These magazines' circulations far surpassed those of the "old guard" magazines. In February 1903 the *Ladies' Home Journal* became the first magazine to circulate more than one million copies an issue, and in late 1908 the *Saturday Evening Post* also topped the million mark. By 1913 five other monthly magazines also had circulations of over 500,000 (Schneirov, Appendix One). This type of magazine dominated the field until World War I, and some of them remained potent cultural forces even afterward.

Why did mass-market newspapers and magazines make their appearance at this particular point in American history? The confluence of a number of related techno-logical, social, and other developments was chiefly responsible. In the 1880s the sulfite process of converting wood pulp to paper greatly added to the papermaking industry's production capacity and dramatically decreased prices for the industry's primary raw material. Also in this decade, the more widespread use of Ottmar Mergenthaler's linotype machines made it possible to typeset much greater quanti-ties of print more easily, quickly, and cheaply than before. Possibly the most important technological development, though, was that between 1865 and 1915 American peri-odical publishers added to their plants more rotary and web perfecting presses and continuous-roll paper dryers. During the 1880s especially, newspaper publishers and, later, magazine publishers, began to install large, automated presses manufactured by R. Hoe & Company of New York that churned out not only words in great number but also illustrations. The infrequent periodical illustrations of the 1860s and early 1870s were woodcuts, but in the 1870s there began a long procession of innovations in illustration reproduction: first zincographs (line cuts etched by acid on zinc plates), then photoengravings in the 1880s, and finally the widespread use of halftone photo-graphic reproductions in the 1890s. By 1915 most modern American newspapers and magazines were graphic cornucopias, appealing to less literate readers with numer-ous illustrations in advertisements, news stories, and features.

But technological innovation was not solely responsible for the increased number, production, and circulation of periodicals. Thanks to the introduction and enhance-ment of free public schooling in many states after the Civil War, along with the soci-etal imperative to teach new immigrants English as quickly as possible, there were more potential readers. In addition, the distribution system expanded its capacity in many ways, thus permitting periodicals to reach more readers than ever before; without this expansion, there would have been no point in producing more periodi-cals. In 1869 the transcontinental railroad was completed, and the total number of railroad miles greatly expanded in the following decades. "Special" or "fast" trains were often engaged, too, to rush Sunday newspapers from New York City to other parts of the country for sale either on that day or the next. A number of wholesale periodical distributors—such as the American News Company, founded in 1864—also increasingly streamlined periodical distribution throughout the country. The U.S. Post Office, however, acted as probably the most important periodical distributor of all. By 1890, 19 million of the nation's 76 million people had mail delivered free to their door, mainly in urban areas, and by 1911 over a billion newspapers and maga-zines were already being delivered along Rural Free Delivery routes (Fuller, 295). Postal rates favored the circulation of periodicals, especially of magazines; under the 1879 Postal Act, first-class postage cost three cents per half ounce or fraction thereof, while second-class matter, including all periodicals, could be mailed for only two cents *per pound* (Postal Laws, 72, 74).

Finally, the growth of national advertising for name-brand products in the 1890s also helped fuel the rise of the great newspapers and magazines of the period. Before the Civil War, most newspapers relied on political parties for start-up capital and operating expenses, and most magazines subsisted on subscription revenues. By the 1880s, however, advertising revenues were the chief sources of income for most periodicals. Serendipitously, department stores were being established at this time in major cities across the country and manufacturers were trying to supplant locally known and/or generic products with nationally known name-brand products. To achieve their aims, both types of businesses needed to advertise heavily in specific metropolitan areas and also to geographically widespread audiences; in doing so, they provided the funds necessary to establish and operate periodicals of all types.

Periodical publishing thus became an industry in the 1880s and 1890s and continued to be one after the turn of the century. Its managers, not surprisingly, began to act much as the managers of other industries of the period did, attempting to control the procurement of materials and the production, distribution, and consumption of their printed products. As one 1908 article in the *Independent* magazine put it, "The modern editor does not sit in his easy chair, writing essays and sorting over the manuscripts that are sent in by his contributors. He goes hunting for things" ("An Editorial," 797). The works of popular and/or well-respected fiction authors were especially desirable yet hard to obtain for editors. As Edward W. Bok testifies in "The Modern Literary King," many periodical editors made contracts with such authors to deliver future, yet-unwritten works by certain dates. In an attempt to help ensure a reliable, steady flow of nonfictional material, almost all major newspapers and magazines also began to construct large staffs that included salaried writers.

Periodical publishers also attempted to control the sales and consumption of their products as much as possible. Assuring the readership of one's periodical was vitally important, because advertisers wanted guarantees that a particular periodical would reach a sufficient number of certain types of readers. And publishers well understood that without adequate advertising revenues, there would be no money to pay for the expensive machines, vast amounts of printing supplies, salaries of staff writers and illustrators, and payments to freelance authors that were required to operate a modern, large-scale periodical.

What, though, were the consequences for authors and readers of these attempts at controlling the production and consumption of periodicals? On the one hand, because of the periodicals' demand for material, thousands of Americans had begun to write nonfiction and fiction, both as freelancers and as regular paid employees. The occupation of "writer" afforded a growing number of people a respectable income, with fewer of the problems inherent in other lines of work. Readers, too, were afforded greater opportunities; there was certainly a wider variety of periodicals available in 1915 than there had been in 1865. On the other hand, many critics have charged that the vast majority of authors who provided material to the newspaper syndicates and mass-market magazines were little more than factory workers who happened to work with pen, paper, and/or typewriter. These critics argue that most authors enjoyed little autonomy and were forced by editors—who always had an eye on what would "sell" to readers and advertisers—to write works on certain subjects and with specified treatments, lengths, and delivery times. Critics have also charged that readers were manipulated by periodical editors and publishers, who supposedly wished them to accept compliantly the messages contained in the various written pieces and advertisements that they published.

Jack London was one of the many authors who saw few advantages in the new conditions. He railed against his treatment by syndicators and magazine editors; it is not surprising that he portrayed his own struggle with them as one of the proletariat versus the capitalists. In numerous advice columns to struggling authors published between 1900 and 1910, as well as in his largely autobiographical novel *Martin Eden* (ironically, first serialized in *Pacific Monthly* magazine in 1908–9), London repeated the common lament that authors were greatly restricted by syndicators and magazine editors who wanted fiction that would please readers and advertisers rather than challenge them. He wrote bitingly of "the inhuman editorial machine" and his belief that "[s]urely there were no live, warm editors at the other end. It was all wheels and cogs and oil-cups—a clever mechanism operated by automatons."

Yet one should not necessarily take contemporary authors' complaints at face value. For example, what London wrote about Martin Eden's experiences with syndicators and magazine editors did not always match the reality of London's own experiences as a struggling author. London himself had two short stories published by the Tillotson and Son newspaper fiction syndicate in 1899 that, contrary to the formula spelled out by Martin Eden in the artifact presented above, jarred the lovers apart at their conclusions, with no marriage bells or happy endings in sight. Upon further investigation, a number of authors' complaints—although not all—turn out not to be completely justified, or at least to demonstrate little understanding of the financial considerations constraining periodical editors and publishers. As can be seen in Mary Wilkins Freeman's letters to Harper and Brothers, at least some authors could deal with their periodical and book publishers (frequently one and the same) from a position of power, successfully negotiating financial terms to their advantage. One scholar, Daniel Borus, has persuasively deconstructed the analogy of writer to worker by concluding, "Unlike the emerging industrial proletariat, writers did not suffer erosion of work skills, sell their labor, punch a time clock, or toil under direct supervision. For all the editorial intervention of the Gilded Age, they kept control of their work process and retained the ability to initiate production" (66).

One should also be careful to distinguish between the conditions under which fiction authors operated and those which governed the work of nonfiction authors. Salaried periodical staff writers were, indeed, expected to write what they were assigned to. With fiction, however, there is little evidence that editors were able to dictate unilaterally the subject, treatment, and length of works. Many authors, as Edward W. Bok notes, signed contracts that stipulated, for example, the length, subject, and treatment of future works. However, these contracts were rarely imposed on authors; rather, they usually resulted from negotiations between the author and the editor. And although Bok decried the way authors had "mortgaged" their works, most authors welcomed these contracts because they paid advances and reduced the insecurity of having to shop a manuscript around to publishers after finishing it.

Bok was one of those in the periodical publishing industry who strongly disliked the new conditions of the 1890s and nostalgically hearkened back to the days when "good" authors supposedly cared little for money. Most of those who shared his viewpoint, though, were editors and publishers who did not like having to pay the high prices created by greater competition for desirable authors' works. Authors, in contrast, generally remembered the earlier days with less enthusiasm, because there had been few outlets available and American authors had their works crowded out of the magazines by pirated British material that could be printed for free. In 1888 Julian Hawthorne had pessimistically concluded, "if our native authors are not to find an outlet in the [newspaper] syndicates, the prospect for them is dark. The magazines are all overstocked, and no author can live on the royalties of his books" (4). As William Dean Howells observed in "The Man of Letters as a Man of Business," the majority of authors undoubtedly benefitted financially from the new competition and thus would have been reluctant to turn back the clock.

And how did the new mass-market periodical industry affect readers? Most had gone from being "intensive" readers of a relatively small number of periodicals in the 1870s to being "extensive" readers who had time only to skim the greater numbers of periodicals being published. Were these readers more informed and empowered by the flood of print that caused this change in reading habits, or were they being trained and manipulated by these periodicals to accept certain values against their will?

Newspapers, the most omnipresent form of mass-market periodical, were often demonized by contemporary critics for having supposedly deleterious effects on readers. In his book *American Nervousness: Its Causes and Consequences* (1881), George Beard proposed that the proliferation of newspapers contributed to the high anxiety levels of many Americans (96, 117, 134). Margaret Lawless of Toledo, Ohio, posited in 1891 that the syndicated materials in most papers were "teaching [readers] to fritter, to idle, to gossip, to be vulgar, pushy, greedy, and crazy for notoriety." Other contemporaries worried that newspapers were training readers to read superficially, for diversion and titillation rather than for education or edification. As "The Newspaper Side of Literature" (1887–88) argues, the new type of newspaper was "too often training its readers out of all knowledge of or care for educational standards," offering instead "a phantasmagoria of unconnected facts relating to every part of the universe." The Sunday editions, supplied with their smorgasbords of print by newspaper syndicates and read on the Christian sabbath, allegedly constituted an even greater threat to the old order, as A. H. Plumb proclaimed in 1891. One 1888 news report indicates that in Downingtown, Pennsylvania, the local chapter of the Women's Christian Temperance Union "classed together whisky and the Sunday newspaper" as societal evils ("Fighting the Sunday Papers," 2). As seen in the artifact "Sunday

Newspapers Eulogized" (1896), however, not everyone shared this view. The benefits and drawbacks for readers of syndicated newspaper materials were also much disputed. Some, such as Margaret Lawless, saw only negative results, while Adelaide Cilley Waldron defended the syndicates for having exposed readers to a better class of materials than they had read previously. This often heated debate about the effects of newspapers on readers, and the numerous suggestions as to how readers should deal with the flood of print, clearly indicate a society in a state of disequilibrium, trying to negotiate a comfortable, proper relationship between new and old authorities.

The newspapers that collectively became known as the "yellow press" came in for especially voluminous criticism in the 1890s. The *Boston Globe*'s Charles Taylor and the New York *World*'s Joseph Pulitzer championed this type of journalism, in order to boost readerships into the hundreds of thousands and reap huge profits from increased advertising. Large-type headlines, copious and sometimes lurid illustrations, a strong emphasis on sex and crime, and numerous articles on pseudoscientific discoveries filled such newspapers' pages. Yellow-press papers also appealed more to the emotions than to the intellect. Consequently their reporters frequently bent the facts to make their copy more sensational. After William Randolph Hearst, editor of the *San Francisco Examiner*, purchased the New York *Journal* in the fall of 1895, the competition between the *Journal* and Pulitzer's *World* became legendary. In fact, these papers' overly sensationalistic, often minimally factual stories about the 1895 Cuban insurrection may have laid the groundwork for the 1898 Spanish-American War. In part because of growing criticism of the press's irresponsible wartime behavior, Pulitzer recoiled from the excesses of yellow journalism and toned down the *World*'s sensationalism. Many other newspapers soon followed suit. By 1910 most metropolitan dailies began to espouse the modern journalistic values of reportorial accuracy and objectivity.

From their very inception, the mass-market magazines, too, were viewed as extremely powerful cultural agents. As one commentator put it in 1908, "They have, to a large extent, fallen heir to the power exerted formerly by pulpit, lyceum, parliamentary debates and daily newspapers in the molding of public opinion, the development of new issues, and dissemination of information bearing on current questions" ("An Editorial," 797). After 1900 some magazines, such as *McClure's Magazine*, *Collier's*, and *Everybody's*, wielded their influence in very positive ways, publishing articles about municipal corruption or corporate greed that encouraged readers to demand the reform of city governments and the regulation of various industries. Some of the most prominent appeared in *McClure's Magazine*: Ida Tarbell's series on the history and practices of Standard Oil (1902–3), Lincoln Steffens's investigations of midwestern municipal corruption (1902–3), and Ray Stannard Baker's "Railroads on Trial" (1906). Although linked to the Progressive political movement, this reportage got the pejorative nickname "muckraking" in 1906 from President Theodore Roosevelt, who welcomed the journalists' aid but wanted them to stop short of causing radical unrest. Like Progressivism, muckraking waned as a concerted effort shortly before World War I.

In recent decades scholars have focused on the potentially negative roles of mass-market magazines in shaping their readers' views. It is still an open question, however, whether or not such magazines truly had the power to create specific socioeconomic classes, restrictive gender roles, conservative racial attitudes, or a culture of passive consumption. We do not know, for instance, whether rural readers reacted differently to the magazines than did urban readers. Quite possibly, rural Americans with a paucity of printed materials found these periodicals liberating: the magazines offered glimpses of a world news and entertainment outside the drudgery of their local, mundane lives, perhaps broadening their horizons and improving the quality of their lives.

The birth of America's mass-market, periodical-suffused society occasioned much debate and even consternation. For better or for worse, American print culture had forever shifted its focus away from books and periodicals directed toward a few socio-economically and geographically select groups of readers and toward periodicals that reached large, heterogeneous audiences nationwide.

SOURCE NOTES

[Unless otherwise indicated material is considered to fall under fair use or to be in the public domain, or a good-faith effort has been made to locate the copyright holder.]

1. "Books, Magazines, and Newspapers," *Journalist* 4 (June 25, 1887): 6.

2. [Allan Forman], "The Journalistic Centralization," *Journalist* 5 (September 17, 1887): 8.

3. *American Magazine* 76 (August 1913): front cover, [1].

4. Lincoln Steffens, "The Shame of Minneapolis," *McClure's Magazine* 20 (January 1903): 227–39.

5. Edward W. Bok, "The Modern Literary King," *Forum* 20 (November 1895): 334–43.

6. William Dean Howells, "The Man of Letters as a Man of Business," *Scribner's Magazine* 14 (October 1893): 429–45.

7. Mary E. Wilkins Freeman, *The Infant Sphinx: Collected Letters of Mary E. Wilkins Freeman*, ed. Brent L. Kendrick (Metuchen, N.J.: Scarecrow Press, 1985), 155–56. Reproduced courtesy the Scarecrow Press, Rowman and Littlefield Publishing Group, Lanham, Md.

8. Jack London, *Martin Eden* (1909; reprint, New York: Macmillan, 1973), 172, 184, 225–26.

9. A. H. Plumb, "Use and Abuse of Newspapers," *Our Day* 8 (September 1891): 209–21.

10. "Sunday Papers Eulogized," *Newspaper Maker* 2 (April 1896): 11.

11. "The Newspaper Side of Literature," *Century* 36 (May 1888): 150–51.

12. Margaret Lawless, "A Reader's Protest Against Syndicates" (letter to the editor), *Writer* 5 (April 1891): 72–73.

13. Adelaide Cilley Waldron, "Business Relations Between Publishers and Writers," *Writer* 1 (June 1887): 56–57.

14. "The Point of View," *Scribner's Magazine* 14 (November 1893): 657–60.

15. W. R. Leigh, "Interior of a Newspaper Train," in J. Lincoln Steffens, "The Business of a Newspaper," *Scribner's Magazine* 22 (October 1897): 454.

16. W. R. Leigh, "A Modern Composing Room," in J. Lincoln Steffens, "The Business of a Newspaper," *Scribner's Magazine* 22 (October 1897): 457.

WORKS CITED

Advertisement. *Boston Globe*, November 1, 1899, 1.

Beard, George. *American Nervousness: Its Causes and Consequences*. New York: G. P. Putnam's Sons, 1881.

Borus, Daniel H. *Writing Realism: Howells, James, and Norris in the Mass Market*. Chapel Hill: University of North Carolina Press, 1989.

Dill, William A. *Growth of Newspapers in the United States*. Lawrence: University of Kansas Press, 1928.

"An Editorial to Order." *Independent* 65 (October 1, 1908): 796–98.

"Fighting the Sunday Papers." *Journalist* 6 (February 25, 1888): 2.

Fuller, Wayne. *RFD: The Changing Face of Rural America*. Bloomington: Indiana University Press, 1964.

Hawthorne, Julian. "Syndicate Matter." *Journalist* 7 (July 14, 1888): 4–5.

Mencken, H. L. *Prejudices: First Series*. 1919. Reprint, New York: Alfred A. Knopf, 1929.

North, S[imon] D[exter]. *History and Present Condition of the Newspaper and Periodical Press of the United States with a Catalogue of the Publications of the Census Year*. Washington, D.C.: Government Printing Office, 1884.

The Postal Laws and Regulations of the United States of America. Washington, D.C.: Government Printing Office, 1879.

Schneirov, Matthew. *The Dream of a New Social Order: Popular Magazines in America, 1893–1914*. New York: Columbia University Press, 1994.

FOR FURTHER RESEARCH

Baldasty, Gerald. *The Commercialization of News in the Nineteenth Century*. Madison: University of Wisconsin Press, 1992.

Bullock, Penelope. *The Afro-American Periodical Press, 1838–1909*. Baton Rouge: Louisiana State University Press, 1981.

Damon-Moore, Helen. *Magazines for the Millions: Gender and Commerce in the Ladies' Home Journal and the Saturday Evening Post, 1880–1910*. Albany: State University of New York Press, 1994.

Garvey, Ellen Gruber. *The Adman in the Parlor: Magazines and the Gendering of Consumer Culture, 1880s to 1910s*. New York: Oxford University Press, 1996.

Hochman, Barbara. *Getting at the Author: Reimagining Books and Reading in the Age of American Realism*. Amherst: University of Massachusetts Press, 2001.

Johanningsmeier, Charles A. *Fiction and the American Literary Marketplace: The Role of Newspaper Syndicates in America, 1860–1900*. Cambridge: Cambridge University Press, 1997.

Mott, Frank Luther. *A History of American Magazines 1885–1905*. Vol. 4. Cambridge, Mass.: Harvard University Press, 1957.

Noel, Mary. *Villains Galore. The Heyday of the Popular Story Weekly*. New York: Macmillan, 1954.

Ohmann, Richard. *Selling Culture: Magazines, Markets, and Class at the Turn of the Century*. London and New York: Verso, 1996.

Scanlon, Jennifer. *Inarticulate Longings: The Ladies' Home Journal, Gender, and the Promises of Consumer Culture*. New York: Routledge, 1995.

Sedgwick, Ellery. "Magazines and the Profession of Authorship in America, 1840–1900." *Papers of the Bibliographical Society of America* 94 (September 2000): 399–425.

West, James L. W., III. *American Authors and the Literary Marketplace since 1900*. Philadelphia: University of Pennsylvania Press, 1988.

Wilson, Christopher. *The Labor of Words: Literary Professionalism in the Progressive Era*. Athens: University of Georgia Press, 1985.

———. "The Rhetoric of Consumption: Mass-Market Magazines and the Demise of the Gentle Reader, 1880–1920." In *The Culture of Consumption: Critical Essays in American History 1880–1980*, edited by Richard Wightman Fox and T. J. Jackson Lears, 39–64. New York: Pantheon Books, 1983.

13

Print and the Creation of Middlebrow Culture

Trysh Travis

SINCE 1900 demographic and technological changes have made books and reading ubiquitous in the United States. The growth of near universal public education created a nation of diverse readers. New methods of paper making, printing, and publishing meant this mass of readers could choose from among increasingly cheap books, magazines, and newspapers. Beginning early in the century, books appeared in a variety of new packages. Hardcover books began sporting dust-jackets that featured short summaries of their contents and brief author biographies. Series publication also took new forms, beginning with Charles W. Eliot's "Five-Foot Shelf of Books" in 1909. Eliot, the president of Harvard, envisioned a series of "great books" that would provide a liberal education to anyone who read them for fifteen minutes a day. For readers who wanted fancier home libraries, companies such as Random House and the Heritage Club produced serial "fine editions" in elaborate bindings, often with new, specially commissioned illustrations. In 1926 New York advertising agent Harry Scherman founded the Book-of-the-Month Club to bring books to would-be readers far removed from good bookstores. In its first year the Book-of-the-Month Club numbered 4,750 members. Within three years it had grown to more than 110,000 and, expanding every decade, now boasts over one million members. In the 1930s and 1940s a number of aggressive publishers ushered in the so-called paperback revolution, and these cheap books quickly achieved mass-market status. Given the phenomenal growth of new institutions like these, it is not surprising that the elite critics who had long claimed "the literary" as their exclusive domain felt threatened. They took aim at these products of the modern age, deriding the new print culture as "middlebrow."

The term "middlebrow" derives from the popular nineteenth-century pseudo-science of phrenology, which claimed that sophisticated mental capacities (reason, logic, dispassionate appreciation) were located in the foremost part of the head, while the lower part housed sensual and emotional capacities. Not surprisingly, phrenological science found that high brows were most common among wealthy, cultivated, Anglo-American elites, while low brows predominated among immigrants, dark-skinned ethnic groups, and the poorly educated working class. In the twentieth century the term "middlebrow" appeared, used by literary and cultural critics to describe the modern texts, readers, and print culture institutions that they believed threatened a long-established hierarchy of genteel and avant-garde literary value.

Critics reached back to the vocabulary of phrenology to express their displeasure with these upstart readers and reading practices because "brow" terminology tied the aesthetics of new print forms to the powerful—and threatening—social changes of the twentieth century.

This chapter explores how the cultural value of print media evolved (or at least seemed to) in response to demographic and technological changes that made books and reading ubiquitous, rather than rare. The near omnipresence of reading affects how historians of the book study the twentieth century. What counts as evidence of twentieth-century print culture differs considerably from what counts as evidence of earlier periods. Print is no longer treated as a precious resource by those who produce and consume, collect and catalog it. Therefore, we cannot count on the carefully assembled household libraries of "average" Americans, the marginalia of devoted but nonprofessional readers, or the painstakingly compiled receipts of mainstream printers to register what reading means in the twentieth century. These kinds of private evidence no doubt still exist, but they are too young yet to have been dignified as "representative" and hence "collectible" by historians and the libraries, depositories, and vaults that serve them. Until the commonplace print culture of the present becomes remarkable for having outlived its moment, we must look to the public domain for illustrations of, invitations to, and definitions of mainstream reading in the twentieth century. The provenance of the artifacts in this chapter reflects this fact.

ARTIFACTS

The artifacts in this chapter represent the middlebrow print culture that emerged around the beginning of the twentieth century, elite critics' attacks on that culture, and individuals' responses to the developments those critics attacked. The first three documents illustrate the ways that middlebrow institutions offered to mediate literary culture for modern audiences in need of guidance. DeWitt Wallace's (1889–1981) 1920 prospectus for the *Reader's Digest* and the 1927 advertisement for the Book-of-the-Month Club (BOMC) demonstrate strategies for attracting members who believed themselves too overwhelmed by the burgeoning literary marketplace to make time to read anything. Random House's 1934 ad "How to Enjoy James Joyce's Great Novel *Ulysses*" shows the ways publishers tried to provide instructions for (and thus attract buyers to) a seemingly difficult piece of literature. *Ulysses* was hardly a new novel; Joyce had written it in Paris two decades earlier, and it had been banned in the U.S. as obscene. Random House purchased the rights to the novel in 1933, and argued for the right to publish it in a highly publicized court case. The publisher's ad drew on public awareness of this controversy and of the novel's complex literary style to attract readers.

DeWitt Wallace, Prospectus for *The Reader's Digest* (1920)[1]

The Reader's Digest:

1. The easiest way in which to learn something really worth while every day.

2. Because of its "boiled down" interest and pocket size—the most practical and the pleasantest means of utilizing odd moments.

3. The one magazine containing articles only of such permanent and popular interest that each issue will be of as great value a year or two hence, as on the date of its publication.

4. The Magazine of 100% Educational Interest—no fiction, no advertisements, no articles on purely transient topics and no articles of limited or specialized appeal.

5. The Reader's Digest in condensing its articles, eliminates unessential and less interesting "filler" which is found in many magazine articles—often simply that reading matter may accompany the advertisements.

6. The one magazine that is preeminently worth keeping—and binding—for future reference and enjoyment.

If it is desired to remove any article, that is an easy matter, there being but one article on a page.

7. The biggest magazine value—regardless of price—on the market. You find one or two articles, perhaps, of enduring interest in the ordinary magazine. The Reader's Digest contains 31 such articles in each issue—"one a day"—each one a "feature" article digested from some periodical.

8. The Reader's Digest believes that a thing really worth reading is worth remembering—which is possible in most cases only if the article is kept for occasional reference in the future. For this purpose, the numbered sub-heads at the beginning of the article will be found helpful.

Many of the "popular" magazines are too bulky to preserve—and not worth it for the little good matter which they contain.

Advertisement for the Book-of-the-Month Club, from *The New York Times Book Review* (1927)[2]

Why Over 40,000 Sensible People Have Already Subscribed to This Service

You miss reading the new books you intend to read! For one reason or another, *you never "get around to them."* That is the chief reason why you should subscribe to the Book-of-the-Month Club,—why over 40,000 individuals, representing every walk of life and constituting probably the intellectual elite of the country, have *already* subscribed.

The purpose of this unique service is not to have someone choose your reading for you or to give you "book bargains." It merely aims to insure *that you will read the books you intend to read*, but which you neglect to read. How does it do this?

You know that out of the thousands of books published, there are only a few you are interested in. You want the outstanding ones. But what are they? The Book-of-the-Month Club has engaged a group of five critics, who select what *they* consider to be the outstanding book published each month. The choice is made, not from manuscripts submitted by a few authors, *but from all the books published by all the publishers.*

The book chosen is sent to you, if you are a subscriber. It comes by mail, *like a magazine.* You can't miss it, by oversight or forgetfulness. When it comes, however, it may prove to be a book you would not have purchased of your own volition. For the judges do not consider their combined opinion any more sacred than yours.

Any book they choose, you will admit, is *very likely* to be one you would not care to miss. But sometimes you may disagree with their choice. For that reason, they recommend and report every month *on all other important readable and outstanding books.* And you may exchange the book you receive any month *for any other book you prefer.*

Note that the final effect of this service is—not that outsiders choose the books you will read—but *that you at last obtain and read* the books you promise yourself to read, but which heretofore you have never "got around to." That is the chief *raison d'etre* of the Book-of-the-Month Club. It explains its surprising growth. The service fills a need long felt by busy and intelligent people, who find themselves "drifting behind the time." Send for our prospectus, which explains how smoothly and conveniently it is operating for over 40,000 people. *The cost of the service itself is nothing.* You pay the same price for your books (no more) that the publisher himself charges. A request for our prospectus will not obligate you to subscribe. Please use the coupon below.

Advertisement for Random House edition of James Joyce's *Ulysses,* from *Saturday Review of Literature* (1934)[3]

How to Enjoy James Joyce's Great Novel *Ulysses*

For those who are already engrossed in the reading of *Ulysses* as well as for those who hesitate to begin it because they fear that it is obscure, the publishers offer this simple clue as to what the critical fuss is all about. *Ulysses* is no harder to "understand" than any other great classic. It is essentially a story and can be enjoyed as such. Do not let the critics confuse you. *Ulysses* is not difficult to read, and it richly rewards each reader in wisdom and pleasure. So thrilling an adventure into the soul and mind and heart of man has never before been charted. This is your opportunity to begin the exploration of one of the greatest novels of our time.

Stuart Gilbert, in his masterly essay on ULYSSES, says: "It is like a great net let down from heaven including in the infinite variety of its take the magnificent and the petty, the holy and the obscene. In this story of a Dublin day we read the epic of mankind."

This monumental novel about twenty hours in the life of an average man can be read and appreciated like any other great novel once its framework and form are visualized . . . just as we can enjoy *Hamlet* without solving all the problems which agitate the critics and scholars. The structure of Ulysses is composed of three elements: the symbolic narrative of the Odyssey, the spiritual planes of the Divine Comedy and the psychological problem of Hamlet. With a plot furnished by Homer, against a setting by Dante, and with characters motivated by Shakespeare, Ulysses is really not as difficult to comprehend as critics like to pretend.

The real clue to Ulysses is simple: the title itself. Just as the Odyssey was the story of Odysseus, Telemachus and Penelope: the father who tries to find his home; the son who seeks the father; the constant wife who puts off her suitors and waits for her husband's return . . . so Ulysses is the story of Leopold Bloom, Stephen Dedalus and Molly Bloom: the father, an average man whose life is incomplete because his only son died in infancy and whom no one will honor or remember after his death; the son, a young poet who finds no spiritual sustenance in art or religion, and who is looking for a symbolic father—a certainty on which he can base his life; the wife, who is the earthly element, a parody of Penelope in her inconstancy, her bawdiness, her animal existence. The theme of the Odyssey has been called "the dominance of mind over circumstance"; and the theme of Ulysses, "the dominance of circumstance over mind."

Each of the characters in Ulysses exists on three different planes of reality. First, the naturalistic which involves the adventures of Stephen and Leopold during one day in Dublin; second, the classical which concerns the parallelism between Ulysses and the Odyssey in respect to the characters, events, and pattern; third, the symbolic which brings in the allusions to philosophy and to Irish history which have given Ulysses a special esoteric significance to a few learned readers. Here Joyce makes every chapter represent a color, a science or art, a symbol, an organ of the body, and a literary technique. But these things need not concern the general reader whose enjoyment of Ulysses depends on its humor, its wisdom, and its essential humanity. Beyond the esoteric significance of parts of the book, and beyond the tremendous wealth of details it offers about manners, morals, customs, thoughts, gestures, and speech, there lies as the solid basis of it one of the most exciting stories offered by modern fiction: the complete, unexpurgated record of a man's uninhibited adventures, mental and physical, during the course of one full day.

THE BOOK-OF-THE-MONTH Club was an established American institution by the mid-1940s, when it published *Black Boy*, Richard Wright's memoir of his hardscrabble youth in the Jim Crow south. *Black Boy* was only the second BOMC selection by an African American author (the first had been Wright's 1940 novel *Native Son*), and it became a bestseller overnight. The letters reprinted here—between a reader and Wright's publisher, Edward Aswell (1900–1958)—show the complex dimensions of the relationship between cultural producers, brokers, and consumers. The selection from Henry Seidel Canby's *American Memoir* elaborates on that relationship. Canby (1878–1961), a professor of English at Yale, was editor of the *Saturday Review of Literature* and one of the original judges of the BOMC. Here he recounts how the judges envisioned their relationship to readers. An additional dimension of the relationship between book purveyors and potential readers is revealed in a letter from Irene Rakosky, who describes the responsibility the book trade has to spread democracy by reaching out to isolated rural readers. Rakosky was executive secretary to the Council on Books in Wartime, a group of trade publishers who promoted books and reading during World War II. Warder Norton, to whom Rakosky wrote this letter, was chairman of the group.

Exchange of letters about Richard Wright's *Black Boy* (1945)

April 22, [1945][4]
Wilmington, NC

Dear Sirs:

I have just tonight read RICHARD WRIGHT'S *BLACK BOY*. It is the first of his works I have read. I'm convinced—from it alone—that he is the deepest, most genuine American writer since Tom Wolfe.

I do not know, of course, how he feels towards 'white Southerners' now. I suppose he must be somewhat inwardly emancipated after years of contemplation and passionate inward struggle over the ever-alive racial issues. But I can say—'white Southerner' though I am—I am aware today that I have discovered a brother in Richard Wright. The realm of the soul transcends race and sex, transcends the detached moments of time and space, transcends even the dependence on a mass-producing publishing house! Ha.

If you think he will give a damn, pass this on to him. It is sometimes good to know when communion genuinely exists even among strangers by accident and friends by nature.

Thanking you, I am
Yours sincerely,
W. A. McGirt, Jr.

April 26, 1945[5]

Dear Mr. McGirt,

Your letter is an unusual one and I want to thank you for it. I shall send it to Richard Wright, who, I am sure, will appreciate it as much as I do. Let me add that I, Wright's editor, am, like yourself, a white Southerner. I was born and brought up in Tennessee. A whole combination of circumstances, which includes your letter, makes me feel that there is real hope for a solution of the most difficult problems as long as men of good will can find a way to speak to one another man to man.

Sincerely yours,
Edward Aswell

Henry Seidel Canby, *American Memoir* (1947)[6]

It took us a long while, too long, to learn a very simple truth. We could not choose a book on the basis of what we thought the public liked and wanted. We did not know. The publishers did not know, as was proved by their frequent (and expensive) attempts to make best-sellers by advertising, and their surprise when some Cinderella on their list was married to the prince of popularity. I should make some qualifications. There is a standardized type of light romance that the people will always take as they will take breakfast-food or sugar. Occasionally a masterpiece or near-masterpiece conforms to this type—a *Treasure Island*, for example—and will sell as well as a synthetic product intended to appeal to the simpler emotions (including the sexual). When minor masterpieces came our way, we welcomed them; but the standardized type did not appeal to us and so did not tempt us to play down to what we knew to be popular taste. Yet sometimes in the earlier years we would take, in a lean month, a just pretty good book, fiction or non-fiction, because we all agreed that this was what the general reader, if not our superior selves, wanted. Such choices often failed, and never succeeded with any emphasis whatever. And we began to see that there was only one safe procedure, which was to choose what we ourselves liked. If we liked a book well enough, the public, whose taste was perhaps less discriminating but at least as sound and healthy as ours, seemed to like it also. The only qualification was common sense. There were books upon which we, as highly experienced readers, might agree which were obviously too erudite, too esoteric, too specialized, or as in modern poetry, too difficult for the intelligent general reader. Yet it proved to be less dangerous to err in this direction than in a choice of the commonplace. . . .

We learned that the general intelligent public, about whom writers and publishers were always talking, wanted leadership even more than advice in their reading. If we gave them a skillful machine-made article from the production line, they were vaguely disappointed, for they wished to read books they liked, but better books, and to some extent, different books from those they had been reading. Why ask to have books chosen for them which they obviously might have picked for themselves? If they were told a book was good and why, and the report was honest, and the book when it came was not out of their range of interest, why then they gave it just that extra ounce of interest, the fillip of expectation, which, as everyone knows, makes the difference between indifferent and satisfactory reading. And furthermore, carries the reader over and through the difficulties of a packed, an elusive, or a subtle book. Many an excellent volume, I am convinced, has failed to circulate as widely as it deserved because of the reader's sluggishness rather than from any fault of the author.

Irene Rakosky to Warder Norton, Council on Books in Wartime (1945)[7]

October 10, 1945

Dear Mr. Norton:

In my three years at the Council, I have always felt that the book industry as a whole could do more than it has to further reading in the United States. The book world seems to be content to sit back complacently and reach the same audience it has since publishing began; namely, the people in large cities who have access to libraries or bookstories, etc. One thing that has not been taken into consideration is the fact that these people will buy and read books anyway. The potential book readers—people living in small communities or farms like the one I came from where there aren't any libraries or bookstories—have been completely ignored. These are the people who have the time to read on long winter evenings when you can't drive twenty miles to the nearest movie or go visiting. Simon & Schuster has taken a stride in getting country people aware of books through their "People's Book Club." Our high school library held all of twenty motheaten books ranging from the "Bobbsy Twins" to "The Campfire Girls" mainly because our School Board didn't feel it important to appropriate funds to provide a library that would whet the appetite for further reading instead of leaving a sour taste in the student's mouth.

The book industry concentrates on advertising and publicity in the book pages of metropolitan newspapers. The people who stop to read this section are undoubtedly interested in books already and confirmed readers. The average person in a large city has other forms of entertainment and probably picks up a book only when there is nothing better to do; or unless it's a "Forever Amber" or a "Leave Cancelled. . . ."

There are any number of projects that could be taken up which would eventually become self-supporting after they were launched, but you need money to launch them. The sending out of radio scripts regarding important books to small radio stations, setting up a service of newsreels to schools, getting a radio program back on a large network, are a few methods by which the idea of reading could be put across. I feel strongly that these mediums of reaching the general public are much more important than the usual reading lists, posters, etc.—which line is more than sufficiently covered by publishers themselves. . . .

This isn't written to criticize what has already been done but in the hope that if the industry does anything in the future, it will want to do more and on a larger scale than we have to date. In three short years, I haven't earned the right to criticize. This is merely the expression of opinion of someone vitally interested in books and who believes they have a value beyond that of newspapers, motion pictures, and magazines, and of a hope that more people can be made aware of them.

Sincerely yours,
Irene Rakosky
Executive Secretary

THE CRITIQUE of the middlebrow was in full bloom by the end of the 1940s, when *Life*, America's most popular pictorial magazine, published the chart "Everyday Tastes from High-Brow to Low-Brow" (based on a *Harper's* article by Russell Lynes) and Winthrop Sargeant's (1903–1986) article "In Defense of the High-Brow." The chart illustrates the modern American obsession with finding one's place in the cultural hierarchy. Sargeant's essay, like Vladimir Nabokov's lecture "Good Readers and Good Writers," exemplifies the powerful ways that elite critics defined the middle-brow: as a modern phenomenon linked to the mass production and consumption of texts and a consequent failure of individual imagination. Nabokov (1899–1977), an internationally renowned novelist, professor of literature, and lepidopterist, usually delivered a version of this lecture at the first meeting of his Masters of European Fiction course at Cornell University, where he taught from 1948 to 1958.

Winthrop Sargeant, "In Defense of the High-Brow," from *Life* (1949)[8]

Though I have some middle-brow tendencies I am, I think, fundamentally a high-brow. I take my culture with a capital C. I wear baggy tweeds. I eschew Roquefort in my salad. I like ballet and Picasso. Sports bore me to death. Aside from a few symphony and opera broadcasts, I consider the sounds that issue from my radio a personal affront. The thing that really stamps me as a high-brow, however, is my atti-tude toward tobacco. I belong to the distinguished minority of chain pipe smokers. I smoke a somewhat obscure but "adequate" tobacco which, I am convinced, is the best in America. But that is not the reason I smoke it. I smoke it because its maker has never insulted my intelligence a) by claiming it is good for my throat, b) by assur-ing me that countless millions of my fellow men smoke it and therefore it is good. I admit that there is more emotion than common sense in this attitude. I would even smoke an inferior tobacco if that was the only way I could have the pleasure of ignoring mass opinion and mass salesmanship. Low-brows would call me a sore-head, and middle-brows would say I was leaning over backward to prove a point. Most high-brows are, in fact, soreheads, and nearly all of them lean over backward.

But look at what they are sore at and what they are leaning away from: in Mr. Lynes's categories, one fact about our contemporary environment is obvious. What culture and civilized living we have today is provided by the interaction of two groups—the esthetically radical high-brows and the somewhat more conservative and stable upper middle-brows. Beneath the upper middle-brows there yawns an awful chasm peopled by masses whose cultural life is so close to that of backward children that the difference is not worth arguing about. Lower middle-brows and low-brows may be bank presidents, pillars of the church, nice fellows, good provid-ers or otherwise decent citizens, but, culturally speaking, they are oafs. Unfortu-nately these cultural oafs make up some 90% of the population.

The thing that burns high-brows like me is that the dominant feature of our mental and spiritual life is the overwhelming flood of cultural sewage that is manufactured

	CLOTHES		FURNITURE	USEFUL OBJECTS	ENTERTAINMENT	SALADS
HIGH-BROW	TOWN Fuzzy Harris tweed suit, no hat	COUNTRY Fuzzy Harris tweed suit, no hat	Eames chair, Kurt Versen lamp	Decanter and ash tray from chemical supply company	Ballet	Greens, olive oil, wine vinegar, ground salt, ground pepper, garlic, unwashed salad bowl
UPPER MIDDLE-BROW	TOWN Brooks suit, regimental tie, felt hat	COUNTRY Quiet tweed jacket, knitted tie	Empire chair, converted sculpture lamp	Silver cigaret box with wedding ushers' signatures	Theater	Same as high-brow but with tomatoes, avocado, Roquefort cheese added
LOWER MIDDLE-BROW	TOWN Splashy necktie, double-breasted suit	COUNTRY Sport shirt, colored slacks	Grand Rapids Chippendale chair, bridge lamp	His and Hers towels	Musical extravaganza films	Quartered iceberg lettuce and store dressing
LOW-BROW	TOWN Loafer jacket, woven shoes	COUNTRY Old Army clothes	Mail order overstuffed chair, fringed lamp	Balsam-stuffed pillow	Western movies	Coleslaw

"Everyday Tastes from High-Brow to Low-Brow,"
from *Life* (1949)[9]

LOW-BROW ARE CLASSIFIED ON CHART

DRINKS	READING	SCULPTURE	RECORDS	GAMES	CAUSES
A glass of "adequate little" red wine	"Little magazines," criticism of criticism, avant garde literature	Calder	Bach and before, Ives and after	Go	Art
A very dry Martini with lemon peel	Solid nonfiction, the better novels, quality magaziner	Maillol	Symphonies, concertos, operas	The Game	Planned parenthood
Bourbon and ginger ale	Book club selections, mass circulation magazines	Front yard sculpture	Light opera, popular favorites	Bridge	P. T. A.
Beer	Pulps, comic books	Parlor sculpture	Jukebox	Craps	The Lodge

especially for the tastes of the low-brow and lower middle-brow. It is difficult even for a high-brow to escape its influence. Only eternal vigilance keeps it from converting us into a 100% low-brow people. This flood exists only for one reason. The oafish classes, being overwhelmingly numerous, are the biggest consumers of everything from salad to music, and an investment in their tastes is correspondingly profitable. They therefore dominate taste in nearly all our big industries where taste is a factor, the most horrible examples in point being the radio and the Hollywood movies. It is, of course, true, that good things sometimes appear by accident even among the products of these industries. But this happens so seldom that high-brows are apt to assume that widespread commercial success is a sure sign of inferiority. Ninety percent of the time they are right. High-brows therefore devote themselves to fostering a type of culture that is not commercially successful. It is lucky they do. Without them this type of culture would probably not exist.

I am not wholly uncritical of my fellow high-brows. Their opinions are sometimes preposterous. They are inveterate faddists. But I find their opinions interesting even when they are wrong. I find them continually turning up new facets of culture that would never occur to their esthetically duller-witted contemporaries. I find them responsible for many of the influences that guide things like the ballet, opera, poetry, modern art, the high-brow novel and the higher-browed productions of the theater—and these things are very important to me. I sometimes get irritated by the preciousness and perversity of my fellow high-brows' ideas and conclude that, after all, my brow may be slipping. But one look at the sheer mass and volume of what we euphemistically call our popular culture suffices to put me squarely back in their camp.

Vladimir Nabokov, "Good Readers and Good Writers" (ca. 1950)[10]

Time and space, the colors of the seasons, the movements of muscles and minds, all these are for writers of genius (as far as we can guess and I trust we guess right) not traditional notions which may be borrowed from the circulating library of public truths but a series of unique surprises which master artists have learned to express in their own unique way. To minor authors is left the ornamentation of the commonplace: these do not bother about any reinventing of the world; they merely try to squeeze the best they can out of a given order of things, out of traditional patterns of fiction. The various combinations these minor authors are able to produce within these set limits may be quite amusing in a mild, ephemeral way because minor readers like to recognize their own ideas in a pleasing disguise. But the real writer, the fellow who sends planets spinning and models a man asleep and eagerly tampers with the sleeper's rib, that kind of author has no given values at his disposal: he must create them himself. The art of writing is a very futile business if it does not imply first of all the art of seeing the world as the potentiality of fiction. The material of this world may be real enough (as far as reality goes) but does not exist at all as an accepted entirety: it is chaos, and to this chaos the author says, "go!" allowing the world to flicker and to fuse. It is now recombined in its very atoms, not merely in its visible and superficial parts. The writer is the first man to map it and to name the natural objects it contains. Those berries there are edible. That speckled creature that bolted across my path might be tamed. That lake between those trees will be called Lake Opal or, more artistically, Dishwater Lake. That mist is a mountain—and that mountain must be conquered. Up a trackless slope climbs the master artist, and at the top, on a windy ridge, whom do you think he meets? The panting and happy reader, and they spontaneously embrace and are linked forever if the book lasts forever.

One evening at a remote provincial college through which I happened to be jogging on a protracted lecture tour, I suggested a little quiz—ten definitions of a reader, and from these ten the students had to choose four definitions that would combine to make a good reader. I have mislaid the list, but as far as I remember the definitions went something like this. Select four answers to the question what should a reader be to be a good reader:

1. The reader should belong to a book club.
2. The reader should identify himself or herself with the hero or heroine.
3. The reader should concentrate on the social-economic angle.
4. The reader should prefer a story with action and dialogue to one with none.
5. The reader should have seen the book in a movie.
6. The reader should be a budding author.
7. The reader should have imagination.
8. The reader should have memory.
9. The reader should have a dictionary.
10. The reader should have some artistic sense.

The students leaned heavily on emotional identification, action, and the social-economic and historical angle. Of course, as you have guessed, the good reader is the one who has imagination, memory, a dictionary, and some artistic sense—which sense I propose to develop in myself and others whenever I have the chance.

There are . . . at least two varieties of imagination in the reader's case. So let us see which one of the two is the right one to use in reading a book. First, there is the comparatively lowly kind which turns for support to the simple emotions and is of a definitely personal nature. (There are some subvarieties here, in this first section on emotional reading.) A situation in a book is intensely felt because it reminds us of something that happened to us or to someone we know or knew. Or, again, a reader treasures a book mainly because it evokes a country, a landscape, a mode of living which he nostalgically recalls as part of his own past. Or, and this is the worst thing a reader can do, he identifies himself with a character in the book. This lowly variety is not the kind of imagination I would like readers to use.

So what is the authentic instrument to be used by the reader? It is impersonal imagination and artistic delight. What should be established, I think, is an artistic harmonious balance between the reader's mind and the author's mind. We ought to remain a little aloof and take pleasure in this aloofness while at the same time we keenly enjoy—enjoy with tears and shivers—the inner weave of a given masterpiece. To be quite objective in these matters is of course impossible. Everything that is worthwhile is to some extent subjective. For instance, you sitting there may be merely my dream, and I may be your nightmare. But what I mean is that the reader must know when and where to curb his imagination and this he does by trying to get clear the specific world the author places at his disposal. We must see things and hear things, we must visualize the rooms, the clothes, the manners of an author's people. The color of Fanny Price's eyes in *Mansfield Park* and the furnishing of her cold little room are important.

We all have different temperaments, and I can tell you right now that the best temperament for a reader to have, or to develop, is a combination of the artistic and the scientific one. The enthusiastic artist alone is apt to be too subjective in his attitude towards a book, and so a scientific coolness of judgment will temper the intuitive heat. If, however, a would-be reader is utterly devoid of passion and patience—of an artist's passion and a scientist's patience—he will hardly enjoy great literature.

WHILE CRITICS deplored the middlebrow, readers experienced it differently. Like the earlier exchange of letters about *Black Boy*, two letters to the *New Yorker*—the popular magazine that published a range of fiction, poetry, and nonfiction—demonstrate the different ways that reading shaped middlebrow individuals' intellectual and emotional, as well as cultural, lives. Like the writings of book trade workers, these personal, historical voices from within the communications circuit complicate and challenge the unflattering picture of middlebrow culture that critics have painted over the years. The final two selections bring the debate over middlebrow culture into the age of electronic narrative. Dwight Macdonald (1906–1982), whose "Masscult and Midcult" became the most famous analysis of the middlebrow, began his career as a film critic. By mid-century he had broadened his iconoclastic critical gaze to include what he considered the crucial problems of the modern age: work, leisure, sex, and art. Like Macdonald, William Shawn (1907–1992), editor of the *New Yorker* from 1952 to 1987, was perturbed by changes in America's communications media. Both men consider what kind of meaning-making remains possible in the modern world.

Reader letters to *The New Yorker* (1951–52)[11]

Dec. 9, 1952
Pines Lake, NJ

Dear Sir:

I don't know how many people who never hesitate to yell when they're annoyed, ever praise as loudly when they're pleased—darn few, I'd imagine. Well, here is a love letter to the New Yorker from one *very* pleased reader.

We first met when I was an extremely sophisticated junior in high school. My dearest girlfriend (and you'll never find closer attachments than those between two extremely sophisticated high school girls) and I used to buy old copies of New Yorker at a bookstore for a nickel apiece. See what a nickel used to buy? I must mention that this was in California—just how those old copies migrated there I can't imagine, but we read them all with great relish, feeling that only the New Yorker could arouse that subtle and sophisticated humor we possessed.

Eventually, of course, I grew older and I hope wiser, but I have never tired, even for a moment, of reading your wonderful magazine.

It trailed my husband and me around to various army camps. Back out to California for a few months, then to Amherst where he finished college, and now in New Jersey where we will live forever, I hope. (I'm tired of sending in address changes.)

I know my love well, but, as in any affair, there are surprises and sorrows. One wonderful issue was John Hersey's Hiroshima. I read it three times through before I could put it down. I was enchanted with James Thurber's learned thesis on the soap operas, saddened, as we all were, by the death of Helen Hokinson. Then, saddest of all by the death of Harold Ross. He was truly a great man, the real spirit of the New Yorker. I felt I'd lost a personal friend. He must have been great to have left behind to others the ability to carry on as he would have. I detected no change of pace or alteration in the quality I had come to expect. I'm a faithful reader, but a critical one.

Other things have delighted me—Rachel Carson's profile on the sea, E.J. Kahn's stories and his wonderful reports from Korea.

What more can I say? Thanks, thanks for past pleasure and the anticipation of more to come.

I love you all, Mr. Minor, Mr. Gibbs, Mr. Coates, and a Very Merry Christmas to all.

Affectionately,
Thelma White

* * *

May 5, 1951
Washington, D.C.

Dear Sir,

I have thought many times of writing the "New Yorker" a fan letter, but have been deterred in the main by a feeling that such a letter ought to be worthy in style of the magazine, and realizing it wouldn't be.

However, I must tell you that I feel more than admiration for a stimulating, satisfying, amusing, and generally delightful combination of articles, comment and cartoons such as you produce each week. The "New Yorker" has become a sort of symbol to me as well as good reading matter. It means intelligence, liberalism, sanity, tolerance, and humaneness—all spiced with wit. I know you know this; you work for that achievement constantly, and doubtless realize you have attained it. Nevertheless, it seems important to me to tell you so.

After I have read my copy, the world's confusion does not seem so unmanageable and hopeless because you and those on your staff have put a firm finger on several essential points in the muddle. I feel I have shared, too, in a cosily human but never sentimental understanding of the doings of our time. You have said what I think and feel as I should like to have said it, and I feel comforted.

In real sincerity, as long as you keep printing the "New Yorker," there are many Americans who have a spokesman, and have fun and have their thoughts given a work-out. The documentary material is unmatched for thoroughness and variety and interesting choice. The cartoons have a quality specially yours (and most appealing to me); the little end-of-page features are wonderful.

But most of all and really important is your ability to puncture the false and, with simplicity and good humor, to exalt the true. You are appreciated.

Sincerely yours,
Constance Moremus

Dwight Macdonald, "Masscult and Midcult," from *Partisan Review* (1960)[12]

We are now in a more sophisticated period. The West has been won, the immigrants melted down, the factories and railroads built to such effect that since 1929 the problem has been consumption rather than production. The work week has shrunk, real wages have risen, and never in history have so many people attained such a high standard of living as in this country since 1945. College enrollment is now well over four million, three times what it was in 1929. Money, leisure, and knowledge, the prerequisites for culture, are more plentiful and more evenly distributed than ever before.

In these more advanced times, the danger to High Culture is not so much from Masscult as from a peculiar hybrid bred from the latter's unnatural intercourse with the former. A whole middle culture has come into existence and it threatens to absorb both its parents. This intermediate form—let us call it Midcult—has the essential qualities of Masscult—the formula, the built-in reaction, the lack of any standard except popularity—but it decently covers them with a cultural fig leaf. In Masscult the trick is plain—to please the crowd by any means. But Midcult has it both ways: it pretends to respect the standards of High culture while in fact it waters them down and vulgarizes them.*

The enemy outside the walls is easy to distinguish. It is its ambiguity that makes Midcult alarming. For it presents itself as part of High Culture. Not that coterie stuff, not those snobbish inbred so-called intellectuals who are only talking to themselves. Rather the great vital mainstream, wide and clear though perhaps not so deep. You, too, can wade in it for a mere $16.70 pay nothing now just fill in the coupon and receive a full year six hard-cover lavishly illustrated issues of *Horizon: A Magazine of the Arts*, "probably the most beautiful magazine in the world . . . seeks to serve as guide to the long cultural advance of modern man, to explore the many mansions of the philosopher, the painter, the historian, the architect, the sculptor, the satirist, the poet . . . to build bridges between the world of scholars and the world of intelligent readers. It's a good buy. Use the coupon *now*." *Horizon* has some 160,000 subscribers, which is more than the combined circulations, after many years of effort, of *Kenyon, Hudson, Sewanee, Partisan, Art News, Arts, American Scholar, Dissent, Commentary*, and half a dozen of our other leading cultural-critical magazines.

Midcult is not, as might appear at first, a raising of the level of Masscult. It is rather a corruption of High Culture which has the enormous advantage over Masscult that while also in fact "totally subjected to the spectator," in Malraux's phrase, it is able to pass itself off as the real thing. Midcult is the Revised Standard Version of the Bible, put out several years ago under the aegis of the Yale Divinity School, that destroys our greatest monument of English prose, the King James Version, in order to make the text "clear and meaningful to people today," which is like taking apart Westminster Abbey to make Disneyland out of the fragments. Midcult is the Museum of Modern Art's film department paying tribute to Samuel Goldwyn because his movies are alleged to be (slightly) better than those of other Hollywood producers—though why they are called "producers" when their function is to prevent the production of art (cf., the fate in Hollywood of Griffith, Chaplin, von Stroheim, Eisenstein, and Orson Welles) is a semantic puzzle. . . . Midcult is the Book-of-the-Month Club, which since 1926 has been supplying its members with

---

*It's not done, of course, as consciously as this suggests. The editors of the *Saturday Review* or *Harper's* or the *Atlantic* would be honestly indignant at this description of their activities, as would John Steinbeck, J. P. Marquand, Pearl Buck, Irwin Shaw, Herman Wouk, John Hersey and others of the remarkably large group of Midcult novelists we have developed. One of the nice things about Zane Grey was that it seems never to have occurred to him that his books had anything to do with literature. [Macdonald's note]

reading matter of which the best that can be said is that it could be worse, i.e., they get John Hersey instead of Gene Stratton Porter. Midcult is the transition from Rodgers and Hart to Rodgers and Hammerstein, from the gay tough lyrics of *Pal Joey*, a spontaneous expression of a real place called Broadway, to the folk-fakery of *Oklahoma!* and the orotund sentimentalism of *South Pacific*. Midcult is or was, "Omnibus," subsidized by a great foundation to raise the level of television, which began its labors by announcing it would "be aimed straight at the average American audience, neither highbrow nor lowbrow, the audience that made the *Reader's Digest, Life*, the *Ladies' Home Journal*, the audience which is the solid backbone of any business as it is of America itself" and which then proved its good faith by programming Gertrude Stein and Jack Benny, Chekhov and football strategy, Beethoven and champion ice skaters. "Omnibus" failed. The level of television, however, was not raised, for some reason.

William Shawn, "The Word" from *The Magazine for Readers* (proposed advertising campaign for *The New Yorker*, ca. 1970)[13]

In recent years, language has been debased by politicians, bureaucrats, academics, advertising people, professional writers, and ordinary men and women. A whole new generation has grown up with a distrust of words. In this same period, the visual image, as employed by television and the films, has come into its own, and has come to be indiscriminately trusted by this same generation; the screen has come to be regarded as a mirror of reality. Rational discourse has fallen into disfavor. Words have come to be regarded as poor substitutes for action. The verbal realm has widely come to be subordinated to the realm of sensation, yet the world of pure sensation is regressive, chaotic, lonely, and ultimately unbearable. It is through words that we organize and master our sensations, and impose some kind of order on our experience. It is words that enable us to reconcile our sensations, our emotions, and our thoughts. It is words that enable us to store knowledge, to pass knowledge on from one person to another and from one generation to another, to instruct each other, to reinforce each other, to comfort each other—to build communication. At its best, television can be respected; even at its worst, it has an important function, and it is here to stay. Films can do things the printed word can't do and shouldn't attempt to do. But the printed word is the life blood of our civilization, is crucial, and it is to the printed word that *The New Yorker* dedicates itself. *The New Yorker* is founded upon the word. By an insistence upon precision in the use of words, and by devoting itself to good writing, it tries to do what it can to maintain the integrity of the English language and to help restore confidence in words. The magazine is read by *readers*—people who continue to find pleasure in the act of reading, and to find sustenance in the printed word. A third of them never look at television, and the rest of them look at it erratically. Since they are also among the country's most thoughtful people, and tend to be the men and women who play leading roles in science, technology, industry, law, medicine, scholarship, and the arts, they constitute a small, concentrated, extraordinary public that certain advertisers wish to address themselves to but cannot count on reaching through television.

COMMENTARY: MIDDLEBROW: THE "PECULIAR HYBRID" OF THE TWENTIETH CENTURY

IN APRIL 1949 *Life* magazine published a lighthearted article entitled "High-Brow, Low-Brow, Middle-Brow." The article was accompanied by "In Defense of the High-brow," an essay by Winthrop Sargeant, one of the magazine's resident intellectuals, and a chart that mapped "Everyday Tastes from High-Brow to Low-Brow" through clothing, home furnishings, charitable causes, and dinner salads. The article announced to *Life*'s readers that "gone are the days . . . when class distinction was determined by wealth, birth or political eminence. Instead . . . true prestige now belongs only to scientists, writers, critics, commentators and thinkers of global thoughts. We have a society of the intellectual elite, run by the high-brows." The article then gave brief descriptions of the different brows and their habits: the high-brow is "basically a critic rather than an artist," a "cultural snob of the worst sort," while the lowbrow's "attitude towards the arts is strictly live and let live. . . . If other people like the ballet it's all right with him as long as he doesn't have to go." These two opposite two ends of the cultural spectrum enjoyed a harmonious relationship. Both were united against "the hated middle-brows," who first usurp and cheapen "pure, non-commercial" highbrow culture, and then "try to sell it" to lowbrows.

The *Life* article brought to the attention of millions of readers a quarrel that had been raging in intellectual and artistic circles since the 1910s: How would the mass-marketing of art and literature affect American cultural life? What would the spread of print culture—the expanded reach of newspapers and magazines, rising literacy rates, and new developments such as book clubs, digests, and paperbacks—mean for literature? Beginning in the late nineteenth century, changes in technology allowed for increased reproduction and distribution of print texts and artifacts, while an increasing standard of living meant that more people had more money to spend on them. Buying, displaying, and understanding books had been for centuries the privilege of the elite. They now became activities for the rapidly growing middle classes, who sought both the intrinsic pleasures of the reading habit and the social power that came with its acquisition. This upset of a centuries-old measure of cultural distinction set off a flurry of criticism. From the early twentieth century on, elite critics writing in specialized journals discussed the disintegration of the traditional order, and speculated despairingly about what new hierarchies of cultural consumption would take its place.

The appearance of "High-Brow, Low-Brow, Middle-Brow" in *Life* magazine illustrates that a new hierarchy of taste, one responsive to the mass production and consumption of culture, had indeed come into being. And since it appeared in such a popular magazine, the article demonstrates the extent to which mapping this hierarchy—and finding one's place within it—had become an obsession for many Americans by the late 1940s. The article brought the language of brows into the popular lexicon of American culture. Ironically, it popularized the term "middlebrow," putting into the mouths of millions of readers the very term elite critics had coined to disparage them and their interest in high culture.

The *Life* magazine chart of the brows gives vivid examples of upper and lower middlebrow culture, but stops short of defining it. What exactly is middlebrow culture? Our commonsense understanding of it as watered-down (or "wannabe") high culture has remained largely unchallenged since the beginning of the twentieth century. The vivid illustrations and authoritative rhetorical stances of the critics who coined and popularized the term "middlebrow" have meant that their *opinions*—which have been overwhelmingly negative—have been taken as *facts*. Consequently, much of our understanding of middlebrow culture, or of what we might call the culture of the educated middle class, has been skewed almost past the point of objective analysis. Recent scholarship in the history of the book, however, has begun the archaeological project of arriving at a more complete and balanced picture of middlebrow institutions, texts, and readers, and their places in American life. This essay first explores the commonsense notion of middlebrow culture as it appears in several classic critiques. It then turns to historical documents to complicate the elite critics' monolithic descriptions. Nonprofessional responses to the evolving print culture of the twentieth century reveal the accuracies and the blind spots of our received definitions of the middlebrow, and suggest some directions that book historians might take in the future.

The phrase "middlebrow culture" has never been neutral. As employed first by elite critics and then by average individuals who internalized their arguments, "middlebrow" did not simply denote a middle point in the spectrum of culture, nor simply the culture of the middle classes. No one and no thing ever wanted to be middlebrow; it was a category to which things and people were consigned. Middlebrow culture was failed culture. But what, exactly, had it failed at? And why did the consequences of this failure seem so serious to some people?

The literary and cultural authority figures who noted the presence of the middlebrow early in the twentieth century, and then bemoaned its growing importance for the next fifty years, were almost exclusively well-educated, white, male, professional critics. Many of them had personal ties to the modernist avant-grade of the 1910s and 1920s and/or the socialist Popular Front of the 1930s. These intellectual genealogies meant that many cultural critics believed art and literature to have radical social potential—the ability to effect progressive change not merely for the individual, but also for the culture as a whole. This potential, they believed, was what made great books great, and it was precisely this quality that the mass-marketing of literature drained away. The politics and the aesthetic tastes of different critics may have varied radically, but they agreed on one thing across the board: modern innovations in literary and artistic production, distribution, and consumption compromised artists, texts, and audiences to the point that literature could no longer serve its historic redemptive, progressive function. In this way, the critics of middlebrow print culture were some of the first historians of the book: attention to (and disgust with) the way modern texts circulated in society formed the basis of their critique.

From this antimodern baseline, elite critics indicted an ever-expanding variety of texts, institutions, and techniques as the twentieth century progressed. Beginning in the 1920s they derided new literary institutions and print forms such as book clubs, literary and news digests, abridged editions, cheap reprints of classics, mass-circulation literary magazines, adult education programs, radio and television programs about literature, and of course, radio, film, and television themselves. Critics' complaints about all these cultural forms were remarkably consistent. One strand of criticism focused on modern audiences, the other on institutions.

The problem with audiences was this: while middlebrow cultural institutions claimed to democratize print culture by making it more available than ever before to large audiences, the individuals these products reached were so diverse, fragmented, and unsophisticated that they could not be dignified by the term "audience." Rather, inhabitants of the middlebrow strata were merely "consumers" of culture, indiscriminate masses with tastes so undeveloped they could not recognize the limitations of the art set before them. Critics scoffed at readers who read for what they believed were the wrong reasons: for moral instruction, or emotional identification, or, worst of all, to prove they possessed the cultural capital required for membership in the new middle class. College educated but not classically trained, these readers were ill equipped to deal with great literature—and it was by no means clear that writers could produce such literature any more.

Critics levied their second major complaint less at readers than at the institutions that served them. New cultural institutions such as extensive book advertising, book clubs and reviews, literary talk shows on radio, and digests and outlines of "great" ideas mediated the relationship between texts and readers. This mediation, which prevented readers from having a direct and honest reading experience, took a variety of insidious forms. It might be distant, as in the pre-selection of "great" books for a book club, or immediate, as in the "digesting" or abridgment of a month's worth of news. In whatever guise, it prohibited the face-to-face meeting of reader and author that the text was meant to bring about. To add insult to injury, middlebrow cultural brokers sold these mediation services for a profit, making it unclear whether their true allegiance lay with art or commerce. With such mixed motives and messages coming from the supply side of the communications circuit, the poor public could hardly be blamed for not knowing what they were reading or why.

Critics' attempts in the first half of the twentieth century, then, to define and explain the culture of the growing middle classes fixated on it as a debased, mechanized version of their own authentic, humane culture. Mass-produced for profit without thought for artistry, mindlessly consumed as a form of social display without attention to meaning, middlebrow culture bore an external resemblance to high culture but was hollow inside. It did not raise the level of the society in which it appeared, but served merely as "a cultural fig leaf" to cover the ignorance and embarrassment of the *arriviste* individuals who produced and consumed it. Elite critics claimed for themselves the privilege of defining and describing this new set of cultural arrangements. It is not surprising that they chose to do so in universally unflattering terms.

For good or ill, elite critics hostile to the new middle classes' modes of literary production and consumption set the terms for the discussion of those modes until well into the twentieth century. Having made ourselves aware of that prejudicial fact, however, we might well ask, is there anything in that first-wave critique of middle-brow intellectual life worth keeping? Perhaps its most powerful and prescient aspect is its suggestion that modern book culture was losing its characteristic humanity and becoming instead a self-sustaining machine. In what was called the "culture industry," humans served two simple functions: first, they staffed a vast, interlocking apparatus for the production and distribution of literary goods; then they consumed those goods and thereby generated profit, which was necessary to keep the machine running. In this machine metaphor, the human sparks that had long been seen as the center of the reading experience—sparks of political empowerment, spiritual transport, intellectual inspiration, or emotional sympathy—were extinguished. Those connections, it seemed, had been replaced by cold cash transactions that benefitted neither the individual mind or spirit, but only the regime of capitalism itself.

While this view exaggerated both the changes in the modern literary marketplace and the effects that they wrought, the image of culture as a machine in which humans were mere cogs resonated profoundly through Western culture in the first half of the twentieth century. The increasing importance of science, industry, and technology, the decline of organized religion and spiritually rich local cultures, and the collision of these trends in two devastating world wars suggested that traditional notions of the book's power within culture might be exhausted. At the same time, as books struggled to compete with new leisure goods and services for the time and discretionary income of potential readers, the print trades were trying to become more like modern business and less like traditional art. Increasingly, they borrowed from other industries the modern techniques of hierarchy, routine, and rationalization. The culture-as-machine model seemed an apt, if dispiriting, way of describing the changed nature of modern book culture.

Not only did this metaphor neatly describe a set of historical forces at work in the world, it also had a satisfyingly poetic quality to it. Critics who compressed the complexity of modern life into vivid derisions of middlebrow culture represented it as a total system from which there was practically no escape. Unlike those trapped within it, however, brave and discerning critics could control this world (to the limited degree of control possible) by naming and describing it. This ability to name and to describe reasserted the power of the critical imagination—the very thing besieged by the modern culture industry. Critics' vivid dismissals of the middlebrow imparted a sense of intellectual and psychological superiority to their audiences as well: Anyone reading, understanding, and agreeing with their denunciations surely could not be a part of what was being denounced! This subtly seductive elitism, coupled with the considerable intellect, creativity, and wit that many critics of the middlebrow brought to their writing, may account for some of the staying power of the highbrow critique of the middlebrow.

But what is missing from the elegant machine metaphor for the changed nature of print culture in the world, and the changed modes of literary production and consumption within print culture, is any attention to nonelite individuals. Readers, writers, and book trade workers inhabited and animated the structures of modern print culture just as they had for centuries. What more do we learn about middlebrow culture if we try to retrieve some of the individual producers and consumers of modern print, whom critics willfully overlooked?

Recovering the individuals who shaped middlebrow culture both reinforces and undercuts the elite critique of that culture. Many of the original middlebrow institutions themselves reflected the idea that culture was a machine, capable of producing more texts than could ever be acknowledged, much less absorbed. Book and magazine production had increased exponentially over the course of the early twentieth century. Readers had to struggle to keep up with the seemingly endless proliferation of print material, mastery of which was a prerequisite for both private well-being and public status. Services such as the Book-of-the-Month Club acknowledged the twin dilemmas of the modern white-collar reader: the inability to keep up with the proliferation of information, and the simultaneous need to do so in order to preserve socio-economic (and personal or psychic) well-being. In its first print ad, the Club asked: "How often have outstanding books appeared, widely discussed and widely recommended, books you were really anxious to read and fully intended to read when you 'got around to it,' but which nevertheless you *missed*! Why is it you disappoint yourself so frequently in this way?" (Sackheim, 118). Middlebrow brokers comforted readers by acknowledging and sympathizing with the increasing complexity—logistical, intellectual, and moral—of print culture. They met the modern problem of overabundance with the modern solutions of delegation and prioritizing. Summary series such as Dr. Charles Eliot's Five-Foot Shelf of Books, outlines such as *The Story of Philosophy* series, and clubs such as the Book-of-the-Month and its many offshoots presented themselves as labor-saving solutions for the harried modern reader. Overburdened professionals (or would-be professionals) could turn the grunt work of sorting, categorizing, evaluating, and choosing among literary goods over to the trusted authorities behind the middlebrow institution, thus freeing themselves up for the necessary (and pleasurable) task of reading the books and learning from them.

The need for these new mediating forms supported critics' contentions that modern print culture, like so much of life, had become massive and overwhelming. The reasons and the ways that readers and producers *used* those new forms, however, show the shortcomings of the culture-industry model. Individual readers did not mindlessly consume machine-generated texts, but turned to texts to find the human within the machine. As their letters to writers and editors suggest, they turned to reading to mediate and to transcend the alienation, impersonality, and moral confusion around them. Individual texts—a book or magazine, or even a particular passage—became talismans, signs that meaning could still be wrung from human existence, and that similarly questing individuals existed somewhere out there in the anonymous modern world.

For even as they offered themselves as appropriately modern solutions to the problems of modern culture, middlebrow institutions announced their allegiance to an enduring tradition of books and reading. Readers' letters suggest that individual texts and the institution of print culture itself retained a powerful symbolic charge that distinguished print from the surrounding world. To many consumers of middlebrow book culture, the linearity of print, the familiar form of the material book, and the continuing elasticity and grace of language itself were reassuring in the face of a world increasingly committed to electronic communication and disposable culture. Book culture, while affected by the conditions of impersonal modernity, symbolized for many readers a different, better set of aesthetic, intellectual, and moral values than those that prevailed around them.

This feeling was shared by book trade workers as well, many of whom saw their chosen profession as a protest against the most dehumanizing aspects of the modern age. Print culture became more regimented and profit driven around the turn of the century. Job titles and duties became more specific, and hierarchies of authority within both individual workplaces and the industry as a whole became more rigid. Pay scales stabilized and improved as part of this professionalization, but workers at all levels experienced a loss of autonomy as print culture became increasingly driven by "market anticipation"—the urge to guess what the reading public wanted and provide it for them before they had a chance to look for it elsewhere (Wilson, 19).

Despite these industry-wide changes, however, the various sectors of print culture actually lagged far *behind* other white-collar professions in their embrace of modern business structures and practices. This was particularly true of the book industry, as distinct from journalism and magazines. The diversified structure of the book trade made it stubbornly resistant to the vertical integration that characterized much modern cultural production. The Hollywood studios of the 1930s and 1940s exemplified perfectly the ideal of an integrated cultural production machine: through their contract system, the studios owned the talent of actors, directors, and writers as well as the means of film production, fabrication, publicity, and distribution. In the book trade, by contrast, distinct individual contractors handled writing, editing, design, fabrication, distribution, marketing, and sales. This segmented business structure forced the industry to tolerate individual input and initiative at many different points in book production.

If the industry was structurally resistant to the "management science" and regimentation that characterized modern mass production, books themselves resisted that other crucial twentieth-century business revolution: national advertising. Books could not (and to this day, cannot) be marketed effectively through long-term advertising campaigns: each title is a completely different entity, and thus requires a different approach. Marketing individual products under a recognizable brand name had effectively increased individual consumption, especially of household goods, since the turn of the century. But when the book trade tried to replicate this strategy, marketing a given publisher as a "brand," with individual titles as "products," the results were remarkably lackluster: as one publisher observed, "the reader doesn't say, as he lays down *Hugh Wynne*, 'Give me The Century Company's books or none!'" (Sheehan, 187). These structural peculiarities of the book industry did not prevent it from modernizing, but they did keep it from doing so wholeheartedly or efficiently.

It is probably not the case that any person chose to enter the book profession because it lagged behind other white-collar fields in its embrace of modernity, and plenty of book trade workers (or "bookmen," as they called themselves) chafed at and tried to overturn its inefficiencies. But many bookmen took a certain pride in the trade's anachronistic idiosyncrasies, which they saw as links to a more contemplative, humane time. Like readers, they were drawn to print culture's rich tradition, its heritage of respect for individual thought and expression. The comparatively antiquated business structure of the industry, combined with this historical residue, allowed book trade workers to see their jobs as more meaningful than other white-collar professions.

This sense that print culture had a unique and distinguished place in the modern world took an explicitly political turn during and after World War II. The book industry threw itself into the war effort. Early on, librarians and wage workers in book manufacturing coordinated donations of more than 10 million books for troop libraries through the Victory Book Campaign and the Book Mobilization Committee. Later in the war, the heads of established publishing houses formed the Council on Books in Wartime, which produced 123 million paperback books for free distribution to GIs at home and abroad. This work was self-interested in one sense: publishers hoped that free books would cultivate new readers, who would then become book buyers in peacetime. At the same time, however, promotional slogans like the Victory Book Campaign's "Praise the Lord and Pass the New Editions!" and the Council on Books in Wartime's "Books are Weapons in the War of Ideas!" dignified books and reading by giving them a privileged place in America's history, and therefore in its war against totalitarianism.

The book's uniqueness was heightened by the fact that totalitarian regimes abroad relied heavily on mass-produced entertainment technologies such as photography, radio, and cinema to disseminate propaganda. By stressing America's history of a free press, and their own role in that history, bookmen identified themselves as stewards of democracy and linked their work to the preservation of America's liberal heritage and its spread across the globe. From this perspective, modern, large-scale book production and distribution and a net increase in the size of the reading public seemed signs of a triumphant, not a dispiriting, modernity. During the Cold War of the 1950s and 1960s, publishers worked with private philanthropists and the federal government to establish programs such as Franklin Book Programs, Inc., and Books U.S.A. This "cultural diplomacy," as it was called, sought to win adherents to America's version of capitalist democracy by showing the citizens of developing nations the rich cultural benefits of that system of government. What better object than the book—inexpensive, accessible, and free of the taint of propaganda—to symbolize the virtues of life in a modern democracy? In this way, even as intellectuals debated whether cultural democracy made for banal reading and weak readers, books remained at the center of the nation's thinking about political democracy.

Like their readers, bookmen embraced the sense of historical tradition they saw embodied in the American book, as well as the power of the written word in general. Because of this, the making of books—as opposed to other cultural products—seemed a particularly meaningful kind of work. Also like readers, book trade workers gained a sense of personal integrity through their connection to print culture, in part because of the relatively autonomous structure of their day-to-day work lives, and in part because of the sense—reinforced by readers—that the texts they produced did good work in the world. Far from mere cogs in a culture industry machine, bookmen saw their commitment to publishing as a means of resisting what was worst and championing what was best in the modern world.

Recovering the actual middle-class producers and consumers of middlebrow culture, then, suggests that the mass-market print forms and institutions lumped together under the label "middlebrow" provided many individuals with answers to the confusions of the twentieth century. This starkly contrasts with the elite critics' powerful view, which saw those same forms and institutions as symptoms of modernity's cultural decline. Both views register the enormous economic, demographic, and social changes that wrenched society from the late-nineteenth century onward, bringing into being dozens of new print forms and thousands of new readers. Otherwise, however, these two views of the middlebrow and what it means have little in common.

Scholars and members of the general public alike continue to disagree as to which assessment of modernity's impact on publishing, writing, and reading is more correct. Is it the view of elite critics, who saw (and see) a qualitative decline in print culture and literacy as "great literature" gives way to digests, comics, and book clubs? Or is it the perspective of nonprofessional readers, who looked (and look) to biographies, reviews, and genre fiction for instruction and inspiration in how to navigate a confusing world? As the history of the book evolves as a field, it may move toward one or the other of these interpretive poles. In the meantime, however, much work remains to be done in defining and understanding the two groups that meet on the contested terrain of the middlebrow: the anxious, despairing critics who popularized the category, and "the curious intelligent readers" who for so long have inhabited it (Fadiman, 2).

SOURCE NOTES

1. DeWitt Wallace, Prospectus for *The Reader's Digest*. Collection of Dr. Stephen Lomazow, Montclair, N.J. Reproduced courtesy of the Reader's Digest Association, Inc. Copyright © 1920 the Reader's Digest Association, Inc., Pleasantville, N.Y.

2. *New York Times Book Review,* January 30, 1927, 19. Reproduced courtesy of the Book-of-the-Month Club, New York, N.Y.

3. *Saturday Review of Literature* 10 (February 10, 1934): 474–75. Reproduced courtesy of Random House, Inc. Copyright © Random House, Inc., New York, N.Y.

4. Harper & Brothers Archives, Manuscripts Division of the Department of Rare Books and Special Collections, Princeton University Library. Reproduced courtesy of the Princeton University Library, Princeton, N.J.

5. Richard Wright Papers, James Weldon Johnson Collection, Yale Collection of American Literature, Beinecke Library, Yale University. Reproduced courtesy of Mary Aswell Doll.

6. Henry Seidel Canby, *American Memoir* (Boston: Houghton Mifflin, 1947), 361–63. Reproduced courtesy of Houghton Mifflin Company. All rights reserved. Copyright © 1934, 1936, and 1947 by Henry Seidel Canby. Copyright © renewed 1975 by Edward T. Canby.

7. In Public Policy Papers, The Council on Books in Wartime Archives, Seeley G. Mudd Manuscript Library, Princeton University Library. Reproduced courtesy of the Princeton University Library, Princeton, N.J.

8. *Life* 26 (April 11, 1949): 102.

9. Ibid., 100–101.

10. Vladimir Nabokov, *Lectures on Literature*, ed. Fredson Bowers (New York: Harcourt Brace Jovanovich, 1980), 2–5. Reproduced courtesy of Harcourt, Inc. Copyright © 1980 the estate of Vladimir Nabokov.

11. *The New Yorker* Records, Manuscripts and Archives Division, The New York Public Library, Astor, Lenox, and Tilden Foundations. Reproduced courtesy of the New York Public Library.

12. Dwight Macdonald, *Against the American Grain* (New York: Vintage Books, 1962), 36–40.

13. *The New Yorker* Records, Manuscripts and Archives Division, The New York Public Library, Astor, Lenox, and Tilden Foundations. Reproduced courtesy of the New York Public Library.

WORKS CITED

Fadiman, Clifton. "To the Curious, Intelligent Reader." Remarks in Acceptance of the National Book Foundation Medal for Distinguished Contribution to American Letters, November 17, 1993.

Sackheim, Maxwell. *My First Sixty Years in Advertising.* Englewood Cliffs, N.J.: Prentice-Hall, 1970.

Sheehan, Donald. *This Was Publishing: A Chronicle of the Book Trade in the Gilded Age.* Bloomington: Indiana University Press, 1952.

Wilson, Christopher. *The Labor of Words: Literary Professionalism in the Progressive Era.* Athens: University of Georgia Press, 1985.

FOR FURTHER RESEARCH

Adorno, Theodor, and Max Horkheimer. "The Culture Industry: Enlightenment as Mass Deception." In *The Dialectic of Enlightenment,* translated by John Cumming, 120–67. New York: Herder and Herder, 1969.

Benton, Megan. *Beauty and the Book: Fine Editions and Cultural Distinction in America.* New Haven, Conn.: Yale University Press, 2000.

Bonn, Thomas. *Heavy Traffic and High Culture: New American Library as Gatekeeper in the Paperback Revolution.* Carbondale: Southern Illinois University Press, 1989.

Bourdieu, Pierre. *Distinction: A Social Critique of the Judgement of Taste*, translated by Richard Nice. Cambridge, Mass.: Harvard University Press, 1984.

Coser, Lewis, Charles Kadushin, and Walter Powell. *Books: The Culture and Commerce of Publishing*. New York: Basic Books, 1982.

Ehrenreich, Barbara and John. "The Professional-Managerial Class." In *Between Labor and Capital*, edited by Pat Walker, 5–48. Montreal: Black Rose Books, 1978.

Hurley, Cheryl. "The Story of the Library of America." *Publishing Research Quarterly* 12 (Winter 1996/97): 36–49.

Kaestle, Carl, and Helen Damon-Moore et al. *Literacy in the United States: Readers and Reading since 1880*. New Haven, Conn.: Yale University Press, 1991.

Kammen, Michael. *American Culture, American Tastes: Social Change and the 20th Century*. New York: Alfred A. Knopf, 1999.

Levine, Lawrence. *Highbrow/Lowbrow: The Emergence of Cultural Hierarchy in America*. Cambridge, Mass.: Harvard University Press, 1988.

Medovoi, Leerom. "Democracy, Capitalism, and American Literature: The Cold War Construction of J. D. Salinger's Paperback Hero." In *The Other Fifties: Integrating Midcentury American Icons*, edited by Joel Freeman, 255–87. Urbana and Chicago: University of Illinois Press, 1997.

Ohmann, Richard. *Politics of Letters*. Middletown, Conn.: Wesleyan University Press, 1987.

Preer, Jean. "The Wonderful World of Books: Librarians, Publishers, and Rural Readers." *Libraries & Culture* 32 (Fall 1997): 403–26.

Radway, Janice. *A Feeling for Books: The Book-of-the-Month-Club, Literary Taste, and Middle-Class Desire*. Chapel Hill: University of North Carolina Press, 1997.

———. "Reading Is Not Eating: Mass-Produced Literature and the Theoretical, Methodological, and Political Consequences of a Metaphor." *Publishing Research Quarterly* 2 (Fall 1986): 7–29.

———. *Reading the Romance: Women, Patriarchy, and Popular Literature*. Chapel Hill: University of North Carolina Press, 1984.

Rubin, Joan Shelley. *The Making of Middlebrow Culture*. Chapel Hill: University of North Carolina Press, 1992.

Stefferud, Alfred, ed. *The Wonderful World of Books*. Boston: Houghton Mifflin, 1953.

Strychacz, Thomas. *Modernism, Mass Culture, and Professionalism*. New York: Cambridge University Press, 1993.

Susman, Warren. *Culture as History: The Transformation of American Society in the Twentieth Century*. New York: Pantheon Books, 1984.

Travis, Trysh. "What We Talk About When We Talk About *The New Yorker*." *Book History* 3 (2000): 253–85.

Wilson, Christopher. *White Collar Fictions: Class and Social Representation in American Literature, 1885–1925*. Athens: University of Georgia Press, 1992.

Wright, Paul. "The Library of America: An American Pléiade." *Antioch Review* 44 (Fall 1986): 467–80.

14

Out of the Mainstream and into the Streets
Small Press Magazines, the Underground Press, Zines, and Artists' Books

ELLEN GRUBER GARVEY

MANY OF the chapters in this book focus on readily visible, large-scale developments in publishing. They show how early American printers influenced daily life, how they affected the political course of empire and nation, how in the nineteenth century new technologies and economies increased print production and distribution, how American publishers helped to bring a national literature into existence, and how the massive reach of periodicals helped to create a national reading culture. Much of this book, then, addresses what we might call "mainstream publishing," that part of the publishing world which is most heavily capitalized and commercial, which distributes its products most widely.

The mainstream, however, is not the only current. This chapter explores the ways in which many Americans have expressed themselves in print without using the dominant publishing establishment. The means of print production have become so ubiquitous, so common, so inexpensive in our time that print itself cannot be controlled—or even effectively regulated—by a particular profession, industry, or class. Various nineteenth- and twentieth-century technologies for print reproduction—typewriters, photography, hobby printing presses, mimeograph machines, desktop publishing software, and photocopiers—have made it easier for people to put their ideas into print. Typically, print productions outside the mainstream have reached a limited and specialized audience, but today a new technology, the World Wide Web, promises that every electronic text has the potential to reach millions of readers.

Publishing outside of the mainstream is not a new development. For instance, in the second half of the nineteenth century, hobby printers all over the country published "amateur newspapers" and even founded associations to promote their passion. And a little later, many artists, authors, and printers founded "small presses" that published works perceived to have little chance of succeeding in the commercial publishing world. Much though not all alternative publishing has been produced on a shoestring and has featured the voices of those who might not otherwise get a hearing: gays and lesbians, members of dissident political groups, racial and ethnic minorities, avant-garde artists and authors, and so on. Alternative publishing, then, demands that we see print culture from a new and challenging perspective, to appreciate both the diversity and power of a print-oriented world.

ARIFACTS

"Little magazines," a type of literary magazine that began to appear in the 1890s, typically reached small and specialized audiences. They were often—and continue to be—conduits for experimental or politically challenging literature. The first artifacts in this chapter come from their founding statements and public rationales. In 1912 Harriet Monroe (1860–1936) introduced *Poetry: A Magazine of Verse*, an influential periodical that she edited and published until her death. In "The Motive of the Magazine," Monroe envisioned her journal as an alternative to "the popular magazines." In 1929 Margaret Anderson, who founded the *Little Review* fifteen years earlier as a journal that would make "no compromise with the public taste," looked back on her reasons for starting the monthly and described why she decided to discontinue it. A quarter century later, the novelist William Styron (b. 1925) framed the *Paris Review*'s introductory remarks as a letter *to* its editors. Self-consciously playing with the convention of the first-issue manifesto, Styron discussed the process of hammering out the journal's intentions. He positioned the journal as anti-political and free of the current jargon of literary criticism he found infesting other literary magazines. While the *Paris Review* of the Cold War sought to place literature outside of political beliefs and activism, several artifacts from the 1960s and 1970s demonstrate the political potential of these organs. The editors of *Freedomways*, which appeared in 1961, a year after the first sit-ins, announced that it would serve the cause of African American rights by providing "a vehicle of communication" for a people struggling against discrimination and segregation. In 1962 Ed Sanders founded *Fuck You: A Magazine of the Arts*, a mimeograph journal that featured poetry and political advocacy. With a nod to Allen Ginsberg, Sanders hoped to publish the work of the "Best Minds" of his generation; Harry Smith (b. 1936), who began publishing the *Smith* in 1964, fronted a kindred sort of rhetoric of the "finest" to claim aesthetic high ground. *Aphra*, a feminist journal that began publication in 1969, was named after Aphra Behn, a seventeenth-century professional woman writer. The "Preamble" to *Aphra* announced that the journal would confront dominant cultural and media stereotypes about women. In a special black women's issue of *Conditions* in 1979, a feminist magazine that emphasized lesbian writing, Lorraine Bethel and Barbara Smith called attention to the shortcomings of other feminist publications that had not sought out writing by African American feminists and lesbians.

Harriet Monroe, "The Motive of the Magazine," from *Poetry: A Magazine of Verse* (1912)[1]

In the huge democracy of our age no interest is too slight to have an organ. Every sport, every little industry requires its own corner, its own voice, that it may find its friends, greet them, welcome them.

The arts especially have need of each an entrenched place, a voice of power, if they are to do their work and be heard. For as the world grows greater day by day, as every member of it, through something he buys or knows or loves, reaches out to the ends of the earth, things precious to the race, things rare and delicate, may be overpowered, lost in the criss-cross of modern currents, the confusion of modern immensities.

Painting, sculpture, music are housed in palaces in the great cities of the world; and every week or two a new periodical is born to speak for one or the other of them, and tenderly nursed at some guardian's expense. Architecture, responding to commercial and social demands, is whipped into shape by the rough and tumble of life and fostered, willy-nilly, by men's material needs. Poetry alone, of all the fine arts, has been left to shift for herself in a world unaware of its immediate and desperate need of her. . . .

The present venture is a modest effort to give to poetry her own place, her own voice. The popular magazines can afford her but scant courtesy—a Cinderella corner in the ashes—because they seek a large public which is not hers, a public which buys them not for their verse but for their stories, pictures, journalism, rarely for their literature, even in prose. Most magazine editors say that there is no public for poetry in America; one of them wrote to a young poet that the verse his monthly accepted "must appeal to the barber's wife of the Middle West," and others prove their distrust by printing less verse from year to year, and that rarely beyond page-end length and importance.

We believe that there is a public for poetry, that it will grow, and that as it becomes more numerous and appreciative the work produced in this art will grow in power, in beauty, in significance. . . .

We hope to publish in *Poetry* some of the best work now being done in English verse. . . . [W]e shall be able to print poems longer, and of more intimate and serious character, than the popular magazines can afford to use. The test, limited by ever-fallible human judgment, is to be quality alone; all forms, whether narrative, dramatic or lyric, will be acceptable. We hope to offer our subscribers a place of refuge, a green isle in the sea, where Beauty may plant her gardens, and Truth, austere revealer of joy and sorrow, of hidden delights and despairs, may follow her brave quest unafraid.

Margaret Anderson, "Editorial," from *The Little Review* (1929)[2]

I began *The Little Review* because I wanted an intelligent life.

By intelligent I didn't—and don't—mean (1) the ability to follow an argument, (2) the capacity for documentation, (3) the gift of erudition, authority, strong physical vibrations, or any of the other primary signs by which people seem to get labelled intelligent at the moment when I am finding them particularly uninteresting.

By intelligence I meant=creative opinion.

There was no creative opinion in Indianapolis, Indiana, in 1912. So I went to Chicago and tried to produce it, in 1914, by founding *The Little Review*.

It was the moment. The epoch needed it, the modern literary movement needed it. But this was of relative unimportance to me. I really began *The Little Review* the way one begins playing the piano or writing poetry: because of something one wants violently. The thing I wanted—would die without—was conversation. The only way to get it was to reach people with ideas. Only artists had ideas . . . and of course only the very good ones. So I made a magazine exclusively for the very good artists of the time. Nothing more simple for me than to be the art arbiter of the world.

I still feel the same way—with a rather important exception. . . . [E]ven the artist doesn't know what he is talking about. And I can no longer go on publishing a magazine in which no one really knows what he is talking about. It doesn't interest me.

Bill Styron, "Letter to an Editor," from *The Paris Review* (1953)[3]

Dear ———:

The preface which you all wanted me to write, and which I wanted to write, and finally wrote, came back to me from Paris today so marvelously changed and re-worded that it seemed hardly mine. Actually, you know, it shouldn't be mine. Prefaces are usually communal enterprises and they have a stern dull quality of group effort about them—of Manifesto, Proclamation of Aims, of "Where We Stand"—of editors huddled together in the smoke-laden, red-eyed hours of early morning, pruning and balancing syntax, juggling terms and, because each editor is an individual with different ideas, often compromising away all those careless personal words that make an individualistic statement exciting, or at least interesting. Prefaces, I'll admit, are a bore and consequently, more often than not, go unread. The one I sent you, so balanced and well-mannered and so dull—I could hardly read it myself when I finished it—when it came back to me with your emendations and corrections I couldn't read it at all. This, I realize, is the fault of neither or none of us; it's inevitable that what Truth I mumble to you at Lipp's over a beer, or that Ideal we are perfectly agreed upon at the casual hour of 2 A.M. becomes powerfully open to criticism as soon as it's cast in a printed form which, like a piece of sculpture, allows us to walk all around that Truth or Ideal and examine it front, side, and behind, and for minutes on end. Everyone starts hacking off an arm, a leg, an ear—and you end up with a lump. At any rate, I'd like to go over briefly a few of the things you questioned; we'll still no doubt disagree, but that's probably for the better. There are magazines, you know, where a questioning word amounts to dishonesty, and disagreement means defection.

First, I said, "Literarily speaking, we live in what has been described as the Age of Criticism. Full of articles on Kafka and James, on Melville, or whatever writer is in momentary ascendancy; laden with terms like "architectonic," "Zeitgeist," and "dichotomous," the literary magazines seem today on the verge of doing away with literature, not with any philistine bludgeon but by smothering it under the weight of learned chatter." . . .

All right, then I said, "There is little wonder . . . that, faced with Œdipus and Myth in Charlotte Bronte, with meter in Pope and darkness in Dante, we put aside our current quarterly with its two short poems, its one intellectualized short story, in deference to *Life,* which brings us at least "The Old Man and the Sea." This, of course, as you remember, was only by way of getting to the first brave part of the Manifesto: that THE PARIS REVIEW would strive to give predominant space to the fiction and poetry of both established and new writers, rather than to people who use words like *Zeitgeist.* Now in rebuttal, one of you has written that it is not always editorial policy that brings such a disproportion of critical manuscripts across the editors' desks, pointing out that "in our schools and colleges all the emphasis is on analysis and organization of ideas, not creation." The result is that we have critics, not creators, and you go on to suggest that, since this is the natural state of things, we should not be too haughty in stating our intention of having more fiction and poetry in THE PARIS REVIEW.

To this I can only say: *d'accord.* Let's by all means leave out the lordly tone and merely say: dear reader, THE PARIS REVIEW *hopes* to emphasize creative work—fiction and poetry—not to the exclusion of criticism, but with the aim in mind of merely removing criticism from the dominating place it holds in most literary magazines and putting it pretty much where it belongs, i.e., somewhere near the back of the book. . . .

Among the other points I tried to make was one which involved THE PARIS REVIEW having no axe to grind. In this we're pretty much in agreement, I believe, although one of you mentioned the fact that in the first number of *The Exile* there were "powerful blasts" by Pound, among others, which added considerably to the interest of the magazine. True, perhaps. But is it because we're sissies that we plan to beat no drum for anything; is it only because we're wan imitations of our predecessors—those who came out bravely for anything they felt deeply enough was worth coming out bravely for? I don't think so. I think that if we have no axes to grind, no drums to beat, it's because it seems to us—for the moment, at least—that the axes have all been ground, the drumheads burst with beating.

Editors' statement, from *Freedomways* (1961)[4]

IT'S A JOURNAL!

We are here.

Conceived of necessity and with impetuous ardour, born in travail, this newest, youngest publication is yet a lusty, bawling infant. This is a good world and a good time in which we are born. For we are African-American, and our name is FREEDOMWAYS.

In scope, militancy and effectiveness the Negro Freedom Movement is attaining maturity. This fact of determined effort to "walk with dignity" is the most vital reality in Negro life today. It stands out on every level and in every segment. Over a half million Negroes in the United States are participating in organizations formed to do away with discrimination, segregation and to demand full citizenship right. Hundreds of thousands more are giving moral and financial support to the legal battles being waged throughout the country. The push from below is forcing heads of organizations and leaders of groups to take more and more advanced positions. And, at this moment our valiant Negro students are braving German police dogs, clubs and harrowing jail sentences as they carry their Sit-Downs into the most benighted and vicious bastions of White Supremacy. . . .

Yet, awareness, determination and valor are not enough. . . .

FREEDOMWAYS is born of the necessity for a vehicle of communication which will mirror developments in the diversified and many sided struggles of the Negro people. It will provide a public forum for the review, examination, and debate of all problems confronting Negroes in the United States.

FREEDOMWAYS offers a means of examining experiences and strengthening the relationship among peoples of African descent in this country, in Latin America, and wherever there are communities of such people anywhere in the world. It will furnish *accurate* information on the liberation movements in Africa itself.

FREEDOMWAYS will explore, without prejudice or gag, and from the viewpoint of the special interests of American Negroes, as well as the general interest of the nation, the new forms of economic, political and social systems now existing or emerging in the world.

FREEDOMWAYS provides a medium of expression for serious and talented writers—for those with established reputations as well as beginners seeking a reading audience for the first time.

"Ye shall know the Truth—and the Truth shall set you free."

This is our precept. We invite historians, sociologists, economists, artists, workers, students—all who have something constructive to contribute in this search for TRUTH—to use this open channel of communication that we might unite and mobilize our efforts for worthy and lasting results. . . .

Lift every voice and sing—of Freedom!

THE EDITORS

Ed Sanders, discussing *Fuck You: A Magazine of the Arts* (1998)[5]

In February of 1962 I was sitting in Stanley's Bar at 12th and B with some friends from the *Catholic Worker*. We'd just seen Jonas Mekas's movie *Guns of the Trees*, and I announced I was going to publish a poetry journal called *Fuck You, a magazine of the arts* . . . the next day I began typing stencils, and had an issue out within a week. I bought a small mimeograph machine, and installed it in my pad on East 11th, hand cranking and collating 500 copies, which I gave away free wherever I wandered. . . . *Fuck You* was part of what they called the Mimeograph Revolution, and my vision was to reach out to the "Best Minds" of my generation with a message of Ghandian pacifism, great sharing, social change, the expansion of personal freedom (including the legalization of marijuana), and the then-stirring message of sexual liberation.

Harry Smith, "Issues on the Anvil: Chaos and Creation," from *The Smith* (1964)[6]

The arts today are as chaotic as careening nations and uncertain sciences. Ostentatious ingenuity is confused with true creation, and trumpeted frustration is regarded as great wisdom. The fool heaven of a century ago has been superseded by the fool hell.

THE SMITH has come to forge new order, to fuse all arts and to choose what is finest in all mind's ordering. It is the greatest magazine, for it is the most general: anything goes as long as it's good.

"Preamble to *Aphra*," from *Aphra* (1969)[7]

Tired of Bellowing and Rothing, Mailering and Malamuding, we looked around at the current literary scene and decided that, for whatever reasons of history and economics, it is still, or perhaps more than ever, dominated by the Judeo-Christian patriarchal ethos. Women have more to give the world than babies. Whole areas of life, of consciousness and feeling are crying for recording and interpretation from within. Too long have women been seen from outside and from afar. Too long have we been brainwashed with male stereotypes of what they are like and what we are like. The view from the bottom may not be wide, but it is deep and upward, and for centuries women have had unique opportunities for practicing observation.

Works of art are bigger than theses, subject to multiple planes of interpretation. We propose a magazine that will give outlet to the feminine consciousness, a magazine free of ulterior motives, interested only in giving women a chance to express themselves and to see themselves. In these days of artistic confusion when the words avant-garde and arriere-garde have lost meaning, leaving fashion as the dominator, we shall seek work that will speak to women on an esthetic level. We submit that one reason for the form of the current upsurge in feminism—the rap session, the group meeting with individuals bearing witness, the opportunity for community and identification—is that the mass media provide such biased and commercially oriented material. The literary and entertainment scene are dominated by male stereotypes, male fantasies, male wish fulfillment, a male power structure. In consequence women have begun spontaneously to band together and create their own consciousness. Groups have been springing up all over the country, multiplying by division. This is all well and good, but there is a need for a less evanescent form of expression. We shall meet on paper, offering work in which women can see themselves, offering them the identification and shock of recognition which art traditionally gives, but which is clearly underexpressed in the current scene—be it book publishing, television, theatre, magazine or film.

The idea then is to encourage women as women, not in terms of male syndromes nor with preconceptions imposed from outside, whether by Freud or Madison Avenue market researchers. If we have a special bias for women it is because they need it: they have been getting a raw deal for centuries, and the reform movement of the nineteenth century and early twentieth centuries has suffered from the backlash of the forties and fifties. The emphasis will be on art, not ideology. We shall publish what we like and what we respond to, with the idea that we shall be speaking directly to women so that they can say, "There am I" and feel stronger and more doing.

Lorraine Bethel and Barbara Smith, "Introduction," from *Conditions: Five: The Black Women's Issue* (1979)[8]

The process of editing *Conditions: Five* began when the *Conditions* collective asked Barbara Smith to guest edit an issue of the magazine. Barbara agreed to do this in collaboration with Lorraine Bethel. We have worked together for over a year in the creation of this work.

One of the most exciting aspects of this issue of *Conditions* is that so many new Black women writers are being published in a feminist publication for the first time. So often women's publications, presses, and organizations have claimed that they could not find any women of color as an excuse for their all-whiteness. . . .

This issue, however, clearly disproves the "non-existence" of Black feminist and Black lesbian writers and challenges forever our invisibility, particularly in the feminist press. It is important to share how we made contact with our contributors.

Of course we used our own extensive networks of personal contacts, but we also distributed flyers announcing the issue and soliciting manuscripts from all over the country. These flyers were sent not only to other feminist publications, but to Black publications that Black women read. Flyers also went to bookstores, women's centers, organizations and individuals. In other words, we and the ongoing editors of *Conditions* made a huge effort to locate Black women outside of usual "feminist" networks.

Another aspect of this process was our encouraging Black women to write who had never published before. Several of our contributors are being published here for the first time and we feel there is a connection between our being Black women editors, creating an entirely Black women's issue, and motivating new Black women writers. . . .

We tried to maintain a consciousness of the way that traditional white / male literary standards have been used oppressively against Black / female writers, and worked to set these standards aside as much as possible. We realize that Black women's writing is generally grounded in a tradition of oral expression, and tried to establish artistic guidelines appropriate to the aesthetic criteria intrinsic to Afro-American culture. . . .

Conditions: Five already has an herstoric place in women's publishing as an all Black women's issue. Its uniqueness suggests how it may be used at a time when Black feminist and Black lesbian materials are still discouragingly scarce. Not only will it function as a resource for exposing individual women to Black feminist thought; we also suggest that it be considered and used as a text in a range of women's studies courses. . . . For the first time teachers of women's studies can integrate a body of positive and explicitly Black feminist material about Black women into their classes. By using *Conditions: Five* in this way they also will greatly support a feminist small press publication which needs it, as opposed to a multi-national trade publisher which does not. Individual readers, especially white women, can also make a commitment to make sure that Black women they know find out about the issue and have an opportunity to read it.

IF SMALL PRESS magazines sometimes took commercial magazines as both their model and their target, other alternative publications imitated and critiqued the mainstream newspaper. Several covers from underground newspapers of the late 1960s and early 1970s suggest how these papers adapted a traditional print format to challenge dominant ideas and established powers. For the cover of the second issue of the *Berkeley Tribe*, which had split from the *Berkeley Barb* over sex ads and money, the staff members posed nude. The underground press even had its own version of the Associated Press: *Liberation News Service* distributed news stories, photographs, and graphics to alternative papers all over the country. The last artifact in this section challenges a different precursor: underground comic books such as *Gay Comix* were often sexually explicit, directly repudiating the "Comics Code" enacted by the mainstream comics industry in the 1950s to fend off attacks on their publications as promoting violence. Underground "comix" featured the work of R. Crumb, Harvey Pekar, and others. By the 1970s underground comix included feminist and gay comix and often complex or experimental work like that published in Art Speigelman and Francoise Mouley's magazine *Raw*.

Cover, *Berkeley Tribe* (1969)[9]

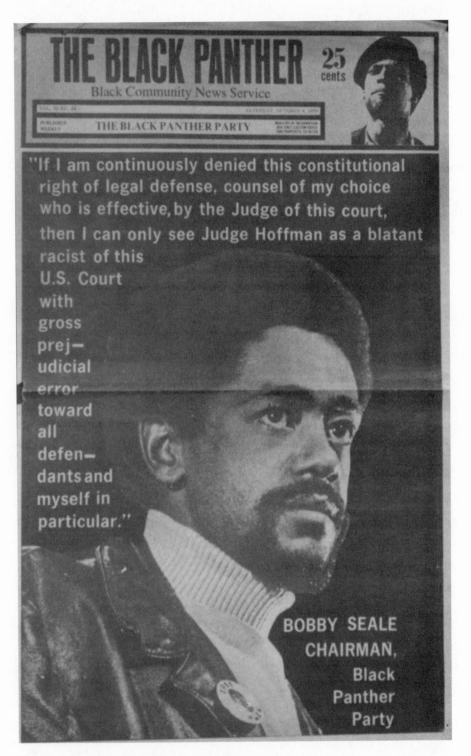

Cover, *The Black Panther* (1969)[10]

Cover, *Liberation News Service* (1970)[11]

Cover, *Las Vegas Free Press* (1970)[12]

Cover, *Liberation News Service* (1980)[14]

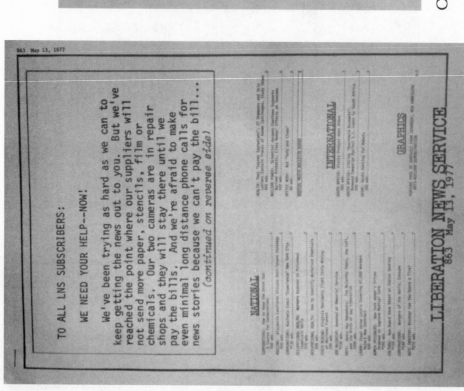

Cover, *Liberation News Service* (1977)[13]

Cover, *Gay Comix* (1982)[15]

THE THIRD SET of artifacts represents the more recent "zine" tradition. While a poster for *Modom* suggested an intriguing plan for group publication and distribution, most zines are written, illustrated, and produced by very small groups, even by a single person. In *Doris*, Cindy O. provided a glimpse into the celebratory self-expression that is the hallmark of the zine. Pagan Kennedy (b. 1962), recollecting how she began producing *Back to Pagan*, likewise detailed a personal path to artistic expression, one that allowed her to bypass credos she had acquired at school of what literature and art should be.

"Modom: Phase 2," ad in poster form, *Modom*, produced by Jake Berry (c. 1990)[16]

All sentient beings are encouraged to participate. If you want to do an "issue" of MODOM all you have to do is write the word MODOM in capital letters on an object, publication, building, street, WHATEVER, and assign it a number above 50. This number could be a fraction, decimal point, or any other kind of number. Then send a letter to the address on this page documenting your MODOM, be sure to include a description of your MODOM, and the number you assign it, and your name (if you wish). If you like, keep a log of your MODOMs and send in documentation of many at one time. All documentation will in turn be placed in the megalog of all MODOMs, and at some point in the future, published in stages as the documentation arrives. If your MODOM is a publication or a collection of objects, please send one to the MODOM address and one to Factsheet Five. Remember, anything can be a MODOM, a thought, other creatures ("real" or imaginary), ANYTHING. Simply record each one & send documentation.

> MODOM is an idea spawned by the happily dysfunctional intelligences at 9th Street Laboratories. Metasemantic Literature for Pandimensional Realities. No deadline—MODOM never stops. MODOM p.o. Box 3112 Florence, AL 35630

> This ad is MODOM #932.615 ½

Cindy O., "i like things to be small. . . ," from *Doris* (1996)[17]

i like things to be small, to fit in my pockets, magazines, paperback books, strings and rocks, gum and photographs. i want this thing here to be smaller, maybe you could fold it twice and it would fit snug in the back of your blue jeans like doris number one did, getting dirty and ratty and torn.

i was on the bart train the other day and there were these four girls, high school girls, three of them looked just like TV, long hair that they would brush back with their fingers, all four had practiced facial expressions, small noses, lines drawn around their eyes. but one girl, she was too tall and gangly and it looked like she just got her braces off, the way she kept feeling her teeth with her tongue. her back-pack had paintings of suns and moons and flowers that you could tell she painted on there, and you could tell her friends made fun of it behind her back. she was the one i watched, her backpack was unzipped part way and i snuck doris number one in. number one, full of my secrets, i couldn't hand it to her because i knew she wouldn't take it, not with her friends watching. i snuck it into her life for her to find later, alone, in her bedroom. the people on the train who saw me do it glared at me, mean and suspicious, like i'd stolen something from that girl, and maybe i had. i got off at the next stop.

but the truth is, i don't hand it out like i used to: watching people on the train, on buses, on the street—handing one to this girl who is laughing with her friend, one to that girl sad and alone on the last train of the night, the girl with the red boots, the one sitting on the wet curb, the boy who pulled his hair in front of his eyes and chewed on the ends. i still want the same things, to break—with this one small gesture—the crazy things we are taught; to keep distant and distrustful, alienated, lonely, and safe. i still want to know stories whispered and yelled and coughed out between too much laughing, but i live in these cities now and i know too many people, all half-way and california style. and i never got winter, cold sun, and thick blankets
cINDY o., DORIS

Pagan Kennedy, 'Zine: How I Spent Six Years of My Life in the Underground and Finally . . . Found Myself . . . I Think (1995)[18]

That year [1988] it seemed as if everyone I knew had suddenly decided to produce a homemade Xerox magazine (or "zine"). My roommate Dona collected the ravings of insane people and turned them into pamphlets; Seth published a cartoon 'zine; Jason color-copied his psychedelic collages; Tony made comic books; Rob was working on a surrealist literary thing; and on and on. At the highest pitch of the scene, the 'zine publishers formed the Small Press Alliance. (The group fell apart after Shiva, the god of destruction, whispered into the ear of an anarchist pamphle-teer that he must destroy the alliance and sue its members for "harassing" him.)

My friends couldn't understand why I didn't have my own publication. I often contributed cartoons and essays to other people's 'zines, so why didn't I just buckle down and start my own? I kept trying to explain that I couldn't do a 'zine because—no offense—I was a real writer. *The Village Voice* had started publishing my reviews and short stories. And I was still working on that novel in progress, which I had begun calling my "nov in prog" because I felt the need to make fun of it in front of my slacker peers.

And then, I don't know, one day something in me snapped. Boredom, really, that's what I should attribute it to. I had to do something with myself, because God knows my fiction wasn't going too well; some days I found I couldn't write at all. So I started a 'zine, telling myself it would be just a little Xeroxed thing to send to friends far away, a kind of letter. Maybe, too, I'd hand out a few copies to acquaintances in Boston. But that was all. Just for fun. . . .

Almost instinctively I broke every rule of respectable fiction. I published my own work (for serious literary types, self-publishing is considered a sign of rank amateurism). I drew pictures. I wrote unpolished sentences and hardly went back to revise. I even scribbled in last-minute notes. And most important, I talked endlessly about myself.

Rule number one of fiction is this: Try not to write an autobiographical story, but if you do, then make sure you "write against yourself," that is, show yourself as a loser, a jerk or whatever. This has the paradoxical effect of making you, the writer, look like a great person because you understand and admit to all your flaws.

Well, life is too short. So in my fanzine, I dispensed with all the wise head-shaking at my own folly. Instead, I let my ego out of the box. I indulged in an orgy of self-adulation. I wallowed in the mud of narcissism. What a relief after so many years of self-effacement!

I did everything they'd told me not to do and I loved it. My fanzine was a fuck-you to *The New Yorker* and the University of Iowa and the Bread Loaf writers' colony and Ticknor & Fields and Raymond Carver and agents named Bitsy and John Updike and the twenty-two-year-old novelists that *Newsweek* told me hung out in the hottest clubs and English Comp jobs. The whole respectable writing crowd could gather in their country club, sip tea on the long green lawns, and discuss elegant style without me. Once I discovered my 'zine, I no longer wanted to belong.

Besides, in some backward way, I had finally learned how to write the Great American Underground Novel—though it ended up being a 'zine instead. And why should it be a novel? What literary masterpiece could have captured my life as well as a Xeroxed pamphlet full of scrawled cartoons?

Once I started doing the 'zine, I knew I was on to something. I was happy here in my room—drawing a cartoon about summer camp, writing about my trip to Knoxville, choosing cheesy illustrations from clipart collections. It reminded me of when I was a little kid, eight or nine, and I used to make my own books. I had rediscovered the sheer delight of creating something. How had I forgotten that this—this absorbed, tongue-between-the-teeth, little-girl feeling—was the essence of art? Oh calloo-callay I had found it again, hidden tide pool of my own thoughts, secret garden, kiddie pool.

ARTISTS' BOOKS, the subject of the final artifacts, sometimes resemble zines. Many, however, are one of a kind or limited editions carefully produced for art and rare book markets. Often created by artists who meditate on the place of books in our culture, such works may challenge our notion of what a book should be, how it should look, and how it should function. Winifred McNeill's *Listen/Whisperer* comments on the book's hinged form, and also its function as repository. Denise Mullen's *Na Pali* employs the accordion or fan structure from which the modern codex may have developed to create a fitting setting for landscape art. Kelsey Osborne's *Beauty Intensive Series 1, Beauty Intensification Procedure* is reminiscent of interactive children's books, but its ironic point is clearly aimed at adults. David Stairs's *Boundless* forces us to think about the book as material object: to open this book entails destroying its binding. Finally, Melissa Zink's (b. 1932) *Story Painting: Mme. B,* rather than being formatted like a book, draws from elements of print to create a complex artwork.

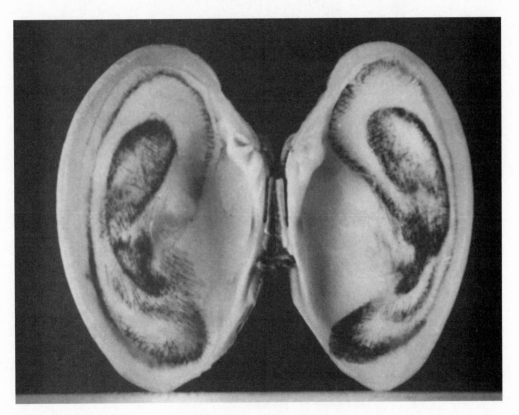

Winifred McNeill, *Listen/Whisperer,* etching on paper, clamshell, beeswax (1997)[19]

Denise Mullen, *Na Pali*, embossed Islamic leather bound book with loose guard and accordion of palladium photos: handmade papers, letterpress, leather endbands (1998)[20]

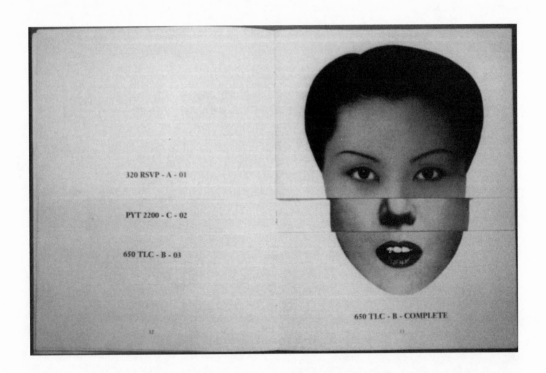

Kelsey Osborn, *Beauty Intensive: Series 1, Beauty Intensification Procedure*, offset, paper, saddle stitched (1995)[21]

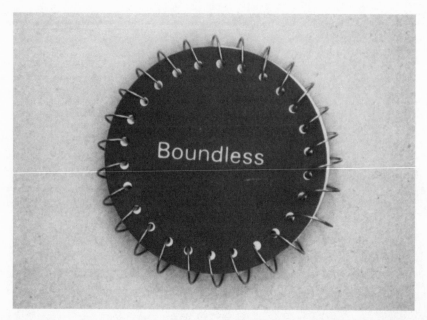

David Stairs, *Boundless,* spiral bound paper (1983 and 1990)[22]

Melissa Zink, *Story Painting: Mme. B,* mixed media (1996)[23]

COMMENTARY: OUT OF THE MAINSTREAM AND INTO THE STREETS: SMALL PRESS MAGAZINES, THE UNDERGROUND PRESS, ZINES, AND ARTISTS' BOOKS

Periodicals and books with small runs, limited readerships—and, often, no profits—had existed since the early days of the nation. The rise of advertising-supported mass-circulation magazines in the 1890s, and of blockbuster bestsellers as an institution shortly thereafter, made such small-circulation productions visible as a special category of publishing. The category of alternative press has included small press literary magazines (also called "little magazines"), chapbook publishing, underground or alternative papers (often with a political slant), fanzines and the zines they grew into, and artists' books. Sometimes surprisingly young, producers of such publications have managed to run them on a shoestring, in part by using the cheapest reproduction methods available. The alternative press has often pushed the bounds of permissible printed speech and has met with censorship for political and sexual content. For the book historian, these publications highlight questions of access to print, access to financing for publication, censorship, and distribution.

The literary monthlies of the 1910s and 1920s such as the *Little Review* and *Poetry* defined themselves as upholding high art against the commercial magazine and book publishing of their era. They claimed to offer access to a purer art elsewhere shunned, misunderstood, and censored, and to hold out a personal editorial vision against the increasingly bland and impersonal face of the commercial magazines. There had been nineteenth-century literary magazines with little or no advertising, but in the twentieth-century publishing scene the sense of taking a principled stand in opposition to a commercial press often defined the little magazines. Later generations of literary magazines such as *Partisan Review* and *Paris Review* distinguished themselves not only from the commercial press, but also from earlier little magazines and university-supported literary journals such as *Kenyon Review*. By the 1950s magazines also asserted their sense of upholding the tradition of earlier maverick magazines, even as they claimed to be original.

When editors announced why or how they began their magazine or published a particular issue, they positioned themselves among and against other publications—even if their pronouncements may not have accurately described the magazine they actually produced. Some statements, like those of the *Smith* and *Paris Review*, ring with the certainty that they represent "the best" literature, even as they gather material from predominantly white men who already confidently define themselves as writers. Others explain the need to find and encourage a particular group of writers (such as black feminists in *Conditions: Five*) and demystify the editorial process by showing how they did so. Statements of what magazines intended to accomplish are very much of their time, and create a fascinating chronology of aspirations.

Some of the publications conventionally included in the little magazine category focused on belletristic writing; others, such as *Phylon*, mixed social science and poetry. The 1970s saw a proliferation of literary magazines, some overtly addressed to different ethnic, political, and racial groups. This development was met with hostility from some little magazines that defined their mission as publishing "the best" literature and imagined their audience as somehow both universal and limited to those of compatible literary tastes. One problem for the researcher addressing little magazines is that there are too many to do justice to. The familiar solution has been to narrow the definition to make the category more manageable, thereby defining a canon of the "important" literary magazines, with the magazines closest to the high modernist tradition usually placed at center.

But if we broaden this narrow and insular definition, new connections and a richer understanding of the world of writers, readers, and publishers appear. If we include a magazine of essays, stories, and poetry such as the *Forerunner* (1909–16), which Charlotte Perkins Gilman not only published but wrote herself, a new line of ancestry for the more personal, self-published, single-author zines of the 1980s and 1990s appears. Newspapers have been the chief component of the foreign-language immigrant press of various communities, with 3,444 begun between 1884 and 1920, many of which published fiction and poetry (see Miller). But immigrants also published literary journals equivalent and sometimes responsive to the English-language small press. *Tsukunft* (Future) and *In Zikh* (In Oneself, the journal of the Introspectivist movement, 1920–40) were notable among those in Yiddish (Harshav, 36–38). Polish journals included *Przyjaciel Ludu* (Friend of the People, begun in Chicago in 1876 as a literary magazine but later changed to a general newspaper), *Latarnia* (Lantern, 1902), and *Przeglad Polsko-Amerykanski* (Polish-American Review, 1911–13). Kahlil Gibran's literary society, the Pen League, had an Arabic journal, *Al-Fanun* (Arts), founded 1913, and other Arabic literary magazines included *Al-Sayeh* (Traveler, begun 1912) and *Al-Sameer*. The publishers of the Latvian arts magazine *Perkons* (Thunder, 1909–11) went on to edit a political, scholarly, and literary journal, *Gaisma* (Light, 1912), which in turn spun off *Dekadentu Gaisma* (Light of Decadents). These journals were as widely read as many little magazines in English, and at least as opinionated and contentious. Placing them within the little magazine tradition establishes that the 1970s proliferation did not fragment a previously shared cultural ground but rather developed from earlier practices. Though they sometimes defined their audience in universal terms, the mainstream literary magazines too represented their own constituencies.

If we include political journals that incorporated fiction or poetry or literary criticism, along with the literary journals that contained opinion pieces but nonetheless have been conventionally included in the "little magazine" category, we gain a better sense of how these publications spoke to their readers and helped to create a sense of literary and political community. Such political/literary journals include those edited by Emma Goldman, *Mother Earth* (begun 1906), and notably the periodicals that W. E. B. Du Bois edited or encouraged over a long career—*Moon* (1905), *Horizon* (1907–10), *Crisis* (1910–34), *Phylon* (begun 1940), and the Marxist-oriented *Freedomways*, edited by his wife Shirley Graham (Johnson and Johnson, 228). All had in common their dependence on readers, patrons, organizations, and often the staff, rather than advertisers, for most of their support. They were thus able to publish material that would not have found a home in the advertising-supported press, either because it would not have been sufficiently popular, or would have been too controversial or subject to censorship, or would have undercut the interests of advertisers. (In their dependence on patrons and organizations and their interest in making converts and creating a community of activist readers, the political magazines had much in common not only with such nineteenth-century publications as abolitionist papers, but with nineteenth-century religious publishing.) A few small-press magazines, such as Elbert Hubbard's *Philistine* (1895–1915) and Harry Smith's *The Smith* in the late 1960s, were run as a kind of hobby, supported by a wealthy publisher's money.

Conversely, some journals, such as the *Chap-Book* of the 1890s or later the *Evergreen Review* (1957–73), were in a sense advertisements themselves: as the flagship journals of book publishers, they excerpted and promoted their press's authors. They are in that sense similar to more commercial magazines like *Harper's* and *Scribner's* when those were owned by book publishers. All have much to tell us about the process of book promotion and the making of literary reputation.

The English-language little magazines of the 1910s and 1920s are widely credited with nurturing principal figures of modernism, such as H.D., T. S. Eliot, Marianne Moore, Ernest Hemingway, and Ezra Pound. Although one of the wealthy founders of the *Dial* originally set up his magazine as an alternative to a fund for supporting artists directly, small press magazines did not by any means coddle authors. Most magazines paid little or nothing; many editors complained of the quality of work they received. Margaret Anderson, for example, ran the September 1916 issue of the *Little Review* blank (except for cartoons of herself and her partner at play), explaining that no art was being produced, and so she would publish nothing. She was, however, willing to serialize James Joyce's *Ulysses* over a period of three years, though for four of those issues the post office, charging obscenity, seized and burnt the press run.

The literary magazines of this tradition were generally of two types. Political magazines such as the *New Masses* (1926) became increasingly prominent in the 1930s; they reappeared in greater numbers with 1960s magazines such as *Freedomways,* and in new permutations by black arts–movement periodicals such as *Umbra* (1962) and *Nommo* (1969), the journal of a Chicago black writers' workshop, whose antecedents also included the independent black arts periodical *Fire* (1926). The quarterly or magazine reviews, such as *Prairie Schooner* (1927) and later the *Paris Review* (1953), some of them supported by universities, became the more common form of the 1940s. These were printed using letterpress and conventionally bound. Styron's *Paris Review* piece complains of the academic slant of the university-based reviews; university sponsorship and other grants left magazines vulnerable to institutional interests. Since schools often undertook to sponsor literary quarterlies to enhance their university's and state's reputation, as in Louisiana State University's ample support of the *Southern Review* (begun 1935), they may have been less willing to risk controversy. The *Chicago Review* (1946–present), for example, was attacked in a local paper for publishing a selection of Beat writing in 1958. A planned subsequent issue was suppressed by the university administration; the staff resigned in protest when a new editor was chosen to put the review on a noncontroversial footing; and the suppressed issue appeared as the first number of *Big Table* in 1959 (Chielens, 74).

The Beat poets of the 1950s and poets allied with or following them created a rich lode of publications in what was called the Mimeograph Revolution—a pungent though slightly inaccurate term since many were photo offset. Mimeograph machines were cheap and easy to use without special training. Stencils were cut directly by a typewriter or stylus, so that production costs beyond the purchase of the machine and paper were minimal, though only a limited number of copies could be run from one stencil and reproduction quality was low. Such publications were well suited to the Beat preference for spontaneity, collaboration, and experimentation in production as well as poetry.

Motives for starting a literary magazine varied. Many were begun by writers and editors who felt that work of a particular type was not being taken seriously. Groups of like-minded friends started others, while some were founded to find such groups. Aram Saroyan, son of William Saroyan, began the mimeographed magazine *Lines* (1964–67) at age twenty-one. He explained, "I was eager to make contact with my literary contemporaries, and the little magazine was a nice entree into the milieu. Young poets need a place to publish, and the magazines gave me an excuse to make contact with anyone whose work I liked" (Padgett and Saroyan, 211). But many mimeoed magazines grew out of a larger vision and a passionate commitment to social change, not to mention the ambition to shake things up, even with their titles, like Ed Sanders's *Fuck You: A Magazine of the Arts* (1962–65). Beat magazines continually sprouted and mutated into other magazines. Titles might reflect the connection or indebtedness editors felt to other publications: Ron Padgett's *White Dove Review* (1959–60), begun when Padgett was a high-school student, was named after an issue of *Evergreen Review* that had a girl holding a white dove on the cover. As Padgett recalled, he worked in a bookstore at fifteen, found out "about *Evergreen Review* and suddenly started reading all these modernist poets such as LeRoi Jones [later Amiri Baraka] and Frank O'Hara, and I subscribed to the magazines advertised in *Evergreen Review*, like LeRoi Jones's *Yugen* and Wallace Berman's *Semina*. And when I looked at *Yugen*, I saw they were just little things stapled together, and so I went down to a local printer and asked, How do you do this? and he said, how, it's nothing—it's real easy. So I decided to start my own magazine" (Padgett and Saroyan, 159).

Unlike commercial magazine producers who define a market niche—a group advertisers will want to reach—before they begin, small-press publishers in the late 1960s and 1970s, like those of Beat publications, began with writers, not with readers and certainly not with a market. (New technology—cheaper computer typesetting, offset and xerox reproduction—made it easier and cheaper to produce attractive magazines.) Authors' desire to be published and the difficulty of finding an audience led editors to complain that they received submissions from many more writers than they had subscribers. An early 1970s survey found that most readers of small-press magazines were writers themselves, with teachers, librarians, and students rounding out the list (Anania, 10). Organizations of small-press publishers such as the Committee of Small Magazine Editors and Publishers attempted to improve distribution and increase readership. Beginning in 1976 the Pushcart Prizes were awarded for the best work in the small press, garnered some mainstream attention, and collected winning works in an annual anthology. Other attempts to promote the small press included placing magazines in libraries, establishing distribution cooperatives, and setting up a bookmobile of small-press magazines.

Women had been involved in American little magazines all along as editors or publishers. The growth of a new feminist movement in the late 1960s inspired new magazines for women's writing that asserted that publishing women was itself a political act. Such publications started with the sense that they were addressing a community of readers and writers that needed them. The 1960s and 1970s saw an increase in African American literary journals, such as *Yardbird Reader*, as well as the appearance of feminist, gay, and lesbian magazines, such as *Aphra* and *Conditions*, that connected to and helped constitute communities of readers. Grants from the National Endowment for the Arts helped support the proliferation of publications, though their apportionment also led to bitter infighting among magazines, in part based on some editors' claims that a magazine addressed to a "general" audience, however tiny, was more legitimate than one addressed to a "special interest" group such as women. The claim that a small readership implied a more select and enlightened audience was another remarkable twist in the complicated aesthetic politics of modernism and elitism.

Like the small-press magazines, the weekly and monthly newspapers that made up the 1960s and early 1970s underground press arose out of commitment and belief rather than commercial drive. While literary magazines of the era often celebrated their opposition to what was called "the Establishment," they also maintained an allegiance to literary writing, however they defined it, rather than reportage. Some of the same writers, such as Allen Ginsberg, Ed Sanders, and Marge Piercy, could be found in both literary magazines and the underground newspapers, but the underground press aimed to spread news not available in the mainstream and to organize, or at least provide communication links for, the communities it addressed.

While the term "underground press" suggests an illegal, hidden status, these papers were generally not covert publications in the same sense as papers put out by the French Resistance under Nazi occupation, or Russian samizdats. Rather the term expressed a sense of opposition and advocacy: opposition to the Vietnam War and other government policies, and by extension to conventional power relationships and authority structures; advocacy of sexual and artistic freedom, communal living or the simple life, and other features of the New Left and the counterculture. They offered a place to publish information, graphics, or writing that other papers would avoid or censor. The term expressed the sense that such material was subversive. For some publications the term "underground" was more literally applicable: the clandestine production and distribution in the mid-1970s of the Weather Underground's publications surrounded them with a sense of value and hardship that probably gained them wider readership than they would have otherwise had. In another camp, by 1970 about sixty papers of the antiwar GI movement, such as *Your Military Left* of San Antonio, *Fight Back* of Heidelberg, and *Anchorage Troop,* were in production and faced government harassment.

The *Los Angeles Free Press* was the first underground paper to publish on a sustained basis, beginning in 1964. By 1967 there were about twenty such tabloids, and by 1969 at least five hundred (Peck, xiv–xv). Many started within the student movement, in reaction to inadequate coverage of antiwar demonstrations in the mainstream press. As they came to define "politics" more broadly, they included articles and papers by and about exponents of gay liberation, black power, Native American struggles, prisoners' rights, children's rights, and mental patients' rights. On the local level, they addressed such issues as local corruption, tenants' rights, and nuclear power and waste.

The way papers were run was sometimes as important to the staffers as what they covered, with many papers experimenting with collective organization. Papers were usually supported by record and concert ads, but sometimes by explicit sex ads, and created by volunteer or low-waged staffs. This arrangement caused the largely volunteer staff of the *Berkeley Barb* to walk out and form the *Berkeley Tribe* when it was revealed that the *Barb*'s owner had made $250,000 a year from sex ads. The new wave of feminism in the late 1960s was both a topic of debate in the papers and a movement among women on staff, awakened to the sexism in their own work lives. Some women staffers responded by taking over a paper where they had previously felt subordinate: *Rat*, in New York, became a women's paper. At least one publication, *Liberation News Service* (LNS), decided in 1970 that its collective should be two-thirds women, both to allow women to learn nontraditional skills like printing and to make sure that women had a voice in the organization's meetings—on the theory that if two-thirds of the staff were women, about half of the airtime in meetings would be taken by men. Numerous papers specifically devoted to feminist news and commentary sprang up as well, such as *Off Our Backs*, *Big Mama Rag*, *Broomstick*, and dozens more.

More than the little magazines, the underground press was regionally based, with papers serving a town or city. Their common identity as a national community of publishers, producing a particular kind of paper, stemmed partially from their shared origins in the student movement and the counterculture. This identity was also shaped by exchanges between the papers, systematized through the lists issued by one exchange network called the Underground Press Syndicate, another called the Cooperative High School Independent Press Service, and a loose agreement to disregard copyright and allow free copying from one another. A tie connecting many of the papers was the *Liberation News Service*. From 1967 to 1981, LNS produced twice-weekly photo-offset packets of news and graphics for several hundred papers across the country. LNS's graphics were particularly popular; the same photo or drawing, put to different uses, often circulated through the underground press for years. The underground press's loose attitude toward copyright also aided the diffusion of stories and graphics around the country—a system like the nineteenth-century practice of "exchanges" between papers. But it also may have backfired in making it harder for nonstaff cartoonists, especially, to make a living at their work and to have the resources to produce it.

Underground papers, press services, and syndicates encouraged others to join in creating their own papers. Such publishing access was not just a tool for spreading radical ideas. Publishing itself could be a radicalizing activity. Participating in demonstrations and taking over buildings, and then seeing newspaper and TV coverage drastically at odds with what the demonstrators had experienced, spurred antiwar activists to question media coverage and put out their own papers. Publishing a paper often led to further radicalization via confrontation with censoring authorities: print shops that refused to print certain material, or high-school or college administrators. "All of a sudden you might find strange school rules being enforced to ridiculous extents. Administrations have been known to suspend underground staffers for conspiracy to litter on school property," one high-school underground-press booklet explained (Al-Fadhly and Shapiro, 12). While authorized military media were censored by military authorities, dissident GI papers were consistently targeted for government harassment and intimidation, including court-martial, transfer, and reduction in rank of editors and distributors on minor disciplinary charges. Copies were opened and impounded (Rips, 140). Federal, state, and local government agencies worked to suppress and disrupt other underground papers as well. FBI visits severely discouraged many printers, distributors, and landlords from working with underground presses. Obscenity or pornography charges and vice-squad raids became weapons against papers that used four-letter words. Though prosecutors often had weak cases, the attacks consumed the papers' time and money. The *Columbus Free Press* was hit with incitement-to-riot charges when its writers covered a riot. The FBI made the *Black Panther Party Paper* a special target, sending anonymous letters complaining of the paper's presence in libraries and classrooms. FBI tactics were responsible for drying up some papers' revenues. In 1969 FBI memos reveal the agency considering using contacts to dissuade Columbia Records from advertising in the underground press. Columbia ads disappeared from, among others, the *Free Press* in Washington, D.C., and the paper was dead within the year. Other papers, like the *Berkeley Barb*, turned to sex ads for survival.

Such tactics contributed to the demise of the underground press. So did the end of the Vietnam War, as well as economic changes such as rising rents, which made it harder for paper staffs to live on the margins by the late 1970s and early 1980s. It may be, as one critic puts it, that "from the start, reporters and writers envisioned a better world; publishers envisioned a better return on their investment" (Bates, 12). By the late 1990s that was certainly publishers' predominant vision, with alternatives increasingly owned by chains, and often carrying stories little different from the mainstream press.

The underground press of the 1960s and 1970s left other progeny besides the alternative papers. Discontented with and feeling frozen out of the mainstream media, but no longer connected to mass political movements, zine producers of the 1980s created a form smaller and more personal in scale. Like some of the underground and alternative papers, zines celebrated the homemade clip-art aesthetic and drew from underground comic art books ("comix") as well. Zine writers' and producers' ties were at least as likely to be to cartooning, punk bands, and performance art as to literature. The writing tended to be edgy and personal, with great value placed on spontaneity or a spontaneous appearance. While the little magazines had claimed to be a bulwark against popular culture, zines more often embraced it, with detailed "Star Trek" scenarios (Jenkins, 17), musings on Barbie dolls, and fantasies about the Partridge Family. Although the practice of gathering to develop stories based on another writers' characters goes back more than a century, judging from the March sisters' Pickwick Club in *Little Women*, late-twentieth-century readers who appropriate and extend licensed characters with corporate owners (like the *Star Trek* characters) trespass on commercial culture through their wholehearted embrace of it. They challenge it in ways that corporate owners, at least, find more threatening than they found the *Little Review*.

As part of a lively history of self-publishing and correspondence circles, zines foreground issues of access to print and access to audience. They both prefigure and coexist with the proliferation of personal Web pages, on which thousands of writers bare their souls without anyone necessarily reading; other zines (and Web pages) attract loyal communities of readers. Little magazines defined themselves against the mainstream press primarily in their content; for zine producers, unorthodox distribution avenues are themselves part of the process of producing the zine or building its community, and mark the difference between the zine and the commercial press.

The word "zine" is not derived directly from magazine, but from "fanzine," a term from the science-fiction magazines of the 1920s and 1930s. Science-fiction fans, who first corresponded through these magazines' letters columns, formed clubs and correspondence groups to continue their discussions of stories, the science behind them, and the authors whose work they admired or excoriated. The first amateur publication to grow out of these groups sprouted in 1930: the *Comet*, later renamed *Cosmology* (Friedman, 10). Such fanzines also had roots in the late-nineteenth-century popular pastime of creating amateur magazines, whose editors organized into amateur journalism associations and exchanged publications. Fanzines appeared in other genres, including mysteries and comic books, and to some extent became the tryout grounds for more commercial magazines. Unlike the commercial, press-release-filled fan magazines put out by the film and music industries, fanzines were by and for fans: often self-published by an individual or community with an intense sense of involvement with its subject. Mimeographed or, at the high end, photo offset, their runs were in the hundreds.

In the 1960s the underground press helped displace fanzines: people who might in the 1950s have put out a fanzine could instead contribute to a press that also spoke from and to a community formed by cultural interests, but whose concerns were politically urgent and encompassed broader issues. But as underground papers either folded or grew into advertising-supported, more conventional alternative papers, fanzines—now for punk rock and *Star Trek* fans as well as the earlier genres—again occupied a unique niche, and came to include both political newsletters and more personal documentation. This new spurt of self-publishing was facilitated by the availability of cheap photocopying, which allowed for more versatile layouts than mimeograph stencils, and for lower prices for short runs than photo-offset lithography had allowed. Some zine producers reduced costs further by making copies on the sly at work. Formats reflect their production history: many zines are folded or stapled permutations of copying paper. The ability to photocopy directly from a pasted-up original allowed for a visual aesthetic of collage, which often favored commercial images from the 1950s.

The freedom from commercial and editorial constraints allowed for a profusion of subject matter, from discontent at work (*Wage Slave World News*) to products of consumerism (*Beer Frame: The Journal of Inconspicuous Consumption*) to parenthood (*Hip Mama*) to adolescent angst (*Teen Fag*) and to reviews of zines (*Factsheet Five*). Fine writing per se was not valued or highlighted; spontaneity and creative response to the world were. These often took the form of personal writing, such as interviews, brief memoirs, or memoirs extended over many issues, sometimes in sharp, hard-edged language, sometimes in a litany of soul-baring complaints. While there were self-published African American and Latino/a publications, those that classified themselves as zines, or connected via a network of exchanges with other zines, seemed to be largely white. The line between political newsletter and zine often blurs, as in a publication such as the *Disability Rag*, by disability activists, or *Diseased Pariah News*, created by people with AIDS and HIV. In an outpouring of feminist "girl zines" or "grrrl zines," such as *Doris*, even very young women have found voice for their own experience and connected with a community of other girl zine producers.

Although producing and mailing a magazine has become easier and cheaper, reaching potential readers remains an issue, if not a problem, for zine producers. A few were sold in independent bookstores, but the bookstore that took them was more likely to offer a carton of assorted zines to rummage through than to yield much shelf space to displaying them. More were exchanged between zine producers. Zines like *MODOM* have fused the question of distribution with the magazine as conceptual art. While many zine producers have embraced the Web as the solution to production and distribution costs, others remain loyal to print for reasons of the sort that Cindy O. of *Doris* articulates. Zines, because of their nonslick format, their embrace of the personal, the idiosyncratic, and the unedited, make the assumptions behind conventionally produced and marketed books and magazines more visible.

In this, zines are like artists' books, which they sometimes resemble and overlap with. Artists have illustrated texts for centuries. In the twentieth century some took on the task more self-consciously and tried to define a new status above that of the illustrator or illuminator. The late nineteenth century had seen increasing interest in the book as finely made object. Enterprises such as William Morris's Kelmscott

Press in England and the Merrymount Press and many other hand-presses in the United States sought to enhance worthy texts with fine book design, illustration, and production.

Artists took another kind of interest in publishing with what have become known as artists' books: books that both use the traditional forms of books—such as scroll, codex, various types of folded materials—and play against them to question or defamiliarize them. Some of these are issued or constructed as "multiples," and may be cheaply made and indistinguishable from zines. Others are handmade, sometimes one of a kind or in very small editions, sometimes using materials, such as clay or wood, not usually associated with books, or using special papers or unconventional binding materials. As a genre, artists' books thus embrace cheaply made and sold pamphlets, as well as works costing thousands of dollars.

Artists' books demand that viewers see the book as an entirety, not just as words presented in a convenient form. In a sense, they answer a complaint often made about beautifully designed and illustrated books: that readers are made so aware of the type and ornamentation that they find it impossible to lose themselves in the text. Artists' books turn this complaint into the basis of an artistic genre that cultivates hyperawareness of the form. In some artists' books, text is subordinate or nonexistent; in others, it is integrally combined with the form of the printing and binding. An artists' book may single out one aspect of the book to foreground or play with, as David Stairs's *Boundless* (1983) does with binding. Winifred McNeill's *Listen/ Whisperer* (1997) draws a connection between a book as hinged object containing words and the hinged clamshells as ears, a receptacle into which sounds fall. In Kelsey Osborn's *Beauty Intensive: Series 1, Beauty Intensification Procedure* (1995), supposedly a guide for plastic surgeons, the masquerade of one kind of book as another is used as parody. Osborn takes up the familiar children's toy book, in which features from different faces can be re-sorted to form new ones, allowing the reader to play, while implying that the cosmetic surgeon's work is equally bizarre and arbitrary. (A price chart for different faces follows the sortable facial features.)

Some artists' books refer to pre-codex forms. Scrolls and accordion-folded books are among the forms that allow for stricter control of sequence and points of access than the codex, which can be opened to any page. Jumping off from the book's characteristic ability to present a sequence of elements, some book artists disrupt sequence, highlight it, or offer different entry points into it. Denise Mullen's *Na Pali* (1998) embodies an experience of travel and exploration. As it sends the reader paging through the landscape, it controls the sequence of what is to be seen, and yet allows all the pictures to be seen simultaneously, like a panorama. At the same time, it draws on associations to other printed forms in its resemblance to a souvenir folder of postcards.

Examining artists' own descriptions of their work can be a fruitful approach to artists' books and related works. Melissa Zink, in a series of works, explains that she has circled around a private aesthetic formed from books and by books. That aesthetic developed from the act of reading, the memories of reading, the literal companionship of books the enchantments of photography, typography, graphic design, paper, leather, et cetera, et cetera. . . . Everything I find most beautiful and moving is in some way connected to books. Books are how I know the world: travel is better in books, biographies more desirable than personal contact, novels preferable to movies, and best of all time is exquisitely controllable. It does not pass, then is now. Consequently, the trance state which I associate with reading is central to my private aesthetic.

In mixed-media works such as *The Art of Biography, Fabricating History, The Files, The Files* and *Story Painting: Mme. B* she therefore seeks to "create a visual match for the internal experience of my reading trance" (Zink). The works mix references to the physical book—worn bits of binding, barely legible spines—with pages and fragments of print, and faces or fragments of faces. They create a sense of a hidden story within or behind exploded book parts and the printed page.

Book artists have taken as their medium all aspects of publishing, so distribution itself can be part of the artwork. In the late 1980s a vending machine dispensed xeroxed, pamphlet-sized artists' books in a New York cinema lobby, shaking up the process of buying books, of buying art, and maybe of buying popcorn, too. "Mail art," in which distribution is itself incorporated into the artistic act, overlapped with Beat magazines such as *Semina* (1955–64), which appeared in many different formats and sizes; copies could not be bought, but rather the edition of several hundred was sent to readers selected by the editor.

The work of book artists raises pertinent questions for the study of publishing in general, for example, by highlighting the embodiment of texts. We often use the word "text" to mean the author's words or even pictures, untethered to a particular typesetting or binding, and the word "book" to refer to a specific material embodiment of a text. Artists' books destroy this neat distinction by making binding and form as crucial as the words. They thus remind us that reading experience for "ordinary" printed works too may be tied to a specific book, and not just to its text. The work of book artists also poses a puzzle in the literary world: What is the relationship between cost and literary "value"? This question receives a new spin (though no answer) in artists' books, which may be sold within the art market, with its orientation to the unique or limited-edition object, where assumptions about value are drastically different from those played out in the literary marketplace. Artists' books again highlight production methods and materials—no longer incidental, but now integral to the assertion of the artist's control.

Alternatives to the mainstream are as numerous and varied as publishers in the mainstream. There are many more modes of alternative publishing, among them such independent small-press book publishers as Zoland, City Lights, Kitchen Table, and Dalkey Archive, and works distributed as posters or as leaflets. New categories have emerged, such as papers distributed and written by homeless people. Even smaller publications fly below the radar of our usual notions of publishing: xeroxlore that makes its way around offices; copied holiday letters; books full of invented spelling made in elementary school classrooms—all worth study.

SOURCE NOTES

[Unless otherwise indicated material is considered to fall under fair use or to be in the public domain, or a good-faith effort has been made to locate the copyright holder.]

1. Harriet Monroe, "The Motive of the Magazine," *Poetry: A Magazine of Verse* 1 (October 1912): 26–28.

2. Margaret Anderson, "Editorial," *Little Review* 12 (May 1929): 3.

3. Bill Styron, "Letter to an Editor," *Paris Review* 1 (Spring 1953): 9–12.

4. Editors' statement, *Freedomways* 1 (Spring 1961): 7–9.

5. Ed Sanders, quoted in Steven Clay and Rodney Phillips, *A Secret Location on the Lower East Side: Adventures in Writing, 1960–1980* (New York: New York Public Library and Granary Books, 1998), 167.

6. Harry Smith, "Issues on the Anvil: Chaos and Creation," *Smith* 1, no. 1 (February 1964): 6. Reproduced courtesy of Harry Smith. Copyright © Harry Smith, Brooklyn, N.Y.

7. "Preamble to *Aphra*," *Aphra* 1 (Fall 1969): 2–3.

8. *Conditions: Five: The Black Women's Issue*, no. 5 (1979): 11–14.

9. Cover, *Berkeley Tribe*, July 10–26, 1969. Author's collection.

10. Cover, *Black Panther*, October 4, 1969. Author's collection.

11. Cover, *Liberation News Service*, April 11, 1970. Author's collection.

12. Cover, *Las Vegas Free Press*, April 23–30, 1970. Author's collection.

13. Cover, *Liberation News Service*, May 13, 1977. Author's collection.

14. Cover, *Liberation News Service*, September 19, 1980. Author's collection.

15. Cover, *Gay Comix*, no. 3 (1982). Author's collection.

16. Jake Berry, "Modom: Phase 2," *Modom* (c. 1990).

17. Cindy O., "i like things to be small. . . ," *Doris* (1996).

18. Pagan Kennedy, *'Zine: How I Spent Six Years of My Life in the Underground and Finally . . . Found Myself . . . I Think* (New York: St. Martin's Griffin, 1995), 8–10.

19. Winifred McNeill, *Listen/Whisperer*, etching on paper, clamshell, beeswax, 1997. Courtesy the artist.

20. Denise Mullen, *Na Pali*, embossed Islamic leather bound book with loose guard and accordion of palladium photos, handmade papers, letterpress, leather endbands, 1998. Copyright © Denise Mullen. Courtesy the artist.

21. Kelsey Osborn, *Beauty Intensive: Series 1, Beauty Intensification Procedure*, offset, paper, saddle stitched, 1995. Courtesy the artist.

22. David Stairs, *Boundless*, spiral bound paper, 1983 and 1990. Courtesy the artist.

23. Melissa Zink, *Story Painting: Mme. B*, mixed media, 1996. Courtesy the artist.

WORKS CITED

Al-Fadhly, Waleed S., and Gary Shapiro. *How to Publish a Highschool Underground Newspaper*. Los Angeles: Al-Fadhly and Shapiro Bank Note Company, 1970.

Anania, Michael. "Of Living Belfrey and Rampart: On American Literary Magazines since 1950." In *The Little Magazine in America: A Modern Documentary History*, edited by Elliott Anderson and Mary Kinzie. Yonkers, N.Y.: Pushcart Press, 1978.

Bates, Eric. "Chaining the Alternatives: What Started as a Movement Has Become an Industry." *Nation* 266 (June 29, 1998): 11–18.

Chielens, Edward E., ed. *American Literary Magazines: The Twentieth Century*. New York: Greenwood Press, 1992.

Friedman, R. Seth. *The Factsheet Five Zine Reader: The Best Writing from the Underground World of Zines*. New York: Three Rivers Press, 1997.

Harshav, Benjamin, and Barbara Harshav. *American Yiddish Poetry: A Bilingual Anthology*. Berkeley: University of California Press, 1986.

Jenkins, Henry. *Textual Poachers: TV Fans and Participatory Culture*. New York: Routledge, 1992.

Johnson, Abby Arthur, and Ronald Maberry Johnson. *Propaganda and Aesthetics: The Literary Politics of Afro-American Literary Magazines in the Twentieth Century*. Amherst: University of Massachusetts Press, 1979.

Miller, Sally M., ed. *The Ethnic Press in the United States: A Historical Analysis and Handbook*. New York: Greenwood Press, 1987.

Padgett, Ron, and Aram Saroyan. Quoted in Steven Clay and Rodney Phillips, *A Secret Location on the Lower East Side: Adventures in Writing, 1960–1980*. New York: New York Public Library and Granary Books, 1998.

Peck, Abe. *Uncovering the Sixties: The Life and Times of the Underground Press*. New York: Carol Publishing, 1985, 1991.

Rips, Geoffrey. *UnAmerican Activities: The Campaign against the Underground Press*. San Francisco: City Lights Press, 1981.

Zink, Melissa. "A Private Aesthetic." Taos, N.M.: Parks Gallery, 1997.

FOR FURTHER RESEARCH

Bury, Stephen. *Artists' Books: The Book as a Work of Art, 1963–1995*. Brookfield, Vt.: Scolar Press, 1995.

Castleman, Riva. *A Century of Artists Books*. New York: Museum of Modern Art, 1994.

Dettmar, Kevin J. H., and Stephen Watt. *Marketing Modernisms: Self-Promotion, Canonization, Rereading*. Ann Arbor: University of Michigan Press, 1996.

Drucker, Johanna. *The Century of Artists Books*. New York: Granary Books, 1995.

Duncombe, Stephen. *Notes from Underground: Zines and the Politics of Alternative Culture*. London: Verso, 1997.

Glazier, Loss Pequeno. *Small Press: An Annotated Guide*. Westport, Conn.: Greenwood Press, 1995.

Glessing, Robert J. *The Underground Press in America*. Bloomington: Indiana University Press, 1970.

Green, Karen, and Tristan Taormino. *A Girl's Guide to Taking Over the World: Writings from the Girl Zine Revolution*. New York: St. Martin's Griffin, 1997.

Gunderloy, Mike, and Cari Goldberg Janice. *The World of Zines: A Guide to the Independent Magazine Revolution*. New York: Penguin, 1992.

Hamilton, Ian. *The Little Magazines: A Study of Six Editors*. London: Weidenfield, 1976.

Higgins, Dick, and Charles Alexander, eds. *Talking the Boundless Book: Art, Language, and the Book Arts*. Minneapolis: Minnesota Center for Book Arts, 1996.

Hoffman, Frederick J., Charles Allen, and Carolyn F. Ulrich. *The Little Magazine: A History and a Bibliography*. Princeton, N.J.: Princeton University Press, 1946.

Kessler, Lauren. *The Dissident Press: Alternative Journalism in American History*. Beverly Hills, Calif.: Sage, 1984.

Kruchkow, Diane, and Curt Johnson. *Green Isle in the Sea: An Informal History of the Underground Press*. Highland, Ill.: December Press, 1986.

Lyons, Joan, ed. *Artists' Books*. Rochester, N.Y.: Visual Studies Workshop Press, 1985.

Marek, Jayne E. *Women Editing Modernism: "Little" Magazines and Literary History*. Lexington: University Press of Kentucky, 1995.

Rowe, Chip, ed. *The Book of Zines: Readings from the Fringe*. New York: H. Holt, 1997.

Wachsberger, Ken, ed. *Voices from the Underground, Vols. 1 and 2: Insider Histories of the Vietnam Era Underground Press; A Directory of Resources and Sources*. Tempe, Ariz.: Mica's Press, 1993.

DOCUMENTARY FILMS

Weinberg, Wendy, director. *Margaret Anderson and the Little Review: Beyond Imagining*, 1991.

Zwigoff, Terry, director. *Crumb*, 1994.

15

Newspapers since 1945

GLENN WALLACH

LOOK AT a daily urban newspaper from 1945 next to one dated today. The two share only the barest formal similarities: both have headlines, stories laid out in columns, obituaries, and advertisements. Everything else has changed. Color suffuses the front pages of even "traditional" papers such as the *New York Times*. Graphics, layout, and content look more toward the twenty-first century than they do to the twentieth. Newspapers have adapted, one way or another, to a changing world. The process has not always been smooth; still one should not move too swiftly to embrace the claims of technological enthusiasts who see the end of newsprint in the electronic dissemination of news.

Throughout the twentieth century newspapers faced a series of technological challenges that appeared to supplant the papers' primacy in news distribution. In the 1920s radio rapidly entered American culture, becoming a household staple for drama, comedy, music, and, of course, news in the course of a single decade. By mid-century radio was pressing its temporal advantage in reporting breaking news as it happened. In the later 1940s television emerged. This burgeoning technology went further than radio with its ability to broadcast both sound and image, but not until the 1960s would this medium begin its significant challenge to newspapers. By the 1990s television's growing dominance was joined by a new force: the World Wide Web. The Web offers media consumers news when and how they want it from multiple information sources of fluctuating authority and reliability.

Technological change affected the look of newspapers even more than their content. Cultural transformations shaped the form and approach of newspapers in other ways. The artifacts that follow review some of the challenges faced by newspapers and reveal that issues that seem quite recent have, in fact, been evolving for many years.

ARTIFACTS

After World War II, Robert Maynard Hutchins (1899–1977) was concluding his sixteen-year presidency of the University of Chicago, where he had championed liberal arts education and the importance of critical thinking. At the behest (and with the financial support) of Time, Inc., founder Henry Luce, Hutchins became the chairman of the Commission on the Freedom of the Press. The commission's 1947 report addressed mass communication's role in post-war civic culture; the excerpt reproduced here worries about the dissolving distinction between news and entertainment. By the early 1950s new issues had come to the fore. In a lecture from 1953, newspaper editor E. Palmer Hoyt (d. 1979) dismisses the impact of radio and television before turning to the major dilemma facing newspapers at the moment: McCarthyism. Hoyt's discussion shows how the techniques employed by McCarthy took advantage of entrenched news-gathering practices. Hoyt spoke from his experience reviving the *Portland Oregonian* before becoming editor and publisher of a struggling *Denver Post* in 1946. He stayed there until 1970. A. J. Liebling (1904–1963) was the principal author of the *New Yorker*'s "The Wayward Press" column from 1945 until his death. He carried out this responsibility with the same gusto he brought to his coverage of everything from boxing to war to the life of everyday people. His May 14, 1960, column, "Do You Belong in Journalism?" raised an issue he discussed frequently: the increased consolidation of newspaper ownership in the post-war years. Technological change was already coming to newspaper production by 1964 when Richard L. Tobin (1910–1995) wrote a surprisingly prescient essay, reprinted here, about the ways newspaper technology would change in what was for him the future, but is our present day. Tobin had years of experience in newspapers, primarily at the *New York Herald Tribune*, and was managing and executive editor of the *Saturday Review* in the 1960s and early 1970s. His closing paragraph still serves as an important caution to those who believe in technology's inevitable power for change.

Commission on Freedom of the Press, *A Free and Responsible Press* (1947)[1]

The American press probably reaches as high a percentage of the population as that of any other country. Its technical equipment is certainly the best in the world. It has taken the lead in the introduction of many new techniques which have enormously increased the speed and the variety of communications. Whatever its shortcomings, the American press is less venal and less subservient to political and economic pressures than that of many other countries. . . . The economic logic of private enterprise forces most units of the mass communications industry to seek an ever larger audience. The result is an omnibus product which includes something for everybody.

The American newspaper is now as much a medium of entertainment, specialized information, and advertising as it is of news. A solid evening of radio adds up to something like the reading of a mass-circulation newspaper except that the percentage of reporting and discussion of public affairs is even lower. It goes as low as zero in the case of some local stations, as low as 2 per cent in many, and up to 10 per cent in some network affiliates. . . . information and discussion regarding public affairs are only a part, and often a minor part of the output of the communications industry.

Information and discussion regarding public affairs, carried as a rider on the omnibus of mass communication, take on the character of the other passengers and become subject to the same laws that governed their selection: such information and discussion must be shaped so that they will pay their own way by attracting the maximum audience.

Hence the word "news" has come to mean something different from important new information. When a journalist says that a certain event is news, he does not mean that it is important in itself. Often it is, but about as often it is not. The journalist means by news something that has happened within the last few hours which will attract the interest of the customers. The criteria of interest are recency or firstness, proximity, combat, human interest, and novelty. Such criteria limit accuracy and significance.

The eager pursuit of these qualities is undoubtedly captivating to the participants, but to the world at large it seems often to lead to unfortunate excesses. . . . To attract the maximum audience, the press emphasizes the exceptional rather than the representative, the sensational rather than the significant. Many activities of the utmost social consequence lie below the surface of what are conventionally regarded as reportable incidents: more power machinery; fewer men tending machines; more hours of leisure; more schooling per child; decrease of intolerance; successful negotiation of labor contracts; increase of participation in music through the schools; increase in the sale of books of biography and history.

In most news media such matters are crowded out by stories of nightclub murders, race riots, strike violence, and quarrels among public officials. The Commission does not object to the reporting of these incidents but to the preoccupation of the press with them. The press is preoccupied with them to such an extent that the citizen is not supplied the information and discussion he needs to discharge his responsibilities to the community.

The effort to attract the maximum audience means that each news account must be written to catch headlines. The result is not a continued story of the life of a people, but a series of vignettes, made to seem more significant than they really are. The sum of such discontinuous parts does not equal the whole, because the parts have not been represented in their actual size and color in relation to the whole.

People seldom want to read or hear what does not please them; they seldom want others to read or hear what disagrees with their convictions or what presents an unfavorable picture of groups they belong to. When such groups are organized, they let the press know their objections to remarks concerning them. The press is therefore caught between its desire to please and extend its audience and its desire to give a picture of events as they really are.

Palmer Hoyt, "New Dimensions in the News,"
The William Allen White Lecture (1953)[2]

I was graduated from the University of Oregon School of Journalism in 1923. Just before commencement day, a great and good friend of mine who had loaned me money to finish school, expressed extreme regret that I was going into the newspaper business. . . . The gentleman said, and he was an outstanding success in his own field, "I am sorry you are going into newspapers because in ten years there will be no newspapers."

And I asked, "Why not?"

He said, "The radio will supplant them. There will be no more newspapers."

History now reveals that the greatest boon to the development of newspapers was this same radio. Certainly it is true that the radio did furnish some competition . . . but the advent of radio forced the newspapers to become better, to become more readable, and to more completely fulfill their obligation to their circulation areas.

I see no threat to newspapers in the advent of television. It is virtually impossible for television to enter into competition with newspapers in the presentation of news because of the difficulties of picturization. Of course, there is always the commentator reading a news report. This, however, is hardly so exciting that it becomes a necessary part of the life of any person who is genuinely interested in news and its background.

Right there in that word "background" is one of the obvious responsibilities of the press. It is increasingly necessary for newspapers, without departing from their highly held standards of objective news reporting, to give adequate background about important stories and events so that the reader will be informed and can, in due turn, make his own judgments.

Today more than 50 million daily newspapers are being circulated to and being read by the public. . . . at the beginning of 1952 there were 1507 evening papers, 363 morning papers and 564 Sunday papers in the United States. . . . Figuring the normal three readers for every paper, it is easy to come to the realization that our daily and Sunday newspaper readership more than equaled our total population of approximately 150 million persons. This . . . brings clearly to point the fact that the American public is the best informed public in the world.

There is impact for you, impact every day of the year, Sundays and holidays included. There are readers equal to our total population.

This same impact, of course, connotes tremendous responsibility, particularly in this era when new dimensions are entering the news picture. There is the dimension of completeness, more necessary than ever because of the partial and suggestive treatment given the news by radio and television.

Then, of course, there are the dimensions of the news itself brought sharply to mind by McCarthyism. . . . McCarthyism to me has several meanings. First it is a synonym for irresponsible charges. Second, it is a description of an era: An era in which the charge becomes more important than the trial, the proof or the acquittal.

Under the operational plan of McCarthy, plain proof is not essential to his purposes; because each new charge produces a trial in the public prints. . . . Twenty minutes before the press time of a given newspaper, Joseph McCarthy accuses John Jones of being a Communist. It just happens that John Jones is not a Communist, but the charge, made under senatorial immunity, is flashed over the wires of one or all of the news services. Then the bannerline. McCarthy says: "John Jones is a Communist."

As I said, this particular John Jones is not a Communist, so eventually he gets around to a factual denial of these charges and a documentation of his innocence. What happens to the story then? Does it have a banner line? I am afraid that it does not. It gets a small space inside, perhaps on the first classified page.

Today, men "with a grievance against his fellow men" are ignoring the courts of law to spread their charges with despicable recklessness under the protective cloak of congressional immunity. . . . They are challenging editors . . . to re-examine their consciences.

A. J. Liebling, "Do You Belong in Journalism?" from *The New Yorker* (1960)[3]

My bed-table book for some months past has been a volume called *Do You Belong in Journalism?* (Appleton-Century-Crofts). "Eighteen Editors Tell How You Can Explore Career Opportunities in Newspaper Work," the subtitle says, but none of them tell how you can manage to have your own paper, like William Randolph Hearst, Jr., or Mrs. Dorothy Schiff, or Marshall Field, Jr., or even John Hay Whitney. All of them warn the aspirant that he won't get rich (nine of the editors are still in shirtsleeves, according to the illustrations), but they offer other compensations.

"Other advantages," J.M. McClelland, Jr., editor and publisher of the Longview, Washington, *Daily News* (circulation 17,147), says, "include employment in a remarkably stable industry. The income of newspapers is generally quite even, and the sudden danger of losing one's job due to sudden perhaps temporary slumps is remote." When Mr. McClelland wrote that, he must have been thinking of a job on the only newspaper in town—which in fact, the Longview *Daily News* is. If a journalist is working in a town where there are two ownerships, he is even money to become unemployed any minute, and if there are three, has two chances out of three of being in the public relations business before his children get through school. The loss of the job will be due not to a sudden slump but a merger; the effect on the fellow who thought he belonged in journalism will be the same.

American cities with competing newspapers will soon be as rare as those with two telephone systems. . . . The recent annual convention of the American Newspaper Publishers' Association in New York . . . reaches here at the same season as the Ringling Brothers and Barnum & Bailey Circus (Circuses were hit by mergers even earlier than newspapers). Like the Big Show, the convention always bears a certain basic resemblance to its predecessors.

I last commented on New York newspaper coverage of the A.N.P.A. in 1953—a memorable year for the publishers because most of them (84 percent, by their own proclamation) were celebrating their first winner in a national presidential election since 1928. . . . The *World-Telegram* ran the headline ONE-PARTY PRESS CHARGE DENIED over a story quoting the then president of the A.N.P.A., a Mr. Charles F. McCahill, general manager of the afternoon Cleveland *News*, who, "denied charges by some followers of Adlai E. Stevenson, the Democratic candidate, that the press was too lop-sided in its support of President Eisenhower." Just lopsided enough, he must have meant. What impressed me when I reread the 1953 story the other day was that the Cleveland *News* is no more. Another potentate I quoted then was . . . the general manager of the Boston *Post*, which had the largest circulation (302,000) of any standard-size newspaper then in Boston. The *Post*—which had an unforgettable habit of running a front page of headlines in assorted type sizes, none under an inch high, and then leaving you to burrow inside the paper for the stories—is as dead as yesterday's *News*. [He lists several more.] That is quite a lot of nationally famous newspapers to go out in the space of seven years that have been far from lean. The list does not pretend to be a complete catalogue of decedents; come to think of it, the Brooklyn *Eagle* still breathed in 1953, although feebly, and there probably are at least a score of less illustrious cadavers. Each of these shipwrecks tossed a hundred or a few hundred people who thought they belonged in journalism out onto the stormy seas of pressagentry or ghostwriting. Mortality among newspapers has been high from the twenties on, but the last years have brought a quickening of decimation. The worst of it is that each newspaper disappearing below the horizon carries with it, if not a point of view, at least a potential emplacement for one. A city with one newspaper, or with a morning and an evening paper under one ownership, is like a man with one eye, and often the eye is glass.

What you have in a one-paper town is a privately owned public utility that is constitutionally exempt from public regulations, which would be a violation of freedom of the press. As to the freedom of the individual journalist in such a town, it corresponds exactly to what the publisher will allow him. He can't go over to the opposition, because there isn't any. . . . That there are some competent newspapers in monopoly cities changes nothing. It is not right that a citizen's access to news should be completely aleatory, depending on the character of the monopoly publisher in the city where he happens to live.

Finally, the moguls elected a new president . . . a Mr. Mark Ferree, of the Scripps-Howard newspapers, [who] "has done about everything there is to do on a newspaper except set type. . . ." His last immersion in editorial ink . . . was as Sunday editor of the Miami *Herald* in 1927; he has been on the side of the house where they keep the money ever since. This is the side of journalism that it pays best to be on. In fact, it is the lop side.

Richard L. Tobin, "The Man with the Pencil of Light," from *Saturday Review* (1964)[4]

What will a newspaper be like in the next forty years? Let's pay a visit to tomorrow's editorial office. It won't be difficult to find the editors, for their chairs will be beside consoles on which are a great number of pushbuttons and a typewriter keyboard. The editors may be completely surrounded by screens similar to television sets, and instead of pencils they'll have slim tubes in their hands—light pencils and erasers that look like pencil flashlights.

The legmen, the reporter, and the rewrite man will not have been replaced entirely, and somewhere along the line an original story will still be typed out by someone. Human beings will still be at the core of the newspaper operation. But from that point on, electronic machinery will have taken over. As a rewrite man finishes each sentence, what he has written will be recorded in an electronic morgue where all of the day's news is being stored on computer tapes, along with the tapes of the news of other days. At the same time, the electronic story is also appearing on one of the editor's viewing screens. All the rewrite man and editor will have to do to receive available background material and available photographs on that particular subject is to dial the electronic news library. The material will appear on the editor's viewing screen or, if preferred, it will be electronically printed out for the rewrite man.

The layout department will then begin electronically choosing which story will go in which space on page one and the inside pages; the photographs will be sorted and, after selection, their images projected on the photo editor's screen; and the captions will be written. Headlines will be chosen and the story projected on a screen to a copy editor who will type out his head after reading the material via TV. . . . every transaction, each communication will be done by flicking one switch or another between one editor or another.

Not only have the computer and electronic screen taken over in the editorial office, but all copy has been set . . . and the whole edition delivered in suburban streets dozens of miles away where additional presses have responded to the electronic button marked "Print." In many homes, electronic devices will have acted as their own printing presses.

Is this fantastic hardware far to our future? Not at all. Variations of it already are being used in the assembling, editing, and dissemination of information by intelligence and military headquarters. Will the human being be dropped completely from the newspaper forty years hence? On the contrary, there will be more demand for editing skills and creativity, but considerably diminishing demand for printers, pressmen, compositors, stereotypers, and other mechanical functionaries now prevalent in the relatively unautomated newspaper business of the 1960s.

The chief question is not, however, one of mechanical advancement or automation or futuristic presswork. The morals, the power, and the responsibility of the editor, the reaction of his reader-viewers, their self-control as citizens of a greatly advanced atomic age—these are the matters that will count far more than editing with electronic pencil or printing by laser beam. It's what the reader-viewers of mankind do with the information that has been communicated to them that will matter most.

THE 1960s were a decade of freedom and experimentation for newspapers as for much of American culture. Sometimes this was the result of legal decisions, as shown in Richard D. Yoakam and Ronald T. Farrar's analysis of a critical Supreme Court case that redefined the boundaries of libel suits against newspapers. Yoakam (1924–) and Farrar (1935–) had long careers as professors and deans at several schools of journalism. In other instances, as with the rise of the underground press, freedom came as the result both of changing technology (it became possible for the first time since the mid-nineteenth century for people without much cultural or financial capital to mount a challenge to the corporate giants who ran most big-city newspapers) and a cultural opening brought on by the explosion of youth enclaves in major cities. Jesse Kornbluth (1946–), a recent graduate of Harvard University in 1967, had already edited a book, *Notes from the New Underground,* when he wrote the essay reproduced here, which reveals the fragile nature of the underground press and the ease with which mass culture appropriated those elements that served its own interests. Kornbluth has since had a successful career as a freelance writer and is currently editorial director of AOL Networks. Press freedom meant something else to a newly elected presidential administration in 1969: potential damage. A memo written by White House aide Jeb Magruder (b. 1934) reveals a deeply antagonistic view of the press and shows that the roots of the infamous Watergate scandal ran far deeper than the failed 1972 burglary of the Democratic National Committee headquarters. The press, of course, is heralded as the hero in uncovering the Watergate scandal. A 1973 essay by Haynes Johnson (b. 1931)—a reporter in Washington since the 1950s and a national political correspondent for the *Washington Post* since 1969—challenged the self-congratulatory attitude of the national press: despite all that freedom coverage remained essentially as uncritical of the establishment as it had always been.

Richard D. Yoakam and Ronald T. Farrar, "The *Times* Libel Case and Communications Law," from *Journalism Quarterly* (1965)[5]

The United States Supreme Court's decision in the *New York Times Co. v. Sullivan* libel case has already become a symbol of a larger trend in all the courts to liberalize the sweep and scope of interpretations of libel.

The *Times* case, and some subsequent lower court actions since then, appear at first glance to be smashing blows for libertarianism; actually, these decisions may have pushed the nation's press, radio and television closer to—not farther away from—a concept of social responsibility.

The case stemmed from a full-page advertisement that appeared in the *Times* on March 29, 1960, in an attempt by integrationist leaders to raise money for Dr. Martin Luther King's civil rights crusades throughout the South. The ad copy contained some harsh statements—many of which proved untrue—about the treatment accorded some Negroes and white sympathizers in several southern cities. The ad copy, signed and paid for by some well-known public figures, was accepted without question by the *Times*. . . . when some Montgomery city officials sued, the *Times*—which, unhappily, had not bothered to check the facts in the ad—could not plead truth as a defense. The first of 11 suits against the *Times* was filed by L. B. Sullivan, one of the three elected city commissioners of Montgomery. . . . The jury found for Sullivan, and awarded him a judgment totaling $500,000.

On March 9, 1964, the Supreme Court unanimously reversed the case, and in so doing pronounced the doctrine that malice was the key to the extent and character of the libel of a political figure. The *Times* had run the ad in question without malice, the Court held, and in effect was doing the very job a newspaper is supposed to do—that is, discussing public officials in the public interest:

> Thus we consider this case against the background of a profound national commitment to the principle that debate on public issues should be uninhibited, robust, and wide open, and that it may well include sharp attacks on government and public officials. . . .

The old notion of "truth" as an acid and airtight test of libel is not nearly as inclusive, or even as relevant, as it once was in cases involving libel on public officials. Instead the test has largely become one of malice—of printing a deliberate lie or with *reckless* disregard of whether the statement is true or false.

The emphasis has been shifted from legalistic to ethical grounds. Social responsibility is now the better test. Instead of saying "don't publish this because if you do you can be sued . . . " the framework now is "you can publish this if you want to, but do you want to?" The decision here is much more difficult. It puts the responsibility on the shoulders of the editor, takes it somewhat further away from the company lawyer, and calls upon the teacher to provide the future editors with an even firmer ethical basis for the making of such decisions.

Jesse Kornbluth, "This Place of Entertainment Has No Fire Exit: The Underground Press and How It Went," from *The Antioch Review* (1969)[6]

The interesting thing about the phenomenon we've come to call the underground press is that it seems quite dead these days. Most of the papers are printing the same ritualized reports of drug busts, leftist paranoia, and catch-all astrology, badly designed and graphically artless. It's winter everywhere, especially in our heads, and the universe seems to have slid into sludge—no one has anything to say that urgently requires saying. The underground press was at best a reflection of the lives of its creators; now that those lives have been maimed by the experience of the last two years, the papers are cynical, exclusive, and cater to an increasingly ingrown audience.

It's not made easier, of course, by the peculiarly macabre proclivity of midcult to "discover" a trend as it's starting to fade; the mass media serves simultaneously as executioner and alchemist. So the underground press that's finally beginning to Make It isn't the underground press I loved, the underground press that suffered and fought just to exist but always kept a sense of humor about the war—no, of those original 125 members of the Underground Press Syndicate, about half have folded and most of the rest have been completely transformed.

Once upon a time, about a generation ago—that is, back in 1967—a feeling flashed through America. For the first time, a lot of young people had the same sense of life. And the same message came to many: It's beautiful. You can do more to enjoy it. And free yourselves, because the Crazies control the planet.

At that time, on the flip side, LBJ was dominating the straight media with his Vietnam freakout and his daily announcement that the Emperor had clothes and someone was twisting the arms of the communications Biggies (or do they twist their own arms?) to get them to say that the Emperor's suit never looked better. . . . So the first priority was to get our own news networks and broadcast our version of The Truth. And the message was poster-simple then: LOVE.

Considered as a movement in itself, the high point of the underground press was the Winter-Summer of 1967. . . . It was a wonderful and amazing circus. . . . If you had something to say, if you were doing something you wanted to show the world, you just walked into your local underground paper and more frequently than not your message was circulated.

The papers were printed with varying degrees of care. [Boston] *Avatar* and the San Francisco *Oracle* were the products of thousands of man-hours and the attention of dedicated artists; the more typical papers were paste-up montages. . . . But it didn't really matter what was said; the point was that these toys were our own and everything worked.

It's difficult to say what destroyed this spirit. It's fashionable to argue that too much acid, too many undisciplined kids, and too much publicity made the underground press so self-conscious that it began to devour itself.

What happened, I think, is that too many papers started to take themselves too seriously. For $200 almost anyone could start a paper and almost anyone did—this flooded the hip media scene until the local underground paper became as institutionalized as the head shop. Underground editors became mini-celebrities. It meant something to put out a paper, and the informal symposia conducted in the *Look* and *Time* articles on the hippies elevated the papers to the position of spokesmen for a movement.

The survival of the underground press as it now exists doesn't strike me as central to the experience of many young people I know. Most of the papers still publishing could disappear tomorrow, and the only true mourners would be the editors and advertisers.

White House Memorandum (1969)[7]

October 17, 1969
MEMORANDUM FOR: H. R. HALDEMAN
FROM: J. S. MAGRUDER
RE: The Shot-gun versus the Rifle

Yesterday you asked me to give you a talking paper on specific problems we've had in shot-gunning the media and anti-Administration spokesmen on unfair coverage.

I have enclosed from the log approximately 21 requests from the President in the last 30 days requesting specific action relating to what could be considered unfair news coverage. . . . In the short time that I have been here, I would gather that there have been at least double or triple this many requests made through various other parties to accomplish the same objective.

It is my opinion that this continual daily attempt to get to the media or to anti-Administration spokesmen because of specific things they have said is very unfruitful and wasteful of our time.

The real problem that faces the Administration is to get to this unfair coverage in such a way that we make major impact on a basis which the networks-newspapers and Congress will react to and begin to look at things somewhat differently. . . . we should begin concentrated efforts in a number of major areas that will have much more impact on the media and other anti-Administration spokesmen and will do more good in the long run. The following is my suggestion as to how we can achieve this goal:

1. Begin an official monitoring system through the FCC [Federal Communications Commission]. . . . If the monitoring system proves our point, we have then legitimate and legal rights to the networks, etc., and make official complaints from the FCC.

2. Utilize the anti-trust division to investigate various media relating to anti-trust violations. Even the possible threat of anti-trust action I think would be effective in changing their views in the above matter.

3. Utilizing the Internal Revenue Service as a method to look into the various organizations that we are most concerned about. Just a threat of a IRS investigation will probably turn their approach.

4. Begin to show favorites within the media. Since they are basically not on our side let us pick the favorable ones. . . . I'm not saying we should eliminate the open Administration, but by being open we have not gotten anyone to back us on a consistent basis and many of those who were favorable towards us are now giving it to us at various times.

. . . we seem to march on tip-toe into the political situation and are unwilling to use the power at hand to achieve our long term goals which is eight years of a Republican Administration. . . . If we convince the President that this is a correct approach, we will find that various support groups will be much more productive and much more cooperative; and at the same time I think we will achieve the goals this Administration has set out to do on a much more meaningful planned basis.

Haynes Johnson, "The Press: A Lack of Vigor," from
The Washington Post (1973)[8]

In these post-Watergate days of self-congratulation among members of the American press, it is popular to hear all the old journalistic chestnuts about rugged independence and the people's right to know and the special adversary role that must exist between journalists and public officials. Watergate, it is being said, was the press' finest hour, a classic example of what freedom of the press is all about.

The Nixon administration, ironically, is lending credence to this impression of an all-powerful press performance. . . . A presidential propagandist, Pat Buchanan, has mounted a familiar administration counterattack. In his view, the liberal, elitist, Eastern press axis is up to its old conspiratorial tricks. It is carefully orchestrating a campaign designed to discredit the President.

And . . . this private word is being passed from some people in the Executive Mansion: The polls are wrong, the President is still immensely popular, and the press will pay the penalty for its excesses in the Watergate coverage.

All this is heady material for the American press, particularly as the accuracy of so many Watergate reports continues to be confirmed. The trouble with these accolades is that, with a few shining exceptions, they aren't deserved. Far from being the fiercely independent government interrogator of vaunted legend, by and large the press has been a permissive tabby-cat.

Writing in the *Washington Post* recently, William Greider spoke of the mentality and attitudes of those implicated in the scandal. Watergate, he said, was crime-by-the-group. Well, it seems to me that when the definitive book on Watergate is written . . . the American press must share in the collective guilt.

For the press, Watergate is only a symptom of a larger pattern of behavior, a pattern that permitted it to be used by government, a pattern that exalted and sanctified the presidency into an office that could do no wrong, a pattern that led many in the press to think of themselves either as important adjuncts of government policy-making or key components of a patriotic team.

In spite of its breast-beating stance of independence and unrelenting government criticism, for years the Washington press corps was a willing accomplice of government secrecy, official trial balloons and justifications for policy failures. It was, for the most part, a staunch supporter of government policies, especially in foreign affairs.

Anyone who thinks the present state of the press in America is outrageously critical of everyone in government from the President on down should look at the earlier record. The modern American press comes out of a tradition of savage independence and caustic, often unfair, criticism characterized by a belief that no official is above rebuke or harsh examination. . . . I think it fair to say that such pugnaciousness has not been hallmark of the American press in recent years.

So pin no laurels on the press as a whole for Watergate. Salute a few, if you will, but remember that for large segments of the press the Watergate story was basically unexplored. . . . In the end, the press has done its job, but like so many others involved in Watergate, it has been a most reluctant hero.

WHILE HAYNES JOHNSON criticized the press's "tabby cat" relationship with the government, others were starting to observe social arenas that had been over-looked within the newsroom itself. Robert C. Maynard (1937–1993) was a reporter at the *Washington Post* for ten years before he led the purchase of the *Oakland Tribune* in 1983. He remained as the *Tribune*'s publisher until his death. Maynard's 1972 essay assailed the fact that most reporters and virtually all decision makers and managers were white. This observation would soon be augmented to specify that they were white men. Women employees of the *New York Times* charged the paper with sex discrimination in the mid-1970s during an era when similar struggles were underway in other work sites and in collegiate athletics. *Times* reporter Betsy Wade's 1993 essay about the lawsuit underlines how quickly progress can be taken for granted even as those struggles for equality changed the women involved and the profession they loved. At the time of the lawsuit Wade (1929–) was married to journalist James Boylan, hence her "payroll name."

Robert C. Maynard, "Perspective: A Black Journalist Looks at White Newsrooms," from *The Washington Post* (1972)[9]

> "... the total professional figure nationally (for all minority group members in daily newspaper journalism) may reasonably be estimated at approximately 300—or three fourths of 1 percent of total writer-photographer-editor employment."—*From a report to the American Society of Newspaper Editors by its Committees on Minority Employment and Education in Journalism*

If the figures for minority participation in American newspapers are not shocking in and of themselves, I invite you to imagine how those white newsrooms appear to the eyes of a black journalist. What he sees is not just a pervasive whiteness that can only suggest racism in the raw. He also sees hypocrisy in this. . . . If government infringes on some right of the media, those who own them waste no time in reaching for the First Amendment. . . . What is forgotten in these times is that we have some other Amendments—the 14th for some reason comes readily to mind—that would make a stranger to these shores assume something very different about the performance of American institutions with regard to the hiring and promotion of minorities.

There is no place to go with figures such as these, except up. . . . After all, before the advent of the urban uprisings, which demanded the hiring of people who could at least gain safe passage to the site of the story, that percentage was probably one sorry fifth of what it is today.

Because we were mostly hired to face down the urban rebellions, the black journalist's position was in yet another way unique. To the police, he was a nosy snoop appearing on the scene of disturbances to ask the kinds of questions police officers are not accustomed to being asked. . . . Then there were the young blacks who were certain our purpose was to "spy for the man" and they were often just as hard to deal with.

Many of us looked about to ask where the blacks who knew and understood the city were working during those times of urban stress. They were all out on the street eating tear gas and ducking bricks and nightsticks almost simultaneously. The writers, the editors, the people with ultimate responsibility for portraying the event to the world were all white.

I am among the least convinced that the problem of finding "qualified" blacks accounts by itself for these appalling statistics.

When white editors are faced with the challenge of making judgments about white candidates for newsroom jobs, they seem to be able to do that with very little problem. But when they must make the same judgments about blacks, it's Jackie Robinson or no go. They want a surefire hitter, a dynamite dude, a winner in all fields. Much as that is racism it is also a function of the uncertainty that racism produces. If you know no blacks, on what basis would you judge the first one you had met?

When I began at age 16 to become a journalist, it was not a calling that cared very much about college degrees. In fact, I remember the first editor who sized me up and decided to take a chance on me. I told him I had no college degree. "Look," he said, "skip all that. Can you write or can't you?" Had he and a few others like him not decided they could make a decision, I too, would no doubt find myself today among the ranks of the "unqualified." It is a galling and terrifying realization in a multicultural society.

Betsy Wade, "Surviving Being a Survivor, Or, Whatever Became of What's Her Name?" from *Media Studies Journal* (1993)[10]

It's a small and diminishing club I belong to: women who put themselves on the line as lead plaintiffs in the media sex-discrimination suits of the 1970s and then stayed on with the same employers. By virtue of my payroll name, I was alphabetically the first of the named plaintiffs at the *New York Times* and thus became the eponym of *Boylan v. Times*. The next to youngest of the seven, I still work there.

We remain proud. Though we may walk invisible among our legatees, we know that we opened doors for a new generation that may not know they were ever closed.

I myself once belonged to a generation that neglected the admonition Alice Duer Miller gave about her woman's college: Do not ever take it for granted; people whose names you will never know broke their hearts to get it for you.

When I went to the intimidating composing room of the *Times* as (I have been told) the first woman to do make-up. . . . I recalled only a sole woman Linotype operator—the already venerable daughter of a printer—who proudly came by to greet me but, by union protocol, from the printers' side of the stone.

When I went to work for the *Times* in 1956 I was 27. Miss Huger appeared to me then to be 150, although she proved to be 53. . . . she had a figure a lot like my ninth-grade English teacher's. I saw her but did not identify with her.

How arrogant that I should recall young Miss Wade trotting into that blocklong composing room with her proofs . . . bringing the fight for equality to the heartland of the International Typographical Union. Miss Huger had joined that battle well before me. . . . A college graduate, she went to the paper in 1927, before I was born, and worked her way into editing and makeup from the stenographers' pool.

When I stand in the *Times* elevator . . . anonymous and ignored by the perky women who have come to the *Times* since 1978, when *Boylan v. Times* was settled, I can claim no right to be angry, hurt or hostile. I am 150 years old and shaped like a ninth-grade English teacher. These young women know that they all made it on their own, and I hear them assert that these discrimination problems have been resolved. We knew what we did could benefit only those who followed, but we have become as invisible as Miss Huger.

In the settlement, we won an affirmative action plan for promotion and hiring that was supervised by the court for four years, and a cash settlement of $350,000 of which $233,500 went to the women—an average of $454 each. . . . [Fellow plaintiff Grace] Glueck believes that the disdainful attitude of her colleagues derived from their belief that money was the objective, and the yield was poor.

The terms of the settlement were not widely known, but that was no accident. The *Times* came in with money offers in the last days of a strike that still had the *Times* and [New York] *Daily News* shut down; there was coverage of the case as it ended, but a shadow of what it might have been.

Ten years after the settlement, in 1988, we held a party for ourselves, to enjoy the pat on the back that we all felt had not been forthcoming from our co-workers. . . . Women holding jobs as photographers, art directors, sports reporters, mapmakers, assistant news editors, columnists—jobs never held by women before the suit—turned out.

[Times staffers Joan] Cook, [Grace] Glueck and I . . . share the belief that our work together and the process of the suit, rather than its outcome, formed us.

Glueck says it was the most important action of her professional life. . . . Cook says, "it was my source of sense of history and a sense of principle. It gave me a sense of self."

I started out afraid, but with friends like that, who can remain timid? *Boylan v. Times* made me a tiger.

DESPITE THE many upheavals in newspapers in the three decades since 1945, the physical layout and makeup of the paper itself seemed to have reached a somewhat stable form. A series of transformations that began in the 1980s changed everything. *USA Today* was the harbinger of change. Its national scope and eye-catching graphics (and, its critics argued at the outset, little "hard" journalism) have made it a ubiquitous presence since its founding in 1982. Soon after its launch Charles Kaiser (1950–), who has written for the *New York Times*, the *Wall Street Journal*, and *Newsweek*, offered an early reflection on this new approach and provided one of the first uses of the phrase that would soon come to be associated with objections to *USA Today*'s mass-produced aura: McPaper. David Remnick (1958–) was a reporter at the *Washington Post* when his analysis of the long-term implications of *USA Today*, reprinted here, appeared in 1992 (he became editor of the *New Yorker* in 1998).

The revolution begun by *USA Today* continued. Three final artifacts suggest the complexities involved in forecasting the future. Jon Katz (1947–), media critic for *Rolling Stone* when the article here appeared in 1992, introduced a distinction between "old" and "new" news—although a reader might ask how his depiction of "old news" compares to the evidence provided throughout this volume. "New news" was proclaimed before the online revolution really took off and made the distinction even more stark. In a 1997 essay, John V. Pavlik (1956–), executive director of the Center for New Media at Columbia Graduate School of Journalism, assessed the rush to online editions of newspapers. John F. Sturm (1947–), president and chief executive officer of the Newspaper Association of America, contended in 1998 that newspapers are in better shape than they have ever been and that they will weather any challenge that the Internet can muster. A perspective somewhere between the sunny industry forecast and the dark predictions of technological inevitability might lead to a different question—not whether the newspaper will adapt to this wave of change, but how?

Charles Kaiser, "The Big Mac of Newspapers," from *Newsweek* (1983)[11]

General-interest national newspapers never work. For decades that has been the conventional wisdom of the news business. As a result the launching of the Gannett Co.'s USA Today last September was greeted with a virtually universal snort of skepticism. Four months later, to the astonishment of almost everyone except Gannett chairman and president Allen H. Neuharth, USA Today seems to be working very well indeed.

Neuharth's marketing flair has played a major role in the paper's initial success. To make it seem ubiquitous to the nation's opinion-makers, thousands of copies have been given away to passengers on the shuttle between New York and Washington. Millions of dollars were spent on the paper's distinctive blue and white television-shaped vending machines, which are cropping up on sidewalks across the country from Punxsutawney, Pa., to Portland, Ore. This week Houston joins the rapidly growing list of big cities where the 25–cent paper is available; next week it's Denver, and a week after that it will be Los Angeles. Everywhere it goes, USA Today's appearance is preceded by a lavish promotional campaign—$200,000 was spent in Pittsburgh alone.

Clever promotion is only a small part of the story. The four-section format (News, Money, Life and Sports) seems to have something for everyone—though in very small doses: a huge first-section weather map, well-designed color graphs that bring statistics to life and short, gossipy stories. . . . "we want stories about the nation's trends and things that work," explains . . . editor John J. Curley. The paper's mostly male readers enjoy its comprehensive sports section and the money section is particularly impressive. . . . USA Today's state-of-the-art technology, which includes transmission by satellite, also gives it the best color reproduction of any newspaper being printed in America.

USA Today's news section at least provides its readers with the illusion that they are receiving comprehensive national and foreign coverage, though most of its stories have no more depth than a 30–second item that flashes by on the evening news. Last Friday's "A" section, for example, contained 236 separate news items—but most of these were no more than three sentences long. The main result is a loss of nuance. "You cannot show shades of gray," says one . . . reporter. "Even if the facts are correct as they appear it can be very misleading because you can't tell the entire story." All this has earned USA Today the nickname "MacPaper"—the fast food of the newspaper business.

Neuharth naturally dismisses such criticisms explaining that they mostly come from journalists, and "USA Today is designed for readers." Despite their disparagement, editors in many markets where the new paper has arrived are already emulating its style. In Pittsburgh, both of the local papers started adding four-color pages in October, and Atlanta Constitution publisher David Easterly admits he "stole" USA Today's color weather page for his own newspaper.

Even though the paper now seems to be prospering, it will be many months before anyone knows for sure whether it's just a passing curiosity or a serious commercial success.

David Remnick, "Good News Is No News," from *Esquire* (1987)[12]

There are few major newspapers in the world that show such unyielding optimism, such an overwhelming desire to please and unite the citizenry, such an obdurate unwillingness to face the sorrows and complexities of the modern world. Most prominent among them are *Pravda* and *Iszvestia*. But compared with *USA Today*, Soviet newspapers face an identity crisis.

USA Today is a more blithe, confident production. . . . From the beginning, *USA Today* was more than a new business. It was a new institution, in perfect sync with its times, a newspaper that would see the world the way Ronald Reagan does, as a television show that We Are All Enjoying Together.

Ask staffers, from Neuharth down, what journalism they are proud of after five years, and many, Neuharth included, will talk only glancingly of certain stories, preferring to stick with "packages," "the philosophy of easy-to-find, easy to read," and how it is "harder to write five inches than fifty." Several stories and projects are mentioned repeatedly: coverage of the Los Angeles Olympics and, above all, coverage of the *Challenger* disaster, which included the headline PERFECT ISN'T POSSIBLE, FUTURE BELONGS TO THE BRAVE.

Tone controls the emphasis, even the content of *USA Today*. An environmental reporter decided it was getting absurd trying to write "happy news" about dioxin. Editors would say that everything should have an "up," "today" angle.

In a period when scores of papers have gone out of business, *USA Today* is the only major newspaper to begin publishing in the past decade. . . .*USA Today* is now the most widely read paper in the country having passed *The Wall Street Journal*. . . . Last June, the company announced that *USA Today* had moved into the black for the first time, showing operating profits of $1.1 million and surprising many Wall Street analysts who saw no opening for a new national paper.

Airplanes are laboratories of America's elites. Somewhere a sociologist is working on "The Curse of the Flying Class." Because of the cost involved, people who fly regularly are likely to have an education and income well above the national average. . . . And like all people who travel, they at times feel as if they are everywhere and nowhere, disconnected. How could they relate to any local paper? And who among them has time for two thousand words about any one thing?

No one understood that new class better than Neuharth. His early market research told him that 850,000 people travel each day on the airlines . . . that 1.75 million people stay in motels or hotels every night. These disembodied, well-to-do souls he felt, cried out for attachment, for news of the old places they were nostalgic for. They would be his audience.

Neuharth has contributed something to the culture that is at once cheery and cynical, a newspaper that imitates and celebrates the vacuity of television. . . . There is no sense of public mission in Neuharth's paper, only private enterprise.

In recent times, the New Journalists, the underground press . . . and dozens of other talents and publications have changed the language of American journalism. Neuharth, too, sees himself as an innovator. But *USA Today* is a product and nothing more. In the end, even its optimism has dangerous moments. Sometimes *USA Today* tries so hard to please that it distorts. AIDS CASES MAY BE ON DECLINE was the head for a recent story, A few paragraphs in, the story says, ". . . and the finding doesn't mean AIDS cases will decline." Doesn't that matter?

Neuharth is a new kind of Citizen Kane. But Kane's . . . was an era of newspaper wars, and the paper that screamed most shrilly often won. Neuharth doesn't have to scream. Instead he coos to his reader, "Everything is all right." His influence, his tone, can be felt in dozens of papers around the country. . . . Other papers have adopted his brevity, and even the Good Gray *Times* is studying the wonders of color. Nearly everyone has stolen the *USA Today* weather map. It is a fine weather map. Neuharth does not raise the old sort of Kane. He offers sugar.

Jon Katz, "Rock, Rap and Movies Bring You the News," from
Rolling Stone (1992)[13]

Straight news—the Old News—is pooped, confused, and broke. Each Nielsen survey, each circulation report, each quarterly statement, reveals the cultural Darwinism ravaging the news industry. The people watching and reading are aging and dying, and the young no longer take their place. Virtually no major city daily has gained circulation in recent years. . . . In the last decade network news has lost nearly half its audience. Advertising revenues are drying up.

In place of the Old News something dramatic is evolving, a new culture of information, a hybrid New News—dazzling, adolescent, irresponsible, fearless, frightening, and powerful. The New News is a heady concoction, part Hollywood film and TV movie, part pop culture and celebrity magazines, tabloid telecasts, cable and home video.

Once the borders were clear and inviolate: Newspapers, newscasts and newsmagazines covered serious events; pop culture entertained us. But in the past generation, the culture sparked by rock&roll, then fused with TV and mutated by Hollywood, ran riot over the traditional boundaries between straight journalism and entertainment.

The country's ascendant magazine is not a newsmagazine but a New News magazine. *Entertainment Weekly* focuses on what editors used to call back of the book—the arts and culture material once ghettoized behind the important stuff. But today, the back of the book is the book.

Emerging cable technology gave viewers and programmers vastly more choices, breaking open the New News. Pop culture—America's most remarkable invention since the car—had spawned a new information culture.

The modern news media—the Old News—was formed in the years after World War II. Major newspapers and . . . network-news divisions chose Washington and New York as their headquarters, and presidential politics, the economy and foreign affairs—the cold war mostly—as their preeminent beats. In its heyday, the Old News showed us the murder of John Kennedy, took us to the moon, then helped drive a president from office and end a war.

Other stories, the sexual revolution, the role of race, dramatic changes in the relationship between people and their jobs, the evolution of pop culture, a rebirth of spiritualism—were covered sporadically and incompletely by the Old News. . . . They were a sideline, never the main event.

But for the New News—and for much of America—they were the event. Women, blacks, Hispanics, gays and Asians had launched an ongoing political and cultural revolution against middle-class white males, who continue to dominate most institutions, including the news media. In some countries, revolutions are violent, bloody affairs settled in the streets. In America, they are slugged out in music videos, movies and cable shows.

The newspaper industry's most dramatic response to the New News—*USA Today*

—was greeted by the business with the same enthusiasm with which the human body greets a foreign invader. It was dubbed McPaper and dismissed as insubstantial, shallow and, worst of all, TV-like.

All the facts add up to a story that . . . journalism doesn't want to hear. . . . Rap and rock—music listened to by the same kids the Old News is fretting about losing—are describing a different world than the one reflected on evening newscasts and in daily papers.

A youthful audience is no guarantee that a New News product is journalistically superior; what is significant is that younger viewers and readers find conventional journalism of no particular use in their daily lives. In fact, given that the media make so much out of fairness and objectivity, it's a puzzle why so few people of any age trust it or its conclusions.

Mainstream journalism frequently checkmates itself. In worshipping balance over truth, objectivity over point of view, moderation over diversity and credibility over creativity, the Old News gives consumers a clear choice. Consumers can have a balanced discussion with every side of an issue neutralizing the other, or they can turn to singers, producers and filmakers offering colorful, distinctive, often flawed but frequently more powerful visions of their truth. More and more, Americans are making it clear which they prefer.

John V. Pavlik, "The Future of On Line Journalism, Bonanza or Black Hole?" from Columbia Journalism Review (1997)[14]

If you build it they will come—at least some of them. Imagine a library that carries the equivalent of 1,600 daily newspapers from all over the globe. Now stop imagining. It's here: the Internet provides more news content than that every day, most of it free. So it's not surprising that increasing numbers of the world's forty million to fifty million Internet users are going online for their news.

The wild Internet provides a lot of information of dubious value, of course, which is part of what makes going online an adventure. But the digitally up-to-date also know that the quality of much of the news online is as high as that of leading newspapers or newsmagazines or TV or radio outlets, because much of it comes from those media.

Yet, that fact leads to a question: If online journalism is little more than another delivery system for "old" media—even if it's a potentially better delivery system—what's all the fuss about? In terms of journalism, what's the point?

For many of us in this field, the point is to engage the unengaged. Some of us envision a kind of news that, as it upholds the highest journalistic standards, will allow news consumers to understand the meaning of the day's events in a personalized context that makes better sense to them than traditional media do now.

Since networked new media can be interactive, on-demand, customizable; since it can incorporate new combinations of text, images, moving images, and sound; since it can build new communities based on shared interests and concerns; and since it has almost unlimited space to offer levels of reportorial depth, texture, and context that are impossible in any other medium—new media can transform journalism. . . .

Yes, the potential to customize content also means readers may select only what appeals to their narrowest interests. This "You News" kind of journalism could thus become a force for atomization, for further civic decay.

But the optimists, and I am one of them, don't believe it. Research for half a century indicates that people use media, new or old, to connect to society, not separate. People go online primarily to connect with the news of their community, whether a geographical community or one formed around some other common bond. . . . So, rather than fracturing society, new media—with online journalism at its core—can help to keep us connected. . . .

News content on the Internet has been evolving through three stages. In stage one, which still dominates most news sites, online journalists mostly repurpose content from the mother ship. In stage two, which gained momentum last year and characterizes most of the better news sites, the journalists create original content and augment it with such additives as hyperlinks (with which a reader can instantly access another website); interactive features such as search engines, which seek out material on specific topics; and a degree of customization—the ability to choose what categories of news and information you receive.

. . . Stage three will be characterized by a willingness to rethink the nature of a "community" online and, most important, a willingness to experiment with new forms of storytelling. Often this is "immersive" storytelling, which allows you to enter and navigate through a news report in ways different from just reading it. . . .

But the promise of new media is not merely about dazzling technology. Most serious news organizations know that young people are turning to online media.

News organizations know too that audiences for online news in the future will be drawn by a site's unique content and perspective, and by its quality. New media represents the future. For editors and publishers, a commitment to quality online news today is the best way to ensure that your news organization will be there when the online business matures a decade or more from now.

John F. Sturm, "Looking to a Bright Future" (1998)[15]

The newspaper industry has weathered varied business conditions over the past several years, but as it prepares for the new century, it finds itself in perhaps its strongest position in a decade, facing the future with renewed gusto and élan.

One barometer of this strength is advertising, most newspapers' primary revenue source . . . daily newspapers continue to reap nearly a quarter of all U.S. advertising expenditures, more than any other medium.

One reason for this outstanding growth is that readers overwhelmingly turn to newspapers for information when they're ready to shop. The Newspaper Association of America's Media Usage Study, "So Many Choices, So Little Time.". . . showed that newspapers overwhelmingly beat all other media as consumer's primary advertising source for most major products and services.

The newspaper industry also is watching its readers show a continued and growing interest in what it has to offer . . . newspapers in the top 50 markets gained nearly 700,000 new readers between 1996 and 1997, while viewership for broadcast and cable TV declined. . . .

While newspapers' traditional print product is doing extremely well on all fronts, the industry also is experiencing exponentially fast growth in another medium—the Internet.

More than 800 newspapers now offer an online product. An unrivaled link to the local community, these newspaper online sites offer everything from local news and entertainment, to links to important government information and even game sites. They offer chat rooms and forums for citizens to speak out on issues, and many of them link to wire services and other news organizations to bring users the world. Consumers also can now take advantage of a one-stop link to daily and weekly online newspapers . . . online products and online newspaper classified ads.

Another important key to the future is a strong and diverse workforce. Industry professionals have taken a proactive role in promoting diversity at newspapers through numerous programs. . . .

Our eyes are keenly trained on the future but we haven't stopped improving our traditional product. The new presses are lighter, quicker and allow us to print a higher-quality newspaper, in many cases with better color. Computer-to-plate systems take advertising and editorial material directly from the PC to the back shop. Improved technology has also enabled us to put out the paper more quickly, pushing back deadlines and getting more late breaking news into every edition.

All of this adds up to an exciting, dynamic, vibrant and growing industry that is posting unprecedented revenue and readership gains. The less-informed like to call us dinosaurs, but there's no extinction on the horizon, only continued growth and a bright future.

COMMENTARY: NEWSPAPERS SINCE 1945—DEADLINE USA?

In the opening of the 1952 movie *Deadline U.S.A.*, the viewer sees a vivid montage of the newspaper at mid-century. A collection of mostly middle-aged white men (and a few tough-talking women) ply their trade throughout the skyscraper headquarters of a metropolitan daily. In the newsroom, editors argue with reporters, the rewrite man gets word from the police station, the political correspondent pleads with a source, the gossip columnist gathers the latest dirt. In the basement, mammoth presses print the early edition, and on the top floor, in the executive boardroom, heirs to the newspaper's founder discuss the sale of the paper to a business conglomerate.

Many American newspapers in 1950 were vertically integrated, compartmentalized operations and faced similar challenges. About 1,700 newspapers were being read by about 58 million Americans nationwide. In the next half century, the number of readers would continue to grow, but the number of newspapers would slowly decline. The ownership of those papers would increasingly be held by chains and conglomerates so that by the 1990s a very few companies dominated circulation. Interurban competition between newspapers, already fading by the early 1950s, would be virtually eliminated except in a few instances.

At the height of their popularity, then, newspapers were threatened with impending collapse. In some respects, the story of the newspaper since 1945 has been a decades-long meditation on the decline of the newspaper in an age of mass communication. Its enemies seemed endless: consolidation burying real competition, human interest stories forcing hard news from the front page, new production methods threatening staff, and new media diluting readership.

Predictions of newspapers losing the struggle with new forms of technology are woven deeply into the last fifty years of newspaper history. The rapid expansion of television would take the timely reporting of events away from newspapers and provide new challenges for holding an audience. Meanwhile, other technological changes affected the physical look of the newspaper and the way it was produced every day; for instance, satellite transmission of pictures and advances in composition would eventually permit the color and graphic saturation of *USA Today*. The rise of computer-networked communication and the World Wide Web presents the latest challenge to the newspaper's form and scope. Beginning in the 1950s new printing and typesetting processes threatened to put pressmen and linotype operators out of work and brought decades of conflict between management fearing rising costs and labor unions trying to protect their craft and their jobs.

Amidst these technological changes, transformations in thought and culture would affect the content of the newspaper's columns. Newspapers in the 1940s and 1950s brought their readers the latest information from the world around them. Radio had headlines and the occasional on-the-spot report, but readers still bought newspapers on the street for the real story, and many big cities had several different papers to choose from. Afternoon papers were popular, as they had been in earlier decades, because they provided sports scores, racing results, and other timely information. But critics now worried that newspapers would change—because the world had changed.

World War II brought home the importance of "the agencies of mass communication in the education of the people in public affairs," said the Commission on Freedom of the Press, a panel of public officials and intellectuals. The editor of *Time* magazine Henry R. Luce had sponsored the commission's study of the press during the early days of the war. It published its findings shortly after the war ended and suggested that the volume of information was simply too much for the average American to absorb without some assistance. The commission called for more professional methods in the activities and training of journalists and suggested that journalism become a subject of academic study.

In the postwar environment of impending "cold" war in international affairs and rapid economic expansion and heightened tensions about internal security at home, popular publications had a different answer. "If Mr. John Q. Public is confused by the abundance and complexity of the news, if he is curious about the goings-on of the great or near-great . . . if he is not satisfied with news of what has happened, but wants a forecast of what is to come, he can select a columnist or commentator who will fill his every need" (Bulman, vi). Syndicated columnists such as Walter Lippmann brought analysis and opinion from the nation's capital to several hundred newspapers, while Drew Pearson told the inside story of politics, and Walter Winchell revealed the inside and underside of all walks of life to readers in more than 600 papers. Columnists offered a sampler of interpretation and entertainment. Their popularity, along with the increased presence of feature stories like those that appeared in mass-circulation magazines, represented a grave threat to some observers: "the subversion of the newspaper's primary function of presenting the news" (Wolseley, 32).

The fear of political subversion dominated many front pages. Coverage of Wisconsin senator Joseph McCarthy's charges in 1950 that communists had infiltrated the Department of State and subsequent House and Senate investigations of federal agencies and civil institutions put many editors to the test. Not all newspapers simply repeated the senator's reckless claims. But by the time McCarthy had been censured by his colleagues in the United States Senate in 1954, many editors regretted the hysterical headlines they had published. Some reporters who scrutinized McCarthy too closely also felt the sting of having their loyalty questioned. Many in journalism were developing a sense of skepticism about the assertions made by public officials.

Despite the profound impact of the Cold War, it was the business of news that seemed to have the biggest influence on newspapers. Conglomerates were already on the march. As the *New Yorker*'s A. J. Liebling had commented in the late 1940s, America has a free press in the sense that "[a]nybody in the ten-million-dollar category is free to try to buy or found a paper" (Liebling, 265). A newspaper historian found that in 1962 "there were 1,769 English-language dailies, but only 155 were in competition and many of these were losing money." Twenty-five years later, the number of dailies had held relatively steady, but "of all cities with a daily paper 98 percent had only one newspaper management" (Tebbel, 262; Bagdikian, 74).

The great social transformation that typified 1950s America, the dispersal of population to the suburbs, had particular impact on newspapers' business prospects. Long accustomed to a densely packed urban readership, the city dailies had to change to home delivery of their paper. They now competed for advertising not only with other communications media but over a broader geographical area. Meanwhile, papers that had served large rural readerships began to scale back. Ad pages swelled the size of papers, now more easily picked up from suburban driveways than from urban newsstands. A historian found that "[t]he solid news is to be found on page one, two and three. For the remainder of the paper it forms an inconsequential border around the advertising on those pages which are not entirely occupied by ads" (Tebbel, 262, 266). It was at this moment of a shrinking news "hole" that there seemed to be too many events throughout the world to fit in a publication of any size.

The manifold upheavals of the 1960s took many in the press by surprise. Editors sent reporters to cover social, political, and cultural conflicts following a set of news-gathering routines that had always worked in the past. In time, events would strain and shatter some of their assumptions.

The civil rights movement in the American south and urban unrest in northern cities left many editors wondering whether their definition of "political action" was too narrow and whether they had a staff and editorial policy sufficiently sensitive to the social changes occurring around them. They had few appropriate models to tell stories about the seeming explosion of a youth counterculture or unrest on college campuses prompted at first by debates over freedom of speech and later by clashes over military service. Foreign war gave newspapers in the 1960s their greatest test.

Press coverage of American involvement in Vietnam is shrouded in mythology, and both its content and consequences remain a hotly contested issue in debates over the conflict. Contrary to some popular claims about unfair and negative coverage, the vast majority of stories from Vietnam never questioned the underlying assumptions for the assignment first of military advisors and later of combat troops to the Southeast Asian nation. Reporters initially followed styles of coverage learned in earlier wars. Correspondents struggled to understand a war in which measures of military success seemed unclear and whose overall trajectory resisted the traditional frames for war correspondence. Even a group of journalists who won awards for their "critical" reports in 1962–63 (and opprobrium from the Kennedy administration) did not denounce the motivations behind U.S. policy. The substance of their reporting expressed skepticism only about the effectiveness of particular tactics.

Grumblings over a "credibility gap" in Washington during the early stages of the war's escalation grew to a roar at home by the conflict's end. Reporters had other difficulties covering dissent against the war. Scholars argue that several fundamental journalistic attitudes distorted coverage: "news involves the novel event, not the underlying enduring condition; the person, not the group; the visible conflict, not the deep consensus; the fact that 'advances the story,' not the one that explains or enlarges it" (Gitlin, 263). This resulted in an emphasis on violent or raucous antiwar protesters and on extremist messages.

By 1968 it seemed that the establishment media could no longer comprehend America's social and cultural turbulence. When Chicago police at the Democratic National Convention clubbed several reporters, it was evident to some observers that "[t]he 'orthodox' press . . . has resisted or ignored the inequities of our society and has attempted to perpetuate governmental, economic, and social abuses" (Blumberg, 151). Either the establishment would have to change, or the modes of journalism would have to be changed.

The mainstream press reeled, but it did not collapse. Many papers handled the turmoil with courage and clarity. At the same time, coverage *was* changing—not in basic news coverage at first, but in feature stories. The *New York Herald Tribune*'s Sunday supplement "New York" (which later became an independent magazine of the same name after the *Herald Tribune* closed in the middle of the decade) and mass-circulation magazines such as *Esquire* became outposts for reporters who could use storytelling techniques usually employed in fiction to describe countercultural phenomena and the lives of sports stars and political figures. By the early 1970s this approach was dubbed "the new journalism" and would influence narrative styles in most newspapers. While the establishment press began to evolve from the edges, underground weeklies emerged in youth enclaves across the nation from 1964 into the early 1970s that challenged the essential legitimacy of daily papers. "Why an underground newspaper? Because the truths they tell cannot be told in the mass media, because they serve the needs that are not being served, because a generation in rebellion and facing rebellion needs a voice," an editor wrote in 1970 (in Glessing, 161). Both the new journalism and the underground press revealed growing fissures in conventional wisdom.

Richard Nixon's election in 1968 brought a further cooling of relations between the mainstream press and "the establishment." Nixon believed the news media was predisposed against his policies, and his staff sought ways to gain favorable coverage. The winding down of the Vietnam War seemed to bring daily evidence that earlier official predictions and assertions had been false. In 1971 a former Defense Department official gave a reporter for the *New York Times* a copy of a secret Pentagon history of the war. First the *Times* and eventually twenty papers published excerpts of the report, soon known as the Pentagon Papers. There were hard lessons in the text. A *Washington Post* column noted: "The substance and in some cases the precise details of virtually everything . . . printed from the Pentagon papers is ancient history. It was nearly all published while it was happening. And it was largely a futile enterprise; neither the public nor the congressional politicians were listening" (Harwood, 84). The Justice Department moved to stop publication of the report and the *Times* and other papers that had received a copy of the study went to court to continue. A *Times* columnist wrote: "For the first time in the history of the Republic, the Attorney General of the United States has tried to suppress documents he hasn't read about a war that hasn't been declared" (in Pember, 404). The Supreme Court swiftly ruled that publication should continue.

The release of the Pentagon Papers was one event that led the Nixon White House to conclude that it needed firmer control over leaks of information to the press. The establishment of a secret group known as the Plumbers to prevent such leaks led eventually to a break-in at the Democratic National Committee headquarters in the Watergate apartment complex in Washington, D.C. Links between the burglars, the Nixon re-election campaign, and White House officials were revealed through investigations by the House and the Senate, but journalists, principally two reporters for the *Washington Post*, played crucial roles. The revelations about abuses of government power, enemies lists, and secrecy that emerged in the Watergate scandal led to a popular identity for newspapers as investigators of public misdeeds and a belief that the press needed protection and access to information. Congress passed an expanded Freedom of Information Act in 1974 to give citizens broader access to previously secret information and enshrined the notion of "the people's right to know" as fundamental to civil rights and journalistic responsibility.

The struggle for equality that had stirred the nation also affected those who had reported voter-registration struggles and racial unrest. Some papers organized investigative teams to cover "urban affairs," a topic that only a few years earlier would have simply been the police beat. A city editor noted in the early 1970s, "Fifteen years ago, the iron-handed city editor dealt out assignments like a stud poker player. . . . Today, the team concept gives the reporters the option of . . . dealing himself a new hand, or calling the game" (Stein, 50). Women and minorities, long underrepresented in reporting and especially in management, began to take legal action. A sexual discrimination suit brought against the *New York Times* showed that these issues would be faced at all levels of the newspaper business. Professional organizations such as the American Society of Newspaper Editors tried to respond by setting goals for diversity in the newsroom and in news coverage of racial and ethnic groups. Reporters began to form their own associations drawn from racial and gender communities to press for equality, educate their editors and colleagues, and transform the profession of journalism.

While the journalistic establishment absorbed these tidal shifts, publishers tried to keep their papers on sound economic footing. Newspapers entered into joint-operating agreements (JOA), merging production operations while still maintaining separate editorial staffs. The Supreme Court ruled in 1969 that such arrangements violated antitrust laws, but Congress in 1970 passed the Newspaper Preservation Act, which exempted papers from those regulations. The law was enacted only after intense pressure from the heads of large newspaper chains. One scholar has shown that several publishers wrote to President Nixon and offered a blatant exchange: his support for the law in return for their editorial endorsement in the upcoming 1972 presidential election. The administration reversed its opposition to the legislation and the papers in several chains gave unanimous endorsements to Nixon in 1972 (Bagdikian, 90–101). While its sponsors argued the Newspaper Preservation Act would protect independent journalistic voices, in subsequent years the law became a means by which chain newspapers eliminated competition in cities. A paper had to demonstrate that it was on the brink of failure before a joint-operating agreement could be approved, but critics charged "the business of getting the U.S. attorney general to approve a new JOA has become a racket of manufactured 'failure'" (Barnett, 47).

Meanwhile, manufacturing the paper itself offered another set of challenges. While newspapers had reported with satisfaction the latest medical breakthrough or astronauts orbiting the earth, other advances in technology led to paralyzing labor disputes when applied to their own industry. Automation promised a more efficiently produced paper. The replacement of linotype or "hot type" production by "cold type" methods, which used various electronic means to feed information to a photo-composition system, promised a cleaner, brighter looking newspaper page. It also meant that many of the technicians who had kept newspapers running in the age of mechanical reproduction would no longer be needed in the era of digital publishing.

Newspaper craft unions believed they were fighting for their lives against the onset of automation and other cost-cutting measures. A strike in 1962–63 brought New York City's newspapers to a standstill for almost four months. One account estimates that by its end, the newspapers had lost nearly $1 billion (in 1990s dollars). The strike "caused a permanent erosion in both circulation and advertising," one journalist concluded, and it led to the demise of several New York dailies (Raskin, 63). The onset of automation continued and similar labor struggles erupted periodically until the adoption of computerized production was complete in the 1980s.

Struggles between the press and the state during the 1960s and early 1970s raised questions about the place of objectivity in newspaper coverage. Even though a large percentage of journalists now had some kind of professional training for their jobs, some sought to revive the proposals made by the Commission on Freedom of the Press about rationalizing the work of journalism. The methods of quantitative social science—data analysis, surveys, opinion polls—offered the possibility for accuracy in gauging public opinion and bringing some measure of "truth" to coverage. The promise of social-scientific expertise transformed a way of journalistic seeing. Comments earlier in the century had emphasized the importance of interpretation and context. The belief that hard social science would ground public-opinion forecasts led to an expansion of what came to be called "precision journalism." The emphasis on social-scientific certainty reduced the reliance on anecdotal opinions from the proverbial man on the street and led to thoughtful analyses of public opinion. It also increased trust in sampling methods and led to debates about whether changes in public opinion drove polls or vice versa. The sociologist's and anthropologist's technique of immersion in another culture as a participant-observer began to appear in lengthy explanatory series, such as one in the *Washington Post* that explored a single family's life in poverty and won a Pulitzer Prize in 1995. Together, these transformations changed the very nature of journalistic understanding.

One unexpected consequence of the prevalence of polls and social-science methods in news reporting was the use of those same techniques to determine readers' needs and develop standards to respond to them. "Newspapers may well be hastening their own decline by emphasizing the more traditional forms of political and social news, rather than attempting more functional—and to much of the public, more engaging, life style coverage," argued a study that urged newspapers to recognize their readers' interest in "personal satisfaction" (Schwartz, 401).

In 1982 a national newspaper published by one of the largest chains in the nation and driven by audience surveys appeared in television-shaped newsboxes around the country. *USA Today* changed expectations for news presentation by presenting compressed news stories, lifestyle features, and masses of colorful photographs and charts. In response, more papers from big cities to small towns hired "specially trained design experts. . . . Whereas 35 percent of the dailies" had them in 1983, half did by 1989 (Utt and Pasternak, 626–27).

Competition from *USA Today* and the dominating presence of network and cable television news have led to claims that a "new media" of radio and television talk shows, sensationalized programs, and online information sources has made "old media" outlets such as newspapers less relevant. Twenty-four-hour news programs and online information sources certainly accelerated the news cycle to breakneck speed. The newspaper of the 1950s covered a major story by publishing details as they became available in subsequent editions every day. Editors and reporters tried to act as "gatekeepers" for unverified information. That filter grew frayed over the years and finally evaporated by the end of the 1990s. It sometimes seemed that the papers embraced sensation and presented it as interpretation. In a movement that seemed reminiscent of the Commission on Freedom of the Press fifty years earlier, observers in schools of journalism and elsewhere argued that newspapers needed to create new links to the communities they served and become active forces in the promotion of democratic principles. This movement, known as public or civic journalism, has generated considerable discussion and a few much-discussed projects. But it has not seemed entirely clear exactly how its proponents define community or democracy, or how newspapers should accomplish these lofty goals. Many newspaper executives and editors came to the conclusion that "to avoid . . . 'marketing myopia'— for example, the railroads thinking they were railroads rather than transportation companies and thus losing their markets—newspapers must become information-marketing companies" (Denton, 33).

Changes in the business of newspapers had also transformed the character of journalistic careers. "Reporters seem somewhat cynical about the subjects of their stories and sentimental about themselves," the historian and former newspaper reporter Robert Darnton observed. His colleagues at the *New York Times*, he remembered, tended to dress like businessmen, "but they had a trenchcoat image of themselves" (Darnton, 83–84). The memoirs of celebrated journalists and popular accounts of the scoops of fabled reporters probably do not give the most accurate portrait of the work of the average newspaper employee. A series of sociological studies beginning in the early 1970s revealed a newsroom that had changed its demographic character, but had also by the 1990s experienced a dramatic decline in individual reporters' sense of their autonomy. The popularity of investigative reporting teams that had seemed to indicate a new era for reporters proved to be short-lived. The teams remained, but primarily as vehicles for generating stories suitable for entry in prize competitions. A sense of increasing management control, and the fear that many executives were primarily interested in profit rather than quality, led to critical assessments with titles such as *When MBAs Rule the Newsroom*. And so, at the dawn of a new century, news people and newspaper executives continued to wrestle with the dilemmas of the past fifty years.

In an imaginary movie remake—let us call it *Deadline U.S.A. 2001*—the newsroom is filled with a much more diverse staff of writers and editors. Most of them have received some kind of professional training in journalism. Although the numbers of minorities have not yet reached the parity goals set in the 1970s, there has been substantial progress. Similarly, women are closing in on equal representation, although major gaps remain. Some reporters are still on the telephone talking to sources, but instead of pounding their story out at typewriters, they tap computer keys. Some are doing research that will never be turned into words; instead they provide material for the sophisticated graphics that illustrate most major stories. Others scan the World Wide Web for hot new scoops or send e-mail to a source around the world, while others design that day's online edition of the paper. Editors transmit entire pages of copy electronically to composing rooms and printing facilities far away from the newsroom. The executive boardroom might still be at the top of a sky-scraper; only that building is probably hundreds of miles or many states distant from the newsroom itself.

The deadline for the newspaper as a medium has not arrived yet.

SOURCE NOTES

[Unless otherwise indicated material is considered to fall under fair use or to be in the public domain, or a good-faith effort has been made to locate the copyright holder.]

1. Commission on Freedom of the Press, *A Free and Responsible Press* (Chicago: University of Chicago Press, 1947), 52–57. Reproduced courtesy of the University of Chicago Press, Chicago, Ill.

2. Palmer Hoyt, "New Dimensions in the News" (1953), reprinted in *The Press and the Public Interest, The William Allen White Lectures*, ed. Warren K. Agee (Washington, D.C.: Public Affairs Press, 1968), 40–43, 47.

3. A. J. Liebling, " Do You Belong in Journalism?" originally published in the *New Yorker,* May 14, 1960; reprinted in *The Press* (1961; 2d rev. ed., 1974), 27–35, and numerous times thereafter. Reproduced courtesy of Russell and Volkening, New York, N.Y., as agents for the author. Copyright © 1960 A. J. Liebling, renewed 1988 by Norma Liebling Stonehill.

4. Richard L. Tobin, "The Man with the Pencil of Light," *Saturday Review* 47 (August 29, 1964): 138–39, 194.

5. Richard D. Yoakam and Ronald T. Farrar, "The *Times* Libel Case and Communications Law," *Journalism Quarterly* 42 (Autumn 1965): 661–64. Reproduced courtesy of *Journalism Quarterly*, Columbia, S.C.

6. Jesse Kornbluth, "This Place of Entertainment Has No Fire Exit: The Underground Press and How It Went," originally published in the *Antioch Review* 29 (Spring 1969); reprinted in *Mass Media: A Casebook*, ed. Richard F. Hixson (New York: Thomas Y. Crowell Co., 1973), 230–35. Reproduced courtesy of the editors, *Antioch Review*. Copyright © The Antioch Review, Inc.

7. In William E. Porter, *Assault on the Media: The Nixon Years* (Ann Arbor: University of Michigan Press, 1976), 244–46. Reproduced courtesy of the University of Michigan Press, Ann Arbor, Mich.

8. Haynes Johnson, "The Press: A Lack of Vigor," originally published in the *Washington Post*, June 24, 1973; reprinted in *Of the Press, by the Press, for the Press and Others, Too*, ed. Laura Longley Babb (Boston: Houghton Mifflin, 1976), 114–17. Reproduced courtesy of the Washington Post Writers Group. Copyright © *The Washington Post*.

9. Robert C. Maynard, "Perspective: A Black Journalist Looks at White Newsrooms," originally published in the *Washington Post*, April 26, 1972; reprinted in *Of the Press, by the Press, for the Press and Others, Too*, ed. Laura Longley Babb (Boston: Houghton Mifflin, 1976), 144–46. Reproduced courtesy of the Washington Post Writers Group. Copyright © *The Washington Post*.

10. Betsy Wade, "Surviving Being a Survivor, Or, Whatever Became of What's Her Name?"

Media Studies Journal 7 (Winter/Spring 1993): 105–15. Reproduced courtesy of *Media Studies Journal*, New York, N.Y.

11. Charles Kaiser, "The Big Mac of Newpapers," *Newsweek* 101 (January 17, 1983): 48. Reproduced courtesy of Newsweek, Inc. Copyright © Newsweek, Inc., New York, N.Y.

12. David Remnick, "Good News Is No News," *Esquire* 108 (October 1987): 156–65. Reproduced courtesy of *Esquire* and the Hearst Corporation.

13. Jon Katz, "Rock, Rap and Movies Bring You the News," *Rolling Stone*, no. 625 (March 5, 1992): 33–37, 40, 78. Reproduced courtesy of Jon Katz.

14. John V. Pavlik, "The Future of On Line Journalism, Bonanza or Black Hole?" *Columbia Journalism Review* 36 (July/August 1997): 30–31. Reproduced courtesy of the *Columbia Journalism Review*. Copyright © *Columbia Journalism Review*, New York, N.Y.

15. John F. Sturm, "Looking to a Bright Future," in "It all starts with newspapers," special advertising supplement to the *New York Times*, September 14, 1998. Reproduced courtesy of John F. Sturm.

WORKS CITED

Bagdikian, Ben H. *The Media Monopoly*. 5th ed. Boston: Beacon Press, 1997.

Barnett, Stephen R. "The JOA Scam." *Columbia Journalism Review* 30 (November/December 1991): 47–48.

Bayley, Edwin R. *Joe McCarthy and the Press*. Madison: University of Wisconsin Press, 1981.

Blumberg, Nathan B. "The 'Orthodox' Media under Fire: Chicago and the Press." *Montana Journalism Review*, no. 12 (1969). Reprinted in *Mass Media: A Casebook*, edited by Richard F. Hixson. New York: Thomas Y. Crowell Co., 1973.

Bulman, David, ed. *Molders of Opinion*. Milwaukee, Wis.: Bruce Publishing, 1945.

Darnton, Robert. "Journalism: All the News that Fits We Print." Orig. "Writing News and Telling Stories." *Daedalus* (Spring 1975); reprinted in *The Kiss of Lamourette*. New York: W. W. Norton, 1990.

Denton, Frank. "Old Newspapers and New Realities: The Promise of the Marketing of Journalism." In *Reinventing the Newspaper*. New York: Twentieth Century Fund, 1993.

Gitlin, Todd. *The Whole World Is Watching: Mass Media in the Making and Unmaking of the New Left*. Berkeley: University of California Press, 1980.

Glessing, Robert J. *The Underground Press in America*. Bloomington: Indiana University Press, 1970.

Harwood, Richard. "Lessons from the Pentagon Papers." *Washington Post*, November 30, 1971. Reprinted in *Of the Press, by the Press, for the Press and Others, Too*, edited by Laura Longley Babb. Boston: Houghton Mifflin, 1976.

Liebling, A. J. *The Wayward Pressman*. Garden City, N.J.: Doubleday, 1948.

Pember, Don R. "The 'Pentagon Papers' Decision: More Questions than Answers." *Journalism Quarterly* 48 (Autumn 1971): 403–11.

Raskin, A. H. "Dynastic Journalism Dies in New York." *Saturday Review* 49 (April 9, 1966): 62–63, 79–80.

Schwartz, Stuart. "A General Psychographic Analysis of Newspaper Use and Life Style." *Journalism Quarterly* 57 (Autumn 1980): 392–401, 431.

Stein, M. L. "Everything Changes—Even the Newsroom." *Saturday Review* 54 (July 10, 1971): 45–46.

Tebbel, John. *The Compact History of the American Newspaper*. New York: Hawthorn Books, 1963.

Underwood, Doug. *When MBAs Rule the Newsroom.* New York: Columbia University Press, 1993.

Utt, Sandra H., and Steve Pasternack. "How They Look: An Updated Study of American Newspaper Front Pages." *Journalism Quarterly* 66 (Autumn 1989): 621–27.

Wolseley, R. E. "The Threat to American Newspapers." *Saturday Review* 28 (June 30, 1945): 7–8, 32.

FOR FURTHER RESEARCH

Bagdikian, Ben H. *The Information Machines.* New York: Harper & Row, 1971.

Benjaminson, Peter. *Death in the Afternoon.* Kansas City, Mo.: Andrews, McMeel and Parker, 1984.

Downie, Leonard, Jr. *The New Muckrakers.* New York: New American Library, 1976.

Emery, Michael C. *The Press and America.* 8th ed. Boston: Allyn and Bacon, 1996.

Gans, Herbert. *Deciding What's News.* New York: Pantheon Books, 1979.

Halberstam, David. *The Powers That Be.* New York: Alfred A. Knopf, 1979.

Hallin, Daniel C. *The Uncensored War: The Media and Vietnam.* New York: Oxford University Press, 1986.

Hynds, Ernest C. *American Newspapers in the 1970s.* New York: Hastings House, 1975.

———. *American Newspapers in the 1980s.* New York: Hastings House, 1980.

Kluger, Richard. *The Paper: The Life and Death of the New York Herald Tribune.* New York: Alfred A. Knopf, 1986.

Leonard, Thomas C. *News for All: America's Coming-of-Age with the Press.* New York: Oxford University Press, 1995.

Manoff, Robert Karl, and Michael Schudson, eds. *Reading the News.* New York: Pantheon Books, 1986.

Meyer, Philip. *Precision Journalism: A Reporter's Introduction to Social Science Methods.* Bloomington: Indiana University Press, 1973.

———. *The New Precision Journalism.* Bloomington: Indiana University Press, 1991.

Prichard, Peter S. *The Making of McPaper.* Kansas City, Mo.: Andrews, McMeel and Parker, 1987.

Robertson, Nan. *The Girls in the Balcony.* New York: Random House, 1992.

Roschco, Bernard. *Newsmaking.* Chicago: University of Chicago Press, 1975.

Schwarzlose, Richard A. *Newspapers, a Reference Guide.* New York: Greenwood Press, 1987.

Sigal, Leon V. *Reporters and Officials.* Lexington, Mass.: D. C. Heath, 1973.

Smith, Anthony. *Goodbye Gutenberg: The Newspaper Revolution of the 1980s.* New York: Oxford University Press, 1980.

Stinnett, Lee, ed. *The Changing Face of the Newsroom: American Society of Newspaper Editors Human Resources Committee Report.* Washington, D.C.: The Society, 1989.

Talese, Gay. *The Kingdom and the Power.* New York: World Publishing Co., 1969.

Ungar, Sanford J. *The Papers & the Papers: An Account of the Legal and Political Battle over the Pentagon Papers.* New York: E. P. Dutton, 1972.

Wolfe, Tom. *The New Journalism.* New York: Harper & Row, 1973.

16

The Once and Future Book

SCOTT E. CASPER, JOANNE D. CHAISON, AND JEFFREY D. GROVES

FOUR EPISODES in the history of the book in America, late-1990s style:

In September 1996 Oprah Winfrey—host of the nation's most popular talk show and one of America's most admired women—launched "Oprah's Book Club." Every month since she has announced her latest selection. Millions of people read the book in time for Winfrey's on-air discussion the following month, which features the author and several readers. The first selection, Jacquelyn Mitchard's *The Deep End of the Ocean*, had sold 100,000 copies before Winfrey recommended it. It was the kind of literary fiction publishers call "mid-list," a solid performer but not a block-buster. Oprah's Book Club made Mitchard's novel a bestseller, topping Stephen King and Danielle Steel on the *New York Times* bestseller list. Since then, Oprah's Book Club has continued to make bestsellers of books that otherwise would not be. Toni Morrison's *Song of Solomon* sold more copies after Winfrey selected it than it had after Morrison won the Nobel Prize for literature in 1993.

On Friday, September 11, 1998, special prosecutor Kenneth Starr released his report on the scandals involving President Bill Clinton and Monica Lewinsky. Within days, paperback editions of the report hit bookstores and supermarkets, but countless Americans had already downloaded the lengthy document from a congressional website. Subsequently posted around the World Wide Web, the digital Starr Report was in such demand that numerous sites crashed as too many users tried to access them. Printed as a special supplement in Saturday's newspapers across America, the report probably spiked paper sales for at least a day, and it generated debate about whether its details belonged on families' kitchen tables. It is impossible to tell how many people did not buy the book because they had already read the report on the Web or in the newspaper, but all three paperback editions made the bestseller list at the online bookseller Amazon.com—whose buyers necessarily have Web access. (Meanwhile, a classic of American literature, Walt Whitman's *Leaves of Grass*, sold briskly in its newfound status as the book the president had given to Lewinsky.)

On March 9, 1999, the National Endowment for the Arts revoked funding for the publication of a children's book. *The Story of Colors/La Historia de los Colores: A Bilingual Storybook* had been written by a leader of Mexico's Zapatista Army of National Liberation—even though he had long since sold the rights to a Mexican publisher, which then sold them to Cinco Puntos Press of El Paso, Texas. Worried about the political response, NEA chairman William Ivey canceled Cinco Puntos's $7,500 grant himself. The next day, the story made the front page of the *New York Times*, and within weeks Cinco Puntos had sold out its first edition of 5,000 copies and ordered a second, 8,000-copy run. A small, family-run press, Cinco Puntos specializes in bilingual children's books. Thanks to its own website, and now to the NEA controversy, it maintains a specialized, growing clientele without considerable advertising or distribution expenses.

A different series of children's books was the surprise blockbuster of 1999. The Harry Potter books had sold 5 million copies worldwide by October; they held three of the top four spots on the *New York Times* bestseller list by December. Their author, J. K. Rowling, has become a celebrity—making the rounds of talk shows and book tours. Like Sir Walter Scott's and Charles Dickens's novels 150 years ago, these most popular books in America appeared originally in Britain. (In fact, it was Rowling's British publishers who decided to use her initials, in an attempt to appeal to both girls and boys.) When the American editions altered British words and phrases to American ones, many Americans ordered the original British versions instead—possible now more than ever before thanks to Amazon.com. Children who never wanted to read before are reading Harry Potter. Parents are reading it to their children, and reading it for themselves. But because the series deals with witchcraft and the supernatural, some school districts have banned it.

As these examples suggest, the present holds great interest for book historians, while the future will certainly offer them significant challenges and problems. The technologies, economies, and social practices of writing, publishing, and reading are multiplying and changing quickly. Consider authorship. Over the last few decades, numerous technologies have enabled authors to assume some of the traditional functions of the publisher. Photocopiers have allowed for the creation and distribution of an immense amount of literature and other printed material, the vast majority of which no library catalog or published bibliography describes or enumerates. No one knows, in other words, how much of this kind of print has been or currently is in circulation. The computer and word processor have given authors more control over their manuscripts. (The word "manuscript," which literally means "written by hand," is still used in spite of the fact that today most text is composed at the keyboard. Our technological advances, it seems, far outpace our lexical innovations.) Given that cramping fingers and dull pencils no longer function as brakes on the writing process, some pundits have argued that the great benefits of the word processor—ease of textual alteration, speed of composition—have contributed to the staggering length of many contemporary books. Such arguments, however, must be qualified: in fact, readers and publishers have been complaining about wordy authors and interminable texts for centuries. Still, there is some truth in the observation that computers have changed the way we write. The most significant new technology, the World Wide Web, threatens to steal the very function of the publisher. With small investments in a computer and an Internet service provider, authors can now electronically publish their works—with illustrations if they like—on the Web, with the promise, although hardly the guarantee, of an audience of millions.

In addition to these technological changes, authors now have rather different social relations and standing than they did a century ago. Some authors enjoy a celebrity that is built on the back of modern broadcast media, most notably television. A nineteenth-century publisher like James T. Fields could not in his wildest dreams have imagined a promotional vehicle of such dynamic possibilities. And the nineteenth-century, Romantic ideal of authorship—the inspired writer, such as Hawthorne, working out narratives of genius and lasting value alone in his attic study—is no longer very convincing, if it ever was. Best-selling and mid-list authors today are frequently influenced by literary agents who help them craft their work with "marketability" in mind—both in placing the manuscript with a publisher and in anticipating how the book will sell. Publishers themselves frequently dictate the form and content of their publications, and many literary authors participate in writing groups or attend workshops in which their texts can be directly fertilized with the ideas and responses of others.

Authorship, of course, is not the only arena of change. The economics of publishing are shifting momentously. Over the last two decades, many publishing houses and newspapers have been purchased by media conglomerates—corporations whose business is not book, magazine, or newspaper publishing per se, but rather the profitable distribution of "communications" through a vast array of media. In 2001 a merger joined America Online, the nation's leading Internet provider, and Time Warner, a publisher of books and magazines (among them, *Time, Sports Illustrated,* and *People*) and the owner of CNN, HBO, Warner Bros., and other communications companies. The resulting corporation, AOL Time Warner, is arguably the most far-reaching purveyor of words and images in human history. As of this writing, their website proclaims that this communications giant "is uniquely positioned to connect, inform and entertain people everywhere in innovative ways that will enrich their lives." Many media critics have bemoaned the increasing control of a few large, often multinational, companies over the books we read, the magazines we enjoy, and the news we consume. These critics also suggest that the corporate demand for significant profitability may change publishing (never a very profitable trade) for the worse. The emphasis on monetary return is not restricted to trade publishing. The market for textbooks has become fierce in the last two decades, and educational publishers have also been acquired by media corporations intent on "maximizing" their investments. Even university presses are feeling the competitive squeeze. Many have cut back drastically on the scholarly monograph, the traditional staple of such publishers, in favor of more marketable wares. Complicating such developments even further, the book market itself seems somewhat unstable. The sale of mass-market paperbacks, for instance, began to diminish significantly in the 1990s, a reversal of a trend that had shown remarkable growth since the "paperback revolution" of the 1930s and 1940s. As more and more American households become equipped with computers, publishers worry that their potential readers will turn their attention (and their money) away from books, magazines, and newspapers and toward the Web, video games, and interactive media. And it is not just the publishers who are worrying. Many print workers are also concerned that their jobs may soon be made obsolete by new technologies for the distribution of information, technologies that they are not trained to support or take advantage of.

Academics, publishers, and journalists have made the current situation sound so dire that some media critics have even predicted "the end of the book." Such predictions, however, are certainly overstated. In some ways, the time has never been better for books, print, and publishing. Books are more available to more people than they have ever been before. Trade publishers continue to produce tens of thousands of titles each year, and, taking into account the large extent of publisher backlists, there are currently more than a million titles in print. The growing number of small presses, like Cinco Puntos, are finding niche markets for their publications. The Internet has created new marketing and distribution opportunities for companies like Amazon.com and organizations like the United States Congress. The Web is also changing the rare and used book market. Where once collectors had to scour bookstores for wanted titles, today they can locate books through online searches. Some bookstores even post pictures of their rare items on their websites and allow buyers to purchase books online. Magazines seem to be thriving, especially those that fill specialized needs. At large newsstands, general-interest magazines jostle with those devoted to skateboarding, needlepoint, antique guns, and so on. Many magazines are also placing their content on the Web, a practice that may ultimately make them more widely read. And we should not lose sight of small-scale publishing. Print artifacts such as newsletters, corporate manuals, underground zines, and so on may be virtually uncountable, but they are nonetheless important examples of the way in which our culture is permeated by print.

Along with the producers of books, we must also consider those who read printed products. For authors and publishers the "Oprah's Book Club" label means more sales—but why? Why do people buy books after seeing them on a bestseller list? The reasons may be as numerous as the readers. Or perhaps not: after all, these readers are modeling their choices on other people's selections, so perhaps their reasons and objectives have certain common threads. One thread, surely, lies in interests: Amazon.com suggests books to customers based on what the company's records show they have already bought. Readers have favorite authors, topics, or genres. At the same time, book buying and book reading (which are not synonymous) are part of a process that literary critics and cultural theorists describe as the formation of "cultural capital," in which people derive personal or social value from their cultural possessions and accomplishments. Advocates of great-books courses invoke the notion of cultural capital: Here is what you should know to be an "educated" person and participate in certain kinds of conversations among certain sorts of people. Publishers follow suit, packaging great books as *Great Books*: in series with uniform bindings and with titles such as Penguin Classics. Indeed, the capital may often derive from owning, as much as reading, the books: having the right books on one's shelves suggests a degree of education. Some companies now sell books "by the foot" to individuals, or to commercial establishments or filmmakers, who want their shelves to look distinguished.

What is different about books and cultural capital today, though, is that the flow is not simply top-down, with elite critics and scholars prescribing which books make the well-read person. Bestseller lists register in large measure popularity, not quality. Winfrey's selections make waves because they are hers, and because she has legions of admirers and viewers. When the New York Public Library and other cultural organizations publish lists of the greatest books of the century, their words enter the marketplace of print beside but not necessarily above Winfrey's in readers' minds. The American Library Association has concluded as much—and now regularly announces her selections on its website.

The missing last words of the question, "Have you read . . .?" depend on the community of readers asking it. Within the past decade, communal reading has enjoyed a resurgence in America. By one estimate, there are more than half a million book clubs in the United States today, almost double the number in 1994. Reading clubs are centuries old: Benjamin Franklin started one with his friends in 1720s' Philadelphia; thousands of women formed book groups in the late nineteenth century. Today's book clubs, no less than those earlier ones, reflect their own particular context. Many meet in bookstore coffee bars—in Borders or Barnes & Noble—and those stores sponsor reading groups of their own. Publishers produce guides for book clubs: how to form a club, what sorts of questions get a good book discussion going. Some book discussions occur online, where participants chat anonymously. Even so, most book clubs are ultimately local affairs. Groups of friends or acquaintances meet to talk about common reading, and new communities develop out of shared reading interests or personal background and circumstances.

Still, even granting that the cultural extent of reading is impressive, the future of reading looks unsettled and, for many traditionalists, unsettling. A growing market for books-on-tape (or, more and more commonly, books-on-CD-ROM) suggests that our dominant reading practices may be substantially augmented by an increasing tendency to listen to the written word, to engage it aurally rather than visually. Reading and listening, of course, are very different ways of experiencing text. Perhaps the fact that ears can be engaged while eyes take care of other tasks (like driving or data entry) may return us to something like the experience in former ages of having someone read aloud in the workplace. The development of so-called "e-books"—electronic platforms for distributing text and image—worries many book readers. Not only has the computer spawned a new place to see text (the monitor), it has also encouraged new ways of authoring and constructing text. The Web, for example, is hypertextual and nonlinear: it allows readers to follow their own interests with the click of a button, a practice that some have argued empowers the reader and subverts "the tyranny of the author." (Others have argued that the book always functioned this way in relation to other books, that computers merely enable such browsing at greater speed and with wider range.)

Such developments have encouraged extensive debates about whether the book as we know it—a "codex" consisting of gatherings of pages or sheets bound on one edge and with paper or cloth covers—will soon be rendered obsolete. Book lovers have often responded to this debate with a question: Would you take your laptop to bed (or to the beach, in the Southern California variant) in order to read a novel? The usual answer is "no." As a technology, books are currently superior to other technologies for certain uses. A well-printed page is less tiring for the eyes than a computer screen, books do not need batteries to make them run, and a paperback novel is much cheaper than even the most inexpensive computer. "Would you take your laptop to bed?," however, is a loaded question. We do not know whether in the coming decades computers will continue to look and function the way they do now. Current technologies that seem limiting to us—the monitor, batteries that too quickly lose their charge—may be replaced by others that we are only beginning to devise. Companies are already developing "digital ink"—which mimics real ink on a page but can be transformed instantly from one text to another—and "digital paper," a kind of interface no bulkier than a traditional book. Such technologies might lead to a machine that looks and functions like a traditional codex (which, of course, is also a machine, although we do not often think about it as such). Perhaps, then, we will indeed settle down some evening in the not-too-distant future to read a special prosecutor's report with our e-book, and the next day take our new machine to the beach to peruse the latest title in a book-club list.

These are exciting but challenging times for the creators and consumers of text and for a culture that is organized around print. But surely others in the past have experienced similar challenges. Previous generations of Americans wondered whether cheap, mass-produced books and new genres would undermine readers' characters. Workers in the print trades, from journeymen in 1810 to newspaper pressmen in 1970, have feared the loss of livelihood with the advent of new technologies. Are the challenges we face greater than theirs? Here is where book history comes into play. Armed with our knowledge of the history of the book in America, of the place and importance of print culture in the United States, we can approach the present and the future with a clearer sense of how to interpret it, with an informed understanding of how present trends have roots in the past.

17

Resources for Studying American Book History
A Selective, Annotated Bibliography

JOANNE D. CHAISON

EDWIN WOLF was one of the preeminent bookmen of the twentieth century. For nearly forty years he was the renowned scholar-librarian at the Library Company of Philadelphia, a subscription library founded by Benjamin Franklin in 1731. Until his death in 1989, he was addicted to bibliographical learning and immersed in all aspects of the history of the book, long before it became a separate field of study. A man of strong feelings and convictions, he loved life and loved books. Among his passions was an irrepressible respect for the editors and compilers of bibliographies and reference books. In 1963, on the eve of the electronic age, Wolf wrote candidly on a number of issues. Apprehensive of computing and what he called the "push-button boys," he observed:

> It is amazing to me how much information is available in already published indexes and bibliographies, what a tremendous amount is in the brains of the experts. . . . I love bibliographies. I even write them. Everyday I sing a silent hymn to the memory of a patient soul whose life-work makes my day's work easier. One of my problems as a librarian is that too few people who come a-researching know about these patient souls and their works.[1]

This chapter is a guide to the efforts of some of these patient souls. It introduces students to resources in book history. Far from being comprehensive, it is a selective bibliography—essentially a starting point, a compass of sorts for wanderers in the hallways of libraries. Although several of these sources extend into the twentieth century, most focus on the eighteenth and nineteenth centuries. There are many rare, out-of-print references in the special collections of research and university libraries, but such guides are not included in this selective listing. Rather, this is a sample of the bibliographies, checklists, indexes, and essays that are currently in print or otherwise likely to be found on the shelves of college and university libraries. We hope that public-service and collection-development librarians will find this bibliography a useful guide toward developing core reference materials to support studies in book history.

The bibliography is divided into five broad sections and includes related citations for each. Section A focuses on the most comprehensive bibliographies (i.e., union lists) of books, newspapers, periodicals, and manuscripts. Section B lists guides for studying American literature. Section C contains a sample of sources for selected genres of print, such as dime novels, crime literature, and Indian captivity narratives. Section D cites a number of specific book history sources, including several collections of essays and conference papers, and current periodicals that publish articles on book history. Finally, Section E offers brief descriptions of three book history organizations, along with their Internet addresses for further institutional information.

It seems fitting to conclude this introduction where we began—with the words of Edwin Wolf. In the article cited above, Wolf also exclaimed: "I like books, those four-square objects that you can hold in your hand. . . . I like the people who work with them, know them, care for them, collect them. . ." (Wolf, 438). Wolf had an unrivaled knowledge of books, of references about their authors, readers, publishers, printers, binders, illustrators, and of everything else that now comprises book history. Had he lived through the 1990s, he would be amazed by, and undoubtedly enthusiastic about, the wonders of electronic resources. But he would neither forget nor diminish the contributions of those patient souls who provide us with a veritable cornucopia of published reference sources for studying American book history.

SECTION A: UNION LISTS OF BOOKS, NEWSPAPERS AND PERIODICALS, AND MANUSCRIPTS, WITH SELECTED RELATED SOURCES

Books: Catalog

National Union Catalog, pre-1956 Imprints. A Cumulative Author List Representing Library of Congress Printed Cards and Titles Reported by Other American Libraries. London: Mansell, 1968–81.

> The several hundred volumes in this monumental work are indispensable resources for authorship, verification of titles, bibliographical information, historical notes, subject headings, foreign translations of works, and location of copies for books and pamphlets published before 1956. There are some 10 million entries in this multivolume cumulation. Bookform editions of the *National Union Catalog* ceased in 1982, and a microfiche edition began publication in 1983.

Books: Related Sources

American Imprints

Evans, Charles. *American Bibliography: A Chronological Dictionary of All Books, Pamphlets and Periodical Publications Printed in the United States of America from the Genesis of Printing in 1639 Down to and Including the Year 1800: With Bibliographical and Biographical Notes.* 14 vols. Chicago: Privately printed for the author by Blakely Press, 1903–59.

Bristol, Roger P. *Supplement to Charles Evans' American Bibliography.* Charlottesville: University Press of Virginia for the Bibliographical Society of America and the Bibliographical Society of Virginia, 1970.

Shipton, Clifford K., and James E. Mooney. *National Index of American Imprints through 1800: The Short-Title Evans.* 2 vols. Worcester, Mass.: American Antiquarian Society and Barre Publishers, 1969.

Evans's bibliography, together with Bristol's supplement to it, is the most important general list of American publications printed through the year 1800. The full texts of most titles listed are available in the microform series *Early American Imprints, First Series, 1639–1800*, published by the Readex Microprint Corporation (recently incorporated into NewsBank). The Shipton and Mooney index, known as the "short-title Evans," is an alphabetical index to the microform series of books, pamphlets, and broadsides. Readex, in cooperation with the American Antiquarian Society (AAS), has more recently published a CD-ROM catalog of the microform series. AAS also makes these cataloging records available to libraries holding the Evans microform series, for loading into their online catalogs.

Shaw, Ralph R., and Richard H. Shoemaker, comps. *American Bibliography: A Preliminary Checklist for 1801–1819*. 22 vols. New York: Scarecrow Press, 1958–66.

Shoemaker, Richard H. *Checklist of American Imprints for 1820–1829*. 10 vols. New York: Scarecrow Press, 1964–71.

Checklist of American Imprints for 1830–. Metuchen, N.J.: Scarecrow Press, 1972–.

Several compilers are continuing the work of Charles Evans in creating a national bibliography, although their efforts (cited above) are in checklist form without bibliographical notes. Each volume in these series is a preliminary list and covers a single year. Presently, volumes for the years through 1846 are available. Titles listed in the volumes for 1801 through 1819 are reproduced in the microform series *Early American Imprints, Second Series, 1801–1819*, issued by Readex Microprint Corporation. No comprehensive microform series for American imprints after 1819 is available.

Booktrade Catalogs

McKay, George L., comp. *American Book Auction Catalogues, 1713–1934: A Union List*. New York: New York Public Library, 1937.

Book auction catalogs record the history of American book collecting and are important sources for the history of American booktrades. McKay lists and locates copies of more than 10,000 auction catalogs in chronological sequence. These reflect the interests and tastes of private individuals and institutions as they acquired their collections of books, pamphlets, broadsides, autographs, and bookplates.

Winans, Robert B. *A Descriptive Checklist of Book Catalogues Separately Printed in America: 1693–1800*. Worcester, Mass.: American Antiquarian Society, 1981.

Winans describes 278 printed catalogs issued prior to 1801 by booksellers, auctioneers, publishers, and libraries. He also provides citations to the Evans American Imprints microform series for access to the full text of the catalog. This is a useful source for determining the availability of certain books, including English imports, and for assessing reading interests in early America.

Library History

Barr, Larry J., Haynes McMullen, and Steven G. Leach, comps. *Libraries in American Periodicals before 1876: A Bibliography with Abstracts and an Index*. Jefferson, N.C.: McFarland & Company, 1983.

The volume includes both a list of periodicals that have articles about libraries, and a section with annotated references to types of libraries—e.g. lyceums, mercantile libraries, and temperance libraries. A third section provides citations to studies of libraries by geographic location, a feature helpful to persons studying library history and its relationship to the history of the book.

Davis, Donald G., and John Mark Tucker. *American Library History: A Comprehensive Guide to the Literature*. Santa Barbara, Calif.: ABC-Clio, 1989.

> This guide, the second edition of Michael H. Harris's *American Library History* (1978), provides historiographic essays on various topics, such as private libraries and reading tastes. It is filled with useful references on the history and development of libraries by type (e.g., social, school, academic, and public), along with extensive references to studies of reading interests and the booktrades.

Singerman, Robert. *American Library Book Catalogues, 1801–1875: A National Bibliography*. Champaign: University of Illinois, 1996.

> This volume lists more than 3,300 separately printed catalogs of American libraries published between 1801 and 1875. Singerman's checklist covers an enormous variety of libraries, including libraries of states, legal associations, charitable organizations, mechanics' institute libraries, hospital, lyceum, prison, and religious libraries. The volume is organized by state with excellent chronological, geographical, and topical indexes to the catalogs.

Regional Printing History

"Imprint bibliographies" attempt to record all the printed matter issued from the various presses of a particular city, state, or publisher. Such bibliographies often contain introductory comments about the regional printing history of the place or publisher, and full or partial bibliographical information about individual printed items. The following bibliographies provide a sampling of many such works:

Arndt, Karl John Richard, and Reimer C. Eck, eds. *The First Century of German Language Printing in the United States of America: A Bibliography Based on Studies of Oswald Seidensticker and Wilbur H. Oda*. 2 vols. Göttingen: Niedersachsische Staats und Universitatsbibliothek, 1989.

Felcone, Joseph J. *New Jersey Books, 1698–1800: The Joseph J. Felcone Collection*. Princeton, N.J.: Joseph J. Felcone, 1992.

Gould, Christopher, and Richard Parker Morgan. *South Carolina Imprints, 1731–1800: A Descriptive Bibliography*. Santa Barbara, Calif.: ABC-Clio, 1985.

Jumonville, Florence M. *Bibliography of New Orleans Imprints, 1764–1864*. New Orleans: Historic New Orleans Collection, 1989.

McCorison, Marcus A. *Vermont Imprints, 1778–1820: A Check List of Books, Pamphlets, and Broadsides*. Worcester, Mass.: American Antiquarian Society, 1963.

Miller, C. William. *Benjamin Franklin's Philadelphia Printing, 1728–1766: A Descriptive Bibliography*. Philadelphia: American Philosophical Society, 1974.

Suzuki, Seiko June, Marjorie Pullman, and The Historical Records Survey, comps. *California Imprints, 1833–1862: A Bibliography*. Los Gatos, Calif.: Talisman Press, 1961.

Subscription Publishing

Arbour, Keith. *Canvassing Books, Sample Books, and Subscription Publishers' Ephemera 1833–1951 in the Collection of Michael Zinman*. Ardsley, N.Y.: Haydn, for the Cultural Arts Foundation, 1996.

> This work, the first substantial contribution to the study of American subscription publishing, records nearly 1,800 canvassing books (also referred to as sample books, salesman's dummies, or prospectuses). The collection, formed by Robert Seymour and Michael Zinman,

includes samples of books on the lives of presidents, religion, the Civil War, women, health, exploration and travel, and many other topics. Arbour's historical introduction and his bibliographical descriptions of the sample books make this an essential work for anyone studying the production and marketing strategies of books in the nineteenth and early twentieth centuries. The Zinman Collection is housed in the special collections department at the University of Pennsylvania.

NEWSPAPERS AND PERIODICALS: CATALOGS

Brigham, Clarence S. *History and Bibliography of American Newspapers, 1690–1820.* 2 vols. Worcester, Mass.: American Antiquarian Society, 1947.

Gregory, Winifred, ed. *American Newspapers, 1821–1936: A Union List of Files Available in the United States and Canada.* New York: Kraus Reprint Corp., 1967.

Together these two bibliographies form a comprehensive record of American newspaper files from 1690 to 1936. Brigham lists by state and town more than 2,000 newspapers published between 1690 and 1820 with historical notes for each title, along with information on editors, publishers, and printers. Nearly all of the newspapers described here have been reproduced by the Readex Microprint Corporation in their microfilm series *Early American Newspapers, 1704–1820.* Gregory's checklist, first published in 1937, is regarded as the standard source of information on the location and holdings of newspapers in nearly 6,000 depositories, including libraries, county courthouses, and private collections.

Union List of Serials in Libraries of the United States and Canada. 3d ed. 5 vols. New York: H. W. Wilson Co., 1965.

This extensive list of more than 155,000 titles is an indispensable finding aid for anyone doing reference work with periodicals. Each entry in the *ULS* has information on changes of title, publication life, and holdings statements of cooperating libraries. The alphabetically arranged list of serials covers the span of time from the eighteenth century to 1950.

NEWSPAPERS AND PERIODICALS: RELATED SOURCES

Albaugh, Gaylord P. *History and Annotated Bibliography of American Religious Periodicals and Newspapers Established from 1730 through 1830.* 2 vols. Worcester, Mass.: American Antiquarian Society, 1994.

Albaugh's authoritative bibliography provides detailed information for hundreds of religious newspapers and periodicals whose publishing history began between 1730 and 1830. His introductory essay describes the reasons for the explosive growth of religious publishing. The descriptive bibliography contains more than 900 detailed entries followed by several appendices: for example, chronological and geographical lists of titles, subject lists by denominational interest, an index of editors, publishers, printers, illustrators, and engravers, and a selective bibliography of secondary sources for religious publishing.

Chielens, Edward E., ed. *American Literary Magazines: The Eighteenth and Nineteenth Centuries.* New York: Greenwood Press, 1986.

In this handy reference, Chielens provides succinct profiles of major literary magazines published between 1774 and 1900. There are publication histories and selective bibliographies for each entry, as well as a useful chronological appendix of literary history relative to the social and historical events of the day.

Danky, James P., ed. *African-American Newspapers and Periodicals: A National Bibliography.* Cambridge, Mass.: Harvard University Press, 1998.

This bibliography is the most complete record of newspapers and periodicals published and edited by African Americans from 1827 to the present. It provides access to more than 6,500 titles, including literary and historical journals, general newspapers, and feature magazines. The publications represent numerous aspects of African American life and culture, ranging from the abolitionist and religious press of the nineteenth century to contemporary publications by hip-hop musicians, civil-rights activists, and education and community groups. The detailed subject index lists topics found in the newspapers and periodicals, and the bibliography also has indexes of editors, publishers, and geographic locales.

Hoornstra, Jean, and Trudy Heath, eds. *American Periodicals 1741–1900: An Index to the Microfilm Collections: American Periodicals 18th Century, American Periodicals 1800–1850, American Periodicals 1850–1900, Civil War and Reconstruction.* Ann Arbor, Mich.: University Microfilms International, 1979.

This is a single-volume, general guide to a major microfilm collection of American periodicals. It provides cumulative title, editor, and reel number indexes, along with broad subject access. Since 1989 Computer Indexed Systems has been preparing a keyword subject index to all the journal articles in the microfilm sets of the American Periodicals Series (APS). This index to the contents of periodicals is available on CD-ROM as *Index to American Periodicals of the 1700's and 1800's* (Indianapolis: Computer Indexed Systems). Many of the titles in the American Periodicals Series are valuable sources for book history, including booktrade journals such as the *American Publishers' Circular and Literary Gazette*.

Kribbs, Jayne K., comp. *An Annotated Bibliography of American Literary Periodicals, 1741–1850.* Boston: G. K. Hall, 1977.

Kribbs's bibliography lists 940 American literary periodicals published during the period. Entries are based on titles in the *American Periodical Series*, the *Union List of Serials*, and Frank Luther Mott's *A History of American Magazines, 1741–1850.* Citations for each title include publication data and content analysis (e.g., prose, poetry, essays, etc.). The indexes include a chronological and geographical index of periodicals, and an index of editors, publishers, and literary authors. There is also an index for the nearly 5,000 titles of the tales, novels, and drama that appear in the periodicals.

Lathem, Edward C. *Chronological Tables of American Newspapers, 1690–1820; Being a Tabular Guide to Holdings of Newspapers Published in America through the Year 1820.* Worcester, Mass.: American Antiquarian Society and Barre Publishers, 1972.

This is an excellent companion volume to Brigham's *History and Bibliography of American Newspapers, 1690–1820.* The tables are aids for locating, chronologically, issues of American newspapers for the period through 1820, thus providing a convenient way to identify the papers of a particular locality and to determine each newspaper's span of publication.

Littlefield, Daniel F., Jr. and James W. Parins. *American Indian and Alaska Native Newspapers and Periodicals, 1826–1924.* Westport, Conn.: Greenwood Press, 1984.

This guide profiles more than 200 American Indian and Alaska Native newspapers and periodicals, with descriptions of tribal and nontribal newspapers, reform and literary periodicals, native and English-language publications, and titles issued from the government supported press. Each sketch includes a publication history and information sources for further research. The appendices list titles chronologically and geographically as well as by tribal affiliation. Of related interest is *Native American Periodicals and Newspapers 1828–1982: Bibliography, Publishing Record, and Holdings*, edited by James P. Danky (Westport, Conn.: Greenwood Press, 1984), an extensive guide to the holdings and locations of nearly 1,200 periodical and newspaper publications by and about Native Americans.

Mott, Frank Luther. *A History of American Magazines.* 5 vols. Cambridge, Mass.: Harvard University Press, 1938–68.

Though dated, this work remains the essential source for the history of American magazines, covering periodical literature published from 1741 to 1905, and profiling twenty-one magazines published between 1905 and 1930. Mott's detailed indexes, including subject categories, are an invaluable starting point for studying American periodical literature.

Wells, Daniel A. *The Literary Index to American Magazines, 1815–1865*. Metuchen, N.J.: Scarecrow Press, 1980.

———. *The Literary Index to American Magazines, 1850–1900*. Westport, Conn.: Greenwood Press, 1996.

In both of these volumes, Wells provides useful references to writers and important topics in nineteenth-century literary circles. The indexes contain personal names of literary figures, general references on a wide variety of topics (e.g., international copyright, drama and theater, the novel, women, poetry), and numerous citations to British and European writers who published in American periodicals.

Manuscripts: Catalogs

National Union Catalog of Manuscript Collections. Washington, D.C.: Library of Congress, 1959–73.

NUCMC was established in 1959 as a cooperative cataloging endeavor in which libraries throughout the United States report their holdings to the Library of Congress. This multivolume collection reproduces catalog records for manuscripts such as letters, diaries, account books, financial records, registers, and legal papers held in about 1,500 repositories in the United States. Each entry includes a description of the collection, finding aids, and location. The complete set of *NUCMC* volumes through 1994 is also available on the Internet through the *NUCMC* homepage at <http://lcweb.loc.gov/coll/nucmc/>.

Index to Personal Names in the National Union Catalog of Manuscript Collections 1959–1984. 2 vols. Alexandria, Va.: Chadwyck-Healey, 1988.

Index to Subjects and Corporate Names in the National Union Catalog of Manuscript Collections 1959–1984. 3 vols. Alexandria, Va.: Chadwyck-Healey, 1994.

These indexes are extremely useful guides to the collections represented in the multivolume *National Union Catalog of Manuscript Collections (NUCMC)*. They bring together, in alphabetical sequence, all the personal and family names, and topical and corporate name headings appearing in the descriptions of manuscript collections cataloged from 1959 to 1984. Users can quickly locate information on authors, publishers, associations, and a wide range of literary affairs in these convenient, comprehensively edited indexes. The personal name index includes references to 200,000 names; that for subjects and corporate names includes nearly 300,000 entries.

Manuscripts: Related Sources

Archives of Harper and Brothers 1817–1914. Cambridge, England: Chadwyck-Healey, 1980. Microfilm, 58 reels.

The extant business records of one of America's most influential publishing houses form an exceptional archive of primary materials, with information on nineteenth-century publishing practices, relationships and correspondence with authors, and improvements in printing technology. An index to the collection was compiled by Christopher Feeney in 1982.

Arksey, Laura, Nancy Pries, and Marcia Reed. *American Diaries: An Annotated Bibliography of Published American Diaries and Journals*. Vol. 1, 1492–1844; vol. 2, 1845–1980. Detroit: Gale Research Company, 1983.

Annotated references in this exceptional resource are applicable to many disciplines, but they are particularly useful for those interested in book history. For example, the volumes contain many citations to the reading habits and interests of diarists, as well as their involvement with literary people and societies. Approximately 5,000 annotations are arranged chronologically by the beginning date of the diary. Publication information is given for separately printed diaries and for those appearing in periodicals and local history journals. The indexes include lists of personal names, geographic locations, and superb subject indexes, which include such headings as book collectors; books and reading; Civil War soldiers' books and reading; newspapers and periodicals; reading aloud; and the names of prominent literary figures. These two volumes revise and significantly expand the edition of William Matthews's *American Diaries: An Annotated Bibliography of American Diaries Written Prior to the Year 1861* (Berkeley: University of California Press, 1945).

Brodersen, Martha, Beth Luey, Audrey Brichetto Morris, and Rosanne Trujillo. *A Guide to Book Publishers' Archives*. New York: Book Industry Study Group, 1996.

Chiefly a directory of the archives of twentieth-century United States book publishers, this also includes the location and description of the records of firms from their founding. For example, the archival records of Charles Scribner's Sons are recorded and located from 1786 to 1971. This finding aid includes business records, correspondence, oral histories, legal records, and other sources. The directory is also available online at <http://www.bisg.org/archives>.

Robbins, John Albert, ed. *American Literary Manuscripts: A Checklist of Holdings in Academic, Historical, and Public Libraries, Museums, and Authors' Homes in the United States.* 2d ed. Athens: University of Georgia Press, 1977.

Though far from comprehensive, this general guide to literary manuscripts includes nearly 3,000 citations for the writings of American authors, and for the institutions that hold their journals, diaries, letters, and manuscripts of their works. Authors range from James Fenimore Cooper (1789–1851) and Lydia Sigourney (1791–1865) to Sarah Orne Jewett (1849–1909), Carl Sandburg (1878–1967), and Jack Kerouac (1922–1970), along with many obscure writers. Nearly 600 libraries reported their holdings. The usefulness of the volume is enhanced by a selective list of manuscript guides based, for example, on genre, ethnicity, and region.

SECTION B: AMERICAN LITERATURE

Bercovitch, Sacvan, ed. *The Cambridge History of American Literature*. New York: Cambridge University Press, 1994–.

This outstanding multivolume history currently includes two volumes for the periods 1590–1820 and 1820–1865. Six more volumes will be published covering poetry and prose writing through 1990. The first two volumes offer thorough treatments of early American literary history with wide-ranging, interdisciplinary coverage of genres and periods such as the literature of colonization, British-American belles lettres, the literature of the revolutionary and early national periods, the literature of expansion and race, the Transcendentalists, and narrative forms. Each volume includes an excellent literary chronology, bibliography, and a detailed index.

Blanck, Jacob, comp. *Bibliography of American Literature*. 9 vols. New Haven, Conn.: Yale University Press, 1955–91.

Winship, Michael, comp. *Bibliography of American Literature: A Selective Index*. Golden, Colo.: North American Press, 1995.

———. *Epitome of Bibliography of American Literature*. Golden, Colo.: North American Press, 1995.

The *Bibliography of American Literature (BAL)* is considered by many scholars to be the basic bibliographical tool in the study of American literature. This is a selective analytical bibliography of nearly 40,000 works by 281 American authors who published from the period of the American Revolution through 1930. Works are arranged chronologically for each author with descriptions of their first editions, reprints, and biographical and critical studies. The *BAL* is available on CD-ROM from Chadwyck-Healey, Inc. (Alexandria, Va.), and is also available on the World Wide Web on a subscription basis from Chadwyck-Healey through its website, Literature Online (LiOn).

Two useful research tools, compiled by Michael Winship, make the mountain of information in *BAL* much more accessible and less overwhelming to researchers. The single-volume *Index* adds depth and context by providing title, date, and publisher indexes for works described in the multivolume bibliography. The *Epitome* is a short-title condensation of the 281 authors represented in *BAL*. These abridged and condensed versions of *BAL* also stand alone as ready reference guides to American literary culture and publishing history.

Dictionary of Literary Biography. Detroit: Gale Research Company, 1978–.

There are more than 200 titles to date in this useful, multivolume series. Individual volumes in the series cover a particular topic or time period. Among the volumes in the series are those for *American Colonial Writers*; *Antebellum Writers in New York and the South*; *American Literary Publishing Houses, 1638–1899*; *Afro-American Fiction Writers after 1955*; and *American Writers for Children*. Each title in the series is edited by an authority in the field; entries vary from brief to comprehensive treatments of the subject, and all include selected references for further reading.

Gohdes, Clarence, and Sanford E. Morovitz. *Bibliographical Guide to the Study of the Literature of the U.S.A.* 5th ed. Durham, N.C.: Duke University Press, 1984.

The standard handbook for students of American literature, this includes nearly 2,000 concisely annotated citations to a wide range of subjects. There are sections, for example, on the booktrade and publishing, literary aspects of women's studies and Native American literature, and special topics, themes, and genres ranging from drama and poetry to utopian writings and the literature of the sea.

Myerson, Joel, ed. *Studies in the American Renaissance.* Boston: Twayne, 1977–97.

For twenty years Myerson edited this annual of scholarly biographical, historical, and bibliographical articles on the general culture of America during the period 1830–60. It is an excellent source of information for those studying the literature, philosophy, and religion of that period. The twenty volumes comprise 265 articles, essays, and transcribed diaries and letters of leading literary figures associated with the American Renaissance. The final volume has a cumulative index.

SECTION C: SELECTED GENRES OF PRINT

ALMANACS

Drake, Milton, comp. *Almanacs of the United States.* 2 vols. New York: Scarecrow Press, 1962.

Drake's checklist of almanacs contains more than 14,000 entries, arranged alphabetically and chronologically by state, from 1639 to 1850 for states east of the Mississippi River and generally to 1875 for the others. Perhaps no single printed document, other than the Bible, was more commonly found in homes throughout the nineteenth century than the almanac. As Drake writes in his introduction, the almanac was one publication that a local printer would unfailingly produce each fall; they were bestsellers everywhere, particularly in areas where reading matter was scarce. There is an enormous variety of almanacs ranging from religious, temperance, and antislavery almanacs to health, labor, and comic almanacs. The content of almanacs extended well beyond the usual astronomical and meteorological calculations to include prose, poetry, essays, history, and general public information, making this an important genre for book historians.

ANNUALS

Kirkham, E. Bruce, and John W. Fink, comps. *Indices to American Literary Annuals and Gift Books, 1825–1865*. New Haven, Conn.: Research Publications, 1975.

Literary annuals were popular nineteenth-century collections of poetry, essays, and fiction, and many prominent American authors contributed to this genre. Kirkham and Fink's index is keyed to the microfilm set of annuals reproduced in 1966 by Research Publications, Inc. The first part of the index consists of a comprehensive list of the annuals' table of contents, including the names of editors, authors, and illustrators. The second part contains important indexes for the printers and publishers of the annuals, and an alphabetical list of the titles of poems and stories. Another source of information about annuals is Ralph Thompson's earlier study, *American Literary Annuals and Gift Books, 1825–1865* (New York: H. W. Wilson Company, 1936).

BIOGRAPHIES

Burkett, Randall K., Nancy H. Burkett, Henry Louis Gates Jr., eds. *Black Biography, 1790–1950: A Cumulative Index*. 3 vols. Alexandria, Va.: Chadwyck-Healey, 1991.

These carefully compiled volumes index the monumental collection of African American biographies reproduced in microform by Chadwyck-Healey, Inc., entitled *Black Biographical Dictionaries, 1790–1950*. They are the largest biographical compilation ever gathered to document the lives of African Americans. The microfiche set reproduces the full text of more than 300 collective biographies of men and women from all walks of life, including hundreds in the literary profession.

The three-volume clothbound index provides an alphabetical list of the 30,000 individuals described in the microfiche set. Included in the cumulative index are brief profiles for each person, as well as additional indexes based on occupations, religious affiliations, and geographic residences. This resource is also available as a database on the World Wide Web. Subscription information is available from Chadwyck-Healey, Inc., at <http://www.chadwyck.com>.

Kaplan, Louis, comp. *A Bibliography of American Autobiographies*. Madison: University of Wisconsin Press, 1961.

This standard reference work includes more than 6,000 entries alphabetically arranged for authors whose autobiographies were published before 1945. A detailed subject index lists occupations of the autobiographers, geographical locales, and important historical events of the times. For book historians, this is a particularly useful source for locating self-published narratives written by ordinary individuals. There are occupational entries for authors, illustrators, poets, printers, booksellers, journalists, and publishers, to name but a few.

CHILDREN'S LITERATURE

Welch, d'Alte A. *A Bibliography of American Children's Books Printed prior to 1821*. Worcester, Mass.: American Antiquarian Society and Barre Publishers, 1972.

Welch's bibliography is the essential reference for studying early American children's books. In his introductory comments, Welch offers a chronological overview of the kinds of books printed for children in the eighteenth and early nineteenth centuries (e.g., sermons, narratives, primers, chapbooks, fairy tales) along with a discussion of American editions of English children's books. The detailed bibliographic descriptions include copious notes; and there is an index of the printers and publishers of early children's books.

Crime Literature

McDade, Thomas M., comp. *The Annals of Murder: A Bibliography of Books and Pamphlets on American Murders from Colonial Times to 1900*. Norman: University of Oklahoma Press, 1961.

This bibliography provides ready access to publications devoted to murder cases occurring in the United States prior to 1900. In his introduction, McDade offers a cogent overview of the criminal process in murder trials and the significance and popularity of published trial reports. The bibliography includes citations to trials, the last words and dying confessions of criminals, and autobiographical narratives. McDade's index lists the names of murderers and victims, along with geographical indexes of crimes. In his introduction to *Pillars of Salt: An Anthology of Early American Criminal Narratives* (Madison, Wis.: Madison House, 1993), Daniel Williams provides an informative essay on the literary significance of the genre.

Dime Novels

Johannsen, Albert. *The House of Beadle and Adams and Its Dime and Nickel Novels: The Story of a Vanished Literature*. 3 vols. Norman: University of Oklahoma Press, 1950–62.

Johannsen's guide is the basic reference for this popular form of American fiction. The handsomely illustrated resource captures all aspects of the dime-novel genre. The first volume includes complete numerical lists of the series of Beadle novels and an extensive history of the firm. The second volume is devoted to the authors and their novels and includes biographies of authors, pseudonyms of various Beadle writers, and a list of newspaper and magazine articles that discuss the dime novel. The third volume is a supplement and addenda, along with an index of songs that appear in the Beadle *Songsters*.

Fiction

Facts on File Bibliography of American Fiction through 1865. Edited by Kent P. Ljungquist. New York: Facts on File, 1993.

Facts on File Bibliography of American Fiction, 1866–1918. Edited by James Nagel and Gwen L. Nagel. New York: Facts on File, 1994.

Bibliography of American Fiction (BAF) lists works published by and about writers in the United States from earliest times to the present. Currently, two volumes have been published, with two more to follow, which will cover the period 1919–1988. BAF provides a record of both primary and secondary bibliographical information to those seeking an introduction to an author's body of work and the criticism it has generated. In addition to bibliographical sources for individual authors, the volumes include a wide range of reference sources for American literary history.

Wright, Lyle. *American Fiction, 1774–1900: A Contribution toward a Bibliography*. 3 vols. San Marino, Calif.: Huntington Library, 1965–1969.

Wright's three-volume checklist is considered the essential guide to novels, romances, fictitious biographies, and travel adventures published in the United States between 1774 and 1900. This is a guide to approximately 11,000 books of American fiction, not a bibliographical description of them. The full texts of works listed in Wright have been microfilmed by Research Publications, Inc. (Woodbridge, Conn.).

INDIAN CAPTIVITY NARRATIVES

Vaughan, Alden T. *Narratives of North American Indian Captivity: A Selective Bibliography.*
New York: Garland Publishing, 1983.

The captivity narrative ranks as among the best-selling genres of American publishing
history. Vaughan's bibliography is a companion volume to Garland Publishing's reprint
collection, *Narratives of North American Indian Captivities* (1977), which includes more than 300
narratives of the experiences of captives among the Indians. Vaughan provides an alphabetical list of all the narratives in the Garland collection, as well as listings of important secondary writings and standard bibliographies of Indian-white relations for further study of the
genre. Another significant guide to this genre is *Narratives of Captivity among the Indians of
North America* (Chicago: Newberry Library, 1912), based on the outstanding personal collection of Edward Ayer.

TRAVEL AND EXPLORATION NARRATIVES

Cole, Garold. *Travels in America from the Voyages of Discovery to the Present: An Annotated
Bibliography of Travel Articles in Periodicals, 1955–1980.* Norman: University of Oklahoma
Press, 1984.

This bibliography contains more than 1,000 annotated citations to travel accounts that
appeared in American periodicals between 1955 and 1980. The narratives range from those of
early explorers, pioneers, and soldiers to those of emigrants, missionaries, itinerant peddlers,
and foreigners traveling in America. These previously unpublished diaries and travel journals
are mostly from the eighteenth and nineteenth centuries. Material is arranged geographically,
and chronologically within each region of the country; and there is a detailed index to
travelers, places, and subjects.

Wagner, Henry R., and Charles L. Camp. *The Plains and the Rockies: A Critical Bibliography
of Exploration, Adventure and Travel in the American West 1800–1865.* 4th ed. Revised,
enlarged, and edited by Robert H. Becker. San Francisco: John Howell Books, 1982.

This superb descriptive bibliography arranges nearly 700 titles chronologically and by
author. There are citations to hundreds of fascinating self-published narratives of western
travel, adventure, expeditions, and explorations. Many narratives were later expanded into
more elaborate publications with maps, advertisements, and illustrations that add rich detail
to the history of the book in the American west. Recently, David A. White has compiled an
anthology of narratives described in the Wagner-Camp bibliography, entitled *News of the
Plains and Rockies 1803–1865: Original Narratives of Overland Travel and Adventure Selected from the
Wagner-Camp and Becker Bibliography of Western Americana* (Spokane, Wash.: Arthur H. Clark
Company, 1996–). Four of the proposed eight volumes in White's series of narratives are currently in print, adding immeasurably to the resources for the study of print culture in the west.

SECTION D: BOOK HISTORY SOURCES

ESSAY COLLECTIONS AND REFERENCE VOLUMES

Albertine, Susan, ed. *A Living of Words: American Women in Print Culture.* Knoxville:
University of Tennessee Press, 1995.

This collection of essays focuses on twelve American women and their role in print culture from the colonial period through the early twentieth century. It is essential reading for

anyone interested in women's careers in printing, publishing, marketing, and book selling. The biographical essays range from studies on Ann Franklin, the first woman printer in colonial New England, to Josephine St. Pierre Ruffin, an African American newspaper publisher, to the literary and business achievements of Sylvia Beach, an American expatriate in Paris and owner of the famous bookshop Shakespeare and Company.

Bowers, Fredson. *Principles of Bibliographical Description*. 1949. Reprint, New Castle, Del.: Oak Knoll Press, 1994.

> Bowers's classic guide to descriptive bibliography is a crucial source for anyone doing bibliographical descriptions of printed books as physical objects. In print since 1949, it covers the analytical principles of describing English and American books from the sixteenth to the twentieth centuries.

Carter, John. *ABC for Book Collectors*. 7th ed. New Castle, Del.: Oak Knoll Press, 1995.

> First published in 1952, this enjoyable, witty, and informative guide is an alphabetical dictionary of bibliographical and booksellers' terms with more than 450 entries, ranging in length from a single sentence to several pages. Concise definitions for technical and bibliographical terms such as imprint, colophon, facsimile, dust jacket, modern firsts, format, wormholes, and wrappers, to mention but a few, make this a useful reference for all bibliophiles.

Danky, James P., and Wayne A. Wiegand, eds. *Print Culture in a Diverse America*. Urbana: University of Illinois Press, 1998.

> The eleven interdisciplinary essays in this volume examine a variety of ways that print culture manifests itself within gender, class, and ethnic groups from the mid-nineteenth century to the present. The papers explore, among other topics, the Italian and Chinese immigrant presses, female African American literary societies, readership in an Iowa public library, and early-twentieth-century hobo self-publication. This book helps to fill a gap in the post-1876 history of print culture by focusing on the multicultural world of readers.

Davidson, Cathy N., ed. *Reading in America: Literature and Social History*. Baltimore, Md.: Johns Hopkins University Press, 1989.

> In this collection of excellent essays, Davidson brings together twelve scholars who explore various aspects of book history from Puritan times to the present. Issues addressed range from literacy, chapbook publications, and magazine reading to publishing practices and the role of books in shaping the lives of immigrants, laborers, and minorities.

Fink, Steven, and Susan S. Williams, eds. *Reciprocal Influences: Literary Production, Distribution, and Influence in America*. Columbus: Ohio State University Press, 1999.

> The insightful and important essays in this volume were originally presented at an Ohio State University colloquium to honor the work of William Charvat. Each original essay focuses on a critical issue in current American book history. Topics include the poetry of Whitman and Melville, the fiction of Hawthorne, Twain, and James Weldon Johnson, the literary careers of Margaret Fuller and Elizabeth Stuart Phelps, advertisements in *Life* magazine, the African American press, and the transatlantic booktrade.

Gaskell, Philip. *A New Introduction to Bibliography*. 1972. Reprint, New Castle, Del.: Oak Knoll Press, 2000.

> Gaskell's work is a history of the printing practices and technology of the hand-press and machine-press periods. He covers printing type, composition, paper, binding, format of books, and other aspects of nineteenth- and twentieth-century book production. This is intended as a successor to R. B. McKerrow's *Introduction to Bibliography for Literary Students* (1927), which covers the period up to 1800. McKerrow's book was reprinted by Oak Knoll Press in 1994 with a new introduction by David McKitterick.

Hackenberg, Michael, ed. *Getting the Books Out: Papers of the Chicago Conference on the Book in 19th-Century America*. Washington, D.C.: Library of Congress, 1987.

These essays on nineteenth-century book history address aspects of book dissemination, the significance of copyright records, institutional book collecting in the old northwest, and publishing practices in the far west. The authors draw on previously unexplored primary sources in thought-provoking ways, particularly for those interested in book history beyond the eastern seaboard.

Hall, David D. *Cultures of Print: Essays in the History of the Book*. Amherst: University of Massachusetts Press, 1996.

In this collection of his own essays, Hall focuses chiefly on print culture in the colonial period, with attention to the transatlantic booktrade as well. Included in the volume are his essays on the world of print in seventeenth-century New England and the Chesapeake, literacy, and patterns of reading and writing in the eighteenth century. Hall's seminal essay, "On Native Ground: From the History of Printing to the History of the Book," is reprinted in this volume.

Hall, David D., and John B. Hench, eds. *Needs and Opportunities in the History of the Book: America, 1639–1876*. Worcester, Mass.: American Antiquarian Society, 1987.

The six essays in this book, originally papers read at a 1984 symposium sponsored by the American Antiquarian Society, address such issues as labor and technology in the booktrades, patterns of American book distribution, popular and elite readership, and the textual study of the book as an artifact.

A History of the Book in America. New York: Cambridge University Press, 2000–.

This five-volume, interdisciplinary history of the book in America will serve as the most comprehensive and authoritative study of American book culture from the colonial period to the present. Volume one, *The Colonial Book in the Atlantic World*, edited by Hugh Amory and David D. Hall, was published in 2000. The collaborative project is sponsored by the American Antiquarian Society with David D. Hall as general editor. Titles of forthcoming volumes are *An Extensive Republic: Print, Culture and Society in the Early Republic* (v. 2), *The Book in an Industrial Age* (v. 3), *Print in Motion: Books and Reading in the United States, 1880–1945* (v. 4), and *The Enduring Book, 1945–1995* (v. 5). *A History of the Book in America* is one of several current national book history projects, which include Britain, Scotland, Canada, Australia, France, and Germany.

Hutton, Frankie, and Barbara Straus Reed, eds. *Outsiders in 19th-Century Press History: Multicultural Perspectives*. Bowling Green, Ohio: Bowling Green State University Popular Press, 1995.

Each superb essay in this collection focuses on a particular group of minorities who are representative outsiders in nineteenth-century American journalism history. Included are studies on the early black press, Jewish journalism, Native American and Spanish-language papers, the women's-rights press, as well as representations of Chinese Americans and Mormons in mainstream publications.

Joyce, Donald Franklin. *Black Book Publishers in the United States: A Historical Dictionary of the Presses, 1817–1990*. New York: Greenwood Press, 1991.

This volume is ideal for anyone interested in African American publishers engaged in book publishing. Joyce profiles black religious publishers, institutional publishers such as cultural, educational, and civil-rights organizations, and commercial publishers of magazines and newspapers. Each entry includes a brief history of the firm, selected titles issued by the publisher, and bibliographic sources for further information. Following the alphabetically arranged entries are a geographical listing of black-owned book publishers and indexes for authors, titles, and subjects.

Joyce, William L., David D. Hall, Richard D. Brown, and John B. Hench, eds. *Printing and Society in Early America*. Worcester, Mass.: American Antiquarian Society, 1983.

The papers in this volume were read at a 1980 conference at the American Antiquarian Society held to encourage new approaches to the study of print culture. The topics include literacy, religious journalism, music publishing, and the relationship between print culture and the rise of the public lecture system.

Karpel, Bernard, ed. *Arts in America: A Bibliography*. 4 vols. Washington, D.C.: Published for the Archives of American Art by the Smithsonian Institution Press, 1979.

Within these four volumes are several thousand annotated citations for works about the arts in America, many of which relate to book history. For example, an extensive section devoted to the graphic arts of the seventeenth through the nineteenth centuries, compiled by Georgia B. Barnhill, provides detailed references for bibliographies, periodicals, dictionaries, and studies about specific printmaking techniques, such as lithography and wood engraving. Topical categories include studies of bookplates, maps, sheet music, broadsides, satirical and political prints, and sources for individual graphic artists. Publications are current through 1975.

Lehmann-Haupt, Hellmut. *The Book in America: A History of the Making and Selling of Books in the United States*. In collaboration with Lawrence C. Wroth and Rollo G. Silver. 2d ed. New York: R. R. Bowker, 1951.

This remains the classic survey in the history of printing, publishing, and book distribution from the colonial period to 1950. Contents include the colonial establishment of the printing press in New England, technological advancements in the booktrade, copyright laws and literary property, and brief histories of leading publishing firms through the mid-twentieth century.

Moylan, Michele, and Lane Stiles, eds. *Reading Books: Essays on the Material Text and Literature in America*. Amherst: University of Massachusetts Press, 1996.

These provocative essays deal with cultural and material history and the textual transmission of books. The authors address a broad range of issues that relate to the book as a physical object. This volume links textual meanings to the material aspects of books, dealing with the latter by examining typography, binding, layout, editing, publishing, packaging, and distribution. Topics range from a study of the physical appearance of antebellum family newspapers and their impact on readers, to the marketing techniques of a prominent Boston publishing house, Ticknor and Fields, and the way they defined literary tastes through their bookbinding styles.

Price, Kenneth M., and Susan Belasco Smith, eds. *Periodical Literature in Nineteenth-Century America*. Charlottesville: University Press of Virginia, 1995.

The fourteen essays in this collection highlight the significance of American periodicals in the history of the book. The essays, arranged chronologically from the 1830s through the end of the century, examine a variety of periodicals such as the *Atlantic Monthly*, *Dial*, and *Southern Magazine*. Several focus on the writing careers of authors whose works were shaped by periodical publication, such as Margaret Fuller, Herman Melville, and Emily Dickinson.

Sweet, Leonard I., ed. *Communication and Change in American Religious History*. Grand Rapids, Mich.: Eerdmans, 1993.

The superbly written essays in this volume explore the role of communications and print culture in shaping religious and social life in America from the eighteenth to the twentieth centuries. The twelve papers range from a study of colonial religious revivalist George Whitfield's brilliant use of the press, to religious publishing and the marketplace in the early nineteenth century, to the pioneering use of radio and television to launch the evangelical, ministerial career of Oral Roberts. The volume includes a detailed, annotated bibliography of reference sources.

Tanselle, G. Thomas. *Guide to the Study of United States Imprints*. 2 vols. Cambridge, Mass.: Belknap Press of Harvard University Press, 1971.

In these two volumes, Tanselle records most of the published research relevant to the study of United States imprints through 1970. This valuable reference source includes citations for bibliographies and checklists in nine categories: regional, genre, and author lists; copyright records; catalogs; book-trade directories; studies of individual printers and publishers; general studies; and checklists of secondary material.

―――. *Literature and Artifacts*. Charlottesville: Bibliographical Society of the University of Virginia, 1998.

Tanselle's fifteen essays provide a critical overview to several basic issues in bibliography, scholarly editing, book collecting, and literary criticism. The essays, previously published in diverse sources, include "The History of Books as a Field of Study," "Reproduction and Scholarship," "Enumerative Bibliography and the Physical Book," "Critical Editions, Hypertexts, and Genetic Criticism," and "Analytical Bibliography and Printing History."

Zboray, Ronald J., and Mary Saracino Zboray. *A Handbook for the Study of Book History in the United States*. Washington, D.C.: Center for the Book, Library of Congress, 2000.

This handbook is an important and timely research guide, particularly valuable for graduate students in the field of book history. Of noted significance is their detailed guide to locating and using a broad range of print and manuscript sources for the "producers," "disseminators," and "consumers" of printed materials. Equally valuable is the extensive bibliography of suggested readings that are keyed to the three major sections of their text.

SELECTIVE LIST OF CURRENT PERIODICALS FOR AMERICAN BOOK HISTORY

American Literary History
American Literature
American Periodicals: A Journal of History, Criticism, and Bibliography
American Quarterly
Book History
Early American Literature
History of Reading News
Libraries & Culture: A Journal of Library History
Papers of the Bibliographical Society of America
Printing History
Proceedings of the American Antiquarian Society: A Journal of American History through 1876
Publishers Weekly
Publishing Research Quarterly
Resources for American Literary Study
Studies in Bibliography

SECTION E: ORGANIZATIONS

A useful directory for centers of book history is found in Maurvene Williams's *The Community of the Book: A Directory of Organizations and Programs*. 3d ed. Washington,

D.C.: Library of Congress, 1993. Preeminent in promoting the study of the history of the book in America are the American Antiquarian Society, the Center for the Book in the Library of Congress, and the Society for the History of Authorship, Reading, and Publishing (SHARP). Among the many other organizations that have an impact on book history are the University of Iowa's Center for the Book; the Penn State University Center for the History of the Book; the Center for the History of Print Culture in Modern America at the University of Wisconsin; the National Yiddish Book Center in Amherst, Massachusetts; the American Printing History Association; and the Bibliographical Society of America.

American Antiquarian Society

The American Antiquarian Society (AAS), a national research library established in 1812 in Worcester, Massachusetts, has comprehensive collections of research materials relating to American printing and publishing history and bibliography through 1876. Its Program in the History of the Book in American Culture, established in 1983, fosters a wide range of programs that relate to all aspects of book history. The society sponsors conferences, publications, and research fellowships. A summer seminar in the history of the book brings together a diverse group of persons concerned with book history, including academics, collectors, librarians, and graduate students. An annual lecture in the history of the book, a thrice-yearly newsletter, *The Book*, and the publication of a multivolume, collaborative history of the book from the seventeenth century to the present, entitled *A History of the Book in America* (see above), make the AAS the leading center of scholarship in the field. Further information about AAS is available on the society's website <http://www.americanantiquarian .org>.

The Center for the Book in the Library of Congress

Established in 1977, The Center for the Book in the Library of Congress maintains an active partnership between the government and the private sector in fostering the significance and understanding of the role of books, reading, literacy, and libraries in American history. A primary goal of the center is the encouragement of the interdisciplinary study of the book. The center sponsors several programs to stimulate interest in books and reading for both scholars and the general public. In 1984 the center began establishing statewide centers to encourage interest in regional print culture. The Library of Congress website <http://www.loc.gov/cfbook> provides further information about The Center for the Book.

Society for the History of Authorship, Reading, and Publishing (SHARP)

SHARP was founded in 1991 as an international and interdisciplinary organization for historians, literary scholars, librarians, bibliophiles, journalists, and others interested in book history. It publishes a newsletter and the annual journal *Book History*, sponsors an annual conference, and maintains an active electronic bulletin board, SHARP-L, on the Internet. To subscribe to SHARP-L, send an e-mail message to <listserv@ listserver.indiana.edu>. The SHARP website <http://www.sharpweb.org> is an outstanding resource, with links to a large number of other sites dealing with book history.

NOTES

1. Edwin Wolf, 2d., "Thoughts on Books and Libraries," *Papers of the Bibliographical Society of America* 57 (Fourth Quarter, 1963): 439–40.

Contributors

SCOTT E. CASPER is associate professor of history at the University of Nevada, Reno. He is the author of *Constructing American Lives: Biography and Culture in Nineteenth-Century America* (University of North Carolina Press, 1999) and numerous articles on nineteenth-century American cultural history. *Constructing American Lives* won the 1999 book prize of the Society for the History of Authorship, Reading, and Publishing. Professor Casper is co-editor of volume 3 of *A History of the Book in America* (Cambridge University Press, forthcoming) and a contributor to volume 2 of *A History of the Book in America*.

JOANNE D. CHAISON is Research Librarian at the American Antiquarian Society (AAS) in Worcester, Massachusetts. She has been active in the AAS Program in the History of the Book and leads its bibliographic workshop on reference sources for book history. She holds an M.A. in history from the University of Connecticut and an M.S. in library and information science from Simmons College, Boston.

NANCY COOK is associate professor of English at the University of Rhode Island. She has participated in the American Antiquarian Society's summer History of the Book seminars, and work from those seminars includes her essay in *Reading Books* (University of Massachusetts Press, 1996) and a double issue that she edited on history of the book studies of nineteenth-century American culture for *ATQ* 12, nos. 3 and 4 (1998).

PATRICIA CRAIN is the author of the *The Story of A: The Alphabetization of America from The New England Primer to The Scarlet Letter* (Stanford University Press, 2001), which won the Modern Language Association 2001 Prize for a First Book. She is a member of the English department at the University of Minnesota. She has written on antebellum authors and on the history of childhood in America, and is currently working on a book about early American literacy.

ANN FABIAN teaches history and American studies at Rutgers University in New Brunswick, New Jersey. She is the author of *Card Sharps, Dream Books, and Bucket Shops: Gambling in Nineteenth-Century America* (Cornell University Press, 1990; paperback, Routledge, 1999) and *The Unvarnished Truth: Personal Narratives in Nineteenth-Century America* (University of California Press, 2000).

ALICE FAHS is associate professor of history at the University of California, Irvine. She is the author of *The Imagined Civil War: Popular Literature of the North and South, 1861–1865* (University of North Carolina Press, 2001) as well as numerous articles on American cultural history. She is currently at work on a project on newspaper culture, especially the writings of newspaper women, at the turn of the twentieth century.

ELLEN GRUBER GARVEY is the author of *The Adman in the Parlor: Magazines and the Gendering of Consumer Culture, 1880s–1910s* (Oxford University Press, 1996), which explores how advertising came to seem ordinary and even natural to American magazine readers through the interplay of fiction and advertising; it won the annual prize of the Society for the History of Authorship, Reading, and Publishing. She has written on women and bicycling (*American Quarterly*, 1995), publisher's advertising (volume 4 of *A History of the Book in America*), and other literary, cultural studies, and publishing history topics. Her current project is on scrapbooks and reading. She is associate professor of English at New Jersey City University.

ROBERT A. GROSS is the Forrest D. Murden Jr. Professor of History and American Studies at the College of William and Mary and book review editor of the *William and Mary Quarterly*. After earning a Ph.D. at Columbia University in 1976, he taught at Amherst College from 1976 to 1988. His many publications include *The Minutemen and Their World* (Hill and Wang, 1976; 2d edition, 2001), which won the Bancroft Prize in 1977. He is currently finishing a sequel titled *The Transcendentalists and Their World*. Professor Gross was chair of the Program in the History of the Book at the American Antiquarian Society and co-editor of *The Book*.

JEFFREY D. GROVES is professor of English at Harvey Mudd College, Claremont, California. He has published articles on American literature in such journals as *New England Quarterly* and *Legacy* and is a co-editor of and contributor to volume 3 of *A History of the Book in America* (Cambridge University Press, forthcoming). He is currently working on a monograph that will explore the relationship of literary promotion to canon formation in mid-nineteenth-century American literature.

JEN A. HUNTLEY-SMITH is a postdoctoral fellow in western traditions at the University of Nevada, Reno. Her dissertation, "Publishing the 'Sealed Book': James Mason Hutchings and the Landscapes of California Print Culture, 1853–1886" (University of Nevada, Reno, 2000), explores the relationship between print and landscape in the nineteenth-century far west. Her article on print technology in the American west appeared in *Western Technological Landscapes* (Nevada Humanities Committee, 1998). She is currently editing *The Miner's Own Publisher: The Diary of James Mason Hutchings, 1855* (Book Club of California, forthcoming).

CHARLES JOHANNINGSMEIER is a member of the English Department at the University of Nebraska at Omaha. He is the author of *Fiction and the American Literary Marketplace: The Role of Newspaper Syndicates in America, 1865–1900* (Cambridge University Press,

1997) as well as numerous articles on nineteenth-century American periodical history and regionalist fiction.

JILL LEPORE is associate professor of history and American studies at Boston University. She is the author of *The Name of War: King Philip's War and the Origins of American Identity* (Alfred A. Knopf, 1998), winner of the Bancroft Prize in American history; *Encounters in the New World: A History in Documents* (Oxford University Press, 2000); and *A Is for American: Letters and Other Characters* (Alfred A. Knopf, forthcoming). She received her Ph.D. in American studies from Yale University in 1995. She has been a Fellow at the Whitney Humanities Center at Yale, the Charles Warren Center at Harvard University, and the Radcliffe Institute for Advanced Study. Professor Lepore edits the online magazine *Common-place* <http://www.common-place.org>.

RUSSELL L. MARTIN is director of the DeGolyer Library at Southern Methodist University. He contributed to volume 1 of *A History of the Book in America* (Cambridge University Press, 2000) and has written articles on newspapers and periodicals for the *Encyclopedia of New England Culture* (Yale University Press, forthcoming) and the *Encyclopedia of New York State* (Syracuse University Press, forthcoming). He is at work on an edition of the poems of Jacob Taylor, compiler of almanacs in eighteenth-century Philadelphia.

TRYSH TRAVIS is assistant professor of English at Southern Methodist University. Her articles on twentieth-century reading and publishing history have appeared in *Book History*, *American Literary History*, and the *Journal of Modern Literature*. She is currently at work on two books, "Reading Matters: Books, Bookmen, and the American Century," and "Recovery and Reading: The New Middlebrow Culture."

GLENN WALLACH's study of national newspaper arts coverage appeared in *Reporting the Arts: News Coverage of Arts and Culture in America* (Columbia University, National Arts Journalism Program, 1999). He is the author of "'A Depraved Taste for Publicity': The Press and Private Life in the Gilded Age," *American Studies* (1998), which was awarded the Stone-Suderman Prize, and *Obedient Sons: The Discourse of Youth and Generations in American Culture, 1630–1860* (University of Massachusetts Press, 1997). He is a member of the history department at the Horace Mann School in New York City.

SUSAN S. WILLIAMS is associate professor of English at Ohio State University. She is the author of *Confounding Images: Photography and Portraiture in Antebellum American Fiction* (University of Pennsylvania Press, 1997) and the co-editor (with Steven Fink) of *Reciprocal Influences: Literary Production, Distribution, and Consumption in America* (Ohio State University Press, 1999). She is currently at work on a book-length project on women writers and publishing culture in nineteenth-century America.

461